Library of
Davidson College

George Frederick Cooke

Thomas Sully's painting of Cooke as Richard III, executed in his Philadelphia studio in 1811. Courtesy of the Pennsylvania Academy of The Fine Arts.

George Frederick Cooke
MACHIAVEL OF THE STAGE

Don B. Wilmeth

Contributions in Drama and Theatre Studies, Number 2

GREENWOOD PRESS Westport, Connecticut • London, England

792.02
C772zW

Library of Congress Cataloging in Publication Data

Wilmeth, Don B
  George Frederick Cooke, Machiavel of the stage.

  (Contributions in drama and theatre studies; no. 2
ISSN 0163-3821)
  Bibliography: p.
  Includes Index.
  1. Cooke, George Frederick, 1756–1812. 2. Actors—
Great Britain—Biography. I. Series.
PN2598.C78W5   792'.028'0924 [B]   79-7589
ISBN 0-313-21487-5

Copyright © 1980 by Don B. Wilmeth

All rights reserved. No portion of this book may be
reproduced, by any process or technique, without the
express written consent of the publisher.

86-5942

Library of Congress Catalog Card Number: 79-7589
ISBN: 0-313-21487-5
ISSN: 0163-3821

First published in 1980

Greenwood Press
A division of Congressional Information Service, Inc.
51 Riverside Avenue, Westport, Connecticut 06880

Printed in the United States of America

10 9 8 7 6 5 4 3 2 1

To Judy and Michael

"Conscience, avaunt! Richard's himself again!"

Cibber, *Richard III*

Contents

Illustrations	xi
Preface	xiii
Introduction	3
1. "Three Kingdoms Claim His Birth"	10
2. London Makes Its Mark	18
3. A Strolling Player	24
4. A Correct Actor	41
5. "The Manchester Roscius"	60
6. "A New Date in My Theatricals"	89
7. Hero of the Dublin Stage	103
8. "I Am Myself Alone"	122
9. Cooke Versus Kemble	137
10. Mr. Cooke of Covent Garden	164
11. "In His Cups"	196
12. Durance Vile	221
13. Fires, Riots, and Farewell	240
14. Among the Yankee Doodles	256
Epilogue: A Posthumous Career	275
Appendix A: Cooke Iconography	287
Appendix B: Table of Cooke's Performances and Receipts in the United States	291

Abbreviations	*295*
Notes	*297*
Selected Bibliography	*345*
Index	*351*

Illustrations

Frontispiece: Thomas Sully's painting of Cooke as Richard III.

1. Joseph Munden (1758-1832). 45
2. A youthful G. F. Cooke. 46
3. William Lewis (1749-1811). 123
4. Painting of Cooke as Richard III (ca. 1800). 126
5. One of the earliest published drawings of Charles Robert Leslie (1794-1859). 172
6. Cooke as Falstaff in *Henry IV, Part 1*. 176
7. Cooke as Sir Pertinax MacSychophant. 178
8. Thomas Abthorpe Cooper (1776-1849). 195
9. John Philip Kemble (1759-1823). 201
10. William Henry West Betty (1791-1874) as Young Norval in *Douglas*. 210
11. Cooke's first appearance in America at the Park Theatre, 21 November 1810. 261
12. Playbill announcing Mr. Morse would appear as Othello on 23 January 1811, in place of Duff. 265
13. Portrait of Cooke painted in Philadelphia. 268
14. Death mask of Cooke. 276
15. Cooke's tomb in 1821. 279
16. Cooke's tomb today. 280

17. Cooke's skull. 284
18. Cooke's tooth given to Edwin Booth; made into a tie-pin. 285

Preface

My interest in George Frederick Cooke was first encouraged by Professor Charles H. Shattuck over a decade ago. Some years later, the late Helen Willard, former curator of the Harvard Theatre Collection, introduced me to the fragments of Cooke's diaries in that collection. To both go my greatest gratitude, not only for helpful suggestions but also for constant encouragement.

The scope of Cooke's career, encompassing almost thirty years in the provinces, ten seasons in London, and a final two years in the United States, has dictated the structure of this study. The focus throughout is on his development as a professional performer and on the nature of his art. While I also deal with his personal life as much as possible, this aspect is treated as secondary to his career as an actor. Because of the scarcity of information previously available on the first phase of his career, five chapters are devoted to his provincial wanderings (3–7). Chapter 1 covers his early life and Chapter 2 the major early influences on his acting. Except for the final chapter on his American tour and an epilogue, the remaining chapters cover his ten London seasons and summer provincial appearances.

It is a privilege to acknowledge my indebtedness to significant research by earlier distinguished scholars. I have tried to indicate my dependence on their work in both the notes and the selected bibliography. My research has taken me to libraries and collections, both public and private, throughout Great Britain and the United States. Without the kind assistance of a great number of individuals and institutions, this work would have been impossible. Those who were especially kind to me include Professor Arnold Hare of the University of Bristol, Miss Beryl Cooke, G. F. Cooke's only living relative and a gracious lady, and Richard P. Sodders, who unselfishly made available to me the benefits of his own research on Cooke. I am grateful to Professors Elmer Blistein, A. H. Saxon, Charles Shattuck, Attilio Favorini, and Barton St. Armand for reading portions of the manuscript and making suggestions. Lois Atwood, a dear friend and perceptive critic, spent countless hours reading the typescript, correcting numerous errors, and offering helpful advice. However, as Dr. Johnson admitted in his final *Rambler* paper, I must apologize to these generous friends for the "obstinacy with which correction was rejected" on some points and "must remain accountable for all faults."

For their constant encouragement, I would like to mention the following: Professors George R. Kernodle, Oscar G. Brockett, Barnard Hewitt, James O. Barnhill, and James Schevill. Professor Kalman Burnim graciously shared his research on Cooke and Alicia Daniels with me, William W. Appleton led me to an important manuscript on Cooke, Burt G. Shevelove granted generous permission to use manuscript material from his private collection, and Raymond Mander and Joe Mitchenson put me in touch with Miss Beryl Cooke.

In Great Britain my work was made both pleasant and rewarding by a great number of people: the staff of the Reading Room and North Library of the British Museum (now called the British Library) and the Newspaper Library at Colindale, the staff of the Enthoven Collection at the Victoria and Albert Museum, Jennifer Aylmer, curator of the British Theatre Museum, Sir Bernard Miles of the Mermaid Theatre, the officers of the Garrick Club, E. H. Lowe, city librarian of the Central Public Library in Lancaster, and Charles Parish, librarian of the Literary and Philosophical Society in Newcastle-upon-Tyne. D. J. Bryant, chief librarian of the Central Library in Kingston-upon-Hull, O. S. Tomlinson, city librarian of the York City Library, John Bebbington, city librarian and information officer of the Sheffield City Libraries, Elizabeth Leach, librarian of the Henry Watson Music and Arts Libraries in Manchester, Muriel H. Simpson, curator of the Berwick-upon-Tweed Library, and W. S. Hough, city librarian of the Bristol Public Libraries. I am also grateful for assistance through correspondence from the Shakespeare Birthplace Trust in Stratford-upon-Avon, the John Rylands Library, the Chester Central Library, and the Liverpool City Libraries. Norma Armstrong, librarian, Central Library, Edinburgh, kindly furnished me the appropriate pages of her thesis, "The Edinburgh Stage, 1715–1820," and A. McLoughlin and Christopher Hyland of the National Library, Dublin, corroborated specific data for me.

My indebtedness to individuals and institutions in this country is likewise enormous: Paul Myers, curator of the Theatre Collection at Lincoln Center, Louis A. Rachow, librarian of the Walter Hampden Memorial Library at The Players, James Gregory, librarian of the New York Historical Society, Jeanne T. Newlin, curator of the Harvard Theatre Collection, and Arnold Wengrow, former assistant to the curator at Harvard, Francis O. Mattson, James Lawton, and John Alden of the Boston Public Library, Donald W. Krummel of the Newberry Library, the late Sam Pearce of the Museum of the City of New York, Marguerite McAneny, former curator of the William Seymour Theatre Collection at Princeton, Dr. Louis B. Wright and Dorothy Mason of the Folger Shakespeare Library, Neda M. Westlake, curator of the University of Pennsylvania Rare Book Collection, John D. Kilbourne, curator of the Historical Society of Pennsylvania, and Marcus A. McCorison, director of the American Antiquarian Society. A special word of thanks must go to Robert Hunsicker, vicar of Saint Paul's Chapel in New York and Robert T. Lentz, librarian of the

Jefferson Medical College Library in Philadelphia. I am also grateful to James Katsaros, director of the Office of Communications Service, City of New York, and Philip Kunkis, deputy chief clerk of the Surrogate's Court of the County of New York.

The editors of *Theatre Survey* and *Theatre Notebook* have kindly permitted the inclusion in more expanded form of materials which I originally published with them: notably "Cooke Among the Yankee Doodles," *Theatre Survey*, 14 (November 1973), 1–32 and "The Posthumous Career of George Frederick Cooke," *Theatre Notebook*, 24 (Winter 1969–1970), 68–74. Portions of chapters were first read at a conference on nineteenth-century British theatre at the University of Massachusetts in May 1974 and at the New England Theatre Conference at the University of New Hampshire in October 1974. I am grateful to both forums for these opportunities.

The University Research Funds of Eastern New Mexico University (in the early stages of my research) and Brown University have provided the necessary financial support for my research time and for travel. Funds from the Ben Brown Memorial Fund at Brown have been used for clerical and typing costs. Without additional financial support from the Brown University Faculty Research Fund, this volume could not have been published.

Specific acknowledgment for quoted material from manuscripts can be found in the notes to each chapter. Finally, my deepest appreciation goes to my wife Judy, who not only encouraged and often shared in my quest, but also undertook the arduous task of typing the final manuscript, and to my parents for their unswerving faith in my abilities.

George Frederick Cooke

Introduction

George Frederick Cooke belongs in the select group of great English actors who flourished during the eighteenth and early nineteenth centuries. In the annals of the London stage he ranks with Charles Macklin, David Garrick, John Henderson, John Philip Kemble, Edmund Kean, and William Charles Macready. He was also the first great English actor to come to America; his presence led to the establishment of the starring system in the United States. During his stormy career he excited enormous enthusiasm on both continents. In the tradition of Garrick and Macklin, Cooke brought a new natural style of acting to the stage. Most important, he deserves to be remembered as the precursor of the romantic style embodied by, and historically credited to, Edmund Kean, whose life and career resemble Cooke's own in myriad ways.

Although Cooke played well over 300 roles during his long career, he limited himself to a small handful after his successful debut at Covent Garden in 1800. Like most prominent actors of the time, Cooke found the role types that he could do superlatively well and thereafter restricted himself to parts that demanded grim humor, sardonic sarcasm, specious menace, baleful guile, or savage ferocity. He excelled in roles like Richard III, Shylock, Iago, Sir Giles Overreach, and Macklin's comic creation, Sir Pertinax MacSycophant.

Curiously, of all the major figures on the English stage during this period of great acting, only Cooke has failed to receive a careful, scholarly treatment. This study is an attempt to fill this void. Space must also be allowed to correct or refute what until now has been the standard source on Cooke's life, William Dunlap's *Memoirs of the Life of George Frederick Cooke*, a pastiche completed in 1813 less than six months after Cooke's death in New York. Cooke, almost in jest, had requested Dunlap, a theatre manager, playwright, and theatre historian, to write his life, and not until friends pressed him did Dunlap actually undertake the project.[1] The aging manager had known Cooke for only eighteen months but had served as his companion and virtual keeper for a couple of months during Cooke's tour of the United States in 1811. The stories told to Dunlap were often exaggerated, facts were romanticized, and even untruths passed from Cooke to Dunlap. Cooke's temperament leaned toward a kind of delirious abandonment that not only led to personal excesses but also helped shape his power in impassioned and often terrible characters. To a staid, priggish gentleman like Dunlap, such uncontrollable behavior was uncouth and immoral. In addition, the deterioration of Cooke's physical and mental powers, after years of alcoholism, was marked by periods of confused thinking. As a result, in Dunlap's rush to complete the book, he took some facts for granted and chose to ignore others. He went only to those sources readily available to him; even with Cooke's diaries in hand, he edited and rewrote them freely.

A contemporary reviewer in England called Dunlap's product a "meagre work" and added that for information "any scene-shifter of Covent Garden could have produced" more.[2] It may be true that Dunlap's study is something of a landmark in the development of the biography in that he gives us less praise of Cooke's acting than condemnation of his intemperance. Nevertheless, the dominant note of Dunlap's work, a moralizing tone that permeates the two-volume, 850-page biography, becomes overbearing and unnecessary—almost didactic. After reading Dunlap, Byron commented: "All green-room and tap-room—drams and the drama—brandy, whisky-punch, and, *latterly*, toddy, overflow every page . . . . the pints he swallowed . . . are too regularly registered."[3] Byron is quite correct: Dunlap's perspective is distorted. The Cooke of Dunlap's acquaintance was one dying of alcoholic disease—he was a blown-up version of the original. The gossip and unproven scandal scattered throughout the biography have been largely responsible for overshadowing the genius and accomplishments of this important and individualistic actor. As a source on Cooke's American visit, however, Dunlap remains obligatory, and the present study, instead of duplicating Dunlap, attempts to complement it. Still, it must be stressed that it was Dunlap who left the impression accepted by too many historians that Cooke was a limited actor, perhaps a potentially great one, but a man simply ruined by alcoholism. In reality, Cooke was more complex than that, and, perhaps because we know altogether too little about him, speculations about this paradox, constantly proving to be a contradiction, become even more fascinating.

Of all the major actors of his time, Cooke is one of the most elusive, despite the fact that he periodically kept a journal recording his activities. Practically nothing is known about his early life or his personal relations. His apprenticeship was one of the longest in the history of the English theatre: he spent over twenty-seven years in the provincial theatre before he was engaged at Covent Garden. In contrast, John Philip Kemble's provincial apprenticeship lasted only seven years. Dunlap's coverage of this segment of Cooke's career is one of the prominent weaknesses of his biography. Whereas he spends over one-quarter of his study on Cooke's two years in the United States, when he knew him, less than one-fifth of the combined two volumes deals with Cooke's twenty-seven years in the provinces. For the modern researcher, dealing with provincial material involves some problems. English provincial material is difficult to locate, little has been written, much has been lost, and what accounts

Introduction

still exist are often of minimal use. It is also a fact that criticism as we know it today was virtually unknown in the provincial press. Small country towns often did not even have newspapers. When criticism did appear, it was often unreliable. Even the London newspapers rarely contained truly honest or dispassionate reviews of plays and players. Leigh Hunt, one of the first modern "critics," made this point clear in recalling his own early efforts: "Puffing and plenty of tickets were ... the system of the day. It was exchange of amenities over the dinner table; a flattery of power on the one side, and puns on the other; and what the public took for criticism on a play, was a draft upon the box office or reminiscences of last Thursday's salmon and lobster sauce." Nevertheless, this study includes the first detailed chronicle of Cooke's provincial career and an evaluation of his reception in London.

Cooke's career was sporadic, and he himself was extremely quixotic. Even during his better days, failure was waiting around the corner after one impropriety too many. His habits and almost schizophrenic personality, one personality when sober and a diametrically opposite one when drunk, spawned many lively, and indeed memorable, anecdotes, and these have been told and retold. Such anecdotes, partially because of the embellishments that accompany them, tell only part of Cooke's story.

Historians have assumed that Cooke is an easily classified actor. In his latter years, he did concentrate on the roles he did best—characters of hypocrisy, jealousy, or villainy in its various forms, both comic and tragic—but it was as much by demand and managerial efficacy as it was by choice. His career as a provincial actor alters any belief in his limitations during those years. Instead, we find a picture of an actor of unusual versatility—running the gamut of broad humor, musical roles, recitations, military and gentry roles, villains, lovers, and heroic parts. As he grew older and his physical instrument became less flexible, such breadth was impossible. Leigh Hunt tagged him "the Machiavel of the modern stage," although Hazlitt and others broadened their estimates, calling him one of the very best actors ever seen on the English stage.

When the audience saw Cooke in his Covent Garden debut as Richard III in 1800, they knew they were observing an original, an actor who, although borrowing from many, had created his own style—an actor who cared little for the classicist's criticism of his impassioned, often indecorous style. Even Cooke's most vociferous declaimers recognized that in him London had found an actor in the mold of Garrick, an actor whose approach was almost the antithesis of the solemn, stately John Philip Kemble, Cooke's principal competitor at Drury Lane. His technique was subjective. He spoke poetry like prose; he delivered soliloquies as if thinking aloud, not declaiming to an audience; his voice was not particularly pleasant—it was even hoarse on occasion; his movements, according to some observers, were awkward and grotesque.

Coleridge's comment that to see Kean act was "like reading Shakespeare by flashes of lightning" is well known. A less-known description of Cooke states that to see him perform was "like reading Shakespeare thro' a magnifying glass."[4] Cooke had seen Garrick, Macklin, and Henderson, and, although his style was often reminiscent of theirs, he became the connecting link between the Garrick period and the Kean period. While his reputation has not been as great as Kean's, he did bring new life and force to the English stage at a time when, under Kemble's influence, it was tending to return to the pre-Garrick artificial days.

It is impossible to demonstrate the tenuous link between Kean and Cooke. We do know that Kean had immense admiration for Cooke. In 1821, on his first U.S. tour, to show his esteem for his predecessor, Kean erected a monument in New York over Cooke's remains. Whether Kean actually saw Cooke act, however, is still open to speculation. In 1817, he told John Howard Payne that he had never seen Cooke; however, he confided to N. P. Willis that in his opinion Cooke had never been excelled and "was a perfect actor—Kemble a very indifferent one; the one had spirit and genius—the other would have been a good teacher of elocution, and no more."[5] Kean certainly had opportunities to observe Cooke during various periods, especially in 1806, when both were in London. Numerous writers have commented on the striking resemblance between their styles. Payne, who saw Cooke in the United States, wrote to his sister after seeing Kean in London in 1817:

If Kean never saw Cooke, and he tells me he never did, the similitude in certain parts of their acting, as well as the conception of the true character, seems to me to be still more wonderful. Their leading features of resemblance in *Shylock* and *Richard* exhibit so marked a correspondence in their genius that it almost proves that both modelled themselves upon similar views of nature.[6]

John Howard Payne, who called Cooke a "discoverer," saw a great deal of Cooke in Kean and Kean in Junius Brutus Booth but found Cooke a more versatile actor than either, an estimation not always shared by other critics and historians. Hillebrand, for example, claims the superiority of Kean "rests on wider range, the intellectuality of his interpretations, and the greater impress he made on his time."[7] Unlike Cooke, however, Kean failed in the comic dialect roles that were Cooke's forte, especially Sir Pertinax MacSycophant in Macklin's *The Man of the World*. Cooke's Richard and Shylock were as great as Kean's, and, as this study illustrates, he was not always as limited to as few roles as Hillebrand and others imply. He certainly did provoke dispute over his unorthodox interpretations, as did Kean. Likewise, Kean's art developed along the same lines as Cooke's, whether by accident, observation, or tradition. Cooke's timing, however, was not as propitious, and he wasted his genius even more completely than did Kean. Still, both were similarly gifted with unusual talents and similar styles; both triumphed in the same or similar roles; both were eccentric in their habits. Kean fittingly received an early warning that he might follow in Cooke's debauched footsteps. Following a drunken spree at Deptford which caused Kean to miss a performance in London, the following appeared in the *New Monthly Magazine* (1 May 1816):

Too often we have had to lament that men, exalted by their genius, should suffer themselves to be precipitated from it by failings and vices which degrade them to the level of the lowest of their species. With the striking example of Cooke before his eyes, we trust that Kean will have the prudence to avoid the fatal rock on which the former perished; nay, we think that a more friendly office could not be rendered by those who value him than to have a starling taught to sing in his ears every hour of the day the emphatic admonition: "Remember Cooke!"

The question of which of these two romantic actors was the superior is a moot point. Kean was championed by Hazlitt, while Cooke had the support of numerous lesser critics during his London tenure but no single strong voice. Thus, Hazlitt asserted that, compared to Kean, Cooke "had only the *slang* and *bravado* of tragedy." Hazlitt, who saw little of Cooke, concluded that Kean had more subtleties and nuances in his performances. Cooke neglected his study and depended on past successes rather than a renewed vigor that comes through constant reexamination and polish. In contrast, Kean, still a young actor when he first gained prominence in 1814, remained for some time an indefatigable student and thus surpassed Cooke in the finer points of character development. Still, we are left with comments such as that of Byron—"Of Actors, Cooke was the most natural, Kemble the most supernatural, Kean a medium between the two."[8] When Kean first visited the United States in 1820–1821, Cooke's memory was still very much alive and comparisons were common. In Philadelphia, Kean's reception was cordial, but the *Aurora and General Advertiser* (20 January 1821) concluded that "Cooke was the greater actor as well as in part the *model* for Kean." Durang concluded that Kean had based much of his Richard III on Cooke, although Kean made "more detached points." His final statement, that their performances were "alike, yet distinct," remains the most sensible conclusion possible, despite its imprecision.[9]

It is somewhat easier to estimate Cooke's greatness in the view of his contemporaries. J. P. Kemble was Cooke's most prominent single competitor. During the ten years Cooke appeared at Covent Garden, however, his popularity was as great as Kemble's and often eclipsed it. For example, Kemble was forced to give up the role of Richard III because of Cooke's superiority. When Kemble resumed the mantle of Richard in January 1811, after Cooke was in America, the audience found the experience an embarrassment.[10] It was some time before Cooke's other great roles were successfully essayed in London; no one would ever revive Sir Pertinax MacSycophant as long as the memory of Cooke's performance remained alive. When Charles Kemble attempted Iago in 1811, *The Dramatic Censor* concluded that he played the role as well as any actor then in London could but added that only two actors within memory had been able to execute the role properly—Henderson and Cooke. When J. P. Kemble tried Sir Giles Overreach, it was simply the "issue of necessity" which gave strong proof of "the potency of Mr. Cooke, as an actor." Indeed, Charles and John Philip Kemble and Charles Mayne Young each, with caution, attempted to "put on his professional *toga*" with only meagre success.[11] More than a year after Cooke's departure from London, the press still mentioned him by name as the only actor capable of filling the enormous house of Covent Garden and condemned Kemble and Harris, co-managers, for resorting to horses, tumblers, rope-dancers, and fire-eaters in lieu of a legitimate attraction like Cooke.

News of Cooke's death was received at Covent Garden with sadness and regret; he was an "original" and the theatre had lost an actor who could not be easily replaced. His peculiar faculties had suited him so completely to a line of acting now missing that a major void was created in the company.

There are questions about Cooke that may never be answered. One that stands out above all others is why he waited so long before applying for a position with a London theatre. Neither Covent Garden nor Drury Lane offered him a position before 1800. Cooke himself, however, states that he was first offered a position at Covent Garden in 1793 but turned it down. No one really knows the answer to this puzzling question, but speculation seems inevitable—and indeed necessary in order to understand Cooke the man. There are a number of plausible possibilities. Consciously or not, Cooke may have been filled with self-doubt, both in terms of his talent as it might be tested in one of the patent houses and in terms of his own understanding of his undependability because of the effects of his drinking. He was clearly aware of his problems, although he often disguised the fact in his diaries. On several occasions throughout his diaries, however, he tried to dissect his confused personality.

There are other possible reasons for his hesitancy. He was a star, a prominent, respected actor in many of the major provincial theatres in England and Ireland. Dunlap implies that Cooke's ambition was not great enough for him to have wanted to rise above this level of fame and prominence. Cooke was also aware that by challenging the London stage, he would come up against a force both revered and long established, J. P. Kemble. He ultimately experienced great satisfaction when he found himself succeeding in this formidable task. But making that initial decision was not an easy one. Cooke's timing was inauspicious, despite his initial success in competing with Kemble at the opposing patent house. Even this advantage lasted only two seasons, when Kemble, in a much stronger position of authority, joined Cooke at Covent Garden. Instead of applying for a position at Drury Lane, Cooke remained at Covent Garden in direct competition with Kemble. The tide of events might have been quite different if Cooke had begun his London career ten years earlier, before the Kemble dynasty was so firmly entrenched, or if, like Kean, he had appeared in

Introduction

London at a time of void, when Kemble was beginning to lose his control and acting powers, and, indeed, the London audience was ripe for a change in style and ideal—a shift from the classical statuesqueness of Kemble to the more passionate romanticism of Kean. Cooke was caught in the middle, unable to sustain his acting powers after years of self-neglect and by his very nature unable to assume managerial control. Any or all or a combination of these factors might have kept him from London. In addition, the London managers knew of Cooke's personal problems, indiscretions, and periodic irresponsibility (although these were much exaggerated), and it was perfectly natural that they would hesitate to accept him into their companies. Nonetheless, Cooke would not have been the first actor with a drinking problem to have a prominent position in a London company. Even Kemble was known to drink heavily on occasion, but he was less public in this respect than Cooke. Later, Kean's drinking would prove as much a problem as Cooke's. But Kean began his career at Drury Lane virtually unknown, and his reputation for drunkenness and general debauchery came later.

One writer who had first seen Cooke as Shylock in 1794 in a small provincial theatre remarked in 1806 that it was lamentable to have seen "so much merit in so much obscurity" for so long.[12] Even so, within ten years Cooke established himself as one of the greatest actors of the century. Although he was often damned and severely censured in the press for his misbehavior, he was also credited for giving a new direction to English acting. He was, as Durang observed, an actor with singular powers. "He could soar to flights of genius without the aid of declamation, or the usual tricks of the art."[13] An admiring poetic partisan summed up Cooke's uniqueness:

> The Rival muses owned the alternate reign,
> With mutual feelings each their feuds forsook,
> Combined their efforts, and created Cooke.
> Pure child of Nature! foster child of Art!
> How all the passions in succession rise,
> Heave in thy soul, and lighten in thine eyes![14]

1

"Three Kingdoms Claim His Birth"

This, the first line of the epitaph on Cooke's tomb in New York, is indicative of the first of many problems which George Frederick Cooke's life poses for the researcher. Cooke's birthplace was variously claimed by Scotland, Ireland, and England. Sources prior to Dunlap's biography of Cooke frequently claimed that Cooke was born on 17 April 1756 in Dublin. On the other hand, his excellence in Scottish roles, as well as his early life in Berwick-upon-Tweed next to the Scottish border, gave impetus to the rumor that he was born in Scotland.[1] Dunlap claims that he was born in Westminster.[2] Of the three, Dublin dominates in the various early accounts of his life.[3] Much of the available evidence, however, is in the form of testimony given long after the fact. Nevertheless, a strong presumption as to place of birth might be made. The date of his birth is also less than conclusive. Only a baptismal registry or some other physical document will ultimately clear up both controversies, but despite diligent investigation, I have thus far been unable to discover anything of the kind. The best that can be done is to set down the possibilities as they do exist.

Although Dunlap says that Cooke told him quite definitely that Westminster was his birthplace, the actor also remarked that "he was generally supposed to be an Hibernian." One must be very cautious in accepting Cooke's word on either supposition; some testimony exists on the alternatives. For example, shortly before Cooke's death, Dr. John W. Francis, one of Cooke's attending physicians, remembered that Cooke had mentioned Westminster as his place of birth.[4] Was this one of those offhand remarks that gained Cooke notoriety, or was it a true deathbed revelation? On the other hand, Cooke never denied the earlier references to Dublin, which were so well publicized during his lifetime.

Cooke's father seems to have been in the military, belonging to one of the regiments that composed the garrison of Dublin. Thus, it is quite plausible that Cooke was born in one of the many military barracks then in Dublin. A rarely cited account of Cooke's birth is the following by a fellow-trouper and friend of Cooke, who called himself simply a "Veteran Stager":

We will endeavor to set the matter at rest: not alone from his own *ipse dixit*, but from more authentic information, from the lips of an ancient lady in the city of Dublin, the wife of a serjeant Graham.... In the year 1806, we saw and conversed with this old man and his still older wife, in company with Cooke, over a glass of Peter Kearney's Inashone whiskey punch,[5] when the old lady declared she well remembered his birth in the barracks of Dublin, some time in the year 1758 [1756?],[6] her husband then being absent with his regiment in America, she being left behind as one of the barrack nurses: the father of Cooke was a non-commissioned officer in the 70th, generally designated at that time, the Black Cuffs, and was a native of Kelso, in Scotland, his mother was born in Drogheda, the daughter of a very respectable inn-keeper in that town, in whose house George's father chanced to be quartered.[7]

The Stager differs somewhat from other sources. Cooke's father's rank in other biographical accounts ranges from a subaltern, a subordinate rank below captain in the British military, to "an officer." Cooke, probably with typical overstatement, described him as "a high Irish officer, and Captain in the 4th Dragoons."[8] Like his friend the Stager, Cooke cannot be taken literally on most details. Dunlap initially accepted Cooke's word but later was forced to retract the assertion. Additional information gleaned in conversation with the widow of Anthony Rock, who had managed the Glasgow and Edinburgh theatres where Cooke appeared while on tour as a performer at Covent Garden, revealed that the captain was more likely a sergeant.[9] If Cooke misled Dunlap in this respect, and he probably did, then certainly his statement to Dunlap concerning Westminster should also be questioned, as indeed it has been.[10]

According to the Stager, Cooke's mother "packed up her tatters, and followed the drums." He suggests that she was a woman of strong mind, "with acquirements and education superior to her station in life, or generally falls to the lot of pretty barmaids."[11] The true status and identity of Cooke's mother is as mysterious as those of his father, although on this issue the evidence is more conclusive. In the first edition of Dunlap's biography of Cooke (London: Henry Colburn, 1813), her maiden name, if Cooke was born within wedlock, which seems unlikely, is given as Renton.[12] Dunlap elsewhere refers to Cooke's mother and aunts as "the Miss Renton Daughters"; he even wrote the name Allison Renton in the notes he used in preparing the biography.[13] Cooke also wrote to a Samuel Renton in Berwick in 1807.[14] Dunlap indicates that Allison Renton was the daughter of the laird of Renton, whose estate was at or near Lamberton.[15] If this is true, then John Renton and Lady Susanna Montgomerie Renton (d. 1754), daughter of Alexander, ninth earl of Eglinton, were her parents and George's grandparents.[16] There is certainly a disparity in status between a granddaughter of the privileged and a common barmaid, although the Stager does say her father was a "very respectable inn-keeper" and thus lessens the discrepancy somewhat. Another contemporary source suggests that Mrs. Cooke's family was displeased with her marriage, if indeed a marriage took place, and thus, by marrying below her station, she may have been disowned.[17]

Cooke's father allegedly died when George was a young boy and left his widow in financial straits.[18] Cooke's mother took young George to live at Berwick-upon-Tweed, where he was educated. When his mother died, he was cared for by her two sisters who bound him apprentice to John Taylor, a printer at Berwick.[19] At some point early in his youth, Cooke spent some years in the London area, but it is unclear whether he was in London before being taken to northern England. The drama critic John Taylor (not the Berwick printer), later editor of the *London Morning Post*, and eventually owner of the *London Sun*, as well as a prolific writer of prologues and epilogues for the stage, remembered young Cooke, who was two or three years his senior. He described him as a "heavy-looking lubberly boy, and the last person I should have expected to turn his attention to the stage, particularly to the assumption of heroic characters."[20]

On one occasion Taylor and Cooke went together to Wandsworth Common, now a few miles southwest of the center of London, to tell a lady visiting a Miss Dunwell there that her house in Rotherhithe had been destroyed by fire. This unidentified lady, distantly related to George Cooke's mother, later inherited Miss Dunwell's mansion and fortune, and, according to Taylor, the same woman also left a legacy to Mrs. Cooke. Taylor considered Cooke's mother "a crazy old woman" and believed that Cooke's later behavior, "inconsistent and extravagant," could be traced to his mother's mental infirmity. After Cooke's death, *The Satirist* claimed that Cooke's mother had died not when he was very young, but rather when he was between seventeen and twenty. She is described by *The Satirist* as "very like her son; and, with a long nose and chin, and an antiquated mode of dressing, she strongly excited the idea of Mother Shipton."[21]

Taylor tells the story of Mrs. Cooke's dealings with the Reverend Mr. Harpur, one of the executors of Miss Dunwell's estate and an officer of the British Museum, a gentleman of learning and most respectable character. Harpur was prevented from paying the legacy until certain legal forms had been processed. Mrs. Cooke was incessant in her applications to Harpur, and one morning called at the Museum, passed without ceremony into the room where Mr. and Mrs. Harpur were at breakfast, and "in a vehement manner demanded the corpse of her son, accusing Mr. Harpur of having murdered him." Harpur coolly told Mrs. Cooke that she should go to the proper authorities, accuse him of murder, and he would then be brought to justice. Mrs. Cooke quietly departed. She must have found her son very much alive shortly after this incident.[22]

Cooke's sojourn in London would appear to be incontestable. Indeed, several early biographical sketches report that Cooke was taken to London by his father at the age of two and remained there until 1763.[23] At the age of seven or so, then, possibly after his father's death, he moved to Berwick with his mother, where her two sisters resided. On his mother's death, George went to live with his aunts, who sent him to school. The exact nature of Cooke's education is not known, although Dunlap tells us that the Renton sisters' library contained no play books. George procured plays elsewhere, including a complete edition of Shakespeare, from a local clergyman, and read them so eagerly that his studies suffered.[24] The stimulus for reading plays seems to have come from the first play he ever read, Thomas Otway's *Venice Preserv'd*. His "first, strange, and incoherent idea of a stage and theatrical representation" was formed from that play, from the study of theatrical prints, in particular a picture of Henry Woodward as Mercutio, and from viewing a puppet show.[25]

Berwick lacked a playhouse, and so the strolling players performed in the town hall. In 1807, Cooke recalled witnessing this company, his first theatrical performance, at the age of ten or eleven.[26] He only saw the company once but recalled that the mainpiece was Colley Cibber's and Sir John Vanbrugh's comedy *The Provok'd Husband, or a Journey to London* and the afterpiece David Garrick's farce *The Lying Valet*. In the mainpiece James Aickin played the character of Lord Townly, a husband who is driven to desperation by his wife and finally decides to separate from her. Aickin, the younger brother of Francis, then a successful London actor and later a manager of the Liverpool theatre, is described as the "hero" of the Edinburgh company at this time. It is most likely that Cooke saw Aickin in the spring of 1767 on Aickin's journey from Edinburgh to London, where in November of that year he joined the company at Drury Lane. Aickin had had a prominent position in a second-rate company under James Dawson and David Beat at the Canangate Theatre until the winter season of 1766–1767. In January 1767, the management did not re-engage George Stayley, a local favorite, and a riot ensued. Aickin had signed a manifesto against Stayley and, fearing further trouble, had left Edinburgh for London, apparently pausing on the way in Berwick.[27] After viewing the Edinburgh actors, Cooke says that "plays and playing were never absent from his thoughts."[28]

In April 1769, another group of Edinburgh actors came to Berwick to perform in the town hall. The company was composed of second- or third-rate actors, but they made a great imprint on the youthful imaginations of Berwick.[29] The first visitation from Edinburgh had inspired Cooke to study the part of Horatio in Nicholas Rowe's *The Fair Penitent* with an eye to presenting the play with a group of schoolmates.[30] Their enthusiasm faded, however, and the production never reached the stage. The second visit, which must have lasted a much longer period of time, led to more fruitful results.[31] With an old deserted barn for a playhouse, the bare floor for a stage, scenery of mat and paper, costumes made up of their street clothes mingled with bits and pieces borrowed from amateur performers, the boys of Berwick staged Isaac Bickerstaffe's comic opera *Love in a Village* and *Hamlet*, played without female roles except for that of Gertrude, which was taken by a very young boy. In the popular opera, Cooke played Young Meadows, his first appearance before an audience, and in *Hamlet*, Horatio. He later recalled the encouragement he received from some of the Edinburgh actors who saw the play.[32]

With little money in their pockets, the young amateurs contrived devious schemes for seeing the Edinburgh troupe perform. Hoping to see John Home's *Douglas*, Cooke and three companions tried to hide under the stage so that they could sneak through an opening into the pit during the production. They were caught by "fat Burk," a member of the company, and "after a fearful interrogatory, most shamefully handed out at the back door." On another occasion, Cooke and his friends slipped into the unguarded back entrance of the town hall. Cooke, seeking a good hiding place until *Macbeth* began, spied a barrel which he quickly climbed into; he soon discovered that he was not alone—his companions proved to be two 24-pound cannon balls. Cooke was now safely hidden in the company's "thunder-barrel," which would usher in the first appearance of the witches. When the cue came, "midst flames of rosin," the barrel was rolled and the noise of the cannon balls rumbling was heard mingled with the shrieks of a thirteen-year-old boy. The stunned property man failed to stop the rolling barrel, so it continued its course onto the stage, where Cooke, in a dazed condition, pushed off the old carpet which had been fastened over the end and found himself before the audience, surrounded by the witches.[33]

If his aunts thought his activity in the printing shop would curtail his theatrical leanings, they were mistaken.[34] His enthusiasm for the stage quickly spread to his "fellow devils" whom he persuaded to rent a room for theatrical performances, hoping that Mr. Taylor would not learn of it. But while Cooke was performing Zanga in Edward Young's *The Revenge*, "the enraged printer dispatched a posse of constables, who rushing in, hurried away the Moorish Chief."[35]

Early in 1770, a Mr. Fisher came to Berwick from Scotland with a paltry company in hopes of establishing the first regular playhouse there. He converted an old malthouse into a playhouse; there Cooke saw "The Earl of Essex, Oroonoko, and other pieces which I do not remember."[36] Certainly, this event rates as insignificant in the history of the provincial stage, but it was an important moment in Cooke's early theatrical education. Meanwhile, Cooke continued his amateur acting. In the autumn of 1770, he claimed that some of the young men of Berwick rehearsed Joseph Addison's *Cato*, and he and a friend from one of the previous theatrical adventures portrayed the two Roman ladies, Marcia and Lucia, Cooke taking the latter. He dated the actual production as 5 November and adds that it received a second performance at the converted malthouse "during the absence of the Regulars."[37]

The chronology of the next twelve to fifteen months in Cooke's life is confusing. A number of possibilities that relate to his earliest theatrical experience are discussed in Chapter 3. It seems clear that sometime in May 1771 Cooke obtained a release from his indentures to Taylor. It is possible that the event occurred even earlier.[38] The Stager says that with the appearance of the first strolling players in Berwick, "the types, the composing stick, all, all, were neglected; in vain were the admonitions, the reproofs of his kind relatives, his mind was made up."³⁹ In June, or possibly even earlier, Cooke and a fellow-apprentice named Colin Mitchell left for London "with a light heart and still lighter purse, their joint stock amounting to 17s 6d."⁴⁰

Dunlap gives no account of this trip or the reasons for it, other than indicating that Cooke witnessed several productions in London.⁴¹ Although the Stager's account is no doubt embellished and possibly laden with half-truths, it sheds some light on this hitherto neglected period of Cooke's life.

> . . . their first visit was to a noted theatrical tavern, in those days the Black Lion, in Russell Street, kept at that time by a retired actor of the name of Waters:⁴² to mine host they told the motive of their visit to London, namely to procure a situation on the stage: the good-natured Waters felt for their condition, procured them beds for the night, and on the morning, painted to them in such doleful colours the misery of a strolling player, together with the impractibility of obtaining a situation on the London boards, as totally dampened their youthful spirits, but what was to be done? to return to Berwick once more to slave at the case, the idea was horrible, however by the friendship of Waters, Colin Mitchell who was in possession of his dentures [sic], obtained a situation in a printing-office in Gray's Inn Lane, and out of his little earnings supported Cooke, who in return occasionally relieved the labour of his friend, by assisting him in his professional duties.⁴³

Soon Cooke and Mitchell met other young men their own age who were also interested in finding theatrical positions. Once more, if the Stager is to be believed, Cooke found himself involved in amateur theatricals. He and his companions decided to prepare a production of *Richard III*, using a hayloft for a theatre, an old carpet hanging over a line for their scenery, and small candles stuck into lumps of clay for their lights. The seats were boards placed over empty beer barrels; a bagpipe served for drums and trumpets. Richard's dress was the "borrowed vestment of a footman, consisting of a scarlet waistcoat, with sleeves of the same colour; a red cloak, obtained of an ancient dame in the neighborhood, fancifully decorated with strips of paper, embellished with Prince's metal, a star and garter made from the same materials."⁴⁴

The cast consisted of a Mr. Briarly as Richard, Mitchell as Richmond, Cooke as Tressel, and Joseph Munden as Buckingham. While there is no way to verify this account, there is no strong reason to disallow it either. One difficulty is that Munden would have been extremely young, at least two years Cooke's junior. The major difficulty involves the remainder of the narrative, in which the Stager describes an engagement made with a country theatrical circuit immediately following. Such an engagement is possible (see Chapter 2), but it must have occurred twelve to eighteen months later than the Stager suggests. It is known, however, that in November 1771, prior to any theatrical engagement, Cooke made a trip to Holland.

Until Cooke's diary was found, the provocation for Cooke's crossing to Holland and the details of the journey were only a matter of speculation. *The Cabi-*

net, 1807, says that Cooke was "embarked in business" and speculated that the trip to Holland may have involved some kind of business scheme. Dunlap, however, misinterpreted *The Cabinet*, since the article in question meant that Cooke engaged in business after returning from sea.[45] A part of Cooke's diary, written while he was in debtor's prison in 1807 and heretofore not readily available (Dunlap did not have it when writing the biography), gives adequate data to settle most significant points.[46]

Cooke went to Holland on the *Brittania*, a ship with about 200 tons of cargo under the command of a Captain Robert Scott. He did not, as Dunlap thought, go to Holland with an uncle, a brother of his mother.[47] Cooke's own words tell the story:

She [the *Brittania*] was one of the constant traders between London and that city [Rotterdam]. We had four cabin passengers, two of which, I remember, were an old jewess and her son. I remained on shore, in Rotterdam, several days; I was ill there, and after being let blood by a French or Dutch surgeon, attended by an English apothecary of the name of Adams. I lodged at a coffee house, kept by an old woman of the name of Dorothy Stevenson, a native of Carlisle, who had resided many years in Holland; & was well known by the English masters of vessels. I remember, after I came home, hearing my Uncle George, who, at that time, was Master of the Griffin, belonging to Yarmouth, in Norfolk, say, he remembered her very well. This uncle was one who was saved out of Admiral Broderick's ship, the Prince George, when she was burnt, I believe, in Gibralter Bay. I was several times ashore at Helvoetsluys, where we lay some days. We had a tedious & bad passage to the Thames; our poor cook, an Irishman, coming on board one night at Rotterdam, hurt one of his wrists by a fall. While we lay at Helboet, he was attended by a barber surgeon, one of the ancient fraternity, who used to poultice his wrist with herbs and shave him.

Cooke completed the entry by telling how, immediately upon their landing in London, the cook was sent to the hospital where it was "found the joint had been all the time dislocated."

Cooke's brief account leaves some unanswered questions, but it does settle several previous speculations as to his activities during this period of early manhood. Dunlap proposes another possible explanation for Cooke's trip: "[Cooke] once said in my presence, that when a boy, he had been midshipman on board of a king's ship;—this may have been the time."[48] Cooke, supposedly on his deathbed, also told Dr. Francis that he had been a midshipman in the Navy.[49] This detail, however, seems to have been another example of Cooke overstatement. Nor is it likely that Cooke made merely a pleasure trip. Although Dunlap misinterpreted *The Cabinet*, he was possibly nearer the truth than he imagined. A number of earlier theatre historians have been justifiably skeptical that Cooke was ever a midshipman, and some have suggested that he probably went as a cabin boy.[50] It appears now that this is a very strong possibility, although Cooke failed to prove a good seaman, being ill on both the trip over and the return.[51] He was back in Berwick early in 1772.

If Cooke entered into business upon his return, no source is available to indicate its nature. Roach claims that Cooke spurned business and came into possession of a legacy bequeathed by a distant relative, which he quickly ran through.[52] If the Dunwell story is at all true, could this have been part of her legacy to Cooke's mother? It is also conceivable that he practiced the craft of printer (compositor) for a short time.[53]

In the summer of 1773, George Cooke saw strolling players in Berwick for the last time. The company included Mrs. J. Brown[54] and her sister (or sister-in-law?) Mrs. Sarah Mills, under the joint management of a Mr. Holland and a Mr. Booth.[55] Both Mrs. Brown and Sarah Mills were later engaged in London.[56]

Cooke's experiences over the next twelve to eighteen months would prove critical in determining the direction of his career. Not only would he leave the amateur theatre, which he would come to abhor, but he would also witness the great stars of the London stage, several of whom would make an indelible impression on him. He himself would become an itinerant player on the long road to fame.

2

London Makes Its Mark

In 1774, quite likely after his first professional engagement (which is examined in the next chapter), Cooke returned to London for the second time, probably after mid-May, and remained there until the beginning of 1775. During this stay, Cooke observed some of the greatest actors on the London stage. Several would have a lasting influence on him. Since he arrived in late spring, Drury Lane and Covent Garden were closed, and the only theatre offering plays on a regular basis was the Haymarket Theatre, where Cooke would soon make his first London appearance.

It was at the Haymarket that Cooke saw Samuel Foote, an actor, playwright, and manager known for his exceptional talent for mimicry and biting satire.[1] Foote was then manager of the Haymarket under a patent granted in 1766 by the lord chamberlain under the Licensing Act of 1737. Foote, a short, fat man with an intelligent face and bright eyes, had been performing with a false leg for eight years. It might have proved a handicap to lesser men, but Foote capitalized on it, making the leg and limp the object of many jokes and an accepted part of his act.[2] His patent actually resulted from the accident that cost him his leg. While visiting the Lord Mexborough at Hampshire, he was urged to try the duke of York's spirited horse. He mounted the animal, which threw him; his broken leg was amputated above the knee. The duke of York, brother to King George III, felt partly responsible and helped Foote obtain a patent for the Haymarket. The patent restricted the Haymarket's period of operation to the summer, 15 May through 15 September, when the other two patent houses were not in operation.[3]

In 1774, the Haymarket had become a summer institution, and Foote was more popular than ever. His brilliance and mimetic powers were devoted primarily to self-exploitation; his most popular vehicles were plays he had written for himself. He was considered rather mediocre in most pieces he himself did not write, and one of these Cooke saw on his arrival: George Villiers' *The Rehearsal*, in which Foote played Bayes, on either 18 or 23 June.[4] Cooke also claims to have seen Foote as Sir Paul Pliant in William Congreve's *The Double Dealer* and as Hartop in Foote's own farce *The Knights*.[5] Foote appeared in these roles in the summer of 1776 rather than 1775. It seems likely that Cooke also spent the winter and spring of 1775–1776 in London. During the summer of 1776 he saw Foote as Pliant and Hartop, as well as Aircastle in his *Cozeners* and Thomas Lofty in *Patron*, both of which he might have also seen in 1775. Dunlap adds that Cooke had frequent opportunities to see and study Foote in many of his own comedies, listing among those roles known to have been performed by Foote in 1774 the Devil in *Devil Upon Two Sticks*, Major Sturgeon in *Mayor of Garratt*, and Cadwallader in *Author*. Cooke never attempted the type of broad topical satire in which Foote specialized (indeed, few did), but his observation probably gave him new insights into the technique of comedy.

With the opening of the winter season, Cooke was able to see the greats of the London stage, including Spranger Barry, David Garrick, and Charles Macklin; indeed, Cooke remarked, "Now I began to see acting." Barry and his wife Ann Barry were the first of the luminaries of the patent houses Cooke saw. In a letter to Horace Walpole on 20 October 1746, Thomas Gray described Barry as "upwards of six Foot in Height, well & proportionately made, treads well & knows what to do with his Limbs; in short a noble graceful Figure."[6] Barry, now approaching the end of an illustrious career, had exemplified the ideal of a tragic hero's appearance and had been one of the great romantic lovers of the age, giving dignity to heroes and passion to lovers. Barry's voice earned him the name "the Silvertoned Barry."[7] Although he had been known for his youthful roles, including one of the most famous Romeos of all times, Barry was now suffering from distemper and the pains of gout and thus principally limited himself to mature parts, including one of his greatest characters, Othello, which Cooke may have seen.[8] The first roles Cooke saw the Barrys perform were Evander and Euphrasia in Arthur Murphy's *The Grecian Daughter*, which they had first performed at Drury Lane in 1772 and were now assaying at Covent Garden. Cooke also witnessed Barry as Lear, Jaques, Sciolto in *The Fair Penitent*, Old Norval in *Douglas*, Orestes in *The Distrest Mother*, Orillon in *The Fatal Discovery*, Lord Townly in *The Provok'd Husband*, and Selim in *Edward and Eleonora*. Cooke was eventually to play many of these roles himself, and the image of old Barry must have remained with him.[9]

Of all Cooke's acting predecessors, he owed most to David Garrick. His career and contributions to the English stage have been too thoroughly studied to need review here.[10] It is significant, however, that Cooke first saw Garrick perform at Drury Lane during this formative period, when he had yet to develop his individual style. In time, Cooke was to become a descendant of the "Garrick" school, but with his own individualities and idiosyncrasies.[11]

When Garrick made his formal debut in London at Goodman's Fields as Richard III in 1741, it was clear that acting was becoming increasingly more subjective in its presentation of dramatic character.[12] The notion that the essence of human nature appears not in action but in reaction was beginning to be felt in the theatrical world of the actor. As Alan Downer points out, Garrick tried to transform the stage, to drive from the stage the exaggerated tendencies of his predecessors that caused them to pay little attention to the corresponding emotions that accompanied the meaning of their lines. Like Cooke, he was not wholly successful, and second-rate actors continued to hang onto the "exaggeration of violence, or of solemnity."[13] Nevertheless, Garrick has been credited with bringing to the London stage a new style of acting, a style that to his contemporaries was of nature. A typical midcentury comment on Garrick rhapsodized that "He restor'd Nature to her lawful Empire upon the Stage, and taught us by the Conviction of our sympathizing Souls, that Kings themselves were *Men*, [and] *felt* like the rest of their Species."[14] Naturalism and restraint are most often associated with Garrick, although theatre historians now feel that he was in fact an actor of the middle ground, "erring on the side of too much, rather than too little fire."[15] Whatever might be the case (and any attempt to reconstruct the style of a past actor is laden with hazards), Garrick undoubtedly belonged to the "Romantic School" as did his three greatest successors—Kemble, Cooke, and Kean. Despite great dissimilarities in their personal styles, all four attempted to interpret their characters on the basis of subjective response.[16]

However natural Garrick might have been, to his audiences he seemed and sounded more familiar than his predecessors, with the possible exception of Charles Macklin. Garrick's intense concentration made his acting seem real, no matter how idealized it was. Apparently, he revitalized the emotional transition, which had been a traditional technique of actors in the past but had been thrown aside in the fervor of declamation. The emotional transition called for the swift changing of one passion into another, utilizing the entire body to express the change, a technique that Cooke would also master.[17] Garrick's facial expressions acted as much as his body or his voice, and his first appearance as Richard introduced a technique he developed over the years.

> The moment he entered on the stage, the character he assumed was visible in his countenance; the power of his imagination was such, that he transformed himself into the very man; the passions rose in rapid succession, and before he uttered a word, were legible in every feature of that various face—his look, his voice, his attitude, changed with every sentiment.[18]

Garrick was not without his tricks; he was particularly fond of starts and pauses in his dying scenes, although he approached these moments with ease and variety. In the tent scene of *Richard III*, for example, Garrick would "start" from his dream in a way which "wakes all the Terrors of an Imagination distracted by conscious Guilt" and then in the brief sequence "Give me a Horse—bind up my Wounds! Have Mercy, Heav'n!" he would pause to change to an expression of dismay before crying out in distress—"Bind up my wounds"—and then pause again before seeking forgiveness, falling to the ground and changing his expression to pitifulness.[19] His most famous start came when, as Hamlet, he saw the ghost and wished to show terror; a sudden expression of recognition would then be followed by a moment of silent emotion, expressed by staggering backwards two or three steps, "his knees giving way under him; his hat falls to the ground, and both his arms, the left most noticeably, are stretched out almost to their full length," and so on.[20] Such "starts" and pauses could stun an audience, but some found that "the start may be too frequent, pause too long."[21]

Despite some vocal deficiencies, Garrick seems to have used his voice well in expressing emotions, but he spoke verse in what was called a "hobble-ti-trot" rhythm. He received a good deal of criticism for mishandling verse, emphasizing the incorrect word or syllable.[22] But he was furthering a reform, begun by Macklin, to tone down bombastic declamation. Cooke was to continue in the same direction, even to the extent of writing verse into prose as he studied his roles. Cooke would learn from Garrick the great importance of listening and reacting to other characters on the stage. Unlike Garrick, however, he would rarely be praised for his elegance of movement, but Garrick felt he had to compensate for his small stature by perfecting his physical appearance. Cooke's movement would most often be tagged as grotesque and crude.

Garrick, like Cooke, was praised for both comic and tragic roles. During this important period in his life, Cooke saw Garrick in several of his most famous parts, including Hamlet (twice), Lear, Benedick (twice), Leon (twice), Kitely, and possibly Iago, all roles that Cooke would later perform.[23] Cooke also implies that he saw Garrick's final performance as Don Felix in *The Wonder* and heard him speak an address on 10 June 1776 at a benefit for the Theatrical Fund.[24]

It seems unlikely that Garrick was a strong direct influence on Cooke, for he could not have seen him act more than nine times. However, Cooke's observations of other actors were strong impulses for him as a young actor and, perhaps unconsciously, he did follow in Garrick's footsteps while creating his own special style. How close Cooke came to Garrick is impossible to ascertain. Garrick's widow, late in her life, told Thomas Dibdin that "I approved Mr. Cooke much; his King Richard was good, and sometimes very fine, and put me in mind of Mr. Garrick." She added, however, that "Mr. Kean—it is like Mr. Garrick himself."[25] Sir George Beaumont, who saw Cooke during his first Covent Garden season and had also seen Garrick, felt Cooke came as near to Garrick as Kean did, "having more of those touches of nature and expression than anybody since his time—He is however coarse in comparison. Garrick might be said to be the Raphael—Cooke the Rembrandt.—Both true to nature, but the former possessing more grace and elegance."[26]

Cooke's own recorded comments on Garrick are few. In August 1798, he recalled "with pleasure and satisfaction Mr. Garrick's excellent performance of Kitely" and added that "Mr. Garrick's powers of discrimination were astonishing."[27] It appears, in fact, that of all the characters shared by both actors,

Garrick's Kitely had the greatest direct influence on Cooke. Dunlap says that Cooke, while in America, told him that he remembered Garrick's Kitely and "profited by his manner of playing it." Cooke gave no other indication of Garrick's influence on his acting, although he had read to Dunlap the "scene with Cash as an exhibition of Garrick's manner of playing it, and certainly it was exquisitely fine."[28] The only other comment of note which Cooke made is one recorded in 1807, while in debtor's prison, in which he predicted that "the taste and genius of Garrick will be recorded to posterity."[29]

Cooke nonetheless excelled in a number of techniques characteristic of Garrick, especially in the use of emotional transitions and "starts." If Cooke was unaware of Garrick's influence or preferred not to admit it, it was more obvious to others. During Cooke's preparation for his debut as Richard III at Covent Garden in 1800, Thomas Harris, the manager, attended every rehearsal and as recorded by Thomas Dibdin, playwright, actor, and close friend of Cooke, "seemed very much delighted, and more than once asked Cooke whether he had not formed himself on observation of Garrick?" Cooke's reply, typical of him, was "that he had never seen the great Roscius in his life."[30]

Cooke also saw Charles Macklin during this period. Although physically he resembled Macklin more than Garrick, Macklin's influence on Cooke was probably minimal since Cooke only saw him perform Shylock and Sir Archy MacSarcasm (on the same evening) two or three times and Iago once. This fact is interesting since Cooke was to inherit two of Macklin's most popular roles, in plays written by Macklin, Sir Archy MacSarcasm in *Love-a-la-Mode* and Sir Pertinax MacSycophant in *The Man of the World*. Indeed, the roles virtually died with Cooke.[31] According to some contemporary commentators, Cooke's Shylock surpassed Macklin's. In Macklin's hands, Shylock was performed for the first time in the eighteenth century as an inexorably evil villain. Macklin, like Cooke, was physically suited for such an interpretation. With piercing eyes, jutting chin, beaked nose, and the addition of a short, red, wispy beard, he seemed the "incarnation of Shakespear's Jew."[32] Since Cooke clearly kept many of the same pieces of business as Macklin, his debt to Macklin in this role seems evident. In his 1807 journal, Cooke mentioned that he had seen not only Macklin in the role, but also Henderson, Thomas King, and Kemble. He clearly preferred Macklin whom he felt fortunate to have seen, admitting that Macklin had been imitated by *all* his successors. Furthermore, Cooke felt that Macklin "fully merited the great reputation he gained by it."[33] Shylock was the role which Macklin chose in his conscious attempt to reform the English stage. Indeed, Macklin seems to have been more dedicated to "natural acting" than Garrick and, as Downer, I feel correctly, concludes: "Garrick has been given credit for more natural acting than he actually practised. But that Charles Macklin was ever anything but a naturalistic performer cannot be questioned."[34] Like Cooke, and possibly the source of Cooke's practice, Macklin wrote out verse lines in prose to avoid sing-song recitation.[35] Critics felt that, compared to Garrick's, Macklin's style was "chaste" and free of trick, without the starts and less obvious preplanned effects common in Garrick's great moments and present as well in Cooke's later style.

Macklin and Cooke suffered from a common problem: both had physical limitations that restricted the range of characters in which they could excel. As is noted in subsequent chapters, this problem had little effect on Cooke's early career. Macklin possessed an ungainly figure: inflexible features, arms, legs, and a hollow-toned voice that was clear but harsh. Like Macklin's, Cooke's movements were not graceful, and his arms, described as similar to a turtle's, were so short as to be out of proportion to the rest of his body.[36] Although Cooke's physical limitations were somewhat different, he likewise found himself increasingly forced into a limited range of roles, but, like Macklin, in these few roles he was rarely surpassed.

During his tenure at Covent Garden, Cooke would find that comparisons with Macklin were inevitable because of their physical resemblance. James Boaden, Kemble's biographer, rarely admired Cooke, but he admitted that "The real excellence of Cooke, like that of Macklin, was a certain sturdy *force* and *cunning* combined, which fitted him for the very parts in which the veteran himself excelled."[37] As Cooke's career progressed, other similarities to Macklin surfaced; these are explored in a later chapter.

During this same period, 1774–1776, Cooke also witnessed the following performers whom he lists in his 1807 journal. Presumably, each was seen in London: William Parsons (d. 1775), Edward Shuter (d. 1776), Thomas Weston (d. 1776), Henry Woodward (d. 1777), John Dunstall (d. 1778), John Lee (d. 1781), Samuel Reddish (d. 1785), West Dudley Digges (d. 1785), David Ross (d. 1790), John Edwin, Sr. (d. 1790), Richard Yates (d. 1796), and Thomas King (d. 1805).[38] Only one of this number, Thomas King, would act on the same stage with Cooke. For Cooke, none made the lasting impression of Macklin and Garrick and later, in 1781, of John Henderson, a third major influence.

3

A Strolling Player

The precise date and occasion of Cooke's first professional appearance are open to considerable speculation. His subsequent early acting career, the details of which are still imprecise, now begins to reveal a definite pattern: that of a youthful strolling player without firm attachments. Cooke apparently preferred the account that he made his first appearance as a "professed actor" in the small town of Brentford, a few miles west of London, in the spring of 1776.[1] It now appears that Cooke may have acted professionally before his second trip to London in 1774. Curiously, however, all major biographical sketches in the eighteenth century, as well as Dunlap, accept the Brentford story without question.

The earliest known evidence is sketchy but intriguing. A playbill (now at Hall's Croft) for a performance of *Hamlet* "at the New Theatre at the Unicorn in Stratford" on 2 March 1771 lists a Cooke in the role of Horatio. Of all performers of this name, on the basis of dates and other biographical data, G. F. Cooke seems to be the best candidate for this Horatio.[2] John Bernard's comment that "nearly forty years previous" to 1811 he had seen Cooke act "when his powers were, perhaps, as far from maturity as was my judgment" is the only eyewitness account that helps corroborate this early date.[3] Records at the Leicester Public Library mention that a Mr. Cooke in 1772 appeared at the Leicester Haymarket Theatre in a tragedy entitled *Zobeide* by Joseph Cradock, a local man of letters.[4] Professor Arnold Hare has recently discovered a half-dozen playbills that place Cooke in the Lincoln circuit, acting professionally in 1773.[5] Dunlap's account of Cooke during each of these periods would certainly allow for such activities. For the spring of 1771 Dunlap is virtually silent, except for mentioning Cooke's release from indentures to John Taylor "previous to the month of June, 1771,"[6] and this could just as easily have been prior to March 1771. In November 1771, Cooke was in Holland and by the early part of 1772, he was back in Berwick. For 1773, there is only Dunlap's story of the strolling company appearing in Berwick during the summer. Therefore, it is distinctly possible that Cooke made appearances in Lincolnshire or some other provincial district. Until more evidence is found, however, the Stratford and Leicester engagements must remain only tantalizing possibilities. As will be seen shortly, the 1773 engagement is quite tenable.

Although the Veteran Stager gives no date, it is intriguing to speculate that his narrative of Cooke's first acting experience coincides with the performances in Lincolnshire and possibly earlier engagements in other country circuits.[7] The Stager claims that during Cooke's outing in amateur theatricals, presumably in London on his visit in 1771, Cooke was seen by Roger Wright (d. 1786), a minor actor employed at Drury Lane for a number of years and described by the Stager as "the best representative of the motley coloured hero that then had appeared."[8] Wright, in the presence of Jemmy [James] Miller, the manager of a circuit in Northampton and Shrewsbury, said "that if he was not much deceived, that long nosed, raw Scotchman, would one day prove to be a d———d good actor."[9] Miller was presumably in London hoping to draft actors into his troupe, and upon repairing to the Black Lion, he saw Cooke and engaged him for his company at 10 shillings per week. As a result of a slump in attendance in his circuit, he had been forced to try a sharing system, common among provincial companies at the time. Cooke accepted the proposition so long as he obtained good parts to act; he gave little consideration to income.[10] If the Stager is to be believed, Cooke "made himself master of the words" of Hamlet, Othello, Romeo, and Hotspur; in Miller's company he acted

Tressel and Buckingham in one night: Orlando, Laertes, Cassio, Poins, Bassanio, Charles Dudley, Manly, Mr. Strickland, and many others of that class: and as they acted but three times a week, he had the others for his own private practice, during which time he applied himself to the studying of such characters as he conceived would one day fall to his lot; every hour, every minute of his time was devotedly employed in close application to study; he was never addicted to card-playing, or gambling of any kind; smoking he abhored, drinking ardent liquers in those days he never indulged in.

This statement is interesting for many reasons. It indicates Cooke's study habits at this early date and gives a possible explanation for the rapid additions to his repertoire in the months at King's Lynn between 1774 and 1775. It also delineates his personal habits early in his career, which later were to change drastically.[11]

Cooke left the Shrewsbury company and joined another one at Canterbury, apparently through the recommendation of Joseph Munden, who, according to the Stager, was then acting in the company, appearing as Lord Hastings in *Jane Shore*. Cooke was unable, however, to make any advancements since the major roles were already in the possession of a Mr. Penn and Billy Swords.[12] Cooke resolved to find a more advantageous position. In this task, he was allegedly spurred on by Charles Macklin, who was then appearing for a few nights in Canterbury. In the presence of the manager, and as the Stager claims, "in Cooke's hearing," Macklin accosted the manager by saying, "Sir, the weeds of your garden you seem to cultivate with care and attention; the only root you possess of value, and likely to flourish, you have planted in a barren soil, and in the shade—mark my words, Sir, that young man (pointing to Cooke) will one day be at the head of his profession."[13] How much of this story placing Cooke at Shrewsbury and Canterbury is true is difficult to ascertain, but it does account for a considerable gap in Cooke's early training and prepares us more adequately for the next step in his apprenticeship, a segment of his early career on which the footing is much surer.

Would it have been possible for a young actor of fifteen or so to have made such early overtures on the professional stage? The question is of minor consideration when it is recalled that such a pattern was common in the eighteenth century, especially in small provincial companies. Kean seems to have been on the road with the Samuel Jerrold company at the age of seventeen, and quite probably he was acting regularly as early as 1802, at age fifteen. John Philip Kemble was in the company of Chamberlain and Crump in Wolverhampton at the age of eighteen. Another contemporary of Cooke, Henry Erskine Johnston, was on the stage at ten and was a professional by age seventeen.[14] It was not unusual, then, for young boys in Cooke's time to run off to be actors, each with visions of becoming the Garrick of his day.

If there is less than conclusive evidence for these early performances in professional companies as outlined above, we are on firmer ground for the years 1774 and 1775 (and probably, with Hare's discovery, 1773),[15] when a Cooke appears on the bills in King's Lynn and Stamford in Lincolnshire playing young leads and even filling musical roles.[16] These performances were in Whitley and Herbert's company; the earliest records place them in the theatre in Checquer-Street, a playhouse built in the late 1760s in the center of St. George's Hall, which itself dates from the sixteenth century.[17] James A. Whitley was clearly the force behind this company, having built a strong reputation as a country manager by 1774. By 1781, he is known to have managed in nineteen different towns, in some of which he was responsible for actually building the first public theatre. The Stamford Theatre, for example, was associated with Whitley and his family for many years, and he doubtless was responsible for building a new theatre there in 1768.[18] *The Thespian Dictionary* credits Whitley with "the most extensive Midland circuit ever known in England: Worcester, Wolverhampton, Derby, Nottingham, Bedford, and Stamford theatres, etc. etc. were his."[19] This company, then, is the one in which young George Cooke seems to have spent two seasons, and possibly a third during the spring of 1773. The two seasons examined here lasted from mid-February to 15 May 1774 and from 14 February to 28 April 1775. Before looking at these seasons, it would be well to look at the evidence which would justify that this Cooke was George Frederick.

The most persuasive evidence is the lack of any other recorded activities for Cooke during these two seasons. Cooke did not arrive in London until the summer of 1774, and, as pointed out earlier, the actual date he left Berwick is unknown. George Frederick Cooke certainly recommends himself as the likely person for the 1774 season. The 1775 time period is less easily resolved, but it appears that Cooke did not see any plays performed in London during this period at King's Lynn and Stamford. The Stager, although attaching this engagement to 1776, seems to confirm the association with Whitley. He mentions an offer to join the company under a sharing scheme, but Cooke balked at the offer after earlier experiences under similar circumstances until the manager "threw into the scale the preponding weight of Richard, Othello, Hotspur, and all the tip-tops in tragedy."[20] Cooke did become the leading male performer in the company, with Miss Glassington as the leading lady, and during the course of his stay with Whitley he performed all the roles the Stager mentioned with the exception of Othello. According to this account, Cooke joined Whitley at Sheffield, but as is true throughout this source details such as this are often confused with other events in Cooke's career.

Cooke began his engagement at King's Lynn in the role of Young Marlow in *She Stoops to Conquer* on Monday, 14 February, with Miss Glassington as Miss Hardcastle.[21] Also listed in the bills is a Mrs. Cooke, the first such mention of a female companion. Cooke's first legal marriage supposedly did not occur until 1796, but as will become evident, actresses utilizing the appellation of Mrs. Cooke cropped up several times during his early career.

Cooke made his first appearance during the beginning of Mart Week, one of the King's Lynn fairs. The company chose this advantageous time to open the theatre, playing nightly except Sunday the first week and five nights its second week. On Tuesday, Cooke appeared as Jaffier in Otway's *Venice Preserv'd*, Mrs. Cooke performing in Francis Gentleman's afterpiece, *The Pantheonites*. On 16 February Cooke did not appear in the mainpiece. Mrs. Cooke took a small role in *The Provok'd Husband* and Cooke sang a cantata after Act IV and appeared as the young romantic hero, Henry, in the afterpiece, Charles Dibdin's *The Deserter*, which had first been performed at Drury Lane the previous year. As Henry, Cooke sang in five musical numbers. On Thursday Cooke took the role of Sir George Hastings in Hugh Kelly's *A Word to the Wise*, with Mrs. Cooke as Miss Willoughby; in the afterpiece, Garrick's *The Irish Widow*, Cooke portrayed Whittle, the old man who falls in love with the young widow (Mrs. Cooke). On Friday he was Jack Meggot, a young man about town in Benjamin Hoadly's *The Suspicious Husband*, after which he played Paris in *The Judgment of Paris*, a new burletta by Abraham Langford. He completed his first week as the young lover in Isaac Bickerstaffe's *Lionel and Clarissa, or The School for Fathers* (1768), a comic opera that had become a standard piece in provincial repertories. By the end of the first week, Cooke had played a variety of roles and had begun to show the versatility that was to be characteristic of his provincial career. Such diversity would show little abatement until Cooke reached London as a star attraction almost twenty-five years later.

During his second week, Cooke added six roles and only repeated Henry in

The Deserters on the 24th. Unless performed earlier elsewhere, he added to his repertoire Granville in Hugh Kelly's tragedy *Clementina* on the 21st; Young Meadows in Bickerstaffe's comic opera *Love in a Village* (22 February); Lord Duke to Mrs. Cooke's Lady Bab in Garrick's farce, *High Life Below Stairs* (23 February), the afterpiece following Hall Hartson's *The Countess of Salisbury*; Epicene in R. Hitchcock's comedy *The Macaroni* (24 February); and Lord Aimworth in Bickerstaffe's comic opera, *The Maid of the Mill*, Mrs. Cooke again appearing in the afterpiece, *The Pantheonites*.

After the Fair Week was over, the company settled down to a more leisurely schedule, performing for three weeks normally on Tuesdays, Wednesdays, and Fridays, and then for the next eight weeks on Tuesdays and Fridays only. During the remaining eleven weeks of the season, Cooke began to add roles of greater stature and demand on his talents. In the light of later criticism of the hoarseness of his voice and suggestions of his inability to sing, it is interesting to note that during his first two weeks, five of his appearances demanded vocal ability. The damage that doubtless occurred to Cooke's voice as he progressed through debauchery and ultimate alcoholism became abundantly clear only a few years after this period, when his voice was still unimpaired and capable of musical ability.

Beginning in March, the size of Cooke's roles increased, and his position as leading man in the company was more evident. He began the month as Wilding in Garrick's *The Gamesters* (1 March) and Damaetas in the burletta *Midas* by Kane O'Hara, followed on Thursday by Hamlet (3 March)—if not the first time in that role, certainly among the first. In addition, he added the following to his repertory: Henry II in Thomas Hull's *Henry II, or the Fall of Rosamond* (5 March); Don Felix in Susanna Centlivre's *The Wonder* (8 March), often repeated during his provincial career, along with Riches in Henry Woodward's *Harlequin Fortunates: or, Cupid's Revels*; Spatter in George Colman the elder's *The English Merchant* (11 March); Zanga the Moor in *The Revenge*, presumably in Dr. Edward Young's version, a role and play that figured prominently in his later career; Ramilie in *The Miser* (18 March); Macbeth (22 March); Revell in the farce *The Note of Hand; or, Trip to New Market* by Richard Cumberland, published that year (25 March); Lord Hastings in *Jane Shore* (5 April);[22] Alexander in Nathaniel Lee's *Rival Queens, or The Death of Alexander the Great* (12 April), fresh from its London premiere, for Mrs. Cooke's benefit night, during which she appeared in *The Irish Widow*; Filch in *The Beggar's Opera* (15 April) and Lovemore in Arthur Murphy's *Way to Keep Him*, plus the recitation of "An Ode To Garrick"; King Lear for his own benefit on 19 April; Lord Hardy the young lover in Richard Steele's comedy *Funeral; or, Grief a-la Mode* (26 April); Ruzee in Gentleman's comedy *The Modish Wife; or, Love in a Puzzle* (29 April); Posthumous in *Cymbeline* (3 May); Lord Trinket in Colman's *The Jealous Wife* (6 May), plus the reciting of "A Picture of a Play-house; or, Bucks! Have at Ye All"; Beau Mizen in Charles Shadwell's *Fair Quaker of Deal; or, The Humours of the Navy* (10 May); Ferdinand in *The Tempest* (13 May), with Mrs. Cooke as Miranda; and Belville in Hugh Kelly's *School for Wives* (17 May), the last night of the season.

It is presumed that Cooke, after completing his ambitious first season at Lynn, went to London, where it has been speculated that he worked for a short time as a printer, or "compositor," at an office in White Friars.[23] Dunlap reports that Cooke arrived in the summer and was able to witness performances only at the Haymarket, where he first saw Samuel Foote.[24] He stayed through the summer and into the 1774–1775 season but left in time to begin a second season with Whitley at King's Lynn, with a few nights at Stamford.

Cooke's first season at King's Lynn had covered three months with thirty-five playing nights and appearances in thirty-six roles in both mainpieces and afterpieces, plus several recitations and the singing of a cantata. Unfortunately, there is no way to assess the quality of these performances, but the activity had been arduous and Cooke was certainly learning his chosen occupation. He had been seen predominantly in the role of the young lover in comic pieces, but he had also performed several roles which would later be staples in his repertoire—Zanga, Macbeth, and Lear.

For the second season, the company remained virtually the same, including Mrs. Cooke, who may have accompanied Cooke to London, probably remaining, as will be seen, for several years with Cooke. The season, with performances on Mondays, Tuesdays, and Fridays, opened on 14 February 1775 with Cooke as Lord Aimworth in *Maid of the Mill*, a role he had played the first season. During the course of this season, Cooke repeated a number of other roles seen during 1774,[25] but as had been true his first season, he continued to add roles at an amazing rate.

Among the major new roles at King's Lynn were Hotspur (17 February), Richard III, postponed from the previous season (7 March); Romeo (21 March); Oroonoko (24 March); and Tamerlane (21 April). The remaining roles were mainly in the comedies of the day: Lord Ogleby in *The Clandestine Marriage* (18 February); Beverly in Colman's *The Man of Business; or, The White Lyar*; Dupely in John Burgoyne's *The Maid of the Oaks* (3 March); Tom, another lover, in Steele's *The Conscious Lovers* (13 March); Beverly in Arthur Murphy's study in jealousy *All in the Wrong* (17 March); Charles Manlove in Richard Cumberland's *The Choleric Man* and Apollo in *Midas* (20 March);[26] Stockwell in Cumberland's *The West Indian* (3 April); Marplot in the popular eighteenth-century comedy by Centlivre, *The Busybody* (18 April), plus "The Toast," a cantata sung by Cooke. For his first benefit on 21 Friday, Cooke performed Tamerlane to Thornton's Bajazet, and on the following Monday he appeared as King Arthur for Mrs. Cooke's benefit in Dryden's *King Arthur; or, The British Worthy* with music by Arne and Purcell.[27]

Cooke completed his Lynn engagement by repeating King Arthur for Mr.

Glassington's and Mrs. Maddox's benefit on 25 April and made his last appearance in Lynn on 28 April as Morcar in Dr. Thomas Francklin's *Matilda*. During the final season with Whitley and Herbert, Cooke made four appearances in Stamford, during Fair Week, repeating roles already performed in Lynn.[28] The unique event of this week in Stamford was the appearance of the equestrian and acrobat Philip Astley and his pupils, presenting songs, tumbling, "double summer sets," the slack rope, and featuring a "Lion's leap over a Garter 6 feet high." To add to the excitement on 30 March a Mr. Porter from Sadler's Wells[29] "will fly over a chair." At this point in his career, before he was to establish his Amphitheatre in London or a permanent base in Paris in 1783, Astley spent most of the year traveling throughout England and Ireland.[30]

Over a period of approximately ten weeks, Cooke appeared thirty-two times in thirty different roles, again many of them young lovers, but adding, possibly for the first time in his career, the role of Richard III, which was destined to become his most popular serious role in England and the United States. Seventeen of the roles performed during that season were not performed during the 1774 season at Lynn.

With such a propitious beginning, why did Cooke claim that his first appearance as a "professed actor" occurred during the spring of 1776 in Brentford? Could it have been because his first seasons in the provinces were so successful and in his own mind he believed that such successes would continue with growing momentum, climaxing with early recognition on the London boards? As we will soon see, this did not happen. In later years, such a setback might have seemed such a blow to his ego that it was simpler to eliminate any mention of these beginnings and rather acknowledge a much more humble beginning. As his diaries show, sublimation of such events in his life was quite common. Or, could the omission of these years have in some way involved the Mrs. Cooke mentioned in the bills? Did Cooke wish to wipe her memory out of his official life? We will probably never know.

In any event, Dunlap, following other earlier biographies and, we would assume, Cooke's own word, isolates the Brentford appearance as the springboard into the provincial theatre and a professional career, a fact that now must be seriously reconsidered.

The Brentford appearance came as a result of Cooke's association with an eighteenth-century spouting club. These clubs, while often ridiculed (as they are in Arthur Murphy's farce *The Apprentice*), provided a place for fledgling actors to rehearse scenes and passages of plays and to criticize each other's efforts. The clubs seem to have produced actors with the type of oratorical delivery that had characterized acting before Garrick and Macklin, but still in a style more conducive to the natural mode. Stagestruck actors paid fees to attend spouting club meetings and, if financially able, additional fees to play parts in a regular theatre.[31] In the Georgian theatre the barriers between amateur and professional were easily lessened through these clubs. Charles Mathews paid 10 guineas to appear at the Richmond theatre, and Pierce Egan describes a whole cast who paid various prices to appear in *Othello* at the Haymarket. Thomas Holcroft, in his autobiographical novel *Alwyn; or, The Gentleman Comedian* (1780), describes his friend Hilkirk who has applied to Samuel Foote for a position in a company bound for Edinburgh. Foote says to Hilkirk: "Well, Sir, I never saw a spouter before that did not want to surprize the town in Pierre, or Lothario, or some character that requires every requisite and address of a master in the art."[32]

Dunlap says Cooke visited a spouting club only once, while Edward Cape Everard, a provincial actor with whom Cooke would perform later, claims to have seen Cooke at several.[33] Just how active he really was we do not know. Although he had limited professional experience already behind him, Cooke, like Hilkirk, evidently took the spouting club route in order to perform at Brentford. The club to which Cooke was introduced by "a stagestruck hero" is not identified by Dunlap but was probably in London, where he had returned after his season at King's Lynn. At Brentford, Cooke performed two nights, first as Dumont in *Jane Shore* and on the second evening as Ensign Dudley in Cumberland's comedy *The West Indian*, both plays familiar to him from earlier performances and possibly both roles performed previously.[34] Cooke recalled that both male and female dressed in one room, the "dressing room was at the audience end of the house, and we had to pass through them to reach the stage, which was no higher than the floor, the whole theatre being a large room in a public house."[35]

My assumption is that Cooke's Brentford appearances occurred sometime after the spring of 1775, possibly during the summer. His whereabouts during the winter seasons of 1775 and 1776 are unknown, but it seems likely that it was during this passage of time that he found his career as an actor at a standstill, the momentum waning, or possibly he was living off a second family inheritance. In the summer of 1777, at approximately the age of twenty-one, Cooke engaged as a professional actor with a small company performing in the town hall of Hastings, Suffolk, on the southeast coast of England. Cooke has little to say of this country engagement, but he did recall that his manager, Standen, was deaf and a "perfect Drawcansir in the theatric field; he used to have a book or part affixed at the side of the stage, to which he coolly resorted when he was at a loss for his author."[36] He also remembered a woman in her seventies, named Woodward, who appeared in male characters and performed Sir Francis Gripe and the Miser. Cooke and the company found rehearsals an ordeal, with Standen following the actors by reading their lips, and "woe to the actor who made a pause for breath or effect, for there ended his speech for that time, and many is the question that by this means was answered before asked, and many were the dialogues that were made inexplicable games at cross purposes."[37]

Eventually, the troupe moved twelve miles northeast to the small community of Rye to perform in an old schoolhouse. At Rye, Cooke became ill "with a fever and ague" and returned to London in November. Apparently, his departure was either unexpected or extremely hurried because he left many of his possessions behind, never to be seen again.[38]

His activities from November to April 1778 are not known, but by spring he had managed to gain roles in three benefit performances at the Haymarket Theatre in London. The customary benefit performance allowed each member of a theatre company and staff one evening's box-office receipts, minus house expenses, including "charges" for the use of the theatre and to defray the cost of candles or other lighting, stage staff, and orchestra.[39] But Cooke did not engage as a regular member of the Haymarket company. In fact, his appearances came during the off-season when the benefit system took on some of its many deviations. When Cooke had observed Foote perform at "the Little Theatre in the Hay" in 1771, Foote had been in full command of the theatre. It now belonged to George Colman the elder, who had leased the playhouse from Foote in January 1777. After Foote's death in October, Colman received a yearly license from the lord chamberlain to operate as Foote had done, opening for a summer season that lasted from 15 May to 15 September. In addition to assuming control of the Haymarket, Colman re-roofed the fifty-six-year-old theatre and carried out other improvements, giving the facility an extra thrust into its second period of prosperity.[40]

With the lord chamberlain's permission, the Haymarket occasionally held productions out of season, as was the case with Cooke's appearances. These added performances were normally benefits for charities or families in distress, but on occasion they were given for spouting club members, other amateurs, or minor actors.[41]

Almost every reference to Cooke's first appearance at the Haymarket on 9 April notes that he played in a benefit for Mrs. E. Massey, whose husband was a member of a club called "Choice Spirits." He played with other notables including George Alexander Stevens, Ned Shutter, and Harry Howard.[42] Mrs. Massey was a member of the Haymarket company. It is possible, however, that both the Masseys shared in the receipts, since Massey's name and address appeared in the advertisements as a location for the purchase of tickets.[43] Nevertheless, the benefit itself was advertised for a Mr. Freeman, possibly an actor listed as Montano in *Othello* at the Haymarket on 1 October 1770, although the bill says this was his "first appearance on any stage."[44] Massey and Freeman played secondary characters in the evening's selection, Otway's blank-verse tragedy, *The Orphan*, with Cooke as Castalio, Mrs. Massey as Monimia, and James Swindall (or Swendall), whose career later crossed Cooke's in Manchester, as Polidore. Cooke's role was a familiar type for him, a tragic heroic lover, virtuous and honorable. In the course of the evening, he would display a spectrum of emotion, from feigned indifference to anger and despair, as well as enact a suicide—certainly a challenging role.[45]

The joint benefit of two virtual unknowns, Silvester and Rae, gave Cooke an opportunity to reappear at the Haymarket on 29 April. Comedy ruled the evening as the mainpiece featured Charles Johnson's *The Country Lasses* (later altered by J. P. Kemble and called *The Farm House*), a farcical plot with two ladies of station, Flora and Aura, who disguise themselves as lasses of the country, and two London travelers, Marian Heartwell and George Modely, who fall in love with them. Just as they had shared male leads in *The Orphan*, Cooke and Swindall did so again, with Cooke as Modely and Swindall as Heartwell.[46] Modely has hints of the villains yet to come in Cooke's repertoire, as he attempts to force his dishonorable intentions on Aura. But as was typical in the eighteenth century, Modely is a repentant villain, a character basically good who temporarily slips from this natural state, but is forgiven in the end. Such a character type became common for Cooke as his proclivity for villainy and ultimate repentance developed.

On the following evening, the Haymarket presented a charitable benefit for the Westminister New Lying-In Hospital, featuring the comedy *The Clandestine Marriage* (George Colman the elder and David Garrick). Cooke was Lovewell, another youthful lover, secretly wed to his employer's daughter, Fanny, but afraid to reveal his marriage because of his modest means—a familiar role to him. Massey appeared as Sterling, the father, and for the first time Cooke appeared with Hannah Robinson, who played Fanny's elder, more materialistically minded sister, Miss Sterling, whose proposed marriage brings complications since her suitor and his uncle fall in love with the already married Fanny. Cooke's acquaintance with Mrs. Robinson, begun at the Haymarket, continued in Manchester.[47]

The three roles Cooke undertook during his first London appearances, and the last for over twenty years except for two additional benefit appearances at the Haymarket in 1779, indicate the major line of business he took during his apprentice years. His initial leanings, perhaps not by choice but assignment, were heavily weighted on the comic side of the scale.

Cooke's next engagement was unique, especially considering the short existence of the theatre to which he would be attached. It thus gives us an interesting glimpse of a small corner of English theatre rarely mentioned in chronicles of the British stage. In May 1778, Cooke traveled from London to China-Hall, located near the town of Rotherhithe. Although a part of London today, it was outside the metropolitan area in the eighteenth century. The public house, or tea house, China-Hall, stood alone in the country on Lower Road, south of the center of London, with a playhouse behind it.[48] The proprietor of the Hall and apparently the theatre as well, a Mrs. Oldfield, dealt in china, hence the name, and sold wines, cider, and other spirits to the public.[49] The actor Edward Cape Everard, who was part of the twenty-eight member company, described it: "In a pleasant spot, about two miles from London Bridge, a commodious house was just built . . . called the China-Hall Theatre, in the center of a large garden, where vast numbers used to repair to tea." Everard, who had hoped to enter

Cooke's intended profession, printer's compositor, recalled that "the playhouse was built of wood, only bricks a yard high, on the outside was the pit-door, with a wooden kind of sentrybox for the money-taker." Unfortunately, Everard has left us little indication of the theatre's interior, only noting that it "could boast of as good scenery as the size would admit of, good dresses and decorations, and really a good company of comedians."[50] Hogan has estimated that the theatre could seat approximately 500 spectators,[51] and if Everard is correct "many persons of the first fashion, from London, condescended to visit . . . , till the Rotherhithe road was almost impassable for carriages."[52]

The tavern's life was to continue for many years, but the theatre behind existed for only three summer seasons and had more than its share of problems for such a short existence. In October 1776, late in the playhouse's first season, the local magistrates closed the theatre; the second year again brought difficulties with the law; but by the third, and as it turned out the last season, when Cooke found himself in the company, the legal problems had abated, and the troupe's future seemed assured for the full season. Then, unexpectedly, after the performance on 26 June the small playhouse was consumed by fire.[53] China-Hall's legal difficulties doubtless evolved because of the theatre's presentation of regular drama, which, under the Licensing Act of 1737, it was forbidden to produce, being within the twenty-mile restricted radius of London. The productions of the 1778 season, however, still included a number of regular dramas and did not limit the theatre's productions to minor forms of entertainment. Indeed, among the plays during the period 25 May–26 June were *Jane Shore, Douglas, Richard III, Romeo and Juliet, Venice Preserv'd*, and *She Stoops to Conquer*. In all, fourteen mainpieces and twelve different afterpieces were presented.[54]

When Cooke joined the China-Hall company, he was not among strangers. The company consisted of a number of performers who had been at the Haymarket during his brief tenure there: Robert Bowles, Mary Sophia O'Reilly, Mrs. Lefevre, Mr. and Mrs. Thomas Wade West, Mr. and Mrs. William O'Reilly, and the Masseys. Also in the company was his leading lady from the King's Lynn seasons, Miss Glassington, as well as her father.

Thomas Wade West, who, with his wife, eventually left England to establish an acting career in various American theatres, played leads in both comedy and tragedy at China-Hall, with Cooke supporting him in several roles.[55] William O'Reilly, who then performed under the stage name of Bailey, acted in comedies. O'Reilly, who later became a favorite comedian in his native Ireland and was praised by Cooke when he performed in Dublin in 1800, probably secured Cooke's services, since he acted as manager at China-Hall its last season.[56]

Of the remaining company members, Cooke remembered Samuel Thomas Russell, later a minor comedian at Drury Lane and then a lad of nine who filled girls' and boys' roles, gave imitations, danced, and even lectured.[57] Another principal performer of the troupe was Kitty Burden, who also performed leads in both comedies and tragedies. Russell, his wife, and his son, Thomas, had all acted at China-Hall since its first season, and Russell had probably been the manager of the theatre for its first two seasons. Cooke was engaged as an actor of second leads in both comedies and tragedies, although in the course of the season a few major roles came his way. The more experienced actors, veterans of the China-Hall stage, had prior claim to the leading roles.

Despite the briefness of this engagement, Cooke continued to demonstrate, as he had under Whitley and Herbert, that he could perform whatever role was available whenever possible. On every evening but two of fourteen nights of appearances, he enacted characters in both the mainpiece and afterpiece, assuming his first roles on the theatre's opening, 25 May 1778, as Frederick in Susanna Centlivre's comedy *The Wonder* and, after, as Charles Gayless in Garrick's *The Lying Valet* opposite Russell's Timothy Sharp, his loyal valet. It can be assumed that the success of *The Lying Valet* prompted the management to repeat the performance later, one of only two repeats during the short season.[58]

Cooke's next role was Glenalvon in Home's *Douglas* (27 May), his largest role of the season and the earliest known reference to his playing this crafty, unrepentant villain.[59] Glenalvon figured prominently throughout his career, in Ireland, England, and America. Because of its prominence in Cooke's career, it might be well to look briefly at *Douglas*, a play that remained popular well into the nineteenth century and one that Sir Walter Scott, as late as 1827, called "certainly one of the best acting plays going."[60] Glenalvon, heir to Lord Randolph, attempts to assassinate him in order to receive wealth and force Lady Randolph to yield to his passion. His plot is foiled by the brave youth Norval (Douglas), later revealed to be the presumed dead son of Lady Randolph by a previous secret marriage to the warrior Douglas, who has been reared by the old shepherd Norval. His identity is kept a secret, and Glenalvon, jealous of his new rival's soliciting of Lady Randolph's favor, plants doubts in Randolph's mind, until the nobleman believes that Douglas is his wife's lover. At a midnight meeting, attended by mother and son, Randolph attacks Norval. Accompanying his benefactor under false pretenses, Glenalvon plans to kill them both. He strikes Douglas from behind, only to be slain himself by the youth. Mortally wounded, Douglas finds his mother and dies. Lady Randolph then jumps off a cliff, and Randolph goes into battle intending to be killed.

Two days after *Douglas* (29 May), Cooke appeared in the role of Young Marlow in *She Stoops to Conquer*[61] and on 1 June 1778 as Lord Hastings in *Jane Shore*, both familiar and previously acted roles. Among the cast for *Jane Shore* was Edward Cape Everard, who joined the company in June, and who also danced between the mainpiece and the afterpiece.[62] Everard and Cooke soon became good friends. In fact, Everard attempted to give the young Cooke valuable tips from his greater experience.[63] During these formative years in Cooke's career, such advice would have been welcomed, and Everard, perhaps gloating a bit over his influence on Cooke, later noted Cooke's enthusiastic admiration for Garrick and his own instructions to Cooke. Everard confessed that he told him of "Garrick's business and manner in some particular characters he intended to play, and I have heard, that when he arrived at the highest degree of his excellence in Covent-Garden, he was not ashamed to acknowledge, that he owed much to my hints, advice, and instructions."[64]

When Cooke portrayed Lord Hastings, he also appeared in the supporting role of Young Wilding in the afterpiece, Arthur Murphy's *The Citizen*.[65] Next came Charles Gripe in Centlivre's comedy *The Busy Body* (3 June) and then a role now familiar to him, Lovewell in *The Clandestine Marriage*.[66]

For the remainder of the season at China-Hall, Cooke appeared in a series of supporting roles, only occasionally stepping into a major character in an afterpiece. West and Russell seem to have used their prerogative to assume more leading roles as the season progressed. Among the more significant parts assigned to Cooke were the honest clerk Truman in George Lillo's domestic tragedy *The London Merchant; or, George Barnwell* (9 June); the quarrelsome Tybalt in Garrick's altered version of *Romeo and Juliet* (10 June); and the bold and stately Earl of Southampton in Henry Jones' tragedy *The Earl of Essex* (19 June). On the same bill with Essex, Cooke appeared as Captain Constant in the farce *The Ghost*, adapted from Centlivre's *The Man's Bewitch'd*.[67]

On 22 June, Cooke took the role of Lord Aberville—a spendthrift, a man of fashion, and a libertine—in Cumberland's sentimental comedy *The Fashionable Lover*. Two nights later (22 June), he played the young lover, Frederick, in Henry Fielding's comedy *The Miser*. Then disaster struck the playhouse. Although Cooke could not recall his role on the night of 26 June, it was Tressel in Cibber's altered version of *Richard III*.[68] He also appeared in the afterpiece, repeating the role of Captain Constant. The fire began shortly after the conclusion of the performance and quickly spread throughout the wooden structure, leveling the playhouse in slightly over two hours.[69] It was apparently caused by arson. Rumors spread rapidly; on 29 June, 1778, the *London Gazetteer* published this account:

On Friday night, about 11 o'clock, a fire broke out at China-Hall Theatre, Rotherhithe, which entirely consumed the same, with all the scenes, &c.

Various accounts are spread concerning the above fire: the performers are said to be of opinion that those of the inhabitants who opposed their performance without effect, have been wicked enough to take this method of silencing them. On the other hand, some of the neighbors say, that the fire was not the mere effect of accident, but in consequence of an opinion that the Magistrates were for stopping the performances, and the property being insured. For the honour of human nature, we hope both reports are void of foundations.

Everard, who omits any mention of magistrates, held the opinion that the arsonists came from one of two possible "inhabitants": "Near to us was the St.

Helena gardens, famous for their tea-drinking, of course our business hurt their's; whether this was occasioned by their means, or by the Methodists harbouring about there, (which, from the threatening papers, I think most likely) we never could discover, but it was clearly a wicked wilful business; it was evidently, as I've said, 'a gunpowder plot.' "[70] Indeed, six hampers of hay had been placed close to the rear of the playhouse,[71] and Everard tells us that the "wooden kind of sentrybox of the money-taker" had been crammed full of straw and other kinds of combustible materials to start the fire. Only two or three chests of clothes could be saved,[72] but the tavern, not attached to the playhouse, received no damage.[73]

During Cooke's thirty-two days of performances at China-Hall, he appeared in twenty-four roles, many previously performed. This is additional support for the supposition that his experience in the provinces was more substantial than it was previously believed to be. He continued to perform predominantly in comedies and added a number of singing roles to his repertoire.

Cooke was caught in the middle of the summer season with no immediate prospect of employment. He remained at China-Hall to assist in the erection of a temporary booth for performances until a new theatre could be built. The landlord "employed a carpenter, . . . obtained the lend of nearly a hundred pounds worth of sailcloth, bays and canvass [sic], and in about a month . . . opened a theatrical tent, or booth."[74] No description of this temporary booth is extant, but it was probably similar to the booth depicted in Thomas Rowlandson's water colour of Richardson's booth at Greenwich Fair. The booth as a center of entertainment was a popular part of London fairs throughout the eighteenth century; thus, the China-Hall management had precedent for their structure.[75]

The first performance there on 30 July was *The Merchant of Venice*, followed by the afterpiece, *The Old Maid*. Few names appear on the playbill for this evening's entertainment, and Cooke's is not among them. It is quite possible, since he had previously appeared in the part that season, that he appeared as Harlow in *The Old Maid*. It would be useful to know what role, if any, he was assigned in the mainpiece, but that, like the other performances and roles on the booth stage, will remain unknown.[76]

Everard gave an additional bit of information on Cooke's acting during the late summer, probably in August. Cooke, he said, wished to play the part of Edgar, and to oblige him Everard took the role of Lear. He added that Cooke "was very perfect in" the role and that "the play . . . was upon the whole well performed, and, considering too that it was almost in London, 'twas wonderful that he played it with great credit to ourselves, to full and genteel houses, no less than three times."[77] It is interesting to recall that it was probably Cooke who had portrayed Lear at Lynn a few years earlier. Nevertheless, at this stage of his career, Edgar was a more fitting role, especially if, as is probable, the company chose the usual eighteenth-century version by Nahum Tate, in which Edgar and Cordelia appear as lovers and the play ends happily.

China-Hall, plagued with problems from its inception, continued to have bad luck. In September, the magistrates ordered the booth closed after "six nights more indulgence," and the actors quickly formed a committee, with Cooke and Everard among the members, to find a way to remain open. Their efforts were to no avail, for after the period of "indulgence" the order still stood. A major part of the company left, not wishing to be arrested. Whether Cooke was among their number we do not know, but Everard says that those who remained presented John Gay's *The Beggar's Opera*. Cooke had played Filch in Lynn, but in this production Everard took the role; no other assignments are known.[78] After the first scene, peace officers rushed on stage to haul away the performers, but Everard managed to escape.[79]

In the meantime, William O'Reilly had been constructing a new theatre and since he had no obstruction he probably believed that the China-Hall Theatre would overcome its jinx.[80] By the end of November, the new China-Hall Theatre was almost completed. But once more it was destroyed. On 25 November 1778, the *London Gazetteer* included the following brief item: "Yesterday morning the playhouse at China-Hall, Rotherhithe, was blown down by the violence of the wind. The said playhouse was burnt down last summer, but it being insured was rebuilt by contract, and the tiling of it completely finished last week." Thus, China-Hall sank into oblivion. The China-Hall chapter, however, meant more experience for George Cooke and added strength to his acting talents, as well as increasing his stock repertoire.

After Rotherhithe, Cooke appeared briefly at the "Tennis Court in the Borough," which he tells us was soon shut up by the Surrey magistrates.[81] It seems most likely that this is the Tennis Court Theatre mentioned by Hogan as a temporary theatre installed in Southwark during the winter of 1778–1779. Its site was probably on what is now Tennis Street, Necomen Street.[82]

In the following spring, Cooke acted twice more at the Haymarket, again for benefits during the off-season. On 22 February 1779, in Edward Moore's sentimental comedy, *The Foundling*, he portrayed the rakish young Charles Belmont for a "Benefit for a Family under Misfortunes," with Hannah Robinson, Everard, and Colin Mitchell, his old friend from amateur days.[83] Mitchell, a friend of Charles Macklin as well, had also performed with Cooke at China-Hall in the temporary booth.[84] Mitchell, Everard, and Cooke also appeared in the afterpiece, *Prejudice of Fashion*, with Cooke portraying Medium.[85] It was Mitchell's benefit, shared with an unknown, Sinclair, that allowed Cooke to reappear at the Haymarket as Glenalvon on 10 May.[86] Despite performances in and around London for several years now, Cooke apparently attracted little or no attention from the two major patent house managers.

Cooke's activities for the next several months are unknown. In September 1779, he joined a company under the management of (David?) Fisher[87] at Sudbury in the eastern county of Suffolk, with Stowmarket and Thetford in Norfolk also part of his circuit of towns.[88] Problems seemed to be following

Cooke, for when Everard came to join the troupe in February 1780 he found only three members of the company left, including Cooke. The remainder of the troupe had evidently deserted with hopes of employment elsewhere. Everard explained the unfortunate circumstances:

I had received a letter, inviting me to join a Mr. Fisher's corps, then finishing their season at Stowmarket, and were about going to Thetford, in Norfolk. I was told by a friend to whom I had shewn this letter, that I should not stay with them a fortnight; "For," said he, "it is not, properly speaking, Fisher's, but Scraggs' company; for he does what he pleases, and the instant that you play any low comedy-part, which is all that he dare aspire to, and even the lowest of the low is much too high for his comprehension and above his abilities, yet the moment that you attempt any character in that walk, depend upon it, that he will leave the theatre. Fisher would be, in fact, very happy at that, if he would go solus; but he and Mrs. Scraggs both known, that in that case he would take Mrs. Fisher along with him."[89]

Scraggs and Mrs. Fisher had secretly left town on at least two occasions, only to be overtaken by Fisher and Mrs. Scraggs, who then persuaded them to return. The rest of the company apparently finding the entire affair distasteful and no doubt disruptive, left, and Cooke had finally reached the same decision when Everard caught up with them. "He told me he would stay no longer with such beings; he had determined, at a venture, to go off to Norwich: wished me to go with him, saying, that if I got no engagement, very probably *he* should, and was almost certain of procuring employment, in his profession as a compositor, and gave me his word that, in either case, I should receive half of his income."[90] Despite the added burden of a heavily pregnant wife, Everard declined Cooke's offer. The generosity of both money and effort in their behalf was not unusual for Cooke, now or later in his career, for whatever weaknesses of character he was to exhibit later, he remained sensitive toward poverty and misfortune in others.

One of several gaps in Cooke's career occurs immediately after leaving Fisher. Perhaps he gained employment in Norwich, but Dunlap simply says he "ceased to tread the boards" and has no additional explanation of the next twenty months.

Dunlap introduces the next stage in Cooke's strolling career by saying that it was "little else than marchings and countermarchings from Nottingham to Loughborough, from Loughborough to Derby, from Derby to Stamford, and then to Nottingham again."[91] Such country experience could only have added to Cooke's training and growing repertoire. In October 1781, he appeared at Nottingham in the company that had belonged to James Whitley, who had died a month earlier in Wolverhampton. Whitley's family had assumed the responsibilities of the company, although the actor O'Brien was made manager on behalf of Whitley's daughter. By the time of Whitley's death, his contributions to the provincial theatre—the numerous playhouses that dotted the Midland and his skillfulness in management—were widely recognized.[92] For Cooke it might have proven more advantageous if Whitley had been still living, and could have remembered and rewarded Cooke for his contributions six years earlier, but the treatment he received there remains unknown. For the next two years, Cooke stayed with the new Whitley company, touring the Midland Circuit.[93]

While with the Whitley company, Cooke made several trips to London and had his first chance to see John Henderson, then in his mid-thirties, perform at Covent Garden.[94] Henderson had begun his career with a brief apprenticeship under John Palmer at Bath in 1772. Thanks to a letter of recommendation from Garrick, he had been engaged by Colman at the Haymarket in June 1777. When Cooke observed him at Covent Garden, Henderson had only recently left Drury Lane and had become London's reigning tragic actor.[95] Since he had clearly inherited Garrick's mantle, it is even more regretful that so little is known about him.[96] Henderson's acting style seems to have been similar to Garrick's; indeed, he began his career giving imitations of his mentor. His reputation had developed as a result of his fine speaking voice, combining passion and judgment, although his voice was not considered to be as flexible, sharp, or pleasing as Garrick's. He was known especially for his ability to make the author's meaning his own; he gave the impression that he was thinking it himself for the first time but was retaining all the facets of meaning. He was a "chaste" actor, with restrained actions. To his credit, he refrained from vocal tricks or other means to gain easy applause. Davies, Henderson's biographer, concludes that his greatest asset was his intense identification with his character, combined with his fine speaking voice and the spontaneity of his expression.[97] During his all too brief career, Henderson played a wide range of characters, including Hamlet, Iago, Lear, Richard III, Shylock, and Falstaff. Cooke remembered seeing him as Macbeth, Hamlet, Shylock, Falstaff, and Benedick.[98] Eventually, Cooke was to play all these roles himself. While in America, almost thirty years after seeing Henderson, Cooke still acknowledged his indebtedness to him and claimed, just prior to performing Falstaff, that "his best points were only copied from" Henderson.[99] Cooke, like Henderson, would closely identify with his roles, giving the audience a strong impression of revealing the author's thoughts for the first time, notably in soliloquies. As Cooke's talent gained greater notice, Henderson, along with Garrick and Macklin, would most frequently be cited as standards of comparison to Cooke's own performances. Such a comparison was inevitable, for the triumvirate of Garrick, Macklin, and Henderson served as principal influence and inspiration for the youthful George Frederick Cooke, who, by the end of 1783, was ready for a new chapter in his career.

4

A Correct Actor

In December 1783, Cooke left Whitley's company and came "to a more important era in my theatrical career," a position in the Manchester company—his first major engagement.[1] After acting sporadically for almost twelve years in relatively minor country playhouses on the fringe of London, he was about to act in one of the major provincial theatres in England.[2] Cooke gives the following account:

Having obtained an engagement for the Manchester Theatre from Mr. James Miller of Shrewbury, who was then acting manager, I left Louth on Saturday the twenty-seventh of December, 1783, and arrived at the Lower Swan Inn in Manchester (at that time kept by Dixon) on Tuesday evening the thirtieth. The next day I went to private lodgings.[3]

This, of course, is the same Miller who had managed the circuit in which Cooke had appeared only a few years earlier, and doubtless such prior contact aided him in gaining this most important engagement. Miller had succeeded as manager of the Theatre Royal, Manchester, during the previous summer of 1783. Tate Wilkinson, manager at York and a future employer of Cooke, considered Miller a "man of friendly and honest intentioned principles, and possessed of property, but unfortunately infatuated with two galloping hobby-horses—Managing a company of unruly actors, and also much more fond of his own acting than his auditors were."[4] Nevertheless, Miller inherited a theatre with a growing reputation.

The grant for a Theatre Royal in Manchester, made to Joseph Younger and George Mattocks, their executors, administrators, and assigns, for a term of twenty-one years, was dated 3 July 1775. A theatre measuring 102 feet by 48 feet was erected at the junction of York Street and Spring Gardens, opening on 5 June 1775 with a production of *Othello*. In 1776, Mrs. Siddons appeared at the new Manchester theatre, and a few months later her brother, John Philip Kemble, performed there. During the winter of 1781, Younger's health was failing, and the theatre was given over to a company controlled by Joseph Austin and Charles Edward Whitlock. (Cooke would first cross paths with Austin and Whitlock during the summer of 1784.) After Race Week, in 1783, they gave up their interest in Manchester and the lot fell to Miller.[5]

Miller quickly set about making extensive repairs on the seventeen-year-old playhouse, as well as decorating the interior "with a variety of new scenery and machinery by a very eminent artist."[6] During this first and only season of Miller's management at Manchester, Karl Gottlob Küttner, a German who between 1791 and 1796 published a monumental work of 2,324 pages on England, resided in Manchester.[7] Although he nowhere mentions Cooke, his earliest letters from Manchester give an interesting first-hand appraisal of the theatre, which then had the reputation of being one of the best outside of London.

The local theatre is small and hardly bigger than the former wooden one at Leipzig, but graceful, warm and comfortable, and the scenes, curtains and effect machines are very good indeed. The proscenium consists of six Corinthian pillars and above it is written: Spectas ut tu spectaberis. In spite of its size, the house has three different entrances, none of which are in connection with the others.[8]

Küttner found the actors "on the whole rather good than mediocre" and observed that tragedy was given more than comedy, "because not only those here, but English actors in general represent the former better than the latter." He found several drawbacks in Shakespearean performances, including one common in the provinces, the reviving of corpses for later appearances. Perhaps most useful in sensing the atmosphere at the Manchester theatre during Cooke's tenure there is his vivid description of the audience:

The gallery is here, as everywhere in England, unbearably unshamed; They throw apples, pomegranates, nut-shells on the stage, in the pit and the boxes; they cry out and make a lot of noise; I know people who refuse to sit on the front seat of the boxes. With ladies they are more polite. Many years ago a flask flew from the gallery into the pit, striking a man's skull. This shrieking and din and all this bad behavior is difficult in the intervals, but during the play itself the gallery is quieter than I have heard in any other place, and the applause and laughter in the middle of speeches does not last so long that one loses the thread or misses a climax. But here, too, it is the gallery which sets the tone, either booing or applauding or calling for an encore. Of battles and murders are they especially fond, and when the theatre is full of bodies, as at the end of *Hamlet* there is no end to the applause and trumpeting. In England, no one is allowed on the stage.[9]

This was not exactly objective criticism at its best, but critical comment, especially in the press of the day, was almost nonexistent in the provinces. Thus, Küttner's comments give us one of the most complete contemporary glimpses of the Manchester stage in 1783.

Miller's company numbered between thirty and thirty-five, which was the average size for an eighteenth-century provincial company. With the change in management, a few of the troupe left, being replaced with Cooke, his old acquaintance Hannah Robinson as principal leading lady, and Thomas Grist, who was to become a great favorite in Manchester. They first appeared on 10 December.[10] Cooke was assigned secondary leading roles, while Grist garnered most of the major parts throughout the season.

After playing with Cooke at the Haymarket, Mrs. Robinson had performed in Portsmouth; she had spent the previous season of 1782–1783 at Covent Garden.[11] She remained at Manchester for two seasons and then moved on to York, where Wilkinson capitalized on her prominence at Manchester, calling her "the Siddons of Manchester." Grist, who had made his "first appearance upon any stage" as Othello at Drury Lane in October 1775, is remembered for the prompter William Hopkins' comment on that first performance, recorded in his diary: "[Grist's] figure is well enough,—a good Voice, and Power enough when he knows how to manage it.—He is awkward, but it was a very fine first Performance, and, if there is proper Care taken with him, he may make an Actor."[12] Grist also left for York, and Wilkinson observed that he "has received much fame in almost every provincial theatre; he is social in every town with many of the most creditable inhabitants, and is entertaining, without recourse to scandal; is in general master of his bottle, and the bottle not master of him."[13]

Another mysterious member of the company was a Mrs. Cooke who played minor roles. Was this the first or second Mrs. Cooke? A Mrs. Cooke, it will be recalled, also appears on the bills at King's Lynn in 1774–1775. What was their relationship? Had she been traveling with Cooke since Lynn? It is quite likely that they were both members of the later Whitley company; possibly she had been left behind in 1775, and Cooke had then reestablished their relationship shortly before coming to Manchester. Her roles at Manchester were quite similar to those at King's Lynn, though there they were more prominent, and in both cases she appeared as a singer. Her position as a utility actress in Manchester would be reasonable considering that the company was more prominent than that at Lynn. At any rate, we have no further knowledge of this Mrs. Cooke from contemporary sources, nor does Cooke later mention a wife prior to his marriage to Alicia Daniels in 1796. It is well to remember that during the eighteenth century it was fairly common for a young actress to assume unofficially the name of the actor with whom she was living in an effort to avoid scandal. Joseph S. Munden, a close friend of Cooke and a well-known comedian in the provinces and later in London, had a mistress for many years, Mary Jones, who not only performed as Mrs. Munden but also had four daughters by him. She finally left Munden, eloping with the actor John Hodgkinson, which caused considerable trouble for Munden when the truth became known.[14]

Cooke's first role at Manchester, on 2 January 1784, was as Philotas in Arthur Murphy's *The Grecian*, with Grist as the deposed King Evander and Robinson in the role of his devoted daughter, Euphrasia.[15] Cooke recalled that he was received with much applause but realized that it

was not a very favorable character for a first appearance, for the *then* heroes of Manchester did not seem inclined to participate or even lend their "blushing honours," for they were all strangers, having only the advantage of me in priority of standing by about a month. This is a courtesy [the choice of role] which has long been established in well-governed theatres; but the Manchester Theatre, at this time under Mr. Miller, who had been chiefly used to small detachments, was really governed by a cabal, not one of whom are now living, or even mentioned in theatrical society.[16]

Is there a faint echo of something less than satisfaction from his first round with Miller?

On 6 January, Cooke played Antonio opposite Grist's Shylock, Robinson's Portia, and John Banks' Bassanio. Banks became part of the management at Manchester in 1788, and his appearance at the Theatre Royal this season marked the beginning of a long association with Cooke.

The *Manchester Mercury* of 20 January 1784, records the first leading role for Cooke this season, the now familiar Young Marlow in *She Stoops to Conquer*. The Tony Lumpkin that night was an actor named Connor, who also became one of many managers at Manchester and for whom Cooke later performed. On 27 January, Cooke supported Grist's Richard III as King Henry VI, which in Cibber's version takes on greater proportions with the stabbing of Henry by Richard. Kuttner found this Richard quite excellent and admired Grist's portrayal of the title role, "with a crooked back, a growth on his right shin, heavy black eyebrows and a black wig, and with his whole figure somewhat stooped."[17] On 3 February, Cooke appeared as Douglas in Home's tragedy.

Before appearing in the first benefit of the season—and they seem to have been plentiful that season—Cooke performed for the first time in his career as Prospero in the altered version of *The Tempest*.

The first benefit, early in March, belonged to the manager, who chose James Thomson's tragedy *Tancred and Sigismunda*, Cooke taking the supporting role of Siffredi, Lord High Chancellor of Sicily and father of Sigismunda. The role was repeated on 7 May. Next came Don Alonzo, the brave soldier in Edward Young's *The Revenge*. In mid-March, benefits came rapidly and afforded Cooke some of his more prominent roles, including Benedick opposite Mrs. Robinson's Beatrice and Claudius for Grist's benefit.[18] Küttner describes a portion of this latter production. He was shocked to see farcical elements introduced into the gravedigger's scene, especially when one of the diggers removed his ten or twelve waistcoats one by one before beginning to dig, while the gallery shrieked with laughter. Then they dug up five skulls and a heap of miscellaneous bones, which Küttner found disgusting. When Hamlet (Grist) finally examined Yorick's skull, he became sickened. Since the grave was on the apron, stage hands came out, swept all the skulls and bones back into the grave, replaced the boards, covered the stage floor with a rug, and left. Küttner adds, "The English can stomach such things without taking the slightest offense."[19]

At the end of March, Cooke was assigned the leading role of Orestes in Ambrose Philips' *The Distrest Mother*. On 2 April, he took his first benefit, shar-

Joseph Munden (1758–1832). Cooke's friend in London and the provinces. Author's collection.

A youthful G. F. Cooke. Since Cooke became a London star late in his life, few early drawings of him are extant. Frontispiece to the *Thespian Dictionary*. Brown University Library.

ing the performance with Mrs. Cooke.[20] Prior to the benefit, Mrs. Cooke had for the most part performed utility parts, although earlier she had enacted Ariel (with songs) to Cooke's Prospero and had been given the role of the beautiful Selima in *Tamerlane*. The Cookes chose Addison's *Cato* for their mainpiece and concluded with Leonard Macnally's new comedy adapted from Laurence

Sterne's novel *Tristram Shandy*. In *Cato* Cooke appeared, probably for the first time in his career, as the Roman senator opposed to Caesar's designs against the Republic. The role of Cato was to have a unique place in his subsequent career.

Since the Cookes' benefit was the "last night of the company's performing till Easter Monday," Cooke did not reappear until 12 April and then as Hotspur, followed by at least four more appearances before his second benefit on 17 May: Ranger in Benjamin Hoadley's sentimental comedy, *The Suspicious Husband*; the title role of Barbarossa, the repentant villain, in John Brown's play; Cardinal Wolsey in *King Henry VIII*; and Don Felix in *The Wonder*.[21]

For some unexplained reason, a second benefit was given the Cookes, with *The Orphan* as the mainpiece, followed by *The Indian Chief*, presumably the entertainment by John Williams.[22] No cast is given for the mainpiece, but Cooke no doubt appeared as Castalio, the role he had performed in the play at the Haymarket. In the afterpiece he portrayed a gambler, a minor role, but the piece, popular that season, was repeated at least three times during the course of the season.[23]

On 21 May 1784, Cooke was Sir Peter Teazle in one of the few productions that receives specific comment in the *Mercury*. Hannah Robinson played Lady Teazle, John Banks was Joseph Surface, and Grist appeared as Charles Surface. On 25 May, the critic, possibly the proprietor of the *Mercury*, Joseph Harrop, gave one of those less-than-helpful comments common in the provincial papers of the eighteenth century: "Mr. Grist and Mr. Cooke entered fully into the spirit of their Characters, and discovered many conspicuous Talents in the Line of Comedy." If nothing else, the brief statement gives further proof of Cooke's early tendencies toward excellence in comic roles. After Teazle, Cooke performed the leading part of the virtuous hero, Alwin, Lord Salisbury, in Hall Hartson's tragedy *The Countess of Salisbury*.[24]

The annual week of festivities for horse racing began on Monday, 31 May. During Whitsun Week, which was also Race Week, plays were normally performed each night.[25] During the period of Cooke's appearances in Manchester, the theatre was usually opened on Mondays, Wednesdays, and Fridays. Toward the end of the eighteenth century, Thursday often was added as an extra playing night. Prices of admission were 3s. boxes, 2s. pit, and 1s. gallery, so that the theatre owners could capitalize on the extra business in town, as most provincial theatres did. I have located only one definite role and one probable for Cooke during the week. On 1 June, he played the principal role of Carlos in Cibber's comedy *Love Makes a Man*, with Thomas Ward, a local printer turned actor, appearing in the cast. Ward, who had acted on the Manchester stage three years before, returned to play during Race Week and eventually became a partner with John Banks in the management of the Manchester Theatre in 1790.[26] On the third night of Race Week, Joseph Younger, the former manager and one of the original patentees of the Theatre Royal, appeared on the Manchester stage as Falstaff in *Henry IV, Part 1*. Although no other role assignments are listed in the advertisements, presumably Cooke repeated his role of Hotspur.

The Manchester season closed on 7 June. Cooke had spent a busy six months in Manchester, portraying at least thirty-two different characters in forty known appearances.[27] A number of the roles were already part of his repertoire when he arrived in Manchester, and he continued to add new ones. It is interesting that he acted more often in tragedy than in comedy (20 to 11), even though he continued to appear predominantly in the role of the hero or the young lover. The number of characters who were out-and-out villains or had definite villainous overtones seemed to be on the rise, however. Most significantly for Cooke, he had finally arrived at an important provincial house where his talents could be tested and observed. The road was beginning to look less hazardous for him. He was to appear on the Manchester stage many more times during his career and on three occasions under three of the actors with whom he had performed that season, Connor, Ward, and Banks.

According to Dunlap, on 15 June 1784, Cooke, having left Manchester, went to Lancaster on the northwest coast of England, then a bustling port town with a population of 8,584 and considerable trade with the West Indies, as well as flourishing businesses in shipbuilding and sailclothmaking. The firm of Gillow, which continued at Lancaster until the 1960s, was already gaining a reputation for good furniture, exporting it to the West Indies and to the London area by sea. Like many growing provincial towns, Lancaster was experiencing a spurt of new construction, including an assembly room and a theatre. Lancaster was typical of the numerous towns chosen by theatrical managers for stops on their circuit, since the race course and the twice a year sessions of the Assize Court swelled the town with visitors. The coastal towns were popular for country managers. There were daily coaches to the north and south, and, in the case of Lancaster, coaches ran daily, tides permitting, over the sands to Ulverston and the more remote parts of the county. Throughout the eighteenth century, managers were careful to time their theatrical performances to coincide with the Assizes, as did the proprietors of the race courses.[28]

It was to Lancaster, then, that Cooke traveled to cast his lot for the summer season with the company of Joseph Austin and Charles Edward Whitlock, for the sum of 2 guineas a week. Joseph Austin, the senior partner, had long been a provincial manager, having first formed a managerial partnership with Michael Heatton in 1766. Prior to management, in 1761, Austin had been a member of a troupe at the new Cork Theatre and later a player at the Crow Street Theatre in Dublin. Whitlock, who had joined Austin in 1778, had been an actor in a number of provincial companies, including Heatton's and Austin's after 1774.[29] By 1784, Austin and his various partners had developed an extensive circuit which included, besides Lancaster, the towns of Preston, Chester, Newcastle-upon-Tyne, and Whitehaven. They had also managed the theatre at Manchester between 1781 and 1783, but had relinquished their interest to James Miller. The Austin-Whitlock company was probably the best organized and most efficient of the companies with which Cooke had thus far been associated. Austin, who ran his company like a well-versed businessman, drew up a list of thirty-one articles covering all phases of the company's activity and gave a copy to each member of the company.[30]

Like most provincial managers, Austin and Whitlock were also performers. Whitlock, who advertised as a dentist in each town where the troupe performed and continued to do so until he gave up management and turned to dentistry full-time, played some leads, but Austin enacted most of the better roles.[31] Austin had performed with Garrick at Drury Lane, excelling as Lord Ogleby in *The Clandestine Marriage*.[32] In the provinces he expanded his repertoire and offered among his roles Richard III, Hotspur, Shylock, Lord Hastings, Benedick, and Sir Peter Teazle.[33] Among the members of the company when Cooke joined was Joe Munden, who had engaged with Austin and Whitlock in 1780 and remained with the company until he went to Covent Garden in 1790 to become a comic staple for over twenty years.[34] Eventually, Cooke and Munden would be performing together at Covent Garden.

Cooke acted with Austin and Whitlock in Lancaster and Preston that summer. Both towns had almost new theatres, which the managers had built in the summer of 1782.[35] The Lancaster theatre, located in St. Leonard-gate, was probably similar to the one in Preston. It is described as "a plain structure" that "displays much neatness within."[36] Previously, Lancaster had only temporary structures serving as playhouses. Unfortunately, I have been unable to locate any indication of the roles Cooke played in Lancaster or Preston.[37] It may be assumed that Cooke obeyed the articles of agreement that summer and proved himself of sufficient worth to the management to be rehired the following summer as the highest paid member of the troupe. At the conclusion of the summer season, while in Preston, Cooke was engaged by George Mattocks to perform in Liverpool that fall.[38]

Like Manchester, Liverpool was fast becoming a major theatrical center in provincial England; it would also be a major city for many of Cooke's triumphs, as well as a setting for degradation and dishonor for him in years to come. From Liverpool he would leave England in little over a quarter of a century, never to return.

Mattocks, in partnership with Joseph Younger, with whom Cooke had performed during Race Week in Manchester, had acquired control of the Theatre Royal in both Manchester and Liverpool ten years earlier. For a brief period, the Manchester theatre had been under the management of James Miller, but it was now back in the hands of Younger and Mattocks. Since Mattocks performed regularly at Covent Garden, Younger had usually been left to oversee most of the local matters. However, on 4 September Younger died, and as a result Mattocks remained in the provinces to become the sole manager of the Liverpool and Manchester theatres.[39]

Cooke had seen the stylish and gentlemanly George Mattocks and his wife act at Covent Garden in 1771, on his first trip to London, and now he was to work professionally with him. John Bernard, an actor-manager who would be among those present to welcome Cooke to the United States, remembered Mattocks when he was a boy and Cooke's new manager had performed in Portsmouth:

> I can remember very well how I used to stand staring at him with a company of kite-flying urchins, as he came sailing down the principal street of a morning to rehearsal, arrayed in a gold-laced suit of green and white, with a bag-wig, three cornered-hat, a silver-mounted cane, and a silver-handled hanger. There was such a swan-like dignity about him, such a fascinating glitter, and "stand-out-of-the-way" consequence; his feather floating, his skirts flying, his sword dangling, and his stick thumping, as he proceeded. . . . He was a pretty singer, and with the exception of [Joseph] Vernon, the best acting vocalist I ever saw.[40]

By this time Mattocks, although still dapper and lively, had turned his attention to management.

Liverpool, "from its trade, situation, and other advantages," was already a successful resort town.[41] Although it was ill-paved, ill-drained, and ill-lighted, it was a pleasant seacoast town with lovely landscapes, fruitful gardens, and picturesque windmills dotting the hillsides, all within a mile of the town hall. Mattocks and Younger had received their Royal Letters Patent for a Theatre Royal on 30 April 1771, and the first theatre with that appellation opened the following year. It was here that Cooke would perform for the next four months. It was a large and handsome building, elegantly furnished inside and out. The front was brick surmounted by an artistic pediment in which was carved the royal arms. The principal entrance was in the middle of the façade, a large door which was led up to by stone steps. Facing this door was the lobby which led to the boxes; on one side a passage led to the pit, while opposite it another led to the gallery. The stage itself was rather shallow, since the back of the theatre abutted an extensive rope works.[42]

Cooke's first appearance at Liverpool was as Frankly in *The Suspicious Husband* on 13 September. For the first time in his career, he appeared on stage with a Kemble, Stephen, the brother of the famous Sarah Siddons, who just two years earlier had been acclaimed in London as a tragic actress without equal, and John Philip, who the year prior had made his debut at Drury Lane as Hamlet. Cooke also first appeared under Mattocks' management with Stephen's future wife, Elizabeth Satchell, and with Isabella Mattocks, the youngest daughter of Lewis Hallam, who in 1752 took the first professional troupe to America.[43] She was already a seasoned Covent Garden performer and had obtained notice as a concert singer outside of the theatre. Stephen and

Elizabeth had acted the previous season at Covent Garden but would spend a number of years in the provinces; in fact, Stephen would become Cooke's manager at Sheffield and Newcastle in 1790–1791. Cooke also found familiar faces in the company, including John Banks, Thomas Ward, and his old competitor from his first Manchester season, Thomas Grist. A Mrs. Cooke is also listed in the bills for that season. The roles assigned to her would suggest that she was the same Mrs. Cooke who was with Cooke in his first Manchester season. It is not clear, however, whether she stayed with Cooke during the interim. Both Cookes appeared in the farce on the thirteenth, *The Citizen*, Cooke as Young Wilding and Mrs. Cooke as Corinna.

Throughout the season, the company played on Mondays, Wednesdays, and Fridays, with an occasional extra night on either Thursday or Saturday. Cooke's assignments were not as taxing as those of the previous season, averaging only two performances a week; still he continued to add new roles to his repertoire. On 14 September, he appeared as Aimwell in *The Beaux' Stratagem*, with Ward as Archer, Stephen Kemble as Sullen, and Mrs. Mattocks as Mrs. Sullen. He did not reappear until the following Saturday, 18 September, on which occasion new strength was added to the company with the first appearance of Banks, appearing for the first time in Liverpool, and Grist, returning after appearances at the Theatre Royal in Dublin. That evening *The West Indian* was chosen to introduce the new company members. Cooke took the role of Young Dudley, while Banks portrayed Stockwell, and Grist, Major O'Flaherty.

Cooke completed his first month in Liverpool with only three additional roles: Lord Raby in *Percy* (20 September), the Abbot in *King Henry the Second* (22 September), and Don Juan in the comic opera *The Castle of Andalusia* by J. O'Keefe (27 and 29 September). The most obvious trend emerging this season was that Cooke was not called upon frequently to appear in afterpieces, nor would he be, but was given substantial roles, though little different from those of earlier seasons.[44]

He began the month of October (4 October) as Villeroy in *Isabella; or, The Fatal Marriage*, with Grist as Biron and Kemble as Count Baldwin, followed on 8 October with Hartson's romantic drama *The Countess of Salisbury*, with Cooke as Raymond, Grist as Alwin, Banks as Grey, and Mrs. Cooke in the role of Eleanor. On 11 October, Cooke appeared as Philotas in *The Grecian Daughter*, with Grist in the more tragic role of Evander. Edward Thompson's comedy *The Fair Quaker*, one of a long series of eighteenth-century comedies altered from earlier plays, followed on 15 October with Cooke as Sir Charles Pleasant. Few significant new roles came Cooke's way during the remainder of October. He repeated roles in *The West Indian* (28 October) and *Henry the Second* (29 October), appeared as Lord Burleigh in *The Unhappy Favourite; or The Earl of Essex* on the 20th, and received his most important role on the 22d, Sciolto in *The Fair Penitent*.

Before the beginning of benefits during the latter part of November,[45] Cooke appeared on only six occasions: Sir John Lambert in Bickerstaffe's comedy *The Hypocrite* (1 November), Moneses in *Tamerlane*, Don Julio in *A Bold Stroke for a Husband* (15 and 29 November), Malville in Arthur Murphy's *Know Your Own Mind* (17 November), and repeated roles in *Isabella* (19 November) and *Percy* (26 November).

Cooke completed his first season at Liverpool with regular appearances in the benefits of his colleagues, first for Mr. Mattocks on 29 November and then as Belarius in *Cymbeline* for Grist and Moss on 6 December. His final weeks included the following: Orestes (10 October), Bellair in Mrs. Hannah Cowley's *More Ways Than One; or, A New Mode to Gain Hearts* (13 December), Glanville in Robert Dodsley's tragedy *Cleone* (20 December), Claudio in *Much Ado About Nothing* (22 December), and Baron Fitzherbert disguised as Friar Tuck in Leonard Macnally's comic opera *Robin Hood* (27 December).[46]

Four months in Liverpool did not advance Cooke's career appreciably. Nonetheless, through his continued relationship with Banks and Ward, as well as his initial association with Stephen Kemble, important professional associations were made. Thomas Grist, however, once more proved to be a strong competitor for major roles. Cooke's parts did not yet suggest the distinctiveness for which he would ultimately be known.

Late in December, Cooke left Liverpool with George Mattocks to open the Manchester season. The company at Manchester included many of the same actors who had performed at Liverpool and some who had been with Cooke under James Miller, including Hannah Robinson, Grist, Banks, Kemble, Fox, Thomas Hollingsworth, Mrs. Maddock from the Norwich Theatre, and Moss, who had joined the company in Liverpool from Dublin.

The season opened on 29 December 1784 with a repeat from the Liverpool season of Dodsley's *Cleone*. Cooke again performed the unrepentant villain, Glanville, to the Cleone of Hannah Robinson and the Sifroy of Stephen Kemble.[47] On 5 January, Elizabeth Satchell, who had joined the company, appeared as Polly opposite Mattocks' Macheath.[48] Cooke and other members of the company may have returned to Liverpool for at least one performance on 11 January, for there is no sign of Cooke in Manchester for a period of almost three weeks.[49] On 19 January, again in Manchester, he played another familiar villain, Raymond in *The Countess of Salisbury*, with Hannah Robinson as Lady Salisbury and the same casting as at Liverpool.[50] Next, in a benefit featuring *Hamlet*, Cooke and Grist performed their familiar roles of Claudius and Hamlet, Stephen Kemble appearing as Horatio with Elizabeth Satchell as Ophelia, a role in which she gained much praise during her career. Following *Hamlet* on the 26th, the company repeated its Liverpool production of *A Bold Stroke for a Husband*, Cooke once more performing as the young lover, Don Julio, who wins Olivia (Isabella Mattocks) after she has pretended to be a boisterous, scolding fool for other suitors.

On 2 February, Cooke repeated his role of Baron Fitzherbert in *Robin Hood*, produced for the first time in Manchester. Thomas Banks, a scene painter, dancer, and actor, was advertised in the bills for several new scenes and decorations which he completed for the production. Beginning the following summer, Banks worked regularly at Birmingham and in 1800 moved on to London where he became the assistant to many of the most famous scene painters of the time.[51]

On 4 February, Cooke abruptly left Manchester. From all available evidence, this appears to be the first difficulty any manager had experienced with Cooke, although the cause was professional pride more than personal indiscretion, which would cause most of the upsets that punctuated his later career. Cooke's explanation seems credible, given the eighteenth-century tradition of "possession of parts." Cooke recalled that "Sir Peter Teazle, which I had acted at Manchester the preceding season with applause, was given at Liverpool to Moss, a doubtful actor, who at Manchester suddenly left us. The part was then sent to me, and I refused it;—the consequence was, I left the company."[52] This turn of events must have created a problem for Mattocks, since the bill for 7 February had already been printed and posted.[53] Cooke left Mrs. Cooke behind to finish out the season, but she would rejoin him the following fall in Chester. Evidently, Cooke was replaced by an actor named Johnson, who appeared 11 February as Baron Fitzherbert and in May as Claudius.[54]

Apparently, Cooke left the stage for a period of almost three months but rejoined Austin's and Whitlock's company at Lancaster in June 1785.[55] It would appear that they at least understood Cooke's reason for leaving Manchester when his role had been taken away and then reoffered. A fellow-player described Cooke's professional good behavior at this time, and at the same time he gave the first known reference to his excessive drinking:

As an actor he was in great estimation; his salary was two guineas a week, the highest then given in that company; he was accustomed to have a given time for study, not unusually long, was always very perfect, and had the reputation of being a *correct actor*. His habits of living were pretty much the same as when in America, only he would sometimes abstain from excess for three months, and behave with the greatest propriety; but when he broke from this restraint, he was not to be heard of for several days: where he hid himself may be easily imagined.[56]

Cooke's avidity for alcohol seems to have begun before the age of thirty. He moved through the classic steps of alcoholism, from addiction to chronic alcoholism which culminated in serious physical disease and death.[57] In 1785, however, the problem was still relatively minor and caused few disturbances in his professional life. Cooke probably was wise to disappear for "several days" rather than carry the results onto the stage, as he was later to do repeatedly.

The roles Cooke performed at Lancaster have not been discovered, nor can the members of the company be stated with assurance. It is known that one of the major events of the summer season was the marriage in June of Charles Whitlock and Elizabeth Kemble, the sister of Stephen Kemble and Mrs. Siddons, at the Priory Church.[58] The new Mrs. Whitlock had just completed two seasons at Drury Lane and would later find an association with Cooke at Newcastle less pleasant than this period of marital bliss.[59] It is also assumed that Munden was with the company throughout the season, since he remained with the company until he went to London, and he is known to have performed for his benefit at Lancaster on 17 August.[60]

In September, the company moved to the Theatre Royal in Chester. The first building there with the name of Theatre Royal opened in 1773, although a patent license was not issued by Parliament until 16 May 1777 to John Stanislaw Townshend. As a result, considerable alterations to the Wool Hall, a structure several centuries old which had served as a theatre for a brief time in 1773, were facilitated. The alterations included the bricking up of several thirteenth-century windows, the removal of the roof, the raising of the walls with 18 feet of brickwork on top of the ancient 3-foot-thick stone walls that had originally stood only 24 feet high, and finally the topping of the structure with a new timber roof.[61]

The company at Chester included, in addition to Elizabeth Whitlock, Munden and Mary Jones, his actress-mistress who performed as Mrs. Munden, Stephen Kemble, his wife-to-be Elizabeth Satchell, Austin, and Mrs. Cooke.[62]

The Chester season opened on 14 September with *As You Like It*. Cooke had the minor role of the old faithful servant Adam, to the Orlando of Whitlock and the Rosalind of Mrs. Whitlock, a role she had performed at Drury Lane. Mrs. Cooke played the minor role of Celia.[63] On the 16th, Cooke was Lord Hastings opposite Mrs. Whitlock's Jane Shore, and on the 19th he repeated his now familiar role of Don Julio. As a rule the company performed three nights a week—Mondays, Wednesdays, and Fridays. Cooke's roles during these weeks began to take on greater prominence.

On 21 September, Cooke played, presumably for the first time, Captain Absolute to Austin's Sir Anthony in *The Rivals*; Munden, in a type of role that was becoming familiar for him, portrayed the bumpkin Bob Acres. Mrs. Cowley's *More Ways Than One* followed on 28 September with Cooke as Carlton and Whitlock taking his previous role of Bellair. For the next few weeks, Cooke appeared in roles familiar to him: Philotas (30 September), Sir John Melville in *The Clandestine Marriage* (5 October), Earl Raby in *Percy* (7 October), and Stukely (11 October). On 19 October, he was assigned his most prominent role to date with the company, Macbeth, with Mrs. Whitlock as Lady Macbeth. The same evening Mrs. Cooke, who had continued to play minor acting and singing roles, was simply listed as having a vocal part. On the 24th Cooke performed Henry II.

A Correct Actor 55

For the Cookes' benefit on 26 October, Cooke chose to play Hamlet, advertised in *Adam's Weekly Courant* (25 October 1785) as "not acted here these two years."[64] Cooke's old role of Claudius was taken by Gloster, while Stephen Kemble and Elizabeth Satchell performed the same roles they had taken at Manchester when Cooke had first played Claudius to Grist's Hamlet. Munden doubled as Polonius and the Gravedigger, still a common practice in *Hamlet* productions. Following the mainpiece, Kemble delivered "Satan's Address to the Sun" by Milton, Munden sang a song, and Cooke recited Garrick's "Ode on Shakespeare."

Cooke completed his October performances as Bertoldo in *Maid of Honour*, as Spatterdash in *The Young Quaker* (the same night), and as Carlton in *More Ways Than One*.[65] Although performances at Chester continued into January 1786, Cooke's last appearance was evidently in the latter part of October. On the bill for *Belle's Stratagem*, 4 November, Cooke is listed for Saville, but his name has been crossed out by Austin and that of Duncan written in; for the rest of the season, his roles were taken over by Platt and Young. No reason is known for Cooke's leaving the company at this point. Could it have been another instance of "lack of restraint?"[66] Mrs. Cooke remained in Chester until the end of January, playing her usual small roles, such as Miss Sterling in *The Clandestine Marriage*, Kathleen in *The Poor Soldier*, second singing witch in *Macbeth*, Lady Capulet, and Regan. This may have been the end of this Mrs. Cooke in George Frederick's life, for only one additional mention of her has been found.[67]

Cooke's next known engagement was with Tate Wilkinson at York in July 1786. Cooke was apparently hired once more to play second leading roles. York, about 100 miles northeast of Chester, was strategically located on the highway to Scotland, about half way between London and Edinburgh. Although its population was only about 15,000, its ease of access was a great virtue for a provincial theatre.[68] The theatre controlled by Wilkinson was remodeled by Joseph Baker in 1769, although the patent was secured by his successor, Wilkinson.[69] The present Theatre Royal in York is located on almost exactly the same site as the one in 1786, although then it was completely surrounded by other buildings, one of them Wilkinson's own dwelling which housed his personal dressing room with direct access to the stage.[70] The patrons entered the theatre through an alleyway. A survey in 1809 gives us a description of the interior. The auditorium was "Fitted up in a neat uniform style, capable of containing a numerous audience." There were two tiers of side boxes, one front box, two front galleries, and two side galleries. Over the front box were the royal arms. The stage boxes were adorned with "emblematic devices, musical and warlike trophies, etc. and edged with gilt mouldings." The length of the stage from the lamps upwards was 37 feet; in breadth, from the opening of the curtain, 18 feet 6 inches or from wall to wall, 42 feet. The height from the pit floor to the ceiling was 34 feet. "In front of the entablature is the following motto, surrounded with ornamental painting,

'Veluti in Speculum
Quicquid Agunt Homines.' "

The interior was colored orange, green, and white, while the seats were covered with crimson cloth.[71]

Tate Wilkinson first came to York as a strolling player in 1763, returned in 1769, and remained until his death in 1803, by which time he had control over a circuit that included not only York, but also Leeds, Wakefield, Pontefract, Doncaster, and Hull.[72] Any actor given an engagement under Wilkinson was fortunate, for, with the possible exception of Bath, York had become the provincial stage where fledgling performers as well as seasoned actors most wished to be seen.[73] Cooke joined the York theatre for performances during Race Week at the end of July and during August.[74]

Cooke had pleasant memories of Wilkinson, recalling that his talents as a mimic enabled him "to copy many characters in a pleasing manner, particularly those of Mr. Foote's writing; and his acquaintance with the London theatres, and the actors and actresses of Garrick's days, makes him an excellent manager of young performers. His theatres are on a respectable footing, and his conduct as a manager very honourable."[75] Later, while in America, Cooke related to Dunlap the following eccentricity of Wilkinson:

... he had a way of writing several letters at a time, sealing them and afterwards directing them, which produced some good games of cross purposes: I received a letter from him soon after my coming to London, telling me that he wondered at my impudence in applying to him for an engagement again, after his having discharged me; and I suppose some poor devil received a hearty invitation to join his company and share half his profits;—for, once his landlady received a letter from him, ordering her to get ready to play Clytus, and his principal performer another, directing him to be sure to have his sheets well-aired.[76]

Cooke's opportunities in York were doubled when he was given the chance to appear opposite Sarah Siddons. Mrs. Siddons was still being acclaimed in London as a tragic actress without equal, although she had not performed regularly at Drury Lane for four years. She would be rarely challenged for this position and had no equals until after her retirement. Sarah Siddons' classic simplicity and overpowering emotional depth, coupled with an emphasis upon grace of movement, dignity, and grandeur, expressed the qualities which a growing romantic revival extolled. Her greatest assets appear to have been her ability to stay always in character, in a way much superior to her brother, John Philip, to react to others on stage even during moments of silence, and to change swiftly from one emotion to another.[77] Mrs. Siddons was a beautiful woman with a natural majesty in her carriage. During her career, she would play a wide range of tragic parts, ignoring comedy almost altogether. At the time of her appearances in York, she was most noted for her portrayals of Lady

Macbeth, Euphrasia, Lady Randolph, Jane Shore, and Isabella. Cooke, who must have revelled in this moment, had no idea that in less than fifteen years he would act with her frequently over a seven-year period at Covent Garden.

Cooke first appeared with Sarah Siddons on 29 July 1786, the opening night of performances during Assize Week and a prelude to Race Week. Cooke as the repentant father, Count Baldwin, supported Mrs. Siddons in her renowned characterization of Isabella in Garrick's adaptation of Thomas Southerne's *Isabella; or, The Fatal Marriage*.[78]

Wilkinson advertised that Siddons would perform six nights during the York Assize Week, held between 29 July and 5 August. In addition to Isabella, she is known to have portrayed Lady Randolph and, after the Assizes, the role of Zara in Congreve's *The Mourning Bride* for Wilkinson's benefit. Although Count Baldwin is the only role I have thus far found Cooke to have performed with Mrs. Siddons during the Assizes, he must have supported her frequently, since he accompanied her throughout her summer provincial tour. In recalling the engagement with Mrs. Siddons, Cooke wrote: "I do not remember whether the prices were raised, but I believe they were; our audiences certainly were very crouded [sic]."[79] The prices were indeed increased. The *Courant* (18 July and 23 January) advertised prices at 5s. for boxes, 3s. for the pit, 2s. for the first gallery, and the upper gallery remaining at its usual price, 1s. An article in the *Courant* (8 August) states that "the Amount of Receipts on the six nights of [Mrs. Siddons'] performing were upwards of 900 [pounds] exclusive of the Gold she received for Tickets on her Benefit." According to the *Yorkshire Magazine*, her performance on 3 August brought in the greatest receipt ever recorded in that city, £192 9s. 6d.[80] Obviously, Sarah Siddons' engagement was a decided success, certainly for the management, and Mrs. Siddons herself received the generous sum of 50 guineas per night.[81] Cooke's opportunity to appear opposite Siddons added immeasurably to his reputation.

In a letter to her lifelong friend, Reverend Sedgewick Whalley of Bath, Siddons reveals the press on the boxes and the excitement in anticipation of her appearance. On 11 August she wrote: "I leave this place for York next Tuesday, where I shall be about a month. . . . It has been impossible to get a place in the boxes for these six months past at York; they were all taken on the supposition of my playing there long before the affair was settled."[82]

Siddons was also persuaded to perform at Wilkinson's theatres in Hull and Leeds,[83] after which she made a return engagement at York for Race Week.[84] In mid-August, Cooke and the entire York company traveled with Mrs. Siddons to complete her engagement.[85] The plays performed, probably at both places, were *The Grecian Daughter, Zara, Belvidera*, and *Isabella*.[86] The company then returned to York for Race Week, where Cooke probably supported Mrs. Siddons for three more nights of performances.[87]

Prior to Cooke's engagement with Wilkinson, Austin and Whitlock had arranged for him to support Sarah Siddons when her summer tour took her to their theatre in Chester in September 1786. Mrs. Siddons finished her provincial tour in time to return to Drury Lane in early October, and Cooke remained with Austin and Whitlock until the close of their season. Although little else is known of this season at Chester, his specific engagement earlier at the same theatre to support Mrs. Siddons would indicate that his reputation as an actor was on the rise.

After leaving Chester, probably in late September, Cooke rejoined Wilkinson's York company at Hull. The Hull season began in late October and was over in the latter part of January 1787. Cooke and the company returned to York on 24 January to begin a season which lasted until May, leaving York on 12 May.[88]

While at York, Cooke's first regular season there, the young actor played mostly supporting roles, while the principal parts were taken either by Wilkinson, appearing in his own favorite characters, or by Alexander Cummins, hired as lead actor for the season. John Bernard has left the following description of the York favorite, Cummins:

In this company I became acquainted with that northern star of the dramatic hemisphere, Cummings [Cummins], who so long, in the opinion of the York audience, maintained a pre-eminence over his tragic contemporaries. . . . he was an actor then of marked originality in characters like Hotspur, Alexander, and Chamont, and possessed a genius for the bold, the rugged, and romantic. . . . If his fame, however, extended beyond the sphere of his exertions, it led to no material results, as he concluded his career where he commenced it, and his name is only recognized now by his great natural qualification—his voice; this was indeed a "most miraculous organ." Barry's had more sweetness and flexibility, but Cummings' the greater compass and strength. My reader from this will infer his great fault—the power he possessed seduced him into a habit of ranting, which the public being pleased with, confirmed him in. Thus, when John Kemble visited York, he was told by the gallery, he "cud na shoot oot laik Coomens."[89]

The York newspaper advertisements tell us that although Cummins took most of the leading roles this season, yielding occasionally to Wilkinson, Cooke did perform a few major roles in comedies and some popular supporting characters. Of the productions known, Cooke enacted the leading roles of the lover Colonel Holberg in James Johnstone's comedy *The Disbanded Officer* in the latter part of March and the jealous husband Sir John Restless for his own benefit in Arthur Murphy's comedy *All in the Wrong* on 17 February.[90] His most important supporting role was in Nathaniel Lee's *Alexander; or, the Rival Queens*, in which he appeared as the faithful old soldier Clytus to Cummins' popular portrayal of Alexander. Cooke's other supporting roles included the repentant villain Sultan in Mrs. Elizabeth Inchbald's *Such Things Are*, the unrepentant villain Malville in Murphy's *Know Your Own Mind*, the cynical but kind-hearted old bachelor Sir Clement Flint in Burgoyne's comedy *The*

A Correct Actor

Heiress, and the lover Ordeal in Leonard Macnally's *The Fashionable Levities*.[91]

Cooke's recitations were also in vogue, gaining considerable popularity as evidenced by the frequent advertisements of them. During the course of the season, he delivered "A Lecture on Oratory," Collins' "Celebrated Ode on the Passions," and Garrick's "Ode on Shakespeare."[92] Although a number of the roles which he performed this season were new to his repertoire, only Clytus reappeared occasionally during the rest of his career.

Wilkinson, like a number of later critics, felt Cooke's talents were greater in comedy than in tragedy, which explains the preponderance of comic roles assigned to him. Wilkinson adds that "The Londoners would scarcely credit the sterling merit Mr. Cooke possesses in a particular cast of parts; for where his character suits, his merit would be undoubted on any stage, however critical."[93]

With the conclusion of the 1787 York season, Cooke ended a period marked by extensive traveling of circuits criss-crossing England. It also marked the conclusion of a period in his career characterized by an apprenticeship in the playing of supporting roles. Although he would spend the rest of the century in the Midlands, northern England, and Ireland, he would rarely take second place to anyone. Thirteen years or more as an apprentice gave him valuable experience and added immeasurably to his confidence. Now that he felt adequately prepared, he could move up to the next step as a featured player. His early associations with Connor, Ward, Banks, and Kemble were key events for him, leading to further engagements throughout provincial England. Certainly, his relationship with the Austin-Whitlock company proved to be the necessary step for a "correct actor" on the rise. His reengagement with them after York officially marks the end of a long apprenticeship and the beginning of a provincial career as a leading actor and tragedian.

5

"The Manchester Roscius"

There is no indication that Cooke joined the Austin-Whitlock company for the summer of 1787. Dunlap states that he "played with various provincial companies," but then Dunlap also fails to record any mention of the reengagement with Austin and Whitlock, a major omission in his narrative.[1] If Cooke did appear that summer, he would have once more played in Lancaster, Preston, and Chester. No evidence has been located to support such a supposition, however. In fact, it is difficult to ascertain exactly when Cooke rejoined the Chester company.

Austin, in his list of performers who had performed under him, recorded that Cooke played Macbeth in Chester on 15 October 1787.[2] There is an extant playbill which lists Cooke as Macbeth opposite the Lady Macbeth of Mrs. Whitlock for that date. On the other hand, on another playbill, apparently for 22 or 23 October (the date is unclear), and the next in chronological order in the volume of bills at the British Museum, Cooke is advertised for Jaffier in *Venice Preserv'd* with the appended note: "[Cooke] who, by way of apology, will give Reasons to the Audience for not arriving at the time he was expected."[3] His first appearance, then, may have been as Jaffier rather than as Macbeth.

The Veteran Stager, who indicates that Munden encouraged Cooke to rejoin Austin and Whitlock, gives an account that may relate to this first season at Chester and the apology that accompanied Cooke's reentry, an occurrence that would become commonplace for Cooke in the future.[4] To the consternation of the company, Cooke had not arrived on the day he was advertised to appear. At 2:00 P.M., a man on horseback arrived with a letter addressed to the managers from Cooke, with a request that they should send by the bearer £10, as he was detained for want of money to defray his expenses.[5] The managers quickly dispatched the property man with the money in a post-chaise, in which Cooke was to return. On reaching his destination, the property man presented his credentials to Cooke who, on learning that he was a property man, replied with great indignation, "What! have those pitiful scoundrels, Austin and Whitlock, those petty directors of coalpit theatricals [Newcastle was a coal-mining center] dared to insult George Frederick Cooke, by sending a property man to usher him into their presence? return to your masters, fellow, and tell them George

Frederick Cooke will not brook an insult." The poor property man, after vain entreaties, returned without Cooke, and an apology was made that evening to the audience. The Stager continues:

... near the finish of the farce a man called upon Munden to come to the watch-house to release from durance vile a friend of his, a gentleman, that would not give his name. From the messenger's description, Joe guessed who the mad gentleman was, and repaired to the watch-house, where he found his friend George surrounded by guardians of the night. The instant he beheld Munden ... he sprang from his seat, and with stentorian lungs, vociferated "The property man, sir—the property man, sir!—tell that tooth-drawing reptile ... and his co-adjutor Austin, George Frederick Cooke will annihilate them; one look of mine, sir, will cause them to shrink into their original nothingness, but eagles war not with sparrows," when he had exhausted his imagination in invective, threats and abuse, he suffered himself to be taken from his confinement, and was conveyed to his apartments prepared for him by Munden. As when in a state of intoxication no man could be more abusive or insulting, so also when in his perfect senses no man could with more elegance, more seeming contrition, atone for errors past; the managers were easily appeased, but it was expected the audience would resent the rememberance of their disappointment or the individual who was the cause of it.

Such was not to be the case, however, for on his first appearance the following Wednesday,

the house was full at an early hour; all hearts beat high with expectation: at length Othello [Jaffier?][6] appeared, and was received with some marks of disapprobation by a few, but by the majority with applause; when silence was at last obtained, he stept forward and addressed them in the following words:—"Ladies and gentlemen; I stand before you self-accused, self-convicted, self-condemned, should your displeasure be added to my own; my punishment, though just, will be more than I shall be enabled to endure." Here several voices were heard to exclaim, "enough, enough! go on, go on! no further apology!" He bowed and proceeded with his character amidst the plaudits and approbation of a respectable and crowded audience.

For many years, audiences, until their endurance was stretched to the breaking point, would accept such apologies from Cooke. On this occasion, which was likely the result of his increasing dependency on alcohol, there seems to have been little after-effect. "During the season his attention to his theatric duties were unremitting, never once deviating into error or intemperance," concludes the Stager.[7] The management certainly found little cause for further concern, for he remained with the company for almost four years.

Since this season proved to be the turning point in Cooke's career, it seems appropriate to cover it in detail. After Jaffier, Cooke appeared as Sir John Restless in Arthur Murphy's *All in the Wrong; or, The Way to be Right*. Restless, the jealous husband, was another major role for Cooke, which he played opposite Mr. and Mrs. Whitlock (Beverley and Lady Restless) and Mrs. Belfil

(Belinda). He chose the same role for his benefit on 12 December. On Monday, 29 October, Cooke was assigned Othello with Platt as Iago, Mrs. Whitlock as Desdemona, and Munden as Roderigo. Hamlet, one of Cooke's few performances of the role, followed on 12 November, with Munden as Polonius, Hugh Sparks as Claudius, and Mrs. Sparks as Ophelia. It will be recalled that at the age of seventeen Cooke had seen Mrs. Sparks, as Sarah Mills, when as a member of a strolling company she had played in Berwick.[8] Apparently, Cooke then played Sir John Melville on the 14th and repeated the role on 30 November. On 16 November, he made his first appearance as Mr. Beauchamp in Mrs. Cowley's comedy *Which Is the Man?*, and on the 19th, he repeated Hamlet. Prior to his benefit, he continued to be assigned major roles: Philotas (23 November), Mr. Oakly in *The Jealous Wife* (26 November), Stukely (28 November), and Don Carlos in *Bold Stroke for a Husband* (7 December).

For his benefit on 12 December, in addition to repeating Sir John Restless (with his friend Munden taking the role of Brush for that night only), there was a comic song by Munden, a solo on the violin by a Mr. Laglace from Paris, a recitation by Cooke of Collins' "Ode on the Passions," and a cantata sung by Mrs. Henderson from the Theatre Royal, Edinburgh, plus as the afterpiece, *Midnight Hour* with Austin and Whitlock. Of all the benefits that season, this was the most ambitious with the most varied bill, and perhaps indicative of the position Cooke was beginning to attain in the estimation of the managers and the public.

Cooke's final six appearances were all in major roles, although he was called upon for Platt's benefit to recite Garrick's "Ode on Shakespeare" and play the role of Young Wilding in the farce *The Citizen*. He concluded the Chester season as Raymond, the Count of Narbonne (17 December), Mr. Vandercrab, a merchant, in Harriet Lee's comedy *New Peerage; or, Our Eyes May Deceive Us* (19 December), Frankly in *The Suspicious Husband* (21 December), Posthumus Leonatus (2 January), and Haswell in *Such Things Are* (9 January).

Newcastle-upon-Tyne was to be Cooke's next engagement, beginning in January 1788. Newcastle, about fifty miles from the Scottish border, was already an industrial center, with mining in coal and lead and extensive manufacturing in iron and glass works.[9] In 1801, the year of the Population Act, there were 28,294 people in Newcastle, excluding seamen, lodgers, travelers, and soldiers, who must have increased its population considerably, along with the 8,000 to 9,000 inhabitants across the Tyne River.[10]

A patent to operate a Theatre Royal had been obtained the summer prior to Cooke's visit (3 July 1787), although Austin and Whitlock had managed the Bigg Market Theatre since 1781.[11] In January 1788, the Bigg Market Theatre gave way to a new playhouse, the Newcastle Theatre Royal, near the post office in the center of town, on the corner of Mosley and Gray streets. Mosley Street was, for the time, a modern street, airy and spacious, running from Pilgrim Street to the foot of the Flesh market.[12] The new theatre structure, almost midway between the street's two boundaries, was leased from the proprietors by Austin and Whitlock. Approximately £6,400 had been spent on the new structure, including land and building. Separate entrances were provided for the gallery, pit, and boxes, which held a total of 1,350 people. At capacity, the theatre would produce £112 10s. at the normal prices of 1s., 2s., and 3s. The Newcastle season opened in January for three months each winter and generally reopened in the summer at Races and Assizes.[13]

On 21 January 1788, the new theatre opened, while the bells of St. Nicholas' and St. John's churches rang in celebration. Cooke had been billed to perform as Lovemore in Murphy's *Way to Keep Him*, with Munden, Austin, and Mr. and Mrs. Whitlock, but for some undiscovered reason did not appear until 28 January when he was advertised to make his first appearance as Othello.[14] In his journal Cooke recalled that after Othello "I met with most flattering applause, which I continued to receive while I remained attached to the theatre."[15] Wilkinson confirms Cooke's remembrances and adds a more personal note: ". . . the infatuation of Mr. Cooke's acting . . . was carried to such a frenzy, that even the ladies languished at that gentleman's making love,—I mean in public,—for I would not dispute his private abilities of pleasing."[16]

For Cooke's first appearance at Newcastle, he was supported by Smith as Iago, Timothy(?) Duncan as Brabantio, Whitlock as Cassio, Munden as Roderigo, Mrs. Norton as Desdemona, and Mrs. Duncan as Emilia.[17] In February he appeared as Macbeth (11 February), Myrtle in *The Conscious Lovers* (18 February), and Jaffier (25 February). In the next few weeks, beginning with Earl Douglas in *Percy* (3 March) and then Mentevole in Robert Jephson's *The Italian Lover* (24 March), he began to move into larger roles, several of which were to become part of his standard repertoire. On 31 March, for the benefit of Mr. and Mrs. Norton, Cooke played Shylock to the Antonio of Smith; on 2 April, he was Haswell and Dupely in *Maid of the Oaks*. Apparently, this was the first time Cooke had appeared with Miss Maria Duncan, a young actress and vocalist of five, whose parents were in the company. She would make her debut at Drury Lane as Lady Teazle in 1804.

By 1 April, the company was well into benefits and Cooke appeared often: for Mrs. Whitlock on 7 April, he was Leonidas in Mrs. Cowley's *Fate of Sparta; or, The Rival Kings*; for Mr. Hill and Miss Richardson, he performed the familiar role of Sir John Melville on 9 April; for Mrs. Belfil's night, he was Romeo (11 April); on 16 April, for the first time, he attempted Clerimont in Richard Sheridan's comic opera *Duenna* for Mattocks' night. On the *Duenna* bill was a Mr. Kean who "gave imitations of all the capital actors at Theatres Royal in London." This may have been the father of Edmund Kean or his father's brother, Moses.[18]

On Friday, 18 April, Cooke took his own benefit night as Richard III, one of the few times thus far he had played the role that would become his most famous.[19] Before the season closed on 30 April, Cooke appeared three more times, in addition to reciting on 28 April "The Picture of a Play-House, or Bucks Have at Ye All" and "The Grecian Fabulist, or the Story of the Man, the Boy and the Ass." On Friday, 25 April, he appeared as Don Felix, and as Stukely on Monday. He completed his first Newcastle season on 30 April when, for the benefit of Austin, he took the role of the lover, Inkle, in George Colman the elder's popular comic opera *Inkle and Yarico*.[20]

The playbill for Austin's benefit also announced that this was the last season for Austin as manager, for he wished to retire to Chester. His share in the company was sold to Cooke's friend Joe Munden.[21] Perhaps the season had proven a disappointment to Austin, for after forty-one nights of performances, the revenue was only £2,700 or about £65 per night, which meant they had played to an average of only over half a house.[22] On the other hand, for Cooke the season must have been euphoric: he had reached a high point in his popularity and, in one season, had played such roles as Othello, Shylock, Macbeth, and Richard III, reaching the status of leading actor and tragedian. He was still being called upon to fill comic roles, lovers, and occasionally, as was true this season, a few musical roles, but such assignments were fewer than ever before.

In early May, the newly formed Whitlock and Munden company performed at the Chester Races. After the week in Chester, Cooke left the company briefly to appear in Manchester for the first time in three years. Indeed, he had not been back to Manchester since his dispute over the role of Sir Peter Teazle with George Mattocks in 1785.

Mattocks' management had been taken over by the partnership of Sydney and Connor. Apparently, Mattocks was engaged as the star attraction for Race Week, coaxed to appear, no doubt, by Connor, with whom he had previously acted. Plays were presented every night of the week of 11 May, but only one role is known for this engagement, Hamlet.[23] Supporting Cooke were second-rate actors, although one, Samuel Ryley, who took the role of the First Gravedigger, has left us a first-hand account so representative of Cooke's intemperance and its effects, that despite its anecdotal nature, it deserves retelling.

Cooke and Ryley had gone to a public tavern one evening where Cooke, as usual, was the life of the party. "Mirth and good humour prevail'd till about ten o'clock, when I perceived a something lurking in his eye, which foretold a storm." Ryley was anxious to get Cooke home and tried to entice him out of the tavern; instead, Ryley's worst fears were realized. With a "haughty, supercilious look," Cooke flew into a rage, shouting, "I see what you are about, you hypocritical scoundrel! You canting, methodistical thief! am I, George C———, to be controll'd by such a would-be puritan as you? I'll teach you to dictate to a tragedian." Cooke then pulled off his coat, threatening to fight Ryley. With no small effort, Cooke was pacified and put his coat back on—but all was not well yet. Straddled before the fire, and completely monopolizing it, stood an unwashed, grimy faced man with matted hair "under a round, greasy hat, with narrow brims, conceitedly placed on one side of the head, which nodded under it, like a shaking mandarin." The man, with his coat skirts under each arm, finally caught Cooke's eye. Cooke stared in amazement at the "filthy fop" for the space of half a minute, examined him from top to toe, and finally "burst into a hoarse laugh, and roar'd out, '*Beau Nasty*, by ————." The "insensible puppy took little notice" of Cooke until

C———— now rose from his seat, and taking up the skirts of his coat, in imitation of the other, turn'd his back to the fire, "warm work in the *back settlements*, sir, said he;" then approaching still nearer, as if he had some secret to communicate, whisper'd though loud enough for every one to hear,

"Pray sir, how is soap?"
"Soap?"
"Yes sir, soap; I understand it is coming down."
"I am glad of it sir."
"Indeed sir, you have cause, if one may judge from
your appearance."

General laughter from the tavern guests followed. The butt of Cooke's ribbing pretended to ignore the uproar. Instead, he rang the bell with an "air of importance, and enquired 'if he could have a *weal kitlet*, or a *matton chip*?'" Cooke quickly interjected, "What do you think of a *roasted puppy*?" and reaching for a poker, interjected "I'll spit you, and roast you in a minute." The dirty beau, visibly shaken, began to retreat toward the door, Cooke close behind, saying, "avaunt and quit my sight, thy face is dirty, and thy hands unwash'd; avaunt! avaunt I say!" Replacing the poker, Cooke continued, "being gone, I am a man again!"

When intoxicated, Cooke rarely knew when to stop irritating others; this evening was no exception. One customer at the tavern, whom Ryley called "Perrins, the noted Pugilist" and described as a "remarkably strong man, and possessed of great modesty and good nature," laughed "immoderately" at the scene he had just witnessed. Cooke took offense at Perrins' laughter and once more pulled off his coat ready to fight. Perrins, a man of mild disposition and familiar with Cooke's habits, simply responded to Cooke's anger with a smile, until

aggravated by language and action the most gross, he very calmly took him in his arms, as though he had been a child, set him down in the street, and bolted the door. The evening was wet, and our hero, without coat or hat, unprepared to cope with it, but entreaty for admission was vain, and his application at the window unattended to. At length grown desperate, he broke several panes, and inserting his head through the fracture, bore down all opposition by the following witticism. "Gentlemen I have taken some *pains* to gain admission, pray let me in, for I *see through my error.*" The door was open'd, dry clothes procured and about one o'clock in the morning we sent him home in a coach.²⁴

Dunlap states that Cooke read the story in his presence at Philadelphia in 1811, and, although "he did not much relish it," he did not deny it. Cooke was actually mortified more by Ryley's introduction to the anecdote, a character sketch that he called "a bitter pill" to swallow.²⁵ Although Ryley was writing long after the event described in his wandering memoir, Ryley and Cooke were evidently fairly close associates in 1788 and their friendship doubtlessly continued when a few years later Ryley became the landlord of the Angel Tavern in Oldham Street, while continuing to dabble in theatre.²⁶ Cooke must have frequently visited his old acquaintance at the tavern on future engagements in Manchester. Ryley's comments, then, are especially revealing since they come from close personal observation. He praised Cooke as an actor and his ability to perform some characters in a manner superior to that of his contemporaries, but added that "they are limited to such parts as suit his figure, which wants grace and proportion; where these can be dispensed with, he has no competitor." Ryley found Cooke, when sober, "the gentleman, the scholar, the friend, the life of every party, an enemy to scandal and detraction, and benevolent, even to imprudence." However, when intoxicated, Cooke became a different person entirely.

No two men, however different they may be, can be more at variance than George C———, sober, and George C———, in a state of inebriety. At these times, his interesting suavity of manners changes to brutal invective; the feelings of his nearest and dearest friends are sacrificed; his best benefactor wounded, either in his own person, or in that of his tenderest connexions, and the ears of delicacy assaulted by abuse of the grossest nature. Such are the unfortunate propensities of this singular man—unfortunate, I say, because he seems incapable of avoiding them, although they have a tendency to ruin his health, injure his property, and destroy his social connexions. No one can more regret these failings than he does, in his hours of sanity, or make more handsome apologies; and if at night he creates enemies, his conciliatory manners in the morning are sure to raise double the number of friends.²⁷

It is well known that such aggressive outbursts as those described by Ryley are not uncommon in alcoholics and, in fact, signify one stage or sign of alcohol addiction. Ryley seemed to be sympathetic in describing Cooke's symptoms and, as we will see, many shared his interpretation of Cooke's Jekyll and Hyde personality. Dunlap, unfortunately, did not and thus shows an intolerance that permeates his book. He felt, as did many at that time, that drinking was only a matter of vice and virtue and "is at the choice of every man."²⁸

One additional statement by Ryley in his *Itinerant* is worthy of quotation, for it gives an insight into Cooke's acting technique and its effects on an audience. Ryley explained, "I have known a respectable actor cry like a woman, through an affecting part, without producing any similar sensation in the audience; whilst Cooke would drown them in tears, and, at the same time, be slily [sic] winking at his friends behind the scenes."[29]

Evidently, Cooke resumed his position with the Whitlock and Munden company after the Manchester Races, although little evidence has been found for Cooke's summer season. It is known that he was in Lancaster in June, for a playbill in the Central Public Library of Lancaster for 10 June lists him as Archer in *The Beaux' Stratagem* with Munden as Scrub. It is likely that Cooke first performed at Newcastle early in June during Race Week and then moved on to other stops on the circuit—Lancaster, Preston, Chester, and perhaps Warrington and Sheffield, which also belonged to Whitlock and Munden.[30]

Somewhere during these strollings, and certainly prior to May 1789, another instance of Cooke's mounting alcoholic problem occurred. Munden wrote:

On the occasion of the company's removal from one town to another, Cooke accompanied Mrs. Munden in a post-chaise. He was exceedingly sentimental; decried the fatal effects of liquor. "Never, my dear Mrs. Munden," said he, "permit my friend Joe to drink to excess, but above all things make him refrain from spirits; brandy and water has been my bane." They separated for the night to their different quarters. In the morning Cook [sic] did not come to rehearsal. Search was made after him in every direction; and with some difficulty, he was discovered lying dead drunk on the floor of a subterranean wine vault.[31]

Cooke was clearly aware of the consequences of heavy drinking for himself and others. This anecdote attests to this awareness. Moreover, about six years later, Cooke recorded in his diary an event that made a strong impression on his sensibilities. While partaking of brandy and water at a tavern, Cooke observed a clergyman, "dirty, drunk and foolish." Cooke felt pity for the man, "a real, sorrowful feeling," and observed:

In viewing him, I thought of others. Drunkenness is the next leveller to death; with this difference, that the former is always attended with shame and reproach, while the latter, being the certain lot of mortality, produces sympathy, and may be attended with honour. From the general temper of the world it is too probable, with respect to the gentleman I am writing of, that a long and faithful discharge of the duties of his office will be almost forgotten, while the hours of his frailty, or to speak stronger, the periods of his vice and folly, will be clearly remembered and distinctly related. I think and hope I shall never forget him.[32]

Such a commentary is ironic in light of Cooke's own alcoholism and the opinion history has tended to have of him. Munden's son also recorded, however, that at about this period Cooke was in the prime of his life, "with powers said to be superior to those he afterwards evinced, and a voice as mellifluous as it became, in the end, hoarse from intemperance." [3]

The Newcastle season began on 5 January 1789 in the midst of a severe winter, with considerable snow and wind, and the Tyne River dangerous with ice.[34] Newcastle's proximity to the North Sea often made for bad winter seasons, but this one appears to have been especially frigid. No doubt it affected audience attendance at the beginning of the season, despite assurances from the management that the theatre would be warm for productions. For opening night, the newspaper advertisement (*Chronicle*, 3 January 1789) informed the patrons that "constant fires have been kept in the theatre for six weeks." Attendance was still poor, and to gain public interest and support the managers produced a benefit on 17 January for "the poor and the needy at this severe and inclement season." Even this strategy only produced a disappointing £17 6s., or about one-sixth capacity.[35]

Cooke had made his first appearance on 12 January as the villain Don Manuel in Bertie Greatheed's tragedy *The Spanish Regent*, with John Hodgkinson, a twenty-four-year-old actor, as Gomez.[36] Hodgkinson had joined the company during the summer season, but left at the end of the Newcastle season when he eloped with Joe Munden's common-law wife, Mary Jones, and eventually established a career in America. During his brief tenure at Newcastle, he was assigned young romantic leads in comic and musical productions. For Cooke's appearance, the audience must have been sparse, but by the end of January, the *Newcastle Courant* (31 January 1789) noted that "a very splendid audience" had attended the performance on 26 January. By mid-February, attendance had apparently returned to normal; the *Chronicle* (21 February 1789) announced that for *The Merchant of Venice* the audience had been "more numerous than on any preceding evening this season, and receipts amounted to upwards of 100 pounds."

Cooke's position was clearly on the rise throughout this season, and excellent roles continued to come his way. On 19 January, he played Macbeth to Mrs. Whitlock's Lady Macbeth, followed by Sir Clement Flint in *The Heiress* on the 26th, Jaques in *As You Like It* with Munden as Touchstone, Hodgkinson as Orlando, and Mrs. Whitlock as Rosalind on 2 February, and Lovemore in *The Way to Keep Him* on 9 February. *The Merchant of Venice* was presented on 16 February, "by desire of the gent¹ of the Shakespear Club," with Cooke as Shylock, Hodgkinson as Bassanio, and Mrs. Whitlock as Portia. Afterwards, Cooke recited Garrick's "Ode." On 23 February, he appeared as the kindly Duke in *Measure for Measure* and on 2 March as Benedick in *Much Ado*.

Benefits began in March, and apparently the audience became rowdy during some of the productions early in the month. On 7 March, the *Chronicle* printed a letter which complained of the theatregoers' noisy behavior and added that everyone acknowledged that "this season's company is infinitely superior to any in the kingdom, London excepted, and is generally supposed to contain performers who must, in a few years, make a leading figure in those theatres" of London. This could, of course, be nothing more than managerial puffery sneaking into the pages of the press.

For Munden's benefit, on 16 March, Cooke took the role of the lover Colonel Feignwell in *A Bold Stroke for a Wife*. He played Prospero and recited Collins' "Ode on the Passions" for Miss Butler on 18 March. He then prepared for his own benefit, 23 March, choosing Addison's *Cato*. A minor incident, however, arose over the assigning of roles. Elizabeth Whitlock refused to perform the part of Cato's virtuous daughter, Marcia, on the grounds that Cooke's choice of play was one "in which no one could appear to any advantage but himself."[37] Frances Butler was persuaded to assume the role, and on 21 March 1789, the *Chronicle* listed her in the part. The next day, a Sunday, Mrs. Whitlock issued a notice saying she would play the part. It was arranged to have Joe Munden inform the audience of the shift in cast, and then immediately after Mrs. Whitlock would unreservedly apologize. On the following evening, however, although the audience refused to hear her, she courageously made her entrance as Marcia and after "much clapping and hissing" completed her performance.[38] In order to offset any additional furor, especially since her benefit was to follow in two days, Mrs. Whitlock issued a leaflet on the 24th apologizing to the public and reiterating that the greatest pride and pleasure of her life was to obey and please them. The pamphlet did not completely quell the controversy. A writer in the *Chronicle* (28 March 1789) commended her for refusing the role; on the 11th, the same paper advertised for sale a twenty-page pamphlet entitled *Thoughts on the Late Disturbances at the Theatre-Royal, Newcastle*, in which Mrs. Whitlock was severely criticized and her figure, which resembled her brother Stephen's, was satirized.[39]

Cooke played Cato, advertised as the first time in the role. Actually, he had used the role for his benefit at Manchester in 1784, delivering the original prologue by Pope, and afterwards appeared as Clerimont in Murphy's farce *Old Maid* and recited Collins' "Ode." The *Chronicle* (28 March) reported that the receipts for Cooke's benefit totaled "upward of 115 pounds, a striking proof how great a favourite of the town this inimitable actor is." The controversy over the role of Marcia, although certainly minor, doubtlessly helped crowd the house that night, and the theatrical gossip surrounding the incident, a popular form of entertainment itself during the eighteenth century, must have spread Cooke's name throughout the surrounding provinces.

James Fennell in his autobiography, which contains one of the strongest attacks on Dunlap for his treatment of Cooke, claims to have first met Cooke about the time of the Cooke-Whitlock fracas, having stopped briefly in Newcastle on his way from Edinburgh. There seems to be little evidence that he actually performed for Mrs. Whitlock's benefit, unless he was not listed on the bills and performed in the afterpiece, *The Pannel*. Cooke, prior to seeing Fennell in Philadelphia in an evening of recitations, said he had never seen him perform.[40] *Cymbeline* was the mainpiece that night, with Whitlock as Imogen, Cooke as her husband, Posthumus Leonatus, and Hodgkinson as Iachimo. Apparently, Cooke did not harbor a grudge or at least was very professional about his responsibilities. *Cymbeline* was repeated for Smith's benefit on 1 April with the same cast.

During his brief visit, Fennell "wished much to see Mr. Cooke, but had not an opportunity till accident presented it, and then but for a few minutes. I was anxious of becoming intimately acquainted with him, but failed in my endeavor." Indeed, Fennell would not become well acquainted with Cooke until years later in Philadelphia. Fennell, who had appeared for a short time at Covent Garden the previous season under the name Cambray, returned there in October. Eventually, in 1792, he left England for a career in the United States. Fennell's one observation on Cooke at Newcastle is nonetheless an important one in that it characterizes Cooke's vocal instrument several years before detailed commentary on his voice appeared in the press and journals, and confirms Munden's estimation. Fennell corroborates that "Mr. Cooke was then celebrated for the extraordinary and beautiful intonation of his voice, which was considered to be his principal excellence."[41] Years of heavy drinking took their toll on his vocal apparatus, as is evident from later comments, but in 1789 there seemed to be no noticable difference from descriptions cited earlier.

During the remainder of March and April, Cooke performed the following roles: Mr. Belville (30 March), Bevil Junior in *The Conscious Lovers* (13 April), Edgar in *King Lear*, "By desire of Sir John, the Officers and Brethren of the Lodge of Free and Easy Johns" (15 April), Captain Plume in *The Recruiting Officer*, Colonel Standard in George Farquhar's *The Constant Couple* with Mrs. Smith in the famous breeches role of Sir Harry Wildair (22 April), Alexander in the *Rival Queens* (24 April), Collins' "Ode" and Petruchio in the afterpiece *Catherine and Petruchio* (27 April), and for Whitlock's benefit on 29 April, Loveless in Miles Peter Andrew's comedy *Reparation; or, The Libertine Reclaimed*.

At the conclusion of the season, the *Chronicle* (2 May) reported that "the company has been universally well received during this season, and has been acknowledged one of the strongest this circuit has seen, or we can ever expect to visit us."

During this season at Newcastle, Cooke appeared in nine Shakespearean roles, or more correctly, altered roles in eighteenth-century adaptations. Consistently, he continued to play the largest number of major parts in the company, and his position in the community was well established. During the remainder of 1789, Cooke made two additional appearances in Newcastle, both a week in duration. For the Newcastle Races, usually held in June, he supported Sarah Siddons once again, and then, according to Dunlap, after visiting

Berwick and Edinburgh in a nonprofessional capacity, he returned to Newcastle to perform during the Assizes with Dorothy Jordan. Mrs. Jordan had made her London debut in 1785 at Drury Lane and for four years had delighted her audiences in such comic parts as Priscilla Tomboy in *The Romp*, Miss Hoyden in *A Trip to Scarborough*, Sir Harry Wildair, and Miss Prue in *Love for Love*. Cooke also performed with her in Chester in the summer or early fall.[42]

It may be possible, for little is actually known of these engagements, that Cooke did not appear with her at Newcastle at all. If the Veteran Stager is correct, he did not. Once more, this rare source is so appetizingly close to known facts, that it cannot be ignored. He tells us that Jordan was to debut at Newcastle as Lady Bell in *Know Your Own Mind*, with Cooke performing Dashwould, "a character certainly as opposite to his general style of characters as it is possible to imagine; a gay, lively, volatile, young man, constantly playing upon the follies and eccentricities of all around him." The managers were probably aware that the role was not ideally suited for him, but since he was a decided favorite in Newcastle, they felt it would do him no damage. The Stager's narrative continues:

... on the morning of the last rehearsal he read the character, a circumstance in opposition to theatrical usage, and also to his own former practice. Mrs. Jordan became alarmed, the managers surprised; however, they possessed a perfect reliance of his perfecting himself in the words in the course of the day; in this however they were deceived, for George left the house before the fifth act began, and though diligent search was made for him, he was *non est inventus*.

Six o'clock arrived, the usual call for the actors before performance, but still no Cooke. At 7:00 P.M., curtain time, he was still missing. Searchers were sent out looking for him, but with no success; the company became alarmed for his personal safety. It was decided to play the farce first in hopes that Cooke would show up. The farce was performed, which necessitated a change of costume for Mrs. Jordan, and he was still nowhere in sight. As a result, Hodgkinson read Cooke's role to the crowded house.

On the following day the search was renewed, but still to no avail. A reward of 10 pounds was offered, and "every means that the kindness of his friends could suggest, or the managers effect, was put in active motion, but all in vain, no tidings of Cooke." Ten days later he was at last found in an obscure public house in the village of Swalwell, a few miles from Newcastle, "in a state of delirium the effect of intoxication; he was conveyed to his lodgings, when by the attention of his medical adviser, he was so far recovered as to be enabled to try the power of the Buxton waters, which in a very short time restored him to perfect health and vigour." Whether this anecdote is true, or even partially true, is difficult to ascertain. The author does indicate, correctly, that Cooke rejoined the company in Chester and "was received by the friendly managers with much kindness." The reason for his action was, as told to the Stager, because he did not like the part and "could not brook the idea of disgracing himself before his generous friends and benefactors."[43]

Cooke was definitely performing in Sheffield for a short season from mid-December to the end of January 1790 at the theatre between Sycamore and Norfolk streets on Arundel.[44] During this month and a half, he acted mostly familiar roles: Shylock (18 December), Major Oakly in *The Jealous Wife* (21 December), Iachimo (28 December), Loveless in *The Reparation* (30 December), Hamlet and Petruchio (1 January), Sir John Dormer in *Word to the Wise* (4 January), Alexander in *The Rival Queens* (6 January), Prospero (8 January), Exeter in *Henry V* (11 January), Colonel Standard (13 January), Lord Hildebrand in *Carmelite* and Modely in Kemble's altered version of *The Country Lasses, The Farm House* (15 January), Gondibert in *Battle of Hexam* (20 January), and Leonidas in *The Fall of Sparta*.[45]

Although Cooke apparently remained with this company for the next year and a half, details about his activities prior to November 1790 are scarce. In September, he was in Lancaster, where a bill in the Central Public Library for 17 September includes Cooke in Whitlock's benefit, reciting the poetical piece "British Loyalty or a Squeeze for St. Paul' " by George Colman, Jr.[46] Back in Newcastle, his second benefit there in 1790 was *Henry VIII* with Mrs. Whitlock as Catherine, her husband as King Henry, Cooke as Wolsey, and Munden as Bishop Gardiner.[47]

In September 1790, Joe Munden sold his share in the management to Whitlock and went to London to join the company at Covent Garden. Early in 1791 at Sheffield, Whitlock relinquished the entire management to Stephen Kemble, with whom Cooke had already performed.

Cooke apparently did not join the Sheffield company at the outset of their season there, for a news item in the *Sheffield Advertiser* (26 November 1790), which is unclear as to whether the theatre had opened on 22 November or 19 November, praises Kemble's Hamlet and Shylock, Mrs. Kemble's Ophelia, mentions Miss Satchell and Mrs. Whitlock, but fails to mention Cooke. It appears that Cooke did not appear as advertised for 22 November, when his name appears in the *Advertiser* (19 November 1790) as Lord Hastings in *Jane Shore*. Instead, *Hamlet* was substituted and Cooke arrived the following week, rescheduling *Jane Shore* for the 29th. His first appearance, then, must have been as Loveless in *A Trip to Scarborough* on 26 November, then Lord Hastings, followed by Captain Cook in the pantomime *The Death of Captain Cook* on the 29th.[48] He next appeared as Sir William Douglas in *The English Merchant* on 3 December, although *Henry IV, Part 1* had been originally announced. *Henry IV* was apparently postponed until 20 December, when Cooke appeared as Hotspur, Betterton as Hal, and Kemble as Falstaff. Subsequently, in London, Cooke would take the role of Falstaff, and Kemble, when he attempted the role in the metropolis, would lose in comparison to Cooke. On 10 December, Cooke played Sir Clement Flint in *The Heiress*, on the 17th, Sir George Touchwood in *The Belles' Stratagem*, and on the 24th, the title role of the Earl of Warwick.

On 27 December, after the mainpiece, *The London Merchant*, in which Cooke did not appear, Kemble presented a sight that, as Dunlap observes, "makes us suspect that there was something rather barbarous in the taste of the Sheffield audience, or of Mr. S. Kemble, the new manager," when he tells us that

> among other strange modes of entertaining the town, Mr. Kemble introduced a travelling Jew in the dress of a North American Indian, who pretended to shew the method of scalping, and to add to the amusement of the spectators, the savage Israelite devoured raw mutton, for the gratification of their appetite and his own.[49]

The advertisement for this phenomenon reveals his billing as Anamaboah, the Indian king, who is described at some length by Ryley in another appearance at Newcastle.[50]

Cooke's only other known role in Sheffield was as Bevil Junior in *The Conscious Lovers*. Since Sheffield's newspapers were published only on Friday, complete bills for the full week's offerings are rarely available and bills of the day have not been located. It is known, however, that before January also advertised were *The Count of Narbonne, Tamerlane, The Tempest, Macbeth,* and *The Way to Keep Him*, all of which Cooke had appeared in before.

Benefits began in January, and for Elizabeth Satchell's (now Mrs. Kemble), Cooke appeared as Neville in Frederick Reynolds' comedy *The Dramatist; or, Stop Him Who Can*, which had premiered the preceding spring at Covent Garden. The repercussions of the French Revolution were beginning to be felt in provincial theatricals, so Mrs. Kemble concluded her benefit with a new spectacle called "Gallic Freedom; or, Vive la Liberte." Cooke's night followed on 5 January, and he chose Falconbridge in *King John*, with Kemble as the king, and recited "A monody on the Death of Garrick," whom he clearly still held in esteem.[51] For the next two weeks, Cooke was extremely active, appearing again as Neville in the popular play *The Dramatist* (12 January); Zamor in *Alzira; or, the Conquest of Peru*, translated from Voltaire by Aaron Hill (10 January); Hammond in Henry Siddons' "prelude" *Modern Breakfast*, which was followed by a recitation of "British Loyalty; or, a Squeeze for St. Paul's," and at the conclusion of a long bill, the title role in *The Guardian* (17 January) for Whitlock's night; and Mr. Clerimont in Richard Steele's *The Tender Husband* (19 January). The last night of the Sheffield season occurred on 21 January, Kemble's benefit night. Whether Cooke participated in *Such Things Are* is not indicated, but most likely he did.

From Sheffield the company moved back to Newcastle. Cooke had not been given the leading roles in Sheffield that he had grown accustomed to in the season before Kemble assumed command. Perhaps for this reason, his low esteem for Kemble's bill of fare, or a series of "indispositions" on Cooke's part, he did not long remain with the company under Kemble's management. The Stager suggests an additional factor. The personages he mentions did indeed belong to the Newcastle company on occasion, and Cooke did, as the Stager indicates, move from Newcastle to Manchester. The Stager tells us that Cooke became too "sensible of the tender passion, and paid to a Mrs. Marshall more attention than was warranted by the strict laws of propriety, she being the wife of an actor in the same theatre." The result was that the good Northumbrians became alarmed and neglected attendance at the theatre. Cooke saw an "impending storm" and left Newcastle.[52] If not the entire reason for Cooke's early departure, such a situation would have complicated matters for Cooke and the management. It is clear that he and Kemble had not found their relationship a pleasant one. In June 1793, another actor in the Newcastle company, John Edwin, Jr., began a paper skirmish with Kemble, accusing him of promising one salary and giving another, and in general misleading him about financial matters.[53] Kemble came back with six pages of rebuttals and denials, claiming that prior to taking over the company no actor had received more than a guinea and a half per week.[54] Finally, on 12 June 1793, Edwin, in a last attempt at "justice," printed one last appeal, accusing Kemble of forgetting promises, letters, etc. In this last missile, Cooke's name enters the debate:

A manager has it always in his power to controul [sic], and be revenged on a comedian. Tho' obliged to us for an existence, their policy in keeping us in poverty, and their property and interest, must keep us eternally in aw [sic]. An actor in favour with the public, is often considered by the manager as his enemy: Mr. Cook's [sic] dispute is an example of that.[55]

This does not exactly pinpoint what the dispute with Cooke was about, but evidently, in addition to the other problems mentioned above, Cooke and Kemble disagreed on financial matters, presumably salary. Certainly if we take all problems into consideration, it seems wise that Cooke would soon separate himself from Stephen Kemble's employ.

On 26 January 1791, Cooke played Hamlet to the Ophelia of Elizabeth Kemble, as he had previously done in Chester in 1785; on 21 March, he played Sir George Touchwood;[56] but by April his sudden "indispositions" and "recoveries" began to be observed. On 6 April, he disappointed the Newcastle audience, and Kemble had to read Cooke's part of Dorimont in *The School for Arrogance*; later in the month Kemble had to assume the role. By May, Cooke's name no longer appeared on Newcastle bills. Since Cooke's reputation was not apparently affected by this sudden departure, it is safe to assume that the Stager is quite correct in saying that Cooke left prior to a "real storm."

His reputation in Manchester was certainly intact, for by June he was engaged to star during the Manchester Races to continue with the company for the upcoming season.

On the evening of 12 June 1789, Thomas King, who had come to Manchester for a brief engagement, completed for his benefit performance and the last night of the summer season two of his most famous roles, Scrub in *The Beaux' Stratagem* and Puff in *The Critic*. A week and a half later, the Manchester theatre was reduced to a shell from a blazing fire that quickly spread throughout the structure and the adjoining buildings.[57] A new theatre was built and opened in February 1790. By the time Cooke arrived in June, the company was also under partial new management. Connor had withdrawn after the fire and had been replaced by John Banks' brother-in-law, Thomas Ward. The new joint management also gained control of Whitlock's Chester Theatre. Banks, partly from ill health and partly from severe criticism, left management in 1800, whereas Ward remained a joint manager until 1807, adding Thomas Ludford Bellamy to the ranks of provincial managers on Ward's retirement.[58] Apparently, the new management flourished in its early years, for Samuel Ryley, who had written a song for the opening of the new theatre and was also performing that season in Manchester, recalled that under Banks and Ward the theatre was "conducted with regularity and propriety" and that Banks proved to be "a complete man of business, and suffered nothing to interfere with this duty."[59] Cooke, of course, knew both men well, having performed with them during his prior engagements in Manchester. In 1796, Cooke would find himself further indebted to them after his first Dublin engagement. For now, however, his position was secure, and the future continued to hold promise.

Although only two parts are known for Cooke during the Manchester Races, he probably performed each night of the week. On 13 June, he appeared opposite Mrs. Powell, a sister to Mrs. Ward, as Romeo. Both Mrs. Powell and Mrs. Ward had previously made appearances at Drury Lane. On the next evening, Cooke played Dumont to Sarah Ward's Jane Shore.[60]

At the conclusion of the Races, Cooke became a member, in his own words, of "an Errant Strolling Company" at Buxton in Derbyshire.[61] Buxton had for centuries been a popular health resort for baths in the warm springs in the area, thought especially beneficial for "billious cholics and rheumatic complaints." The major amusements in the town, other than the baths, were "hunting and taking the air," although the evenings sometimes offered dancing in the "Grand Room" of the Great Hotel and plays. The cardroom adjoining the "Grand Room" possibly proved most popular, since it was opened every night.[62]

Cooke was not impressed with Buxton's amenities, found the theatre a "mean, ill-constructed, thatched building, and the performers . . . worthy of their covering." The church Cooke considered "a wretched hovel, worse than the theatre."[63]

One wonders how Cooke got himself involved with such a company, and in such a place. However unpleasant the lack of professionalism might have been, Cooke made the most of the solitude in the small country town. He took long solitary walks, often with a book or the role he was studying in hand, and he no doubt paused in his walks to read and contemplate. Apparently, it was during this lull that he began a habit that remained with him until the end of his life—he read vociferously and almost anything that fell into his hands, often with little or no discrimination. He would then spend hours writing excerpts or making comments from the books he had been reading in his journal or in a "waste" book. This was especially true during moments when his drinking was in an extreme stage, perhaps as a means of taking his mind off his physical misery or his personal problems.[64]

The roles he played in Buxton are included in his journal. I have not been able to confirm them, but there is no reason to doubt the authenticity of his entries. Performances in Buxton took place in August and included Tancred in *Tancred and Sigismunda*, Major O'Flaherty in *The West Indian*, Joseph Surface in *School for Scandal*, Moody in Garrick's *The Country Girl*, and Rover, the spirited strolling actor, in John O'Keefe's *Wild Oats*.[65]

While in Buxton, he wrote down his opinion of the playwright O'Keefe, and it is characteristic of his critical insights into the hack and mundane playwriting of his time. It demonstrates a good deal of critical judgment and a taste superior to much he was called upon to perform.

By a comparative view with true English comedy writers, or indeed with those of any other nation, O'Keefe's pretensions as a dramatic author can be allowed no higher praise, than that he is an agreeable farce maker, or in other words, an ingenious and pleasing arranger of nonsense, and one degree removed above a pantomime maker. Confusion and improbability of plot, if indeed there is any, ignorance of character, trite sentiment, most absurdly misplaced, low and vulgar conceits, sometimes bordering upon indecency, form a comedy by Mr. O'Keefe.[66]

On 2 September 1791, Cooke left Buxton to join the Ward and Banks company at Chester, where their newly acquired theatre opened for a brief season of one month. While at Chester, Cooke and a few of his colleagues made a short trip to Liverpool to perform one night for a benefit for Mrs. Arnold, a vocalist from London's Covent Garden. She had chosen for her night William Mason's *Elfrida*, basically a dramatic poem written in the form of a Greek tragedy. Cooke and his friends, however, knew nothing of her choice and thus had made no preparation. Without apology or announcement of a selection change, the hastily assembled company performed instead *Tancred and Sigismunda*, with Cooke playing Tancred. Cooke's reaction to their efforts was simple—they "murdered" the tragedy.[67]

As unsuccessful as the night was, the trip was more productive for Cooke. The Liverpool manager, Francis Aickin, brother of James whom Cooke had seen perform as a boy in Berwick, hired him to perform the following summer at Liverpool.

The regular Manchester season opened on 14 November with Hartson's *The Countess of Salisbury* with Cooke in the familiar role of Alwin.[68] The company that season was a relatively strong one, with, in addition to Cooke, Banks, and Ward, Mrs. Ward, Richardson, John(?) Barrett, Davis, William Bates, Mrs. Simpson, Mrs. Powell, and Garret Tyrrell.[69] Following Alwin, Cooke performed the role of Floriville in *The Dramatist*, which he repeated in February, and then, for the first time, Sir George Splendorville, the reforming libertine in Elizabeth Inchbald's latest comedy *Next Door Neighbours*. The latter production was successful enough to be repeated at least three times during the season. On 6 December, when *Next Door Neighbours* was first repeated, a one-act afterpiece was offered entitled *The Prussian Festival*, presented "In Honor of the late Royal Marriage between The Duke of York and Princess of Prussia," in which Cooke appeared as a Prussian officer.

As popular as *Next Door Neighbours* was, the first notable event of the season was the performance of O'Keefe's *Wild Oats*, just prior to the second revival of Inchbald's comedy. Despite Cooke's own dislike for the comedy, it became the most popular offering of the season. For this production, however, Cooke played Harry Thunder, alias Dick Buskin, instead of Rover. The success of *Wild Oats* resulted in at least six more performances during the regular season.

Just before Christmas, Cooke played Captain Jack Absolute, and on 11 January 1792, he took the role of Haswell in *Such Things Are*. Prior to benefits in February, he played the supporting role of the French lover, Count Ribaumont, in Colman the younger's musical drama, *The Surrender of Calais*, which was repeated early in February.

For Mrs. Powell's night, Cooke portrayed the proud lover Count Connolly Villars in Thomas Holcroft's *The School of Arrogance*, and undoubtedly he appeared in other benefits in February and early March. His next known role was not until 19 March when he played the reforming rake Harry Dornton in Holcroft's latest comedy hit, *The Road to Ruin*, presented for John Banks' benefit. He repeated the role again on 9 April for Bates' benefit.

Cooke's own benefit came on 26 March 1792, for which he chose *Henry V* as adapted by J. P. Kemble as his mainpiece and *The Citizen* as his afterpiece.[70] Two days after his own benefit, Cooke recited Collins' "Ode on the Passions" for another benefit, and then on 11 April he gave his fourth performance of Sir George Splendorville for young Thomas Dibdin's benefit. Dibdin, then nineteen or twenty, was the illegitimate son of the playwright, actor, and songwriter Charles, but called himself S. Merchant. Later, he assumed the name of Dibdin, much to his father's annoyance. Eventually, he became the composer of 2,000 songs and the author of numerous plays, pantomimes, and operas.[71] He would resume his association with Cooke at Covent

Garden. At Manchester in 1792 Dibdin painted scenery, prompted, acted small roles, and was beginning to write and compose.[72] Dibdin, who became an intimate friend of Cooke, wrote in his autobiography that he "had the pleasure of being on particular terms of friendly intercourse" with Cooke until the end of Cooke's life. He recalled:

> Cooke was perhaps a greater favourite in Manchester than in any other town in England: his powers of acting were at this time in their zenith; his love of conviviality still superior to his powers of acting. Many an hour have I passed with him in his penitential days; when, in the moment of sickness, induced by intemperance, he has sworn amendment; he lodged next door to me; and on all differences between him and the managers, as agent and counsel for both parties, I have often experienced the sincere pleasure of reconciling quarrels where reconciliation had seemed almost hopeless.[73]

Cooke was obviously beginning to be a trial to managers, although Dibdin writes that Cooke's drinking did not become a major problem for Banks and Ward until late April of this same season.

After Dibdin's benefit, Cooke appeared as Carlos in *Love Makes a Man* and Petruchio in *Catherine and Petruchio*. Then on 25 April, for a production of *The Provok'd Husband*, Cooke gave his "first cause of offense," having been announced as Lord Townley. According to Dibdin, Cooke

> had not arrived at the theatre at eight o'clock; we had entreated the indulgence of the audience; sent little Barret . . . to sing comic songs; the public were patient and lenient in the extreme: but when Cooke did appear, rather (as sailors say) a few sheets in the wind, he was received with three deafening rounds of applause; and began his part by saying, with an accompanying hiccup,—"Why did I marry, especially a woman?" and then he stopped, and staggered, and laughed,—and that with an air of so much drunken independence, that John Bull could hold no longer, indignation came down in torrents, and George was quite as indignant; which was not half so extraordinary, as that the audience were rather subdued by it. "Go on, George!" "Never mind them, lad!" and "Bravo, Cooke!" were heard on all sides; so that the whole of his first scene was inaudible, and he was suffered to make a parenthesis of all but the last, which he played with every appearance of sobriety; went home out of humour, and left word at the door that he would never set foot on that stage again. "Where's Merchant?" was the manager's inquiry; and in half an hour I was at Cooke's bed-side, for he had wisely, for once, retreated to his chambers.

Cooke, says Dibdin, promised to pay the management 45 pounds if this estrangement could not be readily resolved, but no money passed hands. The managers readily forgave him, and the audience was easily placated "on Cooke's merely commencing an attempt at an apology two nights afterwards" prior to performing Count Villars.[74] Dibdin's narrative paints a familiar scene repeated often during Cooke's career, and it is certainly an indication of Cooke's continuing popularity that at a time when audiences were quick to condemn, he could gain forgiveness with very little effort. On one occasion Stephen Kemble is reported to have asked "if Cooke did not owe much of his celebrity to his vice and his utter disdain of public opinion." Thomas Munden answers in a revealing statement:

There might be something in this insinuation. The crowds who flocked to see [Cooke perform in London] . . . were always in doubt whether they should have value for the price of their admission; since it was an even chance that, before the curtain rose, an apology would be made for Mr. Cooke, who was suffering under "violent spasms." This, unquestionably, created excitement, and rendered him a rarity, which his more regular rival [John] Kemble was not. When he *did* appear, the rapture of the audience knew no bounds.[75]

There were exceptions, of course, when the audience was not enraptured, as we shall see.

Cooke apparently remained on good terms with Ward and Banks, and stayed with the Manchester company for two more regular seasons. If other indiscretions occurred, and Dibdin implies they were frequent, we have indication of only one other the next season.

The regular season ended the night of Cooke's attempted apology, although the company gave two charity benefits and played for Race Week before closing the theatre. On 28 May, in a benefit for "the Infirmary, Dispensary, Lunatic Hospital and Asylum," Cooke repeated his role of Captain Absolute, the first night of the Races. The next night, Cooke repeated Dick Buskin with Ward as Rover and Banks as John Dory, and on 30 May he reappeared as Count Ribaumont.[76] For the final performance, 4 June, a benefit for the "Manchester Lying-In Hospital," Cooke took the role of Oakly.

Cooke arrived in Liverpool for his summer engagement with Aickin in June 1792 and found himself in a company which included a number of London actors, among them his old friend Joe Munden and George Holman. Many of those appearing with Cooke had come with him from Manchester, and Holman, when asked by John Bernard later in London to give his estimation of the Manchester company, had replied, " 'There was one clever man amonst them, a Mr. Cooke, a good country actor, John,—but he'd never do in London !' " Bernard quipped back, "This was precisely Garrick's opinion of Henderson."[77]

Cooke's first appearance on 8 June was as Sciolto with Holman as Lothario and Mrs. Fawcett from Covent Garden as Lavinia.[78] On the 11th, he portrayed Stukely, followed on 18 June with Captain Absolute, Dionysias in *The Grecian Daughter* with Mrs. Powell as Euphrasia on 21 June, and on 25 June the Ghost in *Hamlet*. On 27 June, he performed Grey in *Chapter of Accidents* and Banquo on 28 June, followed on 2 July by Clytus, Carlos on 5 July, the Earl of Southampton in *The Earl of Essex* on the 6th, Sir John Melville on the 11th, King Henry in *Richard III* on Holman's last night, 12 July, and Joseph

Surface on 13 July. On the 16th, he took the small role of Adam in *As You Like It* and another small part, Mr. Wingrove, in Joseph Richardson's *The Fugitive* on 18 July. During July, he was also appearing with Tom King, the original Peter Teazle, Puff, and Sir Anthony Absolute in *The Rivals*, in which Cooke had already played opposite him as Captain Jack. King's last night was 20 July and Cooke reappeared with him in *The Fugitive*. On 23 July, he appeared as Sir George Airy in *The Busy Body*,[79] and on 25 July he played Harry Dornton in *Road to Ruin* which he repeated on 6 August and 24 August. With Holman and King gone, Cooke's roles increased in size in August, beginning on 1 August with Count Ribaumont for Mrs. Ward's benefit, followed by Prospero on 3 August and Richard in the historical romance *Richard Coeur de Lion*.

For his own benefit on 15 August, Cooke chose *King Lear* with John Whitfield as Edgar, Mrs. Powell as Cordelia, and Aickin as Kent, plus assorted songs and farces for afterpieces.[80] For Charles Dignum's night on 17 August, he appeared as Count Almaviva in the afterpiece *The Follies of a Day; or, The Marriage of Figaro* by Thomas Holcroft, and on 20 August he played Orloff in Mrs. Cowley's *A Day in Turkey; or, The Russian Slaves*, followed on the 22d with Inkle opposite Mrs. Powell's Yarico, which he repeated on 29 August for Mr. and Mrs. Sparks Powell's benefit. He completed his Liverpool engagement with Don Carlos (23 August), Clairville in Reynolds' *Notoriety; or, The Fashions of the Times* and Carlos in *Love Makes a Man* (30 August), which he had previously played on 5 July, and Iachimo (3 September), which appears to have been his last night in Liverpool.

The Manchester theatre opened for a brief season in September 1792 prior to its regular season in December. Returning after a two-year absence and appearing opposite Cooke was Hannah Robinson, now remarried and acting under the name of Mrs. Taylor. Also appearing in the company list is Miss Alicia Daniels,[81] a young singer and actress whose first recorded stage appearance in a named role was as Leona in *The Padlock* at Drury Lane on 26 May 1791. She had no doubt appeared earlier in the provinces and had performed chorus roles at Drury Lane prior to the 26th.[82] This was her first time in Manchester and her first encounter with George Cooke, whom she would marry in 1796 and leave only a few months later, nullifying the marriage in 1801. Dibdin remembered her as "a good singer and a good girl,"[83] although the author of a pamphlet entitled *The Thespian Mirror, or Poetical Strictures; on the Professional Characters of... the Theatres Manchester, Liverpool, and Chester* characterized her in 1793 differently:

> Of some execution and science possess'd
> Behold little Daniels a singer profess'd,
> Her vanity often mistaking the cause,
> Interprets encouragement into applause,
> The portion of favor she's thought to inherit,
> Is more the effect of her youth than her merit . . .[84]

During his brief season, Cooke portrayed the familiar role of Harry Thunder in *Wild Oats* at least twice, with Ward in his usual role of Jack Rover, and performed Shylock to the Portia of Hannah Taylor, with Alicia Daniels as Jessica.[85]

After Manchester Cooke seems to have spent some time in Chester, where he is listed on a bill for Mrs. Whitlock's benefit on 29 October in the title role of Percy and as Petruchio in the afterpiece, with some other members of the Manchester company, including Tyrrell, Congdon, Bates, and Davis.[86]

The regular Manchester season began on 5 December 1792, but Cooke did not appear until later, perhaps owing to another drinking bout, for on 11 December the *Manchester Mercury* announced that "the Managers have engaged *Mr. Ryley*, to perform Four Nights; Mr. *Grist* will appear in the Course of next Week; and Mr. *Cooke* as soon as his Indisposition will admit." Cooke did reappear on 19 December as Sir George Splendorville.[87] His performances this season seem to have been mostly in familiar roles, including Harry Thunder, Clytus, and Count Ribaumont. *The Surrender of Calais* was presented for Daniels' benefit in March and, although no cast list was given in the advertisment, Cooke probably played the Count as he had in the past. He also appeared as Prospero with Alicia as Ariel and Harry Dornton on at least three occasions.[88] Cooke also appeared as Hamlet on 1 January with Grist as the Ghost. This was a decided reversal for the two actors, since Cooke had previously played the smaller role when appearing with Grist.[89]

On 21 January 1793, Louis XVI was executed. The Revolution had already created some patriotic showmanship in provincial theatres, but with this development it reached its high point. In Manchester, as elsewhere, effigies, of Thomas Paine were burned, public meetings were held, and witch hunts were begun for "real or alleged Jacobins." Because of the prevailing patriotism, *Henry V* received a revival, as it would later during similar historic moments, such as during World War II when Sir Laurence Olivier performed his famous *Henry V*. Cooke appeared as King Henry on 11 February and repeated the role for Mrs. Powell's benefit on 27 February, as well as for his own benefit on 18 March, when he also delivered the prologue and recited Collins' "Ode on the Passions." After the play, Alicia Daniels sang, and Cooke brought the evening to a close with a loyal address to the audience, followed by a playing of "God Save the King."[90] The patriotic trend infiltrated almost all benefits that season.

Cooke had only three other new roles this season: Alonzo in Thomas Morton's historical drama *Columbus* for Banks' benefit (5 March) and possibly again for Mrs. Banks' benefit on 26 April; Edward in *Edward the Black Prince; or, The Battle of Poictiers* (3 April);[91] and the supporting role of Mr. Worthy in Samuel Ryley's comic opera *Roderick Random*, adapted from Tobias Smollett's novel.[92]

Cooke enacted several other roles this season, including one that would become a major part in his later repertoire, Kitely in Jonson's *Every Man in His Humour* (8 April).[93] Of those roles known to have been played by Cooke, the most singular trend that emerges in Manchester is a movement away from the portrayal of lovers and toward an increasing number of villains and rakes, although his comic appearances still outnumbered his appearances in tragedies or historical dramas.

Cooke's exact whereabouts during the summer of 1793 have been a mystery. In fact, Dunlap dismisses the entire year of 1793 by saying it was passed "much as the preceding, and at the same places."[94] It is now possible to speculate on this summer by turning to the Veteran Stager, who is more reliable on this period of Cooke's life than probably any other, since it was at this point that he first became personally acquainted with George Cooke. Because of the void previously existing at this stage of Cooke's career, it is appropriate to quote the Stager at some length.

At the close of the season he joined the management of a Mr. Welsh, where we first beheld him in the town of Bolton, Lancashire; his dress was a grey frock-coat, scarlet vest, buckskin breeches, white silk stockings, long quartered shoes, and an enormous pair of buckles according with the fashion of the day; his hair fashionably dressed and powdered; he appeared in Petruchio. As he did not arrive in the town until after the play had begun, he was consequently not provided with private lodgings, which we procured for him in the same house with ourselves; from this circumstance commenced an intimacy and friendship, which we feel proud in being able to affirm, we had the felicity to enjoy during his life; . . . From Bolton we accompanied him one afternoon to see his old friend Bill Bates [with whom he had performed in Manchester], and a joyous night we passed; it was the first time we had seen him intoxicated, but he was good-humouredly so; he repeated some passages from Macbeth, and asked us if we thought black Jack (John Kemble) could repeat them better; ending with an oath, "I will shake the black rascal on his throne before I die."[95] In the course of the day we returned to Bolton, and at night we acted Jaffier to his Pierre. During his stay in Bolton, he performed Iago, Richard, Macbeth, Petruchio, Aubrey in The Fashionable Lover, Sir Robert Bramble [*sic*] in Every One has his Fault, Sir Charles Racket, in Three Weeks after Marriage, Shylock, and Faulkland in The Rivals [several of these roles do not seem correct for Cooke, but in this respect the Stager may have forgotten exact facts]. We repaired for the season to Buxton, Derbyshire—again we were inmates of the same house, and boarded together; here he was particularly noticed by Mr. Cummins, the landlord of St. Ann's hotel . . . and Mr. James Hall, another proprietor of a very large hotel in the Crescent. The late Mr. Alderman Skinner chanced to be at Buxton that season, and was highly gratified by Cooke's excellence in the character of Shylock, and asked him to sup with him, but he would not accept of any invitation in which his chum was not included. We attended the great alderman, and on our arrival found the table prepared for three; after a short delay a gentleman appeared, not our host, but our host's valet, who apologized for the absence of the alderman from indisposition, but he was deputed to do the honours of the table; George surveyed him with a look of anger and contempt, and seizing his hat, said, "Sir, tell your master, we were invited to sup with a gentleman, and not with a gentleman's gentleman!" We then left the house. George had some strong antipathies, but one in particular was to all drummers; we remember him reading some dispatches from the Continent in which the wounded and killed were enumerated, and among the killed was one drummer: he dropped the paper, clasped his hands, and with the same feeling and triumph of exultation, as he could have exhibited in Shylock, when informed of Antonio's losses, exclaimed, "thank God! thank God! there's one b———d drummer gone at last." There was at this time, in Buxton, a performer of great celebrity on the musical glasses, of the name of Cartwright, who warmly pressed Cooke to attend his performance, to which George readily assented, and as he played some very beautiful Scotch airs, which were prodigious favorites with Cooke, he seemed highly delighted, and expressed himself in the warmest terms of gratification, and invited the performer to take supper with us in a tavern; the glass went freely round, when on a sudden our ears were assailed by a Scotch piper, who had entered the house for the purpose of procuring a bed for the night, and had began to give the customers in the kitchen a specimen of his abilities; now, though George was not a Scotchman, he had all the prejudices of one; he sallied into the place where the piper was, and ordered him something to drink, then returned to us; the brandy and water had by this time sensibly affected him, and forgetting all the praise he had but a short time before bestowed on the performance of Cartwright, exclaimed, "Sir, I have received from that poor piper more pleasure than from all your humbug glasses;" this, poor Cartwright took with seeming good humour; Cooke proceeded to abuse, which provoked from Cartwright a becoming replay, when Cooke very deliberately walked to the corner of the room where stood a certain pewter utensil, which he instantly seized and emptied the contents on Cartwright, leaving the vessel on his head, who, as soon as he could extricate himself from the encumbrance which George had honoured him with, proceeded to inflict condign punishment on the delinquent; poor Cooke's eyes soon bore ample testimony of the prowess of Cartwright. We forced Cooke out of the room, and with considerable entreaty got him to bed; in the morning we found him full of wrath and valour, and nothing would satisfy him but an ample apology from Cartwright, or honourable satisfaction from the explosion of a pistol; fully aware of Cooke's disposition, we felt little dread as to the result: having obtained an interview with his opponent and delivered our message, he laughed heartily at the rememberance of the circumstance, and expressed his concern of being obliged to disfigure the face of Cooke, but at the same time positively declined any thing in the shape of an apology, but would willingly over a friendly glass, bury in oblivion all that had occurred. The more unwillingness Cartwright exhibited towards ending the quarrel in the way proposed by Cooke, the more anxious the latter seemed to proceed; however, by a little skill in our negociation [sic], we prevailed on Cooke to make the first advances toward a reconciliation, which was effected by an if, "if you said so, then I said so; oh! oh! did you so," as Touchstone says "there is much virtue in an if." We left them together in perfect harmony and friendship; but as the wine began to operate, Cooke again became abusive, when Cartwright was, we believe, reluctantly compelled to bestow on the body of poor George such chastisement, as obliged Cooke to call for quarter; but next day he talked no more of pistols. From this time, then the middle of June, to September, his only beverage was porter or cyder, and of either but sparingly; but one night we went to witness an exhibition of fireworks on the hill opposite the Crescent, which when finished, he proposed as the night was damp . . . to fortify against the cold by one glass of brandy and water. We entered the tavern of

Darby Logan, a facetious Irish landlord that George was extremely partial to; here he soon forgot his recent abstemious mode of living, and yielded to the potent draught, nor could all the solicitations of ourselves or others prevail upon him to desist, until he was no longer able to sit or stand, and in that condition we conveyed him to bed, where he was, in consequence of his intemperance, confined for ten days, attended by Dr. Buxton. On his recovery he was solicited by Tom Grist, then acting in Sheffield, to grant him his services by performing the part of Iago for his benefit, which Mr. Welsh, the manager, consented he should do; but on the day prior to his appearing in Sheffield, Grist was seized with an inveterate hoarseness, which rendered him totally unfit to represent the sable Moor; in consequence we were applied to, and having procured the necessary leave from Mr. Welsh, accompanied Cooke in a chaise Grist had sent for our conveyance. When within a mile of Sheffield, Cooke felt assured some of his old friends would be upon the watch for his arrival, and perhaps induce him to do that he should be sorry for; he said he would leave the chaise and enter Sheffield by another route, to avoid temptation. We offered to accompany him, this he resisted; he left us with an assurance of his arriving in half an hour; we were met by Grist, who seemed much surprised at not seeing Cooke, but when the motive was explained to him he was satisfied; this was at four o'clock: we proceeded to the inn: five o'clock, no Cooke: another hour elapsed and no tidings; messengers were dispatched in various directions to find him out; they returned without obtaining the least information. Grist from indisposition was unable to make the proper apology; the manager volunteered his services, and explained as far as he was able to do, the cause of disappointment, and requested Mr. Cunningham, many years a member of the Bath theatre, might be allowed to perform the character of Iago: the request was reluctantly complied with, and we were suffered to proceed; when about the commencement of the 5th act, in staggered Cooke, his cloaths torn and covered with filth, his face marked and bloody, his entire person exhibiting the utmost stage of derangement, and in that condition was laid on a chest behind the scenes, until the play concluded, when he was conveyed into the same chaise that brought us to Sheffield, nor did he once awake until we were within a short distance of Buxton, when he inquired with much eagerness how the audience received him throught the part of Iago, as he believed he was devilish tipsey. We did not at that time conieve [sic] it necessary to state all that had occurred, but in due time he was informed the particulars, nor could he by any possible means call to his recollection, how or where he had passed the time, or what he had done with his money, eight pounds being gone: so ended our Sheffield excursion. At the close of the Buxton season Cooke returned to Manchester.[96]

I have found no way to verify conclusively the validity of this long gossipy account. However, if even the bare outline is correct, then Cooke spent the summer of 1793 in Buxton and its environs, both in a professional capacity and in a series of personal escapades. He did, indeed, return to Manchester for the winter season.

In November, Cooke once more performed with Sarah Siddons in Manchester. During her brief engagement, which occurred before the regular season began, Cooke performed Biron, the presumed dead husband, to her ever popular Isabella[97] and also Shylock to her Portia on 23 November in a benefit produced for "the fund for the warmer clothing of the English soldiery in France."⁹⁸

Before the regular Manchester season began in late December, Cooke made a brief trip to Chester. This type of excursion would normally be considered rather insignificant, but it appears that during this sojourn for the first time in his career he performed the role of Sir Pertinax MacSycophant in Macklin's comedy *Man of the World*. Sir Pertinax became one of Cooke's most popular roles on the London stage, *the Monthly Mirror* acclaiming his acting to be "the most perfect piece of acting on the English stage."⁹⁹ I have located no additional data on Cooke's appearances in Chester at this time, but certainly the introduction of Sir Pertinax to his repertoire marks a significant moment in his career. Appearing on this night, 20 December, with Cooke was the leading lady of the Manchester company, Mrs. Taylor as Lady Lumbercourt (her benefit), Davis as Lumbercourt, Tyrrell as Egerton, and Mrs. Powell as Lady MacSycophant.¹⁰⁰ It is possible that Cooke had appeared in the role previously, but this is the earliest reference to it thus far located.

Cooke was back in Manchester for the opening of the theatre on 26 December when he appeared as Percy.¹⁰¹ Manchester had become very much his home base, and it is here that he reached his maturity as an actor. The "Manchester Roscius," as he was now being called, continued to appear in familiar roles, periodically adding new parts to his growing repertoire. In January he appeared as Harry Dornton, and in February he probably repeated Alonzo in *Columbus*. He also made appearances as Harmony in Inchbald's *Everyone Has His Fault*, which he probably repeated (31 December), and Coriolanus in J. P. Kemble's adaptation of Shakespeare's tragedy.¹⁰² In February, Mrs. Crouch, the well-known vocalist and actress from Drury Lane, visited Manchester. Cooke tells us that "for want of a singer who could speak, a want very often felt in all theatre, I had the pleasure of acting Lord Aimworth to her Patty" in *Maid of the Mill*.¹⁰³

On 2 April, Cooke acted Shylock. One critic admitted that he had seen no finer piece of acting than his Shylock "for a long time," and added that it was a performance not "to be equalled by any other actor in this kingdom."¹⁰⁴ On 3 April, he appeared as Edward in *Edward the Black Prince*.¹⁰⁵ Four days later, for his own benefit, he offered for his mainpiece Robert Jephson's tragedy, *The Duke of Braganza*, in which he appeared as the heroic duke who becomes king of Portugal, and for his afterpiece enacted the father, Colonel Talbot, in *He Would Be a Soldier*. In addition, preceding the performance, he delivered a patriotic speech. On 8 April he appeared as Kitely,¹⁰⁶ and on 9 April he was found "sadly too old for Barnwell" by a local critic; his Lord Davenant in *The Mysterious Husband* on 21 April was "very pleasing," but "very wicked."¹⁰⁷ On 23 April, he played Octavian in *The Mountaineers*, and the comment was that "Cooke, in the distracted Lover, almost out-does himself." At the end of the first act, he gave a masterly recitation of Collins' "Ode on the Passions" and "drew forth a just applause." Cooke doubtlessly appeared in more roles this season, but no further newspaper references are available.

In early June, Cooke was in Manchester for Race Week, playing Harmony,[108] and in July he returned to Buxton, beginning a journal on the 6th. A portion of this journal is the first that I have discovered to be extant, dating from 26 July.[109] Dunlap, who seems to have had the entire journal before him, indicates that early in July he performed Octavian in *The Mountaineers*; Cooke recorded that "piece [was] done decently—drank some rum and water during the performance, which I found took hold of me."[110] A few days later he performed Lord Townley. In addition, Dunlap lists, supposedly from the journal, performances of Hotspur, Harry Dornton, Haswell, Freeport, Petruchio, Faulkland, The Guardian, Jaques, Young Wilding, Rover, Sir Robert Ramble, Anthony Euston, and Sir Callaghan O'Brallaghan in *Love-a-la-Mode*. These roles were all familiar for Cooke, with the possible exception of the last, which is especially interesting considering the fame he would gain from performing Sir Archy MacSarcasm in Macklin's comedy. In his diary, now at Harvard, Cooke specifically mentions playing Young Marlow on 26 July and Freeport and Petruchio on 29 July. Faulkland in *The Rivals* was performed on 31 July for "the benefit of the Widows & Orphans of the Sailors, Marines, &c. who fell in the late engagement (June 1st) under Admiral Earl Howe," and he adds that the boxes and pit were the same price and elegantly filled, estimating the total receipts at about £50. He played The Guardian on 4 September, and the next day he went to the theatre to rehearse "2 scenes of Hamlet, 2 of Macbeth, 2 scenes of Mercutio, a part of Falstaff, in the 1st part of Henry 4th, &, as Shylock, a scene in the 3d Act, & the Trial scene," which he then performed the next night. He adds, "Damned bad in Falstaff." On 11 September, after spending the day in studying Sir Callaghan, he performed Sir Robert Ramble, which appears to have been his last performance in Buxton. He mentions that at Macclesfield, on 18 September, a Mr. Slater, "a drawing master," compelled him after dinner to do "what no party could ever prevail upon me before to do; recited 2 speeches from Shakespeare."[111]

In general, Cooke seems to have passed his summer at Buxton much as he had the summer before, taking long walks, drinking brandy and water a great deal of time at various taverns, and reading a wide assortment of materials while extracting or commenting on them in his journal. His nights were restless, and he spent considerable hours sitting up "ruminating." It was during this summer at Buxton that Cooke observed the drunken minister and hoped never to forget the sight, although he was clearly having his own problems, waking up at "3 A.M. with a heat, sourness & oppression at my stomach (much subject to it)" relieved only after vomiting. Throughout the Buxton sojourn he complained of indisposition and low spirits, "mood wandering and very confused,"[112] but would always return to "the Angel" for a bit more brandy and water. He tried to ride a horse but found himself too tipsy to mount. Cooke's state of mind and physical condition at this stage of his career is most clearly revealed in this early journal. Evidently, he had now reached the stage of alcoholic addiction in which his drinking was almost compulsive. The previous year he had already been taken to task by *The Thespian Mirror* for being too partial to "the cheering juice of the Lesbian wine." Now, even with the image of the clergyman reduced to a pitiful object by drink, he seemed incapable of turning from his "brandy and water." [113]

Cooke's reading material was generally not very significant, except for one item. On 1 September, he began reading C. Stedman's *The History of the Origin, Progress, and Termination of the American War*.[114] While in the United States, between 1810 and 1812, Cooke would mention, over the bottle, that he was in the British army "which attempted to subjugate the U.S."[115] He claimed to have fought in a number of battles and once, pointing to the "Heights of Brooklyn," he exclaimed,

That's the spot! *We* marched up! The rebels retreated! We charged! They fled! We mounted that hill—I carried the Colours of the 5th—my father carried them before me, and my son now carries them[116]—I lead—Washington was in the rear of the rebels—I pressed forward—when at this moment, Sir William, now Lord Howe, and the Lord for ever damn him for it, cried Halt!—but for that, Sir, I should have taken Washington, and there would have been an end of the rebellion! [117]

During his time in America, Cooke made other references to the Revolutionary War—e.g., descriptions of Sir Henry Clinton galloping up Broadway, seeing Warren die at Bunker Hill.[118] Although doubting Cooke's stories, Dunlap admits that "his absence from before the public [circa March 1780 to October 1781] . . . in some measure corroborates those tales of his, which would otherwise have only passed for bacchanalian romances." [119] That Cooke served in the United States seems unlikely, although there is no strong evidence to disprove the possibility. It is more likely that in Cooke's advanced stage of chronic alcoholism he fabricated stories out of the recesses of his confused mind, based largely on the reading he had done on the Revolutionary War, beginning with Stedman in 1794. Certainly, his 1794 journal gives absolutely no indication that he responded to his reading from any first-hand knowledge or experience. If, indeed, he had fought in America, it is odd that he would not have made some allusion to it in his various diaries and journals. Instead, a typical comment is ". . . we heard of no murders, no assassinations; no multiplied and terrifying executions, no private gangs of execrable villains marking their steps by blood and rapine."

With the performances in Buxton over, George Frederick Cooke's country apprenticeship ended. From 1787, when he first joined the Austin and Whitlock company as a leading player, to the summer of 1794, Cooke had risen to the status of a provincial star, popular and in demand. He was now thirty-eight years old and had been an actor for at least twenty years, yet he had spent less than five months performing in and around London and never in a winter patent house. Perhaps he found some satisfaction in the knowledge that he had supported Dorothy Jordan and Sarah Siddons, and had been the leading actor for companies in Newcastle, Chester, Sheffield, and Manchester. Unfortunately, between 1787 and 1794, his drinking problem had steadily worsened, and although he was still able to placate his audiences, it would soon become more difficult. But even while conscious of his present difficulty with alcohol, Cooke must have yearned for something better. He claims to have turned down an offer at Covent Garden in 1793, but if so, why?[120] Surely lesser talents came and went in London! Perhaps there is some truth in Dunlap's assertion that Cooke lacked "proper ambition," owing to "his attachment to what he called conviviality."[121] Or possibly the reverse was true—and the London management knew too well of his "conviviality." Whatever the causes for his absence from the London boards, he was about to move on to another capital—Dublin. Although he would never completely forsake the provinces, his new and promising situation would eventually place him at Covent Garden, but not until he had first sunk to the depths of despair and pulled himself up by the boot straps.

6

"A New Date in My Theatricals"

For over a decade the Dublin stage had been in turmoil. In June 1787, the famous Smock Alley Theatre had shut down after one hundred and twenty-five years of theatrical glory. Richard Daly, a Dublin actor educated at Trinity College, had gained control of Smock Alley from Thomas Ryder at the end of the 1779–1780 season and "by strategem [sic] and inducements, got the best part of Ryder's company to join him."[1] At first Ryder competed with Daly, acting at the Crow Street Theatre, but by June 1781 Ryder, whose debts were already great, found his receipts becoming thinner and thus was forced to relinquish his control of Crow Street as well. Ryder, however, had been a popular actor in Dublin so that Daly wisely persuaded him to join his company at Smock Alley.

All seemed to be progressing in Daly's favor. Then, in the autumn of 1781, Crow Street reopened under the direction of Thomas Crawford, a lawyer turned actor and husband of Spranger Barry's widow. For Daly's operation, however, the Crawford management proved inconsequential. The former Mrs. Barry had grown into an eccentric and temperamental actress. She had procured by law the theatre left to her by her second husband, the actor-manager, and then had rented it to her third husband for her own emolument. In addition, Crawford was a well-meaning man but an actor of little consequence. By December 1782, the situation at Crow Street had deteriorated so much that Crawford seems to have voluntarily resigned its management. The theatre was rented for a brief season to five former members of Crawford's company but fared no better. After a great deal of company discord and discontent with the management, the company disbanded and Crow Street was closed down in 1783.

Daly, in the meantime, had managed to keep his head above water, despite the fact that in addition to Crow Street, the Capel Street Theatre, the second of that name built in 1770, had reopened on 11 November 1782. This company lasted only until May 1783; in September it was announced that the ensuing season would be dedicated solely to English opera. By July 1784, this enterprise had proved financially disastrous and Capel Street closed its doors. At last it seemed that Daly would have the theatrical field to himself.[2]

A greater competitor, however, quickly surfaced, and as would be true in the future, Daly could only blame himself for his undoing. Robert Owenson, one of

Daly's actors, unhappy with Daly's treatment, quarreled with him, left Smock Alley, and took over the Fishamble Street Theatre, a music hall that had been converted into a theatre in 1777. Owenson continued to provide competition for Smock Alley until 1786, when Daly finally received a patent in the form of an exclusive license for fourteen years.[3] Bills for the prohibition of public dramatic performances except in a theatre held by patent from the Crown had been presented to the Irish Parliament by Thomas Sheridan in 1758 and 1772 and by Robert Jephson and George Colman the elder in 1779, but Daly had more luck than his predecessors in creating a monopoly. In June 1787, Daly moved his company from Smock Alley to Crow Street, which had been closed since the spring of 1783.

The Crow Street Theatre had been built by Spranger Barry on the site of an old music hall and had opened on 23 October 1758 with Cibber's comedy *She Would and She Would Not*.[4] After five years of total disuse, the theatre underwent six months of preparation for its reopening, including extensive and lavish new decoration.[5] The newly adorned playhouse finally opened on 18 January 1788 with *The Wonder*. The press puffed enthusiastically over its similarities to Covent Garden with its three galleries, the addition of upper boxes, and the novelty of a coffee room.[6]

For a year or two all went well for Daly; he optimistically looked forward to an era of prosperity. In 1789, however, defamatory notices concerning him began to appear in the *Dublin Evening Post*; riots and disturbances became commonplace within the playhouse. As playgoers became fearful for their safety and stayed away from Crow Street, receipts dropped and the position of Daly's theatre became precarious. To add to Daly's troubles, in 1788 a license was granted to Philip Astley "to cause to be represented feats of horsemanship, musical pieces, dancing, tumbling and pantomimes of any nature, provided they be decent and becoming. . . . provided that no regular tragedy, comedy, opera, play, or farce, be performed at his amphitheatre, as shall have been exhibited at the theatre royal."[7] Astley's theatre, located in Peter Street, although approximately a circus, often skirted the definition of its agreement, and as Daly's popularity decreased, Astley's theatre began to draw the fashionable crowd.

Adding to Daly's miseries was not only Astley's enterprise but also a new amateur organization under the leadership of Frederick Jones, an Irishman, who, like Daly, had been educated at Trinity College. Fired by Daly's low standards, Jones, along with other young gentlemen of Dublin, including the earl of Westmeath, established a company at the old Fishamble Street Theatre "for the improvement of scholars and critics."[8] Jones' effort was the natural culmination of a prevailing rage for amateur theatricals in Ireland, which had been gaining momentum for over fifty years. The success and grandeur of the productions at the Fishamble Street Theatre would ultimately spell total ruin for Daly, and Jones would move into the prominent position of leader of the Dublin stage. In the meantime, Daly, whose apathy and negligence had grown intolerable, desperately sought a solution to the deadened direction of his management.

For George Cooke, who would play under both Daly and Jones, the sad state of Daly's organization would give him the opportunity to move into a major metropolis which would in turn thrust him into starring prominence. In his initial Dublin engagement, however, Cooke soon became aware that he was on a sinking ship; while helping to improve the status of Daly's theatre, his first brief stay was not a pleasant one.

During the winter of 1793–1794, Daly's Dublin situation continued to deteriorate. Likewise, his summer operations in Cork and Limerick had been slipping for several years. The first new blood to arrive on the scene was the seventeen-year-old Charles Mathews, who made his stage debut under Daly in June 1794. Although Mathews was a novice actor at this early stage of his career, Daly was impressed with the aspirant and put him on a salary of 1 guinea a week.[9] Mathews had been engaged in London early in 1794 by Robert Hitchcock, who in 1788 had begun the two-volume *An Historical View of the Irish Stage from the Earliest Period Down to the Close of the Season 1788* (Dublin, 1788–1794). Mathews, who had heard that Hitchcock "was a sort of Serjeant Kite to the Dublin corps of Thespians," was informed by chance that Hitchcock was in London recruiting actors for Daly. Apparently, Hitchcock had no power to promise Mathews anything and no money exchanged hands; Mathews later wondered why he had even been given an offer on speculation.[10] Fortunately, Mathews was accepted into the fold. George Cooke was engaged by this same Hitchcock, sometime early during the summer of 1794, apparently at Manchester, although Cooke never specifies the conditions of his engagement.[11] There is no doubt, however, that Cooke's provincial reputation had spread even to Dublin and London, and his appointment to Daly's company was part of Daly's desperate effort to bolster the sagging reputation of the Crow Street Theatre.

Between the summer and winter seasons, Daly traveled to England for further recruiting, which included, for dances and pantomimes, Jack Richer, Thomas(?) King, Smith, and Mrs. Parker from Sadler's Wells, a comic named Davies, Joe Kelly the singer, and William Palmer, who had been a favorite in Dublin at various periods, beginning in 1764.[12] These various attractions were scheduled to follow the appearances of the vivacious Elizabeth Farren who toured under Daly during the summer of 1794; the addition of a male star, as well as Farren, would have been prohibitive to Daly, who was obliged to pay her £50 per night. According to Mathews, however, Farren packed the theatres in Dublin, Cork, and Limerick for a total of twenty-eight nights, making Daly's considerable investment a profitable one.[13]

In order to prevent a slump in attendance in the interim before Cooke's arrival, Daly imported from Drury Lane a strange stage couple, Mrs. Bateman and the Chevalier D'Eon. Cooke would remember the latter as part of his own bills, fencing at the end of a play dressed as an officer of dragoons.[14] Mrs. Bateman, a stagestruck Englishwoman whose husband was said to be in India and to have allowed her £1,000 a year expenses, had met the "chevalier" in London, where they had teamed up. Mrs. Bateman's main role seems to have been as a financial backer of D'Eon, who was the real curiosity of the two.[15] D'Eon, purportedly a woman, was actually Charles de Beaumont, the French secret agent under Louis XV who gained the confidence of Russia's Empress Elizabeth in 1755, and later, dressed as a man, had won the friendship of George III. After six years in France, he returned to England in 1785. The French Revolution brought an end to a pension he had been receiving from France, and circumstances forced him into public appearances beginning in 1787. D'Eon appeared in a "most ludicrous" fencing costume, including a helmet with feather plumes, armor over a satin petticoat, female shoes, and a female wig over his otherwise bald head.[16] Bateman and D'Eon first appeared with Daly at Cork and after creating a stir there with ridiculous novelty, Daly took them to Dublin to open the 1794–1795 winter season.

Early in November, Cooke finally embarked at Holyhead for Dublin. On his arrival he was introduced to Daly and dined with him and some of his friends in Daly's theatre apartment. "And now commenced a new date in my theatricals," wrote Cooke.[17] Cooke had little competition in Daly's company, and although he himself felt the theatre in Dublin was at a low ebb, the performers ill-paid, and "the house, scenes, and dresses, very mean and bad," he "took possession of the Dublin stage without a struggle . . . the throne was his own."[18] Despite the immediate success he enjoyed at Crow Street, Cooke was never fond of Dublin and in several of his journals gave vent to his animosity toward the theatre and the Dublin audience. Certainly his first season under Daly proved to be an ill-spent period in his personal life.

Cooke's first appearance in Dublin was as Othello on Wednesday, 19 November, with Daly as Iago, Hargrove as Cassio, and Miss Maria Campion as Desdemona. Campion would later marry Alexander Pope and, coincidentally, Cooke would support her in the same character in 1803 for her last performance in London.[19] On 21 November, Cooke performed Macbeth, and on the 24th, he repeated Othello with Palmer as Cassio. The night's attraction was bolstered with Richer on the tightrope and Chevalier D'Eon presenting one of his fencing displays. The next week, on Wednesday, Cooke appeared as Frankly to Daly's Ranger in *The Suspicious Husband*, followed the next night by a repeat of *Macbeth*.

When Cooke repeated Othello on 1 December, the press began to take note of his excellence (although critical commentary is rare in the Dublin newspapers), singling out the "unusual eminence" of passages where jealousy or any strong passion was exhibited.[20] Cooke completed the month of December with appearances as Richard III (on 4, 10, 16, 27, 29), Columbus in Thomas

"A New Date in My Theatricals"

Morton's melodrama (3 December), Friar Lawrence in *Romeo and Juliet* with Campion as Juliet and Hargrove as Romeo (8, 15 December), and Harmony in Mrs. Inchbald's *Every One Has His Faults* (12, 17, 21, 31 December). On the 11th Cooke appeared as the Ghost in *Hamlet* and reappeared as Macbeth on the 26th.[21]

Cooke's first month in Dublin brought him nothing but praise. The press predicted his future success, and the *Evening Post* (18 December 1794) claimed that Cooke's performances were breaking all house records. This, however, appears to have been mere puffery, for apparently even Cooke's presence could not save Daly's reputation and the audience's apprehension. On the 30th, the *Evening Post* reported that "Each night's entertainment adds credit to the theatre." Cooke was praised by the reviewer for the unbounded applause he had justifiably received as Richard III and added: "We are ready to admit him an actor of the first eminence. Indeed, the whole play . . . only wants to be seen by a full audience to ensure much profit and honour to the theatre."

The most thorough observer of Cooke at this time was the young Charles Mathews, who, in addition to sharing lodgings with him, watched his acting with a keen and amazingly critical eye for such a neophyte. In a letter to his close friend, John Litchfield, 28 December 1794, Mathews has recorded a most thoughtful and complete estimate of Cooke's talents:

I think him a most excellent actor, and one of the finest declaimers I ever heard. He came out in *Othello*, and was received with a vast deal of applause, though *Othello* was not his choice for a first appearance. He played it most delightfully, but I do not think it by any means one of his best characters. . . . His address to the senate was spoken in a different manner from what I have heard it before, being more familiar, and indeed more natural, than the customary mode of delivering it. The more impassioned parts were wonderfully fine; nor do I think the second scene with *Iago* was ever better played. His second character was *Macbeth*, which is certainly superior to his *Othello*, and he has played it three or four times to very great houses. He has played . . . *Richard*, which is certainly his masterpiece (that is, of the characters he has played here). His figure and manner are much more adapted to the villain than the lover. His countenance, particularly when dressed for *Richard*, is somewhat like Kemble's, the nose and chin being very prominent features, but the face is not so long. He has a finely marked eye, and upon the whole, I think, a very fine face. His voice is extremely powerful, and he has one of the clearest rants I ever heard. The lower tones are somewhat like Holman's, but much harsher, and considerably stronger. The most striking fault in his figure are his arms, which are remarkably short and ill-proportioned to the rest of his body, and in his walk this gives him a very ungraceful appearance. I forgot to mention that he played *Harmony*, which I think was a fine a piece of acting as I ever saw, and I like it much better than Munden's. He played it as a plain gentleman, not at all *outre* in his dress or manner. He delivered the sentiments in a natural and easy style, and his whole delineation of it is so chaste, that it becomes a much more interesting character than it appeared to be before. After playing *Harmony* the first night, he came forward at the end of the play to make the usual announcement, and he had six successive rounds of applause. I am convinced that he will be a very great favourite in Dublin.[22]

Daly, Mathews tells us, was pleased with Cooke, a pleasure no doubt increased since Cooke, more than anyone else in the company, was bringing money into the impoverished theatre. Approximately a month later, Mathews, in response to his friend Litchfield, admitted that to him Kemble was a superior actor. He considered Cooke next in line and informed Litchfield that "he is increasing rapidly in the favour of the Irish audience, and very deservedly."[23]

Although newspaper accounts and playbills are spotty for Cooke's appearances in early 1795, according to Mathews and existing advertisements, he performed Cato, Zanga, Cardinal Wolsey, Sir Archy MacSarcasm, Colonel Talbot in *He Would Be a Soldier*, Sir Anthony Absolute, and Prospero in *The Enchanted Island* (a reworking of *The Tempest*), an unspecified role in Reynolds' comedy *The Rage* (probably Darnley), and Stukely.[24]

The last mention of Cooke's appearances is for 5 March, the delivery of an occasional prologue by Garrick for his *Neck or Nothing*. It is unclear exactly when in March he left Daly's company. Cooke states that it was on the second or third day of the month, although he is advertised for *The Rage* on 2 March and Stukely on 4 March.[25] He was definitely out of the company, however, after the 5th. Cooke's immediate reasons for deserting the Crow Street Theatre are fairly evident. The obvious explanation, however, is complicated by his personal habits and the increasingly debilitating effects of his drinking. In his 1807 journal, he claims to have become "heartily sick" of the miserable conditions of the theatre, the mediocre and undisciplined company, and Daly's penurious management. Apparently, Cooke could stand no more. His own explanation is brief: "being appointed to act Don Felix in the Wonder, and no dress provided, I embraced the opportunity of taking my leave."[26] The most reliable explanation for Cooke's ire comes from Mathews, who related the following in a 31 March letter to Litchfield:

I am extremely sorry to inform you that Cooke has withdrawn himself from the theatre. Daly was advertised for *Don Felix*, Mrs. Parker's benefit: being unable to play, Cooke was applied to the day before, and said he would play it. Daly's name was taken out, his own inserted. The night came—there was no dress for Cooke. He had sworn in the daytime, without a *new* dress, he would not play. No dress; he kept his word. The part was read; he was very much enraged, and swore he would play no more. I am sorry to say that in that particular he has also kept his word. Mr. Daly, thinking himself the injured person, has never attempted to make it up. Cooke expected entreaties. Daly is too proud to make them. And both are too proud to make up the breach; though, I believe, both wish it. Daly was by no means in fault. He was shut up, and would see nobody. The tailor would make no dress without his orders. It is a misunderstanding which ten words would make up. But obstinacy and pride prevent it. So the town is deprived of an excellent actor. Daly could arrest him for 200 [£] breach of articles, but would not distress him for the world. Daly likes him much. Cooke likes Daly. Does not say one word against him. Says he has treated him like a gentleman. Lays the blame on poor Hitchy [Hitchcock]. Cooke is a great loss. The benefits suffer much for want of him. He knows his own consequence in the theatre, and when he is at all slighted is the most resolute man, and most to be dreaded in his resentments.[27]

There is no reason to doubt Mathews' version of Cooke's departure, for by this time they had become close friends, living in the same lodgings, kept by a widow named Judy Byrn. Cooke's absence once more placed Daly's theatre in a critical situation, which reached even greater severity with Miss Campion's exit early in March and the serious illness of Daly's wife, which forced him to spend much of his time with his nine children and away from theatrical concerns.

Although Cooke's principal reason for leaving Daly seems to have been a professional disagreement, there is little doubt that Cooke's habits had also been deteriorating, which on one night, Mathews tells us, led to his destroying the windows and furniture in his lodgings. The anecdote, retold by Mrs. Mathews, is possibly the most famous of all Cooke stories and needs only be summarized. One evening Cooke and Mathews were walking together after performing *Love-a-la-Mode*, and Cooke invited Mathews, who had played Mordecai, into his room for supper, after which whiskey punch, an Irish recipe and so a novelty to Cooke, was passed around. Cooke praised it as "the nectar of the gods!" and kept insisting that Mrs. Byrn refill his cup, until after several hours she entered with the sixth jug, asked if she was needed any further, to which Cooke replied "Nothing more, my good Mrs. Byrn," and then she retired for the night. Cooke then began to lecture Mathews on sobriety, while glass after glass vanished. Cooke attempted to demonstrate to Mathews "the Passions of the human mind."[28] The results, however, due to the whiskey punch, produced only contortions and distortions, and when Mathews tried to guess the emotion being demonstrated, first guessing anger for fear and then revenge when Cooke intended love, the older actor became incensed and Mathews, uncontrollably, broke into laughter. This infuriated Cooke almost to madness. "What, sir! does it make you laugh?" blurted Cooke. "Am I not George Frederick Cooke 'born to command ten thousand slaves like thee!' while you'll never get salt to your porridge, as an actor."

At length, Mathews was able to calm Cooke by blaming his own behavior on the whiskey punch, but Cooke immediately called for another jug from the absent Byrn. While Mathews attempted to escape, Mrs. Byrn in the room below, yelled up that she had gone to bed and no more punch would be forthcoming. In a bemused rage, Cooke replied: "Mrs. Byrn! hear me: if I'm not indulged with some more whiskey, I give notice, I'll destroy all your furniture." Mrs. Byrn still refused to indulge Cooke, and Cooke, in quick response, broke first the jug on the floor and then began to throw chairs, poker, tongs, and shovel down on the floor to get her attention, after which the fragments were thrown out the window. Mathews made one more attempt to escape, fearing that he might be next to be thrown out the window, but Cooke, now in a frenzy, grabbed him violently, dragged him to the window, and roared out, "Watch! Watch!" A watchman, who had already been attracted by the commotion, asked the cause of the disturbance, to which Cooke exclaimed, "I give this man in charge; he has committed a capital offence—he has committed a murder. . . . He has most barbarously murdered an inoffensive Jew-gentleman, of the name of *Mordecai*, and I charge him with it in the name of Macklin, author of 'Love-a-la-mode.' " At last Mathews freed himself and made for the door, with Cooke behind throwing candlesticks after him and crying, "Well, if you will go, you shan't say I sent you to bed without light!" Cooke then spent considerable time explaining to the watchman the account of the murdered "Jew-gentleman."[29] Dunlap adds that Cooke then ventured out into the night "and was brought home next day beaten and deformed with bruises."[30]

Dunlap claims that Cooke was disgraced by his behavior and that this misdeed led him to "further mad intemperance" and the ultimate abandonment of the stage. There may be some truth to this, although Cooke apparently did not, as Dunlap implies, immediately "in a fit of drunkenness and despair" enlist as a private in a regiment destined for the West Indies.[31] This rash gesture did occur and possibly, as the Veteran Stager also agrees, "in a state of intoxication."[32] It is much more likely, however, that Cooke's enlistment occurred toward the latter part of June, for on 5 July, Mathews wrote to Litchfield that "Cooke has enlisted." Cooke doubtlessly spent the period from March to July in various forms of dissipation and, as Mathews says, was indeed drunk when he enlisted.[33] Furthermore, Mathews believed that Daly would have been glad to reengage him, but Cooke's pride was so great that "he would rather turn soldier from real want than to come to terms." A number of Daly's performers saw Cooke in his military garb when he was about to embark for the Isle of Man the first part of July, but Cooke "seemed to wish rather to avoid speaking to them, appearing quite melancholy."[34] The Stager suggests that Cooke's regiment was bound for the Quiberon Bay expedition and that Cooke had been conveyed on board a tender located opposite the Custom House, where recruits were received. He says that this news was sent to Daly who applied to the mayor for a warrant to search for Cooke. The search, however, proved fruitless, for Cooke had concealed himself so completely as not to be found and soon the regiment sailed out of Dublin harbor.

The Stager may possibly be believed when he says that Cooke did not land, being on the doctor's list, but returned by the same transport to Southampton. What happened next is unclear, as are details of Cooke's wanderings until March 1796, when he once more appears on stage in Manchester. There are at least two versions of the events following his landing in Southampton, neither conclusive but both intriguing and both conceivably containing a degree of truth.

The Stager suggests that Cooke, after being transported to Southampton, was tried by a court-martial for insolence to his officer and sentenced to receive

200 lashes. Cooke was then rescued at the last minute by Joseph George Holman, who had known Cooke in Dublin and interceded with the commanding officer. Although Holman was frequently associated with the Dublin stage and performed there in the summer of 1794, it is not known if his path crossed that of Cooke in 1794–1795, although Cooke had met Holman in Liverpool a few years earlier. Holman is also credited by the Stager with Cooke's release from the army and with supplying him with the means of obtaining his discharge.[35] At this point, however, Dunlap is probably more reliable. He claims that at some point after July 1795 Maxwell, the Portsmouth theatre manager, was in Southampton and was accosted by a soldier who turned out to be George Cooke. Cooke asked Maxwell to intercede in his behalf for his discharge. Maxwell promised to appeal to Ward and Banks in Manchester to come to Cooke's aid, which they did. Maxwell heard no more about Cooke for several weeks. One day a young boy came to him at his theatre in Portsmouth and informed him that "a poor, sick man, Sir, who has been a soldier, is now at my mother's, and begs to see you before he dies." Maxwell went to a dilapidated public house and found Cooke in a stage of total dissipation. Banks and Ward had indeed procured Cooke's discharge and in addition had sent him money to pay his way to Manchester. He had squandered the money, however, and, ashamed to apply to them again, had practically crawled from Southampton to Portsmouth to see Maxwell. After receiving medical attention and care from Maxwell, Cooke was sent to London, at Ward's and Banks' instruction, where he would be met by an agent of the Manchester managers who would send him to Manchester. Cooke, however, made another unscheduled stop on the road between London and Manchester for "another taste of his beloved madness" but finally arrived in Manchester, later than expected.[36]

Despite the problems the Manchester management had in getting Cooke back to his old situation, he arrived at a critical time for Ward and Banks. During the 1795–1796 season, *The Monthly Mirror* began publication in London, replete with news of various provincial theatres, including Manchester. The new journal, "Reflecting Men and Manners, with Strictures on their Epitome the Stage," is a major source for this period of Cooke's career. The Manchester correspondent for the *Mirror* was quick to condemn the Manchester management and in January bemoaned the poor state of the Manchester stage: "if this populous town evinced no more liberality in supporting the managers, than they do in entertaining the town, it would be much if they 'got salt in their pottage!'" In fact, the correspondent noted that Cooke's was a great loss, and Hamerton, Cooke's inferior replacement, considered a "lifeless and inattentive" comedian and little better in tragedy. Even the scenery came under attack: "its shattered condition threatens a speedy downfall, and unless a speedy reformation takes place, the managers will, according to the old phrase, 'bring an old house about their ears.' "[37] Cooke's reengagement at Manchester could not have occurred at a more important time.

In the April number of *The Monthly Mirror*, the Manchester correspondent, also shedding some light on Cooke's military escapade, was relieved to report:

> Re-inforcements have arrived—Cooke, whose absence we have so long deplored, made his appearance in Octavian a few weeks ago [15 March in *The Mountaineers*] to a crowded house, and was received in a very flattering manner. His irregularities while in Dublin, procured for him a *private* situation in the army—he was brought over to England, and confined to his bed at Chatham Barracks some time. Nothing but his indisposition could have saved him from the West-Indies, where his regiment was ordered. He has had plenty of employment since his return, for we cannot live a night without him. His Pertinax M'Sycophant, Macbeth, Mark Anthony, etc., etc. have received their usual tribute of applause. . . . Nothing, I suppose, but his ungovernable spirits, and his attachment to the bottle, have prevented the London managers from engaging him.[38]

Cooke's presence gave the management the stimulus needed to draw them out of the doldrums, for the same issue also reports that "the scenery rather improves: two or three new flats having lately been hung, one of which is a view of the celebrated cascade of Tivoli, near Rome."

Cooke continued to be a major attraction in Manchester this season, acting, in addition to those roles mentioned in *The Monthly Mirror*, King John, Hamlet, Posthumus Leonatus, and, for his own benefit on 25 April, Sir Giles Overreach in *A New Way to Pay Old Debts*, after which he recited Dryden's "Ode on St. Cecilia's Day." A member of the company that season was Alicia Daniels, with whom Cooke rapidly renewed relationship, reciting for her benefit Collins' "Ode on the Passions."[39] He also recited Gray's "Elegy" for Tyrrell's benefit.[40]

At Whitsun Cooke renewed his association with Mrs. Siddons who came to Manchester for a six-night season, supporting her Isabella, Mrs. Beverley, Lady Percy, and Lady Macbeth.[41]

In less than three months, Cooke had reestablished himself in the Banks and Ward company and was soon on the circuit again. During Passion Week he accepted an engagement with John Stanton, the manager of the Lancaster Theatre, where he appeared with Miss Sarah Smith. Cooke spent the summer traveling the circuit of Lancaster, Chester, Preston, and Buxton, performing his usual roles at each place.[42] Cooke was in Preston the latter part of July and the beginning of August, where he performed Penruddock in *The Wheel of Fortune* and for Stanton's benefit he "went on" for Tangent in *The Way to Get Married*. Cooke recorded in his diary:

> I never studied the character of Tangent, but from a few readings retained the words, and the business from playing Captain Falkner three or four times, and seeing it once in London, where it was excellently acted. Many of the performers were not only imperfect in the words, but very ignorant of character. It is a common phrase with many on the

"A New Date in My Theatricals" 99

stage, they have *studied* a character, when they even know not what the expression means; their *utmost* idea of studying being a knowledge of the author's words. In all ranks and professions, there are doubtless many whose genius & abilities neither suited nor accord with the situation in which they move, and the stage certainly has its share (the pulpit many more). It is grievous to behold the higher classes of society represented by those whose utmost sketch of abilities [does not] permit them to appear with any grace as their attendents. Some persons would smile were they informed that there are actors and actresses, and some of them who stand in what is called a respectable light; who are not only destitute of what are called the embellishments of education, but are absolutely incapable of reading their native language.—This will ever be the case while the drama remains in its present unprotected stage: the vulgar opinion of a great part of mankind being, that after a person has failed in every attempt they have made in life, even as mechanics and servants, the stage is still open, as a last and sure resource; and such is the petty and absurd ambition of some, that for the sake of strutting their hour before the public, they will starve in little itinerant groups, rather [than] acquire a decent subsistency by following the employment they were bred to.[43]

This is a revealing statement of Cooke's own habits and attitudes. On 6 August Cooke left Preston and traveled the short distance with Stanton to Lancaster, where they were joined by Henry Siddons. From Lancaster Cooke went to his old watering hole, Buxton, where he renewed his reading habits, cultivated earlier there, and revisited old haunts—the Angel, the Red Lyon, the Grave, the Brown Bear, the Swan, and the Bull's Head.[44]

In September, Cooke rejoined Ward and Banks at Shrewsbury, a new acquisition to their circuit. Cooke continued as the principal tragic actor, and Andrew Cherry, who had recently joined the company from Dublin, became the comic hero. On 30 September, Cooke went to Liverpool and appeared as Sir Edward Mortimer in *The Iron Chest* for Banks' benefit, his only appearance there that season. Also in the cast was Henry Erskine Johnston, the nineteen-year-old actor known as "the Scotch Roscius" with whom Cooke later would be associated at Covent Garden. That night Johnston appeared as Wilford.[45]

The Manchester Theatre was not scheduled to open its winter season until January 1797, after being closed for seven months. In the meantime, Cooke traveled with Alicia Daniels to Chester, where on 20 December 1796 they were married at St. Peter's Church. Miss Daniels, Cooke's second or third wife, although possibly his first legal one, had been performing professionally since 1791 or earlier. She appeared in roles such as Ophelia and Ariel opposite Cooke's Hamlet and Prospero, but she was principally a vocalist in rather minor musical parts. During the summer of 1793, for example, at Liverpool, she performed Juba in *The Prize*, Adelaide in *The Prisoner at Large*, Parisatis in *Alexander the Great*, Sally in *Thomas and Sally*, Belinda in *Modern Antiques*, and Phoebe in *Rosina*, among other secondary roles in both musical and straight drama.[46] Prior to joining Banks and Ward, she had been briefly with Drury Lane in 1791 but had been discharged for "non-attendance" by J. P. Kemble.[47] It was shortly thereafter that George and Alicia first became acquainted in Manchester. She apparently spent the summers of 1794 and 1796 singing at Sadler's Wells and probably also sang at Vauxhall during the same period.[48]

Thomas Dibdin, during the period when he served as prompter, writer, and actor for Banks and Ward, recalled that Alicia "had a completely foreign accent," but gives no more details. During an engagement at Chester, probably in 1795, Miss Daniels and her mother lodged in the same house where the father of the great French actor Talma lived with his English wife and practiced dentistry. Alicia's mother, deeply involved in her career, would stand in the wings while her daughter sang; from nervousness she would constantly tug out the pins from her dress. Dibdin tells us: "thus if Miss Daniels happened (as was frequently the case) to be *encored* in a tolerably long song mama was very nearly undressed before her daughter arrived at the end of it."[49]

Later in her career, after leaving Cooke, she became a principal singer at Bath and Bristol, reverting to her maiden name, and in 1804 she made her debut at the Haymarket. On that occasion she was referred to as a very accomplished singer, "perhaps the best on the stage after Mrs. Billington and Mrs. Mountain."[50]

George and Alicia were both present for the opening of the Manchester winter season on 2 January 1797, when he played Hastings to Mrs. Ward's Jane Shore and Alicia was Eliza in the musical entertainment *The Poor Soldier.*[51] On 4 January, Cooke appeared as Sir Pertinax, which *The Monthly Mirror* called "a diamond of the first water," and then observed, "even Glassington's Lord Lumbercourt cannot spoil the effect of it. Hamerton ranted Egerton as usual." His Warwick in *The Earl of Warwick* was considered excellent, as was his Sir Archy. In fact, "If any but political reasons prevent Macklin's pieces from being represented in London, the want of a person to perform the Scotchman must be a principal one. Cooke then would be an acquisition. I am informed of a Scotchman of judgment, that Macklin's brogue was a caricature, but that Cooke's is natural—he was bred in Scotland."[52] Cooke, of course, was probably not a native Scot, but such a misconception would follow him to the grave.

Throughout the early part of the winter season, *The Monthly Mirror* continued to offer rather lengthy accounts of performances at Manchester. When Cooke appeared as Richard III on 16 January, the correspondent proclaimed that the role "exhibited Cooke to great advantage—What indeed does not?" On 30 January, Miss Allingham, a former resident of Manchester and sister of the dramatist John Till Allingham, began a special engagement, in the course of which she played Juliet, Rosalind, Hermione, and Beatrice, concluding on 6 February with a benefit performance of Belvidera and Roxalana. She played to good houses and her last night was called "a bumper benefit." The same critic, however, noted in the March issue that she acted in Manchester under more unfavorable circumstances than she perhaps expected in any provincial theatre, for Cooke decidedly outshone her in every play.[53]

The same issue of *The Monthly Mirror* also gives the following curious report: "Mrs Cooke has been indisposed for sometime—report says, her husband has lately given her too many *striking* marks of his affection for her; but the honey-moon is scarcely over—when he returns to his *sober* senses, he will surely be less *rapturous*." Although the critic was quick to retract this report in April, reportedly as a result of information received from "very good authority, and with very great truth," it is tempting to believe that the earlier report was not all fiction.[54]

Cooke performed Shylock on 14 February and Sir Edward Mortimer in *The Iron Chest* on 9 March, its first local performance. Benefits began on 13 March, and Cooke chose Bajazet for his night and "got through the arduous task with an increase of reputation."[55] Among other roles played this season, Cooke appeared as Sir William Dorrilon in *Wives As They Were* on 19 April and as Random in the afterpiece, *Ways and Means*.[56]

The Manchester company went to Chester for a brief season after benefits, but was back in Manchester by 8 May, when Johnston began a special engagement of four nights. Mrs. Siddons had been announced to appear on 29 May for four nights, but she arrived in time to begin three nights earlier in *Jane Shore*, with Cooke as Hastings. The following week Cooke supported Mrs. Siddons' Isabella as the Duke in *Measure for Measure*, announced as the first Manchester performance.[57] Mrs. Siddons' engagement virtually brought the season to a close and, more importantly, completed Cooke's career as a provincial star in Manchester, although he would frequently return as a London luminary.

Cooke's summer excursions are not clear. He was certainly in Preston during July, accompanied by Mrs. Cooke, appearing in his usual roles.[58] In late August and early September, the Cookes were in Lancaster. A bill for Wednesday, 6 September, indicates: "The last night but three of Mr. and Mrs. Cooke and Mr. Cherry's performing this season. For the benefit of Mrs. Cooke." The mainpiece that evening was Kelly's comedy *School for Wives* with Cooke as Conolly, Cherry as Torrington, and Henry Siddons as Belville. Mrs. Cooke appeared in *Thomas and Sally* and in a musical entertainment of the "Highland Reel" as Jenny. Cooke also recited Collins' "Ode on the Passions." On 13 September, the Cookes concluded their Lancaster appearances with Cooke as Essex in his benefit performance of *The Earl of Essex*.[59]

During the summer, Cooke had once more been engaged to perform in Dublin. His journal records: "In September 1797 I left Lancaster and went to Whitehaven, in which town and Ulverston, I remained 'till in the following month I embarked for Dublin, but owing to rough weather, landed at Waterford. A part of the Dublin company was then acting at that place. I remained five days, and then set forward for the metropolis."[60] Although he fails to mention it, Mrs. Cooke was also engaged for the 1797–1798 Dublin season as a major singer in the company. The omission was undoubtedly intentional, for whatever marital bliss the Cookes may have experienced, the relationship would quickly sour in Ireland and Cooke would once more find himself alone. His second Dublin engagement, however, would prove less volatile than his first. Even so, his opinion of the Dublin theatre remained unchanged: it would never, in his estimation, "be raised to a proper respectability."[61]

7

Hero of the Dublin Stage

During George Cooke's two and one-half years' absence from Dublin, certain events occurred which temporarily seemed to be improvements over Daly's years as manager. Ultimately, however, with additional lackadaisical management and the debilitating effects of the 1798 Rebellion, little gain would be made for the Irish stage until after 1800 when Cooke was well established in London. For Cooke, then, although the three seasons ahead of him would not prove so disgraceful or personally demeaning as his first year in Dublin, despite mounting debts, bouts with drink, and the desertion of his wife, the period would be little more than a lull, a waiting period before moving on to London. Even toward the end of his stay in Dublin, his own estimation of the Irish audience remained negative and hostile: ". . . Dublin is at all times so void of judgment & so much slave of what is called fashion, that the best productions of Shakespeare or Milton shall be neglected, while vitiated minds, under the name of fashion, croud [sic] to rope-dancing or a puppet show."[1]

During Cooke's absence from Dublin, Daly's fortunes had gone from bad to worse, public disapprobation of his management had increased, and Frederick Edward Jones' private theatricals had gained in popularity. Daly was no doubt delighted when negotiations with Jones, which had begun in the early summer of 1797, reached final agreement on 12 August. The result of some collective bargaining was the deeding over to Jones of Daly's patent and his theatres in Dublin, Limerick, and Cork.[2] Immediately Jones officially closed his private theatre on Fishamble Street and for the next twenty-one years confined his managerial efforts to the Theatre Royal, Crow Street, except for a brief interval at Fishamble while Crow Street underwent renovations.

Cooke, who arrived in Dublin on 31 October, found himself under the new management of Jones, whose sole experience had been in amateur theatricals. If the public was somewhat skittish in accepting him as a public manager, as they no doubt were, Cooke, whose contempt for amateur operations was well known, must have felt his fortunes in great jeopardy.

As soon as Jones took over Crow Street, he decided to renovate the theatre extensively, so that temporarily the company would reopen the Fishamble Street Theatre. The *Dublin Evening Post*, 24 August 1797, issued the following progress report:

The Theatre Royal in Crow Street is undergoing many capital alterations; the stage is to be lengthened quite to Temple-Lane, and the roof raised twelve feet, whereby a number of additional seats will be gained in the Boxes, Pit and Galleries. A new box door will be made opposite Crow Street where the entrance for the Lord Lieutenant formerly was. A superb coffee-room will be joined to the box-lobby, and every possible convenience both for seeing and hearing will be made for the accommodation of the audience. The entrance in the divers parts of the Theatre are to be made more easy and commodious and the scenes new painted.

Jones' first company, with Thomas Ludford Bellamy as stage manager, consisted principally of former Dublin performers, including Philip Lamash, Chambers, and King. Cooke and James Middleton, the Irish-born actor trained at Covent Garden, were considered the "foremost" members of Jones' company when the season opened to a crowded house on Monday, 20 November, with *Othello*. Middleton took the title role and Cooke performed a "truly capital" Iago.[3] Ten years later, Cooke fondly remembered Middleton and the Desdemona of the night, Mrs. Yates, but likewise reminisced that "the remainder of the Dramatis Persona, [sic] made such an impression upon my memory, that I have forgot them."[4]

This was an active season for Cooke, who was now considered an established leading actor. During his first season with Jones, lasting approximately six months, Cooke appeared on the average of three nights a week out of the normal six nights of weekly operation, for a total of at least seventy-two performances in over thirty roles.[5]

On Tuesday, 21 November, Cooke performed the comic role of Harmony, which he repeated twice during the season. His first true test, however, came three nights later when he was assigned Penruddock in Cumberland's *The Wheel of Fortune*, a role that John Philip Kemble had performed in Dublin the preceding summer. The *Evening Post* reported that "It was an arduous task to attempt . . . after Mr. Kemble. . . . it is justice to say, he fully satisfied the audience; and comparing him to Mr. Kemble, we declare that he had more nature and less art than that capital piece of human mechanism."[6] On Saturday, Cooke completed his first week as Grey in Sophia Lee's comedy *The Chapter of Accidents*.

On 7 December, Mrs. Cooke made her Dublin debut as Rosina, followed two days later by Clara in *Duenna*. On the 18th, Cooke appeared first at the Fishamble Street Theatre as Shylock, which he would repeat twice more this season. The *Evening Post* (28 December) considered his Shylock at least equal to Macklin's performance, although London critics later would be divided over the superiority of the two great Shylocks.

Finally, on 29 January 1798, Crow Street Theatre, in all its newly appointed splendor, reopened with a performance of *The Merchant of Venice*. Cooke, in addition to acting Shylock, delivered a special address for the occasion by Joseph Atkinson. The *Evening Post* (30 January 1798) reported:

The Theatre Royal opened last night with extraordinary éclat. The numbers who courted admission were greater than we ever remember to have seen about a Theatre. The carriages of the nobility and gentry who got admission, filled Crow-street, the adjacent passages and a great part of Dame-street. The Grand Overture by Handel had the most magnificent effect;—and the Address spoken by Mr. Cooke, was happy and Characteristic.—The brilliancy of the House, etc appeared to surprize every auditor and was indeed a marvelous metamorphosis from what Crow-street was.

Earlier, on 27 January, the same paper had described the "metamorphosis":

The Stage is lengthened to a depth of eighty four feet. Four additional seats in the Pit, which has new entrances with a passage through the middle and sides, overwhich are flap seats and hinges, to put down when the press of company may require it; they are all covered with green morine.—The seats of the first gallery are covered with carpeting: and those of the upper Gallery matted; the iron railing before it richly gilded.

The corridors round the Boxes, Lattices, etc.: are six feet wide, all flagged with Portland stone—and all the stairs also are of Portland stone.—There are also very convenient rooms for walking or taking refreshments—and all the entrances are very capacious.

The orchestra is entirely new modeled—and in it introduced a grand pianoforte.

Jones' future was looking bright, but once more ill fortune struck Crow Street. On 23 May 1798, rebellion broke out in Ireland, precipitated by the League of United Irishmen organized in 1791 to gain Irish independence. Although the rebellion was crushed at Vinegar Hill, 21 June, smaller uprisings continued to take place throughout the summer. The initial rebellion and the aftermath had a direct effect not only on Crow Street, but also on Jones' operations in Cork and Limerick. First, English and Anglo-Irish military forces established a daily curfew. Even after the rebellion,"the uncertain state of tranquility" so upset theatrical operations that when the theatre was not closed altogether the public was afraid to venture out.[7] *The Monthly Mirror* published the sad truth:

The house having been shut up at the commencement of the Irish disturbances, has since been re-opened, but there is scarcely sufficient money received to pay for the *lighting up* and, in fact, who would hazard his life for the sake of a theatrical performance? for the audience have no security for their persons after a certain hour of the night. . . . till we are entirely restored to tranquility, the players, we fear, must continue to perform to empty benches.[8]

For Cooke these events put a damper on his burst of productivity. His performances had been frequent and the roles assigned to him of the first order. In addition to those already mentioned, he performed such major roles as Richard III, Stukely, Zanga, Joseph Surface, Moody in Garrick's *The Country Girl*, Sir George Touchwood in Mrs. Cowley's *The Belle's Stratagem*, Stedfast in

The Heir at Law, Sir William Dorillon and Haswell in Mrs. Inchbald's *Wives As They Were and Maids As They Are* and *Such Things Are*, both new plays from London, and Octavian in Colman's *The Mountaineers*.[9] As was his pattern in the provinces, Cooke's roles ran the gamut: new roles recently introduced in London, comedies, and a fair number of standard tragic roles, including a half dozen that would become stock fare in his London repertoire.

Jones was forced to close the theatre for almost eight weeks, and Cooke tells us, "When the theatre opened again we performed a few nights to thin audiences. We were obliged to have every thing over by nine o'clock."[10]

The Crow Street company, after a difficult Dublin season, was expected to fulfill engagements in Jones' other two theatres during the late summer—the George Street Theatre in Cork and the Theatre Royal, Limerick. Cooke's closest skirmish with stage management occurred this summer, for before leaving Dublin Jones asked him to serve as his deputy, but Cooke, as unqualified as he himself felt Bellamy was as acting manager, wisely "speedily resigned."[11] The company was to learn very quickly that the situation was no better in Cork and Limerick than it had been in Dublin. For Cooke and the other members of the company, salaries had been paid irregularly since the beginning of the Rebellion. Cooke's credit had diminished to such a sad state that he was arrested by his butcher; he was able to escape jail by paying bail and expenses. Cooke's diary reveals his state of mind just before embarking for Cork:

In the whole of my theatrical life, and I have had my share of ill fortune, I never was placed in a more painful and uncertain predicament. Suspense, of all things, is certainly the worst to be endured. A civil, but pressing creditor has just called in. Oh, the misery of being in debt! How I am to set out on my journey [to Cork], I mean with respect to settling accounts in Dublin, I know not.[12]

A fragment of his August 1798 diary now at Harvard reveals that Cooke passed the summer months uneventfully, other than increasing his debts and suffering inconveniences as a result of the rebellion. One night, for example, after spending a quiet evening at a public house, Cooke began walking home after curfew and was stopped by a sentinel at Trinity College, "but on application to the Corporal of the Guard he very politely permitted me to depart.—Challenged immediately after at the Parliament House, but upon informing the centinel [sic] I had been suffered to pass at the college, he also allowed me to walk on."

Cooke arrived in Cork on Friday, 14 September. From 16 September through 28 February, 1799, Cooke's day-to-day activities are generally well known because of one of his most complete and faithfully kept diaries (available in part at the Harvard Theatre Collection).[13] Cooke's diary at this point in his career reveals his professional activities, as well as his physical and emotional state.

In his first entry, Cooke indicated that for the preceding five days he had been much indisposed and spent his first Sunday in Cork catching up on his correspondence.[14]

Having dispatched my letters to the Post Office, was, for a few minutes much indisposed with a violent pain in the stomach. I plainly perceived I must strictly adhere to the careful & temperate plan I have laid down, or my health will be very soon much impaired. After musing some time, sat down to commence writing memorandums for a diary, which, if possible, I intend to continue for one year. I have a particular reason for beginning it on this day, which I may perhaps hereafter mention.

He never does! It would be intriguing to know Cooke's "particular reason" for beginning this diary. Possibly the diary was begun shortly after the culmination of his growing domestic problems. There are no indications that Alicia Daniels continued living with Cooke after the first season in Dublin, and, strange as it seems, there is never even a fleeting allusion to her in any of his diaries or journals. Since she fails to appear in the advertisements with her husband during the period now under scrutiny, it is possible that she had returned to England to spend some time with her mother. Her career does not surface again until October 1798, when she is listed on a Lancaster bill as "Mrs. Cooke from the Theatre Royal, Dublin" as Agnes in *The Mountaineers* [15] on 6 October. In January 1799, she is in the bills at Bath, where she apparently began this engagement as Mrs. Cooke. A bill for 19 February lists Mrs. Cooke as Jessica with songs in *The Merchant of Venice* to Mrs. Siddons' Portia and Harley's Shylock.[16] She was again in Lancaster during August 1799. By fall 1800, she had resumed using her maiden name,[17] and she was legally severed from Cooke in July 1801. Alicia remained with the Bath company for about five years. She also appeared at other provincial theatres, including a summer season in 1803 that took her to Melton Mowbray and Market-Harborough.[18] Alicia also continued her association at Vauxhall Gardens during this period; a number of songs she introduced between 1800 and 1802 were published.[19] On 16 May 1804, she made her debut at the Haymarket as Rosina in *The Spanish Barber* but soon returned to Bath under the name of Mrs. Windsor. It is likely that she had married a musician named Windsor, a member of the Bath Harmonic Society with which Alicia had also been associated. Alicia died at Bath on 30 April 1826. Of Cooke's three to five wives, Alicia Daniels remains the only one for whom any detailed information is available.

The remainder of Cooke's 16 September entry is inspired by a visit from Joe, the caller of the theatre, whom Cooke invited to his room to talk, but Cooke soon grew indifferent and inattentive:

I could not help thinking there was something strange and capricious in my manner, not to say absurd & saucy. Calling a man up, merely to ask a few insignificant questions, & then appearing to be tired of his conversation! Had any person of a superior station to myself, served me so; how should I have felt? It would very like have soured my temper, & sent me home dissatisfied for the evening.

He then went on at some length about servitude and concluded that "do as you would be done unto will in every situation be found a right maxim."

The Cork Theatre, which had been renovated for the first time in its thirty-five-year existence by Daly in 1796, was located on George's (now Oliver Plunket) Street[20] about 100 yards off the Mall, where the beau monde of "the Capital of the South," as Cork was called, promenaded under a long row of elm trees. The Theatre Royal in Cork measured approximately 136 feet long by 60 feet wide, with a stage nearly as capacious as that of Covent Garden, and was consequently the largest playhouse in eighteenth-century Ireland outside of Dublin.[21] By the time of Cooke's first appearance in Cork on 17 September 1798, two days after its belated opening for the season, the population of Cork, situated a dozen miles up the Lee River estuary on an island intersected with canals, had grown to approximately 120,000 creating a blend of cosmopolitan and provincial life.[22]

Fortunately for the Theatre Royal, the military in Cork looked with favor on theatrical performances and modified the curfew so that at first the regulation was changed to accommodate theatre patrons until 11:00 P.M. and later was changed to 12:00 P.M. for the duration of the season. Although Cooke was initially advertised to appear on the 15th, indisposition apparently postponed his Cork debut.[23] He awoke on Monday "after a restless and uneasy night" and "felt dull & unwell; heavy & inclined to sleep." He tried to shake it off by laying out his paraphernalia for Shylock that night. Being Assize Week and the first full week of the season, Cooke realized the importance of his presence that night. His performance was welcomed with "much approbation & obtained considerable applause during the representation. The play, though indifferently acted, went off with spirit. The audience seemed in great good humour."

The following morning, Cooke moved from the hotel to an apartment, no doubt to avoid the awkwardness of his first accommodation and its poor living conditions. After his first appearance, he discovered on his return to his hotel that an officer who had not slept for three nights had been given the room next to his, through which he had to go to get into his own room. The door was so barricaded that he had to move to another room. While waiting for the chambermaid to prepare the room, Cooke stood by the kitchen fire "while the rats frisked" around him like young kittens.

On 19 September, he appeared as Sir William Dorillon in the Inchbald comedy he had appeared in during the preceding winter. During the succeeding days, Cooke spent much of his time reading Fielding's *Tom Jones*, his third such reading, and making lengthy comments in his diary. He also wrote more letters, principally to Mr. Williams, an actor friend from Buxton who would join Jones' company in the winter, and Montague, "an actor, a friend, and a man," who had left the Dublin company in August and gone to Liverpool. Cooke, although on his best behavior, wrote on the 20th:

I am, at times, possessed with a certain restlessness of disposition, & an indecisive turn of mind, that prevents me from adhering to any one object, unless for a very short time. When these fits are on me, I feel and seem perplexed, & nothing but a change of scene will banish them. I cannot exactly account for their intrusion, but observe, I am chiefly visited by them, when affairs or business are a little embarrassed & unsettled.

His first week of performances in Cork concluded with Stedfast on the 21st, the role with which he would begin his second week on the 24th. "The house was a good one (in the Theatrical phrase) & the play went off with applause," but, as usual for Cooke, he found sleep difficult that night until the "clock had struck two" and he resigned himself to "the Arms of Morpheus." After a quiet weekend, playing cribbage and reading, his first performance the second week was greeted with an even larger house than during the preceding week. On Wednesday, 26 September, the "audience [was] thin" when he appeared as Delaval in Thomas Holcroft's comedy *He's Much to Blame*, which, "partly occasioned by some alterations, went off very heavily."[24] Cooke thought little of the play, but found some originality in the characters. As an intelligent actor, he realized that his part had a scene in the last act which made for easy applause; nonetheless, he still dismissed it as too long.

On 27 September, Cooke wrote: "From the particularity of my present situation, I cannot bend my mind to be so attentive & constant to any one object as it ought to be, however I must endeavor to prepare matters for the approaching season in the best manner possible." In the same entry he tries to defend his constant reference to card playing, justifying it as a way to wile away the time. This is an interesting contrast to the Stager's comments on his early provincial habits and complete abstinence from such diversions.[25]

I know it may be objected that in *any* situation you may employ your leisure in a more profitable manner. I will not attempt to deny it, but am contented with basely offering an excuse for it. It will very little assist me in defending myself to say I have frequently wasted my hours in a much worse manner; when a man reconciles himself to himself by making degrees of sin, he is in the utmost danger of advancing to, rather than receding from the utmost depth of iniquity. Mr. Cumberland, in his Tragedy of "The Mysterious Husband," makes a just observation, & a very forceable expression upon the subject.

It is a doubt with me whether a Gamester (here I take the name in its utmost latitude) or a drunkard, be the most vicious character, or the most dangerous to society. The former, without deranging his faculties, exerts them all for the avowed purpose of plundering every one he plays with; his dearest friend is not excepted; (if such a wretch can have a friend) and when, by superior villainy, or some unforseen chance, or change of fortune, he, in his turn is stripped & beggared, his mind, having lost all the fine feelings of nature, is easily wrought on to embrace the most abandoned and wicked project that human nature, depraved, can possibly suggest. He starts not at murder! & his flagitious career often ends in self destruction. Let no one imagine this picture is too highly coloured; there have been too many examples to prove the truth of the painting. The monster which governs the wretched victim I have mentioned laughs at & sacrifices the peace & happiness of parent, wife, & child; nay, it tears asunder & destroys all ties human or divine.

The remainder of this entry is no longer extant. Dunlap cites a section that presumably is the continuation of Cooke's entry, concluding with:

There have been many excellent arguments used against this beastly vice [drunkenness], and many exposures of its dreadful tendency, but none more strong, pointed, and convincing than the following short story: I believe an Oriental one. A young man was decreed by fate to commit some heinous crime. He was to have the choice of three, but inevitably must chuse [sic]. It was left to him to make his election of parricide, incest, or drunkenness. He chose the last; got drunk, and committed the former two.[26]

On Sunday, 30 September, the company left for Limerick, scheduled to arrive in time for the autumn Assizes. At 6:00 p.m. Cooke, accompanied by eleven fellow-players, set out for the overnight journey to the Munster capital. The party of seven women and five men rode in four post-chaises, three to a carriage. Cooke was accompanied by Mrs. Garvey and George Rawlins. At the pretty spa of Mallow, "the Irish Bath," fourteen miles into their journey, they made a leisurely stop for breakfast and a promenade alongside the town's cascades to view various sites seen while entering town. At Charleville the caravan stopped for the night and proceeded the next day to Killmallock, Bruff, and finally, Limerick. At each stop the militia was observed in full complement.[27]

The Limerick engagement had been postponed until the first of October, when the violence and tension had almost subsided in the southwest of Ireland. Cooke reported, however, that on their arrival they discovered that "by military proclamation, no person was allowed to be in the streets after 10 o'clock at night," and the company met with some difficulty in procuring a guard, without whose protection they could not have played for fear of constant interruptions.[28] All difficulties were quickly overcome, and Cooke made his Limerick debut as Shylock on Monday, 1 October. Details of Cooke's stay in Limerick are scant, since his diary for this period does not exist. It would seem most likely that Cooke performed the same roles as those presented in Cork a few weeks earlier.

Cooke's stay in Limerick was not as pleasant as his weeks in Cork, where he adhered to his resolutions and passed his time in reading, card playing, long walks, and good conversation at the "Mess" where the company met for meals. He found himself in the southern part of Ireland longer than anticipated, thus delaying his arrival in Dublin. In a letter to Jones written on 19 November from a mail coach inn in Clonmell, Cooke explained his delay:

On the 29th of Octr. I wrote to you, & also on the 1st of Novr. On the 7th of the latter I rec. a letter, by which I suppose you had not rec. either of those I have mentioned. By reason of an accident I met with at Limerick, I was prevented leaving Cork until Monday the 12th. I arrived here the same evening in the mail (the place being taken by the Post Master at Cork, & Three Guineas paid me.) Immediately after supper, I was taken ill, and was so much worse next morning, as to be unable to proceed to Dublin. I was incapable of writing, but a gentleman, who was a passenger, promised to call on Mr. Villass [?] (whose address I gave him) as soon as he arrived in Dublin which would be on Wednesday last, & inform him of the cause of my delay. Whether he fulfilled his promise, I know not. This is the first day I have risen from bed since, or been able to sit up. I have been well attended by Dr. Pyne, a Physician of this place, & am much better, but still unable to travel. Since I left Dublin I have had one Physician, two Surgeons, & five apothecaries. For any service I was of, either to you or myself, I had much better have remained behind. The excursion has been a miserable one.

I have seized the first opportunity I was able to account for my absence.

In a postscript, Cooke adds: "Were my situation easy, I should be easier myself, but a Mail Coach Inn is not the best sick quarters."[29]

Cooke did not reappear in Dublin until 10 December 1798, when the *Dublin Journal* advertised that he was to appear as Baron Wildenheim in *Lovers' Vows*. The season had opened on 11 November, and *The Monthly Mirror* reported in December that "Under the management of Mr. Jones . . . this theatre has lately been very successful, notwithstanding the distracted state & internal broils of this unhappy country."[30] Little is known of Cooke's personal life during this season, although he seems to have been quite regular in his professional duties through 19 July 1799. His roles included both King Henry and the title role in *Richard III*. George Harley, who had now joined Jones, was most frequently assigned the title role for the next two seasons, an ironic situation since Cooke's reputation in London would begin in 1800 with Richard. Apparently, because of Cooke's lateness in arriving back in Dublin, he had been superseded in some of the roles that would have been given him. Thomas Huddart, who had been at Convent Garden in 1798 and was also a member of Jones' company, together with Harley, shared the tragic heroes with Cooke.[31]

Cooke's other principal roles that season included the Stranger in Kotzebue's play,[32] Sir William Dorillon, Biron in *Isabella* opposite Mrs. Yates, Loveless in *The Trip to Scarborough* with Lamash as Lord Floppington, Lord Salisbury in Hall Hartson's tragedy *The Countess of Salisbury*, Benedick in *Much Ado* to Mrs. Williams's Beatrice (Mr. and Mrs. Williams, his old Buxton acquaintances had joined Jones), Moody in *The Country Girl*, Old Norval in *Douglas*, Friar Lawrence, and the King in *The King and the Miller of Mansfield*. Although not listed specifically, Cooke no doubt appeared in other roles from the preceding season, such as Stedfast and Captain Bertram.[33]

Three days after Cooke's final performance this season in Dublin, he was present in Limerick for the Assizes, 22–26 July, with Huddart, making his first Irish tour, and young Miss Gough (later Mrs. Galindo), appearing for the first time in Limerick. The company also included Michael Fullam and a popular comedian, James B. Stewart.[34] Cooke also accompanied the company to Cork in late July. On 7 September, a benefit for the Cork poor with Cooke as Shylock closed the theatre for the year.[35]

The 1799–1800 season was to be a momentous one for Cooke, for not only would this be his last year as a member of the Crow Street company, but it would also be the turning point in his career. In May 1800, he would appear for the first time with John Kemble, and in less than six months he would be performing in competition with "Black Jack" as a star of the London stage. On the other hand, his diary, extant from 31 December through 28 February, indicates that he slipped back to his old habits, and, as Dunlap suggests, his daily jottings had "more the air of confessions than any of his other diaries."[36] Several months after leaving Ireland, he would write in a letter to Cork that he had lost ground in Ireland, "driven to leeward more by *Dirty Squalls* than steady winds."[37] Both from his comments and the roles assigned to him, it is clear that he was even more disenchanted than he was the preceding season with the continued competition from Huddart and Harley. His letter suggests other difficulties not specified.

Cooke began his last season in a mundane fashion, appearing the third week in November as the King in *The King and the Miller*, Baron Wildenheim, the Count of Carbonne, and Moody.[38] His first new role was Osmonde in O'Keefe's *The Poor Soldier* with Huddart as Percy on 2 December. The month of December was also relatively uneventful. On the 12th he again appeared as King Henry to Harley's Richard, played Captain Ironsides, the bluff, good-hearted skipper, a relatively insignificant role, in Richard Cumberland's sentimental comedy *The Brothers*, and reappeared as the Stranger on the 17th and the 31st.[39]

Cooke's diary indicates that he finished the 1790s discontented but optimistic for the future. The last day of the year he spent trying to resolve debts left in Limerick, reading over *The Stranger*, lunching with his old friend Williams, and passing the afternoon, until 3:00, in the green room. Of the latter he passed judgment:

It is very rare a Green room conversation is worth attending to; though one might imagine from the profession of the persons who meet there, it would often be otherwise. During a representation in the evening, the strictest order and decorum ought to be preserved, particularly when it is considered how much the thoughts of those who really understand and feel their business, must be discomposed and ruffled by the rude mirth and noisy talk, which is too often to be met with.

The Stranger that night "was better acted throughout than many we have done, as we have a very ill assorted & arranged company." Cooke was unaware of the translator of the Dublin version of *The Stranger* but admired it above all of Kotzebue's plays, although he found "the moral is bad, and the conclusion entirely destroys the proper effect the play ought to produce."[40]

Cooke's first entry for 1800 shows a vigorous state of mind but some regret. His energy was being channeled in a more productive way, although this would quickly change.

Habit does much—Custom is second nature.—Absurd as it may appear, I feel a strangeness, something like regret, at parting with the figure 7 in the date of the year. We have now commenced the last year of a century abounding with astonishing and unforeseen events, and have good reason to think, before its conclusion, some wonderful changes may yet take place. . . . commenced keeping my accounts daily and exactly, a method which, had I pursued during a few past years, would, at the present day, have placed me in a very different situation from what I now write in.

He also indicated that he intended to begin some literary efforts, and he alluded to a play he hoped to write, called "The Road to Happiness," altered from a piece by Kotzebue, "The Peevish Man," translated by C. Ludger.[41] On 12 January, he mentioned 200 lines of a poem entitled "The Stage" which he had begun on 4 June, but had not worked on since going to Cork the preceding July. The next day he tried to work on it, but all he could do was erase the last two lines written. He said no more about either project, and the chances are good that neither was completed.

The Crow Street Theatre was closed on 2 January on account of a charity exhibition at Astley's Peter Street Theatre. Cooke, who had recently injured his knee and had missed a rehearsal earlier in the day, was relieved, especially since his salary would not be affected. At the same time, such a decision on Jones' part simply strengthened his view of Dublin ways.

Surely Dublin could have, if inclined, filled Astley's and assembled an audience at the same time at the Theatre; nor could the latter, open [on] such an occasion, [have] been supposed to injure the former. That stage of mountebanks has been too much honoured by noticing any of their proceedings, unless by curbing their insolence, & informing their ignorance, whenever they dared to infringe upon the privileges of the Theatre.

In this same entry, Cooke briefly alluded to a theme that would be repeated often during the next month and a half: "In the former part of the day I experienced much confusion of mind, which I have at times suffered under, but trust air and business tomorrow will entirely remove it." The next day Cooke went to the theatre and rehearsed Captain Faulkner in *Way to Get Married* "in our usual slovenly way." That evening, though still ill, he played the Stranger to a good house. The following evening he had to perform Faulkner opposite the Julia of a Miss Darlington, who had apparently escaped to Ireland from England to avoid "a disagreeable marriage" and to retain her fortune. Cooke continued to abhor such amateurism; he found her "very indifferent, or, to speak properly, very bad" as Julia.

For the next few days, beginning on 4 January, Cooke spent his time drinking and conversing at his favorite Dublin watering-hole, Peter Kearney's. On the evening of the 5th, he met in the street a "tipsey gentleman" by the name of Bereford, and the two drank wine together in Cooke's lodgings until 5:00 A.M. "Thus terminated a *well spent* day, not much calculated to bear reflection."

The following day Cooke remained in bed until 6:00 P.M., after which he played the Stranger "as well as at any other time, but not with equal ease & satisfaction to himself. I felt unwell, confused, & a powerful mutiny among my nerves. 'Every inordinate cup is unblessed, and the ingredient is a devil!'" Ironsides was repeated on the 7th, then he had another night of drinking on the 8th, and the morning of the 9th again found him "indisposed & much unnerved, the sure consequence of dissipation." Another day in bed preceded his performance of Captain Bertram in *The Birth Day* and afterwards, the cycle of the last few days was repeated: Kearney's till 4:00 A.M., the next day in bed, and performance at night. On this evening, 10 January, Cooke, though feeling ill while dressing, went through the Stranger as usual. His last performance of the week completed, Baron Wildenheim on Saturday night, 11 January, Cooke finally sat down on Sunday to evaluate his week:

The debauches of last week, or, at least, the ill spent hours, broke in upon my regularity, & put aside a good practice, I shall not, for some time, return to [i.e., the keeping of his accounts]. A day, or a night, or both, consumed in conviviality (to speak softly) is often the occasion of many succeeding days & nights being spent in the same manner. Few, when the mind is dissipated, thoughts confused, nerves unstrung, & the whole frame weakened and agitated, can put a sudden stop to the flowing evil. To-morrow I will return to my duty—to-morrow comes, with still less capability, & then to-morrow & to-morrow, until some fortunate or unfortunate event closes the period. I will not, I cannot, at this time, touch upon the many instances when a *fatal* conclusion by this rash, unthinking conduct, is put to fortune, reputation, life, or, sometimes to all at once. Such a reflection, Reason says, ought to erect a lasting momento [*sic*].

Such activities as these, though of a heightened nature during that week, had by now become all too common in Cooke's daily life, and no amount of moralizing after the fact would alter the course of his future. By Sunday evening, though still nervous, he felt "entirely freed from the effects of my last week's dissipation."

A new week began with the seventh performance of *The Stranger*: "My first act, bad; my third, not much better; my fourth & fifth tolerable: in short, by much my worst performance of the part, although I received nearly as much applause as ever." Captain Bertram followed the next night. After the performance, Cooke went into the house to observe *Raymond and Agnes*. His comments afterwards on eighteenth-century pantomime are worth recording:

The story, which is now generally known, is, in the pantomime, obscured, mutilated & perplexed. It must certainly differ much from the Covent Garden piece.[42] The music and scenery, *here*, command no particular attention. The dumb acting, Mrs. Byrne excepted, is very inexpressive & defective. The present race of actors, indeed all I remember, with a very few exceptions, would stand no chance of approbation, in competition with the ancient *mimae*. Deprive them of speech, & you are quite in the shade, if not in the dark. Dancers are certainly the best dumb performers, at the present time, but are too extravagant, & retain their profession, particularly in a serious piece, a great deal too much. It is apt to excite laughter to see a person dancing through a distressful situation.

For the next few days, Cooke spent considerable time recording his reactions to *The Complete Irish Traveller*, his most recent reading material, and his own impressions of Ireland.[43] Much of his diary for several days is filled with rather indiscriminate excerpts from the *Traveller*. On the evening of Friday the 17th, he again performed the Stranger: "The audience as usual to this play. Indeed, at present, we draw audiences by no other." On Saturday, he played Loveless in *A Trip to Scarborough*. Appearing with Cooke as Hoyden in Sheridan's rewritten version of *The Relapse* was a Miss Emily Bindon (later Mrs. Montague Talbot). This young Irish actress had joined the Dublin company the preceding season, and although off-stage Cooke found her sensible, well informed, and possessed of a pleasant personality, on-stage he considered her a "bad actress," with little promise.

In his entry for Sunday, 19 January, Cooke gives the first characterization of the company he kept at Kearney's. After dining there he remained till daylight; an inconsequential argument prompted this commentary:

The society, if I may profane the word, with whom I join at this place, is disgusting, at the least. Some individuals I could wish to select, & the time we might be together would, I believe, pass tolerably, but there are others it shocks me even to think of. It may seem strange why I do not withdraw from it. Local convenience, & the foolish habit actors possess of unaccountably associating with each other, though contrary to inclination, must be my plea, however I shall make my visits rare, & shorten their duration.

His resolve, though soon broken, was reinforced the following day. "As the morning was far advanced when I got home, & the voice of reason drowned in a confusion of intellect I did not go to bed, but sat until near ten o'clock." In the evening he dined at the tavern, remaining until performance time. "Played 'The Stranger', for the 9th time; felt weak, low, & in the last act, very hoarse, or rather a failure of voice, from the preceding day and night. I will not affront myself with any reflections upon the matter, as it seems, if I may so express myself, to have the appearance of *self hypocrisy*."

On Tuesday, 21 January, Cooke performed Osmond in "Monk" Lewis's *The Castle Spectre* and made a characteristic remark on the drama of the day:

I hope posterity, if they read it, will not believe it could repeatedly attract crowded houses, when the most sublime production of the immortal Shakespeare, even for one night would be played to empty benches, at least to empty boxes! But it certainly is the best treat for *empty skulls*.

In actuality, this is more an attack on the Dublin playgoer than on Lewis's play. Nonetheless, he clearly considered it claptrap, its success in Dublin resting in large part on "the introduction of a ghost, and the skill of the painter, with a few scraps of music."

Cooke performed the next four nights without a break: Bertram, Baron Wildenheim, and the King in Dodsley's *The King and the Miller*,[44] the Stranger, and Moody. Despite his regularity, he notes that "except playing every night, I have spent the time in an idle & unprofitable manner."

Sunday began in a routine manner with a visit to the riding master of Astley's Amphitheatre, William Davis, and several of the performers. Cooke has left an interesting impression of the comaraderie of equestrian performers and country players: "There seemed, & I have ere this observed it, a sort of cordiality and fellowship not to be found in a company of actors; unless it might formerly be said to have existed in small communities, which the knavery & rapacity of country managers frequently interrupted." The day ended, however, with Cooke at the tavern until "very late next morning, but not very sober or composed." His first entry of the new week reveals another aspect of the man:

On my return home was going immediately to quit my lodgings upon account of some money a servant had embezzled, belonging to me, which I had entrusted to her mistress. Changed my determination, but do not like the people so well as before. Went to the Theatre, & at my return presented the mistress of the house with 3 box tickets. I mention this to shew my versatile mind.[45]

Although he performed the Stranger that night (eleventh time) well, the next morning he awoke "unwell, both in mind and body," and spent the day and night in bed. Once, embarrassed by his behavior, he wrote: "I need not observe my reflections were more painful than pleasant. I almost blush, tho' alone, at staining paper with vice and folly." His condition was little improved the next day. He sent word to the theatre that he could neither rehearse *Wives As They Were, and Maids As They Are* nor perform that evening, but the deputy manager, Jacob Hammerton, persuaded him that no other piece could be substituted and consequently he agreed to perform Sir William Dorillon. Though suffering pain in his knee and "out of spirits & also out of humour," Cooke felt pangs of professional pride as he observed "the natural acting of the charming little Bellamy [Elizabeth, daughter of Thomas Ludford Bellamy], in Miss Doriland [*sic*], rouse me, & I was ashamed not to endeavour seconding her in the best manner I was able."

Philip Lamash, a fellow-actor and at one time a performer under Garrick at Drury Lane, had died the night before, and for Cooke his death took on special meaning. As he records in his diary, Lamash "had been in a declining state for some weeks past, partly, as supposed, for living too fast." As in the case of the drunken minister in Buxton six years earlier, Cooke saw a reflection of himself in Lamash's dissipation.

In a retrospective look at his life on the last day of January, Cooke has left a most revealing and sensitive self-appraisal of his mental condition, a result no doubt of his constant and prolonged bouts with drink. The description approximates a textbook illustration of alcoholic hallucinosis, closely related to schizophrenia.

To use a strange expression, I am sometimes in a kind of mental intoxication. Some, I believe, would call it insanity. I believe it is allied to it. I then can imagine myself in strange situations, & in strange places. This humour, or whatever it is, comes uninvited, but it, nevertheless, [is] easily dispelled; at least, generally so. When it *cannot* be dispelled, it must, of course, become madness, at least be termed so. It is not always preceded by some fortunate event, or pleasing circumstance, for in that case, although it might still be said to come uninvited, it came with pleasing company. On the other hand I am sometimes as much dejected & depressed, without any sensible or apparent cause. Both, I imagine, proceed from the frame of thought, or temperament of the body, & both maybe driven away most successfully, by some immediate application to pleasure or employment.

Lamash's death was still in Cooke's thoughts. He "was in a flighty elevation of spirits, & yet grave & serious images flitted" across his mind. As soon as breakfast was completed, Cooke sat at the table and hastily scrawled a few verses on Lamash's death:

I supposed *Thalia* lamenting his loss, & took occasion to introduce Ryder & O'Reilly.[46] I wrote a fair copy; read it over several times, and was then going to throw it in the fire, but did not. We feel, in a certain degree, as partial to the brats of our brain, as of our loins.

That night, after performing Captain Bertram, Cooke gave the poem to the singer John Addison, with whom he felt a special closeness, although there had been no "particular intimacy" between them. He requested that the verses not be shown to any other person. To my knowledge, this is the last mention of Cooke's creative writing.

Cooke was not pleased with the majority of roles he had been assigned thus far in the season. His dislike for Elizabeth Inchbald's dramatic efforts are echoed a number of times in his diaries. For several seasons now he had played Sir William Dorillon and felt "plagued" having to act in it. His criticism of the play, *Wives As They Were, and Maids As They Are*, a comedy forgotten today, is quite contemporary and incisive in its castigation of Inchbald's treatment of women. He begins with a brief plot synopsis:

Sir Wm. Dorillon, or Doriland [Inchbald's spelling is Dorillon], having, upon his departure for India, left his daughter with a friend in London, for education, upon his return, in order to observe his manner, is introduced to her under the name of Mandred, an acquaintance of her father's. He finds her immersed in all the giddy riot and folly of a fashionable life. This determines him again to return to India. In the interim, hearing no news of her father, & her pecuniary embarrassments, arising from dissipation, increasing, she is arrested, & flying to Mr. Mandred, for concealment in his apartment, he not only refuses it, but suffers her to be conducted *to prison*. In a visit he makes her there, finding her tenderness for her father is still alive, he permits his friend to discover him, & reluctantly, as he himself says, is reconciled to her. At the close of the piece she is given to Sir George Evelyn, the only worthy character in it. This is the maid "as they are", for which picture, & a very indelicate allusion made to girls of the present day, by one of the characters, the young misses are much obliged to Mrs. Inchbald. There is a Lord Priory, who treats his wife, merely as a rational animal, a creature of his pleasure, and a sort of superior domestic. This is the wife "as they were." When, & where? Our great grandmothers would be as far from thanking Mrs. Inchbald for her character of them, as the spinsters of the present world. He exposes her to the addresses of a professed libertine, to prove her virtue, &, after a little alarm, triumphs, in his mode of managing a wife! But, instead of the disgustingly impudent Bronzeley, a character every where to be met with, had he been a man of sense & refinement, & inclined to gallantry, by no means incompatible with such qualifications, where then would have been his Lordship's triumph? I know it may be objected he would not then have exposed her to the temptation; but I cannot allow this to be altogether just.

This is the main outline of the play. The fable is, in most places, improbably conducted. The circumstance of Sr. W. changing his coat with Bronzeley is absurd in the highest degree, nor are we to suppose the fashion of their cloaths to be anything alike. Lord Priory's character is contradictory, & Sir Wm., while under the disguise of Mandred, expecting his daughter to pay him particular respect, while, as a stranger, he is taking extraordinary, &, I may say, improper liberties with her, is extremely ridiculous.

The language is as good as any we have known of Mrs. Inchbald's. The present German stage morality and Mrs. I's seem much upon a par. This comedy, I think, will never be classed among what is called, in a theatrical phrase, the list of stock pieces; indeed its subject may, in some degree, prevent it.[47]

On 1 February, Cooke was summoned to *As You Like It* rehearsals "but did not *like* to attend," no doubt provoked by a severe cold and sore throat which kept him on his best behavior the next day, Sunday. While reading the December issue of *Walker's Hibernian Magazine,* Cooke came across an account of the death of James Middleton, the Covent Garden actor with whom Cooke had acted during his first season under Jones. The thought of Middleton served as one more reminder of his own weaknesses:

> The first season of the present management, he belonged to the Dublin Theatre. I was frequently with him. He possessed a pleasing, harmonious voice; genteel person & address; but his abilities then were much upon the decline, particularly his memory. He seemed good-natured & facetious, a pleasant (perhaps for his own good too pleasant) companion. But for the humanity of a poor mechanic, he would have perished in the streets. When his forlorn condition was known at the theatres, some among the actors hastened to his relief, but their humane endeavours proved in vain. He expired at little more than 30 years of age. Alas!

On 3 February, Cooke's hoarseness persisted, and he again sent a note excusing himself from the rehearsal of *The Guardian*. But he played the Stranger in the evening for the twelfth time, "very hoarse in the last act." The hoarseness that plagued him throughout this season became a chronic problem throughout the remainder of his career.

On the following day, Cooke recorded a curious and unexplained entry: "From the above date [4 February], until Saturday, February 15th, many things happened, which I could wish to forget. I certainly feel myself hurt, & justly, but in defending myself, I took the exact method of putting weapons into the hands of my Adversaries." Whatever the cause of Cooke's distress, it kept him from making additional entries until 16 February.

On the 15th, Cooke appeared as Horatio in *The Fair Penitent*, while Harley played Sciolto, the role which Cooke had played often and would ultimately be associated with in London. Also in the cast was a young lady whom Cooke mentioned in his diary, on several previous occasions, though never by name. In his opinion, she "would have disgraced a barn in the worst strolling company."

His entries for the next two weeks are extremely brief, listing for the most part his performances and little else: on the 17th Haswell, the Stranger two nights later, Captain Bertram the following night (a Government Night which only "children and rabble avail themselves of"), and Iago on the 25th with Mrs. Sparks, wife of the prompter, Richard Sparks, appearing for the first time as Emilia. The most interesting entry, until 28 February, is a brief one on 22 February: "At night an alarm was given of a woman drowning, & I was called to take a light to my bedchamber window. I did so; the people were collected, & it proved to be a dog."

On the 27th, he arranged for his benefit night to be a Wednesday (25 March) before Easter. No performance was given the next night, and Cooke made a characteristic comment:

The Patentee, in imitation of London, which he likes *occasionally* to imitate, shuts up the Theatre on Wednesdays & Fridays during Lent, unless some of the Actors will take their benefits on those nights. Fortunately, I believe, most would be very glad to keep their houses open on those nights, but they cannot; whereas the Dublin one is under no such restraint, & last year was the first season of such innovation. Indeed at that time he had a selfish, but not a just excuse. He let the Theatre on those nights for Oratorios, consequently all but the singers were unpaid. The renter on those nights severely repented his bargain, as he lost a considerable sum by it, which the actors were by no means sorry for.

Cooke' diary ends with his 28 February entry.

The first half of Cooke's final Dublin season was not impressive, although he had played Iago and the Stranger. The remainder of his roles were limited largely to contemporary parts such as Captain Faulkner, Captain Bertram, Baron Wildenheim, Loveless, Haswell, and the role he disliked more than any other, Sir William Dorillon. He gained some accolades in the playing of Earl Osmond in "Monk" Lewis's romantic tragedy *Castle Spectre*, so much so that he chose the role for his benefit in March along with Comus.[48] Osmond, the villain who captures Angela, gave Cooke a chance to thrill the audience with numerous melodramatic effects.

From March until the end of the Dublin season in July, Cooke found his opportunities for more significant roles improved, beginning on 19 March with Stukely in *The Gamester*, which would become one of his most popular roles on the London stage. Later in the month, he played Macbeth to Huddart's Macduff and Miss Gough's Lady Macbeth. In April and May, he was assigned the lesser role of Las Casas in Sheridan's adaptation of Kotzebue's *Pizarro*, which he played at least six times. He stepped into the title role on 22 May.[49]

The climax of the 1799–1800 season in Dublin was the engagement of John Philip Kemble, who had last appeared in Ireland in 1797. Kemble, who was "in high vogue with the Beau Monde" in London,[50] was still delighted to leave London and Drury Lane, where Sheridan's disastrous management had continued to sink the theatre into a dire financial situation. Kemble had triumphed that season as Rolla in *Pizzaro*, but as his star rose, Drury Lane was approaching an irretrievable state of insolvency.

Kemble left for Dublin on 21 May and arrived in time for his first appearance on 28 May as Hamlet with Cooke as the Ghost.[51] The next evening Cooke supported Saunders from Manchester in *The Castle Spectre* as Earl Osmond to Saunders' Father Philip, and on the 31st he played Stockwell in *The West Indian*. A repeat of *Castle Spectre* followed on 3 June; on the 7th Cooke relinquished the Count of Narbonne to Kemble and took the supporting role of Austin. His final supporting role during Kemble's engagement was Edmund to Kemble's King Lear on 30 June, Cooke's first attempt in that role.[52]

Little commentary is available on Cooke's and Kemble's first joint appearances. *The Monthly Mirror* simply reported that Kemble performed all his roles "with the most unlimited applause, to houses full of the most fashionable company—He is well supported by Cooke, Huddart, and Miss Gough."[53] Despite the sad lack of critical comment, one famous story emerges from the brief contact of the two future London rivals. According to a story told by a member of Jones' company present in the wings during the performance of *The Count of Narbonne*, later related to Dunlap, Kemble came up to Cooke while he was waiting for a cue and critically attacked him by saying:

"Mr. Cooke, you distressed me exceedingly in my last scene—I could scarcely get on. You did not give me the cue more than once—you were very imperfect."

"Sir, I was perfect."

"Excuse me, Sir, you were not."

"By ——— I was, Sir!"

"You were not, Sir!"

"I'll tell you what, I'll not have your faults fathered upon me. And damn me, black Jack, if I don't make you tremble in your pumps one of these days, yet!"[54]

The contest would be taken up again in less than six months, and "Black Jack" would remain Cooke's favorite name for Kemble. Kemble could not have found Cooke's threat of much consequence at this stage in his career; besides, his stay in Dublin was too lucrative to let a country actor affect him in any way. Kemble's brief Irish engagement netted him over £1,117 for fourteen nights' acting.[55]

Kemble was not the only London star to be associated with Cooke toward the end of his Dublin years. Visits were also made by John Bannister, Charles Incledon, and his old friend Joseph Munden, who supported Cooke's Sir Philip Blandford as Sir Abel Handy in *Speed the Plough,* first on 21 June.[56] Cooke would become an intimate friend of Incledon in London, later becoming godfather to one of his children.

Cooke's final season in Dublin had been relatively unimpressive, although in the London press he had gained the title "The Dublin Roscius," an appellation no doubt cultivated by the Covent Garden management who had negotiated that winter for his services starting in the autumn of 1800. Nearly forty-five years old, a provincial actor during most of his adult life, he had never faced a challenge like the one ahead of him—the fame and success he had never really sought, or total failure and oblivion back in the provinces. For an actor who had experienced so many personal and professional disappointments and who, through circumstances largely of his own making, had been forced to reestablish himself repeatedly, the acceptance of a London engagement meant Cooke would now truly "stand the trial."

8

"I Am Myself Alone"

On 14 February 1800, Cooke received a letter in Dublin from William "Billy" Thomas Lewis, acting as agent for Thomas Harris, manager of Covent Garden, advising him that there would be an opening for him in that company for the next season. Cooke wrote back immediately expressing his interest in the position. Ten days later, Cooke received a reply with a request for his terms.[1] On 12 March 1800, Cooke responded to Lewis, accepting an offer for three years, with certain stipulations:

The period I mentioned in my last letter was, I thought, as long as a stranger could expect. An engagement for three years would certainly be an object of importance, were it not the risque the actor runs of being discharged at the end of the first; yet, as you offer me two years certain, it appears it would be my own fault should such an event take place. This hesitation, sir, I assure you, arises from this consideration: my endeavours I can pledge myself for, but my abilities may fall very short of expectation; however, I will do, as many others have, and stand the trial. I therefore accept your offer of an engagement for three years upon the terms you mention, Six, Seven, and Eight Pounds, agreeing to the Manager's power of dissolving the engagement at the end of the first Year.

Your answer to my request respecting the business I was wanted for, is perfectly right; it was made without proper consideration [Cooke's reference here is unknown]. I remain here until the 17th of May; as soon as possible after that proceed to England. I have not yet arranged my summer business, as I would wish to be a short time in London, previous to the commencement of the Winter season.

Until the above period your command will be received here, and meet with immediate attention from

                          Sir,

                          Your most obedient,
                                G.F. Cooke[2]

Whether true or not, Cooke records in his diary that he had rejected the same offer from Harris seven years before. The Covent Garden account books for 1800–1801 confirm that after Cooke's arrival his salary was indeed £6 per week, or £1 per day.[3] As Cooke specifies in his letter, his salary increased to £7 in 1801–1802, but the following season jumped to an average of £14 per week, not the £8 that he had originally expected.⁴

Cooke did not arrive, as he had hoped, before the beginning of the winter season; in fact, it appears that he arrived later than the Covent Garden management had expected.⁵ After completing his engagement in Dublin, appear-

William Lewis (1749–1811). Benefactor to Cooke during his early years at Covent Garden. Author's collection.

ing with J. P. Kemble and Joseph Munden, Cooke spent part of the summer performing in Cork. At the conclusion of his final appearance in September, according to theatre lore, he became dead drunk soon after the drop of the George's Street final curtain. He was found in "the Bulk," a cobbler's tenement near the playhouse, and, since he had no money, his friends collected funds which they gave to the packet master who took Cooke—"as happy as a lord"—across to Bristol on 13 October.[6] This report may actually be one of many during Cooke's lifetime that were more slanderous to the actor than they should have been, for on 17 November 1800, Cooke wrote to a Felix Daly in Cork that "his severe delay" was caused by sickness on the road.[7] On the other hand, it is quite possible that this illness came about as the result of another drunken spree following his Cork engagement.

The Covent Garden Theatre that would house Cooke's debut was designed by Henry Holland in 1792, and although it had gone through additional alterations in 1794 and 1796, it was basically as Holland had first designed it. There was a proscenium stage 15 feet by 6 inches deep, flanked by projecting stage boxes for the king and prince, and proscenium doors set at right angles to the stage front. The stage opening was 29 feet wide and 19 feet 7 inches high. The auditorium itself was horseshoe-shaped. At the time of Cooke's arrival, the theatre held 3,013 persons: 632 in the pit, 1,200 in the three circles of boxes, 820 in the "two-shilling gallery," and 361 in the "one-shilling gallery."[8] Cooke had never appeared in a playhouse to equal this great London landmark, and it would no doubt take some time for him to get accustomed to its size. Vocally, however, he had few worries, for he knew that his voice, even if a whisper, could be heard over great distances.

Cooke finally arrived at the One Bell Inn in the Strand on the night of Sunday, 26 October, attended rehearsal on Wednesday, and despite the continuation of his illness for "near a fortnight" after his arrival, made his debut as Richard III on 31 October 1800, appearing before a London audience for the first time in twenty-one years. Those who had known him in the provinces considered Cooke past his prime and only a shadow of his former self; nonetheless, he was a brilliant and immediate success. The management had done its share to assure his success in the way of physical preparation—"new and appropriate Scenery, Dresses, and Decorations—throughout which strict attention has been paid to the Costume of the Age" were provided.[9] Additional supernumeraries were employed for the soldiery and were given more rehearsal time than usual; Thomas Attwood composed new music for the marches. Cooke, advertised as the "hero of the Dublin stage,"[10] was not, however, provided with the strongest of supporting casts. Some critics, like Thomas Dutton, thought all the dramatis personae, with the exception of Murray's Henry VI, Pope's Richmond, and Whitfield's Buckingham, "indifferently cast."[11]

The audience that first night arrived wondering about this provincial favorite. There had been many rumors and conjectures from the first mention in September that he would debut at Covent Garden. For the first time since Holman and Pope had created a temporary stir fifteen years before, Kemble was to have a competitor who might seriously threaten his preeminence in London. Drury Lane audaciously accepted the challenge and chose to open their season with what was then considered Cooke's strongest piece, Cibber's alteration of *Richard III*. The audience that historical night at Covent Garden was ready to observe a true contest. Among the audience was his old boyhood friend John Taylor and in a front box sat Mr. and Mrs. John Philip Kemble. Kemble, reported Taylor, was "very liberal without being ostentatious in his applause," but no doubt realized that Cooke was a formidable opponent.[12]

Cooke was staggered by his reception—"more attention is paid to me in every quarter than I had any right to expect." His success exceeded his "most sanguine expectations. The managers as much pleased as the Public, & I have every prospect of speedily pulling up the lee way I lost in Ireland."[13] Of the night, Cooke recorded in his journal: "never was a reception more flattering; nor ever did I receive more encouraging, indulgent, and warm approbation than on that night, both through the play and at the conclusion."[14]

For the first time in his lengthy career, Cooke received plentiful critical comment. But as the London critics soon learned, Cooke was an "original," and criticism, no matter its nature, would have little effect on him. As could be expected, the critics fell into two parties, "each equally violent, and equally in extremes, though on opposite sides."[15] Some of the early criticism clearly expressed judgments too quickly, disregarding the brief rehearsal time, Cooke's illness, and his unfamiliarity with the large house. Others, like the *Morning Post*, then a champion of Kemble, were so convinced of the correctness of their preference for the more studied and refined style of Kemble that they found it difficult to make any complimentary remark. Others, like *The Times*, the *True Briton*, and *The Monthly Mirror*, were willing to show more objectivity in their appraisals. *Walker's Hibernian Magazine*'s London representative, typical of numerous commentators, simply concluded that Cooke, as he portrayed Richard, "sustained in a very able manner, so far as conception, discrimination, and the truth of the stage were concerned [and] we pronounce Mr. Cooke, a master of his art."[16] There was, however, no general agreement among the critics. Among those praising Cooke, a certain common recognition did emerge. *The Times* (1 November 1800) noted that "his conception of the character had all the merit, of originality, and his originality was without presumption or fastidiousness, masterly, and impressive." The critic explains: "There did not occur from the beginning to the end a single instance of imitation. He evidently acted from his own feelings . . . many of his readings evinced great critical knowledge, & in the most difficult passages he felt so strongly the elements of the character, as to appear completely free from every other consideration." The *True Briton*, in a series of reviews, found his acting

Painting of Cooke as Richard III (c. 1800) by an unknown artist. Used by permission of Norman Philbrick.

based "upon an observation of real life and a full consideration of the character he is to represent. He . . . comes forward with an original air, and with all the force of Truth and Nature. His acting certainly bears a strong resemblance to that of Garrick, but it appears to resemble Garrick only because he draws from the same source."[17] As numerous other observers noted, this same critic was aware that in the soliloquies, Cooke "appears to be delivering the natural workings of his mind and not to be speaking an address to the audience . . . a common error of most actors." A later critic called this Cooke's "power of concealing art."[18] On the 6th, the *True Briton* attempted to single out Cooke's prominent features, listing correctness, force, and spirit, and concluding that he was distinguished "by the happy union of fire and reflection. His judgement directs his imagination and his imagination animates his judgment . . . his gestures indicate the operations of thought and passion. Yet there is no redundance of action. All his attitudes are the result of his feelings, and he never changes those attitudes till there is a change of passion." After the third performance of Richard, the *True Briton* was compelled to add: "Nothing like such excellence as he exhibits has been seen in this Theatre within our remembrance. His mind seems to be wholly engrossed by the character he sustains, and he is also constantly attentive to whatever relates to it, as delivered by every other Agent of the piece, who has any connection in the scenes in which he is engaged."

Cooke's detractors were quick to condemn his interpretation of Richard as "a piece of mechanical low cunning as would cast back the stage to a period of barbarism, if it could become the fashion. . . . the composition, the refinement, that make a performance entire and graceful, are altogether wanting."[19] Another wrote: "In strength of voice, energy of mind, and boldness of manner, he seems capable of depicting the violent passions in the full extent of all their fury; but the manner in which he portrayed the deep, plausible, and subtle hypocrisy of the tyrant . . . afforded little proof of superior excellence in scenes, in which it is not the tongue, but the mind of the actor that speaks, and which require nice discrimination, varied expression, delicacy, and a knowledge of human nature."[20] The most common negative criticism of Cooke's Richard was expressed in 1804 by the *Morning Chronicle* (16 October): "Openness and seeming sincerity he cannot assume, while his cunning and hypocrisy are so glaring, that they could not impose upon the most credulous and unwary. In the scene with Lady Anne, one would think he wished to jeer and to banter her, whereas the author undoubtedly means that he should appear to her a true penitent and an ardent lover." Leigh Hunt was later to question whether such hypocrisy "ought to betray itself to the audience except in soliloquy."[21] This point of view was most ably articulated by Charles Lamb in one of his rare reviews in the *Morning Post* (8 January 1802).[22] Although Lamb found much to admire in Cooke, he condemned his conception. He found Cooke's portrait a forcible one "of the *monster* Richard, as he exists in the *popular idea*, in *his own exaggerated* and witty *self-abuse*, in the overstrained representation of the parties who were *sufferers* by his *ambition*; and, above all, in the impertinent and wretched *scenes*, so absurdly foistered in by some, who have thought themselves capable of adding to what *Shakespeare wrote*." In a letter written 26 June 1801, Lamb elaborated on his reservations:

You despise, detest, and loathe the cunning, vulgar, low and fierce Richard, which Cooke substitutes [for the "awe and deep admiration of his witty parts, his consummate hypocrisy, and indefatigable prosecution of purpose"]. He gives you no other idea than of a vulgar villain, rejoicing in his being able to overreach, and not possessing that joy in *silent* consciousness, but betraying it, like a *poor* villain, in sneers and distortions of the face, like a droll at a country fair; not to add that cunning so self-betraying and manner so vulgar could never have deceived the politic Buckingham nor the soft Lady Anne; *both* bred in courts would have turned with disgust from such a fellow.[23]

For Lamb, the glaring visibility of Cooke's hypocrisy, the "horns and Claws" perpetually obtruding, were distasteful, coarse, lacking in dignity and heroism in the latter scenes, and vulgar.[24] There is little doubt that Cooke's Richard was, as one American critic phrased it, "a high born villain; stooping to temporary dissimulation to obtain his purpose."[25] Apparently, Cooke sustained "the lame mishapen tyrant" throughout, whether standing still, walking thoughtfully, or in a rage.[26]

Counterattacks and rebuttals were common throughout Cooke's remaining years, especially in his playing of Richard. Some simply dismissed comments such as those of Lamb, who hated Cibber's alteration and called it a "wretched acting play." Others considered it unfair to base comments solely on Shakespeare's original. Likewise, such condemnations were based on the standards of modern taste and, in the case of Richard's "wanton countenance in his 'lust fulle' wooing of Lady Anne, when he was not merely assuming the lover," the critic based his comments on manners of women then.[27] An American critic argued that Cooke's Richard "is marked with blunt, uncouth stateliness, and the harsh and brutal pride that may be supposed to have belonged to a ferocious prince of four centuries ago."[28] A later critic and historian, James Murdoch, explained Cooke's "bold and manly defiance" this way: "The removal of obnoxious personages was to him a natural means to the accomplishment of an ambitious end, that end being simply the perpetuation of the kingly rule of the house of York, which of course meant the good of the kingdom wrought through the instrumentality of the axe and block."[29] Even the most severe of his detractors, dwelling on his defects, were forced to acknowledge this bold and manly defiance, his vigorous and impulsive style, his constant energy, his originality, and, above all, his ability to listen to others and to fill moments of silence with meaningful byplay.

Few of the critical comments cited above give any clear indication of Cooke's actual performance. Two lengthy and detailed analyses of his performance, one written shortly after his debut in *The Monthly Mirror* and the other by the American critic Stephen Cullen Carpenter, writing in 1811, who claimed to have seen Cooke first in 1800, give us the best available detailed accounts of his Richard. By excerpting from both, adding specific directions from two extant promptbooks for Cooke's Richard, and citing other random comments, we can get some idea of his performance.[30]

Since Cooke's debut was the most applauded in many years and subsequent performances of Richard created more excitement and received more public attention than those of any actor for some time, detailed examination is appropriate. *The Monthly Mirror* began by praising Cooke's "active and capacious intellect" and his "proufound [sic] knowledge of the *science* of ACTING."[31] The reviewer then amplified his point:

He has read and thought for himself. He appears to have borrowed neither from contemporary nor deceased excellence. He sometimes passes over what have been usually conceived to be *great points* in the character; and he exalts other passages into importance which former *Richards* have not thought significant enough for particular notice. His object seems to have been to form a grand, characteristic, and consistent whole—and that whole is the result of deep thinking, and well-directed study, judiciously adapted to his individual powers of action;—for Mr. Cooke not only *thinks* originally, but he looks, speaks, and walks unlike any other man we ever saw. "*He is himself alone:*"—he is, therefore, in some degree, a *mannerist* but his *settled habits* are not injurious to the characters he has hitherto played, or is likely to play, in Covent-Garden; and his talents are so uncommonly brilliant, that though we cannot be altogether blind to his defects, they are forgotten almost as soon as noticed. . . . the peculiarities, which rather offend at first, grow more pleasing by degrees, and, before the close of his performance, have lost nearly all their weight in the scale of criticism.

Carpenter in *The Mirror of Taste and Dramatic Censor* began his comments by noting Cooke's naturalism, which many in the audience could not understand:

. . . they can see no merit in Cooke as an actor, because he does exactly what a man in real life would do if he were in the situation of the character he represents. To some palates molasses is preferable to sallad [sic] as a condiment. Habit makes it so: and the sarcastic, biting Gloster himself is disgusting unless he be made a very *sweet* fellow. Besides we may see Nature every day in the open streets and fields for nothing; why then pay a dollar, and get a squeezing, for seeing it on the stage? for we see little else in Cooke.[32]

To the Philadelphia critic, such observations demonstrated a complete misunderstanding of both Cooke and the role, for Shakespeare's object, he said, was

to exhibit in the strongest colors the unlimited powers of stupendous intellect when united with stupendous courage. To this end he forms A Monster who, to the pollution of every crime that can make man noxious to man and offensive to God, adds the most disgusting personal deformity, and yet renders him terribly great, and admirable and sublimely attractive, by the mere force of valor, which nothing can dismay, and of intellect capacious of every thing. These are the fundamental parts of the composition which a truly philosophic actor like Cooke will take for his guide; arising from them as corollaries the more minute considerations present themselves; among those are a continual, evident consciousness in Gloster of his own superior powers, and, arising from that again, the most ineffable contempt for the understanding of all other persons.[33]

Commenting on the same quintessential quality of Cooke's interpretation, *The Monthly Mirror* pointed out that four lines added by Cooke from *Henry VI, Part 3*,

> Why I can smile, and murder while I smile,
> And cry content to that which grieves my heart;
> And wet my cheeks with artificial tears,
> And frame my face to all occasions.[34]

"are very suitable to his manner of playing the part." He continued:

In all the subtle, ludicrous, sarcastic turns of the character, he conveyed the poet's intention with uncommon force—this, indeed, seems to be the governing excellence of his performance. We have seen *Richard* rendered more awful and terrific, but never more thoroughly detestable; and this is the proper feeling that he should excite during nearly the whole of the first four acts. In the last he becomes an object of deeper interest—as his fate approaches, commiseration of his sufferings, and admiration of his valour, are blended with our disgust at his crimes. Perhaps Mr. Cooke is somewhat deficient in the *kingly* and heroic part of the character; and his expression of terror, after the dream, is not so vivid and impressive as it should be; but there must always be imperfection somewhere, and Mr. Cooke's merit can afford to suffer some abatement.

The Mirror of Taste concurred with this estimation of Cooke's superiority in the first four acts. In 1807, *The Monthly Mirror* still held to this judgment: "In the earlier parts of the play, it may be almost questioned whether, through his advantages of nature and art, he was ever excelled."[35] Apparently, little change occurred in Cooke's basic interpretation over an eleven-year period.

Cooke's first appearance on stage in the Cibber version followed the scene between King Henry, Tressel, and a Lieutenant. "As the scene changes to another part of the tower" (Folger promptbook), Cooke entered alone from down left and began his first soliloquy, "Now is the winter of our discontent," the first four lines of which he had added for his debut.[36] *The Monthly Mirror* declared that "The soliloquies were all finely given; not addressed, as too commonly is the case, to the audience, like a chorus to explain the play; but they actually appeared to be the secret deliberations of the soul, forming themselves into words as they arose in the mind." *The Mirror of Taste* was more specific, as it frequently was: "Mr. Cooke's face, person, deportment, and utterance of that fine soliloquy were all Richard. . . .In Soliloquy Cooke is allowed, even by his adversaries, to stand wholly unrivalled: he seems really alone." The critic added a significant comment on the first soliloquy: "In this admirable speech Gloster gives a partial view of his nature, and gains a sort of admiration by his total disregard of mere external personal beauty and ornament. This he evinces by the levity with which he treats his own manifold deformity, and his derision of the fripperies of 'this piping time of peace.' " Henry Crabb Robinson, who with his wife went to see "the present *nine day's wonder*," felt this humor was very appropriate and one addition that separated Cooke from Kemble.[37] Lamb, on the other hand, found Cooke's mirth "the coarse, taunting humour, and clumsy merriment, of a low-minded assassin."[38] The 1800 promptbook (Harvard) clearly indicates that Cooke took lengthy pauses after two key lines: "That dogs bark at me, as I halt by 'em" and "And descant on my own deformity." Lamb pointed out that when Cooke made allusions to his deformities they seemed "accompanied with unmixed distaste and pain, like some obtrusive haunting idea—"

Cooke was often criticized for the harshness of his voice, and a number of reviewers found this irritating, beginning with his first soliloquy. It might be noted here that such comments were nonexistent in his early days; indeed, the opposite was true. An unidentified clipping at Harvard says "His utterance is very distinct, but occasionally harsh and grating on the ear; this defect was most perceivable in the declamatory scenes. When it was not necessary to raise his voice, which he sometimes did much too high, it was pleasing, and not destitute of modulation." *The Porcupine* (8 November 1800) explained that some of his "upper notes appear harsh and inharmonious," but that his "lower tones seem distinct and marking, flexible and strong." The *Morning Chronicle* (1 November 1800), in a slightly different stance, stated that Cooke lacked the "fine art of modulation which gives harmony to declamation," although "the volume of his voice makes his whisper audible" and he "has the art . . . of sliding into a falsetto, which has pathos and impression." James Boaden, Kemble's biographer and champion, explained this trait in terms of "two voices, one of which was harsh and acrimonious, the other mild and caressing." Boaden claims his vocal technique was to execute "a rapid transition from one of these sounds to the other: He used the first either to control or convince—the second to soothe or betray."[39] It becomes clear that, because of heavy drinking, the character of Cooke's voice this first season had changed considerably since his early provincial days. Although his lower tones were still clear and penetrating, his upper register, still powerful, was often harsh and grating. It was generally agreed in 1800, however, that Cooke's rough features and "two voices" were often right for Richard and that the harshness of the voice contributed to the perfection of the first soliloquy, especially in the latter third of the soliloquy, beginning with "Then, since this earth affords no joy," etc.

In Act III, Scene 2, in the chamber with Henry, Cooke displayed the byplay so often referred to and detailed admirably in *The Mirror of Taste*:

> . . . his perception must be dull indeed who could not understand the character from the actor's looks alone; yet were these not more expressive or appropriate than his actions. His fiddling with his sword, the quivering of his lip and under jaw, the convulsive start-

ing of his muscles, the clawing with his fingers, and the universal agitation produced throughout his whole frame by the violence of his passion, bid defiance to every attempt at description. His impatience and the fullness of his purpose were marked with more singular emphasis by his play with his sword, than by any other single circumstance: instead of putting his right hand to it every now and then as others do, he fiddled with the hilt with his left, his thumb beating upon it with convulsive agitation.

In the stabbing of Henry, according to Carpenter, Cooke appeared "Not merely insensible to feeling and inaccessible to remorse" but "sportive in the very act of perpetrating murder," and seemed to "laugh in triumph at his own villainies." Having killed Henry, Cooke derides him with "bitter, sneering irony" and through the entire speech, in which he "walks ruminating" (Harvard promptbook), "the concomitant looks, action and expression of Cooke were inimitably great, striking and characteristic."

In Act II, Gloucester begins his first scene in soliloquy after entering from stage right, deliberating on Lady Anne's disinclination to see him and his own personal unfitness for love. A lieutenant enters from stage right, but

> Too intent upon the subject of his contemplation to brook interruption, he takes fire
>   Glost. Begone, fellow, I'm not at leisure.
>   Lieut. My Lord, the king your brother's taken ill.
> No sooner does this intelligence reach his ear than his whole frame and face undergo an instantaneous change. Every symptom of brutal roughness and overbearing ferocity is dismissed from his countenance, and succeeded by a mixed expression of diabolical transport and fawning kindness, while bending to the lieutenant he replies in a softened, friendly tone of voice,
>   I'll wait on him: leave me—*friend*!
> nor was this more impressive than the wild rapture which beamed from him when, the lieutenant being gone, he exclaimed
>   Ha! Edward taken ill! [Cooke changed taken to ta'en]
> or the murderous spirit that broke forth in the tone of voice, the utterance, and the savage look, with which he said
>   Would he were wasted, marrow—bones—and all.

On seeing Anne entering in mourning, Cooke retired to the right side of the stage. His 1807 promptbook specified that the body be brought on at the top of the stage, from the left through an arch, a Yeoman of the Guard preceding the pallbearers, with lady attendants on the left of the body, followed by Anne, Stanley, and Tressel. The body was then placed at the center of the stage with Anne downstage left of the coffin. *The Monthly Mirror*, which, as pointed out earlier, felt the added lines "Why I can smile, and murder while I smile" to be a key to Cooke's interpretation, added that this speech "conveyed the idea of a man, sensible of his personal deformities, and the barriers which separated him from the rest of his brethren, *hugging himself up*, and enjoying a horrible satisfaction in the possession of a faculty by which he hoped to overreach the rest of

"I Am Myself Alone" 133

mankind, and secure the grand object he had in his eye: this was the great preparatory feature of his performance."

In describing the courtship scene with Anne, *The Mirror of Taste* singled out several moments that seemed most prominent. First, his injunction to the bearers of Henry's body to lay it down. The 1800 promptbook (Harvard) indicates that Cooke considered the business with the halbert to be important. He specified that immediately after "My lord stand back, and let the coffin past," the guard bring forward his spear and on the word halbert in Gloucester's "Advance by halbert [after which Cooke places a semicolon] higher than my breast," the point be raised and on "breast" to place it erect. The second "point" noted by Carpenter is

> the sneering archness of his look and voice, when on Lady Anne having panegyrised the deceased king,
> Oh! he was gentle, loving, mild and virtuous:
> But he's in heaven, where thou canst never come;
> he replies,
> Was I not kind to send him thither?
> He was much fitter for that place than earth.
> The hypocritical pathos he threw into his voice and looks when he offers her his sword, and bids her hide it in his breast. . . .

At this point Cooke kneeled and remained down until after "I swear, bright saint, I am not what I was." This scene with Anne was frequently the source of negative criticism, but Carpenter judged it to be "one tissue, nearly uniform, of transcendent excellence."

In Cooke's next scene, in which Gloucester joins the royal family assembled on the annunciation of King Edward's death, he appeared above the others, upstage center, and "sneering at their sorrows" says

> Why ay! these tears look well—sorrow's the mode,
> And everyone at court must wear it now.

which disturbed Carpenter since the words "must necessarily reach the ears of the court before it can reach the audience."

Both *The Monthly Mirror* and *The Mirror of Taste* commented at length on Cooke's soliloquy at the conclusion of the preceding scene. Carpenter first praised the byplay while Buckingham relates what passed between him and the citizens discussing the raising of Gloucester to the throne and putting aside the children. "But that which deserves most praise was the soliloquy. . . . the private effusion in words of his internal thoughts and emotions." He added, "He deliberated;—the pauses between the broken sentences were filled up by the eloquence of his looks. After putting to himself the questions, 'where shall he keep his court?—the tower?' his face exhibited a visible debate; and again seemed to settle the matter definitively when he said 'Ay!—the tower!' during which whole time not so much as a side glance at the audience escaped him." *The Monthly Mirror* noted the same indirectness but added that there was "no grin of malignant delight at the arrangement he had planned. He seemed to settle as a man of *Richard's* policy, studious of his own immediate interest, would *settle* it, and who was satisfied that he had settled it rightly." *The Monthly Mirror* also observed that Cooke delivered the tower line with an extra "the tower" at the end, a point confirmed by the Harvard promptbook in which the words are written in by Cooke.

In the first scene of Act III, Cooke was discovered sitting on a chair on stage. Carpenter found the following confrontation with the mayor and citizens to be handled by an actor "of genius who had investigated his character with the eye of a philosopher. But no sooner has he impressed the magistrates with the persuasion that he condemns their conduct, and has thereby a little alarmed them, than Cooke changes his key, softens the tone of his voice, and relieves them by clothing his seeming refusal in expressions of kindness and good will." The most striking moment was

his transition from pious humility when, as the mayor and citizens are leaving him . . . to the exultation and hellish transport that swelled his bosom when they had gone. His whole frame seemed to swell as if to bursting; his utterance seemed to be smothered with joy; his face was a living picture of damned ambition wild with gratification: and when, at length, after a pause in which his soul seemed to be convulsed with internal enjoyment, he dashed the prayer book from his hand, and exclaimed

Why now my golden dream is out!
the power of the superior actor was felt and loudly acknowledged.

In Act IV, as king, Cooke has a "look of satanic malice and derision" when he finally breaks with Buckingham. "Yielding to the impetuosity of his furious temper, he burst out like a volcano in the words

I'm busy—thou troublest me!"

The Monthly Mirror commented on Richard's habit of gnawing his lip when he was offended ("The king is angry; see, he gnaws his lip"), and "this peculiarity Cooke exhibited with great effect in several parts of the play; indeed, his perturbation, under all circumstances, is extremely natural and forcibly expressed."

The Monthly Mirror also described the scene after Tyrrell is sent off to murder the princes, where Richard for the first time reflects upon the enormity of his conduct and its probable consequences. "Mr. Cooke was highly interesting; and his hesitation and *walking to and fro*, just before the *tent scene*, with some admirable bye-play, . . . finely denoted the misgivings of his mind as to the event of the approaching battle; and suitably prepared the audience for the awful visitation that was at hand, when the ghosts of those he had murdered were to sit heavy on his soul,

> And weight him down to ruin, shame and death."

Carpenter was less timid in his description of these scenes, noting that at the end of Scene 2 of Act IV, Cooke "showed himself... a powerful agitator of the heart in the softer feelings, and evinced masterly skill and force of expression in the pathetic." For the remainder of Act IV, Carpenter found nothing worthy of any particular observation, but he did say that "Cooke bustled away pretty much as other actors do." He felt, as others did, that Cooke's weakest moments were in the last act; that "he falls short in picturing the hero, and gives rather an inadequate idea of military force and grandeur." *The Monthly Mirror*, however, singled out the mingled irony and displeasure in his reply to Stanley in Act IV—"Well—as you *guess*."[40]

Of note, however, in the last act was Cooke's manner of distinguishing between the archers and the cavalry on

> Draw, archers, draw your arrows to the head,
> Spur your proud horses hard, and rise in blood![41]

The tent scene, likewise criticized by a number of other reviewers, Carpenter also considered Cooke's weakest moment in the play. The new scenery in the Covent Garden production, however, was thought especially effective.[42] The 1800 promptbook (Harvard) indicates that Cooke was discovered seated in the tent, the lamps lowered. On the sofa was a cushion with his crown on top, and a table was placed to his right. On the appearance of the ghost, through stage-traps, Cooke sprang from his couch. But despite all efforts in the scene, Kemble and Henderson were consistently considered greater than Cooke. Carpenter conceded that "Cooke is greater than all others in the meditation scene the night before the battle," demonstrating "Doubt—confidence—apprehension—disregard—defiance—and yet misgiving of the event of the next day" by "walking backwards and forwards,—by his sticking the point of his sword in the ground, and then recovering and flourishing it,—by his sighing and silent attempts to speak,—by his unequalled by-play, and by the matchless expression of his countenance, so obvious, so intelligible, so irresistibly eloquent." Likewise, in the death scene, "Cooke may truly say in the words of Richard 'I am myself alone!' " At one point, Cooke tries to rise and failing "dashes away his sword in despair; another time he drops his sword, and, in making a vain effort to recover, falls again; both equally characteristic of the intrepid furious Richard. But that which gives the finishing stroke to the picture is the look which, raising himself on his elbow, he darts at Richmond. It was terrible, it had soul in it; it looked a testamentary curse, and made the death exactly correspondent to the life and living character of the monster Richard." An American critic added that "As he lifted up his left arm over his forehead, and gave the last withering look at *Richmond*, the expression of his eyes—as they for a moment vividly rolled, then became fixedly glazed, and all vision seemed gone—was peculiar, and thrilled the audience."[43] A pro-Kemble reviewer at Cooke's debut found Richard's death scene "a more rugged and hard piece of *caricature* than any in the whole acting—the poorest and rudest stage could produce nothing farther removed from a modest and corrected exhibition of what is in itself too violent for representation."[44]

The Mirror of Taste devoted twenty pages in detailed comment on Cooke's Richard. One last comment from Carpenter, not found in any other critical essay, deserves mention. Throughout the essay a great deal is made of the conscious superiority of talents and the consequent scorn of others in Cooke's Richard. Carpenter isolated the uniqueness of one of Cooke's techniques: "Except when he is flattering or making use of them as agents, Cooke... rarely faces the other persons of the scene." Instead, he keeps his back either turned or half-turned from them, and when he does look at them "it is to read their intentions in their faces, to cut them with a contemptuous sneer, or to knock them down with a terrible frown." To underline a point made earlier in his discussion, Carpenter reiterated the effectiveness of Cooke's reactions and byplay, which "tells plainly the separate effect of every line they utter upon him, while at the same time he appears so rapt up in his selfish purposes, that he seems in reality to confer only with himself."

Richard III was to remain Cooke's most popular serious role until his death and, in his hands, the epitome of malevolence and evil. London was well aware that a true "original" had come to town.

9

Cooke Versus Kemble

The phenomenal success of Cooke's first night as Richard served as a financial catalyst at Covent Garden. On 5 November, when he repeated the role, which he was to do over twenty times that first season, twice as often as any other character, the receipts jumped from £195.7.6 to £241.2.6. The average of the week before Cooke's debut had been only £150.[1]

The second character Cooke introduced to London, Shylock, was an even greater financial triumph, for on its first night, 10 November, the receipts totaled £300. The only competition for Cooke at Covent Garden during the early part of the season was a new comedy by Frederick Reynolds entitled *Life*, which had opened on 1 November and was bringing in as much as £350 to £450 nightly. However, by the end of its run on 1 January 1801, its receipts were down to £200, while Cooke's appearances were still averaging well over £350.

Cooke, who had few initial acquaintances in London, carefully avoided all invitations until after his debut on 31 October. On 1 November, he accepted a dinner engagement with Thomas Dibdin, his young friend from the Manchester days, and Dibdin's wife. Afterwards they all went to the theatre to see Reynolds' new play, after which Cooke rushed out to find permanent accommodations in the area, at Martlett-court, Bow Street, and then returned to the Dibdin's in Goodge Street. Here Cooke remained until 7:00 A.M. Dibdin, concerned for Cooke's safety and reputation, accompanied Cooke back to his new lodgings.

As we crossed Oxford-street from Rathbone-place, Cooke gave me some papers, begging me to take care of them, as being of the greatest consequence in respect to a suit then pending between his wife . . . and himself in the Court of Consistory. . . . I, of course, promised to take great care of these papers, when Cooke turned short round on me, and asked, "What for? give them back: I shall have them used against me else." I conceived I was answerable to Mr. Harris for Mr. Cooke being properly disposed of after having dined and supped with me, and therefore took not the slightest notice of anything he said.

In Greek Street Cooke, who had rubbed his hand along a freshly painted coachmaker's shop front, rushed suddenly into the middle of the street, raised a large stone, and threatened to hurl it through the window in retaliation. Dibdin, unaware of the cause of this outburst, stopped him just in time. In Soho Square Cooke stopped and

> with thundering emphasis uttered the interjection "Hah!" in a tone about ten degrees beyond the strongest aspiration of our stoutest street-paviours. "There!" said Cooke, "tell Harris what my voice effected, after a hard drinking-bout, at seven in the morning, in Soho-Square!—" "I will, my good friend!" said I. "Will you, indeed," replied Cooke, "be such an enemy of your old friend? What business, Harris will say, had Cooke in Soho-Square at seven in the morning? and, thus, through your forward friendship, I shall lose my situation!" More nonsense followed, he compared Harris to the bright moon and Kemble to a dark cloud and swore he'd "play any part by way of wager for-for-yes, for a god."[2]

Thus ended Cooke's first social outing in London.

Although advertised to appear for this second appearance on 10 November as both Shylock and Sir Archy MacSarcasm in Macklin's *Love-a-la-Mode*, Cooke apparently was not prepared for Sir Archy until 13 November when he repeated Shylock. Instead, *Oscar and Malvina* was substituted.

Shylock was to become one of Cooke's most sought-after roles, performed nine times that first season. Interest in Cooke had now spread throughout London, and the reviewers acknowledged this avid interest. The first Shylock notices were generally enthusiastic. The *Times* (11 November 1800) wrote: "His general manner was perhaps somewhat too forcible in the first act, but the beauties which he sometimes elicited from a single word, outweighed every other defect." The *Times*' reviewer particularly praised Acts II and III and the Senate scene, but singled out "the excellence" of Cooke in the passage immediately after the flight of Jessica. "It was given with such exquisite powers as to excite bursts of applause that have been rarely surpassed in any Theatre." The *True Briton* pointed up as distinctions his smothered malignity and artful caution before the signing of the bond and his agonies on the loss of his money and daughter, as well as his "savage exhultation on the misfortunes of Anthonio [sic], open hatred and determined revenges, final disappointment and dejection—All distinctly and forcibly colored." The *Morning Post* (5 February 1801), still his major detractor, continued to attack his lack of dignity and, although his overall performance was not ranked with other parts, the paper admitted that detached passages placed Shylock in a rank with his best. As was true with Richard's obviousness, the *Morning Post* felt Cooke's reading of "I will be assured I may" was spoken with too "complicated cunning and triumph as if Shylock had not only already digested the plan of Anthonio's ruin, but fully anticipated its success." Likewise, his voice, they believed, could not express sorrow or any soft emotion. The *Post* was most complimentary of Cooke's final scene, but went on to explain how he divided "when it is paid" from "according to the tenour," "spreading a snare for the ignorant by a certain strained and affected mode of speaking the former words."

When Gratiano retorts upon the Jew his praise of Portia as a Daniel, and a most rightful judge, Mr. Cooke made efforts to shake himself off. This is a faulty part in the writing, and requires to be managed with the art that softens defects, although in the greatest of writers. But Mr. Cooke aggravated the fault, by making Shylock attend too much to Gratiano. And, it is to be observed, that though Shakespeare has put words into Gratiano's mouth that seem, at first sight, to turn the Jew's attention from himself and other more important objects, yet he does not put any reply in Shylock's mouth, but permits him to go on with that intense regard of what Portia says, and to the consequent yielding up of himself to the emotions of his own heart which form the beauty of that part of the scene, and which were ill interrupted by Gratiano's foppish raillery.

Once more there was no agreement on Cooke's general conception. The reviewer for the *Morning Herald* (11 November 1800) went so far as to say "throughout the whole [he] evinced a justness of conception and a correctness of execution alike credible to his judgment and to his taste."

Shylock's revenge dominated Cooke's performance, as vividly described by the *Times* (27 November 1800): "His savage and inexorable hate against Anthonio [sic], is ever in his thoughts, accompanies him in all his actions, bargains and thrifts. The love of gain itself is outweighed by this consideration and even in his utmost misery, abandoned by his own flesh and blood, and robbed of his treasure, the hope of revenge, proves a sweet and certain consolation."

Despite comments to the contrary, such as those in the *Post*, Cooke was not without moments of "softer emotion." A note appended to "I am a Jew. Hath not a Jew eyes," etc., in a *Merchant of Venice* promptbook at the Folger, states: "Cooke, when he came to the word 'affections,' so informed it with human feeling, so contrasted it with the context, that it remains as the marked point of his performance."[3] Later critics certainly recognized this quality. *The Comet* (4 January 1812), first acknowledging the "smooth usurious villainy, and diabolical spirit of revenge" in his performance, added that among his greatest scenes was the one with Tubal, where the conflict of passions arising from the loss of his daughter and the prospect of revenge on Antonio, "almost overpowered his corporeal faculties," and that in the trial scene he demonstrated pathos and claimed "a large share of sympathy."

It was only natural that Cooke be compared to Macklin, the greatest Shylock of the previous century. The *Porcupine* (13 November) felt Cooke "came as near to Shakespeare as any of his predecessors, if we except Macklin, to whose manner he bears the strongest resemblance." Once more the reviewer for *The Monthly Mirror* came the closest to capturing the overall quality of the performance, while also comparing Cooke to his famous predecessor:

In voice, feature, and external appearance altogether, he was perfectly the Jew of Shakespeare. His general cast of expression conveyed that deep, heart-rooted, diabolical malignity which the poet intended. His caution, cunning, servility, and moroseness were strictly in character; and in the great scene of the third act, he was hailed with shouts of applause:—the break was exquisite—"*Let him look to his bond.*" The gloomy satisfaction that seemed to accompany the recollection of the deed by which he had Antonio "on the hip," and the savage exultation of his *laugh*, when the full amount of his enemy's losses is stated, were frightfully impressive. The transitions were made in a masterly manner, and the speech in which Shylock urges his own wrongs, and vindicates his tribe, formed a climax of as well-wrought passion as can be conceived. The amateur will not soon forget his stifled emotion at the word *"Passions"*—and other fortunate discriminations, which gave value and originality to this part of his performance of Shylock.

In the *Trial Scene*, the "lodg'd hate" of the impenetrable Israelite was observable throughout. And here, likewise, there were some striking novelties which surprised and delighted us: for instance, the abrupt reply to Portia's request that she would let him *tear the bond*—"When it is *paid* according to the tenour;' indicating a degree of apprehension lest she *should* tear it, and, at the same time, a malignant recognition of the penalty due:—the earnestness of his enquiry "Is it so nominated in the bond?" and his triumphant *chuckle*, when he returned it to Portia, "I cannot find it—'tis not in the bond:"—the division in this passage "I take this offer then; pay the bond—thrice:"—and the eagerness with which he adds the last word, lest he should be excluded the benefit of the offer that had been made him—in fact, the whole of this scene was inimitable, and his last look and groan, on retiring from the court, expressed despair, hate, and disappointed malice.[4]

By the second week of his appearances, Cooke had become the established favorite. By midmonth, the press was reporting that "The excellence of Cooke becomes everyday more attractive" and that "his talents have made such an impression upon the public, that a profound attention is paid to every thing he says and he is exposed to no interruption but what arises from the applause which his merit excites."[5]

Although the public had been told that Cooke's talents were not entirely confined to tragedy and that since the death of Macklin, no actor was said to "be so truly excellent" in the characters of Sir Pertinax MacSycophant and Sir Archy MacSarcasm, they were not prepared for an actor who would also excel in comedy, especially after his Richard and Shylock.[6] So on 13 November, his reputation was increased when, as Sir Archy, he first displayed this virtuosity in comedy before a London audience. *Love-a-la-Mode* followed his Shylock, a pattern Macklin had established and one Cooke would return to throughout his career.

Macklin's farce, a kind of comedy of humours, introduces representatives of various races—MacSarcasm (a Scotsman), Squire Groom (an Englishman), Sir Callaghan O'Brallaghan (an Irishman, the hero), and Mordecai (a Jew). All are suitors for the hand of Charlotte, the ward of Sir Theodore Goodchild;

the Irishman finally succeeds in winning her. This had been Macklin's favorite play, and although he had originally intended to play Sir Callaghan, he took on Sir Archy instead. While slight in plot, the play offered numerous actors opportunities for unique characterizations and business, and, indeed, a number of actors had made their reputations in the play. John Moody as Sir Callaghan moved on to many other Irish roles; Thomas King found the role of Squire Groom perfect for his talent of comic characterization; Macklin himself played Sir Archy for many years.[7] Ironically, Macklin had a strong hatred for the Scots, and even his most faithful admirers admitted that his accent was often incorrect.[8] For this reason, if no other, Cooke was considered a superior Sir Archy to Macklin, and on Cooke's death the role virtually disappeared.

The brief comments on afterpieces in the daily press at this time tell us little about Cooke's Sir Archy. It is clear, however, that his impersonation was unique. His broad Scotch brogue was sustained throughout, and many, on the basis of his performance of Sir Archy, and of Sir Pertinax next season, concluded that Cooke had to be Scottish! The role was perfect for him, with "its oily smoothness and craft" visible in every tone, look, and action of the "heartless hypocrite and time-serving politician."[9] The most revealing remarks as regards his inherent ability in the role were made by Thomas Dutton, editor of *The Dramatic Censor; or Weekly Theatrical Report*. Although frequently a champion of Kemble and often critical of Cooke, he acknowledged Cooke's excellence in Macklin's invention:

... in the *gayer* scenes of comedy Mr. Cooke leaves his competitors at a hopeless and immeasurable distance. His very features seem expressly formed by Nature to excel in the *sarcastic*—a line in which he appears to us to stand without a single rival. ... In [*Love-a-la-Mode*] every look, every varied inflexion of feature, every motion, constituted an illustration of the part ... nor has Macklin more successfully depicted the vain, sarcastic, supercilious, overbearing, yet mean, cringing, abject, and fawning Scotchman, with his pen, than Mr. Cooke did by his matchless style of acting.[10]

William Robson remembered that "The dry, sarcastic mirth, the perfect concentration of self-good opinion, the inward triumphant chuckle, and sneering *Scotch* laugh of Cooke, were beyond belief fine!" He also described how "The twirl with his finger and thumb, with which he put Beau Mordecai forth with 'Walk aboot, and shew y're shapes, mon,' was just as if he had been shewing out the tricks of a dancing dog or a monkey."[11] This first season Cooke would repeat Sir Archy five more times; subsequently, it would find a permanent place in his repertoire.

On 26 November, "By Command of Their Majesties," Cooke acted Shylock for the first time before the royal family, with receipts totaling £396.14.0. Two days later, the management announced that "In consequence of the many Ladies and Gentlemen who from the great overflow have been disappointed of

Places on those nights when Mr. Cooke has appeared in the Part of RICHARD THE THIRD, he will appear in that character on Monday next, for the 5th time—and the Tragedy will be repeated every succeeding Monday till further notice."[12] According to the accounts, this was indeed the practice, with the exception of five Mondays, until Cooke's last appearance that season on 15 June.[13]

On 28 November, Cooke made his first appearance as Iago opposite the Othello of Alexander Pope, who had first appeared in that role at Covent Garden in 1784 opposite Henderson's Iago, a production that Cooke may well have seen himself.[14] In addition, Mrs. Pope (Maria Campion) appeared as Desdemona, Mrs. Litchfield as Emilia, and Thomas Betterton as Cassio. Cooke was announced to be appearing in the role for the first time, but, of course, had played it in the provinces. Mrs. Litchfield, although she had first appeared at Covent Garden in 1796, rose this season from obscurity to the front ranks.[15]

Iago, another arch-villain in Cooke's hands, was to become one more of his controversial characterizations, although he had no contemporary competitor, especially since Kemble had wisely left the role out of his repertoire. Cooke's old friend Joseph Munden, according to his son, found Cooke's interpretation "an entire misconception of the character. It was the very reverse of 'honest, honest Iago.' His villainy was so apparent that it degraded Othello from a confiding dupe to a credulous dotard." Munden quotes a "gentleman of great experience in theatricals" who on leaving the pit, said "If Cooke be right, Henderson must have been sadly mistaken."[16] Others, however, immediately tagged Cooke as Henderson's successor. On 4 December, the *Times* stated that his Iago seemed the most effortless of his roles to date, studied in the meaning of the author and evincing superior judgment in his byplay. While comparing him to Henderson, the reviewer noted that he was also innovative, especially in his scene with Roderigo and the following soliloquy (I, 1), the exchanges with Desdemona and Othello in Act II, the drunken scene with Cassio (II, 2), and the "silent but expressive last scene of Iago's," which Cooke's promptbook indicates contains one of his planned "starts" immediately after Emilia's "He begg'd of me to steal it."[17] Dunlap describes the excellence of Cooke's planned byplay at the end of Act III, Scene 1, which he terms "his mode of anticipating, extending and improving the conception of the author." Iago, kneeling, has sworn "to obey shall be in me remorse, What bloody work soe'er." He rises and Othello says "Within these three days let me hear thee say, That Cassio's not alive." Cooke would start, "and the spectator might plainly read in his expressive face, 'What murder my friend, and companion?'" (In his promptbook, Cooke wrote "Iago expresses regret—thinks of his oath," but he included none of the business.) He then covered his face with his hands and then, gradually lifting his head, withdrew his hands with eyes and face turned upward. At this point he would start again, as if remembering the oath he had just taken and, after a second mental struggle, said, as if submitting to necessity and the obligation imposed on him by his oath—"My friend is dead."[18]

In the soliloquies, the *Times* (29 November 1800) suggested "infusing... somewhat more of animation and energy," but added on 12 December that "Even when silent, he does not suffer a look, a gesture, a word, to lose its correspondent effect on his mind, and the meanest of the *Dramatis Personae*, when concerned in the same scene, becomes, for the moment, as instrumental with him as the highest, in promoting the grand object of the Poet." On 9 March, the *Herald* called Cooke the first successful Iago of late and quoted the playwright Richard Cumberland as having said that he had "witnessed three perfect pieces of acting and only three. Garrick in Lear, Henderson as Falstaff, and Cooke in Iago and of the three he . . . gave the preference to the last."

Apparently, Cooke's villainy as Iago had more nuance than his Richard. The *True Briton* on 29 November singled out his management of Roderigo as displaying a "lighter kind of artifice, that was well distinguished from the deeper villainy with which he entrapped the generous moor, and in the two scenes in which he gradually excites the jealousy of the latter his performance exhibited all the art of a master; without any such elaborate display of his subtlety as we have hitherto seen, and such as, in Iago's own words, seemed to say 'take note oh! World how cunning I am!—' " In other words, there was in the performance a "smooth plausibility" while he was consistently "firm, manly, determined, easy, spirited, and natural." A similar estimation appeared in the *Morning Chronicle* on 4 December 1800: "he portrayed with great skill and dexterity the artful, cunning malignity of Iago. He did it with ease and without grimace." The *Morning Post*, in a lengthy retrospect of Cooke's characters, continued its attack on him, urging that he should be more aware of his predecessors and finding the performance the most unequal of his parts. While the same review (24 January 1801) admitted that Iago was suited to his style, it condemned his lack of "gracefulness of deportment" and seemed to abhor the thought of innovation in Iago's characterization.

For the first time, a reviewer commented on a characteristic of Cooke's delivery, as noted in his Iago, other than harshness. Dutton, in a summary of Cooke's appearances as of December, did discuss the harshness of Cooke's voice, which on occasion was "even grating." Although he considered such a quality "inharmonious," he felt the "defect" was heightened by a tendency Cooke had of "*chopping his words* . . . a kind of te—tum—te—ti enunciation." As an example, Dutton singled out Iago's soliloquy where he proposed to poison the Moor's mind against Desdemona. "Cooke gives the passage thus, with a continual break, or pause, at every second syllable, setting out with a kind of half-foot; e.g.

'Tri—fles light—as air—
'Are to—the jea—lous con—firma—tion strong, &c.

And this species of accent he falls into almost on every occasion, when he aims at giving particular weight and cogency to his words."[19] Dunlap, in discussing Cooke's study of a role, mentioned his part of Sir Archy in which he carefully "scored the emphatic words, with one, and sometimes two, and three lines, according to their respective value and importance."[20] That Cooke indeed used this method to study his lines is shown by the same underlining technique in a number of his extant promptbooks, particularly the 1800 *Richard III*. Cooke's basic approach, clearly a subjective, romantic one, was still marked by a certain amount of careful study and planning, as was the role preparation of his successor Edmund Kean.[21] His writing out of verse into prose in order to aid him in his preparation is still another indication of Cooke's concern with naturalness and the elimination of a "sing-song" quality so often associated with his great rival, John Philip Kemble. Although a slight diversion from the discussion of his Iago, the first clearly articulated explanation of this vocal technique is nonetheless mentioned in relation to that character.[22]

Two additional commentaries shed more precise light on Cooke's Iago: one written immediately after his first appearance in the role and the other by Charles Durang, who witnessed his performance opposite the Othello of the American actor-manager Thomas Cooper (who is mentioned further in Chapter 14). The *Porcupine* (1 December 1800), not in complete agreement with Cooke's interpretation, offered these observations:

. . . where he sneers at the coxcombs of *Roderigo*, and his declamation of drowning himself, bidding him put money in his purse, he might have been more lively, for a flippancy there would have rendered his subtlety more subtle, and given a more varied colouring to the part. His description of his wife before *Desdemona*, was artfully managed; it is difficult to give it without offense to his General's lady, and was meant to be what he conceded it, half serious and half gay; and his metrical reply to that lady's request of praising her, was most . . . admirably delivered. When he plies *Cassio* with the wine, it is done rather too palpably, and his song discovers him to have no ear for music.

The latter comment is interesting considering the large number of musical roles Cooke played in his apprenticeship. The *Porcupine* next supported Dutton's analysis of Cooke's emphases but termed it "too much deliberation" and said he "weighs his words before he gives them breath." Some lines seemed "rather too studied for common conversation." Although blaming it on the London stage's lack of foresight for not having engaged Cooke there earlier in his career, this critic, one of the few to make this observation, noted that Cooke's appearance "was somewhat old for 'four times seven years' of age."

Durang, first commenting on English criticism of Cooke's Iago, then agreed with Dunlap that his start and look at Othello before "My friend is dead!" "was irresistible." In Philadelphia this "point" would receive three immense bursts of applause, "succeeded by a dread pause, as if the audience was lost in contemplation of its sudden sublimity." He added that Cooke's Iago was a continual reaction of quiet, yet vigorous points—vigours, not from any overcharged acting, but from the unique expression of the passions, so well, so powerfully delineated in the features, and the excellent emphasis in his readings, with his modulation of voice. There was no effort; there seemed no acting; yet the performance was the most elaborate effort of art. It looked like nature—but it was nature directed by the most skillful playing. It was the philosophy of acting.[23]

If we look back at the two commentaries quoted earlier on Cooke's Richard, we find that the same overall impression of effortless art was noted in his Iago. By 1811, his Iago had matured markedly, with greater depth and even less effort.

Macbeth, which was to be performed seven times that season, was first presented on 5 December, with Pope as Macduff, Mrs. Litchfield as Lady Macbeth in her first major vehicle, Edward Townsend as Hecate, and Thomas Hull as Duncan. Macbeth was not one of Cooke's better realized characters. Kemble, with his intellectual approach, had created a standard of excellence in the role which made it difficult for Cooke to surpass. Although Cooke was considered natural in the role, he seems to have made little discrimination between the characters of Richard III, Macbeth, and later, Kitely. His Macbeth, therefore, would be remembered for the brilliance of isolated moments rather than the total conception.[24]

The initial reaction was more mixed than usual. The *Morning Post* (6 December 1800), endorsing tradition and sameness, reported: "He played *Macbeth* with an attention to the scene so incessant and active, that nature was a little overstepped, and he spoke in a tone rather too familiar for the dignity of tragedy. This he did in attempting something uncommon, and we are sorry to see too many actors fall into the same error." While acknowledging the genius of isolated passages, the reviewer added: "In the pathetic passages, those of remorse, Mr. Cooke's voice failed entirely; but in others he was very successful, particularly in resuming his courage on the disappearance of *Banquo's ghost* . . . he often surprises, but he seldom makes his audience feel." In a similar vein, the *Morning Chronicle* (2 October 1802) recognized the hardened villainy of Cooke's Macbeth and further interjected: "He was worn by remorse after the crime had been perpetrated, but we could not perceive any marks of those keen struggles with his nature, which he must have had before he could work himself up to the horrid purpose of murdering his sovereign and his guest. . . . Mr. Cooke does not succeed well in blending together opposite passions and feelings. He is peculiarly unhappy in marking their transitions, and shewing in what manner they mutually triumph over each other." Earlier, the *Morning Chronicle* (6 December 1800) had declared: "Sometimes . . . he misses the effect he intends, by a thoughtless and injudicious repetition of a turn which has succeeded in other pasages." On 15 January 1801, the *Morning Post* again, and more severely, criticized this failing: "*Macbeth* has passions of distinct natures, mingling in the finest manner of composition. The actor knows nothing of that harmony; and, as to the more refined passions, cannot represent them ever in a detached state."

There is mutual agreement that Cooke's best moments occurred from the banquet scene through to the end of the play. The *True Briton* (6 December 1800), for example, felt his address to the physician and the reflection on life after the death of Lady Macbeth were most exquisitely delivered. The *Porcupine* (15 December 1800) once more provided one of the more complete critical appraisals, finding in Cooke's look at Banquo when hailed by Ross as Thane of Cawdor, a glance betraying "all that had passed in the prior scene and his hopes of the future." The critic then described his excellence in the last three acts. Of special note was his delivery of the soliloquy, "way of life fallen into the sear, etc." and his "throw physic to the dogs, I'll none of it," "repeated in the tone of a schoolboy who was nauseated with favour [*sic*] of a dose, rather than the resolution of a warrior determined on battle." The scene following Lady Macbeth's death, however, revealed a new reading, which is described in detail by Dunlap and once more illustrated careful working out of inflection. After hearing "The queen, my lord, is dead!", Cooke said with "suppressed agitation," "She should have died—" and then, after a pause, with a tone lowered almost to a whisper, "—hereafter." A similar technique of shifting tone and feeling was used in the "out, out brief candle" soliloquy. Cooke would say the lines

———it is a tale
Told by an idiot, full of sound and fury,
Signifying———

He would follow the word "Signifying" with a pause. Then his voice would subside and "with a tone of suppressed feeling and heart-breaking disappointment," he would then add "nothing."[25]

Macbeth's death scene was also one of Cooke's better moments, being neither "vulgar nor insufferable." The *Porcupine* said he died in a style as if "nothing in life became him like the leaving it." Hazlitt was to record: "We recollect that Mr. Cooke discovered the great actor in the death-scene in Macbeth, and in that of Richard. He fell like the ruin of state, like a king with his regalia about him!"[26] Cooke utilized Garrick's version of Macbeth, with a few additions from the original, but eliminated the death speech that had been added by Garrick, returning to the original.[27]

Although Cooke's Macbeth was not as successful as his previous roles in either conception or execution, it lost him no ground in the public's estimation of him as an actor of versatility, even though he was considered to have failed in comparison to Kemble. The role remained in his repertoire, but because of Kemble's dominance, it was rarely seen in London.

Ben Jonson's *Everyman in His Humour* (1598) had seen few performances since Garrick's 1751 revival. Cooke's revival became a favorite of London audiences throughout his tenure at Covent Garden. The play was a natural choice for Cooke, as the role of Kitely was dominated by jealousy, an emotion he easily portrayed. The plot, rife with incident and misunderstanding, revolves around the efforts of Young Knowell (Brunton) and Wellbred (Henry Erskine Johnston) to escape or at least contain the displeasure of their father (Charles Murray) and brother-in-law, respectively. The true interest, however, is in the humour characters: Captain Bobadil (John Fawcett), who brags of his brave deeds and military courage but is put down as a coward by Downright (J. Waddy); Kitely, whose jealousy of his wife is cured by a trick played on him by Brainworm (Munden); the stupid Stephen (Knight), on whom everyone plays; Knowell, who is suspicious of his son; and Dame Kitely (Miss Chapman), who is jealous of her husband, and, like him, is cured by Brainworm's trickery.

Cooke, who first performed Kitely in London on 17 December, had seen Garrick's Kitely and, as noted in Chapter 2, had profited from his approach to the role. Cooke also chose to speak William Whitehead's prologue, which Garrick had first used in 1751.[28]

Cooke had prepared himself well for this role, having often performed such parts as Don Felix and Strickland, scions of the same stock, in the provinces. The critics were universally in agreement that Cooke's Kitely was among his best performances, despite a slight hoarseness on the 17th. Cooke would perform Kitely ten times that season, consistently drawing large crowds. The first repeat, on 23 December, topped all receipts for the preceding three weeks, bringing in almost £400. On 14 January, the receipts hit a high of £515.11.6, partially because of the presence of the royal family who were received "with most cordial testimonies of applause."[29]

The initial response to Cooke's Kitely was the antithesis to that he had received as Macbeth. *The Monthly Mirror*'s account was typical: "The jealousy of *Kitely* sits admirably upon Mr. Cooke, who, in his interview with Cash [his confidential servant played by Charles Farley], exhibited some masterly acting; and his affected ease in subsequent scenes with his wife, when she taxes him with entertaining the passion that 'gnaws his entrails,' bore the legitimate aspect which honest Ben intended."[30] The major critics all found the interview with Cash in Act III outstanding, especially in its byplay and underplay. Dutton commented that "In depicting the restless starts and sallies of the soul, under the influence of green-eyed monster jealousy, he marked every varied working of the mind, every abrupt transition of passion, with most felicitous accuracy, and energetic glow."[31] Even the *Morning Post* (13 January 1801) had to acknowledge that the scene with Cash "was correct and impassioned" and that "the conflict, the hurry, the change of opinions in *Kitely*, during the debate with himself, were made out in the completest manner." The *Post*, in fact, found little to criticize, noting the excellence of the scene between Cob (Charles Thompson) and Kitely, when the latter is called back to his house with the knowledge that Wellbred and his companions are there; and the effectiveness of Cooke's forced laugh, to recover the slip of "Nor will I more be pointed at, as one/ Disturb'd with jealousy," and the blending of "real anguish and affected gaity" in the exchange with Dame Kitely. Ultimately, the *Post* (18 December 1800) found Cooke perfectly free from "the lack of uniformity" they had noted in earlier roles, but credited this more to Kitely's "fixed, firm and steady" passion than to Cooke's acting.

In Kitely Cooke continued to show his ability to reflect the mental processes of his character. The *Morning Chronicle* (21 October 1802) wrote: "[Cooke] seemed ever possible to trace the chain of ideas that passed in his mind; and to observe how one emotion generated another; as his passion rose or sunk; as he worked himself up to the belief that he was indeed a *cornuto*, or as falling back into momentary security, he upbraided himself for his groundless apprehensions." It is likewise interesting that during the second season one critic found him chaste and forcible in the role, but without unnatural starts and gestures, "no distortions of the countenance, no strained vociferation." Apparently, this role came easier for Cooke than Iago or Macbeth. The *Times* (18 December 1800), for example, stated that "The skill and feeling with which he depicted the various transitions of jealousy in its less turbid and destructive state, than that which the muses of a Shakespeare and a [Edward] Young have rendered so terrific and lamentable in the Tragedies of *Othello* and Zanga [*The Revenge*], were productive of the happiest effect." (Cooke would perform Zanga in 1802.)

One last comment from a later issue of the *Morning Chronicle* (18 October 1804) is appropriate because of its succinct appraisal of Cooke's mimicry and total involvement with Kitely:

He ... gives a comic representation of it, and induces us not to pity the citizen, but to laugh at him. He seems ... to labour under the most violent paroxisms of the passion, and to be overwhelmed with conviction as strongly, upon hearing of the assignation at Cobb's, as "the deluded Moor when he is shewn the fatal handkerchief by *Iago*. Indeed every line in his countenance and every muscle of his body indicates [sic] the varying sensations of his mind, and from his sudden sallies and intervening calms, one deaf might tell whether at any particular moment he believed himself cornuted or not, and to what degree he feels apprehension or security.

For the next month Cooke continued to perform his now established roles, until on 27 January 1801 he took his first London benefit.[32] Although most benefits that season were given in March, April, and May, Cooke, as a reward for his resounding successes, had his benefit advanced to a very early date. As a rule, the earlier the benefit the better, and this gesture on Harris's part was quite exceptional.[33] In addition, Cooke was given the benefit free of the normal £160 house charges.[34] Cooke states that the amount taken in was £560, while the account books indicate the total receipts were £532.[35] This still amounted to at least £100 over the other benefits that season and proved to be one of the most crowded houses ever seen at Covent Garden, "the lobbies . . . filled with persons who could not procure seats" and "the house . . . thronged in every part, and vast numbers returned from the doors, who in vain sought admittance into the theatre."[36]

Harris showed a great deal of wisdom in treating Cooke with such consideration; besides, he could afford it. The season, largely because of Cooke, had been a decided financial success for management—so much so, apparently, that later that year Harris was able to buy land adjoining his house at Uxbridge out of the season's profits and to name a portion of it "Cooke's Field!"[37]

Cooke planned his bill for novelty, beginning with *The Stranger*, one of Kemble's strongest roles and one in which Cooke had excelled in Dublin, followed by a recitation of Garrick's "Ode on Shakespeare" with music by Arne and then *Catherine and Petruchio*. The large attendance attests to his popularity that season.

The choice for a mainpiece was a rather unusual one for Cooke, especially since Kotzebue's play in Thompson's 1798 translation had provided Kemble with a role that was peculiarly correct for his style and was considered a great personal vehicle for him.[38] The play, although one of Kotzebue's best, is today all but forgotten. In the nineteenth century, however, this domestic problem drama, as Nicoll terms it, seemed to treat the theme of the sinning wife with a good deal of strength.[39] So Cooke, perhaps because of the rivalry and his earlier success in the part, took the gloomy title role opposite the Mrs. Haller of Mrs. Litchfield.[40]

The critical reactions were clear. There were qualities in the role that seemed to fit Cooke's propensities, but the part was primarily one of pensive grief and misanthropic moroseness that grows out of a character naturally benevolent, an emotional state difficult for Cooke to portray convincingly. The hardness and sourness that have grown from unmerited suffering and disappointment Cooke might have expected to handle effectively. The *Morning Post* (30 January 1801) seemed to relish pointing out that this choice must once and for all convince skeptics that this actor "ascribes to himself attainments he has not reached." The reviewer concluded, however, with the admission that Cooke was received with great and general applause. The *Morning Chronicle*, less biased than the *Post*, wrote on 28 January 1801 that "he was frequently not destitute of tenderness in his tones, though they are naturally harsh, and the expression of his countenance was more than usually animated and interesting," but then observed: "But viewing his acting on the whole, we do not think that his character is one calculated to display him to peculiar advantage. . . . often too violent in the expression of his feelings, and [we] discovered an abruptness in his manner which nothing in the character seemed to require." Furthermore, he tended to show bursts of anger and rage rather than "the settled gloom of resentment softened by an interval of time." In the final scene,

Cooke simply could not reflect a state of mind once resentful but now subdued by love and compassion.

Kemble, perhaps to demonstrate his superiority in the role, performed the Stranger at Drury Lane opposite Mrs. Siddons' Mrs. Haller on 10 February. Cooke had appeared in the role on 31 January, but wisely dropped it for the remainder of the season and appeared in it only rarely throughout the remainder of his career.

Comparisons of Cooke and Kemble would have been expected this season, but, few appeared in any detail before Cooke's appearance in *The Stranger*. After his first appearance in this role, Dutton pointed out that Kemble's saturnine cast of features, his haggard visage, and his deep, supulchral tones gave him a decided physical advantage. Furthermore, the role required an evenness of action which Cooke did not possess, being "unrestricted by the trammels of mechanical discipline."[41] Following the performance on 31 January, Dutton expanded on this latter point, and, although written tongue in cheek, his commentary reveals a great deal about both actors. Dutton still believed Kemble superior in the role and explained why Cooke failed:

... because his habits, his manners, his disposition, and his whole train of thought and action are not so totally absorbed in *self*, as to render him as adequate and perfect a representation of a *misanthrope*.... He fails because he has *passions*! because he is not *constitutionally frigid* ! because he is not obliged to outrage decency by offering violence, by the way of *apology* for his *want* of powers, to a helpless female!... because he does not *croak* ! because he is not the Knight of the Rueful countenance!... He fails, because he can *feel* !—because he is not *insensible to love*! because his *blood runs riot* ! because he is not *deadened to enjoyment* ! because he is *not a Jesuit* ! because our common mother has dealt *honestly with him* !—... he fails, in short, because he is *not* Kemble! Happy discomfiture! enviable, if there be ought to envy in humanity—enviable miscarriage![42]

Even though Dutton was doubtlessly carried away by his own cleverness here, his description does pinpoint much of the difference between Cooke's and Kemble's styles—and suggests a change of allegiance on Dutton's part.

All reviewers in 1800–1801 generally agreed that Cooke and Kemble were both at the head of their profession, and thus many felt that close measurement was senseless, especially with styles so disparate. This notion, sensible at the time, is regrettable in the light of historical perspective. The problem is alleviated somewhat after 1803 when the two appeared together at Covent Garden. One critic, wise enough not to weigh one against the other, recognized that a character such as Richard III could be approached by "very opposite powers" and still be correct. For example, Kemble was "a better dissembler; more pliant, majestic, and graceful, in action and expression," while Cooke was "more crafty, bitter, ferocious, and energetic." They were both Richard, but "The merits of each teach us the defects of the other, and tend to convince us that they are both far short of perfect representatives of *Richard*."[43]

Completely objective comparisons are nonexistent. Approaching objectivity, however, is an essay published in English translation in 1807 by Christian August Gottlieb Goede, a Leipzig jurist, who wrote on travels in Scotland, Ireland, Wales, and England during 1802 and 1803.[44] Other German visitors to England, including Heine as late as 1826, considered Goede to be one of the more objective German language guides to England.[45] As such, Goede's descriptions of Kemble and Cooke are useful and generally reliable:

> The countenance of Kemble is the noblest and most refined; but the muscles are not so much at command as Cooke's are, who is also a first-rate comedian; but Kemble almost wholly rejects the comic muse. Both are most excellent in the gradual changes of the countenance; in which the inward emotions of the soul are depicted and interwoven as they flow from the mind. In this excellence, I cannot compare any German actors, whom I have seen, with them unless it be Issland and Christ; among French tragedians, even Talma and Lafond are far inferior to them.[46]

Later, Goede described them physically:

> Kemble has a very graceful manly figure, is perfectly well made, and his naturally commanding stature appears extemely dignified in every picturesque position, which he studies most assiduously. His face is one of the noblest I ever saw on any stage, being a fine oval, exhibiting a handsome Roman nose, a well-formed and closed mouth; his fiery and somewhat romantic eyes retreat as it were, and are shadowed by bushy eyebrows; his front is open and little vaulted; his chin prominent and rather pointed; and his features so softly interwoven, that no deeply-marked line is perceptible. His physiognomy, indeed, commands at first sight; since it denotes, in the most expressive manner, a man of refined sentiment, enlightened mind and correct judgment. Without the romantic look in his eyes, the face of Kemble would be that of a well-bred, cold, and selfish man of the world; but this look, from which an ardent fancy emanates, softens the point of the chin and the closeness of the mouth. His voice is pleasing, but feeble; of small compass, but extreme depth. This is, as has been previously observed, the greatest natural impediment with which he, to whom nature has been thus bountiful, has still to contend.

On the other hand

> Cooke does not possess the elegant figure of Kemble; but his countenance beams with great expression. The most prominent features in the physiognomy of Cooke are a long and somewhat hooked nose, a pair of fiery and expressive eyes, a lofty and somewhat broad front, and the lines of his muscles which move the lips are pointedly marked. His countenance is certainly not so dignified as that of Kemble, but it discovers greater passion; and few actors are, perhaps, capable of delineating, in more glowing colours, the storm of a violent passion than Cooke. His voice is powerful, and of great compass; a preeminence which he possesses over Kemble, of which he skilfully avails himself. His exterior movements are, by far, inferior in the picturesque to those of Kemble.

The artist Joseph Farington recorded in his diary, 26 April 1802, a similar comparison speculating as well on the reason for Cooke's initial success:

"[Kemble] ... has established a formal and studied manner of acting which was becoming pretty general, and the public mind was accommodated to it.—The 'rough nature' of Cooke is diametrically opposite of it and has had great affect [*sic*], and shewn the other mode to be too systematic."[47]

Unfortunately, the remaining contemporary comparisons of the two are decidedly biased. William Robson, for example, an avowed champion of Kemble, recognized Cooke's energy and genius which placed him "at least upon an equality with Kemble in Shylock, Richard, Sir Giles Overreach, Kitely, King John, Glenalvon, and all other characters whose villainy was meant to create disgust, but in the noble walk, where pity was to be stirred, deep grief was to soften, elegance to charm, or lofty bearing to impose, then Cooke was very, very far below Kemble."[48]

Isolated comments of value, of course, appear in biased reports, such as Thomas Holcroft's well-known observation that Kemble "contends that blank verse demands a recitation peculiar to itself," while Cooke "has a proud honour of being nearly free from this sing-song defect."[49] Most, however, fall into the class of Boaden's even more slanted attack on the biased comparisons of the time. As a result, these prove almost useless, including Boaden's.

Boaden's claim that there existed "a sizeable shelf of pamphlets, full of falsehood," comparing their Richards is a gross exaggeration.[50] Two that were written, however, are interesting as historical documents. A copy of *Remarks on the Character of Richard the Third; As Played by Cooke and Kemble* (London, 1801) at the Folger Shakespeare Library contains a few marginal notes by Kemble, which prove, if nothing else, that the author who claimed to know neither actor was probably acquainted with both. The objectivity claimed by the anonymous author must be approached with caution; clearly, he has a bias for Cooke. The other pamphlet, lacking detail and credible argument, is entitled *Kemble and Cooke; or, Critical Review of a Pamphlet Published Under the Title Remarks*, etc. (London, 1801). In the following discussion, the first pamphlet is referred to as *Remarks*, the second *Review*, and Kemble's marginal notes, *Kemble*.

Toward the conclusion of the fifty-five page *Remarks*, the writer says: "I lament that Mr. Kemble should appear to envy Mr. Cooke the fame his Richard has acquired him" (p. 47). To this *Kemble* has replied: "When was Mr. Kemble such a Fool? Was Mr. Kemble's politeness in not acting this play any more last year after Mr. Cooke came to London a proof of it?" Kemble, however, would not stick to this resolve in the fall of 1801. *Review*, with less good sense, is concerned that *Remarks* might cause Cooke to "yield to indifference" and "Kemble to suspend his efforts to please" (p. 17). Clearly, in this instance at least, Kemble finally realized, as Cooke did with *The Stranger*, that to yield was the better part of valor. Overall, the arguments in *Remarks* seem to have greater validity than those of his attacker. What both articles actually do, perhaps unconsciously, is to illustrate with totally different examples, each with possible validity, their acting; although *Review* uses few exact cases in defending Kemble. Moreover, *Remarks* is more adept with comparisons. For example, in praising Cooke's soliloquies, he says, "You seem... to be listening to a man who is unconscious that you overhear him"—a statement clearly supported by numerous sources previously cited. Kemble, on the other hand, talked to the Pit—"harangues to the house" (pp. 18–19). In the wooing scene, Cooke's "wheedling flattery" was such as may be imagined "possible to succeed in so bold an undertaking." Kemble on the other hand used all "trembling tenderness of studied passion" (p. 22). With Buckingham, Cooke took interest in his information, showed rising anxiety with accompanying gestures, and rapidly exclaimed: "And did they so?" on Buckingham telling him that he urged the citizens to cry, "Long live King Richard!" "Kemble played it stoically" (p. 23). In Act IV, Cooke plays Richard as though he has changed and drops his jocoseness (a point in interpretation that *Kemble* challenges). "Care and distrust" are both seen in Cooke but not in Kemble. Cooke's manner is commanding and fretful, and he carries through these miseries for the last two acts (pp. 23–24). In the scene with Stanley, Cooke's new interpretation "is not merely a novel peculiarity of manner, but justness of feeling now breaking forth into the display of true delineation." The phrase "As you guess?" was delivered by Cooke as a retort "that shews the spectator the extent of Richard's suspicions;" with Kemble it was a mere interrogation (p. 33). Like other reviewers cited in Chapter 8, *Remarks* found the reading of "Why—after be it then" a moment of suspense, Cooke's face expressing irresolution until the lips move, halted by more deliberation, and then at last the words. Although not challenging Kemble's interpretation, he says Kemble "utters with unhesitating rapidity the reprieve of the hostage."

Review chooses to attack *Remarks* by quoting a series of previous newspaper reviews and couches his rebuttal in phrases such as *Remarks* "has not allowed him to betray one solitary defect" (p. 12) and compares Cooke, based on *Remarks'* praise, to Solomon.

Indeed, it is difficult to fault *Remarks* based on *Review*'s feeble counterattack. Stooping to criticism of the writing, punctuation, and style of *Remarks*, *Review* does little to defend or even characterize Kemble's Richard III. On only one point does *Review* overtly criticize Cooke. He calls Cooke's death "too flimsy" and adds that "his stops were so numerous and injudiciously placed, that the chain of sense and beauty was scarcely preserved intire [sic]— that the major and minor emphasis were so confounded as to leave the picture ... very deficient in that high teint [sic] of colouring, which alone can convey an appropriate idea to the minds of the audience ..." (pp. 45–46). The inference is that Kemble's approach is the reverse of this. It is unfortunate that the rebuttal is not of a more descriptive, literate, and thorough nature. Nevertheless, its feebleness does give more validity to the commentary in *Remarks*.

Dunlap quotes Cooke's journal as saying "I was prevented acting for any of the benefits, Mr. Lewis expected."[51] Apparently, rather than waste Cooke's attraction on benefits, the management reserved the right to utilize the novelty of his talents on nonbenefit nights. So, from March until 15 June, Cooke appeared only two to four times a week."[52]

Fortunately, "Gentleman" W. T. Lewis's benefit gave Cooke a chance to add another important role to his London repertoire: Sir Giles Overreach in Massinger's *A New Way to Pay Old Debts*. Lewis, who had been at Covent Garden since 1773 and had served as acting manager for over thirteen years, was well liked by the Covent Garden company, and his diligence and hard work were respected by all. Cooke remembered him as "the model for making everyone do his duty by kindness and good treatment."[53] His reputation as a comedian in harebrained comic roles was well established. Lewis was well suited to comedy, with a staccato utterance, restless gesticulation, and a light voice. Cooke was indeed fortunate that Lewis chose to revive this vehicle in order to introduce him as Sir Giles, for it was to become one of his strongest and most popular roles, although Cooke often felt that it deserved more exposure than it was given.[54]

Alexander Pope had attempted Sir Giles for a benefit in 1796 at Covent Garden, but it was not until Cooke's appearance that the role became a permanent part of a major actor's repertoire. It is true that Kemble had tried the part at Drury Lane, first in 1783, but after 1788 he did not appear in it again until after Cooke's departure for the United States. Even this proved to be a strategic mistake for Kemble, for his new competitor and Cooke's rightful successor, Edmund Kean, soon proved that he was the superior Sir Giles and Kemble did not play the role again.[55]

Massinger's comedy provided a role "exactly suited to the particular cast of [Cooke's] powers."[56] The *Morning Chronicle* of 9 April 1801 typifies the reaction: "It combines in its form nothing of tenderness; but is a mixture of haughtiness, malignity and contempt; these different emotions the actor seemed ably to feel, and forcibly to express." Sir Giles is an avaricious scoundrel who, in order to obtain more money, confiscates the property of his nephew Frank Wellborn (Lewis), and plans to have his daughter Margaret (Miss Murray) marry, against her wishes, the wealthy Lord Lovell (Murray). Margaret, however, loves Tom (Johnston), the stepson of Lady Allworth (Miss Chapman), who offers to aid the lovers. She consequently pretends to be in love with Frank who, on the basis of this match, obtains money from his uncle. Margaret then elopes with Tom, Lord Lovell marries Lady Allworth, and Sir Giles, from rage and despair, loses his mind.

Genest suggests that the actors all appeared in their roles for the first time, although this seems unlikely.[57] Cooke certainly had appeared as Sir Giles in the provinces.

The Dramatic Censor announced that Cooke had added another wreath to his laurels in a role that called for energetic action and uncommon force. Cooke was alternately arrogant and servile, haughty to his inferiors and fawning to those equal or superior. Dutton was even inspired to pen:

> As Overreach Cooke claims to merit lays
> Justly deserving of our utmost praise;
> Here thund'ring plaudits his bright efforts crown'd,
> And Fame's loud trump his excellence may sound.[58]

The *True Briton*, following his second appearance in the role on 8 April 1801 reported that Cooke "gave a specious colouring to the whole which rendered it characteristic and consistent. He was much and deservedly applauded throughout."

Sir Walter Scott, who possibly first saw Cooke as Sir Giles in Edinburgh during July 1801, also witnessed Kemble's attempt at the role, and, although a personal friend of Kemble, he wrote in an 1813 letter:

> he came not within a hundred miles of Cooke, whose terrible visage, and short, abrupt and savage utterance, gave a reality almost to that extraordinary scene in which he boasts of his own successful villany [*sic*] to a nobleman of worth and honour, of whose alliance he is ambitious. Cooke contrived somehow to impress upon the audience the idea of such a monster of enormity as had learned to pique himself even upon his own atrocious character. But Kemble was too handsome, too plausible, and too smooth, to admit its being probable that he should be blind to the unfavorable impression which these extraordinary vaunts are likely to make on the person whom he is anxious to conciliate.[59]

An unidentified critique in the Harvard Collection indicates that at least one reviewer found too much of Richard and Iago in Cooke's Sir Giles. Most, however, seem to have agreed with Scott. One reviewer, apparently writing after Cooke had begun a performance hoarse, pointed first to the strong passions, unprincipled ambition, and dark and daring designs of Sir Giles that Cooke handled in a masterly manner. He then added that although Cooke

> had to exert himself to make his voice audible, the spirit of the character animated him to such a degree, that the defect was scarcely noticed; at the conclusion, the little that remained of it seemed to be the natural effect of the frantic energy and unbroken resolution with which the bold and haughty mind of *Sir Giles* beholds all its projects dissipated, and its fondest designs reversed.[60]

Cooke's last performance anywhere was as Sir Giles, in Providence, Rhode Island (see Chapter 14). Apparently, the American audiences were apprehensive about the malignancy of the horrible villain, and it was not a strong draw during his U.S. tour.[61] Dunlap wrote:

> The character of Sir Giles shocks by his atrocity, and even his punishment, though we rejoice in it, strikes us with horror. The acting of Mr. Cooke at this terrible point, can never be forgotten. His attempt to draw his sword, and the sudden arrest of his arm, palsied and stiffened, and rendered powerless, as if by the stroke of Heaven's avenging thunder—the expression of his countenance at this moment, and his sinking convulsed,

and then lifeless, into the arms of his servants, were so frightfully impressive, and true to nature, as to leave an image never to be erased.[62]

Perhaps it is true that the American audience found Cooke too natural. The following incident seems to support such a claim.

One of the most honoured citizens of the town [Providence] was Thomas Lloyd Halsey, a man of large fortune, of irascible temperament, and great fondness for theatrical entertainments.... On the night when Cooke was playing *Sir Giles Overreach*—at that point where he is overwhelmed by the production of the forged parchment—Mr. Halsey became so excited that he involuntarily arose from his seat, and ejaculated in the presence of a crowded audience, "Throttle the damned infamous villain!" to the amazement and horror of the whole assembly.

This outburst of such an impulsive person as Mr. Halsey is to be regarded as strong testimony to the genius of the matchless Cooke, whose personations of the malignant passions have never been equalled.[63]

There is no doubt, however, that some of the American reviewers considered Cooke's Sir Giles of special merit. The *New England Palladium* (28 January 1812), in a typical commentary, wrote: "The character is peculiarly adapted to Mr. Cooke's talents, and the chaplets which Fame has awarded to him in London have not withered in Boston. No actor who ever trod the American boards, in this character, has any pretensions of rivalry with Mr. Cooke in this piece."

Cooke repeated Sir Giles five times that first spring in London.[64] Toward the end of the season receipts began to drop off, and Lewis's benefit took in only £320. The remaining performances of *New Way* averaged about £200. On 7 May, it brought in £185, whereas *Richard III* four nights later, Cooke's twentieth appearance in the role, was still bringing in an unusually large receipt, £290, well above other attractions about the same time.

Cooke's first season at Covent Garden ended as it had begun with *Richard III*, on Monday, 15 June 1801. "The numerous and brilliant audience which attended his performance afforded, an incontestible proof, that his powers of attraction still operate in full and undiminished force."[65] In all, Cooke had given sixty-seven performances.[66] Cooke would never duplicate this season in terms of adding new, popular roles, for with the addition of Stukely and Sir Pertinax MacSycophant, his great roles were well established by the end of this first season, with the obvious exception of the Stranger. He would gain some reputation with Falstaff, Pierre in *Venice Preserv'd*, Peregrine in the younger Colman's *John Bull*, and Glenalvon in *Douglas*, but his reputation in London, America, and the provinces would rest with this small handful of roles. It was already clear that his audiences would continue to expect to see him in roles of hypocrisy, jealousy, and villainy in its various forms, both comic and tragic.

Evidently, Cooke managed to control his drinking during this auspicious first season. He had begun the season with a lingering cold and once, just prior to his benefit, had found it necessary to defer an appearance when announced for

Macbeth on 22 January due to "Indisposition."[67] I have found no adverse reaction to this event. Likewise, only one other indication of negligence on Cooke's part has been located, in *Walker's Hibernian Magazine* for June 1801. Apparently, his actions on 1 June while performing Richard made a greater impression on the Irish correspondent, which indeed it might after his past actions in Dublin. The London press, as far as I can tell, took no note of this. *Walker's* reported that on that night Cooke spoke in a low tone and the audience requested him to speak louder. "At length his temper was soured, and he forgot himself so far as to shew something like contempt toward the quarter from which disapprobation issued; and, after pausing a few moments, he abruptly left the stage near the close of the fourth act, without finishing his speech." Cooke returned to complete the play, and "he went through the rest of the character without interruption."[68]

The events of the *Hibernian* account possibly followed a one-night stand in Rochester, Kent, described by Dibdin as preceding his "first *faux-pas* of the many which unfortunately succeeded it." Although this has not been confirmed, the circumstances seem correct since the role mentioned in the account was Richard III, and Dibdin remembered it as Cooke's first or second season. Cooke had agreed to perform for Mrs. Dibdin's benefit without any remuneration, and it was with difficulty that Dibdin convinced Cooke to let him pay for his transportation. "He played, and electrified the audience;—never played better, and never was more collected, which we rejoiced at, because Mr. Harris . . . lent him to us at our peril." The next day Cooke left for London with the Dibdins, had dinner with them, and was put in a coach for the theatre at 5:30. At 6:00 Dibdin and some friends went to the theatre but Cooke had not arrived. "When he *did come*, he was so far *gone*, that I am not certain whether some one else did not finish the part of Richard that night for him." (If this event is correctly placed, he did complete the performance.) Dibdin, who had made sure that Cooke had been "abstemious in the extreme" at his home, was concerned about Harris's reaction. Harris finally did respond: "If Cooke don't get drunk oftener than once a month, the odd lapse will do no harm, for when he is *not* inebriated, the audience will not only give him credit for his excellent acting, but they will applaud him for a negative virtue: 'Only see,' they'll cry, 'how very *sober* he is!' a sort of recommendation which a really praiseworthy actor would never aspire to be entitled to."[69]

Cooke was soon to learn that the London audience, although totally forgiving him on this one isolated occasion and often indulgent in the future, would ultimately prove less than patient with him. *Walker's* warned him "to curb his temper, for without some care in this point, Mr. Cooke *may* raise a prejudice in the public mind, that talents *even great as his* will not be sufficient easily to remove." A warning Cooke was not to heed.

Early in the morning of 16 June, Cooke left for Birmingham to begin a round of provincial guest appearances, a practice common for London actors and one Cooke would follow until leaving England.

This would be Cooke's first engagement at Birmingham, a provincial city second only to Manchester in size and one that had flourished in manufacturing with its numerous warehouses located near canal docks.[70] Cooke would also for the first time encounter William McCready, "an ambitious, ill-tempered, modestly talented Irishman" who, prior to 1794, had been a minor actor at Covent Garden for nearly a decade.[71] In 1795, having given up on success in London, McCready had decided to make his mark in Birmingham and had begun with a summer season on 18 June 1795.[72]

The Birmingham theatre had had a checkered history up to McCready's tenure. The first so-called Theatre Royal (Birmingham did not receive a royal patent until August 1807) had opened in 1774 in New Street, on ground formerly known as "Greenwood's Cherry Orchard," close to the finest private houses in the town. On 18 January 1792, the theatre had been set on fire, probably by incendiaries.[73] On 26 November 1794, the proprietors announced that the theatre on New Street would be completely rebuilt and offered it for rent during the summer of 1795. McCready quickly applied.[74] The new theatre was impressive for a provincial playhouse. The structure included a room for promenades (an assembly room) which provided communication with the boxes and a tavern under the same roof. The new auditorium was 112 feet long with a stage 48 feet deep and 50 feet wide. The proscenium aperture was 38 feet and apparently narrow for the house, so that spaces at the sides were filled in with blank piers. The house was fitted with two rows of boxes and a gallery, the total capacity being 2,000, providing a nightly take of approximately £200. There was also a workroom for machinery provided over the stage area, 19 feet 6 inches wide and 18 feet high. The building was classically elegant on the outside, and the horseshoe-shaped auditorium was decorated with elaborate columns, colored pink, crimson, green, and white. For the benefit of the performers, there were a handsome green room, wardrobe, and dressing rooms.

McCready was a spirited manager, engaging for his season from the middle of June to the end of September the principal performers from both houses in London, thus satisfying the town, which at the turn of the century was a fashionable one, with a core of families not aristocratic but prosperous and of some standing. McCready's standards had been high. Sarah Siddons was a regular visitor, along with Thomas King and W. T. Lewis.[75] It was only natural that he should engage the latest rage of the London stage, George Frederick Cooke.

Cooke was preceded to Birmingham by Mrs. Siddons and her son. They had presented a number of her popular vehicles, including *Jane Shore*. Cooke arrived in time to perform the evening of Wednesday, 17 June, as Richard III, supported, according to a playbill in the Birmingham Library, by G. D. Harley as King Henry, Archer as Richmond, McCready as Tressell, Mrs. St. Ledger (her first season there) as Lady Anne, and Miss Fitzgerald as the Duchess of

York. Cooke repeated Richard a number of times, including his benefit on the 29th, receiving £130 that night, according to Dunlap and *The Monthly Mirror*.[76] On Monday, 22 June, he appeared not as Iago but as Othello, the role he had most often played before going to London. Iago was taken by Harley. Desdemona was played by an unnamed young lady appearing for the first time in Birmingham, and thus he agreed to appear opposite her as Othello. Cooke also appeared as Macbeth and Sir Giles. In all, he performed nine nights in Birmingham,[77] "going through my number of nights with good success," he says.[78]

The Birmingham populace, as a result of poor business conditions and the long war with Spain, had not been attending the theatre before Cooke's engagement, despite appearances by John Bannister, Jr., Miss Maria Theresa DeCamp (later Mrs. Charles Kemble), and Mrs. Siddons. Cooke's great popularity, however, "raised the highest expectation," and his performances were well attended.[79]

From Birmingham Cooke went, for the first time, to Edinburgh. The Edinburgh Theatre Royal, the second of that name, had been built in 1769 at the east end of Prince Street in Shakespeare Square.[80] From 1794 to 1800, Cooke's old nemesis, Stephen Kemble, had managed the theatre, but fortunately John Jackson who had managed from 1781 to Kemble's reign, along with Francis Aickin, older brother of James, the Drury Lane actor, returned for a second period of control.[81] Jackson, an actor and author, was the son of a clergyman in the Church of England and was held in high esteem as a scholar and gentleman. There was considerable relief when he purchased the Edinburgh and Glasgow theatres at public auction for £8,020.[82]

In preparation for the summer season, Jackson had enlarged the auditorium and refurbished the interior, as well as giving the scenery a fresh coat of paint and cleaning the wardrobe.[83]

Before Cooke arrived in Scotland, on 4 July, Alicia Daniels, who was singing that summer at Vauxhall in London and as "ci-devant Mrs. Cooke" was apparently prospering apart from Cooke,[84] had her marriage declared null and void after presenting her case at Doctor's Commons before the Right Honourable Sir William Scott.[85] Evidently, Cooke had given her little thought since coming to London, other than his drunken remark to Dibdin in reference to papers relevant to the proceedings and a possible allusion in a letter to a document left in Ireland to be "disposed" of.[86] Cooke did refer to her once in Boston in 1810 as an "infernal ninny," one of the few available recorded estimates of his opinion of Miss Daniels.[87]

Cooke performed sixteen times in Edinburgh, including two appearances each of Shylock, Richard, and Sir Archy.[88] His first Scottish appearance was on 6 July 1801 as Shylock. During the Edinburgh engagement, Cooke appeared with Talbot and Anne Biggs, both from Drury Lane.[89] Included in the cast his first night as Launcelot was a Mr. Anthony Rock, who would figure prominently in Cooke's life in a few years. In general, with the exception of Cooke, Talbot, and Biggs, the company was composed of "the refuse of all the strolling parties in the kingdom."[90] And Miss Biggs, who was not cast in her usual line, should not have been hired. On the 9th Cooke was Iago to Talbot's Othello, and then on the 13th he played Othello to Wood's Iago.[91] Of the roles seen in Edinburgh, Iago, Sir Giles, and Sir Archy were particularly admired, but Cooke as Othello gave the Edinburgh reviewer for *The Monthly Mirror* a rare chance to comment on a part not previously criticized in the London press and one which would soon virtually vanish from his repertoire. Cooke seemed "to acquire grace from the eastern dress," wrote the critic, and was admirably suited to the "sarcastic manner" of Othello's ironical treatment of Desdemona in the presence of the ambassador from Venice. Equally successful were all the scenes in which the workings of his mind "are displayed in his conduct to Desdemona." However, the scene with Iago failed in the violent bursts of despair, as a result of the harshness of his voice. Least effective was the address to the Senate. His "forte certainly is not calm declamation," concluded the *Mirror*.[92]

The only role thought less effective was Penruddock on 16 July, although Cooke's Shylock was not without attack. A letter to the *Caledonian Mercury* on 7 July 1801, criticized Cooke's "perpetual, unvaried grin on his face" which altered with a grimace. However, after appearing in Richard on 8 July, the same correspondent wrote that his role outblazoned his defects in Shylock and that his features were "acute, eyes piercing sharp," and the action was applicable and not redundant. The Edinburgh representative for *The Monthly Mirror*, on the other hand, found his Richard deficient in harmony and softness of voice:

His beauties in the part were almost always blended with faults. The former chiefly prevailed in his soliloquies. Those in the first act, and when planning the destruction of his nephews, were truly excellent. That upon securing the crown had the greatest merit. His transient gleams of remorse, before the interview with Tyrrel, were excellently pourtrayed [sic]. His tent scene, though a powerful piece of acting, is not so impressive as it should be. Upon the whole, his Richard, though a forcible [one], was not a fine representation. It resembled the image of Nebuchadnezzar, described by the prophet Daniel, much iron, much brass, much clay, some silver, and a little gold.[93]

For his benefit performance, given on 20 July, Cooke chose Macbeth and Sir Archy.[94] Neither of the other two visiting London players appeared in his benefit. Cooke, on 21 July, played Jaques and Petruchio in Briggs's benefit performance, and for Talbot's on 22 July he played Hamlet to Talbot's Horatio and Biggs's Ophelia. A Miss Warcup played Lady Macbeth; the *Caledonian Mercury* (23 July 1801) concluded that she "shouldn't be on stage!"

Cooke later wrote in his journal that "The applause I received in Edinburgh was highly flattering." Another correspondent to *The Monthly Mirror*, however, felt that "owing to the bad bargain they had made [Cooke and Biggs], and the parsimonious conduct of the managers, they have gained little by their engagement by empty fame."[95]

From Edinburgh Cooke went to Glasgow for a short engagement and then on to Liverpool, where he was reunited with Samuel Ryley, who had rented the theatre the year before.[96] At Liverpool he found himself in a better company, including Bannister, Charles Murray, Miss Biggs, Miss Murray, and a few old friends from his provincial days, Mr. and Mrs. Mattocks and Mrs. Ward. He began his engagement with Richard III on 10 August, to a house, according to Dunlap, of £240.[97] Shylock followed the next day, with Murray as Antonio and Miss Murray as Portia, then Macbeth on the 12th opposite Mrs. Ward's Lady Macbeth, and the Stranger on the 13th. For Mrs. Mattock's benefit on 14 August, Cooke took an old familiar role, Leon in *Rule a Wife and Have a Wife*. Bannister's benefit on 17 August provided Cooke with Kitely, and for Murray's night two days later he played Earl Osmond in *The Castle Spectre*. On 21 August, he played Jaques, and for his own benefit the next night *Richard III* was repeated, with Talbot, who had also joined the company, reciting Collins' "Ode on the Passions." Cooke's benefit night was not the most popular in Liverpool, drawing only £112, while Bannister took in £214 and Murray £185.[98] *The Monthly Mirror* reported that Knight, Bannister, and Cooke had "reaped both fame and emolument by their performances" in Liverpool and that their appearances were well attended.[99]

Cooke's next summer appointment would be like the return of a conquering hero, for he was scheduled to go to Ward's and Bellamy's Manchester theatre, the scene of his greatest provincial accomplishments.[100] To give his engagement added strength, Mr. and Mrs. Alexander Pope accompanied him to Manchester. The remainder of the company was comprised of leftovers from the preceding season and "a few miserable strollers, apparently swept from neighbouring barns."[101] The Manchester reporter for *The Monthly Mirror* gave a glowing account of his triumphant return: "At length, his 'brows crown'd with victorious wreaths,' came our long expected favourite Cooke, to revisit his Manchester friends; though now a 'bird of passage,' the look and general plaudits which greeted him on his entrance, appeared so many congratulations on his success in a happier clime."[102]

Once more Cooke began with Richard, on Monday, 24 August, followed in succession by Iago (Pope as Othello), Shylock and Sir Archy, Stukely (the Popes as Mr. and Mrs. Beverly), Harmony in *Every One Has His Fault* and Petruchio (*Every Man in His Humour* had been withdrawn due to the weak company), and Octavian in *The Mountaineers*. Cooke did not pause until Sunday and went for five more straight nights, beginning Monday, 31 August, with Hamlet, then Sir Pertinax MacSycophant (the second time in his career?), Mercutio to the Popes' Romeo and Juliet,[103] and Alberto in *Child of Nature*, Iago and Sir Archy to an overflow house, and finally, on 4 September, Macbeth and Collins' "Ode on the Passions" for his benefit. Pope's benefit on 2 September had drawn £92, whereas Cooke brought in £110.[104] One interesting comment was made on his portrayal of Stukely on 27 August: "We are not merely regarding with animation a change of features, but with astonishment are exploring the inmost recesses of the heart." This isolated comment may have encouraged Cooke to add Stukely to his London repertoire the following season.

Cooke lived through eleven strenuous days in Manchester, and, although he must have found great satisfaction in his homecoming, he badly needed a rest. But Stephen Kemble, now in Newcastle, had announced on 5 September that Cooke was expected there for six nights beginning on 7 September.[105] With just enough time to travel from Manchester to Newcastle, Cooke left immediately, arriving in time to appear on Monday, 7 September, as Richard.[106] Until his benefit on 14 September, announced as Stukely plus Sir Archy and Collins' Ode, Cooke performed Shylock, the Stranger, Othello, and Hamlet. He was hailed by the Newcastle audience "with the warmest applause," and all seemed well.[107] His benefit night was well attended; he performed Stukely, and then, in the middle of the ode, he suddenly and unaccountably stopped, and striking his forehead, as if in the act of recollection, he abruptly retired from the stage. After some explanation between the manager and the audience, the intended farce was changed to *The Village Lawyer*.[108] Cooke, ill and exhausted, had retired to his room on Percy Street. Five days later, on 19 September 1801, the *Newcastle Chronicle* carried the following:

Mr. Cooke feels infinite regret that the accidental recurrence of a bleeding from his breast, should have prevented him from fulfilling the whole of his duty on Monday, but more particularly so when he reflects that it prevented him from personally thanking them for their kindness and support which, both now and on former occasions, have left such an impression on his mind that neither time or circumstance can ever efface.

Whatever the cause, true illness or exhaustion, both of which were feasible after such a strenuous summer, or perhaps even another bout with his old habit, Cooke's problems were just beginning. On the other hand, he later remembered this summer as one of the most regular periods of his career: "The summer after my London engagement I play^d 36 nights in 6 weeks & travel'd 2000 miles. I swept the grass this summer."[109] Specifically, as regards his Newcastle engagement and subsequent events, Cooke records in his 1807 journal the following sequence:

I acted here a week and one night, the latter part of the time much disposed. Mr. Stephen Kemble manager. We had a motley group; Mr. K.'s company was at Scarborough, so with himself, one lady, and one gentleman, the remainder were a small undisciplined set in the neighbourhood, engaged for the time. Relying too much upon not being called upon the first night of the opening of Covent Garden Theatre, and a letter of Mr. Lewis being sent to Manchester, and being detained there, I was acting at Newcastle for the last night on the very evening for which I was advertised to open Covent Garden with Richard. (Drury Lane had opened with it the Saturday before.) I did not arrive in London until the fifteenth of October.[110]

If Cooke's difficulties in Newcastle seemed unfortunate, the opening of the London season in 1801 would prove to be the beginning of Cooke's fall from favor in the eyes of the populace. The snowballing set of circumstances outlined in his journal would set the scene for his return to London.

10

Mr. Cooke of Covent Garden

Shortly after Cooke's initial success in London, he received a letter from his old friend Thomas Ward, written from Chester. Ward had warned him:

> The public are your friends;—look to them *alone*; for while you merit their patronage you will ever experience it. Be not, therefore, persuaded into company; that is, tavern company; for there are those, who will, under the mask of friendship, endeavor to obtain your society in such places, or at their houses, knowing the easiness of your temper, (excuse my bluntness, it can only be for your future comfort) to betray you into excess, to undo you with the town. I cannot point out those I allude to—your own judgment must be your tutor—only be aware of what I say.[1]

If Cooke had heeded Ward, his difficulties this second season and in the future might never have occurred. Instead, Cooke, his culpability in question, began the 1801–1802 season inauspiciously.

John Kemble, in one more attempt to challenge Cooke, had chosen to open Drury Lane with *Richard III* on 12 September 1801, with his brother Charles as Richmond. Covent Garden had already announced that Cooke would appear as Richard on 14 September, and Kemble decided to get the jump on the opposition by beginning his season early. Lewis sent remonstrances to Kemble, but to no avail. Meanwhile, the Drury Lane management gave out the story that the early opening and Kemble's Richard had been necessitated because of problems over the engagement of Elizabeth Billington, the singer and actress.

Mrs. Billington had first appeared at Covent Garden in 1786 with sensational success. In 1794, she had gone to the Continent where her reception had also been triumphal. She remained abroad until 1801, when brutal treatment by her second husband, a young Frenchman named Felican (or Felissent or Filessini), drove her back to London.[2] Controversy of this sort was not uncommon for her; indeed, her sexual adventures caused gossip throughout her career. With characteristic disregard of consequences, she signed agreements with both Harris at Covent Garden and Sheridan at Drury Lane. It was finally decided that she should alternately sing at both houses that season. Sheridan was clearly not pleased with this arrangement, although he had initially hoped to preserve Harris's good-will. His ire was increased by Covent Garden's arrangements with John Braham and Signora Storace, which added enviable strength to Covent Garden's musical department. It was not surprising, then, that Sheridan and Kemble would retaliate with such a challenge to Cooke and Covent Garden. Furthermore, as reported by the *Morning Post* (10 September 1801), it was thought that Kemble had allowed Cooke to exhaust the appeal of his novelty during his first season, and Kemble was now preparing "to attack him with Herculean strength, having been training the whole summer at the watering places, and on the mountains, and having answered well in all his exercises, while Cooke had been exhausting his strength on the various country courses."

Clearly, Drury Lane's tactics were working and all London awaited "great sport." On the 12th Kemble performed Richard with perfunctory response.[3] The 14th arrived and all expected Cooke's Richard that evening. At 4:00 P.M., a new bill was circulated announcing that "some accident, as it is apprehended, having prevented Mr. Cooke's Arrival in Town, the tragedy of Richard the Third is oblig'd to be postponed," and *Lovers' Vows* was quickly substituted.[4] That night many arrived not knowing until after the curtain rose and Miss Chapman as Agatha Fribourg entered that Cooke would not appear. Others believed that Cooke was in London but hiding somewhere in a state of inebriety.[5] Miss Murray was greeted with hisses and calls of "off, off," which continued until Murray (Baron of Wildenheim) came out to address the audience. He attempted to appease them with an explanation of the management's fear of harm befalling Cooke on the road and finally appealed to the indulgence "ever received from a British Audience." Such flattery seemed to calm the audience and Murray withdrew. The play continued amidst more hisses and shouting. Once more the performance was halted, and Murray again tried to bring order until the audience shouted for the manager. Lewis finally came forward, bowed to the pit, and amidst loud jeers tried to explain the situation, claiming not to have known that Cooke also had been announced for Newcastle the same night. At last, unable to satisfy the audience, Lewis offered their money back or a continuation of the substituted play. "The murmurs that followed his speech were lost in applause. It was now past seven o'clock; the play was suffered to proceed, and all symptoms of disapprobation died away."[6]

One source indicates that Covent Garden had moved its opening date back from 17 September to 14 September; thus, it was quite possible that Cooke had not been informed and was indeed innocent of wrongdoing. Drury Lane then felt compelled to change its opening to the 12th in order to compete more advantageously. Both theatres had jumped the Haymarket's closing date of 15 September. As noted in the last chapter, Cooke claims that the letter from Lewis notifying him of his opening performance was not received in time, because it went to Manchester rather than Newcastle.

Although Cooke was probably innocent of "drunken insolence," the London audience nonetheless was beginning to acquire some taste of Cooke's misadventures and thus waited anxiously for "the tribe of apologetic letters, certificates from physicians . . . and the prodigy's own excuse."[7] Indeed, the proprietors of Covent Garden wasted no time circulating letters showing that Cooke was suddenly attacked with a serious complaint in Newcastle. A Dr. E. Kentist wrote from Newcastle on 15 September: "From great fatigue and exertion, Mr. Cooke has ruptured a blood-vessel in his chest which renders it unsafe for him to travel." On the same day, the following letter was sent to Harris:

I trouble you with this, at the request of Mr. George Cooke, who is at present so much indisposed as to render him incapable of writing to you. He had been poor for several days past, but yesterday evening was attacked with such excruciating pains in his chest that the Doctor took a large quantity of blood from him, and he hopes in a few days he may be able to travel, if he has no relapse. He received a letter from Mr. Lewis, dated the 5th instant, but it being directed to Manchester, did not reach here until too late. The distress of his mind *on your account*, is beyond anything I can say.—The Faculty, as well as his Friends, will do anything in their power for his speedy recovery in order that he may soon be with you.[8]

This letter, from a George Dunn, and others, helped to settle the furor somewhat. Furthermore, the excitement over Billington's first appearance on 3 October helped to diminish the controversy.

Apparently, Cooke spent a week after his collapse recuperating in Newcastle. His journal indicates that he left on 21 September, arrived the next day at the Matlock Baths in Derbyshire, where he remained until 12 October, and finally reached his apartment, 4 Boulton Street, Piccadilly, on 15 October.[9] During his absence, the Covent Garden management had filled in with such offerings as *Lovers' Vows, The Poor Gentleman, The School for Prejudice, Romeo and Juliet, Speed the Plough*, and *Wild Oats*.

Cooke was finally announced for Richard on 19 October. Anticipating some opposition from the public, Cooke "went on the stage, before the curtain, prior to the commencement of the play, and made what was deemed a sufficient apology."[10] Cooke's first apology speech before a London audience, the first of many, began in an open and candid way, confessing "I had no authority from the proprietors to be absent at the commencement of the season; but I certainly did not think that my services would be required the first night." He then explained that he had missed Lewis's letter and added: "With the subsequent events that happened to me you are already acquainted. I am exceedingly sorry to have been the involuntary cause of disappointment; and though I may be unworthy of the patronage I have experienced, I shall not fail to exert my best abilities in your service."[11]

Although a number of newspapers and journals still did not believe Cooke's explanations, the audience greeted his apology with the "warmest plaudits."[12] Cooke had survived this first skirmish relatively unscathed. According to existing evidence, he seems to have been guiltless of any personal wrongdoing. As his indiscretions became more common, a one-time indulgent audience began to condemn him out of hand, whether innocent or guilty. Even more so, he steadily became the butt of the daily press.

Cooke's Richard that evening went well. The reviewers were extremely complimentary. The *Morning Chronicle* reported that he had "never exerted himself in the character more and with greater effect." *The Monthly Mirror* wrote that "Tragedy, which had languished in this theatre during his absence, now begins to hold up her head."[13]

All went well for Cooke the next few months. On 21 October, he again appeared as Shylock and Sir Archy MacSarcasm. Although he was suffering from hoarseness, he "still seemed actuated by the feelings of the vindictive Israelite," and "the quick transitions from rage to rejoicing, and from rejoicing to rage," were seldom "more ably delineated," reported the *Morning Chronicle*.[14] He was, as always, praised in *Love-a-la-Mode*. On 28 October, he performed Iago opposite the Othello of Henry Siddons, appearing for the first time at Covent Garden. Cooke's hoarseness had lingered, but his performance was nonetheless "most ably" done.[15] On 16 November, Cooke failed to go on as Richard III, according to a comment on the theatre's playbill in the British Museum. No explanations are given, but possibly the hoarseness that he had been experiencing since October still persisted.

On 27 November, Cooke first appeared at Covent Garden as Stukely. Despite his critical success in the role the preceding summer, he played the role only once this season. The production was prepared for the debut of Matthew Campbell Browne (spelled Brown in the playbills), advertised as from the "Theatres Bath and Dublin." Browne's career, dating from 1778, was uneventful, and despite good notices as Beverly in this production of *The Gamester*, his name, for no apparent reason, disappeared from the bills until the end of the season. Cooke's Stukely was greeted with the "warmest approbation." The last Stukely of memory had been John Palmer, Jr., who died in 1798 and had first performed Stukely in 1770–1771 at Drury Lane. *The Monthly Mirror* considered Cooke quite different from this "old school" actor.[16] Cooke's highpoints were typically those moments of hypocrisy, artful insinuation, cunning, and malignity. The *London Chronicle* (26–28 November) found the best part of his performance "that of his detection, when his whole villainy was developed; his shame and disappointment, not remorse were so truly expressed by a dejected countenance, which, indicated the internal operations of a guilty mind." The *Morning Chronicle* (28 November 1801) agreed that rarely had the stage seen "a more finished portrait of this unprincipled monster.... a man will not often be found who is able, like Cooke, to blend these vices together [avarice, hypocrisy, craft, cowardice, cruelty], so as to produce an air of nature and consistency, and to give an idea of a perfect knave."

Leigh Hunt, who called Cooke "the Machiavel of the modern stage" and felt that he was limited to either tragic or comic hypocrites, wrote on Cooke's Stukely in 1807:

[It] is tragic in the effects produced by his villainy, but in the pursuit of this villainy he is merely grave or sentimental; and everything like cheating has a principle of the ridiculous in it: Rochefoucault, perhaps, would account for this in the superiority which we give our own sagacity over the person cheated. With all Cooke's assumed meekness of countenance in this character... with his fits of thoughfulness so inimitably familiar, and his sudden sighs of pitying conviction he is always greater as he approaches comedy.[17]

The Monthly Mirror agreed that he was most effective when, in Act III, he showed his "bold-faced villainy" with Mrs. Beverly (Mrs. Litchfield). Other outstanding moments occurred in the last act where depicting confusion when his schemes were frustrated, in his soliloquies, especially where he intimated his intentions to try the conjugal fidelity of Mrs. Beverly, and whenever planning more diabolical stratagems.[18]

No doubt because of the temporary loss of Browne, it was thought more practical not to replace him in such a major role, so the play was dropped for the remainder of the season.

In December, "at the desire of the managers of the Theatres Royal Bath and Bristol, and permission and concurrence of Mr. Harris," Cooke performed for the first time five nights at these theatres.[19] Since the 1778–1779 season, the Bath and Bristol theatres had operated in circuit from September to July, with three performances a week in Bristol and one in Bath until mid-November; thereafter, Bristol was dark except on Mondays until benefits began in early June.[20] Cooke was engaged by the managers, William Wyatt Dimond and John Palmer (not the actor), to appear four nights at Bath, beginning Thursday, 17 December, with a Monday performance in Bristol.[21]

The management of the Bath and Bristol theatres was held in high esteem, even in London, and only the York circuit could challenge its preeminence. Bath received its patent in 1768, the first outside of London, and Bristol in 1778; both were among the earliest Theatre Royals in the provinces.[22] Both towns had boasted fine theatres for a number of years: the Orchard Street Theatre in Bath had opened in 1750, and the Bristol theatre in King Street in May1766. The Bristol theatre had just undergone extensive alterations prior to Cooke's visit; the Bath theatre would be replaced by a new structure in 1805.[23]

Cooke appeared first as Richard III on 17 December with Pierce Egan as Richmond, Stanwix as Buckingham, and Miss Sarah Smith, who later joined the ranks of Covent Garden and alternated roles with Mrs. Siddons, as Lady Anne.[24] Cooke repeated Richard the next night, followed on 19 December with *Othello*, Cooke playing Iago opposite Robert William Elliston, who had first appeared in Bath in 1791 and since 1794 had been playing second leads to Dimond. Dimond, however, had that year retired from acting, and Elliston had now taken the principal roles.[25] Elliston's place in theatre history would be assured as a result of his future flamboyant management of the Surrey Theatre in London, and, disastrously, of Drury Lane in 1819.[26]

Cooke appeared in Bristol on Monday, 21 December, as Shylock and Sir Archy and then repeated for Bath the same roles the next night, ending the engagement with Richard on the 23d.[27] Little was written on this brief engagement, although Cooke indicated that he received "the greatest applause and approbation from the audiences" and that the management was polite and attentive to him.[28] The *London Chronicle* (22 December 1801) reported that Cooke's Richard III proved a great attraction at Bath and the houses completely overflowed. One contemporary account in manuscript by Richard John "Obi" Smith, then fifteen, indicates that Cooke lodged in the Smith house, since he was an old acquaintance of Smith's father. Cooke "was kind, affable, and gentlemanly in his deportment—rose early—passed a great deal of his time in reading and taking long walks in the delightful neighborhood of Bath."[29] On subsequent visits, however, Cooke would be less the ideal guest. He would return to the Bath/Bristol circuit the next year for three visits; in June, he would make a gratis appearance for the benefit of the Bath Theatrical Fund, founded that year.

Cooke returned to Covent Garden on 26 December as Richard. That evening "a serious riot in the Theatre occurred," but it had nothing to do with Cooke. The afterpiece had been announced as *The Review*, but, because of the absence of a number of performers, it was changed to *The Jew and the Doctor*, and the riot ensued.[30] The rioters began their disturbance during Cooke's Richard, and a ruffian in the 2s. gallery threw a quart bottle on stage at Cooke's feet.[31]

On 2 January, Cooke played Jaques in *As You Like It* for the first time in London, with Brunton as Orlando, Miss Murray as Rosalind (the first time), and Knight as Touchstone. Jaques was not an important role for Cooke, although the reception by the audience and reviews were definitely complimentary. The *Morning Post* (4 January 1802) thought he had "many strokes of original beauty," and *The Monthly Mirror* reported that he was much applauded, particularly in the recital of the "seven ages of man."[32] The role, however, demanded little display of his talent. The *London Chronicle* (2–5 January 1802) found his moralizing over the deer "left and abandoned by his velvet friends" given with exquisite feeling and justly rewarded with a burst of applause. The *Morning Chronicle* (4 January) was perhaps correct in its estimate of Cooke's Jaques. To them he appeared too sturdy and in too high spirits, lacking tenderness. "Instead of the pensive philosophic *Jacques* [*sic*], we seemed to ourselves to behold a ploughman returning from the ale-house." Cooke must have sensed his deficiency in the role and the small merit he could gain by it, for it was not repeated that season and all but disappeared from his repertoire.

On 4 January, he made his only reappearance as the Stranger and discovered, once more, that the inevitable comparison with Kemble added little to his reputation.

Cooke's third new role this season was Zanga in Edward Young's 1721 tragedy *The Revenge*, which had not been seen at Covent Garden in fifteen years. Cooke was familiar with the part from provincial appearances, and, although he would not act it often, Zanga would remain a part of his repertoire until the end of his life. Cooke recognized Young's play as an inferior imitation of *Othello*. The scenes between Alonzo and Zanga were "faint imitations of those between Othello and Iago," and the women's roles (Isabella and Leonora) were "still fainter [imitations] of Desdemona and Amelia." He also knew that it was no equal to *Othello* and "can only keep attention awake throughout by the representative of the two principal characters being possessed of first rate abilities."[33] Cooke underestimated the value of Young's play, which if not a wholly successful imitation of earlier romantic models, was still a significant attempt to break the fetters of classicism in the first quarter of the eighteenth century.

The revival, repeated twice in January, featured Henry Siddons as Alonzo, Mrs. St. Ledger as Isabella, and Mrs. Litchfield as Leonora. Once more Cooke seemed to be following the lead of Kemble, who had just recently earned great praise as the Moor. Where Cooke appeared in scenes similar to those with Othello, previous to the success of his villainous contrivances, "He seemed to feel his injuries strongly, and to burn for revenge," said the *Morning Chronicle* (5 January 1802). Further, "In inflaming the jealousy of *Alonzo*, he shewed great art, and upon the success of his diabolical schemes, his triumph was grand." The *London Chronicle* (2–5 January) agreed that in the stronger passions he had great force and that no man could surpass him in "bold, direct sarcasms." *The Monthly Mirror* noted the energetic and impressive nature of his appeal to Mohamet, but as all the critics were to observe, the latter scenes were deficient in "princely grandeur."[34]

A comparison with Iago was difficult to ignore, and the *Morning Chronicle* saw weaknesses similar to those in his Iago. Zanga, like Iago, is a master of cunning, but "it is not natural to him, and he only has recourse to it to promote his grand design. His sentiments are heroic and magnanimous, and in happier circumstances he would have been the father of his country, and the delight of mankind . . . we never detest him." Iago perhaps can be represented forcibly without "dignity of manner, gracefulness of utterance, without the delicate expression of glowing sentiment," but Zanga requires all these in addition to "artfulness, dissimulation and subtlety." In criticizing Cooke's characterization, none of the reviewers took into account Zanga's inadequate motive for revenge, one of the major weaknesses of the text. Nonetheless, Cooke was less suited to the role than Kemble, but was still given a great deal of credit for attacking his rival in his strongholds. It was clear to all, in the final analysis, that

Cooke could play Zanga the servile slave to perfection, whereas Kemble could also be Zanga the son of Aldullah, the Moorish king.

On 8 January, Cooke appeared in London for the first time as King Lear, a role which a number of reviewers simply dismissed as adding nothing to his reputation or being totally wrong for him.[35] The *Theatrical Repertory*, for example, said that Cooke, with his "robust porter-like figure" and a voice "incapable of soft and pathetic tones, or any expression of tenderness, and a style of action and deportment the least allied to grace and dignity that ever we witnessed in an actor" made him utterly unqualified for the role. The *Morning Post* (9 January 1802) was especially disturbed by his uniformly clear and strong enunciation, firm step, and vigorous deportment, so that "the heart . . . could not feel that pity which the sight of a deserving object, physically unable to contend with unmerited hardships, never fails to produce."

There were numerous other comments like those cited above. A few concluded, as did the *Morning Post*, that this performance justified those critics who felt Cooke did not possess "an elasticity of mind, a pliancy of powers, to enable him to pursue his rival [Kemble] through all the variety of his characters with the same success that he encounters on Bosworth field."

Although Cooke appeared as Lear only once this season, he would not totally eliminate the role from his repertoire. It is likewise important to observe that of the roles he continued to perform, Lear appears to be among those that did change. A comparison of the initial response and a later one in the United States is appropriate in this respect. Excerpts from the *Morning Chronicle* review of 9 January 1802, which was typical of the general tone of the notices Cooke received, seem to contrast vividly with an 1811 review. The *Chronicle* reviewer began with an appraisal of Cooke's physicality of Lear:

He seemed to imagine that *Lear* was a man hole [sic] in body and vigorous in intellect. His step was firm, his action violent, and his whole deportment manly. He wore a white beard upon his chin 'tis true, but as far as this went it only produced an incongruity between his look and his manner. . . . It is only the idea of *Lear's* helplessness that interests us in his fate. . . . This misconception impaired the effect of the whole performance, but was particularly injurious when the old man had lost his senses. Mr. Cooke made his madness resemble that of *Orestes*, and he shewed none of the delicate transitions from insanity to consciousness. He succeeded best in the early scenes. The *curse* he gave with very great effect, and his denunciations of unknown vengence [sic] were admirable, when he renounced both *Regan* and *Gonneril* [sic], and preferred the raging elements to his unnatural offspring.

He lacked tenderness with Cordelia, however, and "there was a coarseness in his exultation upon his victory over the assassins, and the recovery of his crown. He appeared like a jolly old dog, who boasts of the feats of his youth, and insinuates that his powers are not greatly impaired."[36] Contrast this with Dunlap's "I never shall forget the effect produced upon me, by his tottering

One of the earliest published drawings of Charles Robert Leslie (1794–1859). The engraving, used by *The Mirror of Taste,* was drawn solely from Leslie's observations of performances at the Chestnut Street Theatre but was considered an excellent likeness. Author's collection.

limbs while sinking on his knee to pronounce the terrible curse on his unnatural daughters,"[37] or the detailed and sensitive comments in *The Mirror of Taste and The Dramatic Censor*.[38] This reviewer, who had seen Cooke as early as 1800 in London, though not in Lear, did not admire all of Cooke's performance. He quotes a critic who ranked Cooke's Lear after Garrick, Henderson, and Barry but superior to Mossop and Kemble, the latter because of Cooke's "natural expression of feeling," even though Kemble was superior in "the studied graces of action and in dignity of person and deportment." Cooke was first credited by the American critic with originality—creating his own Lear, not a hereditary one. Unlike the London critics, *The Dramatic Censor* found his reading "infuses into the meaning of the words a subtilty [sic] of sense and an energy of expression truly astonishing." He admitted that Cooke was superior in the portion antecedent to Lear's insanity and implied, perhaps unknowingly, that Cooke was more temperate in the madness and wandering abroad of Lear than he had expected. Although he blamed this on the American audience and their tendency to react through misconception and ignorance, it appears that Cooke may have tempered his initial conception. Instead of rushing through mad scenes with little discrimination, Cooke had now found specific moments he wished to stress. Similar comments on the latter scenes are not to be found in any of the early criticism and isolate the most marked change in his conception. *The Dramatic Censor* continued:

From the time Lear's senses begin to be restored, Cooke's personation of him was excellent. His killing . . . was inimitably executed.
    The sudden renovation of strength, occasioned by despair, and the no less sudden relapse into weakness, received from him the highest coloring of nature; and nothing could be more expressive of exultation than his looks when he exclaimed,
        Did I not, fellow?
        I have seen the day, with my good biting falchion,
        I would make them skip:
Or the mixture of painful recollection and compulsory resignation depicted in the shake and decline of his head, and in the feeble sinking of his voice, when he said
        I am old now,
        And these same crosses spoil me.

A key comment follows the quoting of Lear's lines, "For, as I am a man, I think this Lady/ To be my child Cordelia."

This is perhaps the most exquisite pitch of tenderness which the imitative genius of man has ever reached; and here Cooke displayed the extent and versatility of his powers: his voice, his looks and his utterance perfectly corresponding with the purpose of the poet, and sending every work irresistably [sic] home to the heart.

It is, of course, possible that this commentator was so enamored of Cooke that his remarks should be rejected as puffery or at least cautiously accepted. On the other hand, they are more detailed than the typical early nineteenth-century review and, as cited earlier in the discussion of Cooke's Richard III, are generally honest and objective. It would be a mistake to make too much of *The Dramatic Censor*, but the contrast between this description of his tempered handling of Lear's insanity and his tenderness with Cordelia is in marked contrast with almost all early criticism.[39]

Prior to 15 January 1802, Cooke had created no new roles at Covent Garden. Throughout his London career he would be given less than a dozen, and none would be truly memorable or of lasting interest. His first was Orsino in Matthew Gregory ("Monk") Lewis's *Alfonso, King of Castile*, described by Nicoll as a "blood-red drama of revenge," confessedly unhistorical, although "The action is supposed to pass in the year 1345."[40] The plot is simple: Alfonso (Murray), for a number of years, has condemned Orsino. The latter's son and the king's general, Caesario (Henry Johnston), long for revenge. In concert with Melchior, Caesario plans to assassinate the monarch. Complications arise, however, when it is learned that Caesario is secretly married to Alfonso's daughter, Amelrosa (Mrs. H. Johnston), and Orsino unexpectedly returns to aid Alfonso. Caesario is ultimately stabbed by his father and Amelrosa goes mad.

The production, with music by Dr. Thomas Busby and new costumes and scenery, became a relatively popular entry into the season; it was performed ten times, the last on 11 May.[41] Dunlap implied that assigning Cooke a new role was an indication that his popularity was waning, and, although receipts fail to support a sharp decline, there may be some truth to his assertion. Being in a new production would certainly lessen his opportunities to repeat his major roles. Dunlap's conclusion, however, that Cooke was driven to "drown in oblivious draughts his cares and his ambition" seems to have little credibility.[42]

Since it was a new script, almost all contemporary commentaries dwelled on its merits and deficiences, and in this respect Cooke received little attention in Orsino. The *Morning Chronicle* (16 January), for example, filled its columns with a long comparison of the plot and the events surrounding Guy Fawkes, and claimed the plot actually dealt with the Catholics in the time of James I and the progress of the conspiracy. The play clearly is full of defects—the characters are stock, there is an excess of "blood and horror," and the plot is hackneyed. Nevertheless, the character of Orsino—proud, vindictive, irascible—fell clearly into Cooke's province. But Cooke personally thought little of *Alfonso* and regretted his association with it. In September, he wrote the following:

The gentleman's ["Monk" Lewis] imagination seems entirely taken up with murders, ghosts, old castles, and ancient Spanish ballads. There is certainly some good writing in

Alfonso, but both fable and construction are miserably bad. It abounds with so many improbabilities, and even impossibilities, that to point them out would be an endless task. It is a sanguinary tale, for the four principal characters die violent deaths. One lady poisons another, and is stabbed by her lover, who, after mortally wounding his father in battle *by mistake*, stabs himself, and leaves a halfdead king behind to mourn the catastrophe. The Author, resolving to be singular in every respect, published his play, with a conceited, impertinent preface, *before* it was acted; and the last act materially different from the license manuscript. It struggled though nine [ten?] nights to tolerable audiences, partly procured through the interest of the author, and went to rest for the remainder of the season. I hope for ever, at least as long as I remain in the theatre.[43]

In his second benefit, 24 February, Cooke was featured as Falstaff in *Henry IV, Part 1*, with Lewis, poorly cast, as Hal (the following season he was replaced by John Brunton), Murray as King Henry, and Siddons as Hotspur.[44] The Covent Garden playbill at the British Museum indicates that Cooke received a second free benefit of £409.13.6.[45] Cooke recorded in his journal: "... this season, also, Mr. Harris gave me my night entirely clear, and I signed another article for three years, after the expiration of the third year of my first article, and was immediately put upon a salary of fourteen guineas a week." Either Cooke, writing almost five years after the fact, confused this salary with that of the following year, when according to the account books his salary did increase to £14.4.0, or Dunlap misplaced this item in Cooke's journal.[46] Cooke definitely did not receive an increase this season, his salary remaining at an average of £7 per week throughout the season. Whatever the case, Cooke also wrote in his journal: "This season I took the first part of Henry the Fourth, and for the first time in London acted Falstaff. I have several times repeated it, with the Falstaffs of the second part, and Merry Wives of Windsor, but never could please myself, or come up to my own ideas on any of them."

Even though Cooke was not satisfied with his Falstaff, the reviewers were in universal agreement that Cooke was the best Falstaff of his time and certainly the best since Henderson. In 1806, Stephen Kemble, complete with his natural padding, was engaged to play Falstaff at Covent Garden for three nights, but *The Monthly Mirror* found him only tolerable and still considered Cooke, "Whose *Falstaff* is among his least commendable efforts," the best "our stage can boast."[47] Carpenter, in *The Dramatic Censor*, thought that no one since Quin had given the drollery of the fat knight such a rich characteristic expression of malignant and sarcastic spirit.[48] Cooke's interpretation seems to have been one stressing Falstaff's sound sense, a profound knowledge of human nature, without degrading the character by low buffoonery and practical jokes.[49] As a number of critics indicated, they would rather see a cynic than a fool. Cooke's major difficulty was occasionally obscuring humor by too much study, formality, and stiffness.[50] Crabb Robinson, after spending an evening discussing the role with Coleridge, recorded in his diary that Coleridge considered Falstaff an example of the predominance of intellectual power, content to

Cooke as Falstaff in *Henry IV, Part 1* by DeWilde. Used by permission of Norman Philbrick.

be thought "both a liar and a coward in order to obtain influence over the minds of his associates." Robinson suggested that this description seemed to justify Cooke's interpretation, "according to which a foreigner imperfectly understanding the character would fancy Falstaff the designing knave who does actually outwit the Prince." To this Coleridge responded that in his estimation, "Falstaff is the superior, who cannot easily be convinced that the Prince has escaped him; but that . . . Shakespeare has shown us the defeat of mere intellect by a noble feeling; the Prince being the superior moral character, who rises above his insidious companion." Apparently, Coleridge agreed, at least in part, with Cooke's interpretation.[51]

Later this season, on 28 April, Cooke first appeared as Falstaff in *The Merry Wives of Windsor*, with Henry Siddons as Ford, Murray as Page, Mrs. Dibdin as Mrs. Page, and Mrs. Beverly as Anne Page. He did not perform in *Henry IV, Part 2* in London until 17 January 1804.[52]

Sometime in March, Dunlap says Cooke took a "Flying excursion to Portsmouth, and played Richard two nights out of four." However, *The Hampshire Telegraph and Portsmouth Gazette* (8 March 1802) mentions only one performance of Richard, on Monday, 8 March. Dunlap also says that in April Cooke paid a second visit to Bath and Bristol, by permission of Harris, and played a night at each place. Genest records that Cooke acted Shylock and Sir Archy at Bath on 6 April, presumably presenting the same bill at Bristol on 5 or 7 April.[53]

On 16 March, the Covent Garden management announced in the bills that *The Man of the World* was in preparation and that Cooke would appear for the first time in London as Sir Pertinax MacSycophant. Thomas Dibdin had recommended to Harris in 1800 that because of his excellence in the role, Cooke should perform Sir Pertinax during his premiere season. Harris, however, demurred, fearing that the memory of Macklin in the role would make it unwise "to run a risk of blasting his newly-won laurels by attempting what might be a step beyond him." As a compromise, it was decided to let Cooke perform the smaller role instead, Sir Archy MacSarcasm.[54]

For the second season, Lewis's benefit would offer Cooke another unique opportunity to introduce to London one of his most important roles and the one most seen during his London career. Harris would repeatedly thank Dibdin for first indicating the possibilities.

Macklin's *Man of the World*, produced first in London at Covent Garden in 1781,[55] was initially censored by the lord chamberlain because of its political implications, a perennial portrait of a greedy and hypocritical politician. Macklin, however, had fervently pleaded to the censor that he was attempting "to ridicule and by that means to explode the reciprocal national prejudices that equally soured and disgraced the minds of both English and Scotch men."[56] After several revisions in which the topicality and biting satire were tempered and thus the clear allusion to Lord Bute was lessened, it was finally

Cooke as Sir Pertinax MacSychophant, his most popular comic role. Engraving after DeWilde. Author's collection.

licensed.[57] As late as 1806, however, Elizabeth Inchbald noted that Sir Pertinax embodied the spirit of Lord Chesterfield and exposed him as an example to shun rather than a pattern to imitate.[58] Read today, the play is still an incisive and mordant satire of its times, with unique and original characterizations. Sir Pertinax, as Appleton has noted, is clearly a blood brother of Sir Giles Overreach.

Cooke offered his own opinions of Macklin's play in a diary kept while at Bristol in September 1802:

The fable is simple and well-conducted, the characters, though highly coloured, naturally drawn, and the language nervous and correct. So fastidious was the author in imitation of ancient comedy, that he has not allowed a single change of scene in the whole play. A library from beginning to end: the same scene through his "Love-a-la-Mode." He seems to entertain a strong prejudice against the Scotch in general, yet he appears to make some atonement by pourtraying the knight's family as very different in sentiment from himself. The Scotch are certainly very national, but whether more than the English, Welsh, or Irish, I will not presume to say. They frequently carry their point, whether of good or evil tendency, by a steady perserverance in adapting their behavior to the exigence of the moment. . . . One speech of Egerton's in particular, is a just and glowing picture of the atrocious and flagitious enormities too often practiced at elections by all ranks of people. The province of comedy is to expose and censure, as well as to ridicule. It cannot shew mankind as they are, without exhibiting their vices and deformities. The easiest method of appreciating the just merits of this comedy is to compare it with those of the present time.[59]

Without question, Cooke's Sir Pertinax was considered his most perfect piece of acting. Even the *Morning Post* (29 September 1803) admitted that Cooke was superior to any other delineator of the part including Macklin:

Indeed, the more we attend to the *minutiae* of his performance, the more exactly do we perceive it to coincide not only with the original idea and picture of the author, but with all the additional adventitious colourings with which observation has taught us it may be enriched. The fawning flatterer, the pliant parasite, the servile sycophant, is depicted throughout in his characteristic hues, and that with an ease of nature, a facility of habit, a nicety of discrimination, and appropriate tones and gestures, which not only bespeak a full and just conception of the author's intention, but a perfect portraiture of some living model.

In George III's opinion, Cooke's performance was the most brilliant of the age.[60] Inchbald, who had believed, as many others, that no one could surpass Macklin as the Scotch politician, admitted that Cooke was preeminent. One reviewer felt that while Macklin had too much "spleen and irritability" in prominent passages, Cooke added a "dry mixture of *humour*." John Bernard, who had seen both actors, includes a telling comparison in his *Retrospections of America*:

The great characteristic of "The Man of the World" being that quality in the representation of which Cooke particularly excelled, viz, speciousness, affords the reason why he so much surpassed Macklin in its performance, the latter confusing the light and shade of the character by an invariable roughness, and after attempting to produce effect by a grimacing and bullying altogether inappropriate.[61]

Even William Hazlitt in *The Examiner*, reviewing Mr. Governeurs Bibby from the United States in the role on 21 April 1816, admitted that to compare any actor with Cooke in the part "would be idle; for it was Cooke's very best character, and Cooke was one of the very best actors we have had on the stage."[62]

As late as April 1807, *The Monthly Mirror* was still calling Cooke's Sir Pertinax "the most perfect piece of acting on the English stage" and suggesting that not only would it be impossible to "add a single touch to the picture" but also that after Cooke's death the part would probably cease to be acted, which indeed, with the exception of isolated attempts, it was.[63] If the praise for Cooke's MacSycophant were not so universal, contemporary comment would seem puffery of the most obvious sort. However, when the *Morning Post* (6 October 1802) stated that Cooke's every feature, every gesture "conspire in raising it to the highest pitch" and that not only his Scotch manner is perfect but also "the accent of a Scotsman," the inclination is to accept such an estimate. Macklin's accent was often criticized, one pamphleteer calling it "a very tiresome, drawling, hesitating, repeating, and, on the whole, execrable imitation of the Scots accent, through which breaks out ever and anon the Irish brogue."[64] Such criticism is nonexistent in Cooke's renderings of Macklin's two Scottish characters; this undoubtedly added to the general preference of Cooke over Macklin. Munden claims that the excellence of Cooke's dialect was a result of his long engagement at Newcastle. A more likely explanation is that growing up in Berwick near the Scottish border made such a feat second nature.[65] Cooke's Sir Pertinax and Sir Archy were enthusiastically accepted in Scotland as well.

Cooke's Sir Pertinax prompted Leigh Hunt, in one of the rare detailed and objective reviews of the role, to conclude that Cooke was a better comedian than tragedian. He found MacSycophant Cooke's "most finished performance" and added:

Sir Pertinax would be a perfect piece of acting if Mr. Cooke's action was more various. By giving the person represented a manner, it is sometimes, indeed, more impressive in its effect, especially when the character is an eccentric one; . . . a variety of action would be much more natural, since he is of so various and sanguine a temper, so various in his contrivances, and so various in his behaviour. A monotony of any kind must be unusual with active hypocrisy.

But you may see all the beauties and all the faults of Cooke in this single character; and this proves, perhaps, that it is his favourite one, since he feels inclined to indulge all his habits in its representation. The Scotch dialect which he so inimitably assumes is in vain undervalued by those who persuade themselves that he was born in Scotland. In the first place, to be merely born there is nothing to the purpose, for a man born upon the sea might as well be expected to talk like a dolphin. If he was educated by or with Scotch people, it is merely wonderful that he does not talk Scotch in his English characters, for he gives them none of those compressed vowels and liquified consonants, none of that artlessness and undulation of tone so ludicrous in Sir Pertinax. It is this artlessness of tone that renders a hypocritical Scotchman or Welshman more humourous on the stage than any other hypocrite, and more successful, perhaps, in the world. Sir Pertinax, however, conceals an unavoidable ludicrousness, which might sometimes injure his cause, by apparently delighting in his dialect and by possessing much intentional humour. If Cooke bows, it is with a face that says "What a fool you are to be deceived with this fawning!" If he looks friendly, it is with a smile that says "I will make use of you, and you may go to the devil." A simple rustic might feel all his affections warmed at his countenance, and exclaim "What a pure-hearted old gentleman!" but a fine observer would descry under the glowing exterior nothing but profession without meaning, and heart without warmth.

This sarcasm of Cooke is at all times most bitter, but in this character its ascerbity [sic] is tempered with no respect either for its object or for himself. His tone is outrageously smooth and deep; and when it finds its softest level, its under monotony is so full of what is called hugging one's self, and is accompanied with such a dragged smile and viciousness of leer, that he seems as if he had lost his voice through the mere enjoyment of malice.[66]

The entire opening night cast, each appearing in his or her respective role for the first time in London, was considered excellent. But it was George Cooke, "a rich intellectual treat, and wandering through all the mazy subtleties of life, as the Man of the World, [who] becomes, by the magic of the scene, the Man of the People." that captured the audience's imagination.[67]

In the United States, Cooke's performance took on an added dimension. The more jingoistic reviewers recognized in MacSycophant a parallel with England's "modern great men, such as her members of parliament," and found Cooke's portrayal "a true picture of those men whom America has had most reason to detest, in every period of the present reign."[68] *The Dramatic Censor* offered another detailed analysis, including comments on Cooke versus Macklin. Macklin was "less plausible in his flattery of the peer, less versatile, and infinitely less insinuating," while in Cooke there was "nothing to impair probability."[69] William B. Wood, co-manager of the Philadelphia theatre when Cooke performed there, wrote that a local lawyer, Edward Tighlman, who had seen both Garrick and Macklin, told Cooke that his Sir Pertinax was superior to Macklin's in adding relief to the role through "extraordinary comic powers," whereas Macklin was "too uniformly harsh and severe." Cooke declared this "the highest compliment he had ever received."[70]

One additional observation, significant in its perspective, is offered by Carpenter in *The Dramatic Censor*, a parallel comparison with Garrick.

Carpenter concluded that Cooke's comedy was "as completely distinct from his tragedy, as if they were the workings of two separate men," an excellence comparable to Garrick's.

Both English and American reviewers agreed on Cooke's best moments in *Man of the World*. The most detailed description of these, indicating specific business, is found in Durang. In Act III, Scene 1, Sir Pertinax describes to his son Charles Egerton how he rose from his "beggarly clerkship in Sawney Gordon's counting house" to his present rank, opulence, and importance. Durang described how after

"Sir, I booed, and watched and hearkened... golden claves I had been so long a booing to,".... Cooke rose with great dignity, and a shrewd, impassioned look on Charles—his snuff-box was in his left hand, and a pinch of unused snuff betwixt his fingers—he finished the speech, after a light pause, this: "And was nae that booing to some purpose?"... With great dignity, he continued, "thus, sir, I booed myself into parliament," etc. His manner here was stronger than language could express. His sharp and powerful exultation; his peculiar action and expression of face at once seized the audience with exstacy [sic], and, after a pause of surprise, he was greeted with several rounds of applause.[71]

In Act IV, Scene 1, Cooke created one of his famous "silent points." He complains to Charles that his brother had made some painful political mistakes in opposing the election of a friend of his in Scotland and "effects followed in rapid succession, such as no other representation of character ever made... where the dialogue of the scene runs upon 'conscience' and 'ambition', the *real* value and flimsy pretensions of the former, the conceptions and illustrations of Cooke were those of a transcendent painting." At the end of Charles's speech "Only show me how I can serve my country... and act with unremitting ardor of a Roman spirit," Cooke "raised his hand to ply [his] nasal organ but snuff fell by degrees from fingers to the floor—wrapt astonishment first possessed him, but rising indignation, like inward workings of Etna, became terribly perceptible, until... it burst forth in all its terror in "Why, are you mad, Sir?... you are nae son of mine."[72]

Cooke quickly established his preeminence in Sir Pertinax, and, even though late in the season, it was possible to repeat *Man of the World* six more times.[73]

May was to be a difficult month for Cooke and no less so for his colleagues. He had promised Munden that he would appear in his benefit on 4 May. Munden, to assure his presence, invited Cooke to dinner, saw that he took only a moderate quantity of wine, and walked arm in arm with him to the theatre. At the stage door, Cooke shook his friend by the hand, and said, "I wish you a bumper, Joe! I am going up to dress." When the time arrived for the prologue, Munden began looking for Cooke. "Mr. Cooke, Sir," said the doorkeeper, "Why he left the house the moment he parted from you." Fortunately, Munden had made sure that Cooke's part had been understudied, and Cooke's absence apparently went unnoticed.[74]

On 7 May, Cooke first appeared in London as Edward Mortimer in *The Iron Chest*, for John Fawcett's benefit, to good reviews. Then on 11 May he was announced as Orsino for Mr. and Mrs. Henry Johnston's benefit. *The Monthly Mirror* tells us that Cooke began the performance, although he "was so much disposed [sic] and scarcely able to dress" for the role, but after proceeding a little he was greeted "by some very unreasonable, and we thought cruel tokens of disapprobation." After a few speeches, Cooke declared that he found it utterly impossible to proceed and immediately left the stage, replaced by Claremont.[75] A note written on the theatre's playbill at the British Museum declares that "Cooke attempted to perform but was too inebriated to proceed beyond a few speeches."[76] This is the first publicized occasion of Cooke disappointing an audience because of drunkenness. On 14 May, Mr. and Miss Murray had hoped to present *The Fashionable Lover* but as a result of Cooke's continued indisposition were forced to change it to *Wild Oats*, describing this on the bill as an "UNPLEASING but INEVITABLE EVENT" and pleading for understanding. Compared to previous benefits, well above £450, they did suffer from Cooke's absence, with receipts of only £357.[77] On the 19th, John Henry Johnstone also planned to capitalize on Cooke with a revival of *The Jealous Wife* in order to use Cooke as Major Oakly. Cooke, however, was still indisposed and Waddy took the role.[78] Cooke also had been announced for Sir Pertinax on 17 May, but the performance had to be postponed three times, until Cooke finally reappeared on Monday, 24 May.

For the benefit of Mrs. Mattocks, his old provincial acquaintance, Cooke created the role of Don Estivan in Lumley St. George Skeffington's comedy *The Word of Honour*. He repeated the role for John Brunton's and William Blanchard's benefit on 10 June. The play, never published, was described as one of contrivances, "perfectly in the Spanish style," with dialogue "correct, neat and animated, never debasing itself by dullness, but frequently gaining upon the audience by its interest and pathos."[79] The role, which Cooke accepted after a principal comedian at Covent Garden had declined to do it, added little to his reputation.

Matthew Campbell Browne, it will be recalled, had appeared once earlier in the season with Cooke in *The Gamester* and also as Glenalvon in *Douglas* for Henry Siddons' benefit on 21 May. For his own benefit on 29 May, he chose Otway's *Venice Preser'd*, which had not been seen at Covent Garden since 1790. Earlier in the eighteenth century, Otway had been considered second only to Shakespeare. Thomas Wilkes, in *A General View of the Stage* (1759), had written: "Venice Preserv'd is one of those few Plays which will always speak to the heart of the spectator. . . . when we review the merits of this Play, and The Orphan, we cannot but regret, that we see no more of Otway's dramatic Performances; for his choice of subject is always judicious, his language tender, and his incident striking."

Cooke was able to produce another masterpiece of villainy in the role of Pierre, creating a new tradition for the character. Prior to Cooke, the character had been honest, bluff, and plainspoken, but not hypocritical. Cooke turned away from the old patriot of the Revolution and was

a man of the world, "*a sly, slow, circumspective villain.*" Brave, indeed, and determined to be honest as far as his friend was concerned [Jaffier], but his good qualities were thrown so much into the background, that he appeared in the hands of Cooke rather to exult in the prospect of his personal revenge, than in the success of the pretended cause of general safety and the public good.[80]

Cooke, however, caught the postrevolutionary political mood more realistically. As usual with Cooke, his interpretation grew out of his own peculiar style, and there is little doubt, as Aline Taylor points out, that the English conservative backlash to the French sans-culotte sentiments in 1795 contributed something toward the creation.[81]

Cooke's novelty, however, was not totally accepted. The *Morning Post* (8 February 1803) thought him too much a sneering conspirator, like Glenalvon or Iago, and not enough the bold indignant soldier. "There was a perpetual hunt for novelty, as if the way in which every line of *Pierre* had been hitherto acted must be avoided, such as long pauses and sentences in an under-tone, in the midst of impetuous speeches." A number of reviewers persisted in their belief that Cooke's interpretation was incorrect; nonetheless, he was able to demonstrate a great deal of variety in the role and convince many of his range. Not only did the cold, crafty, sanguinary villain come through but "also the high spirited champion of liberty, and occasionally, the gay, easy, and polished gentleman."[82] Kemble himself attempted Pierre in November 1805, opposite the Jaffier of his brother Charles and the Belvidera of Sarah Siddons. However, this was his last appearance in the role until after Cooke departed for America. Cooke resumed the role on 20 December 1805, opposite Kemble's Jaffier, and continued to be the Pierre of the day. He appeared in the role only once during 1801–1802, but it would remain in his repertoire.

For Hill's benefit on 2 June, Cooke recited Garrick's "Ode on Shakespeare" with music by Arne; on 3 June, he appeared for Mrs. Litchfield's benefit in *Tamerlane*, which had not been seen at Covent Garden for twelve years. Cooke, for the first time in London, appeared as Bajazet, with Siddons as Tamerlane, Mrs. Litchfield as Arpasia, and Miss Murray as Selima. This would be his only appearance in the role this season, and although *The Monthly Mirror* felt that he "increased his reputation by his admirable performance of Bajazet" the role found no place in his repertoire.[83] The following night, Cooke performed Captain Faulkner in *The Way to Get Married* for Waddy's benefit. On 9 June, he appeared as Sir Philip Blanford in Emery's benefit production of *Speed the Plough*.

On 11 June, Cooke traveled to Bath and acted Richard gratis for the Bath and Bristol Theatrical Fund, under the patronage of the duchess of York.[84] On his return he appeared the following Monday, 14 June, in the prompter Glassington's benefit as Sir Pertinax. As a favor to Glassington, Mrs. Jordan appeared as Roxalana in the afterpiece, *The Sultan*. For Whitfield he played Sir Archy on 17 June, completing his second season at Covent Garden.

Although Cooke's behavior had been generally good this second season, the incident in May was a sign of indiscretion that the management had been wary of from the beginning. It is unfair, however, to condemn Cooke too soundly for such a brief period of misbehavior. Cooke was not the only performer to miss performances, as Dunlap implies. For example, on 17 June Munden was replaced by Thomas Blanchard in *The Poor Gentleman*, and Emery was ill so that Charles Moritz Klanert, on short notice, read Stephen Harrow. For the most part, Cooke performed consistently all season in familiar as well as new roles for the London audience. If benefit receipts are any indication, his popularity was not as great as it had been the first season. His benefit ranked well below those of other prominent members of the company, such as Mrs. Billington (£510), Lewis (£549), Incledon (£590), Munden (£585), Fawcett (£471), Knight (£511), and Johnstone (£533).[85] Indeed, he could only boast a sum larger than those of the lesser luminaries in the company. Undoubtedly, other factors, unknown, resulted in his £409 benefit, but it is nonetheless revealing that others did considerably better. The management still must have felt confident of his overall contributions, for it provided him a second free benefit. However, this would be the last season for such a gesture.

During this second season, Cooke performed twenty-one different roles, plus a recitation of Garrick's ode, for a total of seventy-six appearances, including fifteen times as Sir Archy in afterpieces.[86]

Cooke began his summer excursions on Sunday, 20 June 1802, and was in Manchester the next day, after which the Manchester theatre would end its season. Cooke's visit in Manchester had already become an annual event. From Manchester he proceeded to Chester, where it had been announced on 25 June that Cooke, Chester's "old favourite," would perform during Fair Week, his first appearance there in five years.[87] Cooke went through his favorite characters, beginning with Richard III on Monday, 5 July, followed by Sir Pertinax, Shylock and Sir Archy, Falstaff in *Henry IV, Part 1*, and for his benefit on 10 July, Iago and Sir Archy. The few brief comments on his Chester engagement in *The Monthly Mirror* indicate that his opening night was disturbed by the "stirring drum and the ear-piercing fife" as the military was sent out of town because of elections; on the second night the company competed against "Freeman's Septennial feasting and drinking."[88]

Cooke left Chester on 11 July and arrived, indisposed, in Birmingham the next day, having been engaged for eight nights by William McCready. Cooke writes in his journal that "after travelling all night, arrived to breakfast at Birmingham; afterwards went to bed, and in the evening was so ill, I was unable to play Richard, as advertised that night."[89] On Tuesday, 13 July, he went through Iago with Mr. and Mrs. Siddons, Jr., as Othello and Desdemona, and McCready as Cassio, plus Sir Archy, to a very thin house.[90] "Though very far from being recovered he went through his part with great spirit and with his usual happy effect."[91] In addition, Cooke performed Richard, Shylock, and, for his benefit, Hamlet. "On Wednesday the 28th proceeded to Stratford upon Avon. I visited the house and room wherein Shakespeare was born."[92] From Stratford he proceeded to Oxford and arrived back in London sometime around 29 July at the Bath Hotel, Piccadilly.

Cooke had been engaged by Robert Copland to appear for four nights at Margate, during Copland's first season as proprietor.[93] He was scheduled to make his initial appearance at the Theatre Royal on 30 July as Shylock. The company was rehearsed, and all was in readiness. But there was no Cooke or any news of his whereabouts. It was expected that he would be there in time for the performance that evening. The audience arrived, filling every corner of the house, but still no sign of Cooke. In the meantime, a letter had arrived from Cooke stating he was unwell and could not play. Shaw, the manager, kept the letter to himself and after a long delay, finally apologized to the audience and read Cooke's letter. Many were dissatisfied and demanded their money back, but the play was acted with Raymond substituting for Cooke.[94] It is difficult not to believe that this was, indeed, a case of Cooke's drinking. Although he had been ill in Birmingham, he records in his journal that before returning to London he toured leisurely through Stratford and Oxford, and after leaving London again on 1 August on his way to a Plymouth engagement, viewed Stonehenge and the Salisbury Cathedral, and visited the theatre and cathedral in Exeter. After a relaxed trip he arrived in Plymouth on 6 August.[95] The illness which caused him to cancel the Margate engagement was certainly of short duration.

The Plymouth Theatre, under the management of a Mr. Foote, was a relatively small provincial operation but made the most of Cooke's guest appearances. He was engaged to perform seven nights at Plymouth and four at Dock, two miles from Plymouth, scheduled to play Richard, Macbeth, Shylock, Sir Giles, Sir Archy, and Sir Pertinax.[96] A playbill for his first night at Plymouth in *Richard III* on 9 August in the Harvard Theatre Collection indicates how far managerial commendation could go. There is a long paragraph on the greatness of the role and the greatness of Cooke, adding that he "has excited the public Attention more than any Actor that ever appeared on the London Stage." And then, "Such a man is Cooke! who possesses an active and capacious intellect, with a profound knowledge of the SCIENCE OF ACTING. He has read and thought for himself. He has not borrowed either from CONTEMPORARY or DECEASED excellence.... Mr. Cooke not only THINKS originally, but he LOOKS, SPEAKS, and WALKS unlike any other actor on the Stage." As immense as Cooke's ego was, this must have been somewhat embarrassing. In addition, prices were raised for his engagement, except for the gallery, and it was filled first.⁹⁷ Apparently, the management's selling job was successful, for it was reported that most boxes were taken before Cooke arrived and the house was crowded every night.⁹⁸ This same account indicates that before Cooke's arrival, *The Merchant of Venice* had been curtailed and mutilated by the company.⁹⁹

Cooke wrote:

On Saturday the 28th [August], left Plymouth; at Exeter was obliged to wait on the Mayor, to complain of the insolence of the people at the Old London Inn. Late at night left the New London Inn, and about one in the morning arrived at Collumpton. Next day travelled by way of Wellington, Taunton (a handsome town), Bridgewater, and Cross, to Bristol, where I arrived at half past nine in the evening at the Talbot Inn, Bath Street. On Monday removed to No. 56, Queen Square, and that evening played Richard to a full and brilliant audience.¹⁰⁰

Cooke remained in Bristol and Bath until 14 September, performing at Bath on 4 September (*Alfonso* and *Love-a-la-Mode*), 9 September (*Man of the World*), and 11 September (the same). Between 30 August and 13 September, he performed seven nights in Bristol, appearing as Richard, Macbeth, Orsino, Sir Archy, Sir Pertinax, and Bajazet, thus completing his 1802 summer engagements.¹⁰¹

John Philip Kemble and Richard Brinsley Sheridan had been in turmoil for some time at Drury Lane. Kemble had raged and threatened and at last approached Harris at Covent Garden, who was eager to have Kemble and his considerable wealth at the opposition house. Kemble, however, decided that such a momentous decision needed an interval for thought and preparation, so in July 1802, like Garrick before him, Kemble left for an extended tour of the Continent and did not return to London until March 1803. This, then, would be Cooke's last season at Covent Garden before being joined by the Kembles.

Cooke left Bristol on 14 September, the day after Covent Garden had opened the winter season with *Folly As It Flies*. This time Cooke had Harris's permission to miss the opening. Arriving the following morning, Cooke breakfasted, went to the theatre to rehearse Richard, and that evening performed it for the thirty-sixth time in London, after which he returned to his lodgings at No. 4, Boulton Street, Piccadilly. Learning that his rival would be away for the season must have given Cooke a good deal of relief and optimism for success this third season. The season at least was getting off to a good beginning. Cooke's health had benefited from the country that summer, his customary hoarseness was gone, and his voice was clear and strong. The audience flocked to see his Richard his first night; the pit and gallery overflowed at full price, and the boxes were equally full after second price. The receipts swelled to a respectable £320.¹⁰²

On Saturday, 18 September, Cooke signed "a new article for three years, exclusive of this season" and received the first payment of his new salary of £14.14.[103] The next day Harris instructed Cooke to begin preparing Hamlet; with Kemble absent for direct comparison, Harris was no doubt encouraged to give Cooke more leeway in essaying Kemble's great parts.[104]

"On Monday the 27th I acted Hamlet to a very numerous audience. Next day the newspapers, some of whom, I believe, were *prepared* for the business, attacked me in a manner that would have been deemed impossible to have happened to any one who had ever received the slightest approbation from an audience—a London one I mean. I repeated it once [4 October], but never since." Cooke recorded this in an 1807 journal. "I do not doubt," he continues, "but I had faults in abundance; but had I acted it as well as I had seen it acted by Garrick, my reception *in that character* would have been much the same. I believe the second night was worse than the first, and the cause is too obvious to mention."[105]

Cooke should never have been assigned Hamlet; it was never a strong role for him, and now in his mid-forties he was past his prime for the part. Perhaps if he had first attempted the role before a London audience at age twenty-five, when he was not only a more appropriate age but had also been frequently playing young heroic roles and lovers, all might have been different. But now, his failure could have been predicted. Upon hearing that Cooke was going to play Hamlet, George III had remarked, "Won't do, won't do. Lord Thurlow might as well play Hamlet."[106]

If Harris intended to swell the coffers, he was successful on that score. According to the account books, the receipts were almost £510 the first night, one of the largest that season. After the critics' damnation of that night, however, the second on 4 October dropped to an embarrassing £271.

Cooke seemed to hold himself back for the later scenes, but, with the exception of a few moments in the closet scene, no change occurred. "There was a harsh monotony, a coldness throughout, which impressed the opinion, that Mr. Cooke was rather giving an animated reading of *Hamlet*, the acting over all the variety of passions by which he is torn."[107] The large audience had arrived expecting a major event of the season and was disappointed when he failed not only in passages of deep feeling and grief, but also in those of surprise and terror.[108] The audience applauded Cooke enthusiastically after the first night, but only for his past reputation, not for his Hamlet.

There was great surprise when Cooke attempted Hamlet the second time. "After the strong and unanimous condemnation of the former attempt," said the *Morning Chronicle* (5 October 1802) reviewer, "it did not appear probable that he would persevere, unless he had fresh and untried resources. We imagined that he had been prevented from exerting his talents by indisposition or embarrassment, or that by hard study he had discovered the cause of his failure, and had laid up a store of fresh graces with which he was to transport us." Clearly, this was not the case. His second attempt "was as unlike *Hamlet* as ever, and he has proved more completely his insufficiency for what he had undertaken. After this disregard of the public voice, we should feel little tenderness in taking the Performance to pieces, and fairly balancing its merits against what it has defective and absurd." This critic was then compelled to pass severe judgment: "If we were to follow Mr. Cooke from scene to scene, and from act to act, we should only have to remark: 'here he was cold and phlegmatic, instead of agitated and impassioned;' 'here he was boisterous and stormy, instead of displaying wounded sensibility and silent anguish;' 'throughout he appeared a *robustious perriwig pated fellow*; instead of the amiable and accomplished Prince of Denmark.' " Boaden dismissed Cooke's Hamlet with the words "neglectful impudence, or insulting ignorance" and condemned him severely for being imperfect in his lines.[109] Although Cooke had performed Hamlet a few scattered times during his formative days and as early as 1785 had prepared a script thoroughly marked for business with notes on traditional stage practices, it is evident from his diary that after he was assigned Hamlet he spent little time in additional study and preparation.[110]

Cooke appeared on Saturday, 16 October, at Brighton as Shylock and as Sir Archy to "unbounded applause."[111] By 1 November, he had recouped himself somewhat in London with reappearances as Falstaff in *Merry Wives* ("a rich specimen of comic acting"), Sir Pertinax, Macbeth, Shylock, to which he had devoted a more than usual share of energy, and Iago ("super excellent").[112] Until late December, Cooke appeared only in familiar roles—Bajazet, Sir Archy, Zanga, Richard, Sir Giles, Sir Pertinax, Kitely, and Macbeth. On a number of occasions he appeared only in Sir Archy after the successful but slight opera by Cooke's old friend Thomas Dibdin, *The Cabinet*, featuring John Braham and Signora Storace.

Dibdin tells of a dinner one night after *The Cabinet* when Harry Johnston did imitations of Kemble, Cooke, Kelly, Incledon, Braham, and others as Harlequin. His transcription of Cooke's Harlequin is an amusing capsule caricature of Cooke:

Cooke: *Mr. Cooke, making short-armed attitudes—*
To what base uses may we not return! A fool! a motley! I have been a fool all my life! but to change the sword of Richard for a dagger of lath? to make Iago a dom'd blacksheep! This a Toledo! and I, that am not form'd for tricks like these, must caper nimbly in a lady's chamber, fly through trap-doors, tumble on mattresses, and be in danger of my life by the edge of a feather-bed! Here's an aperture for a man of my havings to enter! If't were a bottle of sack, I could get through it well enough (*Tumbles clumsily into the leap*, and presents his face from the *other side of the opening*.) Gentlemen, I see through my error.[113]

On 23 December, Cooke surprised his audience with another of Kemble's roles, Addison's hoary stock piece, *Cato*, which Kemble had first performed in

London in 1784. In fact, it was in the Roman roles that Kemble's classic severity and precision of technique were most admired; *Cato* was the prime example of the Augustan tragedy and presented a stately and almost too perfect character in Cato. Although Cooke was not considered up to Kemble, Booth, Quin, or Sheridan, the reception was generally one of surprise, for despite his lack of majesty and weakness as the moral reasoner upon the state of man, who only toys with his emotions, he was amazingly successful portraying the veteran stoic preferring death to slavery.[114] He exceeded the expectations of the *Morning Chronicle* (24 December 1802) which felt he delivered the sublime and patriotic sentiments "with an energy that made a deep impression upon every heart." Only the *Morning Post* (31 December) found his interpretation totally lacking: ". . . the firmness of a ruffian, not of a sage, a philosopher, a patriot, a hero. . . . He knows not that there should appear, in every tone and word, and look of Cato, a tenderness, a feeling of the woes of humanity, a kindness of affection to others, such as nothing but transcendent magnanimity and wisdom could hinder from overpowering the whole soul, and dissolving it in softness." Nevertheless, the management was encouraged to take greater pains and expense with the production; they might make the piece popular once more. The suggestion was ignored, however, and except for one repeat the production was dropped. With Kemble at Covent Garden the next season, it would be impossible for Cooke to attempt the role again. Ironically, although he rarely performed Cato after 1802, Cooke would choose it for his first benefit in New York eight years later.

In January, Cooke appeared as Iago with a young provincial actor named Carles as Othello. Carles was successful enough to be asked to perform the role on three occasions, but on 7 February when Cooke performed Pierre to his Jaffier he was less effective.[115] Cooke performed Sir Pertinax before the royal family on 14 January. The presence of the royal party, which included the marquis and marchioness of Salisbury, the marchioness of Bath, the earls Harcourt and Morton, countesses of Aylesburg and Harrington, and numerous other lords and ladies and military figures, attracted one of the largest houses that season, the receipts totaling £507.[116]

"Early in March [5]," wrote Cooke, "George Colman the *Younger's* excellent comedy of John Bull made its appearance, and was greatly received." *John Bull, or an Englishman's Fire-Side*, which now seems an inane comedy saved only by a fair Stage Irishman, Dennis Brulgruddery, a role apparently written for John Henry "Irish" Johnstone's special talents, was considered by contemporary critics an excellent comedy. Dunlap judged it Colman's best.[117] Cooke also admired *John Bull*: "In several places there are evident marks of haste, but the characters in general are well drawn, and so much superior to the flimsy stuff of the day, that the faults are hid or passed over." He also recognized, however, that the play possessed little originality.[118]

The plot of *John Bull* is simple: Peregrine, portrayed by Cooke, had run away from England as a lad. At the opening of the play, he is shipwrecked on the coast of Cornwall, learns that he is near Penzance and that his old friend Job Thornberry (John Bull or the Englishman played by John Fawcett) still lives there. Peregrine hears a cry of distress, rescues Mary Thornberry (Mrs. Gibbs) who is running from her seducer Frank Rochdale (H. Johnston), who is engaged to marry Lady Caroline Braymore (Mrs. H. Johnston). She and her father, Lord Fitz-Balaam (Waddy), have just arrived at the manor house of Sir Simon Rochdale (Blanchard), Frank's father. Peregrine persuades Mary to remain at the Red Cow Inn, where Brulgruddery (John Henry Johnstone) is master, until he returns from Penzance. After totally improbable complications, Peregrine reconciles Mary and Job, Frank marries Mary, and Lady Caroline, who learns from Tom Shuffleton (Lewis) that Frank is attached to another, consents to marry Shuffleton. As one might anticipate, Peregrine turns out to be Sir Simon's elder brother.

Cooke later told Dunlap that *John Bull* was delivered act by act, since Colman needed money, but "the last act didn't come, and Mr. Harris refused to advance any more."[119] At last, necessity drove him to make a finish, and he wrote the fifth act in one night, on seperate [*sic*] pieces of paper, and as he filled one piece after the other, he threw them on the floor; then after finishing his liquor, went to bed in the morning of the day he had promised that Mr. Harris should have the *denouement* of the play. Mr. Harris, late in the day, tired of waiting, sent Fawcett to him, and he insisted upon going into his bed-chamber and waking him." There Fawcett found the last act scattered on the floor. "Fawcett gathered together the scraps, and brought them to the theatre in his pocket-handkerchief."[120]

Colman's play was a resounding success that season, running with few interruptions, other than benefits, until the end of the season and accumulating at least forty-five performances. Cooke, however, gained little from Peregrine. Comments on him are sparse, and the general consensus seems to be that the part was unsuited to his "line of acting." As the play went through its repeats, however, Cooke became more mellow in the role, surer of his lines, and began to gain more favor from the audience.[121] The popularity of the play brought the king and queen and three of the princesses to Covent Garden on 17 March, their first visit in two months.[122]

Cooke took his third benefit on Wednesday, 20 April, choosing *The Man of the World* and *Comus*. He took the title role in the afterpiece, and his close friend Charles Incledon, a leading singer at Covent Garden, appeared as the principal Bacchanal. As Dunlap suggests, Cooke's irregularities were beginning to tell, and consequently his night was poorly attended. On 15 April, Cooke did not appear in *John Bull* but was replaced by William Henry Murray, the son of Charles. Earlier that month, Cooke had been so drunk as to prevent *John Bull* from coming off well and had been hissed by the audience.[123] It appears from the playbills that because of continued irregularities Cooke was replaced in *John Bull* for the remainder of the season, appearing in only thirty-three of the total performances. The accounts show that receipts for his benefit were extremely low, only £220, whereas the singer John Braham's on 18 April earned £563 and Lewis's on 2 April £550.

Similar aberrations were to plague Cooke until the end of the season and were all too common for the remainder of his career. Indeed, he seemed to have reached the point of no return. Nonetheless, he managed to get through his own benefit and to appear as Sir Philip Blandford for Munden's night on 29 April. On 4 May, Cooke was scheduled to act in M. G. Lewis's *The Harper's Daughter* for Mr. and Mrs. H. Johnston's benefit.[124] The day before the performance, Johnston received a note from Cooke informing him that his peace of mind was so disturbed, that he was afraid he should not be able to appear the next evening and would probably not perform any more that season. Before the performance, for which Henry Siddons substituted for Cooke, Johnston read an address full of rancor and illiberality against Cooke, and then read and commented on Cooke's note.[125]

Cooke did not reappear until 20 May for Mrs. Litchfield's benefit performance of *King John*, as altered by Dr. Richard Valpy of Reading in 1800. Prior to this performance, it had been given only at Reading School. Dr. Valpy, who tended to moralize Shakespeare, had omitted Shakespeare's first act and replaced it with additions of his own, as well as underplaying Falconbridge and in general correcting Shakespeare "as he would correct a boy's exercise, putting in and putting out as it suited his fancy."[126]

No sooner had Cooke appeared before the audience than he received hisses from several quarters of the house. He stepped forward, quieted the house, and then made what would become a frequent apology. He first stated that he could not "affect to be ignorant of the cause of this disapprobation." He solemnly declared that he had failed to appear in *Harper's Daughter* through no fault of his, for he was confined to bed for twenty-four hours by a "violent disorder." There were many things in the part which he admired; he was never more anxious to come forward. Whatever acts of imprudence he might have committed, or might yet commit, in this instance he felt that his conduct was unimpeachable. The applause which he had received in that house had made the deepest impression upon his mind, and he wished to show himself not undeserving of the public favor. The audience, as they would time and time again, accepted Cooke's story as a satisfactory explanation.[127] Fortunately for Cooke, one of his great talents was his ability to often appease an audience no matter what the circumstances.

Cooke was well accepted that night and repeated King John on 6 June for the benefit of Mrs. Mills and Miss Howells.[128] Comments in *The Monthly Mirror* for May 1803 reflect the general impression of his performance:

Mr. Cooke performed the part in a masterly style. In the scene with Hubert [Carles] where he prompts him to murder Arthur he was particularly great, and indeed in all the character he appeared to infinite adantage. The character . . . is a very arduous one to represent; he is a Tyrant of a different cast to Richard: at one moment brave and scorning superstition; at the other eagerly seeking the influence of the Pope which he had before scorned. . . . Where the genius of the author soared aloft Mr. Cooke kept pace with equal wing, where Shakespeare flagged he bore him up. The contempt with which he treats King Philip at his entrance and his mode of proposing Peace or War; the irony and disdain of these lines "Must I have Philip's sanction to my title?" were admirably given. The scene with Hubert in which he urges him to murder Arthur, his diffidence, his soothing, his breaks, pauses, and manner of giving the distant hints were truly descriptive of nature in such a depraved state of agitation. . . . The dying scene of this weak broken hearted man was well conducted . . . anguish, sorrow and remorse were the attendants of his couch and he breathes his last sigh with the most rapturous applauses—from a crowded audience.[129]

Under Kemble Cooke would be compelled to act the part of Hubert rather than the title role. King John remained in his repertoire in England and America.

Thomas Abthorpe Cooper, an English-born actor, had failed to rise in the ranks as he had expected, despite appearances at Covent Garden in 1795 as Hamlet, Macbeth, and Lothario in *The Fair Penitent*. In 1796, he had gone to the United States on the urging of Thomas Wignell, co-manager of the Chestnut Street Theatre in Philadelphia. By 1803, Cooper had become the leading tragedian in America and a firm favorite. With Kemble's departure from Drury Lane, Sheridan was left with a void in his company, and thus Cooper was invited to appear as a visiting star. Cooper arrived in March and performed Hamlet, Macbeth, and Richard III, but attendance was at first mediocre and then began to fall off. Consequently, Cooper went to the provinces, performing in Manchester, Liverpool, and other cities.[130]

Cooper and Cooke first became acquainted in May. If Dunlap is to be believed, and presumably much of the information on this fragment of their association came directly from Cooper, Cooper was introduced to Cooke by John Dwyer, a principal comedian at Drury Lane, at the desire of Thomas Holcroft, the playwright, who had told Cooper and Cooper's old teacher, the novelist and radical political theorist William Godwin, that he too would like to "become acquainted with a man of Mr. Cooke's notoriety and celebrity in the theatrical world." Consequently, Cooke and Cooper first met at dinner at Wrekin's in Broad Court. Over a bottle they quickly became "warm and confidential friends." During the ensuing conversation, Cooke discovered that Cooper had been given a benefit for 10 June but, being a stranger, had considered not taking it. Cooke offered to play for him, providing Harris would consent. Cooper at first declined but later promised to consult with friends on the suggestion. The two then departed.

Cooper finally assented to Cooke's offer and invited him to dine at his lodgings with friends, including Godwin. Godwin and Cooke had never met and, although total opposites, seemed to get along during the early part of the evening. Before long, however, Godwin became apathetic toward Cooke's incessant talk, made more eloquent by wine, and fell asleep. Cooke stayed until 6:00 A.M. and agreed to meet Cooper at 10:00 A.M. when they would breakfast and travel to Belmont, near Uxbridge, to speak with Harris at his residence.[131] Dunlap's anecdote concerning this meeting is typical of the embellishments and liberties he takes throughout his life of Cooke. Nevertheless, if we delete those "facts" that are known to be incorrect, we get a good deal of insight into Cooke's habits during May 1803. The anecdote is well known and will thus be greatly abbreviated.[132]

Cooper and Cooke arrived at Belmont in the afternoon. Cooke explained his mission to Harris, who questioned such a practice, especially considering Covent Garden's exclusive right to Cooke's services. Cooke combatted all arguments and at last Harris agreed. On Cooke's arrival, Harris had been walking with guests on his grounds, and Cooke had been ushered into the library and left with several bottles of wine. In the meantime, Cooper had waited for Cooke on the commons near the house. Late in the afternoon, Cooke finally rejoined Cooper, and they returned to London. Cooke had become quite intoxicated, and Cooper decided to drive him to Holcroft's, to ply him with tea. Instead, Holcroft offered Cooke more wine. At the last minute, with the management and company in consternation, Cooke arrived at the theatre. Supposedly, these were the events that led to Cooke's extended absence beginning 4 May.[133]

On 10 June, as announced, Cooke appeared at Drury Lane as Iago opposite Cooper's Othello, Mrs. Pope's Desdemona, Charles Kemble's Cassio, and Mrs. Powell's Emilia. This was only one of two occasions in which Cooke would appear at Drury Lane. The most dramatic event of the evening was the collapse of Mrs. Maria Ann Pope, whom Cooke had met first in Dublin as Miss Campion. Cooke led her off stage and a few days later she was dead.[134]

Cooke's third season ended much as the second, with Cooke beginning to demonstrate less and less concern for his professional status and responsibilities. It would be unfair, however, to conclude that he had been a constant problem during any one of these seasons. The success of *John Bull* prevented as many appearances in his favorite roles as he no doubt would have preferred, especially with Kemble absent from London. Nonetheless, he performed all of his most popular roles and added Cato, Hamlet, Comus, Peregrine, and King John. For the first time since coming to London, probably because of the decline in attendance the previous season, Cooke performed Richard less often than other popular roles—only three times. His most performed role, after Peregrine, was Sir Pertinax, seen twenty-one times. In all he performed ninety times, including afterpiece appearances in *Love-a-la-Mode* (five times) and *Comus* once, a total of fourteen more appearances than in 1801–1802.[135]

As tempestuous as his first three London seasons may have been, in comparison with the years ahead, this period would prove to be the halcyon years and the highpoint of his long career.

Thomas Abthorpe Cooper (1776–1849). Co-manager of the Park Theatre. The man responsible for bringing Cooke to the United States. Author's collection.

11

"In His Cups"

As soon as Cooke had completed the Cooper benefit in June, he began his 1803 summer excursions:

> As usual, Manchester, and AS USUAL. Afterward Chester, and then for the first time Cheltenham. I received more benefit from the air and water than from the theatre. I acted a few nights at Worcester, and then proceeded to Derby, Chesterfield, and Nottingham; the weather was fine, and the harvest good. I received every politeness and civility from Mr. and Mrs. Wrench, the principal proprietors. . . . I have just recollected I forgot to mention the pretty little town of Ludlow in Shropshire, where I acted three or four nights, to a very genteel, if not a numerous audience.[1]

The Manchester theatre, Cooke's first stop this summer, had been undergoing the kind of turmoil common in provincial operations at this time. The public, expressing a growing sense of power frustrated by an increasing political self-consciousness and a lack of parliamentary representation, sought any avenue of public assembly to voice its complaints, including the theatre.[2] Consequently, T. L. Bellamy and Thomas Ward had been subjected to a good deal of attack, mostly unfounded. Even Cooke was brought into the controversy. A pamphlet issued in 1803 quoted him as saying "he should not have left this Theatre had he succeeded in his last proposals of an advance of ten shillings and six-pence per week!"[3] But all such controversy was put aside when he, "AS USUAL," more than satisfied the Manchester public with his engagement commencing on 13 June with his old standby, Richard III.[4] During his stay, Cooke also brought out his Cato.[5]

From Manchester he proceeded to Chester with his usual great success and then to Cheltenham, where he "had but a scanty benefit."[6] At the beginning of July he performed three weeks in Nottingham.[7] Although Cooke does not mention it in his journal, he apparently performed in Gloucester at the beginning of August. A handwritten document at Harvard, probably copied from a journal or newspaper, dated 4 August, mentions that he was extremely popular there. "His benefit was a very good one. The house indeed was so very crowded that many went into the pit at Box price and several could not get in at all." At Gloucester he performed Richard, Harmony in *Everyone Has His Faults*, and Sir Archy. It is possible that Cooke, when he refers to Worcester, means Gloucester.

During the second week in August, he was in Ludlow acting Richard on 13 August and Iago on the 15th to the Othello and Desdemona of Mr. and Mrs. Henry Siddons.[8] Toward the end of August, he took his benefit at Derby as Iago and Sir Archy, and then, during the Chesterfield Race Week, beginning on 29 August, performed four nights under Wrench and Robertson.[9] With the conclusion of Race Week at Chesterfield, Cooke completed his 1803 summer tour.

Over the summer Kemble had completed negotiations with Covent Garden, buying a sixth share in the theatre, and consequently was engaged not only as actor but as acting manager as well. In the bargain Covent Garden had also acquired Kemble's sister, Sarah Siddons, and brother, Charles Kemble. The dynasty had moved into Covent Garden in toto. Upon learning of the new arrangement, Cooke must have felt severely mortified, although his only diary comment was to acknowledge their presence.[10] Covent Garden, an inferior theatre compared to Sheridan's eleven-year-old structure, was refurbished over the summer with an alteration of the boxes, the conversion of gallery slips into sixteen private boxes, to be rented to the socially prominent for £300 a season, and new gold and white decorations.[11] *The Monthly Mirror* described the new effect:

The ground boxes, with entrance on Bow Street, were in a beautiful green with panels of white and a gold border. The new private boxes in the third tier consisted of seven on each side, extending from the box near the stage to the gallery, with a narrow gold lattice projecting between each. An upper box was added on each side to those already over the stage door and the boxes converted from the gallery slips were given a raised iron rail, similar to an arrangement at Drury Lane. A green drop curtain was also installed, ornamented in the center with a royal arms in gold. The entire effect was as added lightness, elegance and simplicity.[12]

There was a great deal of suspense among those favoring Cooke as to whether he would be able to act at all under Kemble's management, and if so, whether he would retain his own repertoire. Kemble was welcomed to his new post with a traditional English dinner, which even Sheridan attended to wish him well. Nonetheless, there was considerable ill will toward Kemble among the acting company. When Lewis, the former stage manager and long-time loyal Covent Garden employee, was told that his duties would be taken over by Mr. Kemble, he was naturally unsettled and organized a vigilant opposition; great hatred was worked up against Kemble. Cooke was not the least of Kemble's problems. They had been avowed rivals since their initial dueling over Richard III, and to appease Cooke and the other leading actors at Covent Garden, Kemble, possibly at Harris's urging, entertained them at his home. Boaden attended and found Cooke on his best behavior.[13] As the evening wore on and Kemble got drunker, he began to complain of the newspapers' prejudice towards him, whereupon Cooke, "with a look of the most sarcastic bitterness," quoted the speech about ambition's ladder from *Julius Caesar*. Kemble ignored the recitation and called for more brandy.[14] He may have felt it wise to placate Cooke who retained a strong hold on a large segment of the public.

At first it appeared that all would go well. Kemble agreed that they should play subordinate characters to each other, for even Kemble was aware that the Covent Garden company was now the best in England and he wished to do nothing to jeopardize this strength. The aggregate was, in fact, one of the best in the entire history of the London stage. As the season progressed, however, Kemble gradually withdrew himself from such supporting roles, while Cooke continued to be cast in parts in which he could not but appear at a disadvantage in comparison with Kemble.[15] One of the mysteries of Cooke's behavior is why he did not immediately apply for a position at Drury Lane; in an 1806 journal, he indicated that he had thought about doing so.[16] Dunlap's comment is that "to a mind of common prudence this step would have been suggested the moment J. P. Kemble became a proprietor and acting manager." Perhaps so, but the challenge to Cooke's talents, the retaining of his position in the company now with his great rival in the ranks, must have seemed too much for him to pass up. Besides, Sheridan's financial situation at Drury Lane was more tenuous than ever and of this Cooke was well aware. On the other hand, there is no question that Cooke had been apprehensive. John Taylor had met him in the green room, presumably at the end of the preceding season, and found him "so much affected by liquor, that he was unfit to appear before the audience." Taylor questioned him as to the cause of his melancholy, and Cooke revealed that he had just learned of Kemble's negotiations with the proprietors. "Of course," said Cooke, "I shall be deprived of my characters. There is nobody but Black Jack whom I fear to encounter." Taylor assured him that he was wrong about Kemble. "For his interest," retorted Taylor, "he would rather bring you more forward." As Taylor began to mention roles in which they could support each other, Cooke's spirits rose, and he replied, "If so, we will drive the world before us."[17] Thomas Munden went so far as to suggest that once Cooke realized he was not being assigned roles always equal to those of Kemble, he demonstrated his resentment either by marring a performance through the brandy bottle or by absentia. This indeed may have been the cause of a few missed nights but was certainly an exaggeration of Cooke's reaction to Kemble.[18]

Cooke was given the first entry, on 21 September, as Kitely, and he played his popular role with more skill and effect than ever before. The audience greeted him with an enthusiastic and prolonged burst of applause.[19] Kemble followed on 24 September with Hamlet, the same role in which he had made his debut at Drury Lane twenty years before. In quick succession, Cooke ran through "Thalia's Darling Son in the Scotch Knight" (Sir Pertinax) and Peregrine. On Saturday, 1 October, Cooke made one of his frequent one-night stands, this time at the Theatre Royal, Richmond-Green, for the benefit of Miss F. Drake, playing Richard III to her Lady Anne.[20]

Upon his return from Richmond, Cooke and Kemble were at last announced to appear together on 3 October. Kemble was true to his word; while Cooke played Richard, Kemble consented to play the subordinate role of Richmond. The event drew in receipts of £317, and the audience was spellbound watching the two great rivals on the same stage for the first time in London.[21] Cooke's Richard was well received, although as usual he was criticized for lacking dignity. Kemble's Richmond "was every thing which the audience could have wished," and the partisans greeted him with great applause, resolved to convince him that, by stooping to perform a subordinate part, he could not lower himself in their esteem.[22] *The Monthly Mirror*, however, felt Richmond's animated speeches came "but tardily off" and that throughout Kemble's entire performance there was a languor.[23]

On 6 October, in Home's *Douglas*, Kemble, Cooke, and Sarah Siddons appeared together for the first time. Cooke took Glenalvon, Mrs. Siddons was Lady Randolph, and Kemble took the subordinate role of Old Norval.[24] Cooke's reputation was holding up well. The *Morning Post* greeted him the next day with "his manners and looks have most congenial colours for aptly colouring the gloomy features of jealousy, hypocrisy, and revenge." The *Morning Herald* ranked his Glenalvon among his best performances. The *Times* found a hardness in the performance, and the *Morning Chronicle* doubted that a better Glenalvon could be found but was somewhat disappointed with Cooke. Overall, the season thus far had brought Cooke nothing but plaudits and encouragement.

For Monday, 17 October, Kemble planned the event of the fall, a production of Sheridan's *Pizarro* taken from the German drama of Kotzebue, which had premiered with Kemble at Drury Lane in 1799. For the first production at Covent Garden great pains had been taken: new scenery designed and constructed by Phillips, new costumes made by Mr. Dick and Mrs. Egan, and decorations added by Cresswell and Goostree. Music for the occasion was composed by Kelly. The casting was near perfection. Kemble would play his great role, Rolla the Peruvian warrior; Mrs. H. Siddons was cast as Cora, the Peruvian maiden; Incledon as the High Priest, Las Casas; Charles Kemble as Alonzo, the upright young man; and Mrs. Siddons would resume her role of Elvira, a forerunner of the prostitute with a heart of gold. Cooke was assigned the powerful title role, a villainous type but also the great idealistic hero dragged down by ambition. The public anticipation is evidenced by the large receipts for the night, £471.

The Monday arrived and brought with it near catastrophe. Sarah Siddons, who had not been well for sometime, having had to postpone her first appearance at Covent Garden as Isabella in *The Fatal Marriage*, was so unwell that she had to withdraw from the stage. Kemble addressed the audience, but the house was in a state of confusion.[25] If that were not bad enough, on Pizarro's entrance the "adventurer now added drunkenness" to his other vices.[26] The audience was unable to understand anything Cooke said. He fell back overpowered before the conclusion of the first act, looking pale and reeling in a curve as he tried under considerable agitation to walk. He made several ineffectual attempts to force himself back into action, but after muttering "Ladies and Gentlemen—my old complaint— my old complaint— my old complaint," the audience could not resist what appeared to them a sham.[27] Dunlap says "laughter caught instantaneously through the house, and amidst roars, shouts, and hisses" Cooke was helped off the stage by several attendants.[28] It is, of course, impossible to know the true nature of Cooke's unexpected action. The next morning the *Morning Post* reported:

... from sudden indisposition, of the most alarming indications, he was wholly disabled from proceeding in his part. How vociferously the public disappointment was manifested may easily be conceived. A confused conflict of hissing and applause, of cries of *Go on*; and *Off, off*, for some time alternately prevailed. Mr. Claremont at first came forward to apologize, but to little purpose; Mr. Kemble, in Rolla, then appeared, and obtained an audience, when he explained the unexpected and unavoidable change in the parts. His popularity alone could have stilled the turmult that had arisen, and after some renewed demonstrations of dissatisfaction, the performance was recommenced, Mr. H. Siddons having undertaken to fill Mr. Cooke's place.

Whatever the cause, drunkenness or true illness, Cooke had never disappointed a London audience so early in a season, and none of his earlier actions had received such extensive newspaper coverage. He could ill afford to alienate any audience now or give Kemble reason for dealing with him as he pleased. From this point on, however, Kemble began to show less sympathy toward him, and the assignation of roles favored Cooke to a markedly lessening degree.

Cooke's friends circulated the rumor that his failure had been caused by a sudden attack of a disorder which he had long suffered, but the common belief of the less charitable was that even if this were so, it resulted from "the debilitating influence of the seducing glass."[29] Three days later, Cooke was permitted to appear as Pizarro to generous encouragement, for which he repeatedly bowed respectfully in acknowledgment. *The Monthly Mirror* for November expressed disfavor with the spectacle of the piece compared to that at Drury Lane, where "height and distance" were both among "the sources of the sublime" in a play that depended more on glare and bustle, music and procession, than on individual performances. Nevertheless, it believed Cooke gave a stronger performance than any ever seen.[30] A large audience (receipts were £400) had assembled to see how Cooke would handle himself after his indisposition, and even though there were a few groans and hisses, he quite overcame their censure.[31] Although Pizarro would add little to his reputation, the *Times* (22 October 1803) provided the following analysis:

The character was delineated with all the energy, ambition and undaunted resolution which the Poet has infused into it. He gave it a new complexion, which the London

John Philip Kemble (1759–1823). Cooke's great London rival in the role of Rolla in *Pizarro*. Engraving by Dighton. Author's collection.

audience has not been accustomed to witness, and several lines drew as much applause as the best passages of his Richard the Third. His scenes with Elvira and Alonzo were unquestionably the most successful; and the threat of "Alonzo dies—at sunrise," deservedly called forth reiterating plaudits. If Cooke be rough in his colourings, if he occasionally intermingles with those passages which fall within the sole province of the Tragic Muse, somewhat of the familiar, which all who hear him feel, but which few can define, he has least the merit of thinking for himself, and tracing out a line of acting adequate to his own conceptions. . . . he is "himself alone;" he borrows from none, and shines by no reflected light.

On 27 October, Cooke reappeared in *The Gamester* with Kemble as Beverly and Sarah Siddons in her usual role of Mrs. Beverly, but the novelty of the evening was Cooke's Stukely. "The cool rancour of the soliloquies, and the plausible hypocrisy put on the presence of *Beverly*, were sketched with the hand of a master."[32] While in America Cooke told Dunlap that on one occasion while performing *The Gamester* with Kemble, "we played a scene of the third act in the second. I was frighted out of my wits. 'We're wrong' says I: 'Go on,' says he—and we went through it. When we came off, I exclaimed, 'Do you know what we have done? we have played the scene of the third act.' 'I know it,' says John, very coolly. 'And what shall we do in the third act?' 'Play the second.' And so we did. But the best of the joke was, that the papers never found it out."[33]

Rowe's domestic tragedy *The Fair Penitent*, on 5 November, provided Cooke with his first new role this season, Sciolto, to Charles Kemble's Lothario and John Philip's Horatio. Once more Cooke won the accolades of the evening. *The Monthly Mirror* called his performance the only uniqueness of the production and found him impressive throughout. They were especially taken with him in the final act's conflict between honor and affection; "the rigid duties of the judge and the agony of the parent were powerfully depicted."[34] The *Morning Post* (7 November 1803) reported that he had "enlarged the sphere of his powers, and gave him new claims to the admiration and praise of the public." He was, it appears, highly successful in a role which was believed to be not within his line. The fullest reflection of this success appeared in the *Morning Chronicle* (7 November 1803):

Cooke was extremely well liked in Sciolto . . . the quick feelings and high spirits of the man of honour, he portrayed with much truth as well as boldness. When he presented his daughter with the dagger which was to expiate her crime and to wash away the shame of her family, we saw before us a hero who after the great examples of antiquity supressed [sic] the voice of nature in his bosom, and from a sense of duty did what he knew must render him for ever wretched. It seemed a deed of doubtful morality; but every one admired and approved it in the magnanimity of the motive.

A minor setback for what was otherwise proving to be a most propitious autumn for Cooke after his one earlier major fall from grace occurred on 12 November. As Sandy MacTab in *Three Per Cents*, a new comedy by

Frederick Reynolds, both play and Cooke were damned by all, and the play was quickly withdrawn. Five days later, he totally redeemed himself before a large house, the receipts totaling £410, as Pierre to Kemble's Jaffier and Mrs. Siddons' Belvidera, in *Venice Preserv'd*, dividing with their prior superior claims in their roles the attention and applause of the house.[35]

At this point, Cooke must have felt that everything was going his way and that all his fears of Kemble's predominance was groundless. For the first time that season he came forward as Shylock on 19 November. It was an unusually strong cast, with Sarah Siddons as Portia, Charles Kemble as Bassanio, Munden as Launcelot, and Mrs. St. Ledger as Nerissa. The production was made even stronger with Kemble acting as Antonio, his first time in the role.

By their majesties' command, *Measure for Measure* was presented at Covent Garden for the first time in twenty years on 21 November. The cast featured Kemble as the Duke, Charles Kemble as Claudio, Mrs. Siddons as Isabella, and, for the first time, Cooke as Angelo. The *Morning Post* (22 November 1803) reported that there was "as crowded and brilliant an assemblage as ever graced a Theatre," The account books confirm that it was one of the largest nights of the season, with receipts over £523. A description of the event in the *Morning Post* almost justifies Cooke's later outburst against "Yankee manners" and his frequent references while in America to having stood before his "royal master George the Third, and received his Imperial approbation!"[36] Nothing comparable to the pomp and circumstance of a "Command Performance" would greet Cooke in America. This particular evening began with Incledon, Hill, Martyr, Mrs. Atkins, and Miss Martyr singing "God Save the King," followed by rapturous applause. Between the mainpiece and the farce, *Raising the Wind*, "Rule Britannia" was sung. The royal box was resplendent: King George in the full uniform of a field marshall and the queen in a white and silver robe with a head-dress topped by a plumage of black feathers and ornamented with a tiara fronted with diamonds; Princess Elizabeth in a puce-colored robe studded with stars; and Augusta and Sophia wearing white and silver head-dresses of white plumes and bandeaux of diamonds. Accompanying the royal family were the marquis of Salisbury, the earls of Harrington and Chesterfield, and the countess of Harrington. In the box opposite were the duke of Cambridge and a party of friends, and even the circle boasted the presence of the earl of Uxbridge and his family and the duchess of Leeds. Cooke's performance earned applause from all quarters, and *The Monthly Mirror* once more considered his performance the major novelty of the night; the *Morning Herald* declared that his Angelo had all "the sternness, severity, and pride of the original."[37]

On 28 November, Cooke relinquished Macbeth to Kemble and took the role of Macduff. The only major event of the evening was the elimination of the appearance of Banquo's ghost, which dissatisfied the audience; the evening belonged to Sarah Siddons' famous Lady Macbeth.[38]

Around Christmas time Cooke had been suffering from a cold, brought on no doubt by his usually low resistance, so that in January, although announced for Falstaff in *Henry IV, Part 2*, he was unable to perform. The production was postponed until 17 January; a notice to that effect was posted at 3:00 P.M. on the 9th, the day of the announced performance.[39] This seems to have been the only occasion when Kemble felt it worthy to allude to Cooke in his memoranda book: "Mr. Cooke could not act in Henry 4th P.2d."[40] I have located no corroborative evidence to support Dunlap's explanation that Cooke, although ill, had been intoxicated and attacked in a public house, thus causing the absence as Falstaff and another absence in *Jane Shore* on the 11th. Furthermore, Dunlap claimed that Cooper, apparently serving as his source, had returned to London from Liverpool, found Cooke with the marks of a violent blow on his face, and was urged by Cooke to present a challenge for satisfaction to the gentleman who had provoked him. John Till Allingham, the playwright, was called in as a disinterested party to explain that Cooke had insulted the gentleman, a Mr. Johnson from Dublin, and had gotten what he deserved. Cooke, it seems, was so drunk that he could not recall the circumstances of the blow he had received.[41]

On 17 January, Cooke finally did appear as Falstaff, with Kemble as King Henry, Charles Kemble as the Prince of Wales, and Mrs. Mary Davenport as Mrs. Quickly. Cooke was considered especially effective in the interview with the Lord Chief Justice, played by Murray, and in his panegyric upon the divine powers of sack.[42] A number of reviewers found him more effective in this inferior version of the Falstaff plays than in the other two. The *Courier* (circa 18 January 1806) explained:

He has less occasion for the exercise of that self merriment and almost constant laughter which are so requisite in the other characters. He everywhere depicted him as gifted with nice discrimination, sound sense, and a profound knowledge of human nature, without ever degrading the character, as it is too often degraded, by low buffoonery, and practical jokes. We were even surprised to see Mr. Cooke's countenance, which is rather of harsh and rigid cast, relax into all that soft expansion of feature which should characterise careless levity and genuine good nature.

Three nights later, Cooke appeared as Iago to Kemble's Othello. The performance with Charles Kemble as Cassio and Mrs. Siddons as Desdemona, was praised for the even balance of the cast, especially the four leading roles.[43] Cooke, on the other hand, according to Munden, remarked that it was difficult to make a point opposite Kemble's Othello. "It seemed to me as if I were a snail, which, endeavouring to issue from its shell, finds a large stone impeding its progress."[44]

In February, Kemble called upon Cooke to sacrifice King John, which he had played the previous season, and play Hubert, a change which did him little harm but added no appreciable gains to his season. Even with Mrs. Siddons' Constance and Charles Kemble's Falconbridge, "Mr. Cooke's Hubert is perhaps more skilful than anything in the whole play. If Mr. Kemble was great in the scene where Hubert is tempted to put Arthur to death, at least Mr. Cooke was an equal," wrote *The Monthly Mirror*.[45]

On 23 February, Cooke was given the thankless role of Lieutenant Seymour in a new comedy by Joseph George Holman, *Love Gives the Alarm* (never published), but the production never had a chance. Cooke's role of a stern father was within his province, but by the end of Act V the murmurs in the house had become quite general and the play was quickly removed.[46] Even Cooke later forgot the name of the character he played in this ill-fated comedy but remembered in 1807 that it was "damned [the] first night."[47]

For his benefit on 26 April, Cooke wrote in his journal: "I took 'Such Things Are' for my own night. Why, I know not; it could neither be from *its* novelty, or *my* desire to appear in *Haswell*, but 'such things are.' "[48] A contemporary source states that at the time Cooke said that he chose Inchbald's comedy so that Lewis could appear as Twineall, which is as good an explanation as any, for Inchbald, as indicated earlier, was never a favorite with Cooke.[49] Cooke also performed Sir Archy that night, but the mainpiece, called by the *Morning Post* (28 April 1804) "a very middling dish," was a poor choice. For the second season in succession, Cooke's benefit drew a small house.[50]

The remainder of Cooke's fourth season in London was relatively uneventful. On 1 May, for Munden's night, he took Don Carlos in *A Bold Stroke for a Husband*, and for Mrs. Litchfield's, on 30 May, Osmond in *Castle Spectre*. On the 23d, he played Cohenberg in *Siege of Belgrade* for Mrs. Martyr's benefit.

Cooke also performed again this season at Drury Lane, the last time, for Raymond's benefit; apparently, he gained Harris's permission as he had for Cooper's benefit the previous year. This time, however, he mistakenly let himself be cast in a role for which he was in no way suited or prepared, Coriolanus. Only William Dowton as Menenius and Mrs. Powell as Volumnia came off well. Cooke substituted the boisterous, sneering bully for the noble, ardent, and high-minded Roman. According to *Walker's Hibernian Magazine* (July 1804), he brought laughter from the audience at the wrong moments, especially where Coriolanus "begs the voices of the people," and "Out Heroded Herod" in the scene where Tullus Ausidius taunts him with the epithet of "boy."

On 11 June, he made his only appearance as the Ghost for Kemble's Hamlet and then gave his last performance of the season, on 18 June, as Falstaff in the first part of *Henry IV*.

Cooke performed seventy-nine times this season, including two appearances in *Love-a-la-Mode*. He also delivered a patriotic address on four occasions. The two original characters he attempted were inconsequential, and the plays themselves were damned and withdrawn. In all, he performed twenty-seven roles, including fourteen new for him in London.[51]

Kemble's first season at Covent Garden had been moderately successful. The Shakespearean repertory expected early in the season had been effected with a good deal of care and cost, though not always with satisfaction. Kemble and Harris, however, had continued to depend on the box-office popularity of such trivia as Dibdin's *The English Fleet in 1342*, which packed them in beginning in mid-December, and a carryover of *John Bull*, which tied Cooke up for sixteen performances. The theatre took in £63,182, although true profits were slim, only £3,959. Kemble, on the other hand, did well for himself. He drew some £2,000 from the treasury, shared £1,260 from a private box with Harris, and was paid £315 in lieu of a benefit.[52]

Kemble, with a good deal of finesse, slowly managed to wrestle to a large measure the acting leadership from Cooke. I find nothing, however, to support Baker's conclusion that by the end of the season Cooke "sadder and wiser, was taking what solace he could from strong drink—so much so, in fact, that he was on occasion unable to act."[53] Indeed, for once, Boaden is closer to the mark when he suggests that Kemble and Cooke stood side by side by the close of the 1803-1804 season.[54] It is true that Cooke had the worse press thus far in his career as a result of his drunken behavior or, more correctly, illness resulting from his drunkenness. But unlike the preceding two seasons, the worst instances of such behavior occurred very early in the season. Afterwards he redeemed himself to such an extent that time and time again it was Cooke, and not Kemble or Sarah Siddons, who was considered the novelty of the evening, often in Kemble's own Shakespearean revivals. The cloud that loomed above not only Cooke's head but also Kemble's was a thirteen-year-old boy named Betty, who would shake the professional stability of both tragedians the next season.

Between the fourth and fifth seasons, Cooke once more took to the road. His first stop was Birmingham, where he was joined by Mr. and Mrs. Litchfield. He began his Birmingham engagement on 27 June with Richard III and remained until 13 July, performing, in addition to Richard (three times), Iago, Falstaff, Sir Pertinax (twice), Peregrine, Shylock, Kitely, and Rolla. On 28 June, he performed Iago opposite the Othello of Carles, with whom he had briefly acted in London.[55] Rumors circulated in London that Cooke's conduct in Birmingham had created difficulties, but a Birmingham correspondent for *The Monthly Mirror* quickly squelched the report: "It is sufficient to assert there was not the slightest ground for any such rumour, and that he gave so much satisfaction to the inhabitants by his performances *on*, and by his deportment, *off* the stage, that his benefit [Kitely] yielded near £170."[56] Furthermore, the *Birmingham Gazette* reported: "With this truly great Actor we have been much pleased. His Richard on Wednesday seemed if possible still more popular than on his former representation of the character; indeed to the sensible mind such incomparable acting must prove an inexhaustible source of pleasure."[57] The engagement was so successful that McCready extended it for two additional nights.

From Birmingham Cooke went to Worcester, Hereford, Holyhead, and Dublin on his way to engagements in northern Ireland. During the winter season, Cooke had agreed to act three weeks or ten nights for 300 guineas under Michael Atkins, the manager at Belfast and its satellite theatres of Newry and Londonderry. The previous summer, Atkins had given William Henry West Betty, the "Young Roscius," his first professional engagement of four nights in Belfast.[58] At the end of the 1803–1804 season, he had advertised in his benefit bill that he had experienced heavy losses, and he appealed to the public for relief. These losses apparently stemmed from his efforts to obtain the best performers possible, like Cooke, at rather high prices.[59] Atkins extended his offer to Cooke by proffering him an additional 100 guineas to perform for a week at Londonderry, prior to going to Belfast. So on 5 August Cooke arrived in Londonderry, acted one week and the following Monday. Then he went to Belfast,[60] where for the appointed three weeks he acted at the Belfast Theatre (the Arthur Street Theatre), presenting Richard, Sir Pertinax, and Shylock "with singular success."[61]

Atkins' financial difficulties likely involved Cooke, for Cooke records in his journal that there was trouble in the settlement of accounts. He also states that he was ill at the time, with two physicians and a surgeon attending him. He adds that he declined pressing the debt Atkins owed him because "should any thing happen to me, not having any family, there should not anything be in my possession to appear against him."[62]

On 16 September 1804, Drury Lane opened its winter season with Andrew Cherry's *The Soldier's Daughter*, a holdover from the previous season. The next night Covent Garden dipped into its tried-and-true basket and pulled out *John Bull*. In May 1803, France and Britain had renewed their hostilities after the British refused to evacuate Malta, despite the Amiens Treaty of 1802. Both houses had chosen their opening accordingly.

When the hour of invasion, that is, the hour when England is threatened to see every thing overturned and prophaned, which she has ever held dear and sacred, when the roar of the hostile cannon is daily heard re-echoed by our shores, it well becomes the calm, steady and thoughtful intrepidity of an Englishman, to sit tranquil and composed at *his own fire-side*. Such was his appearance at this Theatre [Covent Garden] last night, where he seemed to enjoy all the honest eccentricities of his own character, and the unostentatious comforts of his domestic hearth as if even the rumour of hostile menace, had never attempted to assail his ear.[63]

Less than three weeks later, on 5 October, Cooke made his first appearance of the season as Sir Pertinax and "was applauded to the very echo that did applaud again."⁶⁴ His performance brought in the largest receipts thus far that season, £315.19.6;⁶⁵ however, on the 8th, *Pizarro*, with Cooke in the title role, topped it with £383.⁶⁶ On the 11th, *The Gamester* had to be postponed because of Mrs. Siddons' illness, so *John Bull* returned and this time Cooke suffered once more through Peregrine. The next day Cooke played Kitely, and on Saturday he traveled to Brighton to play Sir Pertinax, with great success. He was on the go a great deal this month. He returned to London and on Monday appeared for the first time as Richard III. It was on this occasion that Cooke added the lines to the troops and was reported as having improved the fifth act. He immediately returned to Brighton and "with unexampled kindness" played the same role for Mrs. Litchfield's benefit, "which was crowded to the utmost extent of the Theatre."⁶⁷ He played at the Brighton Theatre under the Prince of Wales' patronage throughout the month, traveling back and forth between London and Brighton. An unidentified article in the Harvard Theatre Collection mentions that he played the Stranger for Mrs. Woodfall's benefit on 27 October, Lord Townly for Mr. and Mrs. Wheeler's benefit, and closed the theatre with Penruddock and Sir Archy for the benefit of John Brunton, who had only recently become manager of the Brighton Theatre.⁶⁸

The latter part of October offered no difficulties for Cooke since Reynolds' comedy *The Blind Bargain; or, Hear It Out*, which opened on 24 October, played for fifteen straight nights, until 14 November and then for four more nights beginning 19 November. It proved to be something of a bonanza for the management, drawing in receipts ranging from £288 to £410.⁶⁹ In the meantime, however, Cooke appeared for the first time in London as Strictland, "a bare-faced copy of Jonson's Kitely" but greatly inferior, in Dr. Hoadley's 1747 comedy *The Suspicious Husband*, a play and role he already knew well from the provinces. The cast was doubtlessly strengthened with Cooke's Strictland joining Lewis's Ranger and Brunton's Frankly. But as one reviewer pointed out, "there does not seem to be any great necessity for thrusting a performer of Mr. Cooke's eminence into a part, in the performance of which there may be some risk of his diminishing his acknowledged reputation, and where the highest degree of success cannot add a single wreath to his professional fame."⁷⁰ Cooke did all he could with the role, and the press, although ranking his portrayal of jealousy with his Iago and Kitely, generally agreed that his talents were wasted.⁷¹ The production itself proved to be a weak draw with receipts of only £130; Cooke did not reappear in Strictland.

On 20 November, Cooke made his first appearance that season as Falstaff in *Henry IV, Part 1* and then, two nights later, made one of his now famous slips, almost as if on schedule. That evening he had been called upon to reappear as the Ghost in Kemble's *Hamlet*. A note on the theatre's playbill at the British Museum records that "The Ghost was drunk and found so much difficulty in expressing his 'mission' and in keeping himself above ground that the Pit rose at him indignantly, to which he replied with a motion of defiance where upon a row ensued which for some time interrupted the progress of the Tragedy." Dunlap failed to learn of this event, and one wonders what he would have done with it if he had! Without doubt Cooke was drunk this evening and with no justification except for the stress, fatigue, and possible exhaustion resulting from his schedule that month. He may have been frustrated as well, not only in being assigned the Ghost but also in having to play roles like Strictland and Peregrine. For weeks he had been operating with the alcoholic's contradictory mixture of determination to stop drinking and hopelessness in the endeavor, and probably realized that more and more drink would conquer him. Fortunately, with *The Blind Bargain* running successfully, he had almost a month to dry out and recoup before reappearing on 26 November as Richard. Consequently, his drunken behavior in *Hamlet* passed virtually unnoticed.

What began that night, 26 November, and would plague him throughout the rest of the season could have easily and perhaps justifiably driven him back to the bottle. For this was the year that the "Infant Roscius," Master Betty, took London by storm.

The strange phenomenon of this thirteen-year-old boy wonder and others like him is well known, and it is not my intention to rehash Betty's bizarre career.[72] What is relevant here is that Betty, who had seen Sarah Siddons act in Belfast in 1802, was determined to become an actor and his father, an early and obnoxious example of a stage parent, acquiesced to his desires. By 1804, Betty had built up an enormous following in the provinces, and both patent houses, desiring to capitalize on this novelty, began competing for his services. Kemble and Harris were determined to snatch him up quickly, chiefly "to deprecate his engaging himself anywhere else pending the completion of his engaging with us."[73] Drury Lane's offer of half a clear benefit for seven nights' performances was indignantly turned down; Covent Garden agreed to twelve nights at 50 guineas each, plus a clear benefit, which the elder Betty accepted. Drury Lane at last met the same terms, but Betty would first appear at Covent Garden before dividing his efforts with both houses.[74]

Betty's presence in London had been ushered in with unbelievable fanfare and an extensive propaganda campaign. Puffs in the newspapers kept his name constantly before the public. When Betty and his entourage arrived in London on 25 December, *The Daily Advertiser* (26 November 1804) reported these events under three separate headlines: ARRIVED YESTERDAY—Young Roscius—The Wonder of the Age.[75]

On Cooke's reentry after a month, on 26 November, he received a foretaste of the mortification and insult that lay ahead, for there in the manager's box sat this new wonder. The night would give Cooke an advanced notice of what would become known as Bettymania. The next morning the *Morning Post* reported:

Accomplished as the performance undoubtedly was, the eyes and attention of the greater part of the audience were constantly directed to the manager's box, in which was

Master Betty (1791–1874) as Young Norval in *Douglas*. Author's collection.

seated, the Young Roscius. He was dressed in a dark coloured coat, wore his hat at all time, and occasionally had a silk handkerchief round his neck, as apprehensive of catching cold.

Betty's father accompanied him, but neither appeared interested in Cooke's performance; instead, they spent most of their time conversing with one another. As the *Morning Post* recorded, "Between the acts he came out and approached the lobby, but he was soon discovered and surrounded by crowds.... He soon hastened . . . to resume his seat." Cooke, who received more attention at command performances in the presence of the royal family than with Betty in the house, must have already known that both Kemble and Sarah Siddons had refused point-blank to act with the prodigy and that he, because of his position and reputation, would be compelled to support this young upstart.

Betty's first night at Covent Garden was as Achmet in the now forgotten tragedy *Barbarossa* on 1 December 1804. A tremendous throng rushed to see Betty. The receipts that night came to £638.18.6, the house having been sold out ten minutes after the doors opened.

As anticipated, on 4 December, Cooke was called upon to support Betty in *Douglas*, taking the role of Glenalvon, after the Young Roscius had repeated Achmet on 3 December.[76] The streets around the theatre began to fill at 4:00 P.M., and even the soldiers stationed about Covent Garden could not hold them back. The receipts that night were £573.

It was impossible for Cooke, with his own gigantic ego, not to react negatively to the presence of the boy. Playfair says that Cooke was the only actor who came in contact with Betty who considered him personally disagreeable. This may be true, but then Cooke had more at stake than most, and even his fellow-actors must have resented Betty's elevated position. But Cooke, who spent most of his career in the provinces before gaining the recognition his supremely gifted talent deserved, could not have helped feeling that such an overnight success was somehow a reflection on his own shortcomings. Cooke actually said very little about Betty that is known. In 1811, while in the United States, he met and acted with the young American Roscius, John Howard Payne, and noted: "I was visited by Master Payne, the American Roscius; I thought him a polite and sensible youth, and the reverse of our Young Roscius."[77]

Cooke appeared once more in December as Glenalvon opposite Betty's Young Norval and then was able to put Betty out of sight for a month, while the Young Roscius went on to break records at Drury Lane.[78] Cooke would never be completely free of his connection with Betty, however, and his name would appear in a score of pamphlets and memoirs of Betty written between 1804 and 1808.[79] One publication, James Blisset's *Critical Essays on the Dramatic Excellence of Young Roscius* (London, 1805), contains a typically ridiculous verse by a Joseph Weston of Wolverhampton:

> Nature, one day, with Art was notes comparing,
> 'I cannot bear', said she, 'your vaunts of sharing
> My *sole* creation! If I grant that Kemble
> May, of us twain, yourself the most resemble,
> And that, though I bestow'd the shape and face,
> You added action, energy and grace—

> What then? Exclusively is Cooke my own;
> Of thee regardless—nay, to thee *unknown* !'
> 'Marry come up!' quote Art, 'Since thus you flout me
> And boast that you can do your work without me
> Try! make one *man* (depriv'd of my assistance)
> A *perfect* play'r—and I will keep my distance.'
> 'A *man*!' Dame Nature, in a rage replied,
> 'A child—a very child shall crush thy pride!'
> True to her word, she stamp'd her infant Son
> The faithful miniature of Roscius gone—
> Cooke, Kemble, Holman, Garrick—all in one![80]

The greatest affront to Cooke, however, occurred in May 1805 when Kemble and Harris allowed Betty to perform Cooke's own role, Richard III, in his own backyard. Cooke soon took comfort in the knowledge that the success was minimal at best, that Betty and the foolish antics of his father were beginning to lose him the reverential treatment that followed the initial furor, and that Betty's Richard was not repeated.[81] Even the kindest of reviewers, *The Daily Advertiser*, wrote that "Many may with great propriety, perhaps, insist upon his inferiority to Cooke in the same character."[82] Even though Cooke would have to contend briefly with Betty once again the following season, with the sensation of Betty's presence over it was easier to take it in stride.

On 15 January 1805, Cooke created his sixth new role at Covent Garden, Lord Avondale in Thomas Morton's comedy *School of Reform*. Although the play was successful and was presented twenty-six times (Cooke performed in only twenty of these productions, for in March Hargrave took his role), there was practically no comment on the performance in the press. In fact, after a command performance on 23 January the press gave more coverage to the dress of the royal family than to the entire production. Betty reappeared on 28 January with Cooke once more supporting him as Glenalvon.

On 16 February, Cooke created the role of Lavensforth in Elizabeth Inchbald's moralistic and trivial comedy *To Marry or Not to Marry*. The play revolves chiefly around an inveterate political quarrel between Sir Oswin Mortland (Kemble) and Lavensforth. The latter is banished for his conduct and sentiments. This severe hardship he imputes to the hostile disposition and interference of Sir Oswin. Lavensforth's daughter (played by Miss Shuttleworth from the Margate Theatre) ultimately brings them together and is to marry Oswin.[83] Cooke would play Lavensforth sixteen times that season, including a command performance on 12 March. Although a slight and disagreeable part, Cooke "moulded Lavensforth into a dark revengeful character entertaining high notions of honor with all possible skill" and "left the exertions of all his competitors in the play at an immeasurable distance."[84] The reviewers agreed that the role, while clearly in Cooke's line, represented another waste of his talents.

The remainder of the spring was relatively uneventful, except for 25 March when Cooke barely averted severe censure. He had not performed for a week, and the announced mainpiece for that night, *Out of Place*, was replaced with *Richard III* because of John Braham's illness. On the theatre's bill in the British Museum is this note: "Cooke had not arrived at the time of the performance. The audience began to storm—Kemble came forward and then offered to act Richard himself and was retiring for that purpose when Cooke appeared. He told a story of being upset in a chaise and after much tumult was allowed to get through the part." A familiar Cooke anecdote, if at all true, fits this occasion more than any other. Cooke allegedly sequestered his costume in his lodgings prior to the evening call, dressed there, and upon arriving at the theatre hid himself until Kemble was forced to offer himself as Richard.[85] The preponderance of testimony, however, reveals that Cooke's professionalism, at least toward his comrades in motley, would have prevented such childish behavior, even toward "Black Jack." There is little evidence that Cooke truly delighted in harassing Kemble, despite the uneasy sensation over his status.

The *Morning Post* reported the incident the next day with little fanfare, adding "being *rallied* a little, Richard soon became himself again, and got through his part with tolerable credit."[86]

For Lewis's benefit on 6 April, Cooke took the role of a reduced officer, Mortimer, in search of his wife, in Reynolds' comedy *Laugh When You Can*, which was also given as the tenth command performance of the season. In April, before Easter, Cooke also reappeared as Glenalvon to Betty's Young Norval. After Easter, on 17 April, Cooke was missing for *John Bull* with no explanation, and Kemble had to apologize to the audience, Brunton replaced him as Peregrine.[87] The greatest event of the late spring, however, was Kemble's reentry in a Shakespearean production on 22 May for Mrs. Litchfield's night, in which both Cooke and Kemble reasserted their supremacy in classical roles over Master Betty. Kemble was Othello and Cooke as Iago drew an overflowing crowd, with receipts over £444. The audience repeatedly shook the house with their applause and acknowledged the excellence of Cooke and Kemble with rounds of ovation following each speech in the first jealousy scene.[88]

In June, Kemble granted Charles Macklin's widow a special benefit. She was in financial straits, even though she was eligible for the provisions for widows in the Covent Garden Theatrical Relief Act. *The Wonder*, with Mrs. Jordan making a rare appearance at Covent Garden, and Cooke in *Love-a-la-Mode* were presented. John Henry Johnstone, who had left Covent Garden when Kemble came, appeared for that night only as Sir Callaghan.[89] Although the benefit realized almost £400, Mrs. Macklin's financial troubles were still acute.[90] She died the following year. The circumstances of this benefit became the source of a story illustrating Cooke's generosity. John Moody, the original Major O'Flaherty, wrote in an 1806 letter that Mrs. Macklin had told him of her good fortune in having Cooke appear for her night. "Elated with her good fortune, she mentioned it to some friends, when she was told he would deceive her, for to their knowledge he had a Country engagement for *that* night. She waited on Mr. Cooke, who convinced her to the contrary, for he had put off that engagement for her's [sic], *for which he acted*, and the night was very productive indeed."[91]

This had not been a good season for Cooke. "The season passed at Covent Garden," is all Cooke says. "I did not take any night this season."[92] The 1804-1805 season was clearly a turning point for him at Covent Garden. The appearances he was compelled to make with Betty proved a gnawing frustration; the poor roles assigned to him in new mediocre comedies and the inconsequential diminution of his major roles had their effect. More and more he seemed to turn to the bottle for solace, and on several occasions he either caused disruption of a performance or failed to appear. For the first time since joining the Covent Garden company, he was not announced at all as Shylock and appeared only once as Iago. Without Kemble appearing until the end of the year, Cooke had little chance to essay his greater roles. More than half of his sixty-seven performances, the fewest since his first season, were as Lord Avondale or Lavensforth, and the remainder were scattered among roles like Glenalvon, Pizarro, Peregrine, Mortimer, Cohenberg, the Ghost in *Hamlet*, and Strictland. He appeared as Sir Pertinax on only six occasions and as Sir Archy but four times; Richard was given five performances.[93]

Cooke was once more making his country rounds in July 1805. He failed to appear for an engagement at Brighton in July, and Brunton had to apologize to the disappointed audience.[94] Instead, he began his summer interim at Birmingham under McCready, appearing first on 22 July as Richard III. He was engaged for five nights, through 27 July, and made appearances as Sir Pertinax, Sir Archy, and Shylock.[95] Cooke had been joined at Birmingham by his old friend and fellow-player at Covent Garden, Joe Munden, and the two played together in the afterpiece, *The Farmer*, on 26 July—Cooke as Farmer Blackberry and Munden as Jeremy Jumps.[96] Birmingham had grown steadily over the preceding twenty-five years and in 1805 had a population well over 70,000.[97] No doubt as a result of the demand on Cooke's nights, he was reengaged to return for additional nights in August.

Cooke was still a great favorite in Manchester as well, although he had not appeared there in two years. "That favorite Son of Thespis and unrivalled disciple of Melpomene and Thalia Mr. Cooke is again engaged to display his talents on our boards. It is unnecessary to say anything on the merits of this Gentleman. The lovers of the Drama in this Town having frequently witnessed them with enthusiastic delight."[98] Cooke played in Manchester seven nights, from 29 July through the first week in August, appearing as Richard, Sir Pertinax, Iago, Shylock, Macbeth, and Sir Archy. For his benefit he played Rolla, a strange choice for him, but as he once said, if he "could not take a liberty with his friends, who the devil could he take a liberty with?"[99] *The Stage, or Theatri-*

cal Touchstone reported that his Rolla "was by no means successful," although he had "a very excellent house. His other characters which he had before performed, obtained him much applause, except in the Scottish Tyrant which many of our critics were inclined to think he gave with more *spirit* than Shakespeare had *originally* designed. Some of his lady's speeches made *rather* against him, particularly—

> Think of this good Peers, but as thing of course
> My Lord is often thus.

The audience took these *palpable hits* with much good humour. Cooke is an old favourite, and well deserves the patronage he has always experienced from that spirited town."[100]

According to a playbill in the British Museum, on August 14 he returned to Buxton for the first time since his provincial days to appear for one night in *The Man of the World*, with Fawcett as Egerton and Mathews as Lord Lumbercourt.[101] On 23 August, he was back in Birmingham for benefit nights, appearing as Sir Pertinax, Richard III, Oakly, Lord Hastings, Petruchio, Pierre, Bajazet, and Sir Archy, and on 12 September, for his own benefit, he delivered the prologue to *Henry V*.[102]

From Birmingham Cooke went to Stourbridge and performed two nights for Haynes—Richard III on 6 September and Iago on the seventh. The Litchfield Theatre opened for Race Week on 9 September, and Cooke made one appearance there as Sir Pertinax.[103]

Covent Garden opened the 1805–1806 season on 16 September with *School of Reform* and *The Padlock*. Cooke did not arrive in London at the Bath Hotel until 27 September. In November, Cooke would move to No. 33 King Street, Covent Garden, a street famous for its theatrical ties. James Quin was born in King Street, David Garrick lived there for a brief time, the Falstaff Club was located there, and William Thomas Lewis had lived at No. 35.[104]

Cooke made his first appearance that season as Richard III on 8 October. He had been expected to appear earlier, at least by the public, for some in his opening night house expected a row but were disappointed. Instead, he was received with "long continued plaudits."[105] As the *Morning Chronicle* (9 October 1805) observed:

No apology was made; but upon the scene changing to the Tower, Mr. Cooke stepped forward in the garb of *Richard*. We never recollect to have been present at a more flattering reception. There not only was not the slightest disapprobation manifested, but every one seemed anxious to shew, that in spite of any little irregularities, they were sensible of the merits of this excellent performer. . . . We hope that indulgence and kindness will produce their natural effect—an ardent and sturdy desire to please.

Cooke did attempt to please, for in the next two weeks he ran through Sir Archy, Stukely, Iago, Sir Pertinax, Peregrine, and Sciolto without a hitch. On 29 October, however, a bill was posted at 3:00 P.M. announcing that Cooke had been taken suddenly ill, and William Chapman would replace him as Macduff in *Macbeth*.[106] On 2 November, he was replaced by Hargrave in *Pizarro*; Charles Kemble replaced him as Macduff on 5 November; and for the next month "from various causes," says Cooke, "I did not appear."

"On *Tuesday the 26th* I acted Sir Pertinax MacSycophant, and honoured with one of the most cordial receptions I ever experienced."[107] The *Morning Post*, (27 November 1805) noting his "mysterious absence of several weeks," concurred that he sustained Sir Pertinax "in his accustomed style of excellency and amidst the plaudits of an admiring audience." All went well for the next few months. On 5 December, to celebrate Nelson's victory at Trafalgar, Covent Garden presented *Alfonso, King of Castile*, with Cooke as Orsino, and a special "loyal musical impromptue, Nelson's Glory." On 1 January, Cooke appeared for the first time in London as Dumont in *Jane Shore* opposite Miss Smith in the title role, also for the first time. Cooke was unhappy with the results: "partly from not liking the character, if the audience were pleased with it, I was not."[108] Cooke would soon discover, however, that the audience would also be displeased with his behavior in Dumont.

On 4 January, he gave his only performance of Lord Davenant in Cumberland's *The Mysterious Husband*, a play in preparation since 14 December.[109] Cumberland's play, his first attempt at a domestic tragedy and first seen at Covent Garden in 1783, dealt with the familiar theme of the secret marriages of a father and son to the same woman.[110] In its first outing it had been moderately successful, but even with Cooke's "admirably delineated" Lord Davenant it failed.[111] Its one performance drew receipts of only £180.[112]

On 23 December, Master Betty was back at Covent Garden, performing Achmet, and Cooke would once more support him during the latter part of the season in *Douglas* and *Pizarro*. Bettymania and the attraction of the child prodigy were now beginning to subside. During the same season, a young girl seven or eight years of age, named Miss Mudie, riding on the wave of Betty's success, found herself hissed and booed off the same stage during *The Country Girl*.[113]

Of the major events of that winter, none was more profoundly felt by the British than the death of Vice-Admiral Lord Viscount Nelson. Cooke viewed the funeral procession on the Thames on 8 January; the next day Covent Garden closed in honor of Nelson's funeral at St. Paul's.

Since mid-December, Cooke, on Harris's instruction, had been preparing Iachimo, ostensibly so that Kemble could come forward as Leonatus Posthumous. Cooke appeared first in *Cymbeline* on 18 January 1806 and repeated the role a number of times thereafter, but the new role added little to his fame.[114]

From the latter part of January until the close of the season, Cooke's behavior proved to be a true trial for all concerned. Dunlap seems unaware of these events and simply notes the termination of a diary Cooke had begun on 23 January 1805.[115] There were apparently good reasons for the cessation of his daily records until mid-May. On 27 January, Mrs. Siddons was forced to withdraw from *Pizarro* because of sudden illness and was replaced by Smith; the next night Cooke was taken ill, and Chapman replaced him as Orsino in *Alfonso*. The news was circulated that "Cooke . . . is so much disposed, that it is said to be doubtful whether he will recover."[116] For the next week, despite such unfounded reports, all went smoothly. Cooke played Iago opposite Pope's Othello, Pope's first appearance at Covent Garden in five years, on 3 February; on the 7th, Cooke played Falstaff in *Merry Wives*, but was ill the next night for Betty's *Douglas* and was replaced by William Barrymore. There were a great deal of illness and missed performances at Covent Garden during February. The sick list included not only Cooke but also Kemble, Mrs. Siddons, and Munden. As a result, Cooke's absences went virtually unnoticed. However, on 13 March, when *Love-a-la-Mode* was changed to *Raising the Wind*, things were quite different. A note on the playbill at the British Museum simply reads: "Cooke was 'indisposed'."[117] Indeed, there is no reason to assume that Cooke was anything but ill. Nevertheless, audiences were beginning to resent the frequent changes during the preceding month, and Cooke's latest absence was the straw that broke the camel's back. Even though the bill was changed on account of both Cooke's and Mrs. Humphries' illnesses, John Fawett, who made the announcement to the house, was badly received. Consequently, Lewis came forward and tried to calm the audience but to no avail; the audience called for Kemble, while tossing orange peels and other debris at Lewis. Pope then attempted to assure the audience that Kemble's absence was also from indisposition, which was corroborated by Fawcett and Lewis. The audience would accept no apology, however, and according to one account "scarce a single sentence uttered on the stage could be heard in any part of the house." At last the curtain was dropped "amidst a very general sentiment of disapprobation," and one gentleman spoke aloud from the boxes "on the subject of the disappointments which of late had been so frequently experienced."[118] Another source says that the comedian Thomas Knight, in another box, declaimed that "to his own knowledge Cooke was really indisposed and Kemble had been ill for two days."[119]

Cooke, virtually guiltless in the above events, had received permission from Harris "to act at Bath and Bristol. I played thirteen nights at twenty pounds a night, which was the sum I always received there; but the managers were so satisfied on this occasion, that they paid me three hundred pounds."[120] Cooke remained in Bath and Bristol from 27 March to 19 April. The major reason for his engagement was to help inaugurate the first season of the new Beaufort-Square Theatre, which had opened on 12 October 1805.[121] A contemporary observer on the eve of its opening has left this description:

This elegant edifice . . . is expected to rank among the first buildings of its kind in Europe: its dimensions rather exceed those of old Drury Lane, and the opening space of the green curtain is precisely the same with that of modern Covent-Garden. There are 3 tier of boxes, especially lofty, and affording a great depth of rows towards the centre. . . . The private boxes are, 26 in number, inclosed with gilt letters. The entrance to these is by a private house, and they are accomodated with a suit [sic] of elegant retiring rooms. The colour of the house is a rich crimson, decorated with the antique chaplet, and festoons of oak leaf in gold. But the principal boast of this theatre consists in its ceiling, which runs with one plain unbroken surface, gradually ascending from the summit of the stage to the capitols of the gallery pillars. Here are displayed, 5 beautiful representations of the Heathen Mythology—*chef d'oeuvres* of that celebrated Italian artist, the deceased Caffali. . . . The decorations behind the curtain are upon a scale equally superb.[122]

Cooke filled the new Theatre Royal during his engagement, playing Richard, Sir Pertinax, Macbeth, Shylock, and Sir Archy, and completing his engagement on 19 April as Sir Giles Overreach.[123] Cooke, however, did not completely leave his troubles behind him by escaping to Bath. The *Morning Post* on 24 April 1806 kept questions open. "Many persons are puzzled to think what the object could be, of Cooke, the Actor's visit to *Bath*. Certainly it is, that, however disposed he may be to *play*, he seeketh not the benefit of those *waters*." It is also quite possible that Cooke was less than the sober gentleman during his stay in Bath. Richard John "Obi" Smith recounts in his *Recollections* how Cooke was "flustered with flowing cups" during *Richard III* one night and

the 3rd scene of the 1st act . . . where Gloster no longer able to endure the taunts and reproaches of Henry 6th [Charleton] draws his sword and exclaims "I'll hear no more? Dire prophet in Thy speech!" Cooke assumed such a malignant expression of countenance and flourished his weapon in such a determined manner that the actor who played the part of Henry 6th became alarmed for his personal safety and being naturally of a mild and timid disposition, when Cooke made a desperate lunge at him, he stepped on one side and having no mind to run the risk of a second thrust "more potent than the first," quickly laid himself down and died in peace and charity with all mankind. Cooke staggered across the stage flourishing his sword above his head. Upon this, a critic in the gallery called out, "That's not like the Duke of Gloster." This aroused Cooke's indignation, and with his hat on one side and his wig awry he advanced to the lamps and looking up into the gallery "with lacklustre eyes," in his bold sarcastic manner exclaimed, "That's not like a British auditor!" The audience burst into a roar of laughter and applause, mingled with some hisses, and so ended the first act.[124]

In the second act, when Gloucester makes love to Anne, it was necessary for Miss Jameson to assist Cooke in rising from his kneeling position. In Act III, by the aid of stimulants, Cooke recovered himself a little and "gave occassional [sic] gleams on that genius which like the sun bursting from behind a cloud shone out in the 4th and 5th acts which he acted as no one else ever did or could act them." Smith gives no date for this account, but the previous events at Covent Garden and subsequent events later in the month would justify the possibility of this engagement as the one described. Cooke's drinking in Bath may have resulted in illness that forced him to bed. Smith speaks of a "violent fit of illness," the recovery of which occurred in Smith's house. Smith sat by his bed all night and administered Cooke's medicine. Cooke "read" him a lecture "upon sobriety and temperance": "Never, my dear boy, give way to a propensity to drink. It deprives a man of his health and facilities, and injures his interests and respectability in life: degrades him in the eyes of the world and renders [the manuscript is blank here; possibly Smith meant to add "him contemptible"]. If this illness occurred during this engagement in Bath, it would help explain the events that followed and his tardiness in returning to London.

At any rate, according to Dunlap, quoting from Cooke's journal, "forgetting duty and forgetting himself, he stopped at Marlbro' for nine days" after leaving Bath.[125] When he returned to London he found that all benefit nights had been assigned and declined a late night in May. Cooke's absence in late April, during which time he was announced for two appearances, caused him more anguish than he possibly deserved.[126] As soon as he made his entrance on 3 May as Kitely, a murmur of disapproval for the inconvenience the audience had experienced issued from various parts of the house. The rumors that accompanied his absence had convinced those in attendance that it was because of misconduct. Many demonstrated their feelings by staying away. Several persons in the house hissed and cried "Off! Off!"; however, others strenuously applauded and supported Cooke. He bowed to the audience and in apparent embarrassment, assisted by Charles Farley, came forward and addressed the audience: "Ladies and Gentlemen, my absence the first night was owing to my reading *Thursday* for *Wednesday* in the bill. [The *Morning Post* version, 5 May 1806, states: "The first time, he had no notice whatever to play."] The *second* night (placing his hand on his heart, and speaking in a lower voice), I *have nothing to say*." [*Morning Post*: "He should say nothing whatever on the subject."] This was followed by loud applause, and he went ahead "in a most admirable and masterly style."[127]

For the next few weeks Cooke was regular in his attendance and habits, keeping a daily diary until 17 May, in which he speaks of reading, walking through St. James' Park and areas around Westminster, dining with friends, and sitting for a portrait of Sir Archy with the artist DeWilde.[128] The diary ends abruptly on 17 May. On the 20th, while performing Dumont in Mrs. Litchfield's benefit and retirement night, he "was indisposed and could get no further than the 1st scene."[129] The tolerance and indulgence of the press and the audience were deteriorating quickly. "Cooke proceeds with his usual *potent spirit* to abuse the indulgence of the public," wrote the *Morning Post*. Another reported that Mrs. Litchfield had to apologize for Cooke "who, in the course of the evening, had been found *totally incapable*—from his usual *inebriety*—of performing the part of Dumont."[130] The *Post* added that as soon as he came on the stage

instead of being fit to display the sorrows of an affectionate husband, long divided from a disloyal, but repentent [sic] wife, it was evident that—
"The tears of the tankard were all he could shed;"
and that he was indeed in such a situation as totally disqualified him from discharging his study. The audience testified great displeasure, and he was obliged by his condition, as well as by general indignation, to quit the stage.

On 29 May, although Cooke was still in London preparing to journey to Scotland for a summer engagement, the *Morning Post* reported that Cooke "has sailed, it is said, for Ireland, in hopes of recovering *sobriety*. We never heard of any person sent to the *Fen-countries* for the benefit of the air." Cooke would have to wait until next season to redeem himself. The entire season had been a disappointing and degrading one for the actor, and a "very profitless" one for Kemble and the proprietors.[131] In addition to the poor comedy Cooke had appeared in, Kemble had presented a flood of such undistinguished comedies, seventy-one in all, which had extremely annoyed the critics, including Leigh Hunt.[132] About all Kemble could boast of was a personal triumph as Wolsey in a sumptuous revival of *Henry VIII*.

For George Cooke, this was indeed his most discouraging and unmemorable season thus far—and the press was clearly growing more hostile toward him. He performed no more than fifty times out of a total of 212 nights and presented no role more than six times.[133] And he did not have a benefit night. About all he could look back on with any satisfaction was that *The Man of the World* continued to be almost as popular as when he first stepped into the role of Sir Pertinax, and Richard III would still draw. But the *Post* was correct on one score: Cooke needed fresh air.

12

Durance Vile

In preparation for his 1806 summer excursions, Cooke, on 4 June, wrote in his diary: "Engaged to play 10 nights at the Dublin Theatre, to commence on, or near the 1st of July, 1806. To play a week at Birmingham & the succeeding week at Sheffield, to commence on the 4th of August. To play 13 nights at Liverpool, to commence on or near the 18th of August. Something like a treaty begun with Edinburgh, but nothing proposed on either side; the delay, however, rests with me, as Mr. R. [Rock] expects to see or hear from me."[1] Cooke then posed seven questions that were of concern to him, several indicating his state of mind and desire to make a change in his professional and personal status. His major concerns were: "How to keep the 3 engagements, & what steps to take as to the last?" "How to avoid contracting farther [*sic*] debt in my present residence, & the speediest means of leaving it?"[2] "How to estimate my property, & how to bestow it?" "How to come to some explanation & future determination respecting Covent Garden?" and "How to lay down a plan for the future, as far as probable foresight can enable me to judge?"

Clearly, Cooke was concerned about his future and his position at Covent Garden. He decided to leave London this summer no later than 12 June, leaving behind what was necessary as security for the indebtedness to his landlord. He also planned to write Harris, laying his cards on the table, hoping to return to Covent Garden the next season. If that did not work out, he would try to arrange engagements at Edinburgh, Bath, Bristol, Manchester, and other familiar theatres for the following year. He would then consider applying for a position at Drury Lane.

Cooke added to his diary, in passing, "REMEMBER Sunday, the 20th of April, 1806, at Bath," which was the day after the close of his Bath engagement and the beginning of his trouble at Covent Garden later that month. "Industry & Prudence must be the basis of my conduct," he concluded.

True to his resolve, Cooke left the "Castle and Falcon" in Aldersgate Street about 2:00 P.M. on 11 June on a Manchester coach, accompanied by Anthony Rock, the Scottish manager with whom he had been negotiating. The next evening he arrived in Manchester. Cooke was ill during the remainder of the trip but finally arrived in Glasgow on 15 June to begin his engagement on 18 June.[3] His arrival interrupted the benefits, but business prior to his arrival had been quite bad, and a star of his magnitude was needed just then to bolster the slack season.[4]

Glasgow, like Bath, was operating in a new theatre that had opened in 1805. The new Theatre Royal, located in Queen Street at the extreme west end of the city, was a large one for Glasgow, seating 1,500 people and capable of bringing in £260 when full.[5] Even benefits, however, had not done well; local company members had fared extremely poorly. Toms had £60 for his night and Byrne only £56. Places for Cooke's opening night, however, were soon at a premium.[6] His first role was Richard III, followed by Shylock and Sir Archy, Falstaff in *Merry Wives*, Macbeth, Iago, Sir Pertinax, Sir Giles, Peregrine, and Petruchio, and on 30 June, for his own benefit, Zanga in *The Revenge*. In all, he performed eleven nights, including repeats of Richard, Sir Pertinax, and Sir Archy. Business increased throughout his engagement so that by his benefit night receipts reached £170.[7] Miss Smith succeeded Cooke but proved to be a much inferior attraction.

From Glasgow Cooke traveled to Dublin, where, as he himself had noted, he was expected by July 1. When he had not arrived by then, William Elliston, who had appeared earlier at the Crow Street Theatre under Jones, renewed his engagement for a few nights in order to relieve Lewis, who also had been appearing in Dublin.[8] On Thursday, 10 July, Cooke finally arrived in excellent health and attended the night's performance as a spectator.[9]

Cooke's stay in Dublin began pleasantly for him. On the 15th, when he appeared as Richard, the public rushed at an early hour to see the great tragedian; every part of the house was filled. The *Dublin Evening Post* (17 July 1806) was rapturous over the acting of Dublin's old hero and reported that Cooke had caused a "sudden change in the declining taste for theatricals in this city." Upon his entrance, "an enthusiastic and most rapturous series of plaudits were thundered in all directions."[10] Cooke, alternating evenings with Billy Lewis, went successfully through Shylock, Stukely, and Sir Pertinax, until 25 July.

Despite such a propitious beginning, the result of Cooke's persistent drinking over too many years began to tell on him. His memory would periodically play tricks with him, and although he was not always inebriated on these occasions, his memory lapses were more often than not interpreted as drunkenness. Such was apparently the case on 25 July as Cooke attempted to perform Sir Giles Overreach. The *Evening Post* (26 July 1806) reported on the evening, in a rather charitable manner:

Sir Giles was quite *over-reached* before the termination of the fourth act. In one of the scenes of this act, Cooke seemed, like hounds sometimes, at fault: his memory appeared to forsake him, and, in apparent confusion, succeeded by a degree of confidence—he addressed the audience, informing them, that it was impossible for him to proceed in the part; he then walked off the stage. In the last act, this excellent, this unaccountable Performer, was evidently much affected—in fact, he was not able to pursue the labours of the profession. The audience was somewhat displeased of course; but Mr. Holman appeased their wrath a good deal by saying, that it was impossible Mr. Cooke could have otherwise proceeded in the character, owing to a severe indisposition. The play was finished amidst a mixture of hisses and approbation.

Cooke had not appeared in Dublin since he left for London six years before; no doubt there were still those who recalled some of the displeasure which Cooke's misbehavior had caused them then. Cooke reappeared the next night as Zanga, back in full strength, and was enthusiastically applauded. Although attendance was poor that week, the audience quickly forgave Cooke. On Saturday he played Pierre to Holman's Jaffier and Sir Archy with Lewis as the Groom to benches literally deserted.[11] On the following Tuesday Cooke and Lewis appeared in *John Bull*, but the *Evening Post* (31 July 1806) had to report that "Such is the scarcity of money, and so few are the persons of rank in Dublin at this season, that the receipts at the Theatre-Royal . . . did not exceed £60." Holman's and Cooke's benefit nights were nonetheless welcomed "with the most flattering testimonies of public approbation."[12] The last mention of Cooke in Dublin this summer was for a performance on 4 August. The *Evening Post* (5 August) notes that Cooke was to perform the Baron in *Lovers' Vows* for Mr. and Mrs. H. Johnston's appearance but failed to appear. As a consequence, Mr. O'Reilly read the role.

Cooke notes in his diary that he "made an engagement with Mr. Jones during the winter," no doubt in case things did not work out for the London season.[13] He had probably already left Dublin by 4 August; he had certainly intended to be on his way to England by 29 July at the latest.[14] He was already behind schedule.

According to Cooke's diary, he was expected at DeCamp's theatre in Sheffield by 4 August to play a week. I have located no conclusive evidence to place him in Sheffield, and Cooke states that he went "from Dublin to Liverpool." He was definitely performing in Liverpool by 18 August with Lewis and Emery. For thirteen nights, between Monday, 18 August, and Thursday, 11 September, Cooke performed Richard, Sir Pertinax, the Stranger, Joseph Surface, Sir Archy (the first time in Liverpool), Peregrine, Stukely, Shylock, and for his benefit on 10 September Sir Giles Overreach and the Scotchman in *The Register Office*.[15]

On 18 August, while performing Richard in Liverpool, "Cooke was so overcome with the beauty of Lady Anne (Miss S. Norton), that in recovering himself from his kneeling pastime he made a false step and lost his equilibrium," a story resembling the incident in Bath (1806). The *Dublin Evening Post* (6 September 1806), reporting on this event, added: "We are sorry to add that 'Richard was not himself again;' and that Mr. Archer [King Henry] was obliged to finish the character." It was possibly on this occasion that Cooke, when asked to apologize to the audience, made his famous remark directed at the Liverpool merchants who had made great fortunes from slave trade. "Apology! from George Frederick Cooke'" he cried; "take it from this remark: There's not a brick in your infernal town which is not cemented by the blood of a slave!"[16] Cooke states that he closed his summer campaign with one night at Litchfield.[17]

Even though Cooke did not appear that summer at a number of his normal stops, his reputation in the provinces was so firmly implanted that even absent he was remembered, though not always in a flattering way. Typical are the lengthy verses on him in *The Thespian Review: An Examination of the Merits and Demerits of the Performers on the Manchester Stage* (1806). A great deal of Cooke's reputation for recklessness and improvidence was perpetuated by such journalistic fancies as these:

> To finish characters, read Nature's book,
> And do not mimic, even Shakespeare's Cooke.
> Cooke, who can act—strong skill!—and reach the goal,
> When liquid robbers have his reason stole.
> Cooke never elegant—almost sans grace,
> Trusting to genius to display his face!
> Who, in despite of figure and of voice,
> For *Roscius'* chair, would still be Shakespeare's choice.
> Great as he is, his faults are clear as day!
> Yet we must bear them—they are *part* of Cooke.
> His strong sarcastic grin!—sardonic smiles!
> His bolt-like eyes, when, threat'ning, he reviles!
> His sneer!—his "Guess"—applause will always tax
> And every actor bows to *Pertinax*.
> Think not that Nature's constant to his beck,
> Because George Cooke has been abridg'd of neck!
> Or that his Richard, or his Shylock, charms,
> Because Dame Nature has curtail'd his arms!
> Nor think because he boldly dare depart,
> From grammer's laws to signalize a part,
> That Accents faulty, *Emphases* too high,
> That length'ning qualtities, t'excuse a pause,
> Can e'er be beauties'—E'en in Cooke, they're flaws.
> Cooke, the bright star—the wonder of his age,
> The pride, the libel of the British Stage,
> Whose giant grasp has seiz'd on Roscius' chair,
> And high enthroned, when sober, safe sits there!
> But, when forgetting Common Sense's rule,
> He treads on Reason, drinks, and plays the fool,
> Hard rocks his chair—he falls from Roscius' throne,
> And all his honours in the dirt are thrown.—
> Revere his talents, actors! but reject
> His orgies vile! if ever you expect
> To reap or honour, or the golden need,
> For breathing sweetly on the Thespian reed.

> "Great men have greatest sins!" Cooke's Devil's wine,
> Strange! that through darkness, black like that, to shine!

The last twenty-three lines, beginning with "Think not that Nature's constant to his beck," were addressed to Bengough of the Manchester Theatre who had been imitating Cooke and had been advised that he was excellent enough without such antics.[18] On 22 February 1806, the same author, in more complimentary terms, added:

> There was a time when Cooke subordant [sic] play'd,
> (But Fame his patient merits well repaid)
> And parts rejected both by Grist and Banks
> Were ta'en by him, accepted with his thanks!
> Nor did he fail the characters so low,
> Powers, since acknowledged great, e'en then to shew. . . .[19]

About the same time as the appearance of the verses in *The Thespian Review*, in London the second edition of *Authentic Memoirs of the Green-Room* published another contemporary description of Cooke. He is described as of "middle stature, rather stout, or, to speak with greater precision, of broad proportions." His features are delineated as "strongly drawn, and capable of the most varied and contrasted inflexion. 'Tis in the command of those features, and the forcible expression of his eye, that his superior excellence in a great measure consists. With less gesticulation, and less mechanical trickery, than, perhaps, any other actor on the stage, he draws a bold, decissive [sic] outline, and makes a deep impression on the mind."[20]

Cooke apparently negotiated satisfactorily with the management for the 1806–1807 season, his seventh in London. His first appearance was not until 29 September, after Covent Garden had opened on the 15th with *John Bull*, with Pope appearing as Peregrine for the first time. Betty had been engaged for fifteen nights beginning the middle of September, and Cooke no doubt felt relieved not to have to support him, possibly part of his new reconciliatory agreement with Harris. He remained at his old address in King Street until January when, probably in an effort to economize, he moved to 27, Upper Eaton Street, Pimlico. His salary remained £14.14, the eighth highest among the male members of the company, after Munden, Fawcett, Lewis, Incledon, Pope, Charles and John Philip Kemble.[21] Of the women, Smith and Mrs. Siddons outdrew Cooke. Miss DeCamp would increase her status and worth this year by marrying Charles Kemble.

The fall passed rather uneventfully for Cooke. The press continued to make his life difficult, for on his first appearance that season as Richard on 29 September *The Monthly Mirror* reminded him of his "errors" of the previous season.

Cooke, whose misconduct seems only to increase his attraction, and endear him still more to the public, was saluted, on his *entree* in *Richard*, with repeated shouts and peals of applause, which shook the house to its centre. The errors of last season were not recollected, or if so, remembered only to be forgiven and *rewarded*. He never played better.[22]

The *Morning Post* (30 September 1806) acknowledged his reception and success that night, and added: "Want of grateful feeling does not seem to be among his failings, and gratitude, like charity, covers a multitude of sins." No doubt thankful for public compliments, Cooke still suffered from the press's reminders of his past misdeeds.

On 1 October, Stephen Kemble, engaged to play Falstaff for three nights, made his first appearance at Covent Garden in *Henry IV, Part one*. Cooke must have reveled in the comparisons to himself as the standard, especially with less than kind memories of Kemble from his Liverpool days. "He is far, very far from the mark," wrote *The Monthly Mirror*. "Cooke . . . whose *Falstaff* is among his least commendable efforts, is yet the best our stage can boast."[23] Although a backhanded compliment, Cooke could not help but have been pleased.

Nelson's memory was still very much alive this season, and on 21 October, after appearing as Shylock opposite Miss Smith's Portia, her first time in the role, Cooke recited a new three-stanza ode to Nelson by Pearce and music by Davy, with the concluding lines:

> O Nelson! to thy Country early lost!
> Great was the Final Conquest! Great the cost!

Cooke was situated in front of the orchestra, which had been placed on stage, and "with all the disadvantage of a harsh voice, delivered the ode in a very impressive manner." Each stanza was repeated by the vocal performers. More than one Nelson admirer wiped tears from his eyes on hearing "the solemn dirge which was sacred to the memory of his prototype."[24]

The autumn also saw a revival on 3 November of one of Kemble's greatest roles, Coriolanus, and Cooke, on 15 November, was called upon to create his eighth new role, Prince of Altenburg, in a concocted piece of trivia, *Adrian and Orilla, or, A Mother's Revenge*, by William Dimond, the son of the Bath manager. The operatic drama, with music by J. Attwood assisted by Michael Kelly, was a silly bit of trash and provided Cooke with the role of a lover, for which he was now totally unfit. Unfortunately for him, a drunken spree at a rehearsal would become an oft-repeated anecdote, told first by Michael Kelly. Indeed, his behavior was clearly professionally reprehensible, but I have found no corroborative evidence to support Kelly's claim that Cooke at the first performance forgot nothing "but the whole plot." The reviewers barely took note of him in fact, and one found his pronunciation of "leap" as "lep" the only point worthy of comment.[25] Nevertheless, Kelly says that on 15 November

> Cooke came to rehearsal so intoxicated, that he could scarcely stand. Both the author and myself were on stage, alarmed, as may well be imagined, for the fate of a play, the principal serious character of which, was to be performed by a man dead drunk.
>
> We were determined not to let our play be acted. Mr. Kemble . . . insisted, that the play should be done. In the interim, Cooke was pouring out a volley of abuse against Kemble, calling him "Black Jack, etc" all which Kemble bore with Christian patience, and without any reply. At length, Mr. Harris, with his faithful ally on all emergencies, the late James Brandon, the box book-keeper, on seeing Cooke's situation, decided that the play should not be performed on that night; but that Kemble should make an apology to the audience, on the plea of Cooke's sudden indisposition; which Kemble refused to do.

An argument followed between Harris and Kemble, with the latter responding: "Sir, you are a proprietor—so am I. I borrowed a sum of money to come into this property. How am I to repay those who lent me that money, if you, from ill-placed lenity towards an individual, who is repeatedly from intoxication disappointing the public, choose to risk the dilapidation of the theatre, and thereby cause my ruin? By Heavens, I swear the play shall be acted." Kelly explains how Cooke was coaxed by Brandon to his house, where he slept from 12:00 until 5:00, took strong coffee, and played as scheduled.[26] For the remainder of the performances of *Adrian and Orilla*, throughout November and December, there are no indications of difficulties resulting from Cooke's one-day misadventure at rehearsal.

On 23 November, Cooke began another diary lasting until mid-December. It reveals nothing out of the ordinary: a great deal of reading, some problems with an arm that needed medical attention and embrocation, a visit to the new Olympic Pavilion of Philip Astley, a sitting with the artist Samuel Drummond, and a good deal of pondering over the current political situation.[27]

During December Cooke twice traveled to Norwich with William Roxby Beverley of the Covent Garden company, who also ran a provincial company there, first on 8 December and later on 17 December.[28] On the 10th, Cooke attended Kemble's adapted and ostentatious revival of *The Tempest*. Kemble's new production bore a strong resemblance to his 1789 Drury Lane version. But audiences flocked to see it, perhaps curious to hear Kemble pronounce "aches" as "aitches."[29] Cooke would play Prospero once on 4 May while Kemble suffered from rheumatism and asthma, and audiences would flock to see how he handled the "aches" controversy. When finally forced with a decision on the pronunciation dispute, Cooke delicately circumvented any comparison by simply omitting the passages in which the "aches" occurred. One paper on this occasion printed the following:

> Aitches or akes, shall I speak both or either?
> If akes, I violate Shakespeare's measure,
> If aitches I shall give King Johnny pleasure—
> I've hit upon't—by Jove I'll utter neither.[30]

After his December visit, during which he could bear to watch only part of the first two acts, Cooke agreed with most contemporary critics that the pastiche of a script was tasteless and indecent. (After its opening the play was altered somewhat to be closer to Shakespeare.) Cooke wrote:

... first altered from Shakespeare by Dryden, with the advice and approbation of Sir William Davenant, and now *revised* by Kemble. Dryden was certainly highly censurable for altering and daring to meddle with a piece replete with the flashes of Shakespeare's genius; lowering the beautiful simplicity of Miranda, and adding his own indecent and unnatural characters of Hippolito and Dorinda. ... Since the period when Garrick appeared, to the present, such a despicable piece of patchwork would have met with the reprobation and contempt it so justly merits.[31]

January passed quietly for Cooke, except for a minor incident on 26 January. After playing Richard III, "During [the] pantomime a bottle was thrown from the gallery which severely wounded a person in the Pit. One Sam.l Davis was apprehended and committed."[32]

After three years' absence from his London repertoire, Cooke appeared as Sir Giles Overreach on 7 February to a very respectable house of £339.[33]

Through most of March, Thomas Morton's comedy *Town and Country* was playing to large audiences, so that Cooke sat on the sidelines, with a few country engagements to fill his time. In mid-March, he took his Richard and Shylock to the New Street Playhouse in Salisbury, which was part of a circuit operated by James Shatford.[34] Throughout the remainder of the spring, Cooke found himself very active, filling in often during Kemble's illnesses. In April, he appeared on fifteen nights, including a resumption of Macbeth on 22 and 30 April, a role which because of Kemble's dominance he had not played in London since 1802–1803.

On 21 May Cooke, after missing a benefit the year before, took for his night *King Lear* and *Love-a-la-Mode*, repeating Lear on 1 June. The receipts, totaling £336, while not a large sum, were certainly respectable and indicate a certain endorsement of his regularity throughout the spring. Cooke was strongly supported that night by Charles Kemble as Edgar, Murray as Gloucester, and Miss Smith appearing for the first time as Cordelia.

Cooke performed Sir Pertinax on 30 May in Bath for the Theatrical Fund, for which he "offered to act gratis."[35] Upon his return he continued to carry out his professional responsibilities until the end of the season, appearing for the last time on 9 June for Joe Grimaldi and John Bologna Junior's benefit as Sir Pertinax.

Cooke's seventh season at Covent Garden had been the quietest and least controversial in several years. On the other hand, it had been a relatively nonproductive one for him. He appeared only eight more times than the preceding season, but he did manage to reassert himself in his more important roles.[36] He made nine appearances as Richard and ten as Sir Pertinax, and reappeared after several seasons' absence in Lear and Macbeth.[37] At the end of the season, all was relatively secure for Cooke. He had no idea then that he would not appear in London again until spring 1808. In the meantime, however, he had his summer rounds. By the end of what began as a typical interval for Cooke, he unexpectedly found himself in debtor's prison, and his fortunes took another reversal.

Cooke was engaged for six nights, beginning 14 June, in Manchester, which was to be his first appearance there in two years. *Richard III* had been prepared for him, with Bengough, his imitator, as Henry, Chalmers as Richmond, and Mrs. Ward scheduled to appear as Elizabeth.[38] Cooke did not show. The managers did not give up hope until 23 June when they finally posted the following notice:

Theatre Royal, Manchester. The Managers, in the most respectful manner, acquaint the public that they are under the disagreeable necessity, from Mr. Cooke's not coming to fulfill his engagement, to close the Theatre Royal before the expiration of their term, and not to admit any further disappointment to the town. To the ladies and gentlemen of Manchester, and the inhabitants in general, Messrs. Ward and Young [Charles Mayne Young had joined the management in 1805 after having been a member of the company for several seasons] beg leave to return thanks for their favours conferred, with every assurance of retaining the obligation in their minds with the liveliest gratitude.[39]

According to Rex Pogson, Cooke's action was the more reprehensible in that an advance payment had been made to him. The management would bring suit against him for this amount and, unable to pay, Cooke would pay the penalty.

Cooke was frequently in financial straits during his tempestuous career, and beginning with landlord problems on King Street until the end of this summer, they seemed to have gone from bad to worse. Nevertheless, when he arrived in Glasgow for an engagement in June at the Queen Street Theatre, billed as "the greatest living actor of the day," he had no idea of what lay ahead for him. Until 18 July he entertained the Glasgow public; intense excitement prevailed during the visit. As usual he opened in *Richard III* and appeared as Peregrine, Petruchio, and Sir Pertinax, among other roles.[40]

A number of anecdotes are associated with his three Glasgow engagements, none of which appears to fit his own estimates of these appearances as "productive," "reception favorable," or, for that matter, available notices.[41] On one visit, while playing Sir Archy, he persisted in calling himself Sir Pertinax MacSycophant. When corrected from the audience, Cooke replied: "It's a' the same thing [but] ye've paid yer siller, and ye've a richt to hae what name ye chuse. Sir Archy, then, if ye will hae it so."⁴² On another occasion, according to *The Monthly Mirror*, he appeared on stage tipsy for a second time and was castigated by the audience. Cooke's response was "Gude dom ye, this is the second time I've been insulted in your dom toon of Glascoo, & De'il tak me if I'll ever com into it agen." The report that he marched off stage and that no entreaty could bring him back, while typically Cooke behavior, is not substantiated. Another source, however, suggests that one evening, perhaps the event in question, Rock had to apologize for Cooke, suiting the action to the word when he announced: "Ladies and Gentlemen, Mr. Cooke, I am grieved to say, has been taken with a *bowl* [punch bowl] complaint."⁴³

From Glasgow Cooke traveled to Edinburgh, a treaty with Rock having finally been managed. John Jackson's second period of management in Edinburgh had not proven very successful. The tide of popularity, never in his favor, had irretrievably turned against him. Jackson was old, abused by the press, deserted by the public, and by 1807 his health had so deteriorated that death had come as a kindly relief that year.⁴⁴ Anthony Rock, who had first succeeded Francis Aicken as manager in Glasgow, now moved into Edinburgh. During his engagement, beginning 24 July, Cooke stayed at Rock's, No. 8, Calton Street, opposite the Black Bull Inn.⁴⁵ During his stay, Cooke acted with Miss Smith (later Mrs. Bartley) from Covent Garden; he performed Richard, Shylock, Iago, Oakly in *The Jealous Wife*, Sir Archy, Sir Pertinax, and for his benefit, Macbeth.⁴⁶

In addition to the Glasgow anecdotes, numerous other stories are associated with Cooke's visits to Scotland. One, told by Ryan in his *Table Talk*, is typical. Toward the conclusion of a performance of Richard, the night being very hot, Cooke felt quite fatigued. The manager noticed this, and, between one of the scenes in the last act, he took Cooke into his dressing room, unlocked a corner cupboard, and selected a "*wee thistle* glass, and filling it with native whiskey, presented it to George Frederick, exclaiming, 'Here, Maister Kuke, I dinna think this will hurt ye.' 'No,' says George, glancing at the size of the glass, 'no, my friend, not if it was *vitriol*.' "⁴⁷

Cooke completed his engagement in Edinburgh before 8 August and traveled to his old hometown on the Scottish border, Berwick-upon-Tweed, where he was engaged for six nights. Cooke says "I was to receive one hundred and eighty pounds. I struck off £55. and received £90; the remainder, £35 is still *owing*; I suppose, in the theatrical phrase, to *vex me*."⁴⁸

He was expected in Liverpool on 24 August but again failed to appear. At 4:30 P.M. a bill was issued explaining that a letter had been received saying he was on his way.⁴⁹ Grant substituted for Cooke that evening, but Cooke never materialized. The exact nature of what happened is unknown. The Manchester managers finally located him and sued him for breach of contract. Unable to reimburse them, Cooke found himself in the Appleby Jail in Westmoreland, from 17 August until 30 December.

That Cooke was unable to keep himself out of debtor's prison is not too surprising. Although his salary in London and his provincial fees were well above average, he was never a good manager of his money. His frequent bouts with drunkenness complicated his finances, and he was known to squander large sums with little or no provocation. Dunlap narrates one instance, witnessed by Charles Mathews, which, if not totally factual, must have been typical. After receiving benefit money and the proceeds from an engagement in Manchester, £300 to £400, Dunlap says that Cooke fell into company at a public house with some republican manufacturers of the neighborhood. "The loyalty of our hero was always great, but increased in warmth thermometrically with his stomach and head." Cooke got into a political discussion with one of "the mechanics," words became hostile and abusive, and Cooke finally challenged his antagonist to settle the matter with fists. The man, who knew of Cooke and preferred not to harm him physically, excused himself with "Nah now, Mr. Cooke, you know I would not harm you if I could; you take the liberty of abusing me and challenging me, because you are rich, and know I'm a poor man." "Do I?" says Cooke; "I'll shew you that. There look," pulling all the bank notes from his pocket, "there—that's all I have in the world—there," putting them in the fire, "now I'm as poor as you are—now damn you, come on!"[50]

Cooke was also charitable to a fault. As noted earlier, he frequently acted "gratis" in Bath and elsewhere. There are numerous anecdotes of his giving sums of money to women in distress and to other unfortunates. Mrs. Mathews recalled that "he frequently exerted his rare talents gratuitously for his less gifted brethren of the sock and buskin in the provinces, and when not engaged on the metropolitan stage, occasionally gave 'a night' to the necessities of the 'poorer born'."[51] Even immediately after getting out of jail, he recorded in his diary on 6 February 1808: "visited by an old woman, to whom I gave a pound note."[52] During his American visit, in 1811, according to a protracted anecdote told by Dunlap, Cooke, during an extremely cold and inclement February night in New York, sent a note with a small girl to Dunlap requesting $100. It turned out that Cooke had wandered into a strange house where the mother lay sick, stayed for the night, and became quite drunk. In his delirium, he had promised to pay the rent and to stop the sheriff's officers from confiscating the household goods.[53] While he himself was slowly dying in America, he visited a fellow English actor named Doige, a member of the Park Theatre company during his first season there, who was close to death from dropsy, and made sure there was adequate money to see to his comforts.[54] It has also been recorded that while in New York he "scattered some $400 among the needy and the solicitous."[55] Perhaps as one biographer suggests, Cooke was strongly influenced in his liberality by the account of James Middleton's desperate straits and swore to profit by so severe a lesson in the future.[56] Whatever the motivation of his charity, he was too often liberal to a fault, although his memory deserves this more charitable recognition. One essay written shortly after his death echoed such a sentiment: "... let it not be forgotten, that he was never betrayed into one deed, that indicated the possession of a mean mind, and that his benevolence was of a marked and exemplary sort."[57]

During much of the almost five months in jail, Cooke filled his time writing a diary and a journal of his career, the closest to an autobiography he ever undertook. This became Dunlap's chief source for his biography of Cooke, but, unfortunately, Dunlap took little note of Cooke's own warning: "It is very hastily written, and without a scrap of assistance from any book, note, or memorandum whatever" (*Life of George Frederick Cooke*, 2: 13). Dunlap, as has been indicated throughout this study, did little to check Cooke's facts, and Cooke, as well as Dunlap, often misled his readers. This diary is an interesting document in itself, giving the only true insight into Cooke's mind available and revealing his state of mind through this hiatus. Ironically, he says virtually nothing of his predicament, calling his jailor "mine host of the Anvil," and giving no information on the cause of his imprisonment or negotiations for his release. Throughout the diary, however, there are dozens of references to letters received from Anthony Rock in Edinburgh, Brandon and Glassington at Covent Garden, and others. Apparently, the most serious discussions were between him and Rock, for he simply dismissed a proposal from Glassington. The diary does confirm several important facts, already cited, such as his trip to Holland as a boy and at least the existence of Renton in Berwick, a Mr. Samuel Renton to whom he wrote on 25 November.

Part of this prison diary covering the period 28 November to 20 December, plus the journal, were available to Dunlap. Only recently, another section has been purchased by the Harvard Theatre Collection, covering the period from around 14 November up to the first entry available to Dunlap.[58] The diary entries do devote a lot of space to the transcription of extracts from the few books available to him, but combined, they reveal much of Cooke's native intelligence, melancholy during his confinement, and constant insomnia. On occasion, entries delve deeper than any source into the inner workings of his mind. As an illustration, brief excerpts have been chosen, in chronological order, excluding material previously quoted or irrelevant to the man or of a more general nature. Sections cited in Dunlap have likewise been omitted since they are readily available.

Sunday, November 15th: Arose 20 minutes before ten, breakfasted and dressed. It is a real inconvenience not to be able to shave yourself. When I first, as I thought began to write man, it used to be rather a pleasing occupation, &, I continued it for some time, but, indolence prevailing, to which I am very prone, I left it off, & tho' I have several times attempted it since cannot properly effect it.

Tuesday, November 17th: This is, truly, a November day; dark, raw, cold and foggy. My spirits are, at present, in unison with the weather.

. . . .

While at dinner, received a letter from Mr. Rock, at Greenock. It is impossible to answer from this place, by return, as the mails are gone before you receive the letters they bring.

Friday, November 20th: The afternoon dull & wearisome; the day not "red," but white, with distemperature. . . . Rather indisposed this morning.

. . . .

Between tea & supper, which was about nine, the evening passed dull and stupid; thoughts unsteady, confused & perplexed. Add to this indisposition. . . . Any circumstance, however trival, serves for an anecdote, from a place like this.

Saturday, November 21st: I have been some years in the practice of writing, occasionally, memorandums, & am therefore afraid I may have, unknowingly, made some repetitions, &, if so, not unlikely, given opposite views of the same subject. No doubt, different views of the same situation, call forth different ideas of it.

Sunday, November 22d: I did not arise, owing to a return of my indisposition, until after half past ten; the weather, a frost, but clear & pleasant. After breakfast, much indisposed. Dined some time after one, but eat very little.

Monday, November 23rd: Were men to be read in the same order we read books, or rather in the same order books are taught to be read, I do not think this would be a wrong place to commence the human alphabet in, much farther could not be gone; not even the length of putting two syllables together. Among the mountains the rude simplicity of country life may be found, & the inhabitants are civil & good humoured, but nothing Arcadian within these limits. I have had it hinted to me, that I might receive the visits of some gentlemen, if I were so inclined: but this I *de*clined. Doubtless there are many worthy men round about, but the *gentlemen* of a place like this, are generally comprised in the Parson, or Parsons, the apothecary & the attorney; a supervisor of the excise, if one is resident, & should a justice of peace be added, the circle is deemed great. The general conversation of these gentlemen may be classed thus. The clergyman is either political, or an adept in rural sports, or both; every sentence he utters belongs to one or the other; not a word of divinity; & therein, perhaps he is right. Should the church be at all mentioned, it is only to dwell upon its privileges & authority. The apothecary gives you what little that he may have heard in his round, & the scandal of the whole country. The attorney, if the bent of his discourse be rightly taken, understands the whole science of the law; tells how much a cause was lost, & how it might have been gained; mentions, with an air of superiority, the eminent Council he is acquainted with, whom he has *seen* at the Assizes, & to some of whom, perhaps, he has presented a brief. What the supervisor says, who is also a man of consequence, is complimentary to those present; & so truly orthodox is he in his opinion of the constitution of his country, that after justly asserting the king can do no wrong, he places his *ministers* in the same irresponsible situation. The Justice, if he attends to anything but his glass & his pipe, talks of acts of parliament, the statutes at large, & county or turnpike meetings, where he thought himself a great man; these & anecdotes of the quarter sessions, & toasting the county and borough members, at least one *half* of them, fill up his share of the conversation, "and thus he plays his part."

Thursday, November 26th: From the want of better amusement, fell into a disagreeable, desultory thinking. Among many other things which flitted thro' my imagination, the word independence, or rather the words independence, & independent dwelt a little with me. They are so indefinite with respect to human life, that I do not clearly understand their significant [*sic*]. I have heard a man called independent, that was continually depending upon others; and I have heard an acquaintance of mine, one of the people called quakers, boast, which, by the bye, was wandering from his spiritual tenets, that he did not *care* for any man whatever. He did not comprehend woman; for this independent man was master of a family, & only *second* in authority in that family.

Monday, November 30th: My spirits are sometimes in a pleasing order, but on the sudden, a reverse takes place. My mind is at this time rather oppressed. The minutes are wasting, and nothing positively fixed. The want of books is severely felt.

Saturday, December 5th: I remember hearing a reverend gentleman of Newcastle . . . say, that when a person, on being asked what he was thinking of, replied nothing, he was thinking of a multitude of things, but not any thing distinctly. I have often experienced the remark to be just, and last night was an additional proof of it. I tried to fix my thoughts but in vain. The body would feel a distaste, sometimes approaching disgust, at being long supplied with the same kind of food, and nothing but the craving of hunger would enable it to endure it. The mind is much in the same mental repast, particularly if scantily supplied.

Monday, December 7th: This evening hanging very, very heavy, cast the principal characters of a few plays as they might be done at Covent-garden. I have given as little trouble to the managers respecting plays, the ward-robe-keeper or the property-man, for the time I have been in the theatre, as any one in my situation that ever belonged to it. It may not always be so.

Thursday, December 10th: Passed a cold, dreary, frosty afternoon, in a day-dream by the fire-side. I am afraid too much of life has been passed in the same manner.

Sunday, December 13th: I am uneasy concerning some affairs at Berwick. I have had sufficient lessons of experience to be cautious whom I trust, and perhaps may remember them. I will make no more promises.

Saturday, December 19th: A clear, pleasant, frosty day. Indisposed all the morning, with a disagreeable sensation in my head, and a sickly affection at my stomach. The mind partakes of the body's uneasiness.

And so Cooke ruminated, and while he "wiled away" his time at Appleby, rumors about him were rampant in London. *The Monthly Mirror* first reported in September that "he entered himself aboard a king's ship. It is very probable that he is, at this time, *half seas over*," and then in October changed the story to "Mr. Cooke is said be in durance vile in Kendal."[59] As late as January, after his release, the *Morning Chronicle* (2 January) indicated that a report of Cooke's death was false. Although he was indeed acting again in Scotland, thanks to the manager Rock, apparently the London managers had felt disgraced and thus had left him in jail, even thiough a small sum would have released him. Such inaction was ironic, for a line in *The Cabinet* pointed out that "Cooke still remains, *willy nilly*, at Appleby, notwithstanding the empty benches of Covent Garden."[60] In truth, before Cooke's return to London in March, receipts were constantly in the low £200s.[61]

During the fall season, on 19 December 1807, Kemble attempted Cooke's role of Iago to Pope's Othello, and Cooke's impression was still so prominent that a comparison in the press was inevitable. Both were seen to take extreme approaches to the role: "His [Kemble's] predecessor betrays so much of the workings of cunning and deceit, as makes it seem to the spectators a miracle how *Othello* can be deceived at all—on the contrary, Mr. K. assumed an open, frank, and disinterested air, which would better comport with the shrewd villainy of the character, were it mixed with a little more of the restlessness inseparable from it."[62] This reviewer then rekindled the public's animosity toward Cooke with a stinging review of his past misbehavior. Although absent from London over seven months, he could not escape the wrath of the journalist:

... it is said that he is so much in debt that there is little chance of liberation. Should he die in these circumstances, would it be just to impute neglect of genius to the public? We contend that no people ever stood more perfectly exculpated, since they, for a long period, with unexampled patience, heaped honour and riches on this man, favours which he to the last treated with mad improvidence and ingratitude.... Is the public to be blamed because common sense was not added to his other attainments? Surely not.... If Sir Joshua Reynolds had been idle and drunken, he might have obtained nothing better than a scanty and precarious maintenance, by painting coach pannels, and Birmingham tea-boards.... the inimitable Garrick, if he had possessed Shuter's character, would have acquired little more than Shuter's fame and suffered Shuter's end. So much for Mr. Cooke! He has the reward which his own hands have laboured to prepare!

Cooke, back in circulation by the end of December, had successfully concluded negotiations with Rock to play in Glasgow and Edinburgh. The stay at Appleby seems to have had salutory effects on him, for from December to July he performed his professional duties faithfully and scrupulously.

On 30 December, he performed for the first time since his last night in Berwick on 17 August 1807. On the same day he began another journal, recording his thirteen nights in Glasgow. Supported by Charles Young in such roles as Douglas and Othello, Cooke ran through his usual repertoire—Glenalvon, Sir Archy, Shylock, Iago, Joseph Surface, Stukely, Sir Pertinax, Oakly, Richard III, Macbeth, Peregrine, and Lord Townly.[63] His benefit on 21 January brought in receipts totaling £182.2.6.[64] The next day he left for Edinburgh, arriving Saturday at M'Gregor's Hotel, Prince's Street. He remained in Edinburgh from 23 January to 29 February, during which time he performed twenty-two nights, supported largely by the same company as in Glasgow.[65] He again performed most of his major roles, adding to the Glasgow repertoire Zanga, Kitely, and Jaques. For his benefit on 20 February, he performed Joseph Surface, Sir Archy, and recited "Ode to the Memory of Vice Admiral Lord Viscount Nelson."[66] Cooke records that receipts were £205.[67] On the 25th, he performed for the benefit of the Charity Workhouse and ended his engagement the next night with Iago.[68]

While in Edinburgh, Cooke was often in the company of a Miss Lamb, the daughter of a Mr. John Lamb of Newark, Nottinghamshire. Practically nothing is known of this woman who would become Cooke's second known wife in 1808.

"On Friday, March 4th, at four in the afternoon, left Edinburgh in the mailcoach," writes Cooke. "Supped at Berwick; the next morning breakfasted at Newcastle; in the afternoon dined at Northallerton, and arrived at York between ten and eleven, where I supped and slept. . . . set out the next morning at five in the Highflyer at Stamford. Breakfasted at Ferry-Bridge, dined at Newark, supped at stage between Grantham and Stamford . . . and reached Stamford some time before midnight, where I slept. . . . Set out in a post-chaise for London . . . arrived in London a little after eleven."[69] At first Cooke stayed a few days in a hotel on the east corner of Leicester Square, but on 12 March he moved for the remainder of the season to No. 26, James-street, located almost in the middle of Long Acre, debouching from the southside and crossing what is now Floral Street. Unlike his Pimlico address, it was conveniently located to the theatre, opening into the northside of Covent Garden market.[70]

Cooke was apparently expected by the Covent Garden management as usual in September, since his name remained on the salary list until 7 November.[71] Rumors were certainly circulating as to his reestablishment at Covent Garden. *The Monthly Mirror* even suggested that Sheridan had negotiated with Harris for Cooke's services, but Harris had refused.[72] This was a wise move on Harris's part, for Cooke's welcome on 10 March was tumultuous, when as Sir Pertinax receipts jumped to an unseasonable high of £513.[73] Kemble simply noted the occasion in his memoranda book with "Mr. Cooke returned."[74] Ironically, the London audience seemed "to love him for the dangers he had passed" and greeted him with six rounds of applause. *The Monthly Mirror* reported that "Such a house has not been seen since the *little hour of little Betty*."[75] Furthermore, the *Mirror* swore not to mention Cooke's impudence until "we again suffer by it." Cooke actually gained added stature after such a long absence. The *Morning Post* (11 March 1808), after observing that Cooke was "in the sober and proper sense," added that "the stage at present certainly furnishes no parallel to him." Even though he was suffering from a severe cold, the *Morning Chronicle* (11 March 1808) acknowledged that "he proved that his absence from London had not blunted the edge of his execution."

On 12 March Cooke appeared as Shylock. Once again the house was a large one, well over £400. It was almost as if London had discovered a new star. ". . . He stands at this time unrivalled . . . but we advise the manager not to run Cooke too hard, or he may become broken winded. This present novelty may diminish, but his great merits cannot fail to be always attractive," wrote one reviewer. Another found the audience fixed on him during the court scene, for which he drew repeated bursts of applause.[76] Even the *Mirror*, which had been rather severe on him, wrote: "... taking the character as we find it, and looking for a representative of it, as it is, we discover more qualities in Mr. Cooke, for the just delineation of his smooth, usurious villainy, and diabolical spirit of revenge, then occur in any other actor now living."[77]

When he appeared in his old favorite, Richard, on 14 March, he received the same reception. The *Mirror*, echoing a criticism heard during Cooke's first London season, chastised the management for the poor supporting cast they always seemed to assign for Cooke's Richard, including this night, with Norton as Lady Anne, Brunton as Richmond, Davenport as Stanley, Mrs. Emery as Queen Elizabeth, and Mrs. Leserve as the Duchess of York. Although excellent in comedy, these players were not Covent Garden's strongest performers in serious drama.[78]

From March to early June, Cooke performed at least forty-eight nights, almost as many times as during the entire preceding season. On 9 April, he appeared for the first time in London as Colin MacLeod in Cumberland's comedy *The Fashionable Lover* for Lewis's benefit, the first time the play had been performed at Covent Garden since 1786. The play was repeated once, on 6 May. The only novelty for Cooke in this derivative play was that Colin, considered by some the first Scot used as a central figure in a sentimental drama, and unlike Sir Archy and Sir Pertinax, is not only a buffoon but a moral and sentimental Scotsman, frank, generous, and endowed with every virtue.[79] *The Monthly Mirror* found Cooke "as great in his generous Scot, as far as it goes, as in McSycophant" and praised his dialect in its "ancient purity," as well as the incident in which MacLeod places Miss Aubrey under the protection of a procuress, mistaking her for one of the noble blood of the MacLeods.[89]

The *Mirror* also reported Cooke's first slip-up since returning to London. While performing Richard on 25 April, Cooke appeared drunk, although the audience mistook his "hesitations, hickups, staggering, etc. as just delineations of feeling, and rewarded [Cooke] with applause."[81] The reviewer made one point that was doubtlessly true: as Cooke got older (he was at least fifty-two a few days prior), it became more difficult to sober him up with tea after arriving drunk at the theatre, so that "he loses the power of casting off his disguise, and drunk at first, he is so to the end."

The remainder of the spring passed without incident. On 23 April, he appeared at the new theatre in Gravesend for Mrs. Litchfield's benefit as Sir Pertinax.[82] For his own London benefit on 3 May, Cooke chose *Bonduca, Queen of the Ancient Britons* by Francis Beaumont and John Fletcher as altered by George Colman the elder, plus the farce *We Fly By Night*. The production of *Bonduca*, in preparation by Cooke at least since mid-April, featured new costumes, scenery, and decorations, with music by Purcell, the prologue by Garrick spoken by Cooke, and in Act III "A Solemn Grand Procession to the Temple of the Druids" and "A Grand Triumphal March to the Roman Camp." Cooke took the role of Caratach and Mrs. St. Ledger performed Bonduca. The production was poorly attended, and *The Monthly Mirror* scolded the London populace: "Labouring so much as he lately has in his vocation, and then constantly to crowded benches, makes this respect of the public doubly ungrateful."[83] Nevertheless, the play had little appeal for the public, and although repeated on the 5th, the acting was also reported as mediocre. Cooke's performance, according to the *Morning Chronicle* (6 May 1808), "fell very, very far short of the idea which we have conceived of that generous Prince. His acting was harsh and ferocious in tone, manner and expression," giving more the impression of an "African cannibal" than "a royal Briton."

On 18 May, Cooke first appeared in London as Kent in Charles Kemble's benefit performance of *King Lear*. John Kemble had not played Lear in eight years, and Kent was almost totally unfamiliar to Cooke; yet the production was successful enough for four additional performances. Charles as Edgar, John Philip, and Cooke all received good notices. Cooke was praised principally for keeping the character in balance and in its proper situation in the background, even though Kent's bluntness occasionally degenerated into "vulgarity."[84] Another reviewer felt the role indicated "what a great actor may do with an inferior part. Those who were witness of his performance will not see other Kents with much pleasure."[85] Apparently, Cooke took the role to help out Charles, the only Kemble for whom he felt real affection, even remembering his name on his deathbed.

For Charles' wife's benefit six nights later, Cooke created his last original role in London, the gay, amorous Colonel Vortex in Marie-Therese Kemble's comedy *Match-making; or, 'Tis a Wise Child That Knows Its Own Father*. The play, a trite, contrived piece, offered Cooke very little; he appeared out of his element, except in one scene where in an intended seduction he discovers his own daughter.[86] On 1 June, for Farley's night, he played Clytus in *Alexander the Great*, the first time in London, and the next night, for Blanchard's benefit, he followed with Sir Christopher Curry in *Inkle and Yarico*, also for the first time in London. Five nights later, he accepted the role of Don Felix in *The Wonder* for the last benefit of Mrs. Mattocks, who was retiring after almost sixty years on the stage. Like the role of Curry, Don Felix was a role from his provincial days but had not been seen in London. On this occasion, Boaden made one of the few truly kind remarks of Cooke among all his many comments: ". . . here he would do, and he did do, all nobly. After the play, he recited Garrick's ode to Shakespeare; and, retiring for an instant, returned leading Mrs. Mattocks. Through the whole of her address, which was in plain prose, thanking the audience for the public favour of 58 years, Mr. Cooke supported her . . . . led her off the stage, with all the honours that could crown so valuable an actress."[87] Cooke made his last appearance of the season the next evening, 8 June, as Richard.

Curiously, Cooke's eighth season lasted only three months, but compared to his last full season (1806–1807), it was almost as productive in numbers, and more so in regularity, choice of roles, and frequency of repetition of his better parts. During the three months back in London, Cooke performed fifteen roles, plus reciting the "Ode to Shakespeare," and made fifty-two appearances, including a few combinations of *Love-a-la-Mode* with mainpieces. During his preceding season, from the end of September to the first of June, he had made approximately fifty-eight appearances in eighteen roles.[88] After the vagaries of the fall and winter, Cooke's position and reputation in London had been reestablished to a surprising degree. Without a firm resolve and extraordinary staying power, however, Cooke's future was not secure.

13

Fires, Riots, and Farewell

Cooke's 1808 summer proved as productive as the preceding spring; perhaps his fortunes were looking up. He first went to Bath and Bristol, where an engagement for three nights was expanded to a total of nine. Although ill that month, he never played better and was warmly welcomed by the public.[1] In Bath he performed Sir Pertinax (11 June), Shylock and Sir Archy (13 June), Richard III (16 June), Sir Giles (18 June), and Iago and Sir Archy (25 June). Bristol saw Sir Pertinax (15 June), Shylock and Sir Archy (20 June), Richard (22 June), and Sir Giles (24 June).[2]

On 1 July, he began a six-night engagement at Manchester, also expanded to a total of ten nights. The management and Cooke likely had reached a reconciliation over the events of the previous summer. Between 1 July and 14 July, Cooke appeared as Richard, Iago to Barrymore's Othello, Sir Pertinax (with Mrs. Harlowe from Drury Lane as Lady Rodolpho Lumbercourt), Shylock, Sir Archy, Prince Altenburg, Macbeth, and for his benefit on 11 July, Colin MacLeod and Sir Christopher Curry.[3]

Cooke's next stop was Newcastle, where he had not appeared in five years. Cooke was never fond of Newcastle. In his Appleby diary he wrote the following comment on an advertisement for the theatre with a motto from Shakespeare in it: "This is presumption in the writer, as it supposes that the audience of Newcastle are yet to be informed the use and purport of the stage."[4]

Cooke's engagement, for six nights, began 18 July with Sir Pertinax, supported by Mrs. Samuel Glover (the former Julia Betterton) of Covent Garden. Cooke was ill through part of his stay in Newcastle; the *Chronicle* announced on Saturday, 23 July, that he had recovered and would appear on Monday as Macbeth. He ran through his usual repertoire and renewed his engagement for an additional week, through 5 August, since he was not expected for his next appointment at York before 8 August. That week he supported Barrymore from Drury Lane and William Blanchard and Mrs. Glover from Covent Garden in their benefit nights, appearing as Oakly, Iago, and Richard III.[5] His last appearance was as the Stranger on 5 August with Mrs. Young (the former Miss Biggs) of Drury Lane as Mrs. Haller.

Cooke was preceded to York by his Covent Garden colleague John Emery. It had been twenty-one years since Cooke had performed in York, and now he would appear under John Wilkinson, the son of his old manager Tate Wilkinson. He had accepted the engagement in late May and had agreed to share the first three of a four-night engagement (after £25 had been received) and to take a clear half on the 4th.[6] His first appearance, to universal applause, was as Richard on 11 August. The *York Herald* (20 August 1808) reported that the "audience were delighted with the sarcastic speeches, the dissimulating courtship, the energetic fire, and the remorse and frenzy which he depicted throughout the whole of his masterly portrait of the ambitious tyrant." However, after his second night, as Sir Pertinax, local reaction was less favorable. "We perceived what he might have done, but we were witnesses that he did not do what was expected from him—If he was not cold, he was not animated; if he was not repulsive, he was not brilliant; and a very full house quitted the Theatre, if not displeased, certainly not satisfied." The result of this night was that on Monday, 15 August, Cooke's Sir Giles Overreach "was attended by a few, but how were they delighted? A more masterly representation of Massinger's favourite character we believe was never given. Contrary to the practice of great Stage Heroes, Mr. Cooke could not have acted better had the Theatre been crammed to the uttermost." For his last night, on 16 August, "The inhabitants of York crowded . . . to see his *Iago* and *Sir Archy*."[7]

After leaving York, Cooke traveled to Edinburgh, where on 28 August he appeared with Henry Siddons (Jaffier) and his wife as Pierre in *Venice Preserv'd*.[8] For his benefit on 29 August Cooke played Richard, with Siddons as Richmond and Mrs. Powell as the Queen.[9] For Cooke, the most significant event in Edinburgh was his marriage to Miss Lamb, the young lady with whom he had spent a good deal of time during the previous January and February. Dunlap asserts that "the marriage was agreeable to all parties concerned," but within six months she disappears from mention.[10] Apparently, the marriage was quickly dissolved.

His marriage was greeted with mixed feelings in London. *The Monthly Mirror* announced: "Alas, poor Lamb. Cooke has probably committed this rash act in his *sober* moments. It was shameful to take advantage of a man *disguised*."[11] Others, however, dwelled on the respectability of the lady and wished Cooke well, admonishing him, now that he was married, to play for "fame."[12] Whether this was Cooke's third or fourth marriage may never be known; it was certainly at least his second, since his marriage to and annulment from Alicia Daniels are well documented.

Following his marriage, and presumably a wedding trip, Cooke was expected in Liverpool for a brief engagement. On 12 September, a notice was posted, almost duplicating that of 24 August 1807, announcing that a letter had been received from Cooke saying he was on his way, but since he had not arrived Grant would appear as Richard III.[13] From what I have been able to ascertain, Cooke never arrived to fulfill his obligation, since the following summer he was advertised as appearing there for the first time in three years.[14]

The Covent Garden season opened during Cooke's absence on 12 September 1808 with *Macbeth* and *Raising the Wind*. Eight days later, at 4:00 A.M., Covent Garden was destroyed by fire. The theatre burned like tinder; by 8:00 P.M. the building was gutted, and the roof had fallen in. Everything was lost—scenery, costumes, armor, jewelry, scripts, as well as Handel's organ and scores, which he had bequeathed to John Rich at his death. Between twenty-two and twenty-four people lost their lives.[15] For the Kemble family this was a crushing blow. The property loss alone amounted to more than £100,000 but was covered by only £75,000 in insurance. The cause of the fire was never discovered. It was theorized that a piece of smoldering wadding from a gun discharged during *Pizarro* the night before the fire may have been the cause.[16]

Cooke returned to London to discover that the company had moved to the King's Theatre in the Haymarket, where it would remain until transferring to the Haymarket Theatre on 5 December. The company stayed at the Haymarket until the end of the season in May. In the meantime, Kemble and the patentees scurried about trying to recoup their losses by selling bonds and planning a new Covent Garden, designed by Robert Smirke, to be built on the old site. Kemble, thinking his problems could not worsen, would find them burgeoning when the new Covent Garden finally opened, in September 1809.

Although there had been an opera house in the Haymarket since 1705, Covent Garden's first substitute home had been rebuilt in 1791, officially the second King's Theatre. The opera house, designed by Michael Novosielski, with a capacity of around 2,500, was never intended for legitimate drama.[17] Cooke first appeared here on 13 October as Sir Pertinax:[18]

As soon as his voice was heard from behind the scenes, the applauding began, and as he appeared, he was saluted with three distinct rounds of universal applause. He seemed to be in excellent health, and we never saw his style of acting more vigorous and correct.[19]

With so much on the mind of the proprietors, acting took second place. Although Cooke did appear at the King's Theatre a few times during October and November, the management was lenient with his time and allowed him trips to Richmond, Brighton, and Bath.

On 17 and 21 October, he appeared in Richmond as Sir Pertinax and Richard III.[20] During the latter part of October he appeared at Brighton, and during the latter part of November and early December he performed eight nights in Bath.[21]

The Covent Garden company performed for the last time at the King's Theatre on 3 December, so that on his return from Bath the company had settled in at the small Haymarket Theatre. Beginning 5 December, they would remain there for 144 nights, after a total of 47 nights in the King's Theatre.

The Haymarket Theatre, then in its off-season, was a much more ideal playhouse for legitimate drama, and for Cooke it would mark a return to the site of his first London appearances in 1778. The previous summer another young actor, with whom Cooke had already performed in the provinces, became an overnight sensation at the Haymarket. Charles Mayne Young was immediately snatched up by Kemble for the Covent Garden company, with which he remained, becoming a star in his own right, until his retirement in 1832.[22]

Young and Cooke together were one of the few real drawing cards this season. Young played Othello to Cooke's Iago and Beverly to his Stukely in *The Gamester*, the latter being especially popular. Cooke had received a violent contusion in an accidental fall, which confined him to bed for about three weeks during the end of December and first third of January.[23] Nonetheless, he appeared with Young for the first time as Stukely on 13 January, and the production "attracted a more numerous audience than any at this Theatre during the season. The boxes were filled before half pay, and the lobbies were thronged by persons who expressed the greatest anxiety to get a single peep at the performance." Young was loudly applauded, Mrs. Siddons as Mrs. Beverly was better than usual, and Cooke "displayed his usual ability, and obtained a large share of approbation."[24] The renewed popularity of *The Gamester* resulted in a total of eight performances.

In March, after performing faithfully through February, Cooke again left London for engagements under John Wilkinson at York and Hull. Certain London periodicals would not accept Cooke's absences without assuming misbehavior was the reason. Typical is *The Monthly Mirror*'s report that Cooke, supposedly, had left the following note to the managers:

The wind shifts round to the *north*, I scud before it. If a change take to the *south*, I shall be back by the 6th of March.

Yours, &c. A. Cook and No Scullion!

The editor then added: "This looks like rebellion."[25] There was no provocation for such a remark, however, since Cooke had obviously obtained leave for these engagements. In fact, he had begun negotiations with Wilkinson on 23 January. On 22 February he left his apartment in Great Queenstreet, Lincoln's-Inn-Fields, with his wife, bound for Hull; two days later, the second theatrical disaster of the year occurred, the burning of Drury Lane.[26]

Cooke returned to Hull, the site of one of his provincial triumphs, on 28 February, stopping at the "Cross Keys," a coaching inn in the Market Place, near Finkle Street, the site of the Theatre Royal.[27] Mrs. Charles Kemble had completed a short engagement on Friday, 24 February, as Beatrice in *Much Ado About Nothing*;[28] Cooke appeared first on Tuesday as Richard III, one of four nights, and for his benefit on 3 March took Iago and Sir Archy.[29] As it turned out, this was also the last performance in the old Finkle Street Theatre. In 1810, it was replaced by a new theatre with the same name but on a different site.[30] On 11 March, Cooke returned to York for four nights, beginning with Richard, followed by Iago on 23 March, and Falstaff in *Henry IV, Part One* on his last night, 25 March.[31]

Cooke returned to London during late March and, if Dunlap is correct, dissolved his marriage in early April.[32] *The Monthly Mirror* in March had printed a verse apropos of this dissolution:

> To expiate the sins of yore,
> The fool of custom gave his store,
> 'Perhaps an ewe or ram;—
> So to atone for those of wine,
> Repentent grown, at Hymen's shrine
> Cooke offers up a———Lamb.[33]

As is certainly evident by now, Cooke was unlucky in his domestic affairs. His marriages to Daniels and Lamb seem to have lasted less than a year each. His last marriage, in the United States, ended with his death. Scattered throughout the periodicals of the time are references to his mistreatment of Miss Daniels—allusions to locking her up and physically abusing her. Even if such reports had not been circulated, Cooke was widely known to have been aggressive when drunk. His hostile impulses, which seem to have been concealed under normal social conditions, were released under the effect of alcohol. Although there is no way to prove this, it is even possible that Cooke, like many alcoholics, was not well adjusted sexually and escaped into an alcoholic stupor to avoid recriminations. There is little doubt that he had a self-punitive personality and could, on one night, vilify, strike out, and destroy, while the next morning he would be ashamed of himself and regret his actions. Anne Mathews recalled that a drunken spree "never failed to be followed by shame and repentence [*sic*]."[34]

Despite his domestic difficulties this spring, Cooke completed his performances in April and May with no apparent problems, taking his benefit on 1 May with *A New Way to Pay Old Debts* and *The Miller of Mansfield* in which he played John Cockle the Miller. The receipts for the night were low, only £169. None of the benefits had particularly high receipts: Young's was £210 on 2 May, Munden's £318 on the 3d, and Charles Kemble's £289 on the 5th.[35] For Charles Kemble's night, Cooke had played Gibby in *The Wonder*, and the next evening for Richard Jones' benefit, Baron Wildenheim in *Lovers' Vows*.[36]

During his ninth season, Cooke performed fifty-two times in fourteen roles, not an impressive record, but he had also begun late in the season and the season had ended earlier than usual. He had spent more time than usual out of London.[37] There is some indication that he was restless at the close of the season. Possibly to help cover more debts or simply to eliminate personal attachments, on the morning of his departure from London, Cooke wrote to an unknown party arranging for the disposal of his books and added: "As I have done with playing at *soldiering*, if you could direct me how to dispose of the *Rifle*, I should be obliged to you as I mean to disencumber myself of every useless appendage."[38]

Cooke's final performance at the end of the 1809 season was as Sir Pertinax on 25 May, after which he left for Chichester, arriving on the evening of 26 May. The following night he performed Shylock at the Chichester theatre under the management of Kelly and Maxfield. It had been built in 1792 by William Collins and had a £50 capacity.[39] Arnold Hare, in his excellent study of provincial theatres in the central portion of southern England, includes in an appendix a vivid and amusing account of Cooke's night in Chichester, taken from Lord William Pitt Lennox's *Celebrities I Have Known*.[40] Hare places this incident circa 1810, and not on 27 May 1809.[41] Since Cooke probably had not previously appeared in Chichester (or at least not for many years) and, to my knowledge, did not in 1810, and since Dunlap quotes the May 1809 date from one of Cooke's diaries, that date would seem to be the only possibility.[42] The anecdote gives an excellent sense of a country theatre in the early nineteenth century and reveals a good deal about Cooke at the time.

On the night in question, "the house was crowded to the roof, and the discordant sounds that were being carried on in the gallery nearly deafened me. The good old green curtain . . . was down, and a man in a stage-carpenter's dress was lighting the twelve tallow candles that were stuck into wet clay, and partly screened by tin shades . . . . The two stage doors had been removed and two small private boxes erected in their stead." The pit and boxes were both filled to capacity, almost to suffocation. The orchestra that evening was comprised of "a squeaking fiddle and a spasmodic clarionet." After a good deal of "yelling, shouting, hallooing, cat-calling, during which the roaring of lions, mewing of cats, and hooting of screech owls, with an admixture of howling of dogs, was judiciously imitated," the curtain rose. Following the opening scenes, Cooke finally appeared to an enthusiastic reception. In the fourth act, while whetting the knife in preparation for cutting out Antonio's pound of flesh, Cooke let the blade slip and nearly severed his thumb; in a few seconds his costume was deluged with blood. Lennox, then a young boy, not knowing Cooke had wounded himself, found that "the effect was terrific."

Before the audience could reward Cooke for "the agonizing look, the writhing expression of the suffering man," the curtain dropped. The manager explained that the performance must pause while a doctor examined Cooke's thumb. Buzzing through the house was word that the slip was the result of "A few glasses of toddy, whisky punch, and brandy and water, during the first three acts," which had made him quite inebriated by the trial scene. It was finally reported that the wound had been treated and that it would be possible for the actor to continue.

At the end of the mainpiece, Lennox, with the doctor who had bound Cooke's thumb and the Lennox family physician, went behind the scenes to get a first-hand view of the great tragedian:

Following my guide and medical advisor, I was ushered into the presence of the great George Frederick Cooke. The pencil of Hogarth, a Cruikshank, a Leech, or a Brown could alone give a picture of this curious scene. The apartment was about five feet in breadth, and ten in depth; the floor was covered with a coarse, showy-looking drugget; the walls were distempered a bright amber colour, a wooden stage-chandelier with four "dips" hung from the ceiling; a looking-glass from which a considerable quantity of the mineral fluid had escaped, a deal table, and a few ricketty chairs formed the remaining furniture.

From pegs in the wall hung the Jew's gabardine, his hat, wig, beard, and stick. An embroidered coat and waistcoat, and a powdered peruque were in the hands of the "dresser" and "coiffeur", ready to put on for the farce. The great man himself was seated in a theatrical state-chair, covered with purple velvet and gold tinsel, by the side of the table, upon which were sundry decanters and wine-glasses. Hot water, lemon, sugar, and liquer [sic] case had just been brought in through the public boxes as we entered.

Cooke spoke to Lennox, filling a glass with his "potent beverage" for the lad. Lennox with youthful enthusiasm began giving him a criticism of his Shylock. Cooke continued drinking his punch until the manager indicated that the audience was growing impatient, to which Cooke responded, characteristically, "Tell the Chichester people that George Frederick Cooke will not be dictated to by them; I that have acted before royalty will not stoop to a country audience." More argument and insult followed with Cooke threatening to walk out of the theatre, until Lennox chimed in with "Is Sir Archy as good a part as Shylock?" To that remark Cooke responded: "I forgot. You shall see, and judge for yourself."

I lost no time in returning to the box; and when the curtain drew up for the farce, the actor had so far recovered his senses, that being perfectly "up" in the part, . . . he went through it with the most consummate ability.[43]

The next evening Cooke performed the same roles at Portsmouth billed as "the celebrated Mr. Cooke of the Theatre Royal, Covent Garden."[44]

Cooke returned to London on 31 May and left again immediately for an engagement in Liverpool under Lewis and Knight, his Covent Garden colleagues. After an absence of almost three years, Cooke appeared as Sir Pertinax on 5 June and performed thereafter for fourteen additional nights. He completed the engagement with his benefit on 23 June, for which he presented Kitely and the prologue by Garrick. During his stay Cooke performed Iago, Baron Wildenheim, Falstaff, Shylock, Sir Archy, Richard III, Colin Mac-Leod, Sir Giles, and Lear.[45] At the conclusion of his engagement, two silver gilt cups, dated 20 June 1809, were presented to Cooke "as a token of respect for his superior talent."[46] When *The Monthly Mirror* heard of this, they could not resist another satirical jab at Cooke. They reported that the managers gave Cooke

a piece of plate for his unequalled exertions during the last three weeks . . . having kept sober (Sundays excepted) the whole one-and-twenty days! The *piece of plate*, being "two silver gilt cups," was very satirical of Messrs. Lewis and Knight, for it was as if they had said, "Now, Master Cooke, you have what you like—*a cup too much*."[47]

At the conclusion of the Liverpool engagement, McCready met Cooke and accompanied him to Manchester, where on 26 June he appeared as Richard III, with McCready as Buckingham and Meggett as Richmond.[48] It was most likely that about this time McCready's son, William Charles Macready, saw Cooke and formed his impression later recorded in his diaries. Macready was then about sixteen. The following year he would begin a career as a provincial actor; by 1819, he would be Edmund Kean's only London rival. Macready, after appearing for the first time in London as Richard III during the 1811–1812 season, recalled:

... Cooke, whose peculiarities added so much to the effect of his performance, served to detract from my confidence in assuming the crooked-back tyrant. Cooke's varieties of tone seemed limited to a loud harsh croak descending to the lowest audible murmur; but there was such significance in each inflexion, look, and gesture, and such impressive earnestness in his whole bearing, that he compelled your attention and interest. He was the Richard of the day; and in Shylock, Iago, Sir Archy Macsarcasm, and Sir Pertinax Macsycophant, he defied competition.[49]

Macready also remembered how Cooke, although more popular than Kemble, became the slave of intemperance, "remaining at times for days together in a state of debauch." He recorded stories he had heard relating to Cooke's retorts to his audience,[50] but he also remembered from personal experience an excellent example of Cooke's sober and gentle side, told with Macready's typically snobbish tone. After performing for Macready's father one evening, quite possibly during this engagement, Cooke and a classmate of Macready's at Rugby were part of a dinner party. "Henry Hanmer, then a young man, subsequently a Colonel in the Guards, was quite charmed with his mild and agreeable manners and his interesting conversation." Macready was then compelled to add: "As of many others, it used to be said of him, that he was no one's enemy but his own; a shallow compliment, flattering the easiness of his disposition at the expense of more solid and indispensable qualities."[51] Mrs. Anne Mathews agrees. She remembered Cooke as "a *gentleman* in the most extended sense of the word,—in ideas, words, habits, and actions; perfectly benevolent in his feelings, and moderate alike in judgement and opinion; peculiarly modest of his own merits, and liberal in his estimate of those of others." But then, under the influence of his "punch," "the honey was turned to gall; the *Bottle Imp* mastered his better nature; and he became vulgar, noisy, intolerant, and intolerable; apt to injure, quick to take offense, and still quicker to resent it."[52] Although the more bestial and drunken side of Cooke has been overly publicized, it is historically important to keep in perspective his almost schizophrenic behavior and recall as well those moments of gentleness and humor. Kelly, who helped perpetuate one of the classic anecdotes of Cooke's misbehavior, previously told, also records how "no man, when sober, was better conducted, or possessed more affability of manners, blended with sound sense and good nature, than Cooke; he had a fine memory, and was extremely well-informed." He was even capable, when in good mental shape, of saying no to one more drink, as he did on one occasion after dining with Kelly and Mrs. Crouch at Brighton.[53]

Cooke performed three nights in Manchester, 26 June (Richard III), 27 June (Sir Pertinax), and 28 June (Shylock and Sir Archy), with receipts for the short engagement totaling nearly £400.[54] Accompanied by Rock, his old friend and benefactor, Cooke left on 29 June for the Edinburgh theatre, now under Henry Siddons' management.

From 3 July until 22 July, Cooke performed thirteen nights, including appearances as Richard, Sir Pertinax, Sir Archy, Colin MacLeod, Falstaff (*Henry IV, Part one*), Iago, Joseph Surface, Shylock, and Cato. He had not performed Cato in Edinburgh for many years.[55] The *Caledonian Mercury* (17 July 1809), in its comments on Colin MacLeod, felt that Cooke "speaks the part much superior to its writing, and better than most Caledonians could do—his blunt honesty was finely pourtrayed [sic] in plain homely truths." For his benefit on the 22d, he played Sir Pertinax and the King in *The King and the Miller of Mansfield* to Rock's Miller. Cooke records in his diary that he also "*gave* the managers two nights" during Race Week "which was wrong" and also played Gibby on 7 August for Fawcett's benefit.[56] A playbill at Harvard has him listed as Joseph Surface two nights later for Mrs. Young's night. This was the last season at the Theatre Royal in Prince's Street for almost three years. In the fall, Siddons moved to the circus in Leith Walk, which he refurbished into a more suitable theatre.[57]

On 15 August, Cooke in company with "a young lady of the late Edinburgh Company," left for Perth, by the Queen's Ferry, where the next night he appeared at the Glovers' Hall Theatre as Richard to "a *great* house, £47."[58] It seems that he played six nights, starring as Shylock and Sir Archy, Iago, and, on 22 August, Sir Pertinax.[59] Cooke enjoyed Perth and its situation on the Tay River but found the playhouse "very dirty and inconvenient."[60] On 23 July he returned to Edinburgh.

Cooke intended to travel to Liverpool on Saturday, 26 August, but twenty-two miles from Edinburgh "received so severe a fall, that I was constrained to return thither on the evening of Tuesday the 29th."[61] He was consequently detained until 9 September and did not arrive in London until the 12th, returning to his lodgings of the previous year, No. 8, Panton-Square, near Leicester Square and Haymarket Street.

Cooke's tenth and last season at Covent Garden was catastrophic for Kemble and Cooke. For Cooke, it was both personally humiliating and pitiful, although in the beginning, during the famous Old Price Riots, Cooke was chosen as the people's hero, whereas Kemble was clearly the villain elect.

The New Theatre Royal, Covent Garden, opened with *Macbeth* on 18 September 1809, less than twelve months after the fire. The new theatre, which virtually no one liked, was a massive, squat building, considerably larger than the old one. It was one of the largest theatres in Europe, the design suggested by the Temple of Minerva on the Acropolis. The auditorium had three tiers of boxes arranged in a true horseshoe around the sloping pit, containing twenty-six boxes with three rows of benches. The first two tiers of boxes were open to the general public, but on the third tier private boxes, to be let on an annual basis, had been added. This would prove to be one of the major targets of public outcry; separation of the classes was at the heart of the riots, as was the long-held monopoly of the two patent houses.[62]

To offset the cost of the new building, it was necessary that the prices for pit seats be raised from 3s.6d. to 4s. and the boxes from 6s. to 7s. However legitimate these increases may have been, the patrons jumped on them as an opportunity for revolt. A typical satirical verse on the situation appeared in the *Morning Chronicle* (22 September 1809):

> This is the House that Jack built
> Those are the boxes let to the great, that visit the
>   House that Jack built.
> Those are the pigeon holes over the boxes, let to the
>   great that visit the House that Jack built.
> This is the Cat engaged to squall, to the poor in the
>   pigeon holes
> Over the boxes let to the great, that visit the House
>   that Jack built.
> This is John Bull with a bugle horn, that hissed the Cat
>   engaged to squall to the poor in the pigeon holes
>   over the boxes, let to the great, etc.
> This is the thief taker shaven and shorn,
> That took up John Bull with his bugle horn,
> Who hissed the Cat, etc.
> This is the Manager, full of scorn,
> Who raised the Price to the people for-lorn,
> And directed the thief-taker, etc.

Furthermore, to add fuel to their anger, the celebrated soprano Madame Catalani had been engaged for the new theatre at £75 a night. The public reaction was totally irrational. Such extravagance and for a foreign artist too could not be tolerated. The true causes of the riot were, of course, much deeper. England had been sitting on a powder keg for twenty years. For seventy-two years theatre-going had been restricted by the Licensing Act of 1737; only Drury Lane and Covent Garden were patented to exhibit legitimate drama and had thus created a kind of monopoly. Attempts at reform had proved futile. Covent Garden was now making further demands. To add to the present disgruntled mood, the inveterate London theatre-goers had become progressively less kind to Kemble; his popularity had been in a slump for a number of years.[63]

No one could have predicted the violent reactions that would last until mid-December and would end in Kemble's capitulation. The facts of the Old Price Riot are well known. Cooke was the only actor able to draw a sympathetic crowd. In general, the rioters would greet all the actors with initial applause, to indicate that they were not the culprits, but as soon as they attempted to speak, cries of "Off! Off!," catcalls and hisses, appalling hoots, and the Old Price Dance would begin. The dance was performed with deliberate and ludicrous gravity, each person shouting the letters OP as loudly as possible to the accompaniment of a blow or beat on the floor to underscore each letter.

It all began with the first night, the grand opening. As the evening wore on the tumult grew worse, spreading from the gallery to the pit. Not a word was heard from the stage. At the conclusion of the mute performance, Kemble committed one of the many tactical errors he would make over the next four months. He had the audacity to call in constables who appeared on stage as if to read the riot act. Finally, around 2:00 A.M., after a chorus of "God Save the King," the audience disbursed.

For the second night Kemble tried another tactic—the presentation of *The Beggar's Opera*. In his 1791 memoranda book, Kemble had jotted down: "Whenever there is danger of a Riot, always act an Opera; for musick drowns the noise of opposition," but on this night it did not help.[64] This time the audience came armed with placards and banners, displaying such slogans as "The Devil is black/ And so is Jack."[65]

On the third night, when Cooke made his first appearance that season as Richard III, matters grew worse. The curtain was drawn up and the play began. At first there were loud plaudits which for an instant drowned the voices of discontent, but soon Cooke's every attempt to procure a hearing was overpowered by a louder and more general uproar; hisses, hootings, howlings, roarings, whistles, catcalls, bugle and coachmen's horns, and the clattering of sticks accompanied his words. Placards appeared in the pit with "Persevere and you will conquer," "John Bull's Opposition to John Kemble's Imposition," "No Private Boxes. Let there be no Intrigue, nor Private Performances in the Antiroom behind the Private Boxes!," "It was all *dickey* with the actors." Despite repeated bravos for Cooke and placards reading "Cooke merits our pity, but Kemble our contempt," Cooke went unheard. After half-price, it was even worse.[66]

On the 25th, the bill announced that "THIS THEATRE will be CLOSED, till the committee of GENTLEMEN, to whose Investigation their Books and Accounts are to be submitted, have examined and made up their opinions upon them."[67] Although the management was vindicated and the new prices were obviously justified, it made little difference.

In the meantime, Cooke escaped to Leicester during the first week of October for four nights of performances at the theatre on Hotel Street.[68] He then performed at Birmingham from 11 to 13 October. On the 21st, back in London, he attempted Iago to Young's Othello, but the riot continued. Kemble dared not appear and was greeted by the press, which was having a heyday, with:

> Kemble's the fellow
> Who darn't play Othello,
> Lest on the night
> We shou'd put out the light.[69]

On the 23d, Cooke attempted Sir Pertinax in honor of the fiftieth year of the accession of George III, but despite the celebratory nature of the evening, all was the same. Indeed, the demonstrations were becoming more vociferous and outspoken. One placard displayed a gibbet, a rope, and a figure, with the words "Kemble's deserts for extortion," and another, "This Theatre to be let, Kemble and Company retiring from business."[70] On the 27th, Cooke left town again for one night at Brighton, playing Shylock for Mr. and Mrs. Henry Johnston.[71]

On 30 October, back in London, Cooke appeared before the audience to introduce Mrs. Clarke from Manchester, who was to appear that night in *The Grecian Daughter*. At first the audience listened to their former favorite, but as he began the following prologue, those in the pit could no longer contain themselves.

> Though hostile rage so long within these walls,
> Has rais'd a tempest that each heart appalls,
> A female candidate comes forth to night,
> Who knows your kindness equals all your might.[72]

Throughout the ensuing days, Cooke went through the motions of his major roles but was rarely heard.

Once the slow machinery of the law was put in operation, the entire affair came to an end, and the proprietors bowed in total defeat. Kemble himself met 300 of his leading antagonists on 14 December at the Crown and Anchor Tavern and agreed to all their demands, including the abolition of the private boxes and the dismissal of the old and faithful boxkeeper, James Brandon, who through it all had received a great part of the grief.

By late November, the noise was subsiding. On 1 December, Cooke was able to get through his performance with relative ease; by 13 December, Cooke as Kitely met little interruption, although a few "uproarious chieftains" still wore OP handkerchiefs over their hats. On 20 December, six days after the settlement, Cooke went through Shylock with the "utmost attention, and a perfect calm prevailed."[73]

Cooke seems to have come through the hectic months relatively unscathed and in fact supportive of Kemble. In the green room one night, a fellow-actor said Kemble was indifferent to their plight. Kelly, who was there, asked Cooke what he thought of such an assertion. Cooke replied: "No, Sir, I think him a very great one, and those who say the contrary are envious men, and not worthy, as actors, to wipe his shoes."[74] Kemble may have been Cooke's rival and "Black Jack" on occasion, but in a moment of crisis, Cooke was a faithful member of the profession. In a drunken moment, some two years later in Philadelphia, Cooke confided to Dunlap that "John is an actor! He is my superior, though they did not think so in London—I acknowledge it—and now!"[75]

Although calm reigned once more at Covent Garden, Cooke was about to experience the most unsettling spring of his career in London. The press, without the Old Price Riot as a butt for sensational journalism, turned once more to Cooke. One rather unreliable source even suggests that the renewed attack was in part the result of a cabal that existed against Cooke among John Kemble's admirers.[76] Unfortunately, Cooke gave the press the needed ammunition. On 28 December, he did not appear for a performance of *Merchant of Venice*; bills were posted at the doors announcing that because of his indisposition, Egerton would play Shylock.[77] A large audience, halting the performance, loudly protested, "What, is he drunk again?" After a short interval, Murray came forward and suggested that Charles Kemble take the role, which he did. This, however, failed to satisfy the audience, for they wanted either John Philip or Young, if they could not have Cooke.[78] They would probably have been less vehement if the night before Cooke had not "staggered as the representative of The Roman Father, but was so completely stupified by intoxication, that he was obliged to stagger off again without performing the part."[79]

Cooke's indulgent public had had enough. No matter how great his talent, "he is self-degraded beneath the contempt of the meaning of his audience." The *Morning Chronicle* (29 December 1809) was convinced that he failed to appear as Shylock fearing the indignation of the audience and that his actions had consequently placed the management in a very awkward position. *The Monthly Mirror*, which had grown progressively more hostile toward him, issued a surprisingly mild attack:

... the consequences [of his absence] was [*sic*] that a most ungenerous feeling pervaded the house against him. We call it *ungenerous*, because Mr. Bull should look at home, and recollect how much he likes to spend a *merry Christmas*. On the 26th he got drunk and appeared, for which they abused him (and he who abuses a drunken man, abuses an absent man, which is very unfair); now he gets drunk and decently stays away, for which they also abuse him—What at this season of the year can the poor man do? We have seen Mr. Kemble on the stage as intoxicated as we ever saw Mr. Cooke, but it was certainly not when he had to play a part: however, we are by no means convinced that his getting drunk oftener would not make *John* like him much better.... Every thing is good or bad by comparison, and by this test Mr. Cooke has behaved very well. His cups displeased the audience before, and being in them again, he would not trust himself to return.[80]

In Philadelphia, Cooke told Dunlap: "John takes his bottle sometimes as well as other people; I have had some hard bouts with him. 'Come, Cooke,' says he, 'We don't play to-morrow, let's get drunk;' and if he said so he was sure to do it. Charles is the good fellow. He always used to keep himself steady, and in the morning he'd put John to bed and carry me home in a coach."[81] Kemble was indeed a fairly heavy drinker, but unlike Cooke, he drank largely in private and, although it affected him physically, he apparently never went on stage under the influence of alcohol.

On 9 January, Cooke reappeared as Richard III. A note on the theatre's play bill reads: "Before the play commenced, Cooke came forward to apologize for his late offences. When he came to 'if you will restore me once more to the favours I enjoyed, I promise—' here he was interrupted by unanimous applause and retired without completing a promise not likely to be kept."[82] It had been rumored that Cooke had declared he would never again appear at Covent Garden and had accepted an engagement at Manchester. Cooke had in fact been negotiating with Elliston, now the manager at Manchester, and would leave in February.[83] When it was then announced that he would in fact appear, there was a great difference of opinion as to what his tactics would be and bets were placed that he would not apologize.[84] The *Morning Chronicle* (9 January 1810) provides us with the most complete narrative of that evening. Cooke came forward as soon as the curtain went up and bowed several times. Some of the audience applauded him, others hissed, and some yelled "Off! Off!" Finally there was silence, and Cooke began

"Ladies and Gentlemen—It is impossible for me to express the mortification I feel at the situation in which I stand." (a loud burst of applause, mingled with some disapprobation, prevented him for a short time from proceeding) "When I came to town on the 26th, I did not know I was to play that night, although I acknowledge I had a previous intimation of it. On Thursday, I assure you, I was wholly incapable of playing." (This phrase was immediately applied in a particular sense by some of the audience, and was received with a loud laugh. The remainder of the sentence could not be heard distinctly. We believe Cooke added, "through illness." A mixture of applause and disapprobation again prevented him for a short time from proceeding.)—"Ladies and Gentlemen, I am aware that what I have said cannot be considered as an apology for what has passed, but I hope it will have the effect of restoring me to that favour which I once had."— Applause was here very loudly and generally expressed.

Although the audience accepted Cooke again that night, others considered he had made no apology whatsoever. *The Satirist*, for example, included the following commentary:

... he recently came forward dressed in character as *Richard*, and his address was *in character*, and was indeed as fine *a piece of acting* as we have ever been witness to. The applause was so great as almost to prevent his being heard, and his assumed humility was soon changed to the most barefaced assurance; he even disclaimed all intention of making an *apology*, and having broadly confessed his sins, was scarcely about to refrain from laughing at those who, notwithstanding their late repeated boasts of being the guardians of *public* morals, were yet content to hail with fervent applause, a man who had shamelessly outraged every feeling of decency and decorum, at a season, too, when the bad effects of example were most likely to operate upon the younger classes of society.[85]

There is no way of knowing Cooke's state of mind at this time, or the true nature of his two major bouts with his audience. Doubtless, he deserved strong censure, but continued attacks, even when he was on his best behavior, must have disturbed him greatly. Earlier, before his December illness, a lengthy and prejudicial attack in verse had been made on his acting, in a publication called *The Thespiad*. A note at the bottom of one of the pages declared:

Were we to judge by the fondness of the public, this man would appear to be the best actor we have. . . . And yet no man has treated his audience with such insolence and contempt as this very person. His frequent inebriety, his impertinent speeches, his non-acknowledgment of applause, his unpopular cast of characters, and his extreme want of the *suaviter in modo*—all these circumstances would naturally lead one to suppose, that Cooke must be much disliked.[86]

This same author did hesitantly acknowledge that, when sober, Cooke's Sir Pertinax "is the most perfect representation extant on the stage."

After a difficult December, Cooke performed faithfully and without incident throughout January and February.

At the end of February, he fulfilled his seven-night engagement with Elliston in Manchester, performing his usual fare plus his role of Horatius in Whitehead's *The Roman Father*.[87] Back in London in time to perform Kitely on 6 March, he passed the remainder of the spring season without major incident. Toward the end of April he appeared four nights in Worcester to overflowing crowds.[88] On 5 May, he appeared for the first time as Henry VIII with Kemble as Wolsey and Mrs. Siddons as Queen Katherine, but Cooke, who was compared to Pope, had little success with the role. "Instead of the noble, frank, boisterous look and manners of Harry, he had the look of Richard III or the bearded head of Shylock, and the artful manners of Iago."[89] Cooke would repeat the role only twice more this season; in America he would try it for one last time in New York opposite Cooper's Wolsey.[90]

For his 1810 benefit, which as it turned out would be his last in London, he performed his all-time favorite role, Sir Pertinax, on 16 April, to a respectable house of £398.[91] His career in London ended ignominiously. On 1 June, he was scheduled to play Sir Archy for Jones' benefit, but "at 9—Cooke was discovered indisposed," and on the 5th, Blanchard's night, Cooke was to do Falstaff; at 6:00 it was decided he could not go on, or according to Kemble he simply did not show up that night, and *The Wheel of Fortune* was substituted.[92] The next night, he "would not act" in *Man of the World* for H. Johnston's benefit.[93] His last performance at Covent Garden, after almost three weeks' absence, took place on 22 June 1810 for Mrs. Clarke's benefit as Shylock, to a house of only £230 and no fanfare.

Cooke's last London season ended on a low note. The season had been a tempestuous one for all, and Kemble would never completely recuperate from his experience. The season had offered no particular novelty. *The Satirist* compared the nightly playgoer at Covent Garden to "an ass in a mill," because of the repetition of pieces designed "like the iron bed of Procrustus [*sic*] to suit all customers, who must thus submit for the time to have their understandings cut down to its dimensions."[94] Cooke performed only thirteen roles this last season, for a total of fifty-seven appearances.[95] It is understandable that after such a personally degrading year, Cooke's old friend from America, T. A. Cooper, could steal him away to the United States in less than four months. If Dunlap is correct, Cooke now felt discontented with his London position, and at fifty-four he no longer had the energy to compete with his opposition.[96] There is no doubt that his reputation and status had been undermined by a hostile and negative press.

His final summer in England was passed principally in Liverpool and Preston. Although Dunlap says that Cooper and Cooke first made contact shortly after Cooper's arrival in Liverpool on 7 July, there is no evidence to assume that either was there on that date.[97] Indeed, Cooke was expected in Liverpool to begin his engagement on 23 July, but he failed to appear. A bill was issued at 5:00 P.M. announcing "The Managers have waited with the utmost anxiety until this late hour, in hopes of having the satisfaction of announcing to the Public, the arrival of Mr. Cooke, but they are sorry to say he is not yet come."[98] As a result, the bill was changed from *The Man of the World* to *Lovers' Vows*. Cooke had arrived by Tuesday, 24 July, when he appeared as Sir Pertinax. For the next two weeks, through 14 August, Cooke performed Richard, Iago, Shylock, Sir Archy, Sir Giles, Sir Pertinax, Kitely, Lear, Falstaff in *Merry Wives*, and, for his benefit on 14 August, Luke in Sir James Bland Burges' new drama *Riches; or, The Wife and Brother*, and Sir Archy.[99] If Cooke was still able to add a new role to his repertoire at this date, it would seem his energies had not left him completely.

From Liverpool he went the short distance to Preston, performing Richard III on 16 August and Sir Pertinax on the 17th.[100] So far as I can tell, his last performance in England was before a small country audience, without notice or comment, thus bringing to a close thirty-seven or thirty-eight years on the English stage. Sometime in late July, Cooper had arrived in Liverpool from the United States and had begun the negotiations that would take Cooke away from his native land.[101]

14

Among the Yankee Doodles

The American phase of Cooke's career was a lucrative one, at least for the American managers of the five theatres in which he performed. The receipts for all of his performances in the United States totaled approximately $250,000, which by today's standards would amount to almost $1.5 million.[1] Of this amount, Cooke would receive a paltry $20,000. He was well aware that he was exploited by these "American upstarts." In Philadelphia, during one of his frequent outbursts, he told Dunlap:

I came away, Sir [from England], without preparation—without my stage-clothes—without by books—as if I was running away by stealth from my creditors—like a criminal flying from the laws of the country. Now Holman [the actor Joseph George Holman arrived in the United States in 1812] will come out after making every preparation; after making a bargain by which he will put that money into his own pocket, which I am putting into the pockets of men who treat me as if I was an idiot. They think I am a fool, and that I will receive as a generous gratuity from them, a part of what I enrich them with! Sir, I shall have lost money by coming here—and when I go back, how do I know in what manner I shall be received, or whether I shall be received at all!—To come away without seeing Mr. Harris! my best friend— the man who did everything for me! The man who pitted me against them all![2]

Such resentments, whether true or not, doubtlessly drove him even more to the bottle and produced the consequent paranoia that accompanied his inebriated condition.

What circumstances had placed Cooke in such a wretched predicament? The stratagem by which he was brought to the New World in the first place will probably never be fully known. Most accounts in the standard histories of the American theatre follow William Dunlap's version.[3] Dunlap tells us that Thomas Cooper, then co-manager of the Park Theatre, who was recruiting in London, first approached Cooke in July 1810. It seems more likely, as explained in the previous chapter, that the initial contact was made in late July in Liverpool. Sometime in August, Cooper made Cooke a written offer of 25 guineas a week for ten months, a benefit at each theatre, and 25 cents a mile for traveling expenses between cities.[4]

The negotiations were at a stalemate through September. On 30 September

1810, Cooke, then in Liverpool, wrote Henry Harris that he intended to leave for London on 2 October in the company of his old friend Joseph Munden, who was recovering from a severe case of gout. Munden adds in his own account that early on the morning of 2 October he hobbled to Cooke's lodgings, where he found him dressed, seated in a chair with an empty brandy bottle on the table, and refusing to move. After fruitless entreaties, Munden left to attend to other business.[5]

Dunlap says that Cooke finally did get on the coach but that Cooper overtook him, secretly arranged for another coach to whisk Cooke back to a friend's home about five miles from Liverpool, and finally got him aboard the *Columbia*. The *Columbia* set sail for the United Stares on 4 October. Rumors were already rampant that Cooper had all but shanghaied Cooke, luring him on board when he was too drunk to know what was happening to him. To scotch these rumors, Cooper sent a letter to the Liverpool newspapers declaring that this was a lie, that he and Cooke had simply concluded negotiations which had been underway since 6 August. The author of the Munden biography implies that both Cooper and Cooke were guilty of double-dealing and deceit in an attempt to cheat the Covent Garden management. Cooke, drunk but coherent, recalled in Philadelphia that "Cooper had inveigled him into an agreement when he was drunk, that he was drunk tho' not entirely so when he went on board ship, that he would have return'd to be sure but he was ashamed to return after having gone so far."[6] Even Cooper later admitted that he felt some guilt at the "undue means to get him off" and announced to Dunlap that "he would not undergo again for *any sum* what he did for that purpose."[7]

An interesting version of the Cooke/Cooper negotiations is told by the Veteran Stager in his *Essay on the Science of Acting*. He claims to have been present during the early stages of the negotiations. The "facts" in this essay, as noted earlier in this study, are difficult to verify; nonetheless, they shed some light upon the affair. The Stager says that while in Liverpool Cooke lodged with a Mrs. Delisle in Basnet Street, where Cooper had formerly stayed. Cooper could use visits to his former landlady as an excuse to make contact with Cooke. On several occasions Cooke refused to see Cooper, and, indeed, he rejected his advances with vehemence. Then, says this author, Cooke received a letter from Harris requesting his speedy return to London. Cooke decided to leave by the morning coach. Since the coach was to leave at 4:00 P.M., he planned to go to Warrington, several miles from Liverpool, in order to get a few hours' rest and catch the coach there. Cooke was taking a parting glass at a Liverpool tavern with the Stager and Tom Hollingworth, formerly an actor at Drury Lane and then with the Liverpool company, when Cooper entered. Discovering Cooke's intentions, Cooper informed Cooke that he was going to a place called Mock Beggar. He suggested he would accompany Cooke as far as Prescot, eight miles from Liverpool. Cooke agreed. At this point the author relies on the testimony of a Mr. Holt, the landlord of an inn on the Liverpool-

Prescot road known by the sign of the Legs of Man. He continues: "On the arrival of Cooke at Mr. Holt's, Cooper instantly dismounted, and with considerable difficulty prevailed on his companion to enter the inn; at last he succeeded, Madeira was loudly called for; they were waited on by our host in person." A second bottle was introduced, and soon "Richard was not himself." During these events, Cooper extolled the beauty of America and the advantages it possessed for an actor. Cooke once more took his place in the chaise, but instead of going to its original destination, it was directed to the "seat of Cooper's friend, a Mr. S., a respectable attorney at [near] Liverpool." Cooke was left there while Cooper hastened to Liverpool to arrange for Cooke's passage to America. The narrative concludes:

Things thus having been adjusted to the entire satisfaction of Cooper, he returned that night to Mock Beggar where in the interim an instrument had been drawn up by which Cooke bound himself upon certain terms and conditions to visit for three years the transatlantic shore. A night devoted to Bacchus passed; Cooke was conveyed to bed, and early on the following morning . . . he was conveyed to a chaise in waiting, in which he retraced his steps once more to Liverpool, and was by sagacious and wily manager driven to the water side, where the ship's boat was in attendance to convey him to the vessel which was to waft him for ever from the shore of Britain. . . . All the circumstances were kept in such profound secrecy, and the movements effected with such dispatch, that the first intimation we received of his departure was at 11 o'clock that night from the mouth of the pilot who conducted the ship to the north-west buoy, who called upon us at the theatre, and much to our surprize and regret we learned the above circumstances as far as relates to sailing.[8]

According to this version, although Cooke and Cooper must have conferred and discussed a possible American tour, and finally signed a document of agreement, it is also apparent that Cooper took unfair advantage of Cooke's weakness for the bottle and his subsequent drunkenness. Certainly Cooke was expected for another season at Covent Garden. This is substantiated not only by Cooke's letter to Harris but also by the Covent Garden account books which list Cooke's salary weeks into the season, until it was certain that Cooke had left for the United States.[9]

Forty-three days after leaving Liverpool, Cooke arrived in New York dried out and sober from the long voyage, after first suffering on board the *Columbia* from a fever followed by hemorrhoids and discharge of blood and then total abstinence from alcohol, necessitated by an empty liquor store on board.[10] Cooke would refer to this drying out process as "the water system."[11] One of his New York physicians, Dr. John W. Francis, recalled that on his arrival Cooke "possessed all the physical energies of thirty."[12] Nevertheless, as soon as he found himself in theatrical company, he would quickly be back in his cups.

Although such English actors as James Fennell, Mrs. Whitlock, Mrs. Anne

Merry, and Cooper had preceded him, this was the first American visit of a truly great English star, one whose presence to Francis constituted "the greatest epoch in the progress of the drama."[13] His reception was the greatest ever accorded an actor in the United States.[14] Cooke's presence was to mark the beginning of a new era in the American theatre—the rise of the star system.

The state of theatricals in New York prior to Cooke's arrival was low, as Durang and others have attested. In 1810, it was essential for Cooper and Stephen Price, also a co-manager of the Park, to "invoke some tremendous novelty to arouse the dormant patronage and taste of the playgoing public."[15] It should be noted that in bringing Cooke to America, Cooper endangered his own professional standing, for Cooke was obviously the greater actor. *The Mirror of Taste* gave Cooper credit for magnanimity: ". . . he was perfectly sensible that he was introducing not merely a superior that would outshine him, but an actor whose extraordinary powers must open to the American public a new and far more clear and correct view than they could ever have had before of what is excellent and what censurable in the art."[16] Certainly, Cooper displayed a liberal spirit and "a dignified scorn of those mean jealousies which are too generally found to taint the heart of men in all professions." On the other hand, Cooper must have clearly seen the risk he was taking. Nearly sixty years old, Cooke was ill and was destroying himself with drink; he could not last long. Cooke himself expressed little concern over competing with Cooper—"I'll show those fellows what acting is, they [the American managers] talk of their Cooper, their idol, their wooden God. Haven't I stood the trial with John [Kemble]. What is your Cooper?"[17]

On 17 November, the *New York Herald* announced that Cooke was "engaged . . . to play at New York, Philadelphia, and most of the other large towns; so that it will probably require a year and a half or two years, to complete his series of engagements." The first news of his coming had been doubted, as *The Mirror of Taste* records:

That a performer who has for years been more than any other, distinguished by public favour at home, and had it in his power to acquire there an annual income of five thousand pounds sterling, should in advanced life transverse the Atlantic, and migrate to a country so remote from his own, on a professional speculation, was a thing apparently so much a variance with reason and probability, that any man who but a week before it happened, had hardly enough to suggest a likelihood of its taking place, would be considered either a fool or a banterer.[18]

Once Cooke's presence was certain, however, American journalists did not hesitate to congratulate Cooper and to declare that Cooke's engagement "marks not only the most brilliant era in the stage history of the United States, but holds forth to the old world an incontestible proof of the unexampled advancement of this young country in taste, refinement, and literature, as well as in opulence and prosperity."[19] Wherever Cooke appeared, the journalists repeated this absurd flattery of the audience for its supposed refined taste. Cooke, as is well known, thought otherwise and repeatedly expressed his contempt for the audience. Once, in Baltimore, when he was told that President Madison intended to see him act, Cooke responded, "If he does, I'll be damned if I play before him. What, I? I!—George Frederick Cooke! who have acted before the Majesty of Britain, play before your Yankee President!" He called Madison "the contemptible King of the Yankee Doodles!"[20]

The furor that attended his first New York appearance as Richard III is typical of the excitement and near insanity that characterized his entire tour. A large crowd of men began to gather the evening before the day of performance to wait for tickets. Some brought their nightcaps in order to sleep in comfort. Some brought chairs to sleep in, and others stretched full length and dozed in the street. The next morning the crowd swelled with ticket speculators, servants representing their masters, men hired to procure tickets for others, and so on. Before 9:00 A.M. the area in front of the Park was completely blocked. At 10:00 the box office opened. In the rush some were injured and fights broke out. In an attempt to get nearer the box office, a few individuals climbed up the iron post and along the arm which held the lamp hanging over the theatre door; in the general debacle a burly chap fell from the post on the heads of the crowd. At 5:00 P.M. the entire street in front of the theatre was jammed with people, despite the fact that all the tickets had been sold for hours. When the doors finally opened at 6:00 (thirty minutes past the announced time), a "pell-mell rush ensued." The doors were clogged; the situation got serious. A placard informed ticket-holders that they would be admitted at the stage door. This caused two traffic jams instead of one. The crowd packed the house—"an audience more numerous than had ever before been crowded within the walls of the theatre."[21] The count, according to Dunlap, was 2,200 people and the receipts $1,820.[22]

Similarly wild scenes occurred in Philadelphia and Boston. Charles Durang has left a colorful account of Cooke's first appearance in Philadelphia in March 1811 (see Barnard Hewitt's *Theatre U.S.A.*, pp. 82–85). A slightly different account appeared in Paulson's *American Daily Advertiser* on March 1811:

Those who were most anxious to obtain seats, made regular contracts with the most Sampson like citizen they could find, and indeed in such demand was muscular power during the last week, that any man who would run the risk of being squeezed to death, might readily have obtained a *bonus* of five dollars. . . . at half past six (a.m.) about fifty of the warriors had taken the field . . . a few minutes past nine . . . six or seven hundred spectators and performers were on the spot.[23]

In Boston during the preceding January, despite extremely severe weather, the box office was surrounded from 3:00 A.M. until the ticket sales began at 10:00.[24] Such furor was without precedent in the American theatre.

> The Managers feel extremely gratified by having it in their power to announce the Engagement of
>
> # MR. COOKE,
>
> Of the Covent-Garden Theatre, for
>
> ## TWELVE NIGHTS.
>
> First Night of Mr. COOKE'S Engagement.
>
> On Wednesday Evening, Nov. 21st, 1810,
> WILL BE PRESENTED,
> SHAKSPEARE'S TRAGEDY OF,
>
> # Richard the Third
>
> ## Or, The Battle of Bosworth Field
>
> | | | | |
> |---|---|---|---|
> | King Henry, | Mr. STANLEY. | Catesby, | Mr. CLAUDE. |
> | Prince of Wales, | Miss DELAMATER | Tressel, | —— MORRELL |
> | Duke of York, | —— JONES | Lieutenant, | —— THORNTON |
> | Richard, | Mr. COOKE | Stanley, | —— DOYLE |
> | Buckingham, | —— ROBERTSON. | Tyrrell, | —— M'ENERY |
> | Richmond, | —— SIMPSON. | Elizabeth, | Mrs. STANLEY |
> | Norfolk, | —— HOGG. | Lady Anne, | —— MASON. |
> | Ratcliff, | —— HALLAM. | Duchess of York, | Mrs. HOGG |
> | Lord Mayor, | —— BRAY. | | |
>
> To which will be added,
> THE FAVORITE FARCE OF,
>
> # Fortune's Frolic.
>
> | | | | |
> |---|---|---|---|
> | Robin Rough-Head, | Mr. BRAY | Miss Nancy, | Miss RYCKMAN |
> | Snacks, | —— HOGG | Dolly, | Mrs. OLDMIXON |
> | Mr. Frank, | —— CLAUDE. | Margery, | —— HOGG. |
> | Rattle, | —— DOYLE. | Villagers, &c. | |

Cooke's first appearance in America at the Park Theatre, 21 November 1810. Used by permission of the Harvard Theatre collection.

In each city the system of ticket sales was altered. In New York, after the havoc of the first performance, Price decided "in order to prevent a press upon the Box door" that box tickets would be sold only on the outside of the theatre, at two windows between the pit and box doors.[25] In Boston, during Cooke's first season there (3–25 January 1811) the managers allowed the patrons to purchase tickets in advance for a Cooke performance only if they also bought tickets for the next night when he did not perform. A final twist was that tickets would be resold if not picked up by 4:00 P.M. of the day of performance.[26] For such practices the management was accused in the *Boston Patriot* (5 January 1811) of "avarice, partiality, speculation, and creating a monopoly." To avoid such criticisms on Cooke's second visit to Boston (31 December 1811–30 January 1812), the management eliminated these strictures.[27] Managers William Warren and William B. Wood, who had initiated a procedure similar to that in Boston, devised another system at the Chestnut Street Theatre in Philadelphia after receiving strong censure from the public. They sold places on the day of performance and the morning before, with boxes available for a maximum of twelve people and a minimum of four.[28]

The response to Cooke's acting was extravagant.[29] A letter to the editor of *The Mirror of Taste* declared that "all I have seen before was Boy's play to this night's exhibition [of Richard III]."[30] The editor himself, two months later, explained more fully:

After the tedious, monotonous syllabilizing, dead march speechifying to which this country has hitherto been so much accustomed, the natural acting and familiar colloquial speech of Cooke, seemed at first strange and new; but being comfortable to nature, it stood its ground, and has carried away the crown of laurel.[31]

John Howard Payne, then a nineteen-year-old actor, witnessed Cooke's opening night performance at the Park. Seven years later (19 June 1817), he wrote of it to his sister Eloise:

He made a different impression upon me from any other actor I have ever seen; there was something so exclusively unique and original in his dramatic genius. He always presented himself to me in the light of a discoverer, one with whom it seemed that every action and every look emanated entirely from himself; one who appeared never to have had a model and who depended entirely upon himself for everything he did in the character he represented. Cooke reminds me of no one but himself, and I have never been able to recognize the real *Richard* in any other actor than Cooke. Kean reminds me of Cooke, and Booth [J.B.] of Kean.... He was just as great in dialect parts as he was in the English heroics.... Indeed, I think Cooke (if there is anything in originality) the genius of the English stage.... I deem it a glory for my country to have his remains resting in its soil.[32]

After Cooke's first benefit at the Park on 19 December 1810, in Addison's *Cato*, a strange choice considering his past ill luck with this role, the reviewer for the *New York Journal* (22 December 1810) reported that it was the most crowded house he had ever seen. He continued: "a greater number having been admitted into the Pit than was prudent, occasioned such a tumult that it was impossible for the audience to hear any part of the play during the first act." If one accepts Dunlap's report that because of lack of rehearsal (and probable intoxication), Cooke "hesitated, repeated, substituted speeches from other plays, or endeavored to substitute incoherencies of his own," it was just as well that he was not heard.[33] Cooke's reputation for drunkenness and belligerence toward audiences had preceded him. Receipts dropped slightly during the remaining four nights of his December engagement. Receipts during his second New York engagement in February were also several hundred dollars below those of his first series of performances.

On 29 December 1810, Cooke embarked for Boston; he arrived there two days later. On 3 January the papers announced: "Mr. Cooke has arrived in town, and makes his first appearance on our stage, this evening [as Richard III]. We have never seen this gentleman in the personation of any character, but of this we are assured, by the united testimony of all the English critics, that in the range of characters which he has prescribed to himself, he is unquestionably the greatest actor that ever appeared in England."[34] Indeed, the *Boston Gazette* went so far as to tag Cooke "the finest actor England can produce." Such comments helped to assure a repetition of his New York engagement. During Cooke's visit, on 5 January, a new weekly publication began, *The Cabinet*, which devoted practically its entire first issue to Cooke. Most criticism from his first New York and Boston engagements smacks of puffery, although many superlatives in Cooke's American reviews are in fact substantiated with precise and detailed analyses of individual scenes and lines. Numerous examples have been cited earlier in this study.

Cooke's engagement in Boston was filled with annoyances. Letters to the newspapers complained of management's unfair ticket-sale procedures, of poor stage lighting which often forced the audience to hear Cooke's voice while he moved in semi-darkness, and of the choice of supporting actors.[35] Cooke himself endured the severest criticism he was to experience in America, censure that had little to do with his ability. From 14 to 24 January, the *Independent Chronicle*, a Boston newspaper opposed to everything English, blasted him with sarcasms—indications of a growing nationalistic attitude. The attack began in the form of a letter in two installments, which appeared on 14 and 17 January 1811. In the former issue the *Chronicle* observed: "On the arrival of Cooke the town seemed to have experienced an electric shock"; the mania was so intense that lawyers had written "more eulogies on Cooke than pleas for their clients." Three days later, the paper developed the idea that plays performed by Cooke were "no way appropriate to the temper or habits of our citizens." They would demoralize youth: "A man to get five or six hundred dollars an evening for repeating over the unnatural phrenzies of Shakespeare in his character of Richard III, is certainly a great encouragement for our young men to quit the commercial, for the theatrical stage." As for his performance of Othello, a "white beauty in love with a moor!" was surely the ultimate in moral degradation. "But while American genius is undervalued, English absurdities are extolled." The author then turned to the public and added: "Bostonians think more of Cooke than Bonaparte or the death of the King of England.... A ticket for the theatre is the greatest boon you can obtain."

On 24 January the *Chronicle*, gearing its attack against other of Cooke's roles, stated that in portraying Sir Pertinax MacSycophant and Iago, "a first rate English actor has COOKED up [these portrayals[to suit the taste of the ladies and gentlemen of Boston. These odious pictures of British characters dishonor the nation." It was insinuated that Bostonians really didn't know what was best for them. As a final insult, the following bit of invention was inserted on 21 January 1811:

My friend Mynheer Belch van Butterbox, from his Majesty's Theatre in Amsterdam... communicated to me last night, in pure *Dutch*, the result of his observations at the Theatre.—"In the first place... I have mathematically surveyed this man in the part of Richard, and by just calculation, I have discovered, that without the addition of 1200 cubic inches to the most *fundamental* part of his frame, he can never be a *great* actor.

Such anti-British sentiments appeared only in Boston. Fortunately for Cooke, anglophobia was as yet rare in the Northeast and had little effect on his reception. Even when Congress declared war on Britain in June 1812, maritime New England, New York, New Jersey, and Delaware dissented. The tension of the political situation did not become acute in the Northeast until months after Cooke's death.

Despite the minor issues and controversies affecting Cooke's first Boston season, the season itself was a decided success. The Boston Theatre had not been so crowded for six years and receipts were great. Cooke's share, however, was not as large as the *Independent Chronicle* assumed when it spoke of his receiving $500 to $600 a night.

During his Boston season, Cooke wrote to his old friend Charles Incledon, now a major singer at Covent Garden, acknowledging the satisfaction he had thus far experienced. No doubt Cooke did find much of America backward, and, unquestionably, during moments of drunkenness he threatened to "scourge your Yankee manners!"[36] But no trace of such displeasure occurs in this letter written to an old and close friend and confidant.

Boston, New England, N. America
Jan. 14th, 1811

To Charles Incledon, Esq.
Covent Garden Theatre

Dear Sir,
    This is the first letter I have written to Europe, from which my departure was only the result of a few hours deliberation. On the 4th of October last I sailed from Liverpool,

BOSTON THEATRE.

POSITIVELY THE LAST NIGHT BUT TWO OF
Mr. Cooke's Performance.

PLACES FOR THE REMAINING NIGHTS OF Mr Cooke's Performance, may be taken at the Box Office, at 10 o'clock, on each day of performance.

THIS EVENING, WEDNESDAY, JANUARY 23d, 1811,
Will be presented, the Tragedy, in five acts, of

OTHELLO.

IAGO, - - - - - - - - - - - - - - - Mr. COOKE.

Othello,	Mr. Morfe	Brabantio,	Mr Drake
Caflio,	Mr. Robertfon	Montano,	Mr Darley
Rodorigo,	Mr Entwifle	Gratiano,	Mr. Barnes
Duke,	Mr. Graham	Lodovico,	Mr. Vaughan
Officer,	Mr. Henry		
Defdemona,			Mrs. Darley
Emilia,			Mifs Poole

To which will be added, the favorite Farce, in 2 acts, called, the

LYING VALET.

Sharp, - - - - - - - - - - Mr Bernard

Gaylefs,	Mr. Robertfon	Beau Trippet,	Mr Stockwell
Juftice Guttle,	Mr. Fifher	Dick,	Mr Graham
Meliffa,	Mrs. Doige	Mrs. Gadabout,	Mrs Barnes
Kitty Pry,	Mrs. Drake	Mrs. Trippet,	Mifs Poole

Thursday.....Henry IV.

FALSTAFF, - - - - - - - - - - - - - - Mr. COOKE.

Doors to be open at 5 and the Curtain to rise at 6 precifely.

Playbill announcing that Mr. Morse would appear as Othello on 23 January 1811, in place of Duff. This followed a fierce editorial campaign in Boston to have an "American" actor appear opposite Cooke. Used by permission of the Harvard Theatre collection.

and arrived at New York on the 16th of November. The latter part of the voyage very tempestuous, and many vessels were lost. I was received by Mr. Price, one of the managers, in a very friendly and hospitable manner, and at whose house I remained while I continued in that city. On Wednesday the 21st of November, I made my first appearance before an American audience, and was received by a splendid and crowded assemblage in a most flattering manner. I acted seventeen nights to some of the greatest houses ever known in the New World. My own night exceeded four hundred guineas.

On the 29th of December, in company with Mr. Price, I set out in one of the best passageboats I ever saw, for Newport, Rhode Island, which we reached after a most pleasant trip, in 22 hours, and after a short stay left it in a commodious carriage for this town. We slept on Sunday at Taunton, and arrived here on Monday. My first appearance on Thursday following, in the *new* play of *Richard*, which was repeated the next night. This was also my first play in New-York, where they had it three times, and so will the good people here. The house filled as at New-York, and my reception equally flattering. New-York is the handsomest and largest house. We return to that city on Saturday the 29th; and about the 10th of March journey to Philadelphia, from thence to Baltimore, where my engagement ends; but I shall return to New-York to embark for Liverpool. My time was passed at the last mentioned city in a most agreeable manner, as almost every day, not of business, we had parties at Mr. Price's, or at the houses of some of the principal inhabitants. We are going on the same way here, with this exception, we are lodged at the Exchange Coffee-house, one of the largest and most extraordinary buildings I ever saw, and of consequence, I miss and regret the kind, polite attention of Mrs. P. at whose house I imagined myself in my own, and feel highly gratified at the near prospect of returning to it. Mr. [John] Bernard is one of the managers here, but I believe retires from it at the conclusion of the season. Theatricals are conducted at both Theatres in a very respectable manner, and the companies superior to what I expected to meet. I may add, much so.

I am going to trouble you, my Dear Sir, with a small business, which I request you will be so friendly as to settle for me. If I mistake not the time for paying the [Theatrical] Fund, by absentee, is by the 1st of June, if you would take that trouble upon yourself, you would highly oblige me, & I should gratefully acknowledge it on my return.

To Mrs. Incledon, whom I sincerely hope is well, pray present my best regards. I send my warm rememberance to all the family. Mary and my young godson I suppose I shall find grown out of knowledge.

G. F. *Cooke*[37]

On 26 January 1811 Cooke left for New York, arriving on the 29th. On 1 February he played Shylock, completing his second New York engagement on 8 March as Falstaff in *Henry IV, Part 1*. The management contracted with John Howard Payne to play several nights with Cooke, although because of indisposition Cooke performed only Lear with Payne's Edgar, on 1 March. The receipts for this engagement averaged only about $455 a night, except for the Payne/Cooke night, when it reached $827.[38] By this time, some of his novelty had worn off, and the bitter winter weather kept others away.[39]

Next, Cooke went to Philadelphia, accompanied by Dunlap, where he performed twenty nights at the Chestnut Street Theatre, from 25 March to 30 April. Cooke was loaned to Warren and Wood for a sum amounting to $8,809.16, payable to Cooper and Price. Cooke, however, continued to perform on a weekly salary with clear benefits. Warren states that he considered these terms not to Cooke's best interest.[40] Cooke would obtain better terms on his second visit to Philadelphia in November.

In his *Recollections* Wood writes enthusiastically of the success of this season.[41] Durang, commenting on the receipts of Cooke's nights, which totaled over $23,000, asserted that "these were certainly great receipts for a time when there was scarcely any population in the city much above Ninth Street."[42] Although the management was twice forced to postpone Cooke's first performance because of illness, when he finally opened the engagement on 25 March, again as Richard III, the results were more than gratifying.[43] Receipts exceeded $1,300 nightly, and only five times during the entire run did they dip below the $1,000 mark.

It was during this engagement that Washington Irving wrote his often quoted letter to Henry Brevoort, dated 11 April 1811. Irving had been planning to sail for England but was induced to delay his trip for several days in order to see Cooke's Kitely and Lear. He states:

> The old fellow is in great repute here, and draws excellent houses. I stopped in accidentally at the theatre a few evenings since, when he was playing Macbeth . . . I entered just at the time he was meditating the murder, and I remained to the end of the play in a state of admiration and delight. . . . I place the performance of that evening among the highest pieces of acting I have ever witnessed. You know I had before considered Cooper as much superior to him in Macbeth, but on this occasion the character made more impression on me than when played by Cooper, or even Kemble.[44]

Irving goes on to describe Cooke's style of acting. He finds it unequal from "irregular habits and nervous affections," but when he is in control "there is a truth . . . and a simplicity in his performance, that throws all rant, stage-trick, and stage-effect completely in the background." He compares his best performances to a masterpiece of ancient statuary, "in short, a simple display of nature." *The Mirror of Taste and Dramatic Censor*, a monthly edited in Philadelphia by Stephen Cullen Carpenter, devoted the bulk of its April, May, June, and August issues to Cooke, including lengthy and flattering critiques of Cooke's Sir Pertinax, Shylock, Richard, and King Lear, quoted earlier in this study.

During Cooke's engagement (actually three—the initial engagement of nine nights, a reengagement of three nights, and four additional nights with Cooper), he played all of his better known roles—Richard, Sir Pertinax, Lear, Sir Giles Overreach, Shylock, Macbeth, Pierre, Iago, and Sir Archy MacSarcasm. He had requested old James Fennell to play Othello with him, but Cooper arrived in town on 20 April, and a short season was arranged so that he could play Othello, Beverly, and Jaffier to Cooke's Iago, Stukely, and Pierre.[45] The Philadelphia season closed on 30 April with Cooper's benefit.[46]

Next, Cooke played nine nights in New York with Cooper. The performances in New York occurred without major incident. On 26 May, he left for Baltimore, arriving four days later. During his eight-night engagement, beginning on 31 May, he appeared as Richard, Iago, Sir Pertinax, Pierre, Shylock, and Sir Archy; receipts totaled $5,893.25.

Portrait of Cooke painted in Philadelphia by Thomas Sully in 1811. Courtesy of the Walter Hampden Memorial Library of The Players, New York.

He returned to New York (although in April, to aggravate Cooper, he had sworn he would not) on Wednesday, 19 June. On Thursday evening he was married to his third wife, Mrs. Behn, widow of a German merchant and daughter of James Bryden, keeper of the Tontine Coffee House on the northwest corner of Wall and Water streets, where Cooke had often stayed.[47] Little is known of her. Cooke then appeared for three performances at the Park on 24 and 26 June, concluding with Richard III on 1 July. Thus, he completed his first and most profitable season in the United States, 21 November 1810 through 1 July 1811, having performed eighty-five nights in nineteen roles. Mr. and Mrs. Cooke spent July and August touring upstate New York, with sojourns in Albany, Greenbush, Lake George, Troy, and Saratoga Springs, returning to New York City on 1 September to begin a new ten-month engagement.

The fall season at the Park opened on 2 September 1811 with Home's *Douglas*, Cooke appearing as Glenalvon and Cooper as Young Norval. The engagement terminated on 4 November, when for his benefit Cooke appeared as Sir Pertinax. During this period, Cooke performed nineteen times, missing two performances, 18 September and 7 October, because of indisposition.[48]

While Cooper remained at the Park, performing Rolla in *Pizarro* on 8 November, Cooke opened in Philadelphia as Richard III. Reese James points out that the threat of war with England and the resulting depression in commerce, coupled with the terror caused by the burning of the Richmond Theatre in December, conspired against Warren's and Wood's success in the second Philadelphia season (9 September 1811 to 14 March 1812).[49]

Despite these problems, the Chestnut had been "elegantly refitted, newly ornamented and considerably enlarged."[50] The company had been augmented by the additions of Mrs. Simpson of the Boston Theatre; Mrs. Mason from the Park; Cone and Spiller from the Theatre Royal, Haymarket; and William Duffy of the London and Dublin theatre, via Boston. Cooke himself was to profit more from this engagement than from any other since it was decided that he would receive half of the profits, "that is he divides with us after $390. pr. night for 5 nights the 6th he gets all after 390 and the 13th a Clear Bent.–."[51]

As in Boston, public dissension was raised not against Cooke, but against the actors called upon to support him. *The Cynick*, for example, complained that Cooke as Falstaff (a role relinquished by Warren to Cooke) was forced "to fulfill a new function, that of prompting all the statues and blocks around him."[52]

Having completed his fourteen performances in Philadelphia, Cooke returned to New York to perform seven nights. On 16 December, it was advertised that "the public is respectfully informed that Mr. Cooke will perform in New York, but one night more; after which he departs immediately for Charleston, from where he takes passage for England."[53] This was the second or third time that Cooke's exit to England had been announced. Cooke did not go to Charleston, however, but went to Boston, contracted at $3,200 plus benefits.

His packet boat was forced to land at New London because of a severe five-day gale. Cooke became quite ill and remained in New London while Powell, the co-manager of the Boston Theatre, who was accompanying him, went on to arrange Cooke's first performance for 30 December. On that day Cooke had not yet arrived in Boston, so Powell retraced his steps to find Cooke and bring him on.[54]

During the vacation, the Boston Theatre had been refitted with a new stage, new decorations, and "lamps of American manufacture."[55] On the 31st an eager audience waited for Cooke's appearance as Richard III. The co-manager, Dickson, however, came forward, and in Cooke's name apologized for disappointing the audience on the 30th. He explained "that having just arrived he was much fatigued;—but rather than occasion a second disappointment, he would exert himself to give satisfaction."[56]

On Friday, 10 January, Cooke faltered while performing Sir Archy. Clapp (p. 128) has unfairly accused him of drunkenness on this occasion. Both Dunlap and contemporary reports deny the accusation. Reports similar to that in the *Boston Gazette* (13 January 1812) appeared in all the newspapers:

[Cooke] . . . suffered extremely on board the packet, in his passage through the sound, having been exposed during five days to a gale in this inclement season. After his second night's performance, he was confined to his bed until four of the clock on the afternoon of his third appearance, which was against the positive injunctions of Dr. Jeffries, his physician. His present inability probably arises from his great exertions, in ill health, to gratify the public. On Friday morning, Mr. Cooke, conscious that his performances, saving *Shylock*, had fallen much below his own standard of excellence, went to rehearsal, with an inveterate determination to make the *amende honorable* for his recent deficiencies; but he had no sooner trodden the boards, than he was seized with chills and a dizziness which rendered him unable to rehearse. A species of paralytic affection succeeded, and he continued ill during the day:—nothing but anxious desire to meet the public wishes induced his appearance in the evening. *The public may rely, most positively, that his failure in Pierre and Sir Archy, is attributable to this, and no other cause.* He is still confined to bed and we cannot assure the public when he will be able to revisit the boards.[57]

Although he was scheduled to play Zanga on 13 January, Cooke's illness continued and *The Exile of Siberia* was substituted.

On 20 January Cooke's recovery was announced and he reappeared as Shylock. On 27 January, he was reengaged for seven nights. Business fell off after his illness, but the reasons are undoubtedly more complex than those which Clapp suggests. Powell implies that Cooke's behavior was impeccable during this visit.[58] Cooke was indeed ill during the eight weeks in Boston. Furthermore, growing political tensions drew attention away from theatricals, and the weather during this latter part of his engagement was extremely inclement.[59] The public was also worried about theatre fires, since just before Cooke's engagement opened there had been the terrible fire at Richmond, for which Cooke was given partial blame.[60]

Although criticism was not as plentiful during this engagement—Cooke appeared in only four roles not previously seen in Boston—praise of him still ran high. The jingoistic attacks which attended his first visit disappeared completely. *The Comet* (4 January 1812) suggested: "He who cannot discover the superiority of his acting, even to the best of those who have preceded him on the American stage, will not profit by any thing that we can write." The same issue also recognized that as a result of fatigue his Richard had a hoarseness "which sometimes rendered his utterance indistinct." On the other hand, the *Gazette* of 9 January felt that in his major roles he had improved "in his conception of his text, if improvement can be imagined where supreme excellence was before acknowledged." Even during the latter part of his engagement, when receipts had diminished, the *Gazette* (27 January) exclaimed: "We are decidedly of the opinion that those who have not seen Mr. Cook [*sic*] in *Richard*, have *never* seen the character performed." Commenting on his Sir Giles Overreach, the *New England Palladium* (28 January) stated that "no actor who ever trod the American boards in this character, has any pretensions of rivalry with Mr. Cooke in this piece." On 30 January, an announcement in the *Gazette* stated that the Boston engagement could not be renewed because of an engagement in Philadelphia. On 7 February, Cooke performed for the last time in Boston as Macbeth, for his own benefit.

Instead of going to Philadelphia, Cooke returned to New York. Shortly after his arrival, he informed Dunlap that he had booked his passage for England in a ship to sail from Boston and had left his baggage there. Cooke received a letter from Henry Harris, dated 28 March 1812, three months *after* his statement to Dunlap, offering him a new engagement at Covent Garden and encouraging him to "take leave of the Yankees, and come over and take t'other touch at John Bull, who is as fond of you as ever, and would be most happy to see his favourite again."[61] That such a letter was received and that Cooke's intentions were clear are verified by a note from Cooke to Harris:

New York, May 24th, 1812

Henry Harris, Esq.
Theatre Royal
   Covent Garden

Dear Sir,
   Mr. Newman, the British Agent, yesterday afternoon, delivered to me your welcome and friendly letter. That of your worthy and reverend Father, I have not yet received. [Henry Harris speaks of an offer sent earlier by his father.]
   Mr. N. informed me this will precede the Packet, which is fixed for sailing on the 4th of June, and by that conveyance I shall take my pasage for England. At present, unless by going into Canada, there is no other conveyance, as an embargo is on all foreign bound ships.
   I thank you for your kind invitation to repair to my old Quarters, which I most readily accept, and hope to reach England sometime before the opening of your next campaign.
   Pray present my best respects to your Father, and believe me,

Dear Sir,
   Your much obliged,
   and most obedient,
   G. F. Cooke[62]

Although a formal declaration of war with Great Britain was not made until 18 June 1812, the strained situation between the two countries and consequent embargo combined to make it impossible for Cooke to return to his "old Quarters," as he had obviously planned. He remained in New York until 5 July, appearing for two very brief engagements at the Park, first for five performances in March and then once more on 22 June. During much of this period, Cooke was confined to bed, suffering from liver ailments. His condition had begun to take a turn for the worse during his first Philadelphia engagement, when he was bled several times.[63]

In early July, Powell and Dickson announced "that they have engaged MR. COOKE, to perform in the Providence Theatre for six nights only."[64] The Cookes left New York by the Providence packet on 5 July and arrived on the 8th, the season commencing on 13 July with *The Merchant of Venice* and *Plot and Counter-Plot*.

The Providence Theatre, a relatively small one, was located at Washington and Mathewson streets, fronting on Westminster. Measuring 81 feet long by 50 feet wide, it contained two tiers of boxes, a gallery, and a pit. The proscenium opening was only 16 feet high by 24 feet wide.[65] In order to compensate for the limited capacity of the theatre and the potential audience drawn from the small community, Cooke was to share equally with the managers after $150 and have a clear benefit.[66]

Willard reports that Cooke, temporarily recovered from his "condition," never played better in his life, surpassing his efforts in Boston. Cooke lived at least three-quarters of a mile from the theatre, at the Golden Ball Inn on Benefit Street, and walked to and from it every morning, as well as on the evenings he performed. Willard says that he never missed a rehearsal or disappointed an audience, his eminence in elocution drawing to the theatre "all of the bar, the rector of the church, and pastors of several of the other religious societies of the town."

The impact of Cooke's performances on this small town, later to become a favorite tour stop for theatrical companies and stars, was immense. *The Rhode-Island American and General Advertiser* (17 July 1812) gives a typical reaction: "It would far exceed the limits of a newspaper were we to attempt to criticise or point out the various beauties of this inimitable performer, in his impersonation of these truly arduous characters. Throughout the whole there was nothing to condemn, much to admire, and more to astonish." The rush to the box office far exceeded the capacity of the theatre. On 18 July, in the *Providence Gazette*, the managers advised that in order to prevent difficulty and give an equal chance to the public in general to see Cooke, "a Box-Plan, with the whole of the Boxes regularly numbered, will be opened at the Box Office at the Theatre at 10 o'clock on each Day of Performance, when Places may be taken."

For nine performances (the engagement was extended for three nights beginning 27 July), receipts totaled almost $2,000. Cooke's share, including benefit, was $574. Willard (p. 62) qualifies this by adding that the audiences were larger than the receipts might indicate since many of the best seats were occupied by stockholders.

On 31 July 1812, "Thespis," writing in the *Rhode-Island American*, noted that Cooke would "make his final bow to the Providence audience this evening in the character of 'Sir Giles Overreach,' " and fervently added: "Those who witnessed the 'brilliant performances' of Mr. Cooke, during his visit here, will pay the tribute of respect due to his superior talent, by attending the Theatre this evening, and those who have not yet seen him, will doubtless avail themselves of the last opportunity which will offer of gratifying their curiosity and taste, by beholding this great Actor, justly styled the Garrick of the present day." Unknown to either "Thespis" or the audience that evening, this "tribute" would be the last Cooke would ever receive in the theatre. Although he had followed a strict regimen while in Providence, his health was obviously worsening, and it was even feared that he could not survive a removal to New York. By 1 September, however, after a three-day stay in Boston, ostensibly to regain his luggage, he was back in New York. There he remained, his final days restricted to his attic apartment at the Mechanics' Hall, a well-known New York tavern, until his death on 26 September 1812.

The figure of Cooke had made a lasting impression on those who had seen him both on and off the stage. His close friend and physician, Dr. John Wakefield Francis, remembered him as an old English gentleman, walking down Broadway with his dignified mien and stately carriage. Durang was fascinated by his staid, gray surtout, his stiff hair brushed back, and his upright walk. He reminded Durang of "a retired, half-pay officer" with "all the sternness of the soldier's habit." Although decades of debilitation and the natural wear of encroaching old age had all but destroyed him, Cooke turned eyes wherever he went with his 5'10" frame and stout, broad torso, his prominent nose, in shape between aquiline and Roman, the full forcible expression of his eyes, and when in full control of his faculties, his dignified, self-possessed, and courteous manner.[67] However, in spite of all his public qualities, at the base of his character was a coarseness which would not or could not be forgotten. "We thought of nothing but the indulgence of his passion, particularly devoting himself to the bottle," his old boyhood chum John Taylor was later to write[68]—this, despite the tremendous enthusiasm demonstrated by audiences wherever he played in the New World, the overriding triumph of his short sojourn, and the ultimate influence of his visit on the theatre itself. It was perhaps fitting then, if not wholly deserved, for Cooke to receive an unofficial epitaph such as this:

> Pause, thoughtful stranger! pass not heedless by,
> Where Cooke awaits the tribute of a sigh.
> Here sunk in death those powers of the world admir'd,

By nature given, not by art acquir'd.
In various *parts*, his matchless talents shone;
The one he fail'd in was, alas! his *own*.
                    M.F.[69]

Epilogue: A Posthumous Career

Late in the afternoon of 24 September 1812, Joseph Fay, a New York lawyer, was summoned to a well-known New York tavern at the corner of Broadway and Park Place (then called Robinson Street) to write the will of the actor George Frederick Cooke. In a letter to John Howard Payne written immediately after the event, Fay reflected on his unexpected experience.

He [Cooke] is now in the last stages of his disorder. I went to his room, and received his directions for drawing the will. He leaves all he has (about 2000 dollars only) to his *present* wife. He said he owed a dollar or two to his hair-dresser, but not a cent to any other man in the world—and he half smiled as he said it—adding at the same time he was not afraid to die for he trusted in a good providence. Holman [the actor] was with me, and he and Doc. [name is not clear but according to the will it was Dr. David Hosack] are Executors. If an old woman, who crossed my palm when I was a little boy, had told me ... that I should sit by the bed of the then renowned *Cook* [sic] in the presence of the then admired *Holman* in the attic story of a New York tavern—drawing a will and catching the last look of that great *Richard* as the curtain dropped on him—forever—! I should have called her imposter and been indignant at her attempt to insult my understanding—yet all this has happened to me this day—nay, this evening—and within the last hour.[1]

According to a lengthy letter from Dr. Hosack to Dunlap, Cooke survived until 6:00 A.M. on 26 September and died of dropsy.[2] He had been confined to bed for almost five weeks with a severe and lingering illness, which produced a condition we would now describe as manic-depressive. Hosack says that his liver was badly discolored, the result, probably, of cirrhosis caused by Cooke's excessive drinking. During his illness he was attended with "tender and anxious solicitude" by his last wife, Mrs. Violet Mary Cooke, and various American friends. In his last hours his mind was perfectly clear.[3]

On Sunday, 27 September, Cooke's body was taken to St. Paul's Church two blocks away, where at 5:00 that evening a few friends viewed it. The funeral procession, which had begun at 4:30, was a civic affair. Stores closed, all official bodies adjourned, and flags were at half-mast. A solemn cortege drew up in front of St. Paul's: Governor Daniel D. Tompkins of New York came in a carriage with Mayor DeWitt Clinton and Elisha Jenkins, secretary

Death mask of Cooke. Nothing is known of this mask. Used by permission of the Harvard Theatre collection.

of state; in the procession were representatives of the clergy, the medical profession, the army and navy, science, literature, and the stage.[4] The body was deposited in the Strangers' Vault of St. Paul's.

Thus ended the life of an actor whose professional career spanned almost forty years, beginning with provincial engagements in Great Britain, climaxing with ten seasons at Covent Garden, and concluding with 160 appearances on the American stage over a period of one year and ten months.

If the sum of $2,000 left to his American wife seems slight in comparison to his total income in the United States (approximately $20,000), it should be remembered that for the last eight months of his life (from 9 February 1812) Cooke performed only fourteen times. His health was failing, medical bills were increasing, and he was supporting a new wife. And, as has been noted, Cooke was never known for his care with money.

He did not die a pauper, however, as various gossiping English accounts would have it. Thomas Munden claims that "in the receipt of a large income he was always poor, and he died almost a beggar." A later writer reported that Cooke's body was not found until several days after his death and that his head was severed. Further, that after dying a pauper in a charity hospital, Cooke had been consigned to Potters Field, saved only when a group of "fans" took up a collection and bought a plot in St. Paul's.[5] Such tales should be dismissed once and for all.

A final chapter in Cooke's life, or more precisely afterlife, escaped Dunlap since his biography was completed shortly after Cooke's death.[6] This narrative concerns his subsequent reburial in 1821 and the beginning of a legend. In Dunlap's *History of the American Theatre* (1832), some of the missing points are filled in but a new mystery is created. Dunlap mentions that in 1821 Edmund Kean on his first American tour erected a monument to Cooke's memory, after moving the body from the Strangers' Vault where it had lain since 1812 to its new location in the center of St. Paul's churchyard. He concludes his report with a bizarre, unexplained comment: ". . . it may hereafter be found that his surgeon possesses his scull [*sic*], and his successor, Kean, the bones of the forefinger of his right-hand,—that dictatorial finger,—still the monument covers the *remains* of George Frederick Cooke."[7] Thus began one of the strangest legends in the history of the theatre. What became of Cooke's skull, and did Kean, indeed, leave the grave with Cooke's forefinger? The story of the former can be dismissed now; the latter must continue to be part of theatrical folklore.

In a series of articles appearing in the 1930s, Drs. David Hosack and John Wakefield Francis, who performed Cooke's autopsy, were still being accused of decapitating Cooke in lieu of payment during the postmortem examination. The alleged loss of the head had not been reported, apparently, up to 4:30 P.M. on Sunday, 27 September, when the remains were taken from the hotel to the place of sepulture two blocks away. As noted earlier, his funeral was not a secretive affair.

When Kean visited New York in 1820 he brought with him, according to numerous accounts, the desire to remove Cooke from the Strangers' Vault to a new grave, over which he proposed to raise a suitable monument. The exact location of the spot in which Cooke was first buried is unknown. That it was St. Paul's we have assurance from Dunlap and other testimony. The churchyard was formerly much larger than it is today, and the Strangers' Vaults may have been in a part of the yard no longer in existence, since no Strangers' Vault exists today. Dunlap, however, says definitely (in 1832) that the remains were removed from one part of St. Paul's churchyard to the spot they now occupy. The supposition that Cooke was buried in a vault beneath the church seems quite erroneous since the church neither has nor had a crypt or basement.

Supposedly Kean, along with Dr. Francis, approached Bishop John Henry Hobart at Trinity Church to receive permission to transfer the remains. The bishop gave his permission only after it was agreed that a tablet could not be placed inside St. Paul's.[8] A number of accounts record Kean's reaction to the monument on its completion by the Frazees, 4 June 1821, two days before he left the United States.[9] Kean is supposed to have retired to the spot for a farewell look. Dr. Francis, who accompanied him, said that "tears fell from his eyes in abundance, and as he walked Broadway and heard the evening bells, he returned again to the spot and sang sweeter than ever two of his favorite songs—'Those Evening Bells,' and 'Come Over to the Sea.' " It was on the occasion of the transferral of the remains that Kean, according to tradition, is supposed to have abstracted one of the toebones or the forefinger, which he brought back with him to London as a precious relic. Versions of the fate of that bone are varied and have become part of theatre lore.[10] One story states that on Kean's arrival in England Elliston and several of the Drury Lane company went to Barnet to meet him, where Kean ordered them to fall on their knees and kiss the relic. When he arrived home, Kean's first words to his wife were: "I have brought Charles [his son] a fortune. I have something that the directors of the British Museum would give ten thousand pounds for; but they sha'n't have it." He then placed it on the mantelpiece, not to be touched but to be worshipped. Mrs. Kean held the relic in disgust and finally had it thrown away. Upon missing the bone, Kean stormed, raved, and searched the house and the servants. Finally, realizing that it was gone, he sank into a chair and exclaimed: "Mary, your son has lost a fortune. He was worth ten thousand pounds; now he is a beggar!" The most popular legend is that on missing the bone, Kean left the stage. None of these, of course, can be verified.

The monument erected in the shadow of the steeple of historic St. Paul's is made of dolomite marble, a soft stone with little durability.[11] Above the memorial slab is a small pedestal on two steps, surmounted by an urn, from the top of which a flame issues toward the former side of the Park Theatre where

Cooke's tomb in 1821, painted by I. R. Smith and published in London (1822). Kean is pointing at the monument while Dr. J. W. Francis looks on. Courtesy of the City Museum of New York (J. Clarence Davies collection).

Cooke's tomb today. The bronze plaque faces St. Paul's. Photo by author.

Cooke enjoyed his New York triumph. The monument was "Erected to the Memory of George Frederick Cooke by Edmund Kean of the Theatre Royal, Drury Lane, 1821."[12] At the bottom of the stone was placed this verse written by Fitz-Green Halleck:

> Three Kingdoms claim his birth
> Both hemispheres pronounce his worth.

Epilogue

There is a rather spurious story that on the night before sailing from Liverpool to America, while expatiating on the raising of a monument to Cooke, Kean asked for suggestions for an epitaph. In answer to his request, an actor by the name of Taylor wrote this verse on a card and handed it to him:

> Beneath this stone lies Cooke interred
> And with him Shakespeare's Dick the Third.[13]

Such a suggestion would certainly not have pleased Mr. Kean, who thought so highly of Cooke and modeled his acting after him.

At the time of its erection, the monument stood under the shade of a widespreading horse-chestnut tree. Since then, the monument has suffered the ravages of time. It has been refurbished on six occasions: by Charles Kean in 1846; E. A. Sothern in 1874; Edwin Booth in 1890; "The Players Club" in 1898; Percy S. Bullen of the *London Daily Telegraph* and others in 1912; and by the Edmund Kean Club of New York in 1948.[14] When the Edmund Kean Club wished to have the words recut in 1948, it was thought that the marble was too soft to take recuttings. Hence, a bronze plaque was affixed through negotiations with the Kean Club and their officers, Giles Playfair, George Freedley, Maynard Morris, and Thomas Curtiss.[15] On a pilgrimage to the tomb in November 1967, I first noted that all the original markings were practically gone; a slight shadow of inscription on the east side (E. A. Sothern's) still remains. The sculptured urn is wobbly, and the point of the flame is worn down. There are numerous cracks in the four-sided monument. The tomb is prominently placed in the churchyard, surrounded by crumbling monuments to other illustrious dead, and, although in the heart of New York's financial district, it seems almost isolated on a hill where the wind constantly blows. Birds chirping in nearby shrubs almost give notice that though the grave below is dark and silent, the world above is pulsating with life and will preserve, while life endures, the memory of one who ranks among the greatest of Thespians.

Until recent years the tomb served as a shrine to many great actors. Since an earlier version of this epilogue appeared in *Theatre Notebook*, I have been told by theatre colleagues that they, too, have made special treks to Cooke's monument. In 1826, Macready is said to have stood there as a silent visitor. Charles Kean is reported to have brought a group from the Park Theatre to visit the monument in 1830, renewing his father's homage of ten years earlier. Charles and Fanny Kemble laid a wreath on the base of the monument in 1832, and in 1855, on a cold day in November, Rachel threw some hothouse flowers into the plot. Madame Ponisi said she went with Edwin Forrest to visit the tomb when he was playing in *The Broker of Bogota* (1852) at the Broadway Theatre.[16] The last publicized report I can locate of such honor was in November 1929, when a memorial wreath was placed on his grave by the Reverend Dr. Joseph P. M. Comas, vicar of the church, and the Reverend Harold Weigle,

Jr., chaplain of the Episcopal Actors' Guild of America. This was followed by a vespers service in the church.[17]

This service preceded by one year the announcement that Cooke's skull had been at last located. There is no direct evidence as to when or how the skull was first acquired. It has been suggested that Cooke himself directed that Dr. Francis should have it.[18] Dr. Francis may have obtained it at the time of, or soon after, the transfer of Cooke's remains in 1821. One source suggests that the body had been exhumed in the presence of Dr. Henry Francis, John's brother, and that John shortly thereafter took the skull away in a yellow silk handkerchief.[19] There seems to be nothing on which to base any different supposition. Long popular was the story that Dr. Francis was interested in the study of the brain and, knowing Cooke had been regarded as a genius, desired to learn whether the actor's brain offered from that of other mortals. There appears to be no evidence to support such a theory. Beginning with the disappearance of the skull, revealed by Dunlap in 1832 and reinforced by Francis in his *Old New York*, a long list of legends began to be born;[20] Cooke's career, by the severing of his head, began a last chapter.

Francis himself tells of having loaned the skull to the Park for the gravediggers' scene in *Hamlet* (p. 292). On the following morning, the skull was returned and again locked away. That evening Francis attended a meeting at the old Washington Hall of the Bread and Cheese, a dining club founded by James Fenimore Cooper in 1824. Francis mentioned the skull, and the ensuing interest, increased by the current study of phrenology, caused Francis to have the skull brought for examination by several members, including the club's guest, Daniel Webster. These are the only two stories that seem to have validity, but the tales did not cease here. In 1899, an article appeared claiming that the skull continued to be used at the Park by such actors as Charles Kean (in 1830) and George Vandenhoff (in 1842). It goes on to claim that a few months before the burning of the Park in 1848, Thomas Hamblin, the manager of the Bowery Theatre, took possession of the skull. It then supposedly was carried home by the stage manager and disappeared, only to appear once again in the latter part of January 1873. On this occasion a rather seedy, slim, middle-aged man was reported to have appeared at Augustin Daly's Fifth Avenue Theatre office with a bundle under his arm, claiming it to be the skull of Cooke. Daly, a superstitious sort, turned the man out of his office, only to affirm in 1898 to the same reporter who had originally heard Daly's story in 1873 that indeed the man did have Cooke's skull under his arm.[21]

The truth of Cooke's wandering skull is quite simple. The conclusive answer is found in an unpublished manuscript prepared by Dr. George McClellan (1849–1913), long the owner of the skull. McClellan was a nephew of General George McClellan, commander of the Union Army of the Potomac, and dean of the Jefferson Medical College in Philadelphia. He was also a summer neighbor of Dr. Valentine Mott Francis (1834–1907), son of Dr. J. W. Francis.

Here is Dr. McClellan's explanation, presented orally in Philadelphia on at least four occasions between 1901 and 1907 but seemingly ignored for almost fifty years.[22]

It is curious that since Cooke's burial, there have from time to time been rumours current about his missing head. How it was first ascertained that the skull had been removed at the time the body was placed beneath the tomb which Kean caused to be erected, it is not easy to explain. The fact has been passed about, since that time to this, and many interesting articles have appeared stating more or less fanciful theories, and sitting in judgment, not altogether fairly, on poor Cooke.

Some twenty or twenty-five years ago [ca. 1880], at Jamestown, Rhode Island, I had under my professional care Dr. V. Mott Francis, who had sustained a grave injury to his head. One morning, while he was convalescing, at my usual visit I found a surprise party, which he had invited to be present, consisting of Doctors Sands, Markoe, Samuel Francis [V. Mott's younger brother], and others from New York. My patient, Dr. Francis, was sitting in his bed wrapped in a dressing-gown, with a brown box on his knees. After some expressions of gratitude for what I had done for him, he finished by saying that "as Fate had deprived me of owning *his* skull, he proposed to substitute it by another," and handed me the box. On opening it I found a skull, which Dr. Francis stated that he had received as an heirloom, from his father, Dr. John W. Francis, and that it was the head of George Frederick Cooke, whom Dr. Francis had attended in his last illness, as already stated, so that it was beyond question identified.

Dr. McClellan continues the narrative, clarifying another minor mystery.

On removing the skull from the box, one of the few remaining teeth, an eye-tooth, dropped on the floor [actually a molar]. One of those present said to me "as you have the head won't you let me have this tooth?" I asked what he proposed doing with it? His reply was that he would like to send it to his friend Edwin Booth, the actor. I acceded, expressing at the same time my warm admiration for Booth, and was told in return that, if Mr. Booth acknowledged the gift by letter, I should have the autograph. Unfortunately Booth telegraphed "thanks for Cook's [sic] tooth, deposited in Player's [sic] Club." . . . The skull in its box, was put aside for awhile, and later placed with other skulls in one of the cases at my private school of anatomy. I gathered no fresh information concerning it for some months, beyond the facts related by Dr. Francis as to how his father got possession of it, and that *he* has preserved it with some dread of exposure regarding its whereabouts, owing to a search instituted by Cooke's friends in England, and a reward offered for its recovery.

The tooth that McClellan speaks of is now in the possession of the City Museum of New York. When Dr. McClellan died, the skull was in the possession of his widow. On her death, in 1929, and according to Dr. McClellan's will, Dr. Ross V. Patterson, his successor as dean of the Jefferson Medical College, inherited the skull. Dean Patterson died in 1931 and bequeathed the skull and McClellan's papers to the Medical School. In trying to relocate the

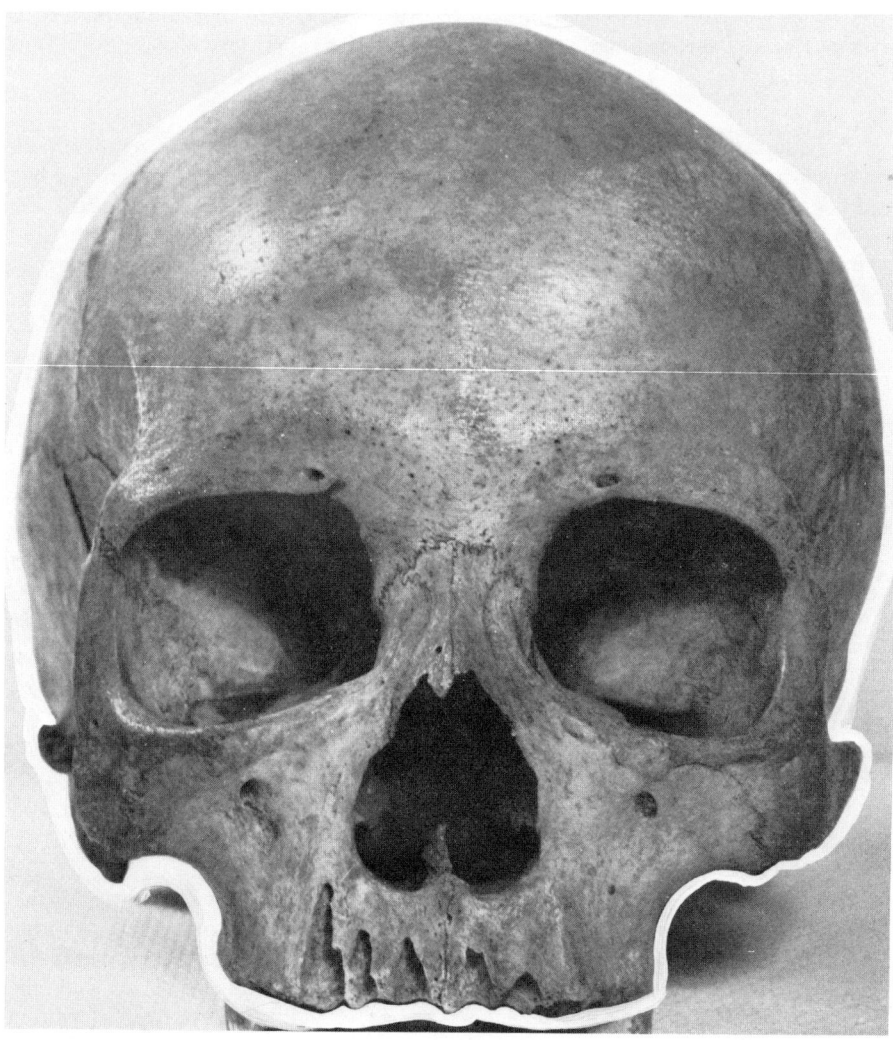

Cooke's skull. Photo courtesy of the Jefferson Medical College, Philadelphia.

skull, I discovered that Dr. A. J. Ramsay, head of the department of anatomy and a member of the staff for thirty-two years, had not been aware that the school owned the skull.[23] Finally, after numerous letters passed back and forth, the skull was located in a display case in the College's library. There is also a death mask of Cooke in the Harvard Theatre Collection, but I have been unable to locate any information concerning it.

Cooke's tooth given to Edwin Booth; made into a tie-pin. Courtesy of the City Museum of New York.

News of Dr. McClellan's bequest stirred new interest in Cooke's skull. A rash of newspaper articles soon followed, again spreading strange tales about the ownership of the skull.[24] According to the reports, the skull had belonged to three generations of McClellans, having been given to the first McClellan by John W. Francis himself. This also marked the first real effort to place the skull back with the remains at St. Paul's. An earlier effort to place the skull in new surroundings, but not in the tomb, was made by Dr. Horace Howard Furness, the Shakespearean authority. Furness, a friend of Dr. McClellan, had attempted unsuccessfully to obtain the skull from Dr. Patterson for exhibition at The Players. Furness told several friends about this attempt, including William A. S. Lapetina, a retired Philadelphia lawyer and director of the Duse Art Theater in Philadelphia. Lapetina wrote to Dr. Patterson concerning the skull's replacement with the body, but the proposal was seemingly refused.

Interest in the skull died down until 1936 when Daniel Frohman, president of the Actor's Fund of America, wrote to Patterson: "I feel that our organization should be intrusted with this honored commission [to disinter Cooke's body and rebury it with the skull]. I would be only too glad to appoint a committee to supervise the replacement of the skull with Cooke's body as a tribute to the first great actor in the American theatre."[25] This attempt, too, was unsuccessful but did succeed in adding one more legend to the many centered around Cooke's skull. The news article announcing Frohman's attempt also gave a fanciful narrative that in the 1880s, while playing Hamlet in Philadelphia, Booth was given a skull shortly before the curtain and was requested to use it as a favor to a patron. According to this account, Booth did so and only afterwards was he informed that it was the skull of George Frederick Cooke. Perhaps Cooke's skull is doomed to create new legends until it finally does rest in its appointed tomb in St. Paul's churchyard.

As a motif of his life, one of paradox and irony, the skull is a fitting symbol. One could suggest in jest that in life Cooke frequently lost his head during moments of tempestuousness; thus as a headless actor after death, his fitful rest is appropriate. But George Cooke, a man of passion and genius, who died from the results of drunkenness, lived with a vision of immortality just beyond his fingertips. George Tichenor has left a fitting conclusion to Cooke's life: "The study of Cooke's botched life is some slight solace for the spiritual frustration of us all. Like Prometheus, the Wandering Jew, and the Flying Dutchman, Cooke is the symbol of eternal scapegoats, men who have held an unquenched fire against their vitals when they could not lift a torch; or perhaps the repeated incarnation of one damned soul, working in and out of a dark loom an unfathomed destiny."[26]

Appendix A

Cooke Iconography

Cooke was painted or drawn by a number of leading artists in England and the United States, including Samuel DeWilde, Robert Dighton, George Cruikshank, Gilbert Stuart, and Thomas Sully. (Copies of the engravings mentioned below can be found in the Harvard Theatre Collection (HTC) unless otherwise noted.) A watercolor of Cooke as Richard III at Cork in September 1800, taken from life by W. Loftis, is in the Folger Shakespeare Library. An engraving by Dighton of Cooke's Richard was published in 1800. James Green painted him as Iago in 1801 and exhibited the canvas at the Royal Academy the same year (in the Garrick Club). An engraving by J. Ward was published in 1801, and a similar engraving by an anonymous artist appeared at about the same time. Cooke as Iago, in an engraving in stipple by W. Ridley, after J. Corbett, was published in *The Monthly Mirror* in 1800; the same picture was also engraved by P. Maquire. A bust portrait by J. Corbett, engraved by J. Whessell, was published by T. Simpson and John Thompson in 1801, and reissued by Thompson in 1804. The same portrait, but reversed, by an anonymous engraver, was published in *The Thespian Dictionary*. Cooke was painted as Shylock by Thomas Phillips in about 1803 (Garrick Club). Also in 1803 an engraving of Shylock by William Skelton, after Phillipe De Loutherbourg, was published by Kearsley, as well as an engraving as Macbeth by Parker, after De Loutherbourg. An engraving as Falstaff in *Henry IV, Part 1* by J. Alais was published in 1802 by J. Roach. Also in 1802 Macpherson published an engraving by Francis(?) Chesham, after Cruikshank, of Cooke as Iago. A miniature of Cooke as Richard III by J. T. Barber Beaumont is in the possession of Robert Eddison of London; it was shown in an exhibition of paintings, drawings, and stage designs arranged by the Guildhall Art Gallery in collaboration with the Society for Theatre Research in 1964. A version was engraved by A. Cardon and published by J. P. Thompson in 1805.

DeWilde's painting of Sir Archy, mentioned in the text, was signed by the artist on 16 May 1806 (Garrick Club) and was variously engraved: by R. Woodman, published by John Cawthorn in 1808; by A. Cardon, published in Cawthorn's *Minor English Theatre* in 1806; and by J. Kennerley, published in *Oxberry's Dramatic Biography* in 1826. (Some of the Woodman issues incorrectly identify the character as Sir Pertinax MacSycophant.) Cooke as Shylock was engraved by J. Alais and published by J. Roach in 1804. An engraving as Richard III by an unknown engraver was published by N. Jones in 1802. A mysterious engraving by Henry(?) Warren after DeWilde's engraving of Cooke as Timon in *Timon of Athens* was published by Kearsley in 1805. I have yet to locate a performance by Cooke as Timon. There is also a promptbook at the Folger with G. F. Cooke in gilt on the spine, but the book was not Cooke's (see Shattuck, p. 464, no. 12). Cooke's Sir Pertinax was engraved by J. E. Walker, after Henry Singleton, and published by Longman & Company in 1806. A portrait of Cooke was drawn by S. J. Stump circa 1807, with engravings by J. Hopwood published in 1807 by Mathews and Leigh and published in the *Cyclopaedian Magazine* by P. Maguire; the same portrait appeared in *The Cabinet* in 1811 by an anonymous engraver. Another portrait was engraved by Ridley & Company and published in the *European Magazine* in 1807.

DeWilde painted a watercolor on paper of Cooke as Richard, and a portrait of Cooke in this part by DeWilde was exhibited at the Royal Academy in 1809. A version of the picture at the Garrick Club was engraved by Francis(?) Cheesman for the *Theatrical Inquisitor* in 1813 and also appeared in *Le Beau Monde*; an engraving by Anderson also appeared. Cooke sat for DeWilde in January 1808 and wrote in his diary: "Mr. DeWilde, according to appointment came, and took a full length drawing of me in Richard III. A part of the dress, &c. I put on. This is a complacency I must give up" (see *Life of Cooke*, 2: 85).

Cooke was painted or drawn by Stuart, Sully, Charles Robert Leslie, and William Dunlap while in the United States. Leslie (1794–1859) was an unknown when Cooke arrived in Philadelphia in 1811. The same year Leslie went to London to study at the Royal Academy and subsequently became a well-known painter of cabinet pictures. Dunlap wrote in *The History of the Rise and Progress of the Arts of Design in the United States* that he first saw Leslie's drawings of Cooke at Edwin's, the engraver, and found the likeness of Cooke "very extraordinary," especially since Leslie had drawn them "merely from seeing them on the stage in character" (see *History of Arts*, 2: 302–303; 3: 2; also Willard, p. 70). Dr. John W. Francis agreed that they were of "most remarkable fidelity" (*Old New York*, pp. 221–212). During the spring of 1811, *The Mirror of Taste and Dramatic Censor* published engravings of Sir Pertinax, Richard III, King Lear, and Shylock by D. Edwin after Leslie. A canvas of Richard was painted by Leslie in 1813 and engraved by Paton Thomson for Oxberry's *New English Drama* in 1818 (painting in Garrick Club). Thomas Sully painted Cooke at least three times at his residence on South Fifth Street in Philadelphia: once for Wood, the Philadelphia manager; once for a Mr. Wilcocks; and once as Richard III (see *Life of Cooke*, 2: 292, 296, 306, 319). The most famous oil painting (Richard III) was sold by the artist for $300 to the Pennsylvania Academy of Fine Arts, Philadelphia, where it still hangs (see *History of Arts*, 2: 268). A portrait by Sully hangs in the Garrick Club, bequeathed by J. W. Wallack. The Garrick Club painting may be one of the other two paintings or a replica made in 1816 from one of the 1811 portraits (see *Catalogue of Pictures in the Garrick Club*, compiled by C. K. Adams, London, 1936, p. 10). The Players' Club in New York owns another Sully portrait (no. 27 in that collection). A bust portrait engraved by Edwin also appeared in *The Mirror of Taste* in 1811.

Gilbert Stuart painted Cooke in Boston in January 1811. Cooke found Stuart one of two people in Boston who pleased him most (see *Life of Cooke*, 2: 211; *History of Arts*, 1: 247). This bust portrait was painted for Stephen Price and was completed on 6 January. It is now in the Garrick Club (*Catalogue*, p. 111).

Various other paintings, drawings, or engravings exist, mostly undated. The Garrick Club possesses a painting of Cooke as Kitely by Henry Singleton; a small panel, head and shoulders; a set of nine silhouettes on paper; and a pencil drawing on paper, head and shoulders, all by unknown artists. HTC, in addition to the engravings mentioned above, has in its collection the following: a vignette engraved by S. Benwell and an engraving by Brook of Richard III; an engraving by E. Sciven of Richard, after G. Bullock from a model in rice paste, published by Zanetti in 1812; King John, in the tent with Prince Arthur, engraved by J. K. Shirwin; engravings as Falstaff in *Henry IV, Part 1* by F. Lambert, after "A.B.," from an original in the Dick Collection, and an engraving by John Taylor Wedgwood, after Singleton, published by Longman & Company; Falstaff in *Merry Wives* engraved by Richard Rhodes, after John Thurston; engraving as Shylock by J. Archer, published by Oliver & Boyd, Edinburgh, and D. Arnott, London; engraving as Sir Archy by an unknown engraver published by Oliver & Boyd in Edinburgh, 1811; engraving by Stalker, after Singleton, of Sir Giles Overreach, published by Longman & Company; engraving as Sir Pertinax by an unknown engraver published by Oliver & Boyd, Edinburgh; and one as Strictland in *The Suspicious Husband*, engraved by J. Archer and also published by Oliver & Boyd. The Folger Shakespeare Library has an oil painting of Richard III by an unknown artist. Another painting of Cooke as Richard by J. R. Lambden, copied after Sully, was first in the Augustin Daly Collection which was sold at the Anderson Galleries in 1912 and in 1962 was sold by the Folger to the American Shakespeare Festival Theatre, in Stratford Connecticut, where it now hangs. A half-length portrait in oil of Cooke as Richard, unsigned and undated, was offered for sale by

Appendix A

I. K. Fletcher in 1964 and purchased by Prof. Norman Philbrick in California. The Boston Public Library has an engraving by Cruikshank entitled "The Whiskey-shop in an uproar; or, the grand climateric of a tragedian!" published by P. Egan in 1813. Cruikshank also drew a caricature entitled "Cook the actor; the Dirty Beau and Big Ben." A miniature by Dunlap was engraved by H. R. Cook and published by J. Miller in 1813, by William S. Leney, and by Richard(?) Cooper for Dunlap's *Life of Cooke*, which was published by Colburn in 1813 (see *Life of Cooke*, 2: 365, 371). There are several other pictures of Cooke at the Garrick Club (see *Catalogue*, p. 207, for details on the eleven original paintings or drawings of Cooke). A miniature painting of Cooke by Dodsworth Peacock is at The Players' Club. A watercolor on ivory by an unknown artist is in the Shakespeare Memorial Theatre Gallery at Stratford-upon-Avon. (See Epilogue, n. 12, on engraving of Cooke's tomb.) There are doubtless other extant portraits, both originals and engravings, and the author would appreciate hearing of any not mentioned in this appendix.

Appendix B

Table of Cooke's Performances and Receipts in the United States

This list has been compiled from published sources cited elsewhere in the text, newspapers from the collections of the American Antiquarian Society and the Rhode Island Historical Society, and playbills in the Harvard Theatre Collection and the Walter Hampden Memorial Library at The Players.

Abbreviations

B—Boston
Balt—Baltimore
NY—New York City
Ph—Philadelphia
Pr—Providence
NK—Not Known

Plays

A—*Alexander the Great*
EM—*Every Man in His Humour*
FP—*The Fair Penitent*
G—*The Gamester*
H IV—*Henry IV, Pt. 1*
H VIII—*Henry the VIII*
KJ—*King John*
KL—*King Lear*

LAM—*Love-a-la-Mode*
MV—*The Merchant of Venice*
MW—*The Man of the World*
MWW—*Merry Wives of Windsor*
NW—*A New Way to Pay Old Debts*
R—*The Revenge*
R III—*Richard the Third*
VP—*Venice Preserv'd*
WF—*The Wheel of Fortune*

City	Date	Mainpiece	Role (if not Title Role)	Afterpiece	Receipts
NY	11/21/10	R III		Fortune's Frolic	$1820
	11/23	MW	Sir Pertinax	The Ghost	1423
	11/24	R III		The Purse	1155
	11/28	MV	Shylock	Honest Thieves	1804
	11/30	MW	Sir Pertinax	The Prize	1180
	12/3	*Douglas*	Glenalvon	LAM (Sir Archy)	1287
	12/5	R	Zanga	Hit or Miss	1605
	12/7	MV	Shylock	LAM (Sir Archy)	1270
	12/10	*Macbeth*		Hit or Miss	1605
	12/12	NW	Sir Giles	The Padlock	963
	12/14	H IV	Falstaff	The Purse	1444
	12/17	NW	Sir Giles	Hit or Miss	798
	12/19	*Cato* (Benefit)		LAM (Sir Archy)	1878

City	Date	Mainpiece	Role (if not Title Role)	Afterpiece	Receipts
	12/21	MV	Shylock	*Ella Rosenberg*	467
	12/24	H IV	Falstaff	*Poor Soldier*	726
	12/26	MW	Sir Pertinax	*Ella Rosenberg*	1126
	12/28	R III		*Poor Soldier*	1264
B	1/3/11	R III		*No Song No Supper*	881.50
	1/4	R III		*Jew & the Doctor*	739.87 1/2
	1/7	MW	Sir Pertinax	*My Grandmother*	887.75
	1/9	MV	Shylock	*Weathercock*	979.37 1/2
	1/10	*Douglas*	Glenalvon	LAM (Sir Archy)	764
	1/11	MW	Sir Pertinax	*The Padlock*	614.12 1/2
	1/14	MV	Shylock	*Sixty Third Letter*	825.75
	1/16	*Othello*	Iago	*Fortune's Frolic*	841.75
	1/17	MV	Shylock	*The Blind Boy*	624.87 1/2
	1/18	*Macbeth* (Benefit)		*Rival Soldiers*	1008.12 1/2
	1/21	H IV	Falstaff	*The Quaker*	867.50
	1/23	*Othello*	Iago	*Lying Valet*	1115.25
	1/24	H IV	Falstaff	*Raising the Wind*	665.37 1/2
	1/25	R III		*My Grandmother*	915.62 1/2
NY	2/1	MV	Shylock	NK	511
	2/4	R III		NK	665
	2/6	VP	Pierre	Lock and Key	368
	2/8	MW	Sir Pertinax	NK	457
	2/11	MWW	Falstaff	NK	627
	2/13	*Macbeth*		*High Life Below the Stairs*	331
	2/15	MWW	Falstaff	*The Budget of Blunders*	345
	2/18	R III		*Twenty Years Ago*	314
	2/20	KL		*Rosina* (bill says *Budget of Blunders*)	634
	2/22	KL		*Twenty Years Ago*	388
	3/1	KL (Payne's Benefit)		*Lock and Key*	827
	3/4	MW	Sir Pertinax	*The Weathercock*	553
	3/6	WF	Penruddock	LAM (Sir Archy)	399
	3/8	H IV	Falstaff	*The Romp*	428
Ph	3/25	R III		*The Review*	1348.15
	3/27	R III		*Matrimony*	1114
	3/29	MW	Sir Pertinax	*The Hunter of the Alps*	1474.34
	3/30	MV	Shylock	*A Budget of Blunders*	1159.62
	4/1	R III		*The Adopted Child*	1187.50
	4/3	MW	Sir Pertinax	*The Weather Cock*	1202.50
	4/5	KL		*Sylvester Daggerwood*	995.76
	4/6	NW	Sir Giles	*Killing No Murder*	1035.06
	4/8	H IV	Falstaff	*Of Age Tomorrow*	1920
	4/10	MV	Shylock	*The Spoil'd Child*	870.50
	4/11	*Macbeth*		*Too Many Cooks*	778
	4/13	*Douglas*	Glenalvon	LAM (Sir Archy)	1196
	4/15	EM (Benefit)	Kitely	*The Highland Reel*	1365.25
	4/17	KL		*Modern Antiques*	678
	4/19	MW	Sir Pertinax	*Prisoner at Large*	948.25
	4/20	R III		*The Scheming Lieutenant*	997.40
	4/26	*Othello* (w/Cooper 1st time)	Iago	*The Old Maid*	1504.76
	4/27	G	Stukely	*Ways & Means*	1193

Appendix B

City	Date	Mainpiece	Role (if not Title Role)	Afterpiece	Receipts
	4/29	VP	Pierre	*Don Juan*	1312
	4/30	*Othello*	Iago	*Irishmen in London*	1292.30
NY	5/6	R III		*The Anatomist*	1380
	5/8	*Othello*	Iago	*Lock & Key*	1620
	5/10	G	Stukely	*The Honest Thieves*	945
	5/13	*Othello*	Iago	*The Apprentice*	1123
	5/15	A	Clytus	LAM (Dir Archy)	935
	5/17	FP	Horatio	*Prisoner at Large*	678
	5/20	VP	Pierre	*Wags of Windsor*	934
	5/22	H IV (Benefit)	Falstaff	*Prisoner at Large*	884
	5/24	*Othello*	Iago	*Wags of Windsor*	1130
Balt	5/31	R III		*The Invisible Girl*	825.75
	6/1	*Othello*	Iago	*The Old Maid*	773.50
	6/3	MW	Sir Pertinax	*The Highland Reel*	801.75
	6/4	*Hamlet*	Ghost	*The Ghost*	320
	6/5	VP	Pierre	*The Scheming Lieutenant*	938
	6/7	MV (Benefit)	Shylock	LAM (Sir Archy)	858.25
	6/8	MW	Sir Pertinax	*Fortune's Frolic*	474.25
	6/10	H IV	Falstaff	*Ways & Means*	901.75
NY	6/24	MW	Sir Pertinax	NK	794
	6/26	EM	Kitely	NK	697
	7/1	R III		*Lock & Key*	657
NY	9/2	*Douglas*	Glenalvon	*Lock & Key*	NK
	9/4	R III		*The Young Hussan*	NK
	9/6	*Othello*	Iago	*The Poor Soldier*	NK
	9/9	KJ		*Fortune's Frolic*	NK
	9/11	A	Clytus	LAM (Sir Archy)	NK
	9/13	EM	Kitely	*Prisoner at Large*	NK
	9/16	G	Stukely	*The Wood Demon*	NK
	9/20*	*Macbeth?*	Macduff?	*Spoil'd Child?*	NK
	9/25	*Othello*	Iago	*Spoil'd Child*	NK
	9/27	MV	Shylock	LAM (Sir Archy)	NK
	9/30	VP	Pierre	*The Wood Demon*	NK
	10/2	H VIII		*The Apprentice*	NK
	10/4	MW	Sir Pertinax	*Love Laughs at Locksmiths*	NK
	10/18	R III		*The Romp*	NK
	10/21	H IV	Falstaff	*Of Age To-Morrow*	NK
	10/23	KJ		*The Bee Hive*	NK
	10/25	MW	Sir Pertinax	*The Romp*	NK
	10/28	*Othello*	Iago	*The Bee Hive*	NK
	10/30	WF	Penruddock	*Paul & Virginia*	NK
	11/1**	KL		NK	NK
	11/4	MW (Benefit)	Sir Pertinax	*Catharine & Petruchio*	NK
Ph	11/8	R III		*Fortune's Frolic*	917
	11/9	MW	Sir Pertinax	*Tom Thumb*	780.41
	11/11	KL		*Ways & Means*	675.95
	11/13	*Macbeth*		*Prisoner at Large*	729.75
	11/15	WF	Penruddock	*Hunter of the Alps*	724.50
	11/16	R III		*Matrimony*	706.75

City	Date	Mainpiece	Role (if not Title Role)	Afterpiece	Receipts
	11/18	H IV	Falstaff	*The Irishman in London*	632.25
	11/20	MV	Shylock	LAM (Sir Archy)	1177.75
	11/22	MW	Sir Pertinax	*The Devil to Pay*	1115.50
	11/23	NW	Sir Giles	*A Budget of Blunders*	646
	11/25	KJ		*The Adopted Child*	546.88
	11/27	MV	Shylock	LAM (Sir Archy)	1041.37
	11/29	R III (Benefit)		*Who's the Dupe*	1121.89
	11/30	MW	Sir Pertinax	*The Lady of the Rock*	571.70
NY	12/6	*Othello*	Iago	*The Apprentice*	NK
	12/9	G	Stukely	LAM (Sir Archy)	NK
	12/11	MW	Sir Pertinax	*The Forty Thieves*	NK
	12/13	*Macbeth*		*Sprigs of Laurel*	NK
	12/14	MV	Shylock	LAM (Sir Archy)	NK
	12/16	MW	Sir Pertinax	*The Forty Thieves*	NK
	12/17	R III		*The Prize*	NK
B	12/31	R III		*Yes or No?*	761.87
	1/1/12	MV	Shylock	*No Song No Supper*	593.87 1/2
	1/3	MW	Sir Pertinax	*The Midnight Hour*	811
	1/6	H IV	Falstaff	*The Weathercock*	703.62 1/2
	1/8	*Othello*	Iago	*My Grandmother*	838.37 1/2
	1/9	WF	Penruddock	*Of Age To-morrow*	736.50
	1/10	VP	Pierre	LAM (Sir Archy)	584.25
	1/20	MV	Shylock	*Turnpike Gate*	470.50
	1/22	NW	Sir Giles	*Music Mad*	417.62 1/2
	1/23	R	Zanga	*The Fortress*	520.12 1/2
	1/24	R III (Benefit)		*The Purse*	704.75
	1/27	*Macbeth*		*Fortune's Frolic*	609.50
	1/28	NW	Sir Giles	*The Weathercock*	451.50
	1/29	R	Zanga	*Tale of Mystery*	365.37 1/2
	1/31	KL		*The Quaker*	557
	2/3	*Othello*	Iago	*The Jew & the Doctor*	376.25
	2/5	MV	Shylock	LAM (Sir Archy)	658.37 1/2
	2/6	KL		*The Ghost*	513.75
	2/7	*Macbeth* (Benefit)		NK	696.25
NY	3/16	MW	Sir Pertinax	*Lock & Key*	NK
	3/18	*Othello*	Iago	*Sprigs of Laurel*	NK
	3/20	R III		*The Romp*	NK
	3/23	*Othello*	Iago	LAM (Sir Archy)	NK
	3/25	H IV (Benefit)	Falstaff	*'Tis All a Farce*	NK
Pr	7/13	MV	Shylock	*Plot & Counterplot*	268.50
	7/15	R III		*The Weathercock*	286
	7/17	MW	Sir Pertinax	*Wags of Windsor*	227.50
	7/20	*Macbeth*		*The Spoiled Child*	259
	7/22	WF	Penruddock	LAM (Sir Archy)	165.75
	7/24	R	Zanga	*Plot & Counterplot*	198
	7/27	KL		*My Grandmother*	157
	7/29	H IV	Falstaff	*Musick Mad*	93.50
	7/31	NW (Benefit)	Sir Giles	*Blue Beard*	285

*Dunlap says he did not play this night; other sources cited in the text disagree.
**Dunlap says 11/3 but must mean 11/1 since the 3d was a Sunday; I have located no bill to confirm.

Abbreviations

The following abbreviations are used throughout the notes. For the full entry, consult the Selected Bibliography.

LC	William Dunlap, *The Life of George Frederick Cooke*, 1815
DD	*The Diary of William Dunlap, 1766–1839*
H & P	J. L. Hodgkinson and Rex Pogson, *The Early Manchester Theatre*
LS	*The London Stage* (Hogan and Stone)
MM	*The Monthly Mirror* (London)
TN	*Theatre Notebook*
TS	*Theatre Survey*
VS	*An Essay on the Science of Acting by a Veteran Stager*, 1825
WP	Tate Wilkinson, *The Wandering Patentee*
BM	The British Museum (now officially The British Library)
HTC	The Harvard Theatre Collection
NYPL	New York Public Library (Performing Arts Collection, Lincoln Center)
V & A	The Victoria and Albert Museum (Enthoven Collection)

Notes

INTRODUCTION

1. William Dunlap (1766–1839) left five major nondramatic works: *A History of the American Theatre* (1832), *History of the Rise and Progress of the Arts of Design in the United States* (1834), *The Life of Charles Brockden Brown* (1815 and 1822), his biography of Cooke (1813 and 1815), and a novel, *Thirty Years Ago; or, The Memoirs of a Water Drinker* (1836). In the latter Cooke appears as a major character. There are numerous biographical details about Cooke, some fictitious, but none adds to our knowledge of Cooke's life. See especially 1:16–21, 119–128; 2:115–136, 145–152, 168–169, 203–204, 207–213, 217, 220.

2. *The Satirist*, 3, n.s. (1 October 1813), 338–351.

3. Lord Byron, *The Works of Lord Byron*, 2:249–250. Byron's comments are in a letter to Thomas Moore, dated 22 August 1813.

4. Quoted in MS, *Recollections of 'O'Smith, Shevelove Collection*. All quotations from *Recollections* are by permission of B. G. Shevelove, London, England.

5. N. P. Willis, in *New York Mirror*, 17 August 1833.

6. Gabriel Harrison, *The Life and Writing of John Howard Payne*, pp. 45–46.

7. Harold Hillebrand, *Edmund Kean*, p. 331.

8. Lord Byron, 5:437, from "Detached Thoughts," 15 October 1821.

9. Charles Durang, "The Philadelphia Stage from the Year 1749 to the Year 1855," *The Philadelphia Sunday Dispatch* (1854–1860). Chapter 44:88. I have used the seven-volume scrapbook of Durang at the University of Pennsylvania, arranged and illustrated by Thompson Westcott.

10. See *MM*, n.s., 9 (January 1811), 63.

11. *The Dramatic Censor or, Critical and Biographical Illustrations of the British Stage*, pp. 171, 255, 291–292.

12. Clipping, HTC, from *The European Magazine*, December 1806. The statement is in a letter to the editor from T. Moody, dated 15 December 1806.

13. Durang, 44:89.

14. From the "Emerald Isle" by Phillips quoted in George O. Willard, *History of the Providence Stage*, p. 71.

CHAPTER 1

1. Such an assumption appeared as early as 1797 in *MM*, 3 (February 1797), 119–120.

2. *LC*, 1:1.

3. See, for example, *The Cabinet*, 2 (October 1807), 133, and J. Roach, *Authentic Memoirs of the Green Room*, 2d ed., 2, Pt. iv, 13. A few standard sources continue to place his birth in Dublin, e.g., John Doran, *Their Majesties' Servants*, p. 379.

4. *LC*, 2:394.

5. During Cooke's engagement in Dublin, between 1794 and 1800, he often refers to visits to Kearney's in his diaries. Cooke did appear in Dublin in July 1806.

6. The "Veteran Stager" appears to be two to three years off in his dating throughout his account of Cooke, which is written in a long footnote. This problem will occur again.

7. *VS*, pp. 106–107.

8. *LC*, 1:2; 2:317. *DD*, 2:441, says "high Irish Gentleman."

9. William Dunlap, *History of the American Theatre*, p. 385. Cooke with an "e" is definitely the Irish spelling of the surname, while Cook is generally considered English. There seems little doubt that his father at least was Irish. Later descendants of this Cooke branch of the family did live in Cork, according to Beryl Cooke, Cooke's last known descendant.

10. See Arnold Hare, "George Frederick Cooke: The Actor and the Man," in *The Eighteenth-Century English Stage*, Kenneth Richards and Peter Thomson, eds., p. 124; Henry Barton Baker, *Our Old Actors*, pp. 270–271; *Dictionary of National Biography*, Sir Leslie Stephens and Sir Sidney Lee, eds. (London, 1887), 4:1007–1009.

11. *VS*, p. 107.

12. See 1:2. In the 2d edition of 1815 the name is spelled Benton.

13. *DD*, 2:462–463.

14. MS Thr 20. 1, HTC. See Chapter 12, n.58.

15. *LC*, 1:2; *DD*, 2:462.

16. William Fraser, *Memorial of the Montgomeries, Earls of Eglinton*, 1:100–114. Lady Susanna was the sixth child of Alexander's third wife, the daughter of Sir Archibald Kennedy of Culzean. Fraser only says she died "leaving issue" and gives no details of children.

17. See Roach above.

18. Dunlap records in his diary that Cooke told him his father "left me a little fellow to the care of my mother but I was soon my own master—that was my ruin" (*DD*, 2:441). *VS* (p. 107) on this account seems to be in disagreement with Cooke and most other sources. He claims that when Cooke was about thirteen months old, young Cooke accompanied his parents to America, where his mother died when Cooke was four. He further states that in 1762 his father returned to England and entrusted Cooke to the charge of his brother, a printer in Berwick-upon-Tweed. He simply may be confusing John Taylor, to whom Cooke was later apprenticed in Berwick, with a relative.

19. *LC*, 1:2,5, 113; John Taylor, *Records of My Life*, p. 113.

20. Taylor, p. 128.

21. A fictitious English prophetess, first heard of in a tract of 1641, in which she is said to have lived in the reign of Henry VIII and to have foretold the death of Cardinal Wolsey, Thomas Cromwell, Lord Percy, and others. See *The Satirist*, 3, n.s., No. 15 (October 1, 1813), 358.

22. Taylor, pp. 130–131. *The Satirist*, p. 359, implies that Cooke was negligent in subsequent dealings with relations. One evening in the green room Cooke was asked "if he had not a relation who lived in one of the narrow streets on the Bank-side of Lambeth. The gentleman knew exactly the degree of kindred, but wanted to discover whether prosperity had rendered Cooke wholly regardless of family connexions. His answer was, 'I should have an uncle there but I know not what has become of him.' It is probable that he never inquired. The relation was his mother's own brother."

23. For example see: *MM*, 10 (December 1800), 347; *The Cabinet* (October 1807), p. 133; *The Thespian Dictionary*, 2d ed. (London, 1805), s.v. Cooke; Thomas Gilliland, *The Dramatic Mirror*, 2:106; Roach, above.

24. *LC*, 1:2–3, 5–6; see Roach above.

25. Ibid., 1:3. Cooke says that he later saw Woodward in fourteen roles, presumably during the period 1775–1777. The roles he lists are Touchstone, Lucio, Marplot, Trappanti, Colonel Feignwell, Clodio (*Love Makes a Man*), Tom, Young Philpot, the Apprentice, Buck, Razor, Petruchio, Trappolin, Squire Groom (ibid., 1:438).

26. Ibid., 1:4–5. Dunlap records in his diary that Cooke claimed to have been a midshipman on a man o'war at eleven (*DD*, 2:441).

27. Philip H. Highfill, Jr., Kalman A. Burnim, and Edward A. Langhans, *A Biographical Dictionary*, 1:49–50.

28. *LC*, 1:5. Most of Cooke's comments are from various diaries and journals quoted by Dunlap. Those documents extant will be cited in the notes and quoted in the text, rather than Dunlap's version of them. Most biographical data were recorded in an 1807 journal.

29. Ibid., 1:7–8. Cooke recalled in 1807 that among the troupe were Mr. and Mrs. King, Mr. Buck, Mr. Dancer, Mr. Smith, Mr. Taplin, Mr. Wills, and Mr. Joseph Reinagle.

30. Ibid., 1:6.

31. He remembered having seen *Alexander the Great, Romeo and Juliet, George Barnwell, The Wonder, Douglas,* and *Macbeth* (ibid., 1:9–11).

32. Ibid., 1:8–9.

33. Ibid., 1:9–13.

34. See Taylor, p. 113.

35. *LC*, 1:13–14. Although Dunlap's telling of this story does not make clear whether it is from Cooke's journal, it is nonetheless a typical tale of early stagestruck youth in Cooke's time. The portion of Cooke's journal covering this early period, written in 1807, has not survived. It is probably part of Cooke's papers borrowed by Dunlap from Cooke's widow while writing the biography. See *DD*, 2:461.

36. *LC*, 1:16.

37. Ibid., 1:16–17.

38. Ibid., 1:17.

39. *VS*, pp. 107–108. In 1811, the editor of *The Mirror of Taste*, 3, No. 11 (January 1811), p. 17, claimed that he had heard from close friends of Cooke that his parents resented his going on stage and carried "that resentment to the grave, to his entire exclusion from the little partrimony [sic] to which his birth intitled [sic] him; & that this circumstance made an impression upon his sensibility which had nearly been fatal to life, & was thought to be the *radical cause of all his subsequent misfortunes.*"

40. See s.v. Mitchell, *The Thespian Dictionary*; *VS*, pp. 108–109.

41. Dunlap quotes Cooke as having seen *Oroonoko* and *Midas*, a burletta by Kane O'Hara, at Covent Garden. Among the cast of the afterpiece were Mr. and Mrs. George Mattocks, with whom Cooke would shortly become more fully associated. See *LC*, 1:19–20.

42. The Black Lion, Russell Court, Covent Garden, was used then as a register office for engaging actors for the provinces. See *MM* (February 1799), p. 67.

43. *VS*, pp. 108–109.

44. Ibid., p. 109.

45. *The Cabinet* (October 1807), p. 133, says: "On his emancipation from school discipline, in 1771, our hero went to sea, and afterwards embarked in business; but less from inclination than necessity." Dunlap, as he was inclined to do, chose the phrase "embarked in business" out of context and wrote ". . . he went to Holland, for what purpose he has not recorded. 'The Cabinet' speaks of his being 'embarked in business,' meaning, I presume some scheme of his friends to engage his mind in mercantile pursuits, or to initiate him in the mysteries of trade" (*LC*, 1:18). The writer of *The Cabinet* must have used as a source *The Thespian Dictionary* of 1805 (s.v. Cooke), since the sentences are almost verbatim. The latter records: "In 1771, he went to sea, and afterward was put to a business. . . ." Neither source, however, mentions Holland, or in what capacity Cooke went to sea. See also Roach, above.

46. MS Thr 20.1, HTC.

47. He makes such a statement in the notes for Cooke's biography. See *DD*, 2:463.

48. *LC*, 1:18; 2:317; *DD*, 1:441, says Cooke was eleven.

49. *LC*, 2:394. Such a speculation was disseminated prior to Dunlap. *MM* (December 1800), p. 347, published the same possibility, which was then reprinted in *Walker's Hibernian Magazine* (January 1801), p. 1.

50. See, for example, *Dictionary of National Biography*, 4 (London, 1887), 10007; and Cecil Armstrong, *A Century of Great Actors*, p. 103.

51. There are numerous indications that Cooke had a very real antipathy to sea voyages. For

example, he became ill in 1795 on board a military vessel, and Dunlap records in his diary that Cooke turned down a party on a sailboat in the United States for the same reason (see *DD*, 2:463). His reputation as an alcoholic naturally sparked other remarks on his dislike for water. Supposedly, when it was confirmed that he had dropsy, he replied, "How the devil doctor should I come by this water—I never drank any" (ibid.).

52. Roach, 2:13. Roach also claims that he received another family windfall sometime between 1778 and 1786. See also *The Cabinet* (October 1807), p. 134 and *Their Majesties' Servants*, p. 379.

53. [Pierce Egan], *Life of George Frederick Cooke*, p. 4, says he did.

54. Highfill, et al. 2:364. Mrs. J. Brown was born Mills, married William Ross shortly after her appearance in Berwick, and as Mrs. Ross acted in Norwich from 1774 to 1780. Since Cooke is speaking of the past, and if he is correct, he must mean Miss Mills when he speaks of Mrs. J. Brown.

55. This Booth is not identified further by Cooke. None of the known Booths fits the time and place satisfactorily, although Cockran Joseph Booth and J. Kennedy did have a provincial company active during the summer of 1773 (ibid., 1:229).

56. *LC*, 1:20.

CHAPTER 2

1. *LC*, 1:21.
2. Simon Trefman, *Sam. Foote, Comedian, 1720–1777*, p. 189.
3. Ibid., pp. 148–151, 155–159.
4. Ibid., p. 280.
5. *LC*, 1:21, 439; 2:91.
6. Quoted in Highfill, et al., *A Biographical Dictionary*, 1:327.
7. See Bertram Joseph, *The Tragic Actor*, pp. 131–148.
8. *LC*, 2:275. Cooke does not include Othello in the listing of roles he saw Barry perform (1:437), but he does mention seeing Barry in *Othello* to Dunlap, who recorded it in his diary (*DD*, 2:425).
9. William Hawkins in *Miscellanies in Prose and Verse* (1775), quoted by Highfill, et al., 1:336, praised Barry lavishly but hesitantly added: "[his action] is sometimes rather flat and unmeaning to the true sense of his words, and likewise a stoop in his shoulders, and a bend in his knees, as if he was ashamed of his superior stature . . . and desirous to level it to the common standards; but I forget that he is bordering on the vale of years, consequently such blemishes as those must be pardoned and forgiven."
10. See, for example, Margaret Barton, *David Garrick*; Kalman A. Burnim, *David Garrick—Director*; David M. Little and George M. Kahrl, eds., *The Letters of Garrick* (Cambridge, Mass., 1963).
11. The term *School* has been used by scholars to designate similarities in personal styles or a certain homogeneity in style. See, for example, Alan Downer's use of *school* as a means of classifying eighteenth-century acting in "Nature to Advantage Dressed: Eighteenth-Century Acting," *PMLA*, 58 (1943), 1002–1037, reprinted in John Loftis, ed., *Restoration Drama: Modern Essays in Criticism*, pp. 328–371, and the same methodology for nineteenth-century acting in "Players and Painted Stage: Nineteenth Century Acting," *PMLA*, 61 (June 1946), 522–576. Although this study is not directly concerned with changing styles and the consequent dominant aesthetic tendencies of their age, I would recommend as an excellent treatment of this subject, which clearly relates to Cooke and his predecessors, Joseph W. Donohue, Jr., *Dramatic Character in the English Romantic Age*, especially pp. 216–242 on Garrick's subjective character and pp. 243–269, "Shakespearean Character on the Early Romantic Stage."
12. See Donohue, pp. 221 ff.
13. Downer in *Restoration Drama*, p. 339.

14. [J.G. Cooper], *Letters Concerning Taste* (1755), p. 109, quoted in Donohue, p. 230.
15. Downer in *Restoration Drama*, p. 340.
16. Donohue, p. 244.
17. See Chapter 6, pp. 95–96.
18. John Genest, *Some Account of the English Stage*, 4:14.
19. This technique and its effects are described in [Roger Pickering], *Reflections upon Theatrical Expression in Tragedy*, pp. 50–51.
20. This description is given in its completeness by a German traveler, G. C. Lichtenberg, in *Briefe Aus England* (1776–1778), W. Grenzmann, ed. (1953), 1:971, quoted in Joseph, p. 110.
21. *The Poetical Works of Charles Churchill*, 1:106.
22. Joseph, pp. 90–92.
23. *LC*, 1:28, 114, 178, 286, 437; 2:275. Cooke does not record having seen Garrick's Iago, but, as with Barry, he did mention this to Dunlap (*DD*, 2:425).
24. *LC*, 2:28.
25. Thomas Dibdin, *The Reminiscences of Thomas Dibdin*, 2:31–32.
26. *The Farington Diary by Joseph Farington*, James Grieg, ed., 1:304. This entry is dated 15 March 1801.
27. *LC*, 1:114–115.
28. Ibid., 1:178.
29. Ibid., 2:23.
30. Dibdin, 1:280.
31. See Chapter 10, n.63.
32. See William W. Appleton, *Charles Macklin*, pp. 43–55.
33. *LC*, 2:26–27.
34. Downer in *Restoration Drama*, p. 339.
35. Joseph, p. 246.
36. James Boaden, *Memoirs of the Life of John Philip Kemble, Esq.*, 2:414.
37. Ibid., 2:417.
38. *LC*, 1:437–440.

CHAPTER 3

1. *LC*, 1:30.
2. I am grateful to Kalman Burnim for this information. Professor Burnim kindly made available to me an early draft of the entry on Cooke which appears in Highfill, et al., *A Biographical Dictionary*, vol. 3.
3. John Bernard, *Retrospections of America*, pp. 368–369. Bernard places Cooke in Chichester circa 1771; this has not been verified. See Chapter 13.
4. I am grateful to W.R.M. McClelland, city librarian of the Leicester Library, for locating this information for me.
5. Professor Hare gave me this information in London, April 1974. His interpretation of these bills and Cooke's early career subsequently appeared as "George Frederick Cooke's Early Years in the Theatre," pp. 12–21.
6. *LC*, 1:17.
7. Roach, p. 17, simply says that prior to 1786 Cooke ran the customary round of Thespian itinerancy, particularly with the companies of Nottingham and Lincoln.
8. *VS*, p. 110.
9. Miller indeed managed such a circuit, including Worcester and Wolverhampton as well, until his death on 14 August 1791. Cooke would deal more with Miller in the near future. See H & P, p. 103.
10. The Veteran Stager claims that in seven weeks each actor obtained only 9s. (p. 110).
11. *VS*, pp. 110–111.

12. I have been unable to verify Munden's location at this time; no source checked contradicts the possibility of his presence in Canterbury. However, he would have been only fifteen or sixteen years of age.

13. *VS*, p. 112.

14. Harold Newcomb Hillebrand, *Edmund Kean*, pp. 24–25; Herschel Baker, *John Philip Kemble*, p. 26; *MM*, 10 (September 1800), 131–132.

15. Hare tells me that they seem to be for the Whitley company and list Cooke in the same roles discussed here under 1774 and 1775.

16. The King's Lynn and Stamford appearances are reconstructed from playbills in the Burney Collection (937.f.2), BM. Charles Beecher Hogan believes the Cooke in question here was William Cooke but offers no concrete evidence to support his contention. His principal argument is that G. F. Cooke was a "totally unknown boy of about seventeen" and thus would not have been given the roles assigned him—i.e., "Hamlet, Macbeth and King Lear." As will become apparent, Cooke did not begin with these roles but progressed from roles nearer his actual age. See *TN*, 28, No. 2 (1974), 88–89.

17. See Richard Southern, "Concerning a Georgian Proscenium Ceiling," pp. 6–12; Sybil Rosenfeld, "Notes on the Theatrical History of St. George's Hall, King's Lynn," pp. 25–26.

18. H & P, pp. 44–52.

19. q.v. Whitley, *Thespian Dictionary*.

20. *VS*, p. 113.

21. Also in the company were Messrs. Adcock, Maddocks, Thornton, Sherborne, Light, Robertson, Mesdames Read, Watson, Light, and the Misses Lowell and Clement; later in the season, Mrs. Reddish from Drury Lane joined the ranks.

22. On 8 April, Cooke was announced to play Richard III for Mr. Glassington's and Mrs. Maddocks' benefit. That afternoon a bill was circulated announcing that Cooke had been taken suddenly ill and was incapable of performing. As a consequence, George Barnwell was substituted. From available evidence, this would appear to be the earliest mention of Cooke advertised for Richard and the first notice of indisposition.

23. [Pierce Egan?], *Life of George Frederick Cooke*, p. 4.

24. *LC*, 1:21. See Chapter 2, pp. 1–3.

25. These were Young Marlow, Macbeth, Ferdinand, Lionel, Jaffier, Alexander, Young Meadows, Paris, Beau Mizen, Henry, Hamlet, Fuzee, and Henry II.

26. The names of Cooke and Mrs. Cooke (as Venus) are crossed out on the bill for 20 March, probably not to indicate that they did not appear but for later printings of the bill after Cooke left the company at the end of the season. The same is true of a number of other bills with Cooke's name on them.

27. On the bill Cooke had added "Mr. Cooke ever grateful for the Favours he has received from the town of Lynn, has made it his Study to get up something new for their Entertainment, and the Public may rest assur'd, that no Expence or Pains have been spared on this Occasion." Although clearly a piece of managerial puffery, Cooke must have been well accepted in Lynn.

28. The Stamford roles were: Lord Aimworth (27 March), Lionel (28 March), Charles Marlowe (30 March), and Henry II (31 March).

29. See Denis Arundell, *The Story of Sadler's Wells*, p. 28.

30. Highfill, et al., 1:147.

31. See Thomas Holcroft, *The Life of Thomas Holcroft*, Elbridge Colby, ed., 1:120–122, 125; V. C. Clinton-Baddeley, *All Right on the Night*, pp. 23–24; Elbridge Colby, "A Defence of Spouting Clubs," *The Nation*, 106 (January 31, 1918), 124–125; Anthony Pasquin, *The Eccentricities of John Edwin*, 1:5–12; Samuel W. Ryley, *The Itinerant*, 1:67–71; and John A. Thieme, "Spouting, Spouting-Clubs and Spouting Companions," 9–16.

32. Quoted in Robert Gale Noyes, *The Neglected Muse*, pp. 77–78.

33. *LC*, 1:29; Edward Cape Everard, *Memoirs of an Unfortunate Son of Thespis*, p. 78.

34. Dudley may have been performed at Canterbury; Cooke appeared as Stockwell in *The West Indian* at Lynn on 3 April 1775.

35. *LC*, 1:29–31.
36. Drawcansir is the character in George Villiers's *The Rehearsal*, a travesty of Almanzor in *The Conquest of Granada*.
37. *LC*, 1:31–32.
38. Ibid., 1:32.
39. See St. Vincent Troubridge, *The Benefit System in the British Theatre*, p. 19.
40. Phyllis Hartnoll, ed., *The Oxford Companion to the Theatre*, 3d ed. (London, 1967), p. 435.
41. Charles Beecher Hogan, ed., *LS*, 5, Pt. 1, cxxxii–cxxxvii, clxxxv–clxxxix. The house charge at the Haymarket, from 1776 to 1796, amounted to 60 guineas.
42. *Gentleman's Magazine*, 82 (November 1812), Pt. 2, 494. This was part of Cooke's obituary. It is also mentioned in *LC*, 1:33 and in an unidentified article from *The Statesman*, in the HTC.
43. The Masseys had a benefit performance of their own two months prior to this one, on 9 February 1778. See Hogan, p. 147.
44. Charles Beecher Hogan, *Shakespeare in the Theatre*, 2:509.
45. The playbill at Harvard also lists in the company Mr. and Mrs. Bailey, Mr. Bowles, and Master Benson, and includes as the afterpiece for the evening *The Irish Widow*.
46. Hogan, *LS*, p. 166.
47. *London Gazetteer*, 30 April 1778; Hogan, ibid., p. 167.
48. Hogan, pp. 8, 113.
49. Charles Beecher Hogan, "The China Hall Theatre, Rotherhithe," p. 76. Hogan gives a fairly complete description of the history and location of China-Hall.
50. Everard, pp. 75–76, 78.
51. Hogan, "The China Hall Theatre," p. 77.
52. Everard, p. 75.
53. Hogan, "The China Hall Theatre," pp. 76–78; Hogan, *LS*, p. 183.
54. Hogan, *LS*, p. 113.
55. Hogan, "China Hall Theatre," p. 78.
56. Ibid., pp. 79–80; Hogan *LS*, p. 177; s.v. O'Reilly (William), *The Thespian Dictionary*. Cooke tells us little about this engagement. He simply records "In the summer of this same year I was a member of the company at China-Hall, and acted something on the night the theatre (a wooden building) was burnt. Mr. O'Reilley (then Bailley) the celebrated comedian of Dublin, at that time was a member of our Rotherhithe corps. Mr. Russel of Drury Lane was then a forward promising boy" (*LC*, 1:33).
57. Hogan, *LS*, pp. 16, 17, 113; Hogan, "China Hall Theatre," pp. 77–78.
58. Hogan, *LS*, p. 180.
59. Ibid., p. 177.
60. Quoted in W. Davenport Adams, *A Dictionary of the Drama*, 1:419.
61. Hogan, *LS*, p. 178. On the 29th he also played Hortensio in *Catherine and Petruchio* (Hogan, *Shakespeare in the Theatre*, 2:623).
62. Cooke had seen Everard at the Haymarket in 1774 performing minor roles. Everard, born in 1755, began as a child actor under the name Master Cape with Garrick at Drury Lane and added the name Everard during the 1773–1774 season. He spent a total of twenty-three years at Drury Lane. A great deal of his time was also spent in the provinces, and occasionally he acted in an out-of-season production at the Haymarket. See Hogan, *LS*, p. 9; G. W. Stone, Jr., ed., *LS, 1660–1800*, 4, Pt. 3, 1832, 1742; Everard, pp. 201–203, 207–214.
63. Everard, p. 78.
64. Ibid.
65. Hogan, *LS*, p. 178.
66. Neither Cooke nor the character of Lovewell is included on the playbill for 8 June 1778, but since other company members are listed in familiar roles, it seems probable that Cooke was the Lovewell. See Hogan, *LS*, p. 179.

67. During the course of the season, Cooke also appeared in the following: Conjurer in the comic ballad-opera *The Old Maid* (9 June), Bedamar in *Venice Preserv'd* (15 June), an unknown character in the unpublished *Comical Courtship* (15 June), Freeman in *A Bold Stroke for a Wife* (18 June), Sir Harry's Servant in *High Life Below Stairs* (18 June), and George Bevil in the farce *Cross Purposes* (22 June). See Hogan, *LS*, p. 182.

68. Ibid., p. 183.
69. Everard, p. 76.
70. Ibid., pp. 76–77.
71. *Morning Chronicle*, 29 June 1778.
72. Everard, p. 76.
73. *Morning Chronicle*, 29 June 1778.
74. Everard, p. 77.
75. See Sybil Rosenfeld, *The Theatre of the London Fairs in the Eighteenth Century*, pp. 150–168, for details on the booth theatre and staging during the eighteenth century.
76. Hogan, *LS*, pp. 179–180.
77. Everard, p. 78.
78. Ibid., p. 80.
79. Ibid., pp. 78–80.
80. Hogan, "China Hall Theatre," p. 80.
81. *LC*, 1:33.
82. Hogan, *Shakespeare in the Theatre*, 2:723.
83. *London Gazetteer*, 22 February 1779; Hogan, *LS*, p. 235.
84. S.v. Mitchell, *The Thespian Dictionary*; Everard, p. 77.
85. *London Gazetteer*, 22 February; Hogan, *LS*, p. 235.
86. Hogan, ibid., p. 256.
87. Adams, 1:519, gives 1761 as Fisher's date of birth. If this date is accurate, he would have been only eighteen at this time. However, Fisher did develop a company that worked the Suffolk and Norfolk circuit and built theatres in Bungay, Beccles, Sudbury, Woodbridge, Newmarket, Lowestoft, etc.

88. Everard, p. 91; *LC*, 1:34.
89. Everard, p. 91.
90. Ibid., pp. 91–92.
91. *LC*, 1:35.
92. H & P, pp. 57–58.
93. *LC*, 1:35.
94. Ibid.
95. Henderson died young, before his fortieth birthday in 1785, of overwork and early privation.
96. See Arthur Colby Sprague, *Shakespeare and the Actors*, pp. 49, 90, 137–145, 168, 241, 289, 382.
97. Thomas Davies, *A Genuine Narrative of the Life of Mr. John Henderson*, pp. 44–46; for an analysis of Henderson's acting, see also Joseph, pp. 177–186.
98. *LC*, 1:438.
99. Ibid., 2:192.

CHAPTER 4

1. *LC*, 1:35.
2. Manchester was beginning the population growth which would rapidly transform it from a quiet country town into a vast center of industry. A population survey made by Reverend John Whitaker in 1773 indicated only 27,246 inhabitants, including those in nearby Salford. Richard Arkwright's patent for spinning by means of rollers, granted in 1769, and improvements by Samuel

Crompton in 1778 plus other inventions helped in the rapid transformation of Manchester. See H & P, p. 76.

3. *LC*, 1:36.
4. Tate Wilkinson, *WP*, 2:67.
5. H & P, pp. 75–104.
6. *Manchester Mercury*, 25 November 1783.
7. See John Alexander Kelly, *German Visitors to English Theaters in the Eighteenth Century*, pp. 92–97.
8. Karl Gottlob Küttner, *Beyträge zur Kenntnis vorzüglich des Innern von England und seiner Einwohner*, 16 vols. (Leipzig, 1791–1796); portions of his section on theatre are translated by Kelly and in H & P, pp. 107–108.
9. Kelly, pp. 94–96; H & P, pp. 104–108.
10. Hogan, *LS*, 5:549, 582.
11. H & P, p. 104.
12. Williams Hopkins, MS Diary (1775) in Folger Shakespeare Library cited by Dougald MacMillan, *Drury Lane Calendar*, p. 189.
13. *WP*, 3:87.
14. Thomas S. Munden, *Memoirs of Joseph Shepherd Munden, Comedian*, pp. 20–23.
15. *Mercury*, 4 May 1784. Cooke reappeared as Philotas on 5 May. Unless otherwise indicated, this season is reconstructed from issues of the *Mercury*.
16. *LC*, 1:36–37. This was written in 1807.
17. Kelly, p. 96.
18. Mrs. Robinson was afterward Mrs. Taylor.
19. Kelly, pp. 95–96.
20. *Mercury*, 30 March 1784, indicates they were living at No. 5, Birchin-lane.
21. He repeated Barbarossa on 12 May.
22. Pseudonym for Anthony Pasquin. See *Biographia Dramatica*, 2:323, and Allardyce Nicoll, *A History of English Drama*, 3:316.
23. In February, March, and May.
24. Probably on 26 May.
25. See H & P, pp. 78–79.
26. *Mercury*, 1 June 1784; H & P, pp. 60, 130.
27. In addition to the roles mentioned in the text, Cooke also performed the following supporting roles: the aged father Lord Raby in Hannah More's *Percy*; Fitzherbert in Cowley's comedy *Which Is the Man?*; the villainous Fairfax in William Howard's *King Charles the First*; Valerius in William Whitehead's *The Roman Father*; Moneses in *Tamerlane*; Southampton in *The Earl of Essex*; the gentleman Villeroy in *Isabella*; Spatter in *The English Merchant* (George Colman the elder); and the villainous Abbot in Thomas Hull's *King Henry the Second*.
28. *LC*, 1:38. I am grateful to Mr. Eric H. Lowe, chief librarian of the Central Public Library in Lancaster, for supplying me with background information on Lancaster during the last quarter of the eighteenth century.
29. For a survey of Austin's managerial career, see Cecil Price, "Joseph Austin and His Associate, 1766–1788," pp. 89–94.
30. The list, apparently in Austin's hand, is at the BM, slipped into Playbills 307, a broadside with writing on both sides. See also Cecil Price, "An Eighteenth Century Theatrical Agreement," pp. 31–34.
31. Price, "Joseph Austin," p. 93; *LC*, 1:38. A typical advertisement in the *Sheffield Advertiser*, 3 December 1790, offered such services as "scaling and cleaning" for 10s.6d. and "filling a decayed tooth with Gold" for the same; silver was 5s. and lead only 2s.6d. Austin's roles are listed in Price, "Joseph Austin," p. 94, from a handwritten list in the BM, pasted in Playbills 308. In addition, although not discussed by Price, there is in another collection of BM bills (307) a list of "well-known performers (some of them First Introduced) under the Management of Austin at

Theatres in Lancaster, Whitehaven, Sheffield, and Theatre Royal in Manchester, Newcastle upon Tyne and the City of Chester" (hereafter cited as Austin, "Well-known performers").

32. Munden, pp. 18–19.
33. Playbills 308, BM.
34. Price, "Joseph Austin," p. 92, and Munden, pp. 32–33.
35. H & P, p. 102, give 1782 for both. "A Short history of the town of Lancaster" (Lancaster, 1807), in the possession of the Central Library of Lancaster, suggests that the theatre was built in 1781.
36. Description in "Short history of Lancaster."
37. Many of the provincial towns of this period had no local newspapers, and the playbills have not survived. The local Lancaster paper did not begin publication until June 1801.
38. *LC*, 1:38–39.
39. H & P, p. 112–113.
40. John Bernard, *Retrospection of the Stage*, 1:3.
41. Thomas Gilliland, *The Dramatic Mirror*, 1:223.
42. R. J. Broadbent, *Annals of the Liverpool Stage*, pp. 53–54. According to Playbills 226 (BM), the price of admission for this season was 3s.6d. for boxes, 2s.6d. for pit, and 1s. for gallery. Details for this season have been reconstructed from these bills.
43. See Philip Highfill, Jr., "The British Background of the American Hallams," p. 5.
44. On 17 December, Cooke appeared as Ensign Maclaymore in *The Reprisal*; he may have performed in the afterpiece on 11 January.
45. I have found no indication that Cooke took a benefit in Liverpool.
46. Cooke is listed on the bill for 11 January as Alonzo in *The Revenge* and Colonel Tamper in the afterpiece *The Deuce is in Him*, which indeed he may have performed, since he was absent for three weeks during his next engagement at Manchester in the same time period.
47. *Mercury*, 28 December 1784.
48. H & P, p. 114.
49. Playbills 226, BM.
50. *Mercury*, 18 January 1785. The remainder of the Manchester season is reconstructed from issues of the *Mercury*.
51. See Highfill, et al., *A Biographical Dictionary*, 1:256–257.
52. *LC*, 1:39.
53. Playbill, HTC.
54. H & P, pp. 114–115.
55. *LC*, 1:39.
56. Quoted by Dunlap, ibid., 1:39–40.
57. See Neil Kessel and Henry Walton, *Alcoholism* (London, 1966), pp. 85–97.
58. "Short history of Lancaster," confirmed by *Adam's Weekly Courant*, 21 June 1785, cited by Price, "Joseph Austin," p. 93.
59. Gilliland, 2:1013, incorrectly says Covent Garden.
60. Broadsheet in the Record Room of the Central Library, Lancaster, records a poem about John Gilpin which is "to be spoken by Mr. Munden at his benefit."
61. Frank Simpson, "Chester's Theatre History," *Chester Chronicle*, 19 May 1932.
62. Playbills 307, BM, and M. St. Clare Byrne, "The Earliest *Hamlet* Prompt Book in an English Library," pp. 22–23.
63. This season has been reconstructed from Playbills 307, BM, unless otherwise indicated.
64. This is a significant Hamlet because of the extant promptbook located in the Newcastle Literary and Philosophical Society, apparently used by Cooke for the first time in Chester. It is discussed, although not so fully as one might wish, by M. St. Clare Byrne in *TN* cited above. It also has the distinction of being the earliest known *Hamlet* promptbook extant in an English library and is one of the earliest of all *Hamlet* promptbooks in existence. Hamlet was never one of Cooke's major roles, however. He played it once in London (27 September 1802) and repeated it only once.

65. The exact dates of these performances have been torn from the playbills, but based on the three-day playing week, they are probably 28 and 31 October, although the advertisement in the *Courant* might suggest that Mrs. Whitlock's benefit, *Maid of Honour*, was on the 31st. The benefit advertisement also gives the addresses where the beneficiaries lodged. The Cookes were at Mr. Tilston's in Foregate Street.

66. *VS*, p. 115, does mention that at some point in Chester, although unclear as to the exact date, Cooke became involved with another actor over a dress, "in which the manager justified the right of Cooke's opponent" and he relinquished his position. He does say his next engagement was at York, which seems to fit this time period.

67. She does reappear in a bill at Chester on 30 December 1786 as Miss Neville in *She Stoops to Conquer*.

68. *A New Description of York*, p. 4.

69. Charles Beecher Hogan, "One of God Almighty's Unaccountables; Tate Wilkinson of York," in Joseph W. Donohue, Jr., ed., *The Theatrical Manager in England and America*, p. 67, says the first theatre was built in 1744 by a predecessor of Baker.

70. *WP*, 3:172.

71. *A Description of York*, pp. 69–70. Although this description was written in 1809 after Wilkinson's death when the theatre was under the management of his son John, the details would be virtually the same. Tate Wilkinson had "newly embellished" the theatre in January 1785 (*WP*, 2:181).

72. Hogan, "One of God Almighty's Unaccountables," p. 65.

73. Hogan has deduced that the theatre held about 550 persons. Tickets were 2s. in the pit, 3s. boxes, 1s.6d. for the first gallery, and 1s. for the upper gallery. As Hogan, pp. 68–73, points out, however, the average nightly income from the sale of tickets at the door was approximately £20, with nightly expenditures in the range of 20 guineas. Two years before Cooke played at York, Wilkinson had initiated a subscription plan for season tickets, which boosted the average about £14 a night. Wilkinson left two long and rambling autobiographical works, *Memoirs of His Own Life*, and *WP*, cited above. Hogan, the author of the essay cited above, has recently published a useful index to *WP* (London: The Society for Theatre Research, 1973). The four sources cited in this note contain the most complete information on Wilkinson currently available and are recommended for further study.

74. The race track was located about one mile south of the city on a large flat plain called Knavesmire. The races at York were established in 1709 during the reign of Queen Anne. See *Description of York*, p. 79. The regular York season was February–May (Hogan, "One of God Almighty's Unaccountables," p. 84).

75. *LC*, 1:117–118. This was written by Cooke in 1796 shortly after the publication of *WP*. Cooke considered the memoir an "incoherent jumble," a feeling he likewise had for Wilkinson's first memoir.

76. Ibid., 2:309.

77. See Bertram Joseph, *The Tragic Actor*, pp. 216–239. The most recent biography of Siddons is Roger Manvell, *Sarah Siddons* (New York, 1970).

78. *York Courant*, 18 July 1786.

79. Mrs. Siddons' roles are listed in ibid., 1 and 8 August 1786. See *LC*, 1:43.

80. *Yorkshire Magazine*, 1 (August 1786), 255.

81. Austin, "Well-known performers," s.v. Mrs. Siddons.

82. Thomas Sedgewick Whalley, *Journals and Correspondence*, 1:479.

83. The theatre at Hull was the Theatre Royal, Finkle Street, which was built in 1768 and gained a royal patent in 1769. It was replaced in 1810 by a new theatre with the same name on a different site. A description of the interior, said to have been written in 1769, and in the possession of the Local History Library in Kingston-upon-Hull, though not too reliable, is nonetheless worth citing: "The interior of this theatre consists of boxes, which are fenced off from the pit, and are at the sides, and the gallery goeth all the way round from the boxes on either side. The exterior has a large piazza in the front, and hath separate entrance for boxes, pit and gallery. The building

standeth back from the street—but doth not look very imposing." Wilkinson had repainted the interior and added paper borderings in 1794–1795 (*WP*, 2:176).

84. *Courant*, 8 and 15 August 1786.

85. *LC*, 1:42–43. I have been unable to discover the particulars of their stay in Leeds (there were no local papers then), but the troupe played for four nights at Hull, 14–18 August. See *WP*, 3:22–23. The box-office receipts were £450 (*Courant*, 22 August 1786).

86. *WP*, 3:22–23.

87. *Courant*, 15 August 1786; 22 August 1786.

88. *LC*, 1:43; *Courant*, 2 and 23 January 1787; *WP*, 3:40. Wilkinson adds that, in addition to Cooke, also leaving the company in May were Mr. and Mrs. Kayne, Messrs. Knight, Lowe, and Stanfield, Misses Farren and Eccles, and Mrs. Warrel.

89. Bernard, 1:175–177.

90. *Courant*, 17 February, 27 March, 1 May 1787.

91. Ibid., 23 January, 3, 10, 17, and 24 April, 8 May 1787.

92. Ibid., 13 February, 27 March, 10 April 1787.

93. *WP*, 3:22–23.

CHAPTER 5

1. *LC*, 1:43.
2. Playbills 307, BM.
3. Playbills 308, BM, are used throughout to reconstruct this Chester season.
4. *VS*, pp. 115–117, says this occurred in Newcastle where he had been advertised to play Othello. Cooke was, indeed, advertised for Othello at Newcastle on Monday, 28 January 1788, and this event may have happened then. Other particulars, however, point more conclusively toward the beginning of his engagement with Austin and Whitlock. Whichever is correct, and the story is heavily embellished in either case, it is significant in that it gives us the earliest account of an apology by Cooke to an audience.
5. Ibid., p. 115, says Cooke was "detained in Chester" and if this did occur in Newcastle rather than Chester, such would have been the case.
6. Ibid. indicates that Othello was again announced, but this was not the case at either Newcastle or Chester.
7. Ibid., pp. 117–118.
8. See Chapter 1; also Thomas S. Munden, *Memoirs of Joseph S. Munden*, p. 20; J. Roach, *Authentic Memoirs of the Green Room*, pp. 157–158.
9. *The Picture of Newcastle upon Tyne*, p. 105.
10. Ibid., pp. 5–7.
11. Harold Oswald, *The Theatre Royal in Newcastle upon Tyne*, p. 7.
12. *Picture of Newcastle*, p. 14.
13. Ibid., pp. 14–17, 26, 28.
14. Oswald, pp. 16–17; *Newcastle Chronicle*, 26 January 1788.
15. *LC*, 1:44.
16. *WP*, 3:23.
17. Unless otherwise noted, the remainder of this season has been reconstructed from issues of the *Newcastle Chronicle*.
18. See Harold Hillebrand, *Edmund Kean*, pp. 4–9.
19. According to the *Chronicle*, 12 April 1788, Cooke's address in Newcastle was Mr. Grey's, High-Friar Street.
20. Playbills 260, BM; *Chronicle*, 26 April 1788.
21. Oswald, p. 28; Munden, p. 16.
22. Oswald, pp. 28–29.
23. *Manchester Mercury*, 13 May 1788; Playbills 252, BM.
24. The preceding quotations all found in Samuel W. Ryley, *The Itinerant*, 3:66–69.

25. *LC*, 1:51.
26. Ryley, 3:90; H & P, p. 139.
27. Ryley, 3:65–66.
28. *LC*, 1:51. Dunlap misinterprets Cooke's action as observed by him later in the United States and fails to understand that his querulousness, character assassination of old and trusted friends, periodic heaping of abuse on America, American ways, and those with whom he worked were clear indications of an advanced alcoholic illness. The examples scattered through the second volume of Cooke's memoirs, if of any great value at all, are clear signs of Cooke's frequent paranoid misinterpretations, self-pity, self-deceptions, neglect of meals, compensatory bragging and generosity, and the like, all known stages in a deteriorating stage of alcoholism. One activity, which Dunlap in one effort to show Cooke charity omits from the biography, is Cooke's frequent visits to brothels while under the keep of Dunlap. These activities are recorded in Dunlap's own diary (2:442–444). All evidence points to the fact that Dunlap had very little respect for Cooke. In his diary he almost always refers to him as "old wretch," "Old man," or "old beau," and condemns him at every turn, rarely exerting a personal effort that might alter the situation. Although I will cite a few examples from Dunlap on Cooke's "indisposition," they are in general of inconsequential use in chronicling Cooke's professional career. If one is interested in these tales of woe, they are readily available in Dunlap's own works. See *DD*, 2:418–469; *LC*, 1:79, 85, 86, 125, 129–135, 172–173; 2:233–238, 302, 352, 409. For a complete guide to *LC*, see my "An Index to: The Life of George Frederick Cooke by William Dunlap," *Theatre Documentation*, 2, Nos. 1 and 2 (Fall 1969 and Spring 1970), 109–120.
29. Ryley, 1:183. Ryley's illustration brings to mind William Archer's essay, *Masks or Faces*? (London, 1888), in which such a story would have been apt. It is not included, however, but see p. 178 in *The Paradox of Acting; Masks or Faces?* (New York, 1957).
30. Oswald, p. 26; Munden, p. 16.
31. Munden, p. 17. This anecdote, if true, happened prior to the conclusion of the Newcastle season of 1789, since Mary Jones, referred to as Mrs. Munden, left Munden at Newcastle in May 1789. See Billy Joe Harbin, "The Career of John Hodgkinson in the American Theatre" (Ph.D. diss., Indiana University, 1970), p. 17, and his essay, "John Hodgkinson in the English Provinces, 1765–1792," *TN*, 28, No. 3 (1974), 106–116.
32. Cited in *LC*, 1:77–79, dated 13 August 1794.
33. Munden, pp. 16–17.
34. *Newcastle Chronicle*, 3 January, and 17 January 1789.
35. *Chronicle*, 17 and 24 January 1789.
36. Ibid., 10 January 1789. This Newcastle season is reconstructed from issues of the *Chronicle* unless otherwise noted.
37. Oswald, pp. 30–31.
38. *Chronicle*, 28 March 1789.
39. See James F. Arnott and John W. Robinson, *English Theatrical Literature, 1559–1900, A Bibliography* (London, 1970), p. 159. A copy of the pamphlet is held by the Newcastle-upon-Tyne Library.
40. James Fennell, *An Apology for the Life of James Fennell*, p. 278; *DD*, 2:422.
41. Fennell, p. 278.
42. *LC*, 1:55.
43. *VS*, pp. 118–120.
44. See John Holland, *The Picture of Sheffield*, pp. 77, 198. Sheffield, renowned for its cutlery industry, had a population of about 31,000 in 1791. The theatre was built in 1762 behind large assembly rooms.
45. From *Sheffield Advertiser* and *Sheffield Register* cited in M. St. Clare Byrne, "The Earliest Hamlet Prompt Book in an English Library," pp. 21–22.
46. The company in Lancaster consisted of Messrs. Betterton, Whitlock, Sheridan, Norman, Stanley, Emery, Ross, Moreton, Whitmore and Munden; Mesdames Sparks, Emery, Leister, Whitmore and Whitlock.

47. Oswald, p. 31.
48. *Sheffield Advertiser*, 26 November 1790. The remainder of the Sheffield season is reconstructed from issues of the *Advertiser* or the *Register*.
49. *LC*, 1:57.
50. Ryley, 3:305–307.
51. *Register*, 31 December 1790, gives Cooke's address as No. 9 Pond lane.
52. *VS*, pp. 121–122.
53. John Edwin, *To the Public* (4 June 1793), pp. 1–4.
54. Stephen Kemble, *To the Public* (10 June 1793).
55. John Edwin, *To the Public* (12 June 1793). I have used copies of the Edwin-Kemble pamphlets in the BM.
56. Playbills 260, BM.
57. *Manchester Mercury*, 23 June 1789.
58. H & P, pp. 130, 156.
59. Ryley, 3:79, 90.
60. H & P, p. 133.
61. *LC*, 1:60.
62. *A Description of Buxton, and the Adjacent Country*, pp. 7–9, 20–21, 56.
63. *LC*, 1:60.
64. A large percentage of the material in his diaries and journals is devoted to this kind of copy. Although it obviously helped Cooke through difficult moments, it is of little use to the biographer.
65. *LC*, 1:61.
66. Ibid., 1:61–62.
67. Ibid., 1:62–63.
68. *Mercury*, 8 November 1791. This Manchester season is reconstructed from issues of the *Mercury* unless otherwise noted.
69. H & P, pp. 135–136; *VS*, p. 122; Playbills 252, BM.
70. *Mercury*, 20 March 1792. Tickets for Cooke's benefit were available at "Mr. Beard's Fountain Street."
71. See Thomas Gilliland, *The Dramatic Mirror*, 1:318–321.
72. H & P, pp. 133–134; *Mercury*, 10 April 1792.
73. Thomas Dibdin, *The Reminiscences of Thomas Dibdin*, 1:119–120.
74. Ibid., 1:120–121.
75. Munden, pp. 29–30.
76. Playbills 252, BM.
77. John Bernard, *Retrospection of the Stage*, 2:199–200.
78. Liverpool season reconstructed from Playbills 226 in BM unless otherwise noted.
79. Playbills, Burney 937.f.2, BM.
80. Playbill, HTC. Appearing on the 23 July bill for *The Busy Body* and Cooke's benefit on 15 August is the name of Miss Charlotte Tidswell, a "walking gentlewoman," who was partially responsible at this time for the infant Edmund Kean and is conjectured by some to have been Kean's mother. It is doubtful, however, that Kean, then about five, would have been with her in Liverpool. See Hillebrand, pp. 1–3.
81. *Mercury*, 11 September 1792.
82. Professor Kalman Burnim made available to me an early draft of an essay on Daniels which has subsequently appeared in Highfill, et. al., *A Biographical Dictionary*, vol. 4. s.v. Daniels, Alicia, later Mrs. George Frederick Cooke, the second and Mrs. Windsor, d. 1826, singer, actress. Some of my information on Daniels comes from this essay. Playbills 227, BM, indicate that she spent the summer of 1793 in Liverpool, where there is also a "Master Daniels" on the bills. Cooke was evidently not with her then.
83. Dibdin, 1:119.
84. C. Censor is given as the author of this lengthy poem, which includes in its full title the names of those performers dealt with, including Ward, Grist, Banks, Mrs. Powell, Francis, Ryley,

and others. It is forty pages in length and of no value as poetry; nevertheless, it is an interesting contemporary document. I have used a copy in the BM. Of Cooke, among other things, Censor writes (pp. 3–6):

> Of Cooke whose deportment, spirit, and ease,
> While merits regarded, must certainly please,
> For long had the Muses lamented their state,
> Long sigh'd for an actor whose worth was innate,
> Who the secret possess'd of improving their charms,
> Whose judgment informs and energy warms,
> Who gives to each feature the tint it requires,
> Who even the bosom of apathy fires,
> Whose efforts are govern'd by genius and taste,
> Who dignifies speech with action that's chaste.

Twenty-two lines later he adds:

> ... for one impropriety damn him for ever,
> Not so honest Cooke who to prudence a stranger,
> Most wishes to serve where he sees the most danger,
> Those subtle distinctions to virtue unknown,
> That shakes the foundation of charity's throne,
> He leaves to the learn'd casuistical tribe,
> On their properties merits or ills to decide,
> While prompt to relieve or revenge the oppress'd,
> He proves the real worth that inhabits the breast,
> But they who have shar'd the reward of his merit,
> Can best tell the virtues that govern his spirit. ...

85. *Mercury*, 18 September, 25 September, and 2 October 1792.
86. Playbill, HTC.
87. *Mercury*, 18 December 1792. Unless otherwise indicated, this season is reconstructed from issues of the *Mercury*.
88. In December 1792, February and April 1793. No cast lists are given in the advertisements, but Harry Dornton was normally Cooke's role.
89. *VS*, p. 122, has left a rare personal sketch of Cooke's Manchester competitor: "... this man could not, without fainting, see a leg of mutton cut the usual way, as it gave him a sensation equal to that he conceived he should feel, were the calf of his own leg so cut; he upon all occasions, when that substantial dish was produced, requested to carve it his own way, which he invariably did the venison fashion: he was a noted ale drinker, and neverceasing smoker; would sit up all night, and keep to his bed as long as business did not require his presence."
90. Tickets for Cooke's benefit were available at Mr. Rowland's Fountain-Street.
91. Playbills, 252, BM.
92. From Ryley's account (3:90) it is not clear if his comic opera was ever actually presented. He says that the lord chamberlain's license arrived too late, and it was necessary to change the mainpiece to *King Lear*. H & P, p. 138, imply that it was presented, and indeed it may have been at a later date than first announced.
93. Playbills, 252.
94. *LC*, 2:65.
95. Similar epithets by Cooke are cited elsewhere, e.g., Chapter 6.
96. *VS*, pp. 123–129.
97. *Mercury*, 19 November 1793.
98. H & P, p. 139.

99. See *MM*, n.s., 1 (April 1807); see also Chapter 10.
100. Playbill, HTC.
101. *Mercury*, 24 December 1793. Season reconstructed from the *Mercury*, unless otherwise noted.
102. See H & P, p. 140.
103. *LC*, 1:64. Dunlap mistakenly places this event prior to 1794. See H & P, p. 140.
104. Cited by Highfill, et al., s.v. Cooke.
105. Playbills 252, BM.
106. Ibid.
107. Highfill, et al., s.v. Cooke.
108. *Mercury*, 10 June 1794.
109. MS Thr 20, HTC. Use of Cooke's diaries by permission of the Harvard Theatre Collection.
110. See *LC*, 1:65–82.
111. Also quoted by Dunlap, 1:80, in slightly altered form.
112. Ibid., 1:69.
113. See n.84.
114. The 1794 journal gives a good indication of the diversity of Cooke's reading, now and later. Cooke got his books from Moore's circulating library in the Cresent. They included: Boswell's *Life of Samuel Johnson,* Pasquin's *Life of Lord Barrymore, Goldsmith's Poetical Works, Gleanings by the Rev. J. Moir, The Danish Massacre* (a novel), *Richard Savage's Works* (1729), *Paul Scarron's Comical Works,* Matt. Consett's *A Tour Through Sweden, Swedish Lapland, Finland and Denmark,* Chalmers' *Life of Thomas Ruddiman* (an Edinburgh librarian), *A Survey of the Russian Empire, Travels on the Rhine, Memoirs of Dumourier,* Peltier's *Picture of Paris, Lady Mary Wortley Montagu's Works,* E. J. Eyre's tragedy *Maid of Normandy, The Adventures of a Watch,* Sewell's tragedy *Sir Walter Raleigh,* Captain Tench's *New South Wales,* Drinkwater's *Siege of Gibralter, Jean Francois Marmontel's Tales,* plus Sheffield, Chester, Manchester newspapers, and a bookseller's *Compilation of a History of England.*
115. *LC*, 1:94; 2:158.
116. There is no evidence that Cooke had any children or legitimate heirs, despite Dunlap's invention of a son in *Thirty Years Ago*. However, I have located references to two, possibly one and the same, who claimed to be Cooke's son. A Cooke writing to the editor of the *London Morning Chronicle*, 10 April 1837, from 47 Compton Street, Soho, claimed to be Cooke's illegitimate son and stated that he had been silent in order to protect his mother. At the time of the writing, he furthermore stated that he then held a subordinate position at Madame Vestris' Royal Olympic Theatre. He had written to several London managers but had not been answered. He was of the "Older School," and his applications were ignored because he wrote to them as an actor and in language "more suited to a slave." Furthermore, he claimed that if given the chance he would demonstrate some of his father's "leading characteristics." Letter is in the HTC. A footnote in *Recollections of "O" Smith*, MS in Shevelove Collection, London, records the following, doubtless a reference to the same GFC: "October 31st, 1837. This evening at the Adelphi Theatre [where Smith was appearing] I was accosted by one of the supernumeraries who paid me some very extravagant compliments on my acting, to which I paid very little attention as the man seemed intoxicated. Mr. Yates [co-lease of the Adelphi] afterwards informed me that it was a natural son of George Frederic [*sic*] Cooke's: that from motives of charity he had employed him in the theatre at 1s. per night. Shortly afterwards he was compelled to discharge him for drunkenness and inattention." Quoted by permission of B. G. Shevelove. Richard John "Obi" Smith (1786–1855), a minor actor in Bath and London, does not date his manuscript, although he was apparently still working on it as late as 1854. I am grateful to Professor W. W. Appleton for first calling my attention to this document. A playbill at Harvard lists this Cooke, or another actor claiming the same name, as Richard III at the Park on 18 June 1839, for Mr. Richings' benefit. Odell, in addition to

Notes

this appearance, lists four other appearances by this Cooke: a repeat of Richard on 2 July 1839 (see George C.D. Odell, *Annals of the New York Stage*, 4:288) and 2 October 1839; Shylock on 3 October; and Hamlet on 4 October (Odell, 2:377–378). Odell says this is the last mention of Cooke. There is no reason to assume that Cooke did not have an illegitimate son, but until more conclusive evidence is forthcoming, such a possibility is best served as a footnote.

117. *LC*, 2:201.
118. See ibid., 1:102–103; 2:158, 201–202, 216, 217, 349–350, 359, 374–377. See also Dunlap, *Thirty Years Ago*, 1:16–21, 111–115.
119. *LC*, 1:95.
120. See Chapter 7.
121. *LC*, 1:81.

CHAPTER 6

1. J. D. Herbert, *Irish Varieties*, p. 8.
2. See Peter Kavanagh, *The Irish Theatre*, p. 282; La Tourette Stockwell, *Dublin Theatres and Theatre Customs*, pp. 148–151.
3. Kavanagh, p. 285; Stockwell, p. 156.
4. Stockwell, p. 124.
5. Ibid., pp. 157–159.
6. Ibid., p. 159; *Dublin Evening Post*, 22 January 1788; *Dublin Chronicle*, 22 January 1788.
7. *Liber Munerum Publicorum Hiberniae*, 2 vols. (1824), 1:109, quoted in Kavanagh, p. 285. Stockwell, p. 351.
8. Stockwell, p. 165.
9. William Smith Clark, *The Irish Stage in the Country Towns*, p. 134; Anne Mathews, *Memoirs of Charles Mathews*, 1:96, 106–107.
10. Mathews, 1:74–75.
11. *LC*, 1:81. Mathews, 1:109, states, "I believe Cooke is engaged for the winter, from Manchester."
12. Clark, p. 370; Mathews, 1:121.
13. Mathews, 1:111.
14. *LC*, 1:84.
15. Mathews, 1:118.
16. See Clark, p. 137. The behavior of d'Eon (Charles Genevière Louis Auguste André Timothée, 1728–1810) gave us the term *eonism*, denoting the tendency to adopt the costume and manners of the opposite sex. An autopsy settled all speculations: d'Eon was certified male.
17. *LC*, 1:81.
18. Ibid., 1:83–84.
19. See Chapter 10.
20. *Dublin Evening Post*, 2 December 1794.
21. Mathews, 1:126; performances reconstructed from issues of the *Evening Post* and *Faulkner's Dublin Journal* for the months of November and December.
22. Mathews, 1:128–129.
23. Ibid., 1:140–141.
24. Ibid., 1:129, 131; issues of the *Dublin Journal* for January, February, and March.
25. *LC*, 1:84.
26. Ibid., 1:84–85. *VS*, p. 129, suggests the breaking point came when Cooke was assigned Pizarro rather than Rolla and became so galled that he flew to his old resource, the bottle. This version is little deserving of credence.
27. Mathews, 1:146–147.
28. Apropos of this anecdote, Cooke, in 1811, told Dunlap the following: "I hate drunkenness. I detest it, for its consequences you'll say—true but not alone I dislike it for myself. Many an hour

have I spent in studying my profession—alone—when the world has thought me drinking. I have studied the passions, Sir and all their various grades. There, Sir, is fear, so I distinguish it from surprize, now suspicion. There's attention—now rage—that is the most difficult of all. Anger, the expression is different according to the object—from the wife to the lowest menial." See *DD*, 2:441. Cooke had evidently mastered the ability to shift rapidly from one emotion to another as attested to by the numerous repetitions in his career of Collins' "Ode on the Passions," "a musical pastiche or a exhibition of images." As one early critic pointed out, the abruptness of the transitions in Collins' Ode demands an actor fill in these intervals in recitation, and "hence perhaps we may account for the differences between this *Ode* on the stage, and in the closet." Cooke had attained a good deal of renown early in his career for the effectiveness of his emotional shifts. See *The Flapper*, 47 (23 July 1796), 186.

29. Mathews, 1:131–138.
30. *LC*, 1:91.
31. Ibid.
32. *VS*, p. 129.
33. Mathews, 1:153.
34. Early during Cooke's first London season, Thomas Dibdin accompanied him home after a late dinner and observed "that when in the army he [Cooke] had always been accounted a bad one at a march, from not being able to step in time." Cooke was indignant at this remark and proceeded to march through Soho "at a tolerably steady quick step" while Dibdin whistled a quick march (Thomas Dibdin, *The Reminiscences of Thomas Dibdin*, 1:282–284).
35. *VS*, pp. 129–130.
36. *LC*, 1:92–93.
37. *MM*, 1 (January 1796), 190–191.
38. Ibid., 1 (April 1796), 373–374.
39. A "Master Daniels, junior" played this season the title role in the comic opera *The Adopted Child*.
40. H & P, p. 145; Playbill, HTC.
41. H & P, p. 146.
42. *LC*, 1:97.
43. Ibid., 1:102–103. The original MS, quoted here, is in *Life of Cooke by Dunlap*, extra-illustrated in five volumes, collected and arranged by J. H. Leigh (n.p., 1900), interleaved in vol. 5 (HTC, TS 933.6).
44. Ibid., 1:107.
45. Playbill, HTC.
46. Playbills 227, BM. Although purely fictional, Dunlap suggests in *Thirty Years Ago; or, The Memoirs of a Water Drinker* that Cooke's first marriage was in 1790 or 1791 to a woman later known as Mrs. Johnson, who then escaped from Cooke to the United States with their son (2:116–117).
47. Add MS 31,972, BM.
48. Doane's *Musical Directory* for 1794 lists a Miss Daniels as a soprano at Sadler's Wells, and a Folger Library manuscript notes that she played a lass in *England's Glory* on 31 August. The songs "Absence" and "The Gallant Forty Second" as sung by Miss Daniels at Vauxhall were printed about this time. I am grateful to Professor Kalman Burnim for this information.
49. Dibdin, 2:388–389.
50. *MM*, 17 (May 1804), 351.
51. H & P, p. 146; *MM*, 3 (February 1797), 119.
52. *MM*, 3 (February 1797), 119–120.
53. See ibid., 3 (March 1797).
54. Ibid., 3 (April 1797), 247.
55. Ibid., 247–248.
56. Playbill, HTC.

57. H & P, p. 149.
58. A playbill in Burney 937.f.2, BM, lists him as Sir William Dorillon in *Wives As They Were* for Cherry's benefit; Mrs. Cooke sang acappella "The Streamlet that flow'd round her cot" as part of the performance.
59. Playbills, Central Public Library, Lancaster.
60. *LC*, 1:107–108.
61. MS Thr 20, HTC, dated 27 September 1798.

CHAPTER 7

1. MS Thr 20, HTC, dated 28 February 1800.
2. See William Smith Clark, *The Irish Stage in the Country Towns*, p. 141; also *MM*, 4 (August 1797).
3. *Dublin Evening Post*, 21 November 1797. Cooke performed Iago five times this season.
4. MS Thr 20.1, HTC, dated 30 November 1807, from Appleby Jail.
5. See Arnold Hare, "George Frederick Cooke: The Actor and the Man," in *The Eighteenth-Century English Stage*, Kenneth Richards and Peter Thomson, eds., pp. 128–129. Hare's figures have been checked against issues of the *Evening Post* and the *Dublin Journal*. There are no playbills for these performances in the Dublin National Library. The three seasons covered in this chapter have been reconstructed from the above newspapers unless otherwise noted.
6. *Evening Post*, 30 November 1797. Performed five times this season.
7. Sir John T. Gilbert, *The History of the City of Dublin*, 2:220.
8. *MM*, 6 (July 1798), 49.
9. Cooke appeared in each the following number of times: Richard (4), Stukely (3), Zanga (3), Joseph Surface (4), Moody (3), Touchwood (3), Stedfast (7), Dorillon (5), Haswell (4), Octavian (3). He appeared in nine other lesser roles.
10. *LC*, 1:109–110.
11. Ibid., 110.
12. Ibid., 118–119.
13. There is a gap from 28 September to 31 December. A few fragments which have not survived are quoted in Dunlap, but when possible, the original will be cited. If not otherwise noted, the extractions are from the HTC diary.
14. He wrote to Creswell in Lancaster, Hammerton and Collin at Liverpool, Ryley at Buxton, and Mrs. Ledger at Whitehaven.
15. Playbills 291, BM.
16. Playbills, Burney 937.f.2, BM.
17. *MM*, 10 (October 1800), 260.
18. Playbills 294, BM. A Miss H. Daniels is also listed in the Market-Harborough bills.
19. A bill for Covent Garden, 26 December 1800, lists a Miss Daniels in the cast of *Harlequin's Tour* (V & A).
20. The site is now occupied by the Cork general post office.
21. Clark, pp. 69–70, 81.
22. See ibid., p. 134.
23. *Cork Evening Post*, 13 September 1798.
24. Clark, who is otherwise reliable, mistakenly says that Cooke was the chief guest star of the season at Cork and came there from Covent Garden. He then identifies Delaval as one of his most recent Covent Garden parts (p. 143). The play was first performed at Covent Garden the preceding winter on 13 February, but not with Cooke.
25. See Chapter 3.
26. *LC*, 1:124–125. This is a typical passage from Cooke's diary that has been freely rewritten and edited by Dunlap. In fact, in his transcription of the entry, there are several sentences that clearly do not coincide with the extant portion of Cooke's diary. For example, after Cooke's "if such a wretch can have a friend" Dunlap has written:

and when by superior villainy, or some unforeseen chance, he is in his turn beggared, he is ready fitted for the most atrocious crimes, robbery, murder, or suicide. Drunkenness, in addition to the high degree of wickedness attached to it, has the melancholy and woeful effect of degrading the human beneath the brute creation. What confidence can be placed in those persons who are in the habit of rendering themselves incapable of rational exertion? A crime committed in this state is aggravated by the state itself, and in this light both moral law and religious must view it.

Compare Dunlap's "improvements" with original quoted in the text.

27. *LC*, 1:125–127.
28. Ibid., 128.
29. Letter, Cooke to Frederick Jones, 19 November 1798, HTC.
30. *MM*, 6 (December 1798), 373.
31. *VS*, p. 129, confusing this season with his 1794 Dublin engagement, does suggest that Cooke was mortified with this situation.
32. *The Stranger* is first mentioned in the *Dublin Journal*, 10 December, for performance on the 12th and then postponed until the 17th. It had never been acted at Crow Street. Presumably it was performed as scheduled, although I have not been able to confirm this with bills. Cooke is not mentioned in the newspaper advertisement, but since he performed the role repeatedly during the 1799–1800 season, it would seem logical for him to have taken the role this season.
33. Playbills 211, BM, list him on 24 June as the King in *The King and Miller of Mansfield* and on 9 July as Baron Wildenheim. Few additional bills have been located.
34. Clark, p. 67. Cooke indicates in his 1800 diary that he stayed at Ryan's Inn.
35. Ibid., p. 144. Cooke's only mention of Cork is in his diary on 12 January 1800.
36. *LC*, 1:150.
37. Letter, Cooke to Felix Daly, 17 November 1800, Dreer Collection, Pennsylvania Historical Society, Philadelphia.
38. Cooke lodged this season at a Mrs. Drake's, the widow of a plumber, near the Liffy River.
39. The more interesting roles of Sir Benjamin Dove and Belfield in *The Brothers* were played by Fulham and Jones, respectively, on 21 December.
40. Cooke does note that this was not the Thompson translation used at Drury Lane in 1798 but "no more than an alteration from a printed one, which was offered to Drury Lane & rejected." Versions by Schink and Papendick were also published in 1798, and the Dublin version must have been based on one of these.
41. Published in 1799. Translation of Kotzebue's *Üble Laune*.
42. A "New Grand Ballet Pantomime of Action called Raymond and Agnes; or, the Castle of Lindenburgh" was first presented at Covent Garden on 16 March 1797.
43. Cooke's continuing interest in the printing profession is indicated in his comments on this publication: "The imprint was London, but I soon found the certain marks of an Irish Edition: incorrectness, poor engravings, brown paper & grey ink." In an entry on 24 September 1798, he commented on the edition of *Tom Jones* he was reading: ". . . the paper is bad, and the text most shamefully incorrect. The volumes have more the appearance of being composed of *proof-sheets*, than of ever having undergone a revision; but neither beauty, or accuracy in printing, have yet made their appearance in this island."
44. Cooke described Dodsley's play as "a pleasant, well-written little comedy . . . infinitely too good to be called a farce. The satire is apt, pointed, & while there are kings & nobles, will always remain in full force. The dialogue easy, the subject traditional. . . ." (23 January).
45. Dunlap records a similar event in his diary (2:430). The event occurred in Philadelphia and is possibly the source for another anecdote in Dunlap's notes reported to have occurred in Liverpool in 1809. Cooke is reported to have left his money with his landlady for safekeeping and instructed her not to give him any if he demanded it when drunk. After drinking late one night, Cooke returned and demanded his money; the lady refused to acquiesce. ". . . he entreats and threatens and then goes off and procures a warrant and police officers and returns to demand the money—it was still refused and the doors shut on him. The next day he came back in all the shame of fruit-

less repentance, beg'd pardon and return'd thanks to the lady of the house" (see *DD*, 2:467).

46. Thomas Ryder died in 1791. As mentioned in Chapter 6, he was long associated with the Irish stage as actor and manager. William O'Reilly (Reilly after 1790) is the singing comedian with whom Cooke was first associated at China-Hall in 1778.

47. See Allardyce Nicoll, *A History of English Drama*, 3:146–147, 149.

48. Playbill, HTC.

49. Playbills 211, BM; *Dublin Journal*, 22 May 1800.

50. In a letter of Hester Thrale Piozzi quoted by Herschel Baker, *John Philip Kemble*, p. 235.

51. *Dublin Journal*, 28 May 1800.

52. *LC*, 1:110, also lists Henry to Kemble's Richard III.

53. *MM*, 9 (June 1800), 374.

54. *LC*, 1:111.

55. Kemble's Journal, summer 1800, cited in Baker, p. 238.

56. Also on 28 June and 1 and 8 July. The only other role performed by Cooke in the last half of the 1799–1800 season not mentioned in the text was Cleaveland in Joseph George Holman's *The Votary of Wealth* on 17 June (Playbills 211, BM).

CHAPTER 8

1. MS Thr 20, HTC.

2. Letter, Cooke to W. T. Lewis, 12 March 1800, HTC.

3. Covent Garden Account Book, Add MS Egerton 2299, BM. During his initial season, he was far from the highest paid on the rosters. Lewis made £20 per week, Incledon £14, Dibdin £20, Pope and Munden £12. Other salaries, however, went as low as 10s.

4. Covent Garden Account Books, Add MSS Egerton 2299, 2300, 2301, BM.

5. Add MS Egerton 2299 indicates that Cooke was initially on salary beginning 20 September but that his salary was erased on each successive Saturday until 29 October.

6. J. C. Croker, *Familiar Epistles to Frederick E. Jones, Esq., on the Present State of the Irish Stage*, p. 32.

7. Letter, Cooke to Felix Daly, 17 November 1800, Dreer Collection, Pennsylvania Historical Society.

8. See Richard Leacroft, *The Development of the English Playhouse*, pp. 134–139.

9. Playbill, Folger Shakespeare Library; Playbills, 88, vol. 12, BM.

10. *MM*, 10 (September 1800), 187.

11. *The Dramatic Censor*, 3 (December 1800), 238. Cooke's first supporting cast in London also included: Stanley—Davenport; Tressel—Betterton; Prince Edward—Mrs. Findlay; Lt.—Waddy; Duke of York—Master Standen; Catesby—Claremont; Ratcliffe—Klanert; Lord Mayor—Thompson; Oxford—Atkins; Terrel—Abbot; Norfolk—Seaton; Lady Anne—Mrs. Litchfield; Duchess of York—Miss Leserve; Queen—Miss Chapman. Criticism of Cooke's supporting casts persisted throughout his London career, especially for Richard.

12. John Taylor, *Records of My Life*, p. 132. Taylor attended rehearsals for Richard and noted great change in Cooke; he was no longer the "lubberly boy" (p. 131).

13. Letter, Cooke to Felix Daly.

14. *LC*, 1:145.

15. *The Dramatic Censor*, 3:265.

16. *Hibernian Magazine*, December 1800, p. 326.

17. 1 November 1800.

18. *Boston Cabinet*, 1 (1811), 7–13.

19. Unidentified clipping, V & A.

20. Unidentified clipping, HTC.

21. Leigh Hunt, *Dramatic Essays by Leigh Hunt*, William Archer and Robert W. Lowe, eds., p. xliii.

22. Lamb wrote few reviews in the *Morning Post*. Coleridge introduced him to the proprietor of

the paper in late December 1801, and he was paid 2 guineas a week to contribute dramatic criticisms and other prose or verse. Early in Janaury, Lamb stopped contributing criticism, finding the deadline too difficult. He considered his review of Cooke "the best thing" he had done, although he had not written it on the same night as the performance (letter to John Rickman, 9 January 1802, in *The Works of Charles and Mary Lamb*, E. V. Lucas, ed., 1: Miscellaneous Prose, 1798–1834 [New York, 1903], 292). The review is in vol. 1:36–38.

23. *The Letters of Charles and Mary Lamb*, E. V. Lucas, ed., 1:259–261.

24. See also *Le Beau Monde; or Literary and Fashionable Magazine* (April 1808), pp. 224–225.

25. *New England Palladium*, 18 January 1811.

26. *The Cabinet*, 1 (1811), 7–13.

27. *Porcupine*, 7 November 1800 (Burney 957, BM).

28. *The Dramatic Censor*, 3:197.

29. James E. Murdoch, *The Stage*, pp. 85–86.

30. Professor Charles H. Shattuck has catalogued the two Cooke promptbooks for *Richard III* in *The Shakespeare Promptbooks*, pp. 391–392, as No. 3 and No. 5. No. 3 is the Lowndes edition, 1793, which Cooke apparently marked for provincial managers, signed and dated 1808. It offers alternatives for managers, depending on the resources of the playhouse. It contains a two-page properties list, a great number of cuts and restorations, calls and cues for effects, and limited stage business. The book is at the Folger Shakespeare Library (Rich III, 4), where I examined it. No. 5 is the Roach edition, also marked in Cooke's hand, evidently prepared first for his debut, since a note is made in Cooke's hand to that effect. It also contains stage business, occasional cues for effects, and restorations. In general, it duplicates the material in the Folger book. It also lists performances on 22 March 1805 and 8 January 1810. It was given to C. Smith by W. Clunes in 1842. The book is in the HTC (TS. 2587.64). Ironically, Dunlap had the Folger promptbook in his possession and witnessed Cooke's Richard several times, but had little to say about Cooke's performance. In fact, he says, "I regret, now, that I did not, when I had ample opportunity, note every passage of every character this great actor played, and described minutely the manner of the tone, the movement of the arm," etc.—and then assumes that no one would be interested anyway! (See *LC*, 2:179.) In general, his comments on Cooke's roles are of minimal use. For his remarks on Richard, see 1:147–148, 157; 2:179–181, 399–403.

31. *MM*, 10 (November 1800), 318–322.

32. *The Mirror of Taste and Dramatic Censor*, 3 (March 1811), 182–200.

33. Later, in the above essay (p. 186), he adds:

Habituated to consider his deformity as an exclusion from the pale of human nature, Gloster treats all others as if they were beings of a different species. Varying his means according to the character of each, he, by persuasion, flattery, or terror, makes them the instruments of his policy, and, even while he flatters, despises them. From the constant exercise of dissimulation, and the natural versatility of his genius, he derives such a facility in feigning, that he can assume as many shapes as Proteus.

34. Cooke has added these lines into the Harvard promptbook.

35. *MM*, n.s., 1 (March 1807), 207.

36. Written into the Harvard promptbook. All subsequent stage directions in this chapter are from the promptbooks.

37. Henry Crabb Robinson, *Diary, Reminiscences, and Correspondence of Henry Crabb Robinson*, Thomas Sadler, ed., 1:53.

38. Lamb, *The Works of Charles and Mary Lamb*, 1:38.

39. James Boaden, *Memoirs of the Life of John Philip Kemble*, 2:279. The comments made in the text cover the major observations on his vocal delivery sustained throughout his career from 1800 on. In toto, very little is made of his accent, and those prominent instances will be cited in the

text. One observation made during his second London season is worthy of citation: in a criticism of his Richard, one critic calls his enunciation "northern and provincial," pointing out his pronunciation of Lancaster, with stress on the second syllable, which to this writer was a pronunciation never heard before (*The Theatrical Repertory*, 6 [24 October 1801], 82 ff.). A strange criticism of his pronunciation appeared in 1811 in *The Mirror of Taste*, op. cit., p. 220:

"*Either*," which he pronounced as if it were spelled *yther* instead of *eether*; *Guildhall*, which he pronounced as if sounded like *guile* instead of *Geeldhall*; and *say*crifice which he ought to know is by all gentlemen pronounced *sak*rifice. He pronounces too the final *s* in words ending with *ss* much more hard than in general elegant speakers do; we own it astonished us to hear Mr. Cooke give the French termination to the words "pursuivant" and "odour." These have long been denizened as English words. As to the pronunciation of the letter *R*, which has been so ridiculously censured, we think it not merely correct, but beautiful, as stamping the character of a necessary letter which feebleness and vanity are gradually melting down to nothing.

The *Morning Chronicle*, 16 October 1804, offers another criticism rare in all Cooke criticism. The reviewer felt that Cooke fell into a Scotch accent "on the most solemn occasions" in Richard. As an example he mentions that Cooke, when about to engage Richmond in single combat, pronounced the words "My soul and body on't" in the tone of Gibby in *The Wonder* and "a roar of laughter rang from all parts of the house."

40. A clipping in the V & A, dated 15 October 1804, indicates that by this date Cooke had done some study and had brought Act V up to the level of the rest of the play and "so kept up the point of excellence to the end." It was at approximately this time that he "judiciously introduced some lines from Shakespeare's text, extremely opposite to the patriotic sensations of the present moment." These were lines in the address to the army:

> Let's whip these stragglers o'er the seas again;
> Lash hence these overweening rags of France,
> These famish'd beggers, weary of their lives,
> If we be conquer'd, let men conquer us,
> And not those bastard Bretons, whom our fathers
> Have in their own land beaten, spurn'd, trod on,
> And left on record as the heirs of shame!
> Are those men fit to be the heirs of England?

According to the 1800 promptbook, which was used at least through 1805, the lines came immediately after "To desperate ventures, and assur'd destruction." It is not clear in the promptbook when the lines were first added.

41. James Boaden found much to dislike in this section of Cooke's performance. Being opposite to other viewpoints, Boaden is quoted here:

When, in the 7th scene of the 5th act, the heroic mind of Richard is hurrying on to the grand point, the *charging* of the ENEMY, the following passage occurs, in which two of his *admired* varieties were to be found.

> (Catesby hastily enters, having been dispatched by
> Richard to Lord Stanley)
> K. Ric. What says Lord Stanley? will he bring his power?
> Cate. He does refuse, my lord; he will not stir.
> Ric. Off with his son George's head. [Distant march]
> Norf. My lord, the foe's already past the marsh:
>   After the battle let young Stanley die.

> Ric. Why, after be it then—
> A thousand hearts are swelling in my bosom:
> Draw archers, draw your arrows to the head:
> Spur your proud horses hard, and ride in blood.

At this juncture, his decision as to young George Stanley is a thing of the instant; either his life or death are of little moment; they are as grains of sand whirled from a chariot-wheel in rapid rotation. Mr. Cooke fastened upon this precise point of time to affect *deliberation*, and stood, ... swaying his body backwards and forwards, till he settled the fate of young George, and relieved the almost agonized spectators, by "after be it then." The very next line, the reader sees, makes it impossible that Richard could have been deliberating about a thing so trifling:—"A thousand hearts are...." If Cooke did say "*my* bosom" (I think he did [Boaden is correct],) he was wrong again. Richard does not mean to indulge his *vanity* by an insult to OTHER NATURES: he hoped, perhaps believed, his followers to be as brave as himself. He merely expresses the expanding energy and thick palpitation of the heart, by words that mean, "I feel as if I had a *thousand* hearts within me."

Boaden simply dismisses the archer/cavalry business by saying Cooke should have referred to Shakespeare and the lines:
> Fight, gentlemen of England! fight, bold yeomen!
> Draw, archers, draw your arrows to the head!
> Spur your proud horses hard, and ride in blood.
> Amaze the welkin with your broken staves.

to realize that Richard addressed three parts of his army. Of course, Cooke was speaking Cibber and thus Boaden's attack is not altogether fair (2:280–283).

42. *London Times*, 1 November 1800.

43. Charles Durang, "The Philadelphia Stage from the Year 1749 to the Year 1855," *The Philadelphia Sunday Dispatch* (1854–1860). 44:88.

44. Unidentified clipping, V & A.

CHAPTER 9

1. Add MS Egerton 2299, BM. Subsequent financial data for Cooke's first season are taken from this source.

2. Thomas Dibdin, *The Reminiscences of Thomas Dibdin*, 1:281–285.

3. *Merchant of Venice* promptbook (Merch, 35), Folger Shakespeare Library. No. 45 in Charles H. Shattuck, *The Shakespeare Promptbooks*, p. 284. The book belonged to J. B. Roberts (circa 1860–1900) and contains references to a number of actors in addition to Cooke.

4. *MM*, 10 (November 1800), 321–322. Cooke's supporting cast included Alexander Pope—Bassanio; Knight—Gratiano; Munden—Launcelot; Thompson—Tubal; Miss Murray—Portia; Miss Dixon—Jessica; Murray—Antonio.

5. *London Times*, 25 November 1800; *True Briton*, 25 November 1800.

6. See *MM*, 10 (September 1800), 187.

7. See William W. Appleton, *Charles Macklin*, pp. 117–122.

8. William Cooke, *Memoirs of Charles Macklin, Comedian*, p. 273.

9. James E. Murdoch, *The Stage*, p. 80.

10. *The Dramatic Censor*, 3 (December 1800), 269; see also *Le Beau Monde; or, Literary and Fashionable Magazine* (May 1808), pp. 8–10.

11. William Robson, *The Old Play-Goer*, pp. 59–60.

12. Playbill, HTC.

13. Cooke disliked playing more than twice a week. He later recalled that "at three I grumbled; four I would not do. I complained to Mr. Harris of playing four nights a week: I said, 'it's too much, sir.' 'Why, yes,' says he, 'it's almost as much as playing six nights in the country at race-week.' There he had me. 'But consider, Sir, what I get at the race-week.' 'I do, and I consider that

what you get there comes to you from here; if you had not played here, you would have got nothing there!' " (*LC*, 2:332-333; *DD*, 2:448).

14. See Charles Beecher Hogan, *Shakespeare in the Theatre*, 2:516.
15. See *MM*, 11 (November 1802), 291-294.
16. Thomas S. Munden, *Memoirs of Joseph Shepherd Munden, Comedian*, pp. 38-39.
17. *Othello* promptbook (TS 2493.50), HTC. No. 6 (p. 355) in Shattuck. West issue of Kemble edition, Boston, 1807. Promptbook of the Park Theatre when Cooke played Iago to Cooper's Othello. Very little of Cooke's business is indicated—mostly cuts, calls, cues for effects, and a note on the use of supers.
18. *LC*, 2:397-398.
19. *The Dramatic Censor*, 3 (December 1800), 267.
20. *LC*, 2:405.
21. See Alan S. Downer, ed., *King Richard III: Edmund Kean's Performance as Recorded by James H. Hackett* (London, 1959).
22. Dutton, *The Dramatic Censor*, p. 267, also mentions that "his arms always move in a semicircular direction—his look always fixes on the ground—and he treads the stage to the same measure, and the same distance." This is what a number of reviewers may mean when they speak of his lack of "dignity of deportment" and "grace." See Chapter 44: 89.
23. Charles Durang, "The Philadelphia Stage from the Year 1749 to the Year 1855," *The Philadelphia Sunday Dispatch* (1854-1860). Chapter 44: 89.
24. See Dennis Bartholomeusz, *Macbeth and the Players*, pp. 142-143.
25. *LC*, 2:403-404.
26. William Hazlitt, *The Complete Works of William Hazlitt*, P. P. Howe, ed., 8:207; Bartholomeusz, p. 143.
27. *Macbeth* promptbook (*NCP. 285342), NYPL. No. 12, p. 238, in Shattuck. Inchbald edition; marked in Cooke's hand only for the title role; apparently prepared for his American tour. A number code is used for major crosses and movement. It is of little help in interpretation of the role. Unlike his *Richard* promptbook, it does not contain underlining for emphasis or indication of pauses, and the like. Cooke's major addition is in Act I, Scene 7, the "If it were done" soliloquy. After "the deep damnation of his taking-off," Cooke has added the lines beginning with "—and pity, like a naked, new born babe striding the blast," to the end of the original soliloquy.
28. See Mary E. Knapp, *Prologues and Epilogues of the Eighteenth Century*, pp. 5-6.
29. *Morning Chronicle*, 15 January 1801.
30. *MM*, 10 (December 1800), 401.
31. *The Dramatic Censor*, 4 (January 1801), 23-25.
32. The only event of note in Cooke's performances up to his benefit was the introduction of a new but temporary Othello on 20 December, "a Medical Gentleman of respectable connections and considerable literary talents" [a Mr. Moisey]. *London Times*, 22 December 1800; *MM*, 11 (January 1801), 55.
33. See St. Vincent Troubridge, *The Benefit System in the British Theatre*, p. 37.
34. On benefit bill, Playbills 88, BM. A number of sources, e.g., *Dictionary of National Biography*, s.v. Cooke, incorrectly say £136. The charges had only recently been increased from £140 to £160. See *MM*, 8 (August 1799).
35. *LC*, 1:179; Add MS Egerton 2299. Cooke did not realize it was a free benefit until after the curtain fell (*True Briton*, circa 28 January 1801, HTC).
36. *Morning Post*, 28 January 1801; *MM*, 11 (February 1801), 126-127.
37. *Bath Chronicle*, 15 October 1801.
38. See Herschel Baker, *John Philip Kemble*, pp. 230-231.
39. Allardyce Nicoll, *A History of English Drama*, 3:220.
40. Dutton says Mrs. Pope was rejected for the role and in retaliation, Alexander Pope refused the role of Steinfort which was then taken by H. Johnston (*The Dramatic Censor*, 4 [February 1801], 64).

41. Ibid., 57–64.
42. Ibid., 4 (March 1801), 85–88.
43. Unidentified clipping, HTC, dated circa September 1803.
44. Christian August Gottlieb Goede, *England, Wales, Ireland, und Schottland, Erinnerungen an Natur und Kunst aus einer Reise in der Jahren 1802 und 1803*, 2d ed., 5 vols. (Dresden, 1806); English version, *The Stranger in England*, 3:255–258. See John Alexander Kelly, *German Visitors to English Theaters in the Eighteenth Century*, p. 162.
45. Kelly, p. 52.
46. Goede, *The Stranger in England*, 3:255–258. This was certainly not a universal opinion. George Ticknor, who had seen Cooke numerous times in Boston as a young man, wrote in a letter from Paris, 11 April 1817: "Cooke had a more vehement and lofty genius, and Kean has sometimes, perhaps, flashes of eccentric talent; but in an equal elevation of mind, and in dignity and force, Talma, I think, left them all far behind" (*Life, Letters and Journals of George Ticknor*, 1:127).
47. *The Farington Diary by Joseph Farington, R.A.*, James Greig, ed., 1:342.
48. Robson, pp. 57–58.
49. *The Theatrical Recorder*, 1 (1805), 274.
50. See James Boaden, *Memoirs of the Life of John Philip Kemble*, 2:283–285.
51. *LC*, 1:181.
52. His salary for a number of weeks, because of the diminution of performance nights, was reduced from £6 to £4, according to the account books, whereas the rumor circulating at the beginning of February was that his salary had been advanced to £12 (*Morning Chronicle*, 6 February 1801).
53. *LC*, 2:269.
54. See *MM*, 11 (April 1801), 271–272.
55. See Robert Hamilton Ball, *The Amazing Career of Sir Giles Overreach*, pp. 44–58.
56. *Morning Chronicle*, 9 April 1801.
57. John Genest, *Some Account of the English Stage*, 7:515.
58. *The Dramatic Censor*, 4 (April 1801), 147.
59. J. Gibson Lockhard, *Memoirs of the Life of Sir Walter Scott, Bart.*, p. 235.
60. Unidentified clipping, HTC, probably early 1801 season.
61. See Appendix B for receipts.
62. *LC*, 1:190–191.
63. George O. Willard, *History of the Providence Stage*, p. 64. This story was reported by a journalist, S. S. Southworth.
64. 28 March, 8, 15, 20 April, and 7 May.
65. Unidentified clipping, V & A. Accounts show that the receipts were only £200, but still well above non-Cooke appearances in June.
66. 23 of Richard; 10 each of Shylock, Iago, and Kitely; 7 of Macbeth; 5 of Sir Giles; and 2 of the Stranger. On five occasions he had coupled Sir Archy with Shylock.
67. Note on Playbills 88, BM.
68. Boaden, 2:297, does record the same incident, possibly using the *Hibernian* account as his authority. He dates the event, however, 11 May, clearly confusing this with the first major incident of Cooke's misbehavior on 11 May 1802. See Chapter 10.
69. Dibdin, 1:286–289.
70. See Conrad Gill, *History of Birmingham*, 1:126–128.
71. See Alan S. Downer, *The Eminent Tragedian William Charles Macready*, pp. 5–14.
72. Thomas Gilliland, *The Dramatic Mirror*, 1:206.
73. Gilliland says August 1792, but John E. Cunningham, *Theatre Royal: The History of the Theatre Royal Birmingham*, pp. 22–24, says January. The latter source is my principal authority on the Birmingham theatre.
74. Broadside, 111785.k.31 (22), BM.

75. Downer, *Macready*, p. 8.
76. *LC*, 1:190.
77. 17–19, 22–26, 29 June. Dates confirmed by playbills and newspapers in Birmingham Public Library.
78. *LC*, 1:190.
79. *MM*, 12 (July 1801), 56.
80. The Theatre Royal held about 630; when it opened in 1769, prices were pit and boxes 3s., gallery 2s., and upper gallery 1s., or about £40 in all. See James C. Dibdin, *The Annals of the Edinburgh Stage*, pp. 152, 181–188.
81. Ibid., p. 241.
82. *MM*, 8 (August 1799), 120; Walter Baynham, *The Glasgow Stage*, p. 31.
83. *MM*, 12 (August 1801), 199.
84. *MM*, 12 (July 1801), 59.
85. *The Thespian Dictionary; or, Dramatic Biography of the Eighteenth Century*, p. 2 of Addenda et Corrigenda.
86. Letter, Cooke to Felix Daly, 17 November 1800, Dreer Collection, Pennsylvania Historical Society.
87. John Bernard, *Retrospections of America*, p. 373.
88. Elizabeth Armstrong, "The Edinburgh Stage, 1715–1820" (Thesis, University of Edinburgh, 1969), p. 14, includes a list of Cooke's appearances in Edinburgh. For this engagement she lists only thirteen performances, although my sources disagree (e.g., she mentions no appearances in *Richard III*).
89. *Caledonian Mercury*, 15 June 1801.
90. *MM*, 12 (September 1801), 201.
91. Cooke, *LC*, 1:192, says Woods played on both nights. Advertisements seem to indicate otherwise.
92. *MM*, 12 (September 1801), 201–205.
93. Ibid., 203–204; see also Munden, p. 97.
94. *Caledonian Mercury*, 13 July 1801, gives Cooke's address as Mowat's Lodgings, No. 13 Terrace.
95. *MM*, 12 (August 1801), 140–142.
96. R. J. Broadbent, *Annals of the Liverpool Stage*, p. 110.
97. *LC*, 1:193.
98. Playbills 228, BM; the benefit receipts are written on the back of the bill; Cooke's address is given as No. 17, Tarleron Street.
99. *MM*, 12 (August 1801), 137.
100. *LC*, 1:193, incorrectly says Ward and Banks.
101. H & P, p. 159.
102. *MM*, 12 (September 1801), 201–203.
103. This was not Cooke's first appearance as Mercutio. Nonetheless, Cooke related the following to Dunlap apropos to the performance: "Pope came to him and told him he was at a loss what play to take for his benefit, as he wished one that had not been performed of late, and in which he and Mrs Pope and Cooke could all play. Mr. Pope's choice was fixed on Romeo and Juliet, provided Cooke would play Mercutio. Cooke laughed at the idea, from his general unfitness, and added, 'besides which, I know nothing of the part.' These trifling objections were overruled, and Cooke yielded to the plea that his name would strengthen the bill" (*LC*, 1:194).
104. *MM*, op. cit.
105. *Newcastle Chronicle*, 5 September 1801.
106. Ibid.
107. *Chronicle*, 12 September 1801.
108. *Chronicle*, 19 September 1801.
109. *DD*, 2:446.

110. *LC*, 1:194–195.

CHAPTER 10

1. Letter, Ward to Cooke, 3 November 1800, in *LC*, 1:169–170.
2. See Highfill, et al., *A Biographical Dictionary*, 2:122–129, and *MM*, 11 (May 1804), 337.
3. In late November, Kemble finally gave up Richard, after audiences began falling off at both houses. *The Theatrical Repertory*, 12 (7 December 1801), 177, went so far as to say the audiences were feeling "disgust and disatisfaction" over the repetition of Richard by both actors. Covent Garden Account Books, Add MS Egerton 3200, BM, indicate that the 19 October performance had receipts of £375.36; 26 October £420.5.6; 16 November, £316.7.6; 30 November, £202.16.6. After Kemble relinquished the role, receipts rose: 7 December, £313.12.6; 13 December, £308.15; 19 April, £315.16.6.
4. Covent Garden Playbills 88, BM.
5. *The Theatrical Repertory; or Weekly Rosciad*, 1, No. 1 (19 September 1801), 11.
6. Unidentified article, HTC.
7. James Boaden, *Memoirs of the Life of John Philip Kemble*, 2:299–300.
8. Quoted in the *Theatrical Repertory*, 1, No. 2 (26 September 1801), 31.
9. *LC*, 1:200–201.
10. Cooke quoted by Dunlap, *LC*, 1:202.
11. Ibid., 202–203, and *Theatrical Repertory*, 1, No. 6 (24 October 1801), 81–82.
12. *Morning Chronicle*, 20 October 1801. See also *Theatrical Repertory*, 1, No. 6 (24 October 1801), 81.
13. *MM*, 12 (October 1801), 278–279.
14. 22 October 1801.
15. *Theatrical Repertory*, 1, No. 7 (31 October 1801), 102.
16. *MM*, 12 (December 1801), 422.
17. Leigh Hunt, *Dramatic Essays by Leigh Hunt*, William Archer and Robert W. Lowe, eds., p. 105.
18. *MM*, 12 (December 1801), 422–423.
19. *LC*, 1:206.
20. Kathleen Barker, *The Theatre Royal Bristol, 1766–1966*, p. 46.
21. He was originally announced as Shylock and Sir Archy, but the appearance may have been canceled because of illness.
22. See Guy Tracey Watts, *Theatrical Bristol*, p. 83; Barker, pp. 14, 38; Belville S. Penley, *The Bath Stage*, p. 35.
23. Both the Bath and Bristol theatres represent the best examples of Georgian town theatres and have received extensive coverage elsewhere, so that none needs to be given here. In addition, the 1766 Bristol structure, although altered, still stands. See Barker, *Theatre Royal Bristol* and *The Story of the Theatre Royal Bristol* (Bristol, 1971); Richard Southern, *The Georgian Playhouse*, pp. 28–42; Richard Jenkins, *Memoirs of the Bristol Stage* (Bristol, 1826); M. E. Board, *The Story of the Bristol Stage, 1490–1925* (London, 1926); Penley and Watts.
24. Bath playbill, HTC; see *MM*, n.s. 3 (April 1808), 283–286.
25. John Genest, *Some Account of the English Stage*, 7:563; Barker, *Theatre Royal Bristol*, p. 67.
26. Although a strongly biased biography, see George Raymond, *Memoirs of Robert William Elliston*.
27. Appearances and dates in Bath have been checked with playbills and newspapers (*Bath Journal* and *Herald*), and confirmed by Professor Arnold Hare's research, loaned to the author.
28. *LC*, 2:206.
29. MS, *Recollections of 'O' Smith*, Shevelove Collection.

30. Note written on back of playbill (88), BM.
31. *Theatrical Repertory*, 1, No. 15 (28 December 1801), 244.
32. *MM*, 13 (February 1802), 134.
33. Notes from 1798 diary quoted in *LC*, 1:211–212.
34. *MM*, 13 (February 1802), 134.
35. See ibid., p. 135; *London Chronicle*, 7–9 January 1802.
36. *Theatrical Repertory*, 1, No. 17 (11 January 1802), 273–276.
37. *LC*, 1:212.
38. *The Mirror of Taste and The Dramatic Censor*, 4 (August 1811), 113–141. A thirty-one-page discussion of Colman's and Tate's adaptations precedes the comments on Cooke.
39. There are two extant promptbooks of Cooke's King Lear. I have examined his 1811 book used at the Park Theatre, New York, at the HTC (TS.2355.65), No. 14, p. 208, in Charles H. Shattuck, *The Shakespeare Promptbooks*. It is of little use. A second promptbook, dated 21 May 1807, NO. 10, p. 208, in Shattuck, is at the University of Michigan (PR.2819.A22.K32). I have not been able to examine this book.
40. Allardyce Nicoll, *A History of English Drama*, 4:163.
41. Its highest receipts were £325 on 25 January (Add MS Egerton 3200, BM).
42. *LC*, 1:213.
43. Ibid., 254–255.
44. The *Morning Chronicle*, 23 September 1802, says the entire production was hurt with Lewis as Hal, appearing as "an old buffoon, who, instead of gaining the affection and calling forth the numerous powers of the renowned knight, seemed only fit to dance on a Merry Andrew's stage, or to act *Touchstone* in Bartholomew Fair."
45. Dunlap quotes the same figure; Add MS Egerton 3200, BM, says £409.6.6.
46. *LC*, 1:214.
47. *MM*, 22 (October 1806), 274.
48. *The Mirror of Taste*, 2 (November 1810), 377.
49. *Morning Post*, 18 January 1802.
50. *London Chronicle*, 23–25 February 1802.
51. Henry Crabb Robinson, *Diary, Reminiscences, and Correspondence of Henry Crabb Robinson*, Thomas Sadler, ed., 1:199.
52. A fourteen-page partbook for Cooke's Falstaff in *Merry Wives* is at the Folger (MW, 32), No. 7, p. 304, in Shattuck. It is dated 27 April 1802 and is endorsed on the front from "Boulton Street, (4) Piccadilly, Tuesday, Half past Eleven at Night."
53. *LC*, 1:242; Genest, 7:564. A performance of *Richard III* at Covent Garden is listed in the account books for 6 April, with a notation that Cooke paid back cash advanced him on 15 December last. If Cooke indeed performed in Bath, it is possible that Genest's date is incorrect. Since Bath was normally closed on Mondays, the correct date may be 7 April. He may not have appeared at Bristol at all, although I have yet to confirm this.
54. Thomas Dibdin, *The Reminiscences of Thomas Dibdin*, 1:285–286.
55. First production at Crow Street, Dublin, in July 1764, as *The True-Born Scotsman*.
56. Letter from Macklin, 1779, quoted by William W. Appleton, *Charles Macklin, An Actor's Life*, p. 212.
57. The account of this controversy is well known and is related in several sources. See Appleton, *Charles Macklin*, pp. 210–216; William Cooke, *Memoirs of Charles Macklin*; J. T. Kirkman, *Memoirs of the Life of Charles Macklin, Esq.*; F. A. Congreve, *Authentic Memoirs of the Late Mr. Charles Macklin, Comedian*; Robert R. Findlay, "The Comic Plays of Charles Macklin: Dark Satire at Mid-Eighteenth Century," *Educational Theatre Journal*, 20, No. 3 (October 1968), 398–407.
58. Charles Macklin, *The Man of the World*, pp. 4–5.
59. *LC*, 1:266–267.
60. Clement Scott, *The Drama of Yesterday and Today*, 1:208.

61. John Bernard, *Retrospections of America*, pp. 369–370. G. S. Bibby studied Sir Pertinax from Cooke's own promptbook. It was given to him by Cooke's widow in New York. Bibby gave it to James H. Hackett in 1829. It is now in the V & A, London, (GE.5122, Pr.1810), and consists largely of cuts and additions interleaved into the 1810 Edinburgh edition of the play. Although on his deathbed Cooke had hoped that it go to J. P. Kemble, this request was apparently never carried out (see *LC*, 2:382). *DD*, 2:462, incorrectly says that "Mrs. Cooke has sent the marked book of The Man of the World to Mr. Kemble."

62. William Hazlitt, *The Complete Works of William Hazlitt*, P. P. Howe, ed., 5:299.

63. Actors attempting the role would suffer in comparison with Cooke. In 1811, while Cooke was in the United States, a Mr. Grant tried Sir Pertinax in London and the comments in *The Satirist*, 10 (1 January 1812), 50–51 are typical:

We must confess that the strong impression made on us by the performance of Mr. Cooke, made rather against this actor, as we were the more on the alert to watch his every action, and the more likely promptly to detect his failings, which we expected would be numerous. We were, however, very agreeably disappointed; the style in which Mr. Grant sustained the part, may certainly be challenged as an imitation of Cooke, but though we are not very prone to lift up our voices in favour of imitation, we have no hesitation in saying, that in no other style ought it ever be played. . . . His performance was unquestionably inferior to that of Cooke, but still it will easily be conceived, it might be a very meritorious piece of acting.

Grant was received with admiration but failed to obtain a regular engagement in London. In evaluating Grant, *The Dramatic Censor* (February 1811), p. 467, wrote that "To be brief, this comedy is, without the aid of Mr. Cooke, like the firmament without a sun!" Edmund Kean failed in the role because he was unable to master the Scottish dialect. The only subsequent actor to succeed in the part was Samuel Phelps, who in 1850 first played Sir Pertinax and continued to do so until the end of his career. See Shirley S. Allen, *Samuel Phelps and the Sadler's Wells Theatre*, pp. 267–269. Of course, by the time Phelps found a vehicle in Sir Pertinax, the memory of Cooke was fading or had vanished.

64. *A Scotsman's Remarks on the Farce of Love-a-la-Mode*, p. 11.

65. Thomas S. Munden, *Memoirs of Joseph Shepherd Munden, Comedian*, p. 89.

66. Leigh Hunt, *Dramatic Essays by Leigh Hunt*, William Archer and Robert W. Lowe, eds., pp. 105–106.

67. *London Chronicle*, 5–7 October 1802. See *MM*, 13 (May 1802), 357. The initial cast included: Lord Lumbercourt—John Waddy; Sidney—Charles Murray; Counsellor Plausible—Beverly; Serj. Eitherside—George Davenport; Melville—John Whitfield; Tomlins—T. Abbott; John—William Atkins; Sam—Truman; David Egerton—William Lewis (replaced by H. Siddons the next season); Betty Hint—Mrs. Mattocks; Constantia—Miss Murray; Lady MacSycophant—Miss Leserve; Nanny—Miss Martha Norton; Lady Randolpha Lumbercourt—Mrs. Glover.

68. *Boston Independent Chronicle*, 24 January 1811.

69. *The Mirror of Taste*, 3 (April 1811), 245–254; see also *The Port Folio*, 3 (July 1811), 86–87.

70. William B. Wood, *Personal Recollections of the Stage*, pp. 161–162.

71. In Cooke's promptbook, see n. 61 above, he has made several changes in the text, not only to update a few topical allusions, but also to stress the title, adding two prominent "Man of the World's" into the dialogue and changing several lines to emphasize the word "booing" (bowing), the excellence of Cooke's delivery of which is repeatedly mentioned by reviewers. In Act III, for example, he changes "I never could stand straight in the presence of a great man, but always bowed, and bowed, and bowed . . . as it were by instinct," to "I never in aw my life could stand . . . but I was always booing and booing and booing."

72. Charles Durang, "The Philadelphia Stage from the Year 1749 to the Year 1855," *The Philadelphia Sunday Dispatch* (1854–1860), Chapter 44: 92.
73. 21 and 24 April; 5, 10, and 24 May; 14 June.
74. *MM*, 13 (May 1802), 258.
76. Playbills 88, BM. Arnold Hare, "George Frederick Cooke: The Actor and the Man," p. 133, in *The Eighteenth-Century English Stage*, Kenneth Richard and Peter Thomson, eds., incorrectly says 11 April.
77. Receipts written on playbill (88), BM.
78. *MM*, op. cit.
79. *London Chronicle*, 25–27 May 1802.
80. *The Drama; or, The Theatrical Pocket Magazine*, 2 (February 1822), 163.
81. Aline Mackenzie Taylor, *Next to Shakespeare: Otway's 'Venice Preserv'd' and 'The Orphan'*, pp. 204–207.
82. *Morning Post*, 18 November 1803.
83. *MM*, 13 (June 1802), 421.
84. *LC*, 1:244; Penley, p. 88; *Bath Journal*, 7 June 1802.
85. *MM*, 13 (June 1802), 422. Confirmed by account books, Add MS Egerton 3200, BM.
86. Cooke's season, in addition to these roles, breaks down as: Richard III—12; Shylock—4; Iago—2; Macbeth—2; Orsino—10; Zanga—2; Falstaff—5; Falstaff in *Merry Wives*—1; Sir Pertinax—7; Don Estivan—3. The following, one each: the Stranger, Sir Giles, Stukely, Jaques, Lear, Edward Mortimer, Pierre, Bajazet, Captain Faulkner, Philip Blandford, and Garrick's Ode. Genest, vol. 7, agrees with this count, except for eight performances listed for Sir Pertinax, and is apparently unaware of Don Estivan and Captain Faulkner.
87. *MM*, 14 (July 1802), 62–64; *Chester Chronicle*, 25 June 1802.
88. *Chester Chronicle*, 2 and 9 July 1802. Cooke was supported in Chester by Faulkner, Carr, Hollingsworth, Penson, Bobadil, Bengough, Gordon, Ward and Mesdames Tayleure, Faulkner, Ward, and Bellamy.
89. *LC*, 1:245.
90. Playbill, HTC.
91. *MM*, 14 (August 1802), 136.
92. *LC*, 1:245–256.
93. Theatre Royal, Margate, opened 27 June 1787 and held some 700.
94. Malcolm Morley, *Margate and Its Theatre*, pp. 42–43; *MM*, 14 (September 1802), 208. Morley incorrectly says Othello was to be Cooke's initial role.
95. *LC*, 1:246–247.
96. Ibid., 248. Dunlap says he performed four nights at Dock which I have been unable to confirm. At Plymouth he was scheduled to appear as Richard, Macbeth, Shylock, Sir Giles, and Sir Archy. Dunlap records eight nights at Plymouth, but the bills indicate only seven.
97. Boxes were raised from 3s. to 4s.; pit from 2s. to 2s.6d.
98. Unidentified handwritten account, HTC.
99. The Plymouth company according to a letter in *MM*, 14 (November 1802), 352–353, included Hague, Lovegrove, Mills, Mathews, Freeman, Smith, Gore, Westernly, Grant; Mesdames Forbes, Gore, Westernly, Mills; and Misses Hague, Grant, and Hooper.
100. *LC*, 1:248. This Richard, according to Cooke, was his sixty-fourth since leaving Dublin.
101. Playbills 203, BM, and *LC*, 1:250–269.
102. *Morning Post*, 16 September 1802; Add MS Egerton 2301, BM.
103. Cooke's salary was now just below that of Lewis and above that of Incledon, Munden, and Fawcett.
104. *LC*, 1:272–273.
105. Ibid., 286.
106. Frederick Reynolds, *Life and Times of Frederick Reynolds*, 2:322.

107. *Morning Post*, 28 September 1802.
108. *The Courier*, 28 September, 1802.
109. Boaden, 2:327-328.
110. In *Hamlet* Cooke was supported by Cory as the Ghost (first time), Munden (Polonius), Waddy (Claudius), Brunton (Horatio), Claremont (Laertes), Miss Chapman (Gertrude), and Miss Reeve, daughter of the composer, making her first appearance as Ophelia.
111. *London Chronicle*, 19-21 October 1801.
112. *MM*, 14 (October 1802), 274-276; unidentified clipping attached to playbill for 2 October (Shylock), V & A. *Othello* on 21 October featured a Mr. Braine of the Navy Office, making his first appearance on any stage; he was criticized for his lisp and lack of dignity, and was advised to choose another role. He is listed in the bill as "a gentleman."
113. Dibdin, 2:379.
114. *Morning Herald*, n.d., HTC; *MM*, 15 (January 1803), 56.
115. Carles returned to the provinces and was finally acquired by Drury Lane in 1806 as a replacement for Holland. See *MM*, 15 (February 1803), 128; 22 (October 1806), 276.
116. *Morning Post*, 15 January 1803; Add MS Egerton 2301, BM.
117. *LC*, 1:290.
118. Ibid., 375; *DD*, 2:425-426.
119. The success of *John Bull* brought Colman £1,200. See Nicoll, 4:52. The accounts show £300 paid to him this season.
120. *LC*, 2:277-278.
121. Genest, 7:581 records forty-eight nights of *John Bull*, but I can only account for forty-five from bills and accounts. See *Morning Post*, 7 March 1803, and *MM*, 15 (March 1803), 190.
122. *Morning Chronicle*, 18 March 1803.
123. Unidentified clipping, HTC.
124. Dunlap, *LC*, 1:318-320, incorrectly identifies this event and refers to a performance of Sir Archy, a role in which Cooke did not appear during either April or May. Evidently, Dunlap has fabricated a string of stories out of the *John Bull* incident and *The Harper's Daughter*.
125. Clipping attached to playbill, V & A; undated articles from *True Briton, Morning Chronicle, Times*, HTC.
126. Genest, 7:585-586. See George C. Branam, *Eighteenth-Century Adaptations of Shakespearean Tragedy*, pp. 2, 16, 18-19, 33-34, 140, on other alterations by Valpy.
127. Unidentified clipping, HTC, possibly *European Magazine*, June 1803. See also *LC*, 1:320-321.
128. Dunlap, *LC*, 1:321, incorrectly says 3 June.
129. *MM*, 15 (May 1803), 347-348.
130. Joseph Ireland, *A Memoir of the Professional Life of Thomas Abthorpe Cooper*, p. 25.
131. *LC*, 1:298-303.
132. See *LC*, 1:303-318.
133. Dunlap's version of this story is much more involved. He has Cooke forgetting his errand with Harris, pleading for more money instead, and then, in a drunken stupor, remembering Cooper left on the common. He also chooses *Love-a-la-Mode* for the performance he almost misses and reports that he failed to finish the second act. Another version of the story is even more fanciful: Cooper was left out in a snowstorm for hours, half frozen; Harris, upon reminding Cooke he was scheduled to play Richard III, was answered by Cooke—"Do you know who I am, Sir? Am I not George Frederick Cooke?—without whose talents you would be confined to your own grease-tub; and who will never more darken your inhospitable doors while he lives, or uphold your contemptible theatre any longer after this night!" (Unidentified article, HTC; see also Anne Mathews, *Anecdotes of Actors*, pp. 86-92.) The play, if this happened at all, was *John Bull*. This story illustrates the great problem in accepting most Cooke anecdotes as actual fact. More often than not, they are told in such an exaggerated fashion as to be almost certain fabrications. Of course, anec-

Notes

dotes in general are always in question, but the very nature of Cooke's peculiarities and habits must have given rise to even more exaggerated stories than the norm.

134. Munden, p. 104.

135. Cooke's score for 1802–1803 was Peregrine, 33 appearances; Sir Pertinax, 22; Sir Archy, 5; Iago, 4; Richard and Falstaff in *Merry Wives*, 3 each; Macbeth, Orsino, Hamlet, Cato, King John, 2 each; and the remainder 1 each—Shylock, Sir Giles, Zanga, Falstaff in *Henry IV, Part 1*, Pierre, Bajazet, Sir Philip Blandford, and Comus.

CHAPTER 11

1. *LC*, 1:323–324.
2. See H & P, pp. 161–162.
3. *A Letter to Ward With Critical Review on the Conduct of the Managers with Observations on Some of the Performers at the Theatre Royal* (Manchester, 1803), n.p.
4. Playbills 252, BM. According to the bill, a Miss Daniels performed the Duke of York. This was probably not his former wife, who played that summer in Market-Harborough (Playbills 294) and Melton, Mowbray, in June (Playbills 294). In the former bills, a Miss H. Daniels is also listed in younger roles. This may be the same Daniels who played at Manchester with Cooke. Alicia Daniels was certainly too old in 1803 for the Duke of York.
5. Even company members were involved in the controversies. J. F. White accused the management of forcing him into serious roles for which he was panned, including one in Cooke's *Cato*. See J. F. White, *An Appeal to the Public at Large, of the Town of Manchester, but Chiefly Addressed to the Violent Opposers of J. F. White Comedian*.
6. *MM*, 16 (August 1803), 131–132.
7. *MM*, 16 (July 1803), 60.
8. Playbills 248, BM.
9. *The Derby Mercury*, 25 August 1803.
10. *LC*, 1:327.
11. *MM*, 16 (August 1803), 131; Herschel Baker, *John Philip Kemble*, p. 275.
12. *MM*, 16 (September 1803), 204.
13. James Boaden, *Memoirs of the Life of John Philip Kemble*, 2:381–382.
14. Baker, p. 276.
15. See John Genest, *Some Account of the English Stage*, 7:610, and Anne Mathews, *Memoirs of Charles Mathews, Comedian*, 2:107–108.
16. *LC*, 1:386.
17. John Taylor, *Records of My Life*, pp. 132–133.
18. Thomas S. Munden, *Memoirs of Joseph Shepherd Munden, Comedian*, p. 108.
19. *MM*, 16 (September 1803), 204.
20. Playbill, HTC. Cooke possibly made one other brief trip this fall, to Brighton for the benefit of Mrs. Levendall in *The Man of the World* (unidentified manuscript, HTC).
21. Add MS Egerton 2302, BM, source for all receipts this season.
22. Unidentified clippings, HTC and V & A.
23. *MM*, 16 (October 1803), 278.
24. *Douglas*, by the first Scotsman to achieve success in drama, marked the coming of Romanticism to the English-speaking theatre. See Alice E. Gipson, *John Home: A Study of His Life and Works*, pp. 71–126.
25. Clipping attached to playbill, V & A.
26. James Boaden, *Memoirs of Mrs. Siddons*, 2:345.
27. Boaden, *Life of Kemble*, 2:383–384. It is actually doubtful that Cooke spoke at all, but the phrase "My old complaint" became almost his battle cry and is appropriate to mention here.
28. *LC*, 1:330; Munden, p. 108.

29. *Evening Post*, 18 October 1803.
30. *MM*, 16 (November 1803), 349.
31. *The Courier*, 21 October 1803.
32. Unidentified clipping, V & A.
33. *LC*, 2:333.
34. *MM*, 16 (November 1803), 350.
35. *Morning Post*, 18 November 1803.
36. *LC*, 2:349.
37. Reviews from handwritten copies in HTC; also *MM*, 16 (December 1803), 412–413.
38. *LC*, 1:331.
39. *MM*, 17 (February 1804); *Morning Post*, 10 January 1804.
40. Kemble Memoranda Book, vol. 3 (1801–1807). Add MSS 31, 972–975, BM.
41. *LC*, 1:333–338.
42. There was general agreement on this in the *Morning Chronicle, British Press, Morning Post, Times, Morning Herald,* and *MM*, 17 (February 1804), 131–132.
43. *Morning Chronicle*, 21 January 1804.
44. Munden, pp. 38–39.
45. *MM*, 17 (February 1804), 132–133.
46. *Morning Post*, 24 February 1804.
47. *LC*, 1:437.
48. Ibid., 340.
49. Unidentified clipping, HTC. In 1807, Cooke wrote that Inchbald's "flimsy pages and more flimsy remarks" would sink into oblivion. See *LC*, 2:22–23.
50. Add MS Egerton 2302, BM, indicates that receipts were only £207.18.6. The playbill for 26 April 1804 reveals Cooke's address this season to have been 34, Southampton Street, Covent Garden.
51. Four roles were predominant this season: Peregrine, 16 times; Iago, 6; Macduff, 8; Pierre, 6; and thirteen roles were performed only once each.
52. Add MS Egerton 2302 and Add MS 29,954, BM.
53. Baker, p. 277.
54. Boaden, *Life of Kemble*, 2:394.
55. Playbills, HTC, indicate that Cooke lodged at Colmore Row.
56. *MM*, 18 (July 1804), 61–62.
57. HTC, n.d.
58. Betty had been discovered by Atkins' prompter, Hough, who had resigned in September 1803 to accompany Betty on tour.
59. See Highfill, et al., *A Biographical Dictionary*, 1:165–166.
60. *LC*, 1:348. Information from Cooke's journal.
61. Peter Kavanagh, *The Irish Theatre*, p. 289; *Ireland Mirror; or, A Chronicle of the Times*, 1 (September 1804), 269.
62. *LC*, 1:348–349.
63. Unidentified clipping, 18 September 1804, V & A.
64. Unidentified clipping, HTC.
65. Figure from note on playbill, BM. The account books, Add MS Egerton 2303, say £312.8.6. *The Dramatic Censor . . . for the Year 1811*, p. 99, reported that, when full, Covent Garden receipts would total £600 or 3,044 people; the season's nightly receipts averaged about £300.
66. Figure from note on playbill, BM. Add MS Egerton 2303 says £363.16.
67. Unidentified clipping, HTC; *LC*, 1:350 only mentions these performances but gives no details.
68. In *DD*, 2:420, Cooke is reported as having called Brunton "a clever lad, but you won't say he's an actor; I love Jack, he's my friend but he's a dire dog." Brunton had joined Covent Garden in

1800 as a substitute for Holman. *MM*, 10 (October 1800), 244–248, agreed that he was a deficient actor who was rushed into too many large roles by the managers.

69. Add MS Egerton 2303, BM. Unless noted, all receipts for this season are from this source.

70. Unidentified review, HTC.

71. *MM*, n.s., 1 (February 1807), 144–145; reviews copied from the *Morning Chronicle, Morning Herald, Morning Post,* n.d., but circa 19 October 1804, HTC.

72. See Giles Playfair, *The Prodigy: The Strange Life of Master Betty*.

73. Letter to Kemble from Thomas Harris, Brighton, n.d. Album of Covent Garden letters, 1790–1821, chiefly from Harris Edward Barlow and Henry Harris. 1966/A 1137, British Theatre Museum.

74. See Baker, pp. 277–287.

75. Cited in Playfair, p. 68.

76. For reactions to Betty, see Baker, p. 280 ff.; Playfair, p. 69 ff. Reviews of his performances are of little true value because of the mania built up even prior to his appearance.

77. *LC*, 2:183, 239. Cooke met Payne on 21 November, five days after arriving in the United States. He was obviously taken by Payne and wrote to him the next day in a most polite manner, confirming an engagement to meet James Fennell at Payne's father's house. On 1 March 1811, Cooke performed King Lear for Payne's benefit at the Park Theatre. Cooke's letter to Payne is in the HTC.

78. Betty's first night at Drury Lane, 10 December, brought in £706.8.0. See *Oxberry's Dramatic Biography*, 3, No. 47, p. 268; receipts fell off at Covent Garden until 26 December and a production of *George Barnwell* (£389.8.0) and Cooke's Richard on 31 December brought in the next highest, £343.12.0. Add MS Egerton 2303, BM.

79. See Playfair bibliography, p. 181.

80. Quoted in Playfair, p. 45.

81. Receipts were £415. Add MS Egerton 2303, BM.

82. Quoted in Playfair, p. 132.

83. See Allardyce Nicoll, *A History of English Drama*, 4:185; *Ireland's Mirror*, 2 (April 1805), 184.

84. *Morning Chronicle*, 18 February 1805; *Times*, 18 February.

85. See Cecil F. Armstrong, *A Century of Great Actors*, p. 111.

86. The phrase "Richard's himself again" was often associated with Cooke after a drunken bout. The phrase comes from Cibber's line "Conscience, avaunt! Richard's himself again" in his version of *Richard III* (Act V, Scene 3).

87. Note on Covent Garden playbill 90, BM.

88. Unidentified clipping, HTC.

89. Playbills 90, BM. This was an extra night.

90. Kemble Memoranda Book, vol. 3, indicates it was £367.11.6. Add MSS 31, 972–975.

91. *LC*, 1:359–360.

92. Ibid., 360.

93. Cooke's performances during the 1804–1805 season were as follows: Lord Avondale, 20; Lavensforth, 16; Richard, 5; Glenalvon, 4 to 6; Sir Pertinax, 6; Sir Archy, 4; Falstaff, Mortimer, 2: Iago, Pizarro, Cohenberg, Ghost, Strictland, 1.

94. *Stage or Theatrical Touchstone* (July 20, 1805), p. 21.

95. *LC*, 1:364.

96. Playbill, HTC.

97. See Conrad Gill, *History of Birmingham*, 1:120.

98. Unidentified handwritten comments copied from reviews, HTC.

99. *LC*, 1:364.

100. *Stage or Theatrical Touchstone* (August 17, 1805), p. 100.

101. Playbills 274, BM.

102. Unidentified handwritten report, HTC; *MM*, 19 (August 1805), 136.

103. *LC*, 1:363–364, quotes Cooke's journal (1807?) on this summer, and Cooke mentions two or three nights at Stroud, which may actually refer to the Stourbridge engagement, and he says he was at Litchfield three nights. I have only been able to confirm the one night, however.

104. See E. Beresford Chancellor, *The Annals of Covent Garden and Its Neighborhood*, p. 122.

105. *Morning Post*, 9 October 1805.

106. Playbills 90, BM.

107. *LC*, 1:365. From 8 October, Cooke kept a sporadic journal through 1805–1807, which Dunlap reproduces, with editorial changes. One entry, 4 June 1806, is in the HTC.

108. Ibid., 370.

109. Ibid., 368.

110. See Stanley Thomas Williams, *Richard Cumberland, His Life and Dramatic Works*, p. 193.

111. *Morning Post*, 6 January 1806.

112. Add MS Egerton 2304, BM.

113. Baker, p. 285.

114. Cooke prepared a rehearsal copy of *Cymbeline* on the night of 22 January 1806. It contains little detail, however, and only indicates major exits and entrances and some business. It is at the Folger Shakespeare Library (Cymb, 12). Charles Shattuck, *The Shakespeare Promptbooks*, p. 82, lists it as No. 7 in his catalogue.

115. *LC*, 1:378.

116. *Morning Post*, 1 February 1806.

117. Playbills 90, BM.

118. Unidentified article, Stead Collection, NYPL.

119. Unidentified clipping, 15 March 1806, HTC.

120. *LC*, 1:378.

121. Penley, *The Bath Stage*, p. 95.

122. *Ireland's Mirror*, 2 (November 1805), 597–598.

123. Playbills 177, BM, and Stead Collection, NYPL.

124. *Recollections of "O" Smith*, MS, unpaginated. Shevelove Collection.

125. *LC*, 1:379.

126. Cooke is listed on the bills for 23 April in *The Gamester*.

127. Unidentified clipping, HTC.

128. *LC*, 1:379–384. See Appendix A for notes on other Cooke iconography.

129. Note on Playbills (90), BM.

130. Unidentified review, V & A.

131. Add MS Egerton 2304; Add MS 29,956, BM.

132. Leigh Hunt, *Dramatic Essays*, William Archer and Robert W. Lowe, eds., p. 139.

133. Cooke's scoreboard for the 1805–1806 season is as follows: Sir Pertinax, 6; Richard, Pizarro, 5; Iago, Glenalvon, Iachimo, 4; Sir Archy, Kitely, 3; Shylock, Stukely, Orsino, Peregrine, 2; the various Falstaffs, 1 each; Pierre, Sciolto, Lord Avondale, Dumont, and Lord Davenant, 1.

CHAPTER 12

1. Cooke Diary, MS Thr 20, HTC. See also *LC*, 1:384–386.

2. He was paying £3 per week; his salary was a maximum of £14.14 weekly. According to the Covent Garden ledger at the BM, his total salary that season was £347.14.

3. MS Thr 20, HTC; *LC*, 1:387–389.

4. *MM*, 21 (June 1806), 412 ff.

5. Robb Lawson, *The Story of the Scots Stage*, pp. 208–210.

6. Walter Baynham, *The Glasgow Stage*, p. 60.

7. *MM*, 22 (July 1806), 64; *LC*, 1:389.
8. *Dublin Evening Post*, 3 July 1806.
9. *Evening Post*, 12 July 1806.
10. Cooke was supported by Talbot as Richmond, Foote as Buckingham, and Grant as King Henry.
11. *Evening Post*, 29 July 1806.
12. *Evening Post*, 2 August 1806.
13. MS Thr 20, HTC; *LC*, 1:389.
14. The Harvard diary, not Dunlap, for 4 June, includes this remark.
15. Playbills 230, BM.
16. John Doran, *Their Majesties' Servants*, p. 383; Mrs. Anne Mathews, *Anecdotes of Actors*, pp. 98–99. A parallel story is told by Dunlap when Cooke was in America. Cooke took great delight in deflating pomposity, and on hearing a gentleman bragging about his ancestral links to the first settlers of Maryland, Cooke could not resist asking if he had preserved the family jewels. When quizzed as to his meaning, Cooke replied "the chains and handcuffs" (*LC*, 2:346). For a variant, see Mathews, *Anecdotes*, pp. 93–95.
17. *LC*, 1:390.
18. *The Thespian Review*, No. 2 (February 8, 1806), pp. 12–13. J. M. Benwell in *An Essay on the Danger of Unjust Criticism* (1806) defended Bengough, a five-year veteran at Manchester.
19. *The Thespian Review*, No. 4 (February 22, 1806), p. 26.
20. J. Roach, *Authentic Memoirs of the Green Room*, 2d ed., vol. 2, Pt. 4, 19–20.
21. Add MS Egerton 2305, BM.
22. *MM*, 22 (October 1806), 274. Receipts were £411.16., the second largest thus far that season. *Henry VIII* on 22 September with Kemble as Wolsey and Mrs. Siddons as Katherine had drawn £494.
23. *MM*, 22 (October 1806), 274.
24. Clipping dated 22 October, V & A.
25. Unidentified clipping, V & A.
26. Michael Kelly, *Reminiscences of Michael Kelly*, 2:236–239.
27. *LC*, 1:390–424.
28. Ibid., 1:414–415, 422.
29. Herschel Baker, *John Philip Kemble*, p. 288.
30. Clipping, HTC; *LC*, 1:428.
31. *LC*, 1:419.
32. Note on bill, Playbills 91, BM.
33. Add MS Egerton 2305, BM. The theatre playbill has £353 noted on it. His performances were all well attended that month: Strictland on the 10th (£367), Sir Pertinax on the 14th (£418), Iachimo on the 16th (£438), Major Oakly on the 17th (£357), Richard on the 23d (£408), and Kitely on the 28th (£330). All but Oakly from accounts (Add MS Egerton 2305); the remaining figure on theatre playbills (91).
34. See Arnold Hare, *The Georgian Theatre in Wessex*, p. 161.
35. *Bath Journal*, 25 May 1807.
36. Total performances from first London season to date, 509.
37. Seventh season scoreboard: Sir Pertinax, 10; Richard, 9; Altenburgh, 9; Shylock, Kitely, 4; Sir Archy, Iago, 3; Macbeth, Sir Giles, Lear, Falstaff (*Merry Wives*), Major Oakly, Iachimo, 2; Stukely, Pierre, Glenalvon, Prospero, "Ode to Nelson," 1.
38. Playbills 252, BM.
39. H & P, pp. 174–175.
40. Lawson, p. 214.
41. *LC*, 1:429; 2:38.
42. Baynham, p. 64.
43. *MM*, n.s., 7 (January 1810), 56–57. John Galt, *The Lives of the Players*, 2:201, also sug-

gests that Cooke's comment after appearing in Glasgow in 1801, "We removed to Glasgow, where I finished my number of nights, and quitted Scotland, very sensible of the favors with which I had been received," would indicate this as the occasion of these anecdotes. See *LC*, 1:192.

44. Baynham, p. 58.
45. *Caledonian Mercury*, 30 July 1807.
46. *Caledonian Mercury*, 25 July, 30 July, 1 August 1807.
47. Richard Ryan, *Dramatic Table Talk*, 1:23. Anne Mathews, *Anecdotes*, pp. 96–99, tells the same story but substitutes "thimble-full" for "wee thistle" and gives Cooke's response as "nor would it if were aqua-fortis!," adding that Cooke with an authoritative voice demanded, "*Fill the glass, Sir!* Am I not George Frederick Cooke? 'born to command ten thousand slaves like thee!' *Fill the glass, I say*, and refuse me at your peril!" A third variant of the story, although said to have occurred in Liverpool, as told by Kean is also in Ryan, 2:142–143. See also F. W. Hawkins, *The Life of Edmund Kean*, 2 vols. (London, 1869), 1:74. Not being present for a performance, the manager found Cooke at a "pot-house" near the theatre, where he was drinking out of a very small glass. The manager rebuked him for breaking his promise to quit drinking. Cooke responded: ". . . you can't expect a man to reform all at once. I have given over drinking, in a *great measure*," holding up the small glass under the manager's nose. The phrase left off "drinking in a great measure" became a stock phrase in Cooke's repertoire of "clever" phrases, repeated in another context to Dunlap in April 1811 (see *DD*, 2:433).
48. *LC*, 1:429.
49. Playbills 230, BM.
50. *LC*, 1:434–435; Anne Mathews, *Memoirs of Charles Mathews, Comedian*, 1:153–154.
51. Mathews, *Anecdotes*, pp. 100–104.
52. *LC*, 2:42.
53. *LC*, 2:229–238. Dunlap uses this incident in *Thirty Years Ago; or, The Memoirs of a Water Drinker*, 2:119–136. He fictionalizes that the widow was Cooke's first wife, a Mrs. Johnson, who had escaped from Cooke to America and had raised their son Henry there. This, then, becomes an unexpected reunion, although neither party realizes their true identities.
54. *LC*, 2:353–360.
55. John W. Francis, *Old New York*, p. 210.
56. [Pierce Egan], *The Life of George Frederick Cooke*, pp. 23–24.
57. *The Statesman*, n.d., HTC. Dunlap in his characteristic way wrote that in the United States "People are applying to him for money and he gives merely because he has not firmness to refuse, tho' he regrets parting with the cash" (see *DD*, 2:430, 448).
58. The 14 November to 28 November diary (MS Thr 20.1, HTC) once belonged to Henry Irving. It was then given by Lawrence Irving to Sir Bernard Miles, who in the summer of 1971 sold it to Harvard. Part of the later section is also at Harvard. See *LC*, 2:2–35, for that portion available to Dunlap. The original is used by permission of the HTC.
59. *MM*, n.s., 2 (September 1807), 217; n.s., 2 (October 1807), 290.
60. *The Cabinet*, 2 (December 1807), 353; see also 3 (February 1808), 140.
61. Add MS Egerton 2306, BM.
62. *MM*, n.s., 3 (January 1808), 51–52. *The Cabinet*, 3 (March 1808), 208, summarized the impact of Kemble's Iago:
>How in Iago Kemble shews his art!
>He strikes out all the beauties of the part.
63. Playbills, 30 December 1807 and 4 January 1808, Stead Collection, NYPL.
64. *LC*, 2:38–39. See also *The Cabinet*, 3 (February 1808), 141.
65. *LC*, 1:43. Playbills list Mr. and Mrs. Young, Rock, Mansell, Berry, Evatt, Archer, Shaw, Brown, Forrest, Watson, Mesdames Willoughby, Vining, W. Penson, and the Misses Charteris and Walton.
66. Playbill, HTC; *The Cabinet*, 3 (March 1808), 215.
67. *LC*, 2:42.

68. James C. Dibdin, *The Annals of the Edinburgh Stage*, p. 253.
69. *LC*, 2:42.
70. See E. Beresford Chancellor, *The Annals of Covent Garden and Its Neighborhood*, pp. 248–249.
71. Add MS Egerton 2306, BM.
72. *MM*, n.s., 3 (March 1808), 270.
73. Add MS Egerton 2306, BM.
74. Add MS 31,975, BM.
75. *MM*, n.s., 3 (March 1808), 269–270.
76. Unidentified clippings, V & A.
77. *MM*, n.s., 3 (March 1808), 269–270.
78. Ibid., 271.
79. See Williams, *Richard Cumberland, His Life and Dramatic Works*, pp. 88–104.
80. *MM*, n.s., 3 (May 1808), 401.
81. Ibid., 399.
82. *LC*, 2:45.
83. *MM*, n.s., 3 (May 1808), 401; Add MS Egerton 2306, BM, incorrectly has Cooke's night listed as 21 May and the receipts, presumably correct, as £336.
84. *Morning Chronicle*, 19 May 1808.
85. HTC, unidentified issue of *The Cabinet*.
86. Unidentified clipping, HTC.
87. James Boaden, *Memoirs of the Life of John Philip Kemble*, 2:451–452.
88. Scoreboard for 1808: Sir Pertinax, 12; Richard, 7; Shylock, Sir Archy, 6; Kent, 5; Iago, Kitely, Colin MacLeod, Falstaff (*Merry Wives*), Caratach, 2; Falstaff (*Henry IV, Pt. 1*), Vortex, Clytus, Sir Christopher Curry, Don Felix, "Ode on Shakespeare," 1.

CHAPTER 13

1. *The Cabinet*, 4 (July 1808), 63.
2. Bath and Bristol playbills, HTC; Playbills 177 and 203, BM; *MM*, n.s., 4 (July 1808), 62; *LC*, 2:70–71.
3. Playbills 252, BM; playbills, HTC.
4. Quoted in *LC*, 2:13.
5. *Newcastle Chronicle*, 16, 23, and 30 July 1808.
6. Letter, Cooke to John Wilkinson, 28 May 1808, Folger Shakespeare Library.
7. Ibid.; Playbills 327, BM; typescript, Sybil Rosenfeld, *The York Theatre*, n.d., p. 391, in the York Public Library.
8. *Caledonian Mercury*, 25 August 1808. Elizabeth Armstrong, "The Edinburgh Stage, 1715–1820" (Thesis, University of Edinburgh, 1969), p. 14, says *Venice Preserv'd* was presented on 26 August.
9. Playbill, Stead Collection, NYPL.
10. *LC*, 2:72.
11. *MM*, n.s., 4 (October 1808), 258.
12. Unidentified clippings from *The Cabinet* and *The Satirist*, HTC; see also *The Gentleman's Magazine*, 78, Pt. 2 (October 1808), 951.
13. Playbills 230, BM.
14. Playbill for 5 June 1809, Playbills 233, BM.
15. See Desmond Shawe-Taylor, *Covent Garden*, p. 18; Richard Leacroft, *The Development of the English Playhouse*, p. 177; Herschel Baker, *John Philip Kemble*, pp. 291–292; John Joseph Stockdale, ed., *The Covent Garden Journal*, 1:33–44.
16. Shawe-Taylor, p. 18.
17. See Daniel Nalbach, *The King's Theatre 1704–1867*, pp. 78–85.

18. Cooke's salary rose to an all-time high this season of £20 per week (Add MS 29,631, Covent Garden Ledger 1808–1809, BM). Thomas S. Munden, *Memoirs of Joseph Shepherd Munden, Comedian*, p. 138, says Cooke was scheduled to appear as Glenalvon on 26 September but "was gone to be married and could not come."
19. *Morning Post*, 14 October 1808. See also *The Cabinet*, 4 (November 1808), 357.
20. Playbills, HTC.
21. Brighton playbill, 28 October 1808, HTC; Bath bills, Playbills 177, BM.
22. See W. Macqueen-Pope, *Haymarket: Theatre of Perfection*, pp. 205–208.
23. *LC*, 2:73–75.
24. Clipping, V & A.
25. *MM*, n.s., 5 (March 1809), 190.
26. *LC*, 2:86, 95.
27. "Cross Keys" stood until 1937.
28. *Hull Advertiser*, 25 February 1809.
29. *Hull Packet*, 28 February; *Hull Advertiser*, 4 March; Playbills 401, BM.
30. See Thomas Sheppard, *Evolution of the Drama in Hull and District*, p. 42f.
31. Rosenfeld, p. 393.
32. *LC*, 2:96–97.
33. *MM*, n.s., 5 (March 1809), 181. The verse is dated 25 February 1809 and signed R.H.T.
34. Anne Mathews, *Anecdotes of Actors*, p. 84.
35. Kemble Memoranda, Add MS 31,975, and Add MS Egerton 2307 agree on Cooke's benefit; 2307 gives £285 for Young's night, while Kemble's memoranda give the quoted figure.
36. Playbills, V & A.
37. Scoreboard for 1808–1809 season: Sir Pertinax, 9; Stukely, 8; Shylock, 6; Richard, 6; Iago, 5; Archy, 4; Kitely, 3; Pierre, Falstaff (*Henry IV, Part 1*), Sir Giles, Falstaff (*Merry Wives*), 2; John Cockle, Gibby, Baron Wildenheim, 1.
38. Letter, 26 May 1809, Simon Gratz Collection, Pennsylvania Historical Society.
39. See Arnold Hare, *The Georgian Theatre in Wessex*, pp. 169–170; Francis W. Steer, *The Chichester Theatre*, pp. 5–6.
40. William Pitt Lennox, *Celebrities I Have Known*, 1:269–82; Hare, Appendix IV, pp. 210–217. A slightly revised version of the story appears in Lennox's *Plays, Players and Playhouses*, 1:60–80.
41. Hare, p. 161. In Lennox's later work, p. 60, a bill for the performance, from memory, is reproduced—the date indicated is July 21, 180—.
42. *LC*, 2:97. John Bernard, *Retrospections of America*, p. 368, claims to have seen Cooke in Chichester in about 1771, a statement that lacks verification, despite the intriguing reference to such an early performance date, which now seems conceivable.
43. A similar story is told by Pierre Irving in *The Life and Letters of Washington Irving*, 1:279–280. While in the United States, Cooke was booed by the audience one night after Shylock; he tapped the handle of his sword emphatically and said: " 'Tis but a foil," and shaking his finger at the audience added, " 'Tis well for you it is." The allusion to a sword might suggest that Irving meant Richard III and not Shylock.
44. *Hampshire Telegraph*, 29 May 1809. For a discussion of the physical theatre at Portsmouth and its history, see Hare, pp. 171–172.
45. Playbills 233, BM; playbills, HTC.
46. *Caledonian Mercury*, 8 July 1809.
47. *MM*, n.s., 6 (July 1809), 52.
48. Playbills 253, BM.
49. Sir Frederick Pollock, ed., *Macready's Reminiscences, and Selections from His Diaries and Letters*, p. 51.
50. Macready tells of a young officer who interrupted a performance, to whom Cooke replied: "D—n you, sir! You are an ensign? Sir, the King (God bless him) can make any fool an officer, but it is only the great God Almighty that can make an actor!" Ibid.

51. Ibid., p. 52.
52. Mathews, *Anecdotes*, p. 84.
53. Michael Kelly, *Reminiscences of Michael Kelly*, 2:239.
54. Playbills 253, BM; *LC*, 2:98.
55. Playbills, HTC and NYPL; *Caledonian Mercury*, 3, 8, 10, 13, 15, 17, and 20 July 1809.
56. *LC*, 2:99.
57. The last performance at the Prince's Street Theatre was 12 August; the first at the Circus was 14 November 1809. See James C. Dibdin, *Annals of the Edinburgh Stage*, pp. 254, 259.
58. *LC*, 2:100.
59. Robb Lawson, *The Story of the Scots Stage*, p. 251, incorrectly says he began on 22 August.
60. *LC*, 2:100.
61. Ibid., 101.
62. See Leacroft, pp. 177–185 and Charles Dibdin, Jr., *History and Illustration of the London Theatres*, pp. 24–32, for details on the new building.
63. See Baker, pp. 295–315.
64. Add MS 31,972, BM.
65. *The Covent Garden Journal*, 1:227.
66. *Morning Post*, 21 September and 10 October 1809; *London Chronicle*, 23 September; *Covent Garden Journal*, 1:195–227.
67. Committee composed of John Sylvester, Sir Thomas Plomer, John Whitmore, J. J. Angerstein, and Sir Charles Price (Playbills 92, BM).
68. *LC*, 2:117; *A Walk Through Leicester, Being a Guide to Strangers*, pp. 131–132.
69. *Morning Chronicle*, 7 November 1809.
70. *Covent Garden Journal*, 1:206–207.
71. Playbills 202, BM.
72. *Morning Post*, 31 October 1809; *Covent Garden Journal*, 1:223–224.
73. *Covent Garden Journal*, 1:284; *Morning Chronicle*, 1 and 20 December. During the negotiations, Cooke performed in Portsmouth on 11, 12, and 13 December.
74. Kelly, 2:240.
75. *LC*, 2:284.
76. John Galt, *The Lives of the Players*, 2:212.
77. Note on playbill (Playbills 92, BM); *MM*, n.s., 7 (January 1810), 56–57.
78. *Morning Post*, 29 December 1809; *Morning Chronicle*, 29 December 1809.
79. *The Satirist*, 6 (January 1, 1810), 101. Cooke had been assigned the role of Horatius by Harris in November (Letter, Harris to Edward Barlow, 3 November 1809, British Theatre Museum) and had first appeared in it on 27 November. The initial response was very favorable. The *Morning Post*, 28 November 1810, called him "very great: the patriotic exultation of the aged Roman, when he learns that his sons are chosen the champions of their country, his indignation at hearing of the flight of Publius, and the subsequent transition from rage and despair to admiration and delight, were depicted in a most masterly manner."
80. *MM*, n.s., 7 (January 1810), 56–57.
81. *LC*, 2:309.
82. Playbills 92, BM.
83. Letter, Cooke to Elliston, 15 February 1810, in *The Theatre: A Weekly Critical Review*, 1 (January to July 1877), 266.
84. *Morning Post*, 9 January 1810.
85. *The Satirist*, 6 (February 1, 1810), 199–200.
86. *The Thespiad* (London 1809), p. 19. The poem, apparently by John Joseph Stockdale, Jr., who published it, is fifty pages in length. His verse on Cooke, pp. 19–20, is as follows:

> His Pow'rs confin'd, but lions in their chains,
> Rough, awkward Cooke the second fame maintains.

> In him, no grace, no studious art we find,
> His parts unconn'd, his accent unrefin'd.
> Richard alike in words as actions sins,
> And adds lame utt'rance to mishapen shins.
> His gesture in fore-fingers stretch'd consists,
> In pinion'd elbows or in clenched fists.
> An eye askance, his pride of high descent.
> In ladies' rooms his hatted head we see,
> His pleading love inflects the farther knee.
> Let classic Kemble pore upon his book,
> But nowns [sic] and verbs are fiddlesticks to Cooke.
> Skill'd to perform, the jesting villain's part,
> Whose grave grotesque hides venom in his heart,
> Cooke's sneering nostril, and malignant eye,
> And voice discordant well the wretch supply,
> But in high tragedy, where graceful ease,
> And lofty carriage must conspire to please;
> Unfit to kneel in attitude of love,
> Born to spit fire and curse the gods above,
> Cooke fails—to Anne Richard cannot vow,
> Nor *booing* Pertinax like Romeo bow.

87. Playbills 253, BM.
88. *Morning Post*, 24 April 1810.
89. Unidentified clipping, HTC. There are two extant Cooke promptbooks for *Henry VIII*: the one at Harvard (TS. 2272.100), dated 2 October 1811, Park Theatre, was used when Cooke and Cooper played together; the other, at the Shakespeare Memorial Library in Birmingham (S649.28/526709), belonged to Edward Knight and was a gift of Edward Simpson, a later manager of the Park. It is dated 1827 by Knight. Neither is particularly helpful in reconstructing Cooke's performance, although some stage business is indicated. The Covent Garden production was a good deal more sumptuous than that at the Park, although other differences were apparently minor. The Harvard book is listed as No. 10 (p. 156) and the Birmingham as No. 11 in Charles H. Shattuck's *The Shakespeare Promptbooks*.
90. See Appendix B.
91. Add MS Egerton 2308, BM.
92. Notes on playbills (Playbills 92, BM); see also *MM*, n.s., 7 (June 1810), 457; Kemble Memoranda, Add MS 31,975, BM.
93. Add MS 31,975.
94. *The Satirist*, 7 (February 1810), 200–201.
95. 1809–1810 scoreboard: Sir Pertinax, 12; Shylock, 9; Richard, 8; Iago, 7; Falstaff (*Henry IV, Part 1*), and Kitely, 4; Horatius, 3; Henry VIII, 3; Major Oakly, Stukely, 2; Sir Giles, Sir Archy, Glenalvon, 1.
96. *LC*, 2:125.
97. Ibid., 130.
98. Playbills 233, BM.
99. Ibid.
100. Playbills 298, BM.
101. Cooper acted in Liverpool from 10 September to 19 September, taking a benefit as Hamlet on 21 September. See *MM*, n.s., 8 (November 1810), 397.

CHAPTER 14

1. The figures cited here are at best intelligent guesses. I have utilized quotations of receipts

wherever they have appeared, collating figures whenever possible. Most figures have appeared in published sources cited elsewhere in the notes. See Appendix B.

2. *LC*, 2:314–315; *DD*, 2:439.
3. *LC*, 2:130–169.
4. *DD*, 2:440, 450.
5. Thomas S. Munden, *Memoirs of Joseph Shepherd Munden, Comedian*, pp. 179–181.
6. *DD*, 2:439.
7. Ibid., 435.
8. *VS*, pp. 130–134.
9. Add MS Egerton 2309, BM. Cooke is included in the salary lists for 15 and 29 September, and 6 October. The *London MM*, n.s., 8 (October 1810), 316, bitter over Cooke's defection, exclaimed: "Mr. C. was engaged to Mr. Harris and owed him eight hundred pounds [unverified in the account books]. All this Mr. Cooper knew as well as Mr. C., and—and—but they are both transported, and let justice be satisfied."
10. Letter, Dr. David Hosack to Dunlap, 16 March 1813, quoted in *LC*, 2:384.
11. *DD*, 2:423.
12. John Wakefield Francis, *Old New York*, p. 205.
13. Ibid.
14. Recent doctoral studies on Cooke's predecessors on the American stage only seem to strengthen this conclusion. See N. B. East, "John Bernard, Actor-Manager, 1756–1828" (University of Kansas, 1970); Norman B. Potts, "The Acting Career of James Fennell" (Indiana University, 1969); B. J. Harbin, "The Career of John Hodgkinson in the American Theatre" (Indiana University, 1971). Also see Gresdna Ann Doty, *The Career of Mrs. Anne Brunton Merry in the American Theatre*. Although English, Cooper was fairly well established as an "American" actor by the time Cooke first appeared in the United States. His popularity is unquestionable, but such a hoopla as that preceding Cooke's visit did not occur. Cooper was a seasoned and familiar figure on the American stage when he began his career as a traveling star without management responsibilities in 1815.
15. Charles Durang, "The Philadelphia Stage from the Year 1749 to the Year 1855," *The Philadelphia Sunday Dispatch* (1854–1860), Chapter 44: 87. Cooke developed an intense dislike for Price, and although, like Rock and McCready before him, Price had attempted to lodge Cooke in his own home, Cooke quickly balked and moved into the Tontine Coffee House. See *LC*, 2:188, 197; *DD*, 2:436.
16. *The Mirror of Taste and the Dramatic Censor*, 2, No. 5 (November 1810), 372–373.
17. *DD*, 2:420–421.
18. *The Mirror of Taste*, 2:371–372.
19. Ibid.
20. *LC*, 2:348–349. See also George O. Willard, *History of the Providence Stage*, p. 67 and *LC*, 2:294–295, 342, 346–350, 372–374 for other comments by Cooke on the United States. Cooke, when in his cups, often threatened to write a pamphlet which he intended to publish in England in order to "blow up your Managers and your Theatres and your actors and your blasted Country." Dunlap concluded in his notes for Cooke's biography that he did not think Cooke really "vicious enough" to carry out his threat. See *DD*, 2:455.
21. Joseph N. Ireland, *Records of the New York Stage, From 1750 to 1860*, 1:273. The scene recorded here is based largely on an unidentified newspaper clipping, HTC.
22. Ireland says that only twice did receipts exceed this initial performance at the Park: $1,821 on 12 September 1836, when Forrest played *The Gladiator*; and $1,833 on 24 June 1836, on Placide's benefit as Iago to John Reeve's Othello. Joseph Ireland, *A Memoir of the Professional Life of Thomas Abthorpe Cooper*, p. 38. *LC*, 2:198, however, says that Cooke's benefit on 19 December took in $1,878.
23. See also *DD*, 2:427, 431.
24. Willard, pp. 61–62.
25. *New York Evening Post*, 23 November 1810.

26. *The Cabinet*, 3 (18 January 1811), 33–36.
27. *Boston Gazette*, 30 December 1811.
28. *Philadelphia True American*, 8 November 1811.
29. Major passages from New York newspaper criticism have been quoted by George C.D. Odell, *Annals of the New York Stage*, 2:355–363.
30. *The Mirror of Taste*, 2, No. 5 (November 1810), 374.
31. Ibid., 3, No. 1 (January 1811), 22–23.
32. Quoted in Gabriel Harrison, *The Life and Writing of John Howard Payne*, p. 49.
33. *LC*, 2:197–199; also see *DD*, 2:417–418. As far as I can ascertain, the last time Cooke played Cato prior to this performance was 19 July 1809 in Edinburgh. For London debut, see Chapter 10.
34. *Boston Gazette*, 31 December 1810 and 3 January 1811.
35. *The Repertory*, 8 January 1811. *The Cabinet*, 2 (12 January 1811), 25–28 and 3 (19 January 1811), 36–39, elaborated: "candle snuffers were made, in vile robes, to represent nobility," the army of Richard and Richmond and the citizens of London were represented by about five supernumeraries. The foreground of the stage was hardly illuminated enough to discern the face of a performer the distance of four boxes from the scene. In addition, the lights created a great deal of smoke. *The Cabinet* also remarks on the miserable orchestra, the dirty boxes, and the severe coldness in the theatre during the inclement weather. The regular company was condemned as being poor, while at the same time, Morse, "a very respectable actor," had been soliciting employment the entire season without success.
36. *LC*, 2:295. His behavior had altered little from that described over twenty-five years earlier by Ryley. For example, Dr. Francis wrote: ". . . his mania for drink . . . dethroned his high purpose, and at times degraded him below the dignity of man. In that condition his whole nature was altered and his appearance almost diabolical; you dwindled under his indignant frown; no violence was like his; abuse of kindest friends, extravagance beyond limits, obstinancy invincible." Francis, p. 209.
37. See *LC*, 2:203–205. MS in the Simon Gratz Collection, Pennsylvania Historical Society. The letter was given in part by Incledon to the *London Morning Herald* on 6 March and published the next day; later it was reprinted in American papers. It is reprinted in part by Dunlap. It was first quoted in its entirety in my article, "Cooke Among the Yankee Doodles," pp. 13–14. Dunlap's reaction to the letter was typical of him—"in praise of every thing he curses & condemns" (*DD*, 2:442).
38. Figures taken for this New York engagement from Ireland, *Records of the New York Stage*, p. 276 and *LC*, 2:227–243. Boston receipts primarily from Dunlap and William W. Clapp, Jr., *A Record of the Boston Stage*; Philadelphia receipts from Dunlap and Reese D. James, *Old Drury of Philadelphia*; Baltimore figures from James; both Philadelphia and Baltimore figures also examined in William B. Wood's Account Books and Journal, 1810–1835 (MS Am. 19, University of Pennsylvania); Providence figures from Dunlap and Willard; other New York receipts from Dunlap. Sources differ slightly on receipt figures. See Appendix B.
39. *LC*, 2:284–285; *DD*, 2:450.
40. William Warren quoted in Durang, 44:89.
41. William B. Wood, *Personal Recollections of the Stage*, pp. 133–134, 154, 159–170.
42. Durang, 44:88.
43. Cooke apparently learned of the first postponement in the newspaper in Trenton on his way to Philadelphia. It was also reported that he would play Friday (22 March). Cooke's response was: "I'll be damned if I do! if I am too unwell to play Wednesday how do they know I shall be well enough to play Friday?" *DD*, 2:419; *LC*, 2:255. He was ill during his stay in Philadelphia; on 9 April, he was bled by Dr. Thomas Parke. See *DD*, 2:437.
44. Pierre M. Irving, *The Life and Letters of Washington Irving*, 1:278–279; see also Bernard Hewitt, *Theatre U.S.A.*, pp. 85–86. Irving had met with Cooke at his apartment on 8 April 1811 and was in his presence on a number of subsequent occasions. See *DD*, 2:437.

45. See *An Apology for the Life of James Fennell*, pp. 492–495. Fennell defends Cooke from Dunlap's moralistic pen throughout his discussion of Cooke. See, especially, pp. 279–281. According to Dunlap, Cooke actually thought little of Fennell's talent, calling it "mere school-boy ti-hem hem-ti—schoolboy? Nay, I would have whipt a boy that could not have done better." This comment followed an evening of Fennell's recitations on 22 March (*DD*, 2:423). Furthermore, Dunlap says Fennell "was teazing" Cooke to play Iago to his Othello (ibid., 2:438).

46. Dunlap, since he was with Cooke, gives his most reliable account during this engagement. Nevertheless, as clearly revealed in his own diary, his puritan bias was so intense that even this account must be approached with caution.

47. *DD*, 2:373. As has been pointed out, Mrs. Behn may have been his fourth or fifth wife. Apparently, after Cooke's death, Mrs. Cooke moved to Connecticut. Dunlap talks of going to Greenwich to pick up manuscripts from Mrs. Cooke in January 1813 (*DD*, 2:461). Evidently, Cooke married Mrs. Behn without Bryden's knowledge (ibid., 2:464).

48. *LC*, 2:362, also says Cooke did not play on 20 September, although the playbills, newspapers, and Ireland, *Records of the New York Stage*, p. 280, state that he played Macduff to Cooper's Macbeth.

49. While Cooke was playing in Philadelphia, Placide, co-manager of the Charleston Theatre, came to negotiate a season with Cooke. Although Cooke had completed his Chestnut Street engagement and the Richmond Theatre had been kept open in hope of his fulfilling his contract, Cooke decided instead to go to Boston. See Durang, 41:93; Clapp, pp. 128–129, goes so far as to say that Cooke, by having the theater kept open beyond the normal season, "was, in a measure, the cause of this sad catastrophe" which took seventy-two lives on 26 December 1811.

50. James, pp. 16–17.

51. William Warren's Diary, 30 March 1811, quoted by Calvin L. Pritner, "William Warren's Financial Arrangements with Traveling Stars, 1805–1829," *TS*, 6, No. 2 (November 1965), 87.

52. *The Cynick*, 1 (16 November 1811); see Pritner, pp. 83–90.

53. Odell, 2:379, mentions that on 11 November Cooper dared to appear as Richard III and was advised to "never again . . . appear in this arduous part, until the impressions which Mr. Cooke's Richard have left on the public mind be completely obliterated."

54. *LC*, 2:366, says Cooke was in New London; *New England Palladium*, 31 December 1811, says Providence.

55. Clapp, p. 127.

56. *The Comet*, 31 December 1811.

57. A similar report appeared in the *New England Palladium*, 14 January 1812, with the exclusion of the last two sentences. A letter from Cooke to James Dickenson [Dickson], 7 February [1811?] says: "I wrote to you again yesterday, mentioning why I was delayed. My leg grows much better, and I hope speedily to see you" (Manuscript Collection, Boston Public Library). Nowhere does Dunlap mention any leg trouble, but Cooke's statement would support the report of "paralytic affection" and might possibly have been just one more of Cooke's many afflictions, giving validity to illness other than inebriety. It might be recalled that he had suffered a number of falls and leg injuries during the last twenty years of his life.

58. Quoted in *LC*, 2:367–368.

59. *The Columbian Sentinel*, 11 January 1812, reports that the temperature averaged four to six degrees during this period.

60. See n. 49. On 6 January 1812, a series of letters on the Richmond fire appeared in the *Boston Gazette*. In the same issue, the managers assured Bostonians that their theatre was safe (i.e., an iron curtain, globed lamps, three doors from the boxes, two doors from the pit and gallery, a hose from an aqueduct in the cellar, and all doors leading from the stage made of iron). Obviously, the Bostonians were not assured. *The Satirist* (Boston), 16 January 1812, called the story about a fireproof curtain the most ridiculous hoax of the season, challenging "all the sons of Vulcan or Thespis in Christendom to render it serviceable in case of fire."

61. *LC*, 2:379; Munden, pp. 186–187.

62. The letter is in a portfolio identified as Correspondence of Thomas Harris, Henry's father, British Theatre Museum, London.

63. *LC*, 2:245; *DD*, 2:437, 443, 447.

64. The announcement in *The Providence Gazette and Country Journal*, 11 July 1812, stated: "The managers have the pleasure of announcing to the Public, that they have engaged MR. COOKE, to perform in the Providence Theatre for six nights only. During the Engagement, no play can be repeated. In order to prevent difficulty, and give an equal chance to the Public in general to witness the brilliant Performances of this justly celebrated Actor, a Box-plan . . . , when Places may be taken in any number not exceeding ten, or less than two." It then announces the mainpiece, *The Merchant of Venice*, "for the only time this Season."

65. See Donald C. Mullin, "Early Theatre in Rhode Island," pp. 167–186.

66. *LC*, 2:378; Willard, p. 63.

67. Francis, p. 211; Durang, 44:88; Willard, p. 67.

68. John Taylor, *Records of My Life*, quoted by Durang, 44:89.

69. Unidentified clipping, HTC.

EPILOGUE

1. Miscellaneous MS, courtesy of the New York Historical Society, New York City. Joseph George Holman first appeared at the Park Theatre as Hamlet on 28 September 1812. According to Cooke's will and the decree admitting the will to probate (dated 28 October 1812) on file in the Surrogate Court of the County of New York (Book 50, p. 261), witnesses to the will were Dr. J. W. Francis, J. Robinson, and Joseph Fay. Subsequently, Hosack and Holman, with no explanation given, refused the executorship, and the legal right of executing the will went to Mrs. Mary Cooke, the sole beneficiary. The will itself mentions no specific sums of money or estates, nor does it enumerate outstanding debts. Cooke had requested on his deathbed that a ring belonging to Charles Kemble be sent to him and his marked copy of *The Man of the World* be sent to John Philip. According to Dunlap, Price sent the ring to Charles but, as discussed previously in the section on the 1801–1802 season the text apparently never reached its destination. See *DD*, 2:462. In *Thirty-Years Ago*, Dunlap fantasizes that the ring was sent to Cooke's first wife, Mrs. Johnson (2:212). Cooke also wished to be affectionately remembered to Henry Harris and James Brandon (*LC*, 2:382). In an account of his death in pencil on a page of his Richard III promptbook (R III, 4, in the Folger Library), the name of Dr. Wilson, one of his English physicians, is included with those of Kemble, Brandon, and Harris. It also confirms the request to return Kemble's ring but makes no mention of the script. In *The Shakespeare Promptbooks*, p. 391, Shattuck identifies the four-page account as written by an eyewitness. I have not been able to verify this. The account mentions four physicians who attended Cooke, but only two coincide with accounts in Dunlap (i.e., Hugh McLean and Hosack; Francis' name is mysteriously omitted). Hosack (1769–1835), along with Francis (1789–1861), performed an autopsy on Cooke and subsequently Hosack included his findings in his letter to Dunlap. Later, in *Thirty Years Ago*, Dunlap includes Francis, a Dr. Cadwallader, and Cooke's valet Davenport in his fictionalized account of Cooke's death (2:209). Joseph Dewey Fay (1779–1825) was a native of Vermont and had studied law in the office of Alexander Hamilton. He became a successful attorney and gave much time to advocating the abolition of imprisonment for debt.

2. This letter appears in *LC*, 2:383–393. I have chosen to use Dunlap sparingly in this chapter because of his obvious bias and the distortion throughout the work. Dunlap, now available in reprint, is readily accessible and should be consulted as a supplement to this chapter. See my guide to Dunlap, "An Index to: The Life of George Frederick Cooke by William Dunlap," *Theatre Documentation*, 2, Nos. 1 and 2 (Fall 1969 and Spring 1970), 109–120.

3. See n. 1 above, note attached to *Richard III* promptbook.

4. The funeral was announced in the *New York Columbian*, 26 September 1812, with this last statement: "His friends and acquaintances are requested without further invitation to attend his

funeral from the Mechanic-Hall to-morrow afternoon, precisely at half-past 4 o'clock." See also *LC*, 2:395; *New York Evening Post*, 11 November 1899; and John Wakefield Francis, *Old New York*, p. 210 ff.

5. Thomas S. Munden, *Memoirs of Joseph Sheperd Munden, Comedian*, p. 187; unidentified article, 1 November 1936, HTC.

6. Anecdotes followed Cooke even to his deathbed. One such story says that when nearly dying, he asked a friend who was at his bedside to bring him a glass of water, at the same time saying, "On our death-beds we must be reconciled to our enemies" (unidentified clipping, HTC).

7. William Dunlap, *History of the American Theatre*, p. 393.

8. Francis, p. 233.

9. See Harold Hillebrand, *Edmund Kean*, pp. 222–223, and Francis, p. 234.

10. The variety of this tale is immense. It was probably first popularized in Bryan Proctor's *The Life of Edmund Kean*, pp. 196–202. This present retelling is from *Lights of the Old English Stage*, pp. 146–147.

11. To my knowledge the only other monument in memory of Cooke is in Dublin's St. Patrick's Cathedral.

12. An engraving of Cooke's tomb was made by John Rubens Smith (1775–1849), a designer and etcher. His design and etching of Cooke's monument, with the figures of Kean and Dr. Francis, had some notoriety at the time. The engraving, slightly altered in the lower portion, was published in London in 1822. It is also one of the plates in I.N. Phelps Stokes' *Iconography of Manhattan Island* (New York, 1915–1928), in the American history collection of the NYPL. The building second from left in the background is the Park Theatre.

13. See George Vandenhoff, *Leaves from an Actor's Note-Book* (New York, 1860), pp. 25–27.

14. The original inscription was located on the southside; the northside recorded Charles Kean's repairs and the eastside, Sothern's, with Theater Royal, Haymarket, written underneath his name. The present plaque contains all the original information with the addition of Cooke's dates (1756–1812). Sothern's repair was especially important since, under the direction of T. E. Mills of Wallack's Theatre, the whole structure was bound together in the interior with iron anchors. Through the years it was frequently rumored that other actors were going to repair the tomb; in 1895 there was a report that Wilson Barrett would undertake the chore. Indeed, it is now in need of such repairs.

15. This information was kindly supplied by Father Robert Hunsicker, vicar of St. Paul's, and H. R. Cline of the Office of the Clerk of the Vestry. The data were located on p. 54 of the *Churchyards Booklet*. NYPL has all correspondence relating to these negotiations. The remaining members of the Kean Club in 1948 were Mary Mason, Theodore Leavitt, Mr. and Mrs. Stanley Kauffman, Mrs. Giles Playfair, Donald Buka, Edward Burke, and Mr. and Mrs. Philip Arthur.

16. These visitations were reported in the *New York Evening Post*, 11 November 1899; they can be verified chronologically.

17. Unidentified newspaper article dated 25 November 1929, HTC.

18. Lloyd Morris, *Curtain Time*, p. 12, relates that in 1930, Dr. Francis' granddaughter, Mrs. Louis Francis Lyon, a retired actress, said that Cooke left him his skull for "science's sake" since he had nothing to leave him but "love and gratitude." Unfortunately, I have not been able to verify this account. Morris's book is not documented, and he died shortly after the book appeared.

19. Unidentified article, possibly *Temple Bar*, HTC.

20. Francis, pp. 204–213, should be examined for the doctor's own account of Cooke.

21. *New York Evening Post*, 11 November 1899.

22. McClellan's fifteen-page manuscript is entitled "The Strolling of a Player's Head." On the last page it is dated November 1901; below this is a list of four occasions on which he read the paper: once in 1901, once in 1902, and twice in 1907. There is no indication that it was ever revised. Apparently, McClellan made no attempt to publish his manuscript. Since he died before

the furor over the skull in the 1930s, he was unable to refute all false reports. When he wrote the manuscript, McClellan was on the staff of the Pennsylvania School of Anatomy and Surgery, which he founded in 1881, and was professor of artistic anatomy at the Pennsylvania Academy of Fine Arts. His grandfather founded the Jefferson Medical College in Philadelphia, which McClellan joined in 1906.

23. Letter to author from Dr. A. J. Ramsay, 25 October 1967.

24. The first of these articles was in the *Philadelphia Record*, 11 May 1930.

25. "To Bury the Great Actor's Missing Head with the Body After 124 Years," *Sunday Mirror Magazine*, 1 November 1936, in HTC.

26., George Tichenor, "Odyssey of a Skull," *Theatre Guild Magazine* (December 1930), p. 15.

Selected Bibliography

Adams, W. Davenport. *A Dictionary of the Drama.* Vol. 1. Philadelphia, 1904.
Allen, Shirley S. *Samuel Phelps and the Sadler's Wells Theatre.* Middletown, Conn., 1971.
Appleton, William W. *Charles Macklin, An Actor's Life.* Cambridge, Mass., 1960.
Armstrong, Cecil F. *A Century of Great Actors, 1750–1850.* London, 1912.
Arundell, Denis. *The Story of Sadler's Wells.* New York. 1965.
Baker, Henry Barton. *Our Old Actors.* London, 1881.
Baker, Herschel. *John Philip Kemble.* Cambridge, Mass., 1942.
Ball, Robert Hamilton. *The Amazing Career of Sir Giles Overreach.* Princeton, 1939.
Barker, Kathleen. *The Theatre Royal Bristol: The First Seventy Years.* Bristol, 1961.
———. *The Theatre Royal Bristol, 1766–1966.* London, 1974.
Bartholomeusz, Dennis. *Macbeth and the Players.* Cambridge, England, 1969.
Barton, Margaret. *David Garrick.* New York, 1949.
Baynham, Walter. *The Glasgow Stage.* Glasgow, 1892.
Benwell, J. M. *An Essay on the Danger of Unjust Criticism.* Manchester, 1806.
Bernard, John. *Retrospection of the Stage.* Edited by W. Baile Bernard. 2 vols. London, 1830.
———. *Retrospections of America, 1797–1811.* New York, 1887.
Biographia Dramatica; or, A Companion to the Playhouse. 3 vols. London, 1812.
Blake, Charles. *Historical Account of the Providence Stage.* Providence, R.I., 1868.
Boaden, James. *Memoirs of the Life of John Philip Kemble, Esq.* 2 vols. London, 1925.
———. *Memoirs of Mrs. Siddons.* 2 vols. London, 1827.
Board, M. E. *The Story of the Bristol Stage, 1490–1925.* London, 1926.
Branam, George C. *Eighteenth-Century Adaptations of Shakespearean Tragedy.* Berkeley and Los Angeles, 1956.
Broadbent, R. J. *Annals of the Liverpool Stage from the Earliest Period to the Present Time.* Liverpool, 1908.
Buckingham, Joseph Tinker. *Miscellanies Selected from the Public Journals, 1779–1861.* Boston, 1822.
Bulloch, John Malcolm. *The Playhouse of Bon-Accord* (Aberdeen). Aberdeen, 1906.
Burnim, Kalman A. *David Garrick—Director.* Pittsburgh, 1961.
(Buxton). *A Description of Buxton, and the Adjacent Country.* Manchester, 1790.
Byrne, M. St. Clare. "The Earliest *Hamlet* Prompt Book in an English Library." *TN,* 15, No. 1 (Autumn 1960), 21–31.
Byron, Lord. *The Works of Lord Byron.* Edited by Rowland E. Prothero. 5 vols. London, 1898 and 1901.
The Cabinet, 2 (October 1807), 133–135.
Censor, C. *The Thespian Mirror, or Poetical Strictures; on the Professional Characters of Mr. Cooke et al. of the Theatre Royal, Manchester, Liverpool, and Chester.* 1793.
Chancellor, E. Beresford. *The Annals of Covent Garden and Its Neighborhood.* London, n.d.
Churchill, Charles. *The Poetical Works of Charles Churchill.* London, 1844.
Clapp, William W., Jr. *A Record of the Boston Stage.* Boston and Cambridge, 1853.

Clark, William Smith. *The Irish Stage in the Country Towns, 1720–1800*. Oxford, 1965.
Clinton-Baddeley, V. C. *All Right on the Night*. London, 1954.
Congreve, F. A. *Authentic Memoirs of the Late Mr. Charles Macklin, Comedian*. London, 1798.
Cooke, William. *Memoirs of Charles Macklin Comedian*. London, 1804.
Cotton, William. *The Story of the Drama in Exeter, During Its Best Period, 1787 to 1823*. London, 1887.
Croker, J. C. *Familiar Epistles to Frederick E. Jones, Esq., on the Present State of the Irish Stage*. Dublin, 1805.
Cunningham, John E. *Theatre Royal: The History of the Theatre Royal Birmingham*. Oxford, 1950.
Davies, Thomas. *A Genuine Narrative of the Life of Mr. John Henderson*. London, 1778.
Dibdin, Charles, Jr. *History and Illustrations of the London Theatres*. London, 1826.
Dibdin, James C. *The Annals of the Edinburgh Stage*. Edinburgh, 1888.
Dibdin, Thomas, *The Reminiscences of Thomas Dibdin*. 2 vols. London, 1827.
Donohue, Joseph W., Jr. *Dramatic Character in the English Romantic Age*. Princeton, 1970.
———, ed. *The Theatrical Manager in England and America*. Princeton, 1971.
Doran, John. *Their Majesties' Servants or Annals of the English Stage from Thomas Betterton to Edmund Kean*. 2 vols. London, 1865.
Doty, Gresdna Ann. *The Career of Mrs. Anne Brunton Merry in the American Theatre*. Baton Rouge, 1971.
Downer, Alan S. *The Eminent Tragedian William Charles Macready*. Cambridge, Mass., 1966.
———, ed. *King Richard III: Edmund Kean's Performance as Recorded by James H. Hackett*. London, 1959.
The Dramatic Censor or, Critical and Biographical Illustration of the British Stage. For the Year 1811. Edited by J. M. Williams. London, 1812.
The Dramatic Censor, or Weekly Theatrical Report. Edited by Thomas Dutton, 4 vols. London, 1800–1801.
Dunlap, William. *The Diary of William Dunlap, 1766–1839: The Memoirs of a Dramatist, Theatrical Manager, Painter, Critic, Novelist, and Historian*. Edited by Dorothy Barck. 3 vols. New York, 1931.
———. *History of the Rise and Progress of the American Theatre*. New York, 1832.
———. *History of the Arts of Design in the United States*. Edited with additions by Frank W. Bayley and Charles E. Goodspeed. 3 vols. Boston, 1918.
———. *Memoirs of the Life of George Frederick Cooke*. 2d ed. 2 vols. London, 1815.
———. *Thirty Years Ago; or, The Memoirs of a Water Drinker*. 2 vols. New York, 1836.
Edwin, John. *To the Public*. Newcastle, 4 June 1793.
[Egan, Pierce (?)]. *The Life of George Frederick Cooke, Esq.* London, 1813.
Everard, Edward Cape. *Memoirs of an Unfortunate Son of Thespis*. Edinburgh, 1818.
Fennell, James. *An Apology for the Life of James Fennell*. Philadelphia, 1814.
Fitzgerald, Percy. *The Romance of the English Stage*. 2 vols. London, 1874.
Francis, Dr. John W. *Old New York*. New York, 1865[6].
Fraser, William. *Memorial of the Montgomeries, Earls of Eglinton*. 2 vols. Edinburgh, 1859.
Galt, John. *The Lives of the Players*. 2 vols. London, 1831.
Genest, John. *Some Account of the English Stage, From the Restoration in 1660 to 1830*. 10 vols. Bath, 1832.
Gilbert, Sir John T. *The History of the City of Dublin*. 2 vols. Dublin, 1854.
Gill, Conrad. *History of Birmingham*. 2 vols. Oxford, 1952.
Gilliland, Thomas. *The Dramatic Mirror*. 2 vols. London, 1808.
Gipson, Alice E. *John Home: A Study of His Life and Works*. Caldwell, Idaho, 1917.
Goede, Christian August Gottlieb. *The Stranger in England; or, Travels in Great Britain*. 3 vols. London, 1807.
Greig, James, ed. *The Farington Diary of Joseph Farington, R.A.* 8 vols. London, 1923–1928.

Hare, Arnold. "George Frederick Cooke's Early Years in the Theatre." *TN*, 31, No. 1 (1977), 12–21.
———. *The Georgian Theatre in Wessex*. London, 1958.
Harrison, Gabriel. *The Life and Writing of John Howard Payne*. New York, 1875.
Hazlitt, William. *The Complete Works of William Hazlitt*. Edited by P. P. Howe. 21 vols. London, 1930–1934.
Herbert, J. D. *Irish Varieties*. London, 1836.
Hewitt, Barnard. *Theatre U.S.A., 1668 to 1957*. New York, 1959.
Highfill, Philip, Jr. "The British Background of the American Hallams." *TS*, 11 (May 1970), 1–35.
———; Burnim, Kalman A.; and Langhans, Edward A. *A Biographical Dictionary of Actors, Actresses, Musicians, Dancers, Managers, and Other Stage Personnel in London, 1660–1800*. 6 vols. to date. Carbondale, Ill., 1973–.
Hillebrand, Harold Newcomb. *Edmund Kean*. New York, 1933.
Hodgkinson, J. L. and Pogson, Rex. *The Early Manchester Theatre*. London, 1960.
Hogan, Charles Beecher. "The China Hall Theatre, Rotherhithe." *TN*, 8 (July-September 1954), 76–80.
———, ed. *The London Stage, 1660–1800*. Vol. 5. Part 1. Carbondale, Ill., 1968.
———. *Shakespeare in the Theatre, 1701–1800*. 2 vols. Oxford, 1957.
Holcroft, Thomas. *The Life of Thomas Holcroft*. Edited by Elbridge Colby. New York, 1968 (reprint).
Holland, John. *The Picture of Sheffield*. Sheffield, 1824.
Hunt, Leigh. *Critical Essays*. London, 1807.
———. *Dramatic Essays by Leigh Hunt*. Edited by William Archer and Robert W. Lowe. London, 1894.
Ireland, Joseph N. *A Memoir of the Professional Life of Thomas Abthorpe Cooper*. New York, 1888.
———. *Records of the New York Stage. From 1750 to 1860*. 2 vols. New York, 1866.
Irving, Pierre M. *The Life and Letters of Washington Irving*. Vol. 1. New York, 1868.
James, Reese D. *Old Drury of Philadelphia: A History of the Philadelphia Stage, 1800–1835*. Philadelphia, 1932.
Jenkins, Richard. *Memoirs of the Bristol Stage*. Bristol, 1826.
Joseph, Bertram. *The Tragic Actor*. London, 1959.
Kavanagh, Peter. *The Irish Theatre. Being a History of the Drama in Ireland from the Earliest Period up to the Present*. Tralee, 1946.
Kelly, John Alexander. *German Visitors to English Theaters in the Eighteenth Century*. Princeton, 1936.
Kelly, Michael. *Reminiscences of Michael Kelly of King's Theatre and Theatre Royal, Drury Lane, including a period of nearly half a century*. 2 vols. London, 1826.
Kemble and Cooke; or, A Critical Review of a Pamphlet published under the title of Remarks on the character of Richard the Third, As Played by Cooke and Kemble. London, 1801.
Kemble, Stephen. *To the Public*. Newcastle, 10 June 1793.
Kirkman, J. T. *Memoirs of the Life of Charles Macklin, Esq*. London, 1799.
Knapp, Mary E. *Prologues and Epilogues of the Eighteenth Century*. New Haven, 1961.
Lamb, Charles and Lamb, Mary. *The Letters of Charles and Mary Lamb*. Edited by E. V. Lucas. 3 vols. New Haven, 1935.
———. *The Works of Charles and Mary Lamb*. Edited by E. V. Lucas. 7 vols. New York, 1903–1905.
Lawson, Robb. *The Story of the Scots Stage*. New York, n.d.
Leacroft, Richard. *The Development of the English Playhouse*. Ithaca, N.Y., 1973.
(Leicester). *A Walk Through Leicester; Being a Guide to Strangers*. Leicester, 1804.
Lennox, William Pitt. *Celebrities I Have Known*. London, 1876.
———. *Plays, Players, and Playhouses*. 2 vols. London, 1881.

Lights of the Old English Stage. New York, 1878.
Lockhard, J. Gibson. *Memoirs of the Life of Sir Walter Scott, Bart.* Edinburgh, 1845.
Loftis, John, ed. *Restoration Drama: Modern Essays in Criticism.* New York, 1966.
The London Review. Conducted by Richard Cumberland. 3 vols. London, 1809.
Macklin, Charles. *The Man of the World, with Remarks by Mrs. Inchbald.* London, 1806.
MacMillan, Dougald. *Drury Lane Calendar.* Oxford, 1938.
Macqueen-Pope, W. *Haymarket: Theatre of Perfection.* London, 1948.
Manvell, Roger. *Sarah Siddons.* New York, 1970.
Mason, Louise H. "At the Tomb of George Frederick Cooke." *The Theatre Magazine* (March 1909), pp. 86–87.
Mathews, Anne. *Anecdotes of Actors.* London, 1844.
———. *Memoirs of Charles Mathews.* 4 vols. London, 1838.
Mathews, Brander and Hutton, Laurence, eds. *Actors and Actresses of Great Britain and the United States. The Kembles and Their Contemporaries.* New York, 1886.
Michael, Ruth A. "History of the Professional Theatre in Boston from the Beginning to 1816." Ph.D. dissertation, Radcliffe College, 1941.
The Monthly Mirror. London, 1796–1812.
Morley, Malcolm. *Margate and Its Theatre.* London, 1966.
Morris, Lloyd. *Curtain Time.* New York, 1953.
Mullin, Donald C. "Early Theatres in Rhode Island." *TS*, 11, No. 2 (November 1970), 167–186.
Munden, Thomas S. *Memoirs of Joseph Shepherd Munden, Comedian.* London, 1844.
Murdoch, James E. *The Stage or Recollections of Actors and Acting from an Experience of Fifty Years.* Philadelphia, 1880.
Nalbach, Daniel. *The King's Theatre 1704–1867.* London, 1972.
(Newcastle). *The Picture of Newcastle upon Tyne.* Newcastle, 1807.
Nicoll, Allardyce. *A History of English Drama, 1660–1900.* 6 vols. Cambridge, England, 1952–1967.
Noyes, Robert Gale. *The Neglected Muse.* Providence, R.I., 1958.
Odell, George C.D.. *Annals of the New York Stage.* 15 vols. New York, 1927–1949.
Oswald, Harold. *The Theatre Royal in Newcastle upon Tyne.* Newcastle, 1936.
Oxberry, William. *Oxberry's Dramatic Biography.* 4 vols. London, 1825–1826.
———. *The Theatrical Banquet, or, the Actors Budget.* 2 vols. London, 1809.
Pasquin, Anthony. *The Eccentricities of John Edwin.* Dublin, 1791.
Pemberton, T. Edgar. *The Theatre Royal, Birmingham, 1774–1901.* Birmingham, 1901.
Penley, Belville S. *The Bath Stage.* London, 1892.
Phelps, H. P. *Players of a Century: A Record of the Albany Stage.* 2d ed. New York, 1890.
"Philipi." *A Peep into the Theatre Royal, Manchester; with some remarks on the merits and demerits of the Performers.* Manchester, 1800.
[Pickering, Roger.] *Reflections upon Theatrical Expression in Tragedy.* London, 1755.
Playfair, Giles. *The Prodigy: The Strange Life of Master Betty.* London, 1967.
Pollock, Sir Frederick, ed. *Macready's Reminiscences, and Selections from His Diaries and Letters.* London, 1876.
Price, Cecil. "An Eighteenth Century Theatrical Agreement." *TN*, 2 (January–March 1948), 31–34.
———. "Joseph Austin and His Associates, 1766–1788." *TN*, 4 (July–September 1950), 89–94.
Proctor, Bryan. *The Life of Edmund Kean.* London, 1835.
Raymond, George. *Memoirs of Robert William Elliston.* 2 vols. London, 1846.
Remarks on the Character of Richard the Third as Played by Cooke and Kemble. London, 1801.
Reynolds, Frederick. *Life and Times of Frederick Reynolds.* 2 vols. London, 1826.
Richards, Kenneth and Thomson, Peter, eds. *The Eighteenth-Century English Stage.* London, 1972.
Roach, J. *Authentic Memoirs of the Green Room.* 2d ed. London, 1806.

———. *Authentic Memoirs of the Green Room.* London, n.d. (circa 1815).
Robinson, Henry Crabb. *Diary, Reminiscences, and Correspondence of Henry Crabb Robinson.* Edited by Thomas Sadler. 2 vols. Boston, 1869.
Robson, William. *The Old Play-Goer.* London, 1841.
Rosenfeld, Sybil. "Notes on the Theatrical History of St. George's Hall, King's Lynn." *TN*, 3 (January-March 1949), 24–27.
———. *The Theatre of the London Fairs in the Eighteenth Century.* Cambridge, England, 1960.
Ryan, Richard. *Dramatic Table Talk.* 3 vols. London, 1830.
Ryley, Samuel W. *The Itinerant.* 2d ed. 3 vols. London, 1817.
A Scotsman's Remarks on the Farce of Love a la Mode. London, 1760.
Scott, Clement. *The Drama of Yesterday and Today.* 2 vols. London, 1899.
Shattuck, Charles H. *The Shakespeare Promptbooks.* Urbana, Ill., 1965.
Shawe-Taylor, Desmond. *Covent Garden.* London, 1948.
Sheppard, Thomas. *Evolution of the Drama in Hull and District.* Hull, 1927.
Skinner, Otis. *Mad Folk of the Theatre.* Indianapolis, Ind., 1928.
Southern, Richard. "Concerning a Georgian Proscenium Ceiling." *TN*, 3 (October-December 1948), 6–12.
———. *The Georgian Playhouse.* London, 1948.
Sprague, Arthur Colby. *Shakespeare and the Actors.* Cambridge, Mass., 1944.
The Stage, or Theatrical Touchstone. London, 1805.
Steer, Francis W. *The Chichester Theatre.* Chichester, 1957.
Stockdale, John Joseph, ed. *The Covent Garden Journal.* 2 vols. London, 1810.
Stockwell, La Tourette. *Dublin Theatres and Theatre Customs, 1637–1820.* Kingsport, Tenn., 1938.
Stone, G. W., Jr., ed. *The London Stage, 1660–1800.* Vol. 4, Pt. 3. Carbondale, Ill., 1962.
Taylor, Aline MacKenzie. *Next to Shakespeare: Otway's 'Venice Preserv'd' and 'The Orphan.'* Durham, N.C., 1950.
Taylor, John. *Records of My Life.* London, 1832.
The Theatrical Inquisitor; or, an enquiry into what two worthy Managers have promised, and what performed. Manchester, 1804.
The Theatrical Repertory or Weekly Rosiad. Containing Criticisms on the Performances which were Represented at Drury-Lane and Covent-Garden Theatres, During the Season 1801-2. London, 1801–1802.
The Thespiad. London, 1809.
The Thespian Dictionary; or, Dramatic Biography of the Eighteenth Century. London, 1802.
The Thespian Dictionary. 2d ed. London, 1805.
The Thespian Review; an Examination of the Merits and Demerits of the Performers on the Manchester Stage. Manchester, 1804.
Thieme, John A. "Spouting, Spouting Clubs and Spouting Companions." *TN*, 29, No. 1 (1975), 9–16.
Ticknor, George. *Life, Letters and Journals of George Ticknor.* 5th ed. Vol. 1. Boston, 1876.
Trefman, Simon. *Sam. Foote, Comedian, 1720–1777.* New York, 1971.
Troubridge, St. Vincent. *The Benefit System in the British Theatre.* London, 1967.
(Veteran Stager). *An Essay on the Science of Acting by a Veteran Stager.* London, 1828.
(Ward). *A Letter to Ward with Critical Review on the Conduct of the Managers with Observations on Some of the Performers at the Theatre Royal Manchester.* Manchester, 1803.
Watts, Guy Tracey. *Theatrical Bristol.* Bristol, 1915.
Whalley, Thomas Sedgewick. *Journals and Correspondence of Thomas Sedgewick Whalley.* Edited with a Memoir and Illustrative Notes by Reverend Hill Wickham. 2 vols. London, 1863.
White, J. F. *An Appeal to the Public at Large, of the Town of Manchester, but Chiefly Addressed to the Violent Opposers of J. F. White Comedian.* Manchester, 1803.

Wilkinson, Tate. *Memoirs of His Own Life*. 4 vols. York, 1790.
——. *The Wandering Patentee; or, History of the Yorkshire Theatre, From 1770 to the Present*. 4 vols. York, 1795.
Willard, George O. *History of the Providence Stage, 1762–1891*. Providence, R.I., 1891.
Williams, Stanley Thomas. *Richard Cumberland, His Life and Dramatic Works*. New Haven, 1917.
Wilmeth, Don B. "Cooke Among the Yankee Doodles." *TS*, 14 (November 1973), 1–32.
——. "The Posthumous Career of George Frederick Cooke." *TN*, 24 (Winter 1969–1970), 68–74.
Wood, William B. *Personal Recollections of the Stage*. Philadelphia, 1855.
(York). *A Description of York, containing Some Account of its Antiquities, Public Buildings, etc.* London, 1809.
(York). *A New Description of York*. York, 1830.

Index

Addison, John, 117
Aickin, Francis, 76, 79–80, 159, 230
Aickin, James, 13, 76
Alfonso, King of Castile (Lewis), 174
Allingham, John Till, 100, 204
Allingham, Maria Caroline, 100
Alwyn; or, The Gentleman Comedian (Holcroft), 31. *See also* Spouting clubs
Amiens Treaty, 207
Anamaboah, the Indian king, 73
Angel Tavern (Manchester), 66
Appleton, William W., 179
Apprentice, The (Murphy). *See* Spouting clubs
Archer, [Alexander], 158, 223
Arnold, Mrs. Elizabeth, 76
Arthur Street Theatre. *See* Belfast Theatre
As You Like It, 19
Astley, Philip, 30, 90
Astley's Peter Street Theatre (Dublin), 113
Atkins, Mrs. (singer), 203
Atkins, Michael, 207
Atkinson, Joseph, 104
Attwood, Thomas, 124
Augustan tragedy. *See Cato*
Austin, Joseph, 41, 48–49, 64
Austin and Whitlock (managers), 53, 57, 60–64, 87. *See also* Austin, Joseph; Whitlock, Charles Edward
Author (Foote), 12. *See also* Foote, Samuel
Baker, Joseph, 55
Baltimore, Maryland, 260, 267
Banks, John, 44, 47, 51, 75–77, 99
Banks, Mrs. John, 81
Banks, Thomas, 53
Banks and Ward (managers). *See* Ward and Banks
Bannister, John, 121, 159, 161
Barrett, [John], 77
Barry, Ann, 19, 89
Barry, Spranger, 19, 90, 173

Barrymore, William, 217, 240
Bateman, Mrs., 91–92. *See also* D'Eon, Chevalier
Bates, William, 77, 81, 82
Bath, 40, 168–69, 177, 187, 217, 228, 240
Bath Theatre Royal, 168. *See also* Beaufort-Square Theatre
Bath Theatrical Fund, 169, 184, 228
Beat, David, 13
Beaufort-Square Theatre (Bath), 217–18. *See also* Bath Theatre Royal
Beaumont, Charles de. *See* D'Eon, Chevalier
Beaumont, Sir George, 21
Beggar's Opera, The (Gay), 38
Behn, Mrs. Violet Mary (later Mrs. George Frederick Cooke), 268, 275
Belfast, Ireland, 207
Belfast Theatre, 207
Belfil, Mrs. (actress), 63
Bellamy, Elizabeth, 117
Bellamy, Thomas Ludford, 75, 104, 106, 117, 196
Bengough (actor), 225, 229
Bernard, John, 24, 50, 58, 266; on Cooke's Sir Pertinax, 179–80
Berwick-upon-Tweed, 13, 77, 180, 230
Betterton, Thomas, 72, 142
Betty, William Henry West, 205, 207, 209–12, 213, 214, 216, 225
Beverley, William Roxby, 227
Beverly, Mrs. (actress), 177
Bibby, Governeurs S., 180
Bigg Market Theatre (Newcastle), 62
Biggs, Anne (later Mrs. Young), 159–60, 161, 240, 248
Billington, Mrs. Elizabeth, 100, 164
Bindon, Miss Emily (later Mrs. Montague Talbot), 115
Birmingham, 157–59, 185, 206–7, 214, 215, 250

Birmingham theatre, 158
Black Lion (tavern), 15, 25
Blanchard, William, 183, 198, 238, 240
Blind Bargain; or, Hear It Out (Reynolds), 208
Boaden, James, 23, 131, 152, 197, 206, 238; on Cooke's Hamlet, 189
Bologna, John, Jr., 228
Bolton, England, 82
Booth, Mr. (manager), 17
Booth, Barton, 190
Booth, Edwin, 283, 286
Booth, Junius Brutus, 262
Booth and Holland (managers). *See* Booth, Mr.; Holland, Mr.
Boston, Massachusetts, 260–66, 270–71
Boston Theatre, 264, 269–70
Bowery Theater, 282
Bowles, Robert, 34
Braham, John, 165, 189, 192, 213
Brandon, James, 227, 251
Bread and Cheese Club, 282
Brentford, England, 30–31
Brevoort, Henry, 267
Brighton Theatre, 208
Bristol, 168–69, 177, 187, 217, 240
Bristol Theatre Royal, 168
Bristol Theatrical Fund, 184
Brittania, the, 16
Brown, Mrs. J., 17
Browne, Matthew Campbell, 167, 183
Brunton, John (Jack), 147, 169, 175, 183, 208, 213, 214, 237
Bullen, Percy S., 281
Burden, Kitty, 34
Busby, Dr. Thomas, 174
Butler, Frances, 69
Buxton, 75–76, 82–84, 86, 99, 215
Byrn, Judy, 95
Byrne (actor), 222
Cabinet, The (Boston), 263
Cabinet, The (Dibdin), 189
Cambray, *See* Fennell, James
Campion, Maria. *See* Pope, Mrs. Alexander
Canangate Theatre, 13
Canterbury, 25
Capel Street Theatre (Dublin), 89
Carles (actor), 190, 206
Carpenter, Stephen Cullen, 267; on Cooke's Falstaff, 175; on Cooke's Sir Pertinax, 181-82; on Cooke's Richard III, 128–36
Cartwright (musician), 83

Catalani, Madame, 249
Cato (Addison), 14, 190; Cooke as, in London, 190; Cooke as, in the U.S., 190. *See also* Cooke, George Frederick; first stage appearances as an amateur
Chalmers (actor), 229
Chambers (actor), 104
Chapman, Miss Charlotte Jane, 147, 154, 165
Chapman, William, 216, 217
Cheltenham, 196
Cherry, Andrew, 99, 101
Chester, 54–55, 58, 61–62, 64, 71, 72, 76, 81, 85, 99, 101, 185, 196
Chester Theatre Royal, 54, 75
Chesterfield, 196, 197
Chestnut Street Theatre, 193, 262, 266, 269
Chichester, 245–46
Chichester theatre, 245
China-Hall Theatre, 33–38
"Choice Spirits" (club), 32
Claremont (actor), 183, 200
Clarke, Mrs. (actress), 251, 255
Clinton, Mayor DeWitt, 275
Coleridge, Samuel Taylor, on Cooke's Falstaff, 175–76
Collins, William, 245
Colman, George the elder, 32, 90
Colman, George the younger, 191. *See also John Bull, or an Englishman's Fire-Side*
Columbia, the, 257–58
Comas, Reverend Dr. Joseph P.M., 281
Cone (actor), 269
Congdon (actor), 81
Connor (actor/manager), 44
Cooke, George Frederick; abstinence, comments on, 109–110, 219, acting style of, 5–7, 127, 128, 144, 150–52, 155–56, 267 (*see also* specific roles with separate entries); alcohol, effects on, 53, 64–66, 67, 71, 78–79, 81, 82–84, 87, 95–96, 112, 114, 116, 117, 124, 157, 165–66, 183, 186, 191, 194, 198, 199–200, 204, 206, 208–9, 214, 218–19, 222–23, 224–25, 226–27, 230, 231, 235, 226–27, 230, 231, 235, 237, 244, 247–48, 252, 258, 259, 263, 286; *Alfonso*, comments on, 174–75; American Revolution, claims to have participated in, 87; American tours of, 259–73; Americans, condemnation and praise of, 203, 260, 264–66; apologies to audiences by, 61, 79, 166–67, 192, 200, 213, 219, 223–24, 253–54;

Index

apprentice as a printer, 12; late arrival for second London season, 164–66; Bath and Bristol, first appearances in, 168-69; Behn, marriage to 168; benefit, first London, 148-49; Birmingham, first appearances in, 158-59; birth of, 10; *Castle Spectre,* opinions of, 116; comic excellence of, 47, 59; compared to Charles Macklin, 22-23, 104, 139, 140-41, 179-81; compared to David Garrick, 21-22; compared to Edmund Kean, 6-7, 144; compared to John Henerson, 40, 135; compared to John Philip Kemble, 104, 131, 135, 146, 150-53, 171, 173, 206, 235; compared to Stephen Kemble, 175, 226; Cooper, Thomas A., associations with, 193-94; court martial of, 96-97; Govent Garden debut of, 5, 22; Govent Garden initial negotiations with, 122; Daniels, Alicia, marriage to, 99; Daniels, Alicia, marriage to voided, 159; death of, 272, 275-77; debts incurred by, 106 *(see also* financial straits of); descriptons of, 224-25, 273; diary and journal of, 76, 86, 106-110, 112-20, 179, 185-86, 187, 219,221, 227, 232-35; and "the dirty beau," 64-66; dissolution of second marriage to Lamb, 244; *Douglas,* sees production of, 14; Drury Lane, appearnaces at, 194, 205; Dublin first appearnaces in, 92-94; Dublin, leaves suddenly in 1795, 94; Dublin and Dublin theatre, comments on, 92, 102, 103, 120; earliest professional appearances of, 24-30; early theatrical influences on, 13, 14, 17, 18-40; early years in Berwick-upon-Tweed, 12; early years in London, 12, 18; Edinburgh, first appearances in, 159-61; education of, 12-13; eighteenth-century actors, comments on, 98-99; enlistment in army of, 96; equestrain performers, admiration for, 116; father of, 11; final performance anywhere of, 273; final performance in England of, 225; financial conditions at death, 277; financial straits of, 229, 231, 235, 244 *(see also* debts incurred by); first stage appearances as an amateur, 13, 14, 15; funeral and burial of, 275; greenroom, opinions of, 112-13; Hamlet, comments on his performance of, 188; Haymarket Theatre, appearances at, 32-33, 38, 242-45; Holland, trip to, 15-16; illnesses of, 111, 156, 162, 165-66, 185, 200, 204, 216, 217, 240, 243, 248, 252, 259, 266, 267, 270, 272; in Appleby Jail for debt, 229-35; indiscretions toward London audiences by, 156-57; initial reception in London, 125-28; intention to return to England, 266, 269, 271; Jordan Dorothy, acts with, 71; Kemble, J.P., defends, 252; Kemble, J.P., first appearances with, 120-21; Kemble, J.P., first appearance with in London, 199; Kemble, J.P., under the management of, 198-200, 202-6, 207-14, 215-20, 225-29, 236-39, 242-45, 248-55; Kemble, J.P., and Siddons, acts with for first time, 199; Kemble's *The Tempest,* comments on, 228; Kemble, Stephen, dispute with, 74; King's Theatre, performs at, 242; Lamb, marriage to, 241; Lancaster, first appearances in, 48-49; leaves England for the U.S., 256-58; literary efforts of, 113, 117; Liverpool, first appearances in, 49-52; London (1774–75), stay in, 29; London debut of, 124; London, initial season in, 187-94; London, fourth season in, 198-205; London, fifth season in, 207-14; London, sixth season in, 215-20; seventh season in, 225-29; London, eighth season in, 236-39; London, ninth season in, 242-44; London, tenth season in, 248-54; London residences of, 137, 166, 187, 215, 225, 236, 243, 248; *Macbeth,* sees production of, 14; *Man of the World,* comments on, 179; Manchester, first appearances in, 43-48; Marshall, Mrs., has indiscretion with, 74; Master Betty and Master Payne, assessment by, 211; most prominent roles played by, 3, 156; mother of, 11, 12; Newcastle, first appearances in, 62-64; Newcastle audiences, condemns, 240; O'Keefe, opinion of, 76; on David Garrick, 21-22; on Tate Wilkinson, 56; painted or drawn by artists, 287-89; pantomime, opinions of, 115; philanthropy toward others, 39, 213-14, 231, 247-48; reading habits of, 76, 87, 109, 115; reburial of and monument to, 277-78, 280-82; regimen, lack of, 113; *Revenge, The,* comments on, 170; self-appraisal of mental state or personal status, 117, 221, 232-34; serves as a cabin boy, 16; Siddons, first acts with, 56-57; silver cups presented to in Liverpool, 246-47; skull, legend of, 277-78, 282-86; spouting club appearances by, 30-31; *Stranger, The,* opinions on, 113; trend toward villains and rakes, 82; unhappy marriages of, 244; U.S. response to acting of, 262 *(see also* specific roles with separate entries); visit to London as young man, 15; vocal characteristics of, 28, 68, 70, 100, 119, 131, 143–44, 146, 151, 180, 228, 247; Whitlock (Mrs.), controversy involving, 69; wife, first mention of possible, 27; will of, 274; *Wives As They Were and Maids As They Are*, criticism of, 118; works as a compositor, 17, 29; writes verse into prose, 21, 144; York, first appearances in, 55–57

Cooke, George Frederick, roles played by: Abbot (*King Henry the Second*), 51; Adam (*As You Like It*), 54, 80; Aimwell (*The Beaux' Stratagem*), 51; Alberto (*Child of Nature*), 161; Alexander (*Rival Queens*), 28, 70, 72; Alonzo (*Columbus*), 81, 85; Angelo (*Measure for Measure*), 203; Anthony Euston, 86; Antonio (*The Merchant of Venice*); Apollo (*Midas*), 29; Archer (*The Beaux' Stratagem*), 67; Aubrey (*The Fashionable Lover*), 82; Austin (*The Count of Narbonne*), 120; Bajazet (*Tamerlane*), 101, 184, 187, 189, 215; Banquo (*Macbeth*), 79; Barbarossa (*Barbarossa*), 47; Barnwell, (*The London Merchant*), 85; Baron Fitzherbert (*Robin Hood*), 52, 53; Baron Wildenheim (*Lovers' Vows*), 111, 112, 114, 116, 244, 246; Bassanio (*The Merchant of Venice*), 25; Beau Mizen (*Fair Quaker of Deal*), 29; Beauchamp (*Which Is the Man?*), 62; Belarius (*Cymbeline*), 52; Bellair (*More Ways Than One*), 52; Belvil Junior (*The Conscious Lovers*), 70, 73; Belville (*School for Wives*, Kelly), 29, 70; Benedick (*Much Ado About Nothing*), 44, 68, 111; Bertoldo (*Maid of Honour*), 55; Beverly (*All in the Wrong*), 29; Beverly (*The Man of Business*), 29; Biron (*Isabella*), 111; "British Loyalty, or, a Squeeze for St. Paul" (recited), 72, 73; Captain Bertram (*Birth Day*), 112, 114, 115, 116, 117, 119; Captain Constant (*The Ghost*), 36; Captain Cook (*The Death of Captain Cook*), 72; Captain Faulkner (*The Way to Get Married*), 114, 184; Captain Ironsides (*The Brothers*), 112, 114; Captain Jack Absolute (*The Rivals*), 54, 77, 79; Captain Plume (*The Recruiting Officer*), 70; Caratach (*Bonduca*), 237–38; Cardinal Wolsey (*King Henry VIII*), 47, 72, 94; Carlos (*Loves Makes a Man*), 47, 78, 79, 80; Carlton (*More Ways Than One*), 54, 55; Cassio (*Othello*), 25; Castalio (*The Orphan*), 32, 47; Cato (*Cato*), 46–47, 94, 189–90, 196, 248, 262; "Celebrated Ode on the Passions" (recited), 62, 69, 70, 77, 81, 85, 98, 101, 161, 162; Charles Belmont (*The Foundling*), 38; Charles Dudley, 25; Charles Gayless (*The Lying Valet*), 35; Charles Gripe (*The Busy Body*), 36; Charles Manlove (*The Choleric Man*), 29; Claudio (*Much Ado About Nothing*), 52; Claudius (*Hamlet*), 44, 52; Clerimont (*Duenna*), 63; Clerimont (*Old Maid*), 69; Clerimont (*The Tender Husband*), 73; Clytus (*Alexander; or, the Rival Queens*), 58, 79, 81, 238; Cohenberg (*Siege of Belgrade*), 205; Colin MacLeod (*The Fashionable Lover*), 237, 240, 246, 248; Colonel Feignwell (*A Bold Stroke for a Wife*), 69; Colonel Holberg (*The Disbanded Officer*), 58; Colonel Standard (*The Constant Couple*), 70, 72; Colonel Talbot (*He Would Be a Soldier*), 85, 94; Colonel Vortex (*Matchmaking*), 238; Columbus (*Columbus*), 92; Comus (*Comus*), 120, 191; Conolly (*School for Wives*, Kelly), 101; Coriolanus (Kemble adaptation), 85, 205; Count Almaviva (*The Follies of a Day*), 80; Count Baldwin (*Isabella*), 57; Count Connolly Villars (*The School of Arrogance*), 77; Count of Carbonne, 112; Count Ribaumont (*The Surrender of Calais*), 77, 79, 80, 81; Damaetas (*Midas*), 28; Darnley ? (*The Rage*), 94; Dashwould (*Know Your Own Mind*), 71; Delaval (*He's Much to Blame*), 109; Dionysias (*The Grecian Daughter*), 79; Don Alonzo (*The Revenge*), 44; Don Carlos (*A Bold Stoke for a Husband*), 62, 80, 205; Don Estivan (*The Word of Honour*), 183; Don Felix (*The Wonder*), 28, 47, 64, 147, 238; Don Juan (*The Castle of Andalusia*), 51; Don Julio (*A Bold Stroke for a Husband*), 52, 54; Don Manuel (*The Spanish Regent*), 68; Douglas (*Douglas*), 44; Duke (*Duke of Braganza*), 85; Duke (*Measure for Measure*), 68, 101; Dumont (*Jane Shore*), 31, 75, 216, 219; Dupely (*The Maid of the Oaks*), 29, 63; Earl Douglas (*Percy*), 63; Earl of Essex (*Earl of Essex*), 101; Earl of Southampton (*The Earl of Essex*), 36, 79; Earl of Warwick (*Earl of Warwick*), 73, 100; Earl Raby (*Percy*), 54; Edgar (*King Lear*), 37, 70; Edmund (*King Lear*), 120; Edward (*Edward the Black Prince), 81, 85; Edward Mortimer (The Iron Chest), 183; "Elegy Written in a Country Churchyard," Gray (recited), 98; Ensign Dudley (The West Indian), 31; Epicene (The Macaroni), 28; Exeter (Henry V), 72; Falconbridge (King John), 73; Falstaff (Henry IV, Part 1), 175–77, 185, 205, 206, 208, 243, 246, 248, 266; Falstaff (Henry IV, Part 2), 177, 204; Falstaff (The Merry Wives of Windsor), 177, 189, 217, 222, 255; Farmer Blackberry (The Farmer), 214; Faulkland (The Rivals), 82, 86, 114; Ferdinand (The Tempest), 29; Filch (The Beggar's Opera), 28; Floriville (The Dramatist), 77; Frankly (The Suspicious Husband), 50, 62, 92; Frederick (The Miser), 36; Frederick (The Wonder), 35; Freeport (The Scotch Woman), 86; Friar Lawrence (Romeo and Juliet), 93, 111; a gambler (The Indian Chief), 47; Ghost (Hamlet), 79, 93, 120, 205; Gibby (The Wonder), 244, 248; Glanville (Cleone), 52; Glenalvon (Douglas), 35, 38, 199, 211, 212, 213, 235, 269; Gondibert (Battle of Hexam), 72; Granville, (Clementina), 28; "Grecian Fabulist, or the Story of the Man, the Boy and the Ass" (recited), 64; Grey (Chapter of Accidents), 79, 104; Guardian (The Guardian), 73, 86; Hamlet, (Hamlet), 28, 55, 62, 64, 72, 74, 81, 98, 160, 161, 162, 186, 188–89; Hammond (Modern Breakfast), 74; Harlow (The Old Maid), 37; Harmony (Everyone Has His Fault), 85, 86, 93, 104, 161, 196; Harry Dornton (The Road to Ruin), 77, 80, 81, 85, 86; Harry Thunder, alias Dick Buskin (Wild Oats), 77, 79, 81; Hastings (Jane Shore), 100, 101; Haswell (Such Things Are), 62, 63, 77, 86, 106, 119, 205; Henry (The Deserter), 27, 28; Henry II (Henry II), 28, 54; Henry V (Kemble adaptation), 77, 81; Henry VI (Richard III), 44, 79, 111, 112; Henry VIII (Henry VIII), 254; Horatio (The Fair Penitent), 119; Horatio (Hamlet), 13, 24; Horatius (The Roman Father), 252, 254; Hotspur (Henry IV, Part 1), 29, 47–48, 72, 85; Hubert (King John), 193, 204; Iachimo (Cymbeline), 72, 80, 216; Iago (Othello), 82, 104, 119, 142–45, 160, 161, 167, 168, 185, 186, 189, 190, 194, 204, 206, 213, 214, 215, 216, 217, 222, 230, 235, 240, 241, 243, 246, 248, 250, 255, 267; Inkle (Inkle and Yarico), 64; Jack Meggot (The Suspicious Husband), 27; Jaffier (Venice Preserv'd), 27, 60, 63; Jaques (As You Like It), 68, 86, 160, 161, 169, 235; John Cockle (The Miller of Mansfield), 244; Joseph Surface (The School for Scandal), 76, 80, 105, 223, 235, 248; Kent (King Lear), 238; King (The King and the Miller of Mansfield), 112, 116, 248; King Arthur (King Arthur), 29; King John, 98, 192–93; King Lear (King Lear), 28, 80, 171–74, 228, 246, 255, 266, 267; Kitely (Every Man in His Humour), 82, 85, 161, 189, 198, 206, 208, 219, 235, 246, 251, 254, 255; Laertes (Hamlet), 25; Las Casas (Pizarro), 120; Lavensforth (To Marry or Not to Marry), 212; "Lecture on Oratory" (recited), 59; Leon (Rule a Wife and Have a Wife), 161; Leonidas (Fate of Sparta), 63; Lieutenant Seymour (Love Gives the Alarm), 205; Lord Aberville (The Fashionable Lover), 36; Lord Aimworth (The Maid of the Mill), 28, 29, 85; Lord Avondale (School of Reform), 212; Lord Burleigh (The Earl of Essex), 51; Lord Davenant (The Mysterious Husband), 85, 216; Lord Duke (High Life Below Stairs), 28; Lord Hardy (Funeral), 28; Lord Hastings (Jane Shore), 28, 35, 54, 72, 215; Lord Hildebrand (Carmelite), 72; Lord Ogleby (The Clandestine Marriage), 29; Lord Raby (Percy), 51, 52; Lord Salisbury (The Countess of Salisbury), 111; Lord Townley (The Provoked Husband), 78, 86, 208, 235; Lord Trinket (The Jealous Wife), 28; Loveless (Reparation), 70, 72; Loveless (Trip to Scarborough), 72, 111, 115; Lovemore (Way to Keep Him), 28, 68; Lovewell (The Clandestine Marriage), 33, 36; Luke (Riches), 255; Macbeth (Macbeth), 28, 54, 60, 63, 68, 82, 92, 93, 98, 120, 144–46, 159, 160, 161, 186, 187, 189, 214, 218, 222, 228, 230, 235, 240, 267; Macduff (Macbeth), 202; Major O'Flaherty (The West Indian), 76; Malville (Know Your Own Mind), 52, 58; Manly, 25; Mark Antony (Julius Caesar), 98; Marplot (The Busybody), 29; Medium (Prejudice of Fashion), 38; Mentevole (The Italian Lover), 63; Mercutio (Romeo and Juliet), 161; Modely (The Country Lasses), 33, 72; Moneses (Tamerlane), 52; "Monody on the

Death of Garrick" (recited), 73; Moody (*The Country Girl*), 76, 105, 111, 112, 116; Morcar (*Matilda*), 30; Myrtle (*The Conscious Lovers*), 63; Neville (*The Dramatist*), 73; Oakly (*The Jealous Wife*), 62, 72, 79, 215, 230, 235, 240; Octavian (*The Mountaineers*), 85, 86, 98, 106, 161; "Ode on St. Cecilia's Day," Dryden (recited), 98; "Ode on Shakespeare," Garrick (recited), 55, 59, 62, 68, 149, 184, 238; "Ode to Garrick" (recited), 28; "Ode to Nelson," Pearce (recited), 226, 235; Old Norval (*Douglas*), 111; Ordeal (*The Fashionable Levities*), 59; Orestes (*The Distrest Mother*), 44, 52; Orlando (*As You Like It*), 25; Orloff (*A Day in Turkey*), 80; Oroonoko, 29; Orsino (Alfonso, King of Castile), 174–75, 186, 216; Osmond (*The Castle Spectre*), 116, 120, 161, 205; Osmonde (*The Poor Soldier*), 112; Othello (*Othello*), 62, 63, 92, 93, 159, 160, 162; Paris (*The Judgment of Paris*), 27; Penruddock (*The Wheel of Fortune*), 98, 104, 160, 208; Percy (*Percy*), 81, 85; Peregrine (*John Bull*), 190–92, 198, 206, 208, 216, 222, 223, 229, 235; Petruchio (*Catherine and Petruchio*), 70, 72, 78, 81, 82, 86, 160, 161, 215, 222, 229; Philotas (*The Grecian*), 43, 51, 54, 62; "Picture of a Play-house; or Bucks Have at Ye All" (recited), 28, 64; Pierre (*Venice Preserv'd*), 82, 184, 190, 203, 215, 223, 241, 267; Pizarro (*Pizarro, Sheridan*), 199-202, 208; Poins (*Henry IV, Part 1*), 25; Posthumous (*Cymbeline*), 28, 62, 70, 98; Prince of Altenburg (*Adrian and Orilla*), 226–27, 240; Prologue (*Henry V*), 215; prologue (*Neck or Nothing*), 94; Prospero (*The Tempest*; also *The Enchanted Island*), 44, 69, 72, 80, 81, 94; Prussian officer (*The Prussian Festival*), 77; Ramilie (*The Miser*), 28; Random (*Ways and Means*), 101; Ranger (*The Suspicious Husband*), 47; Raymond (*The Countess of Salisbury*), 51, 52, 62; Revell (*The Note of Hand*), 28; Richard (*Richard Coeur de Lion*), 80; Richard III (*Richard III*), 22, 29–30, 64, 82, 92, 93, 100, 105, 111, 124–36, 142, 150, 152–53, 156, 158–60, 161, 162, 166–67, 168, 169, 185, 186, 187, 189, 196, 197, 199, 206, 208, 209, 213, 214, 215, 218–19, 222, 223, 225, 228, 229, 230, 235, 237, 238, 240, 241, 243, 246, 247, 248, 253, 267, 268, 269, 271; Riches (*Harlequin Fortunates*), 28; Rolla (*Pizarro*), 206, 214; Romeo (*Romeo and Juliet*), 29, 63, 75; Rover (*Wild Oats*), 76, 86; Ruzee (*The Modish Wife*), 28; Sandy MacTab (*Three Per Cents*), 203; Sciolto (*The Fair Penitent*), 51, 79, 202, 216; Scotchman (*The Register Office*), 223; Shylock (*The Merchant of Venice*), 63, 69, 81, 82, 85, 101, 104, 108, 110, 112, 137, 138–40, 141, 159-60, 161, 162, 167, 169, 185, 186, 189, 203, 206, 214, 218, 222, 223, 226, 228, 230, 235, 236-37, 240, 245-46, 248, 251, 255, 266, 267, 270, 272; Siffredi (*Tancred and Sigismunda*), 44; Sir Anthony Absolute (*The Rivals*), 94; Sir Archy MacSarcasm (Love-a-la-Mode), 94, 140–41, 159–60, 161, 162, 167, 169, 185, 186, 187, 189, 196, 205, 208, 213, 214, 215, 216, 218, 222, 223, 228, 230, 235, 240, 241, 243, 246, 248, 255, 267; Sir Callaghan O'Brallaghan (*Love-a-la-Mode*), 86; Sir Charles Pleasant (*The Fair Quaker*), 51; Sir Charles Racket (*Three Weeks After Marriage*), 82; Sir Christopher Curry (*Inkle and Yarico*), 238, 240; Sir Clement Flint (*The Heiress*), 58, 68, 73; Sir Edward Mortimer (*The Iron Chest*), 99, 101; Sir George Airy (*The Busy Body*), 80; Sir George Hastings (*A Word to the Wise*), 27; Sir George Splendourville (*Next Door Neighbours*), 77, 81; Sir George Touchwood (*The Belles' Stratagem*), 73, 74, 105; Sir Giles Overreach (*A New Way to Pay Old Debts*), 98, 154–56, 159–60, 186, 189, 218, 222, 223, 228, 240, 241, 244, 246, 255, 267, 271, 273; Sir John Dormer (*A Word to the Wise*), 72; Sir John Lambert (*The Hypocrite*), 52; Sir John Melville (*The Clandestine Marriage*), 54, 62, 63, 79; Sir John Restless (*All in the Wrong*), 58, 61, 62; Sir Pertinax MacSycophant (*Man of the World*), 85, 98, 100, 161, 177–82, 183, 185, 186, 187, 189, 190, 191, 198, 206, 208, 214, 215, 216, 218, 222, 223, 228, 229, 230, 235, 236, 237, 240, 241, 242, 245, 246, 248, 251, 254, 255, 267, 269; Sir Peter Teazle (*School for Scandal*), 47; Sir Philip Blandford (*Speed the Plough*), 121, 184, 192; Sir Robert Ramble (*Every One Has His Faults*), 82, 86; Sir William Dorrilon (*Wives As They Were*), 101, 106, 108, 111, 117; Sir William Douglas (*The English

Index

Merchant), 72; Spatter (*The English Merchant*), 28; Spatterdash (*The Young Quaker*), 55; Stedfast (*The Heir at Law*), 105, 109, 112; Stockwell (*The West Indian*), 29, 120; Stranger (*The Stranger*), 112–13, 114, 115, 116, 119, 149–50, 161, 162, 208, 223, 240; Mr. Strickland (*The Suspicious Husband*), 25, 147, 208; Stukely (*The Gamester*), 54, 62, 64, 79, 94, 105, 120, 161–62, 167, 202, 216, 223, 235, 243, 267; Sultan (*Such Things Are*), 58; Tamerlane, (*Tamerlane*) 29; Tancred (*Tancred and Sigismunda*), 76; Tangent (*The Way to Get Married*), 98; "The Toast" (sung), 29; Tom (*The Conscious Lovers*), 29; Tressel (*Richard III*), 15, 36; Truman (*The London Merchant*), 36; Tybalt (Garrick's version, *Romeo and Juliet*), 36; Vandercrab (*New Peerage*), 62; Villeroy (*Isabella*), 51, 52; Whittle (*The Irish Widow*), 27; Wilding (*The Gamesters*), 28; Wingrove (*The Fugitive*), 80; Worthy (*Roderick Random*), 81; Young Dudley (*The West Indian*), 51; young lover (*Lionel and Clarissa*), 27; Young Marlow (*She Stoops to Conquer*), 27, 35, 44, 86; Young Meadows (*Love in a Village*), 13, 28; Young Wilding (*The Citizen*), 36, 51, 62, 86; Zamor (*Alzira*), 73; Zanga (*The Revenge*), 28, 94, 105, 170–71, 189, 222, 223, 235
Cooke, Mrs. George Frederick Cooke, 27, 28, 29, 43, 46–47, 51, 53–55. *See also* Behn, Mrs. Violet Mary; Daniels, Alicia; Lamb, Miss.
Cooper, James Fenimore, 282
Cooper, Thomas Abthorpe, 144, 193–94, 195, 196, 204, 254, 255, 256–59, 266, 267, 269
Copland, Robert, 185
Cork, 91, 103, 105, 106–10, 112, 124
Cork Theatre, 48. *See also* George Street Theatre, Cork
Covent Garden, Theatre Royal, 124, 162, 177, 197; compared to the Crow Street Theatre, Dublin, 90; destroyed by fire, 242; new theatre opens, 248–49
Covent Garden Theatrical Relief Act, 212
Cozeners (Foote), 19. *See also* Foote, Samuel
Crawford, Thomas, 89
Critical Essays on the Dramatic Excellence of Young Roscius (James Blisset), 211–12
Crouch, Mrs. Anna Maria, 85, 248

Crow Street Theatre (Dublin), 48, 89–91, 103–5, 222
Crown and Anchor Tavern, 251
Cumberland, Richard, on Cooke's Iago, 143
Cummins, Alexander, 58
Curtiss, Thomas, 281
Daly, Augustin, 282
Daly, Felix, 124
Daly, Richard, 89–96, 103
Daniels, Alicia (later Mrs. George Frederick Cooke), 43, 80–81, 98, 99–102, 104, 105, 107, 159, 241
Darlington, Miss (actress), 114
Davenport (actor), 237
Davenport, Mrs. Mary, 204
Davies (comic), 91
Davis (actor), 77, 81, 85
Davis, William, 116
Dawson, James, 13
Dawson and Beat (managers). *See* Beat, David; Dawson, James
DeCamp, Maria Theresa (later Mrs. Charles Kemble), 159, 225, 238, 243
D'Eon, Chevalier, 92
Derby, 196, 197
Devil Upon Two Sticks (Foote), 19. *See also* Foote, Samuel
DeWilde, Samuel, 219
Dibdin, Charles, 77
Dibdin, Mrs. Thomas, 157, 177
Dibdin, Thomas, 21, 22, 77–78, 137–38, 157, 177; on Cooke in Manchester, 78; on Alicia Daniels, 100; on Cooke's indiscretions, 157
Dickson (Dickinson), James, 270
Digges, West Dudley, 23
Dignum, Charles, 80
Dimond, William Wyatt, 168
Distrest Mother, The (Philips), 19
Dock (England), 186
Doige (actor), 231
Double Dealer, The (Congreve), 18
Douglas (Home), 19, 35; *see also* Scott, Sir Walter
Dowton, William, 205
Drake, Miss F., 198
Drummond, Samuel, 227
Drury Lane, Theatre Royal, 34, 120, 250, 164–65, 169, 187, 197, 200, 207, 209, 249; destroyed by fire, 243
Dublin, 11, 89–96, 102–6, 111–22, 222–23
Dublin theatre history, 89–90
Duffy, William, 269

Duncan, Mrs. (actress), 63
Duncan, Miss Maria, 63
Duncan, [Timothy], 63
Dunlap, William, 3, 4, 8, 16, 112, 144, 174, 204, 217, 231–32, 256, 266; *Memoirs of the Life of George Frederick Cooke*, 3–4, 232; on Cooke's King Lear, 171–72; on Cooke's Macbeth, 146; on Cooke's Sir Giles Overreach, 155–56
Dunn, George, 166
Dunstall, John, 23
Durang, Charles, 267, 273; on Cooke's Iago, 144; on Cooke's Sir Pertinax, 182
Dutton, Thomas, 124; on Cooke's Kitely, 147; on Cooke's Sir Giles Overreach, 154; on Cooke's and Kemble's interpretations of The Stranger
Dwyer, John, 193
Edinburgh, 159–61, 230, 235–36, 241, 248
Edinburgh Theatre Royal, 159, 248
Edmund Kean Club, 281
Edward and Eleonora (Hull), 19
Edwin, John, Sr., 23
Edwin, John, Jr., 74
Egan, Pierce, 31, 158. See also Spouting clubs
Egerton, Daniel, 252
Elfrida (Mason), 76
Elliston, Robert William, 168–69, 222, 253–54, 278
Emery, Mrs. (actress), 237
Emery, John, 184, 240
English Fleet in 1342 (Dibdin), 206
Episcopal Actors' Guild of America, 282
Everard, Edward Cape, 31, 33, 35, 37–38, 39
Everyman in His Humour (Jonson), 146–7
Exchange Coffee-house, 266
Fair Penitent, The (Rowe), 13, 19
Falstaff, criticism of Cooke's portrayals, 175–77, 204
Falstaff Club, 215
Farington, Joseph, comparison of Cooke and J.P. Kemble, 151–52
Farley, Charles, 147, 219, 238
Farren, Elizabeth, 91
Fatal Discovery, The (Colman), 19
Fawcett, John, 147, 183, 191, 215, 217, 225, 248
Fawcett, Mrs. John (formerly Mrs. John Mills), 79
Fay, Joseph, 275
Felican (also known as Felissent or Felessini), 165

Fennell, James, 69–70, 258, 267
Finkle Street Theatre (Hull), 243
Fishamble Street Theatre (Dublin), 90, 103, 104
Fisher, Mr. (actor/manager), 14
Fisher, [David], 38–39
Fitzgerald, Mrs. (actress), 158
Foote (manager, Plymouth), 186
Foote, Samuel, 18–19, 31, 32. See also Cooke, George Frederick, early influences on
Forrest, Edwin, 281
Fox (actor), 52
Francis, Dr. Henry, 282
Francis, Dr. John Wakefield, 10, 258, 273, 277–79, 282–83
Francis, Samuel, 283
Francis, Dr. Valentine Mott, 282–83
Freedley, George, 281
Freeman, Mr. (actor), 32
French Revolution, 81
Frohman, Daniel, 286
Fullam, Michael, 112
Furness, Dr. Horace Howard, 285
Garrick, David, 19–22, 36, 49, 79, 143, 146, 147, 173, 187, 215, 237; roles played by, 21–22. See also Cooke, George Frederick, early theatrical influences on
Garvey, Mrs. (actress), 110
General View of the Stage, A. See Wilkes, Thomas
George Street Theatre (Cork), 106, 108
George III (king of England), 92, 203, 251; on Cooke's Hamlet, 188; on Cooke's Sir Pertinax, 179. See also Royal family's visits to Covent Garden
Gibbs, Mrs. Maria (later Mrs. George Colman the younger), 191
Glasgow, 161, 221–22, 229, 235
Glasgow theatre, 159, 222–29
Glassington, Miss (actress), 27, 34
Glassington, Joseph, 34, 100, 185, 232
Gloucester, 196
Glover, Mrs. Samuel (formerly Julia Betterton), 240
Glovers' Hall Theatre (Perth), 248
Godwin, William, 193–94
Goede, Christian August Gottlieb, records physical description of Cooke and J.P Kemble, 151
Gough, Miss (later Mrs. Galindo), 112, 120
Grant (actor), 230, 241
Gravesend (England), 237

Gray, Thomas, on Spranger Barry, 19
Grecian Daughter, The (Murphy), 19
Grimaldi, Joseph, 228
Grist, Thomas, 42–44, 47, 51, 52, 55, 81, 84
Hallam, Lewis, 50
Halleck, Fitz–Green, 280
Halsey, Thomas Lloyd, 156
Hamblin, Thomas,, 282
Hamerton (actor), 97, 100
Hamlet, as played by David Garrick, 20–21
Hamlet, criticism of Cooke's initial London performances, 188–89
Hammerton, Jacob, 117
Handel, George Frederick, organ and scores of, destroyed by fire, 242
Hanmer, Henry, 247
Hare, Arnold, 245
Hargrove (actor), 92, 93
Harley, George D., 111, 112, 119, 158, 159
Harlowe, Mrs. (actress), 240
Harpur, Reverend Mr., 12
Harris, Henry, 257, 271
Harris, Thomas, 122, 149, 157, 164, 175, 177, 187, 191, 193–94, 205, 212, 225, 227, 236, 256; on Cooke's debut as Richard III, 22
Harrop, Joseph, 47
Hastings (England), 31
Haymarket Theatre, 18, 32–33, 38, 165, 242–43, 269
Hazlitt, William, 7, 180
Heatton, Michael, 48
Henderson, Mrs. (singer), 62
Henderson, John, 22–23, 40, 79, 135, 142, 143, 173, 175
Herbert (manager), 26. *See also* Whitley, James A.
Hill, Mr. (actor), 63, 184, 203
Historical View of the Irish Stage from the Earliest Period Down to the Close of the Season 1788 (Hitchcock), 91. *See also* Hitchcock, Robert
Hitchcock, Robert, 91, 95
Hobart, Bishop John Henry, 278
Hodgkinson, John, 43, 68, 70
Holcroft, Thomas, 31, 193–94; comparison of Cooke and J.P. Kemble, 152
Holland, 15–16
Holland, Mr. (manager), 17
Holland, Henry, 124
Hollingsworth, Thomas, 52, 257
Holman, George Joseph, 79, 97, 223, 256, 274

Hopkins, William, 43
Hosack, Dr. David, 275, 277
Howard, Harry, 32
Howells, Miss (actress), 192
Huddart, Thomas, 111, 112, 120
Hull (England), 57, 58, 243
Hull, Thomas, 145
Hunt, Leigh, on Cooke's Richard III, 127; on Cooke's Sir Pertinax, 180–81; on Cooke's Stukely, 167–68
Iago, criticism of Cooke's initial London performances, 142–44
Inchbald, Elizabeth, on *Man of the World* (Macklin), 179
Incledon, Charles, 121, 191, 199, 203, 225, 264
Independent Chronicle (Boston), 263–64
Irish Rebellion of 1798, 103, 105
Irish Widow, The (Garrick), 27
Irving, Washington, 267
Jackson, John, 159, 230
Jameson, Miss (actress), 218
Jamestown, Rhode Island, 283
Jane Shore (Rowe), 25
Jaques (*As You Like It*), criticism of Cooke's initial London performances, 169
Jenkins, Elisha, 275
Jephson, Robert, 90
Joe (caller at Cork Theatre), 107
John Bull, or an Englishman's Fire-Side (Colman the younger), 190–91
Johnson (actor), 53
Johnston, Henry Erskine, 99, 101, 147, 154, 174, 183, 189, 191, 192, 251, 254
Johnston, Mrs. Henry, 174, 183, 192, 251
Johnstone, John Henry, 183, 190–91, 213
Jones, Frederick Edward, 90, 103–6, 111, 222
Jones, Mary (Mrs. Joseph Munden), 43, 54, 67, 68
Jones, Richard, 244
Jordan, Dorothy, 71, 185, 213
Kean, Charles, 278, 281, 282
Kean, Edmund, 6–7, 8–9, 144, 154, 247, 262, 277, 278–81. *See also* Cooke, George Frederick, compared to Edmund Kean
Kean, Edmund, Sr., 63
Kean, Moses. *See* Kean, Edmund, Sr.
Kean, Mrs. Mary, 278
Kelly, Joe, 91
Kelly, Michael, 226–27, 248, 251
Kelly and Maxfield (managers), 245
Kemble, Charles, 164, 184, 194, 197, 199, 202–5, 216, 225, 228, 238, 244, 252

Kemble, Mrs. Charles. *See* DeCamp, Maria Theresa
Kemble, Elizabeth. *See* Whitlock, Mrs. Charles
Kemble, Fanny, 281
Kemble, John Philip, 4, 5, 8, 22, 41, 50, 100, 104, 112, 120–21, 135, 144, 145, 150–53, 154, 164–65, 170, 184, 189–90, 197–206, 208–9, 211–14, 216–17, 220, 225–28, 234–35, 236, 238, 242–43, 248, 250–52, 254, 259, 267; and alcohol, 252–53; negotiations and shareholder at Covent Garden, 197; on quelling a riot, 250. *See also* Cooke, George Frederick, compared to John Philip Kemble
Kemble, Stephen, 50–52, 54–55, 72–73, 74, 159, 162, 175, 187, 226; and Richard Brinsley Sheridan, 187; compared to Cooke's Falstaff, 175, 226
Kemble, Mrs. Stephen. *See* Satchell, Elizabeth
Kemble and Cooke; or, Critical Review of a Pamphlet Published Under the Title Remarks, etc. (London, 1801). *See Remarks on the Character of Richard the Third; As Played by Cooke and Kemble*
Kentist, Dr. E., on Cooke's illness, 166
King, Thomas, 22–23, 75, 80, 141, 158
King, [Thomas], 91, 103
King Lear, 19
King Lear, criticism of Cooke's initial London performances, 171–74; criticism in the U.S., 171–74
King's Lynn, 26–30
King's Theatre in the Haymarket, 242
Kitely, criticism of Cooke's initial London performances, 147–48
Knight, Thomas, 147, 161, 169, 217, 246
Knights, The (Foote), 18. *See also* Foote, Samuel
Küttner, Karl Gottlob, on the Manchester theatre, 42, 44
Lamash, Philip, 104, 117
Lamb, Miss (later Mrs. George Frederick Cooke), 236, 241
Lamb, Charles, on Cooke's Richard III, 127–28
Lancaster, 48, 53–54, 60, 67, 72, 98, 99, 101
Lancaster theatre, 49
Lapetina, William A.S., 285
League of United Irishmen. *See* Irish Rebellion of 1798

Lee, John, 23
Leeds (England), 57
Lefevre, Mrs. (actress), 34
Leglace, Mr. (violinist), 62
Leicester, 250
Leicester Haymarket Theatre, 24
Lennox, Lord William Pitt, 245–46
Leserve, Anna Maria, 237
Lewis, William "Billy" Thomas, 122, 154, 156, 158, 162, 164, 175, 177, 191, 192, 197, 205, 208, 215, 217, 222, 223, 225, 237, 246
Licensing Act of 1737, 34, 249
Limerick (Ireland), 91, 102, 105, 110, 112
Limerick Theatre Royal, 106
Litchfield, Mrs. Harriett, 142, 145, 149, 168, 184, 192, 205, 206, 208, 213, 219, 237
Litchfield Theatre, 215, 225
Liverpool, 49–50, 52, 76, 79–80, 99, 161, 223–24, 230, 246–47, 255, 256–58
Liverpool Theatre Royal, 50
London. *See* Cooke, George Frederick, London, debut of; initial season in; second season in; third season in; fourth season in; fifth season in; sixth season in; seventh season in; eighth season in; ninth season in; tenth season in; London residences of
Londonderry, 207
Lord Bute, 177
Lord Chesterfield, as compared to Sir Pertinax MacSycophant, 179
Louis XVI (king of France), 81
Love-a-la-Mode (Macklin), 22, 140–41; anecdote in Dublin, 95–96. *See also* Macklin, Charles; Cooke, George Frederick, roles played, Sir Archy MacSarcasm
Love in a Village (Bickerstaffe). *See* Cooke, George Frederick, first stage appearances as an amateur
Ludlow (England), 196, 197
Lying Valet, The (Garrick), 13
Macbeth, criticism of Cooke's initial London performances, 145–46
McClellan, Dr. George, 282–85
McCready, William, 158, 185, 186, 207, 214, 247
Macklin, Charles, 22–23, 25, 104, 177, 179–81; roles played by, 22
Macklin, Mrs. Charles, benefit for, 213–14
Macready, William Charles, 247–48, 281
Maddock, Mrs. (actress), 52
Maddox, Mrs. (actress), 30

Madison, James (president of the U.S.), 260
Man of the World, The (Macklin), 22. See also Macklin, Charles; Cooke, George Frederick, roles played by, Sir Pertinax MacSycophant
Manchester, 41–42, 49, 52–53, 64, 75–79, 80–82, 84–88, 96, 97–98, 100–101, 161–62, 185, 196, 214–15, 229, 231, 240, 247–48, 253–54
Manchester Theatre Royal, 41–42, 75, 97, 99, 196
Margate, 186
Martyr, Mrs. Margaret, 203, 205
Mason, Mrs. (actress), 269
Massey, Mr. E., 32–33, 34
Massey, Mrs. E., 32–34
Mathews, Mrs. Anne, 247
Mathews, Charles, 31, 91, 93–96, 215, 231; estimate of Cooke's talent in 1794, 93–94; on Cooke leaving Dublin in 1795, 94
Mattocks, George, 41, 49–52, 64, 161
Mattocks, Mrs. Isabella, 50–51, 52, 161, 183, 238
Maxwell (manager), 97
Mayor of Garratt (Foote), 19. *See also* Foote, Samuel
Mechanics' Hall (New York), 273, 275
Meggett (actor), 247
Memoirs of the Life of George Frederick Cooke (Dunlap), 3–4. *See also* Dunlap, William
Merchant, S. *See* Dibdin, Thomas
Merchant of Venice, The, Cooke's promptbook of, 139
Merry, Mrs. Anne, 259
Middleton, James, 104, 119, 231
Miller, James, 25, 41, 42, 49, 52
Mills, Mrs. Sarah, 17, 62, 119, 192
Mirror of Taste and Dramatic Censor. See Carpenter, Stephen Cullen
Mitchell, Colin, 15, 58
Montague (actor), 109
Monthly Mirror (London), 97; on Cooke's Othello, 160; on Cooke's Richard III, 128–36
Moody, John, 141, 213
Morris, Maynard, 281
Moss (actor), 52
Mossop, Henry, 173
Mountain, Mrs. (singer), 100
Mudie, Miss (child prodigy), 216
Munden, Joseph S., 15, 25, 43, 49, 54–55, 61–64, 67–69, 72, 79, 121, 147, 180, 182, 192, 198, 204, 205, 214, 217, 225, 244; on Cooke's apologies, 79; on Cooke's Iago, 142; on Cooke's Scottish accent, 180
Munden, Mrs. Joseph. *See* Jones, Mary
Munden, Thomas, 277
Murdoch, James, on Cooke's Richard III, 128
Murray, Charles, 124, 147, 154, 161, 165, 174, 175, 177, 183, 204, 252
Murray, Miss Harriet, 154, 161, 169, 183, 184, 228
Murray, William Henry, 191
Mysterious Husband, The (Cumberland), 109
Nelson, Viscount Horatio, 216, 226
New Street Playhouse (Salisbury), 228
New York, 190, 231, 254, 259–63, 266, 267–69, 271–72
Newcastle-upon-Tyne, 62–64, 68–71, 72, 73–74, 162–63, 166, 180, 240
Newcastle Theatre Royal, 62–63
Norton, Miss S., 223, 237
Norton, Mr. (actor), 63
Norton, Mrs. (actress), 63
Norwich, 227
Nottingham, 39, 196
Novosielski, Michael, 242
O'Brien (actor/manager), 39
Old Price Riots, 248–52
Olympic Pavilion, 227
Orchard Street Theatre. *See* Bath Theatre Royal
O'Reilly, Mary Sophia, 34
O'Reilly, William, 34, 38, 117, 223
O'Reilly, Mr. and Mrs. William, 34. *See also* O'Reilly, William
Owenson, Robert, 90–91
Palmer, John (manager, Bath), 40, 168
Palmer, John, Jr. (actor), 167
Palmer, William, 91, 92
Pantheonites, The (Gentleman), 27
Park Street Theatre (New York), 256, 259–62, 269, 272, 278, 282
Parker, Mrs. (actress/pantomimist), 91
Patron (Foote), 19. *See* also Foote, Samuel
Patterson, Dr. Ross V., 283
Payne, John Howard, 6, 211, 262, 266, 275
Penn, Mr. (actor), 25
Perth (Scotland), 248
Peter Kearney's (tavern), 11, 114, 115
Philadelphia, 252, 256, 257, 260, 262, 266, 267, 269, 271
Pierre in *Venice Preserv'd*, criticism of

Cooke's initial London performances, 184
Pizarro (Sheridan, after Kotzebue), 199, 242
Pizarro, criticism of Cooke's initial London performances, 200–202
Platt (actor), 55
Players Club, 281, 283
Playfair, Giles, 281
Plymouth Theatre, 186–87
Ponisi, Madame, 281
Pope, Alexander, 92, 124, 145, 154, 161, 217, 225
Pope, Mrs. Alexander (Maria Ann Campion), 92, 142, 161, 194
Portsmouth theatre, 97, 177, 246
Powell and Dickson (Dickinson). *See* Powell, Snelling; Dickson (Dickinson), James
Powell, Snelling, 269, 270
Powell, Sparks, 80
Powell, Mrs. Sparks, 75, 77, 80, 85
Powell, Mrs. William, 194, 205, 241
Preston (England), 98, 101, 255
Price, Stephen, 259, 265–66
Providence, Rhode Island, 155–56, 272–73
Providence Theatre, 272
Provok'd Husband, or a Journey to London, The (Vanbrugh), 13, 19, 27
Queen Street Theatre. *See* Glasgow theatre
Quin, James, 175, 190, 215
Rachel (Élisa Félix), 281
Rae (actor), 33
Rawlins, George, 110
Raymond (actor), 186, 205
Reddish, Samuel, 23
Rehearsal, The (Villiers), 18
Remarks on the Character of Richard the Third; As Played by Cooke and Kemble (London, 1801), 152–53
Renton, Allison. *See* Cooke, George Frederick, mother of
Renton, John (Cooke's grandfather), 11
Renton, Lady Susanna Montgomerie (Cooke's grandmother), 11
Renton, Samuel, 11, 232
Revenge, The (Young), 14. *See also* Cooke, George Frederick, first stage appearances as an amateur
Rich, John, 242
Richard III, as played by David Garrick, 20
Richard III, Cooke's promptbooks of, 130–36, 144
Richardson (actor), 77
Richardson, Miss (actress), 63

Richer, Jack, 91, 92
Richmond-Green, Theatre Royal, 198
Richmond, Virginia, Theatre fire, 269, 270
Road to Happiness, The (proposed play by Cooke), 113
Robinson, Mrs. Hannah (Mrs. Taylor), 33, 38, 42–44, 47, 52, 80–81, 85
Robinson, Henry Crabb, on Cooke's Falstaff (*Henry IV, Part 1*), 175–77; on Cooke's Richard III, 131
Robson, William, on Cooke's Sir Archy MacSarcasm, 141; on Cooke's acting specialty, 152
Rochester (England), 157
Rock, Anthony, 11, 159, 221, 230, 232, 233, 234, 248
Romantic School of Acting, 20
Ross, David, 23
Royal family's visits to Covent Garden, 141, 147, 190, 191, 203, 212, 213. *See also* George III (king of England)
Russell, Mr. and Mrs. (actor/actress), 35
Russell, Samuel Thomas, 34
Ryder, Thomas, 89, 117
Rye (England), 32
Ryley, Samuel, 64, 66, 75, 81, 161; on Cooke's acting technique, 67
St. Ledger, Mrs. Catherine, 158, 170, 237
St. Paul's Church (New York), 275, 277
Salisbury, 228
Satchell, Elizabeth (Mrs. Stephen Kemble), 50–51, 52, 54–55, 73, 74
Saunders (actor), 120
Sciolto (*The Fair Penitent*), criticism of Cooke's performances of, 202
Scotland, anecdotes on Cooke in, 229–30
Scott, Captain Robert, 16
Scott, Sir Walter, 35; on Cooke and J.P. Kemble as Sir Giles Overreach, 155
Scott, Right Honourable Sir William, 159
Scraggs, Mrs. (actress), 39
Scraggs, Mr. (manager), 39
Shatford, James, 228
Shaw (manager), 186
Sheffield, 72–73, 84
Sheridan, Richard Brinsley, 120, 164–65, 187, 197–98, 236
Sheridan, Thomas, 90, 190
Shrewsbury, 99
Shrewsbury theatrical company, 25
Shuter, Edward, 23, 32
Shuttleworth, Miss (actress), 212

Index

Shylock, criticism of Cooke's initial London performances, 138–40
Siddons, Henry, 99, 101, 167, 170, 175, 177, 192, 197, 241, 248
Siddons, Mrs. Henry, 197, 199, 241
Siddons, Sarah, 41, 50, 56–58, 70, 98, 101, 158, 159, 184, 197, 199, 202–6, 209, 211, 217, 225, 243, 254. *See also* Cooke, George Frederick, Kemble, J.P., and Siddibsm acts with for first time
Silvester (actor), 33
Simpson, Mrs. (actress), 77, 269
Sinclair (actor), 38
Sir Giles Overreach, criticism of Cooke's initial London performance, 154–55; stage history of, 154; Cooke's U.S. reception in, 155–56
Smirke, Robert, 242
Smith (actor), 63, 70
Smith, (actor/pantomimist), 91
Smith, Miss (later Mrs. Bartley), 216, 225, 226, 228, 230
Smith, Mrs. (actress), 70
Smith, Richard John "Obi", 169, 218–19
Smith, Miss Sarah, 98, 168
Smock Alley Theatre (Dublin), 89–90
Smollett, Tobias. See Cooke, George Frederick, roles played by, Worthy
Sother, E.A., 281
Sparks, Mrs. *See* Mills, Sarah
Sparks, Richard, 119
Spiller (actor), 269
Spouting clubs, 30–31
"The Stage" (poem by Cooke), 113
Stamford (England), 26–30
Stamford Theatre, 26
Standen (manager), 31
Stanton, John, 98
Stanwix (actor), 168
Starring system, rise of the, 259
Stayley, George, 13
Stevens, George Alexander, 32
Stewart, James B., 112
Storace, Signora, 165, 189
Stourbridge, 215
Stranger, The (after Kotzebue), 149
Stranger, criticism of Cooke's initial London performances, 149–50
Stukely (*The Gamester*), criticism of Cooke's initial London performances, 167–68
Sudbury, 38
Surrey Theatre, 169

Swendall, James. *See* Swindall, James
Swindall, James, 32–33
Swords, Billy, 25
Sydney and Connor (managers), 64
Table Talk (Ryan), 230
Talbot, Montague, 159–60, 161
Taylor (actor), 281
Taylor, Aline, on Cooke's Pierre in *Venice Preserv'd*, 184
Taylor, John (critic), 12, 198, 273
Taylor, John (printer), 12, 14
Taylor, Mrs. *See* Robinson, Mrs. Hannah
Tempest, The (Kemble's adaptation), 227–28
"Tennis Court in the Borough" (theatre), 38
Thespian Mirror, or Poetical Strictures; on the Professional Characters of . . . the Theatres Manchester, Liverpool, and Chester, The (1973), 80
Thespian Review; An Examination of the Merits and Demerits of the Performers on the Manchester Stage (1806), 224–25
Thompson, Charles, 147
Tichenor, George, 286
Tighlman, Edward, 181
Tompkins, Daniel D. (governor of New York), 275
Toms (actor), 222
Tontine Coffee House (New York), 268
Townsend, Edward, 145
Townshend, John Stanislaw, 54. *See* Chester Theatre Royal
Trafalgar, Nelson's victory at, 216
Trinity College, Dublin, 106
Tyrrell, Garret, 77, 81, 85, 98
Valpy, Dr. Richard, 192
Vandenhoff, George, 282
Venice Preserv'd (Otway), 13, 183
Vernon, Joseph, 50
Veteran Stager, 10, 14–15, 25, 74, 82–84, 96–97, 257–58
Waddy, J. (actor), 147, 183, 184, 191
Warcup, Miss (actress), 160
Ward, Thomas, 47, 51, 75–77, 79, 165, 196
Ward, Mrs. Thomas (Sarah), 75, 77, 80, 100, 161, 229
Ward and Banks, 97, 98, 99. *See also* Banks, John; Ward, Thomas
Ward and Bellamy, 161, 196. *See also* Bellamy, Thomas Ludford; Ward, Thomas
Ward and Young, 229. *See also* Ward, Thomas; Young, Charles Mayne
Warren, William, 262

Warren and Wood, 266, 269. *See also* Warren, William; Wood, William B.
Webster, Daniel, 282
Weigle, Reverend Harold, 281
Welsh, Mr. (manager), 84
West, Mr. and Mrs. Thomas, 34
Westminster New Lying-In Hospital, 33
Weston, Thomas, 23
Whalley, Reverend Sedgewick, 57
Wheeler, Mr. and Mrs. (actor/actress), 208
Whitehead, William, 147
Whitfield, John, 80, 124, 185
Whitley and Herbert Company. *See* Whitley, James A.
Whitley, James A., 26, 29, 39
Whitlock, Charles Edward, 41, 48–49, 61–64, 72, 73
Whitlock and Austin. *See* Austin and Whitlock
Whitlock and Munden, 64, 67. *See also* Munden, Joseph; Whitlock, Charles Edward
Whitlock, Mrs. Charles (Elizabeth Kemble), 54, 61–63, 68–70, 72, 81, 258
Wignell, Thomas, 193
Wilkes, Thomas, on *Venice Preserv'd*, 183
Wilkinson, John, 240, 243
Wilkinson, Tate, 41, 55–58, 240
Williams (actor), 108, 111
Williams, Mrs. (actress), 111
Windsor, Mrs. (Alicia Daniels), 107. *See also* Daniels, Alicia (later Mrs. George Frederick Cooke)
Wood (actor), 160
Wood, William B., 181, 262
Woodfall, Mrs. (actress), 208
Woodward (actress), 31
Woodward, Henry (actor), 13, 23
Worcester (England), 196, 254
Wrench and Robertson (managers), 197
Wright, Roger, 25
Yates, Mrs. Mary Ann, 104, 111
Yates, Richard, 23
York, 55–57, 58, 240–41, 243
York Theatre Royal, 55–56
Young (actor), 55
Young, Mrs. *See* Biggs, Miss
Young, Charles Mayne, 8, 229, 235, 243, 244, 250, 252
Young, Edward, 148
Younger, Joseph, 41, 47–48, 49
Zobeide (Cradock), 24

About the Author

DON BURTON WILMETH is professor of Theatre Arts and English and chairman of the Department of Theatre Arts at Brown University in Providence, Rhode Island. He is the author of *American Stage to World War I*, in addition to many articles.

LIBRARY OF DAVIDSON COLLEGE

Books on reg.... checked ... for tw... eks. Books
 pres...